Dermot Keogh has written an absorbing, and in many instances surprising, study of Irish relations with Argentina in the last century, through years of turbulence, tyranny and progress ... A fine achievement and a splendid book.

John Banville, Booker Prize winner

This is a great book, combining meticulous scholarship with fine writing to bring a century of Argentine–Irish relations vividly to life. Dermot Keogh's magnificently scholarly and vividly revealing history of Ireland and Argentina in the twentieth century is so well written and, yes, gripping, that I never wanted to stop reading. Here is a history that brings to life the fascinating story of the Irish in Argentina. Professor Keogh reveals much that is unknown in this tour de force that brings the skills of investigative journalism to painstaking scholarship.

Robert Cox, former editor of the Buenos Aires Herald

In this compelling study based on exhaustive original research, Professor Dermot Keogh greatly enhances our understanding of the contribution Irish emigrants made to Argentina.

He succeeds in sustaining a consistently balanced perspective, while devoting particular attention to – indeed examining to unprecedented depth – the extremely strained and often intensely brutal period when the army junta seized power between 1975 and 1983.

Professor Keogh also explores perceptively the challenge the junta posed to the Catholic Church. This inescapably resulted in the deep involvement of both the local clergy and Irish diplomats, many of whom Professor Keogh commends for the exemplary quality of their response to what, even at this distance in time, remains a chilling reminder of the potential for cruelty, indeed savagery, of some of the Argentinian military up to the highest levels.

In doing so, Professor Keogh illustrates with exceptional command of detail the complexities of the circumstances confronting both the Catholic clergy and Irish diplomats in responding to the often horrific cruelties inflicted by the military regime on those it designated as its enemies. It is a story little known in Ireland. But however distant from Irish shores it occurred, it constitutes an important and enduring analysis of an impressive, indeed remarkable, episode in Irish history.

John J. Lee, Emeritus Professor of History, New York University

Ireland and Argentina in the Twentieth Century: Diaspora, Diplomacy, Dictatorship, Catholic Mission and the Falklands Crisis is based on research in archives in several different countries: archives of state, of the Catholic Church and of other bodies, not least those of Irish societies and institutions in Argentina. It also uses the correspondence of key figures, some in private hands, as well as interviews carried out by the author, and is informed by the author's decades-long engagement with Latin America and his personal acquaintance with many of the book's protagonists. A book of extraordinary scope, it substantially advances several areas of research on Ireland and on Argentina. If the book is about relations between two countries of relatively small population thousands of miles apart, it illuminates the intersection of major global forces – diaspora, post-colonialism, missionary religion, international diplomacy and human rights – in a strikingly original way. It is a major achievement.

Diarmuid Ó Giolláin, Professor of Irish Language & Literature and Concurrent Professor of Anthropology at the Keough-Naughton Institute for Irish Studies, University of Notre Dame

Dermot Keogh's *Ireland and Argentina in the Twentieth Century: Diaspora, Diplomacy, Dictatorship, Catholic Mission and the Falklands Crisis* is a ground-breaking book that fulfils a crucial lack in the history of diplomatic relations between Ireland and Argentina and opens up an untracked field of research. Generously acknowledging existing studies, Professor Keogh draws extensively on new sources and develops an analysis from the origins of Irish diplomacy in 1916 with Eamonn Bulfin as first envoy to Argentina, through the rise and fall of Juan Domingo Perón, the dark times of Argentine dictatorship and the Falklands/Malvinas war. He ends up with the restoration of democracy and human rights, giving particular attention to the relevant Rice/Cabrera case. Interlacing twentieth-century diplomatic history with the role of the Irish Catholic missionaries ('soft power') and the previous history of the Irish in Argentina, Professor Keogh has produced a stimulating and challenging transnational assessment of over a century of Irish–Argentine history. This is an insightful landmark book, which deserves to be widely read.

Laura P.Z. Izarra, Professora Titular, Coordenadora da Cátedra de Estudos Irlandeses WB Yeats, Departamento de Letras Modernas, Faculdade de Filosofia, Letras e Ciências Humanas, Universidade de São Paulo

Dermot Keogh takes us on a trans-hemispheric voyage navigating connections over time between Ireland and Argentina. His scholarly pen traces how Irish diplomats helped, at times risking their own safety, to chart responses to populism, military coups and the accompanying contradictions within Argentine Catholicism between liberation theology – of whom there were notable Argentinian-Irish practitioners – and the ecclesiastical status quo.

The book is at its most compelling when Keogh rigorously investigates the state-sanctioned murder of priests and lay workers in the 1970s, and the narrative charts another raging storm when, in 1982, Charles Haughey confronted Margaret Thatcher over her country's invasion of the Malvinas/Falkland Islands. This book is a timely reminder that from the tip of Malin Head to the toe of Tierra del Fuego we Irish and our often generous Argentine hosts continue to sail the ocean of life together thanks to bonds of family, faith and the quest for liberty.

Joe Little – a relative of Patrick J. Little who was sent as a Sinn Féin envoy to Buenos Aires in 1920 – is a writer, and was Religious and Social Affairs Correspondent with RTÉ News and Current Affairs from 1994 to 2019.

IRELAND AND ARGENTINA IN THE TWENTIETH CENTURY:
DIASPORA, DIPLOMACY, DICTATORSHIP, CATHOLIC MISSION
AND THE FALKLANDS CRISIS

Ireland and Argentina in the Twentieth Century

Diaspora, diplomacy, dictatorship, Catholic mission and the Falklands crisis

DERMOT KEOGH
(*with* PATRICK KIELY)

First published in 2022 by
Cork University Press
Boole Library
University College Cork
CORK
T12 ND89
Ireland

Library of Congress Control Number: 2022932567
Distribution in the USA: Longleaf Services, Chapel Hill, NC, USA

British Library Cataloguing in Publication Data
A CIP record for this book is available from the British Library.

ISBN: 978-1-78205-511-2

Printed in Poland by BZ Graf
Print origination & design by Carrigboy Typesetting Services
www.carrigboy.co.uk

COVER IMAGE – From the Laurence Ginnell papers, Mullingar Library, Co. Westmeath. The painting by an unknown artist was given to Ginnell during his time in Argentina between July 1921 and March 1922. It may have been painted by an Irish nun in San Antonio de Areco.

www.corkuniversitypress.com

This book is dedicated to

Ann

Professor John J. Lee

Matthew and Madelaine MacNamara

Justin Harman and Juan José Delaney

The late Patrick Rice, Fátima, Amy, Blanca and Carlos Cabrera Rice
and Celeste and Almendra Quintana Rice

Eoin, Niall, Aoife, Clare, Caroline, Elizabeth, Marco, Barry,
Abigail, Luke, David, Aisling, Darragh, Clodagh, Anna Amy,
Emanuele and Olan

And in memory of Mgr Kevin Mullen, Fr Peter Hinde,
Bernard Davenport, Walter LaFeber, Patrick McKernan,
Art Agnew and Sally O'Neill de Sánchez

Contents

Acknowledgements

The president of Ireland, Michael D. Higgins, whose engagement with Latin America began in the early 1960s, did me the great honour of writing a foreword to this volume. Up to 2022, the president had made three official visits to Latin America. As an academic and a member of the Labour Party, he had written and broadcast on the Irish in Montserrat and played an active role in the 1980s on Central America and Chile. His academic interest in the Irish abroad is reflected in his writing over sixty years.

Without the academic support of Professor Joseph Lee, it is doubtful if I would have had an academic career. As a colleague for over twenty years at University College Cork, I enjoyed his company and his counsel. As a head of department, he encouraged staff to open up new areas of research. In building a school of history, he was courageous and innovative. I remain in his debt.

The late Professor Walter LaFeber of Cornell University encouraged my research on Latin America in the 1980s and remained supportive through the decades, inviting me to teach at Cornell in summer 1989.

Ambassador Justin Harman was a great source of encouragement and support while I was researching this project. Assigned in late 1975 to Argentina on his first foreign posting, he served there until 1978, returning as ambassador in 2014 until his retirement in 2017. He plays a dual role as a prominent actor in this text and as a friend whose support over the years, together with that of his wife Carmen, helped open many doors and introduce me to prominent members of the Irish-Argentine community. My wife Ann and I are indebted to both of them for their hospitality and for the use of their apartment during research trips to Buenos Aires.

This book is the result of an engagement with Latin America which first began in 1963 and continued for nearly sixty years through my undergraduate studies at University College Dublin, as a journalist in the 1970s and later as a lecturer and professor at University College Cork from 1980 until 2010. In 1963, I met Patrick Rice in the Divine Word Missionaries (SVD) seminary in Donamon, County Roscommon. We studied together and became lifelong friends. Our paths first diverged after four years when I left the order. Rice was ordained in 1970 and was sent immediately to Argentina, where he worked with his order as a teacher of philosophy. In 1972–3, he joined the Little Brothers of Charles de Foucauld and became a worker priest in a *villa* (slum) in Buenos Aires. We kept up our friendship throughout that period. On 11 October 1976, he was kidnapped with a catechist Fátima Cabrera in a *villa* in Buenos Aires. Both were taken to a clandestine detention centre (CCD) where they were tortured by agents of the state. Unlike other members of his order in Argentina, he survived, as did Fátima Cabrera, the latter having spent over two years in jail and four years under house arrest. Rice, after nearly three months in jail, was deported to Ireland. He worked in London, Geneva and Washington between 1977 and 1979 with human rights groups to expose what was happening in Argentina. He moved to Caracas in the early 1980s where he helped set up FEDEFAM, an organisation that represents the families of the disappeared throughout Latin America. In 1984, he returned to Buenos Aires to help organise the annual FEDEFAM conference. There he met Fátima Cabrera for the first time since they had been in prison in 1976. Prior to his return to Argentina that year, Rice had decided to leave the priesthood in order to dedicate his life to work in the area of human rights. By that time, his relationship with Fátima Cabrera had changed. They married in Caracas in 1985. Having spent the intervening years as a promoter of human rights at the UN, in Latin America, Africa, Sri Lanka, the Philippines and in the Balkans, he died suddenly in 2010 at an airport in Miami on his way from Ireland to his home in Buenos Aires.

Thanks to the generosity and hospitality of the Rice-Cabrera family, including their children Carlos, Amy and Blanca (my godchild), I had a base from which to work in Buenos Aires.[1] My understanding of Latin America over the decades owes a great deal to them, introducing me to many academics and human rights activists, among them Ana María Lodala, María Adela Antokoletz and members of the Madres de Plaza de Mayo. Fátima gave me access to Rice's personal papers, which are extensive and of significant historical importance. The extended Rice family in Fermoy shared their memories with me of growing up on the family farm. My thanks to his sister Kathleen and husband Tommy Lee and their daughter Amy; his brothers Liam and his late wife Kitty and their son Patrick. I am also grateful to his other brothers and their wives: John and Nuala; Tom and Kay; Edward and Margaret; and Denis and Bríd.

While researching this book, I relied heavily on my friend, computer expert and former research assistant Patrick Kiely, who accompanied me on research trips to Buenos Aires and to Rome. The research for a part of this project was funded by the Irish National Institute for Historical Research founded under the UCC School of History PRTLI 4 programme directed by Dr Hiram Morgan. Mr Kiely's name deservedly appears on the title page of this book for having shared his computer and historical expertise with me over fifteen years. Sheila Cunneen, with whom I worked while in UCC, suggested editorial changes to the different drafts of this volume.

I owe a great debt to my friends Madelaine and Matthew MacNamara, who helped me find the answers to many research queries. Their generosity over forty years has enabled me to draw upon their unrivalled knowledge of international history and modern literature. I also thank the following for their help and support: Tom Boland, Damien Bracken, Angela Cahill, Gertrude Cotter, Joseph T. Carroll, Gary Murphy, Deirdre McMahon, Brian and Laura Miranda Lennon, T.P. O'Mahony, Mary Harris, Jeff Kildea, Peter Kuch, Joe Little, Susan Nugent, Michael O'Sullivan, Andy Pollock and Eibhear Walshe. The outstanding president of UCC, Gerard Wrixon, helped me secure a generous donation towards the cost of publishing this volume. I am also grateful to Professor Nuala Finnegan, University College Cork, director of the Society for Irish Latin American Studies (SILAS), who, with the help of Margaret Brehony, continues to foster the growth of studies of the region across the disciplines.[2]

Juan José Delaney, academic and novelist, is a friend and mentor, who introduced me to his own literary and historical work and to many people in Argentina. His academic work proved of great help, as did the research trips we took together to different towns in the camp (*campo* = countryside), including Mercedes and Venado Tuerto. His uncle, Luis, was a mine of information and a gracious host on our visits to the American Club in Buenos Aires. Through Prof. Delaney's introduction, I am beholden to the Irish Catholic Association (ICA) for the support provided during my research trips and for granting me access to the archives of *The Southern Cross* in Colegio Santa Brígida. My thanks to Lucas Ussher, Federico Richards, John Michel, Michael Flynn, Julio Suppicich and Sandra Beatriz Fusco for their help. James Ussher helped me consult the records of the Federation of Irish Societies in the Argentine Republic (Federación de Sociedades Irlandesas de la República Argentina).

I am grateful to Ambassador Jacqueline O'Halloran and the staff at the Irish embassy in Buenos Aires, in particular Yanina Bevilacqua, Héctor Viavattene, Dermot Fitzpatrick and to former ambassadors James McIntyre, Philomena Murnaghan, Máirtín Ó Faínín, Kenneth Thompson and Paula Slattery. My thanks to the secretary general of the Department of Foreign Affairs and Trade, Niall Burgess, and his colleagues, especially Brendan Rogers, for their help while researching this volume, and to the late Bernard Davenport, who served both as a third secretary and ambassador in Buenos Aires. He shared his knowledge and experiences with me as did his wife Fiamma on a number of my visits to their apartment in Florence. The Davenports also gave me a gift of valuable archives. Colin Wrafter, who served as third secretary in Buenos Aires during the Falklands/Malvinas conflict, answered many of my questions on that period. I am also grateful to the following Irish diplomats for their help at different times over the past forty years: Ted Barrington, Frank Cogan, Thelma Doran, Colm Ó Floinn, Philip McDonagh and the late Patrick McKernan.

My thanks to the following scholars of Irish Latin American affairs: Edmundo Murray, pioneer of the study of the Irish in Argentina; Dr Laura Izarra, professor of literature in English, University of São Paulo, and the founding editor in 1999 of the interdisciplinary journal *The Brazilian Journal of Irish Studies* (ABEI); Prof. Mariela Eliggi, Universidad Nacional de la Pampa, a founder member in 2017 and first president of the Asociación de Estudios Irlandeses del Sur;³ Susanna Taurozzi, the historian of the Passionists in Argentina; film maker, writer and theatre director Oscar Barney Finn; and to historians María Eugenia Cruset, Susan Wilkinson and Viviana Keegan. The leading authority on the Irish in Venado Tuerto, Roberto Landaburu, generously shared his research with me, took me to the museum in his historic farmhouse, and gave me access to his collections of photographs, some of which are reproduced in this book.

The historian Edward Walsh, who worked as a Dominican priest in Argentina for a number of years, generously shared with me his rich archival findings on the Irish in Argentina in the nineteenth and twentieth centuries. His knowledge of the period was a resource on which I relied heavily. Stretching over nearly twenty years, there are a number friends without whose help this book could not have been written. My gratitude to the late Jeanne Winder and Michael Bulfin for granting me access to the papers of their father, Eamonn, and to those of their grandfather, William. That rich family collection, together with material already deposited in the National Library, opens up the history of the Irish in Argentina in a unique way. Those papers also provided limited information about the unofficial diplomatic role of their aunt Anita who helped her brother Eamonn with his work in Argentina between 1919 and 1922. My thanks also to Paula O'Doran, senior executive librarian, Mullingar, who helped me when I consulted the Laurence Ginnell papers. I am grateful too to Aideen Ginnell and to her parents for granting me access to family archives relating to Laurence Ginnell.

Jerome and Austin Mullen, the brothers of Mgr Kevin Mullen, who played an important role while working as a diplomat for the Holy See in Buenos Aires between mid-1976 and 1979, gave me access to family archives.

During numerous research trips to Buenos Aires, I worked for long periods at the Archivo Histórico de Cancillería, where the staff were always unfailingly helpful. María Cecilia Mendoza, administradora gubernamental, shared her academic knowledge and diplomatic expertise with me. Guillermo David, dirección nacional de coordinación cultural, at the National Archives, identified a number of important sources for me and was untiring in answering my questions. He also shared with me his research on Irish Argentines in the Peronist movement from the 1940s. I am grateful to Pedro Bevilacqua and the staff of the Espacio Memoria y Derechos Humanos (ex-ESMA) and the Museo de Inmigrantes. Visiting both institutions helped give me an insight into different periods in the history of Argentina. My gratitude to the late Bishop Guillermo Leaden, brother of the murdered Pallottine priest Alfredo, who granted me an interview despite being in very poor health. The late Emilio Mignone, lawyer, academic, politician and human rights activist, gave me great encouragement to complete this book.

Among those who helped me in Buenos Aires were the late journalist and historian Michael Geraghty, who worked there for over fifty years. His wife Sonia Campbell and his daughters Brenda and Eileen continue to help me, as do also the following: Cristina Abaca; Eduardo and Salomé Clancy; the late Juan Clancy; Jackie, Julián, Edna and Eddy, Henry and Grace Kelly; Silvia Elena Kenny de Cavanagh; Diana Englebert Moody; Dickie MacAllister; the late Patricio Turner; José Wallace; Roberto and Alisú Walshe; and Carlos Findlay Wilson. My thanks also to the journalist Robert Cox and his wife Maud for their help and encouragement; the journalists Sergio Kiernan, Brenda Lynch Wade and the late Andrew Graham-Yooll and the historian Horacio Verbitsky who gave me an interview. The Irish-Argentine painters Guillermo MacLoughlin and Fernando O'Connor shared with me their insights into contemporary Argentina, as did Andrés Waissman and Gachi Prieto. Andrés painted a series entitled *Multitudes*, which records the arrival of the hundreds of thousands of immigrants, including his Jewish grandparents, who made their home in Argentina in the nineteenth and twentieth centuries. One of the series can be seen at Juan Manuel de Rosas station on the Buenos Aires underground.

I am grateful to the staff of the following national libraries and archives: National Archives of Ireland, Dublin; Library and Archives of Canada, Ottawa; US National Archives, Maryland; British National Archives, Richmond, London; National Archives of Australia, Canberra; Archivio Storico Diplomatico, Ministero degli Affari Esteri, Rome; Archivum Secretum Vaticanum, Rome; the National Library of Ireland and the libraries of Trinity College, Dublin; the Archives Department, University College Dublin; NUI

Maynooth; and NUI Galway. My thanks to the staff of the Boole Library at UCC, and in particular those who serve on the check-out and inter-library loans desks; to the head of Research Collections and Communications, Crónán Ó Doibhlin; the head of Special Collections, Elaine Harrington; and to Collette Crowley, Sheyeda Allen and Mary Lombard.

In 2011–12, I was the visiting John J. Burns Scholar at Boston College. Prof. Tom Hachey and his late wife Jean were most gracious and supportive during our stay. My thanks to the former Burns librarian and associate university librarian for special collections Dr Bob O'Neill. His successor Dr Christian Dupont is an ongoing source of encouragement and support. My thanks to other Boston College staff: Liam Bergin, Kevin Kenny, Robert Savage, Joe Nugent, Gustavo Morello and Kevin O'Neill. Anne Kenny, Elizabeth Sweeney and Kathleen Williams provided me with expert research assistance. Professor Diarmaid Ó Giolláin, Department of Irish Language and Literature, University of Notre Dame, arranged for me to lecture there. Mary and Leo Ó Giolláin took care of me during a productive stay which allowed me to work in the archives, where I was helped by Aedin Clements and Erika R. Hosselkus.

I was given access to a wide range of primary sources in Catholic Church archives in Ireland and abroad, including the Pontifical Irish College, Rome; the Dublin Diocesan Archive; Armagh Diocesan Archive; Diocese of Achonry; and Diocese of Killaloe. I found the Association for Church Archives of Ireland's directory of the records of male and female congregations and diocesan archives to be a most helpful research tool. My thanks also to the following: Noelle Dowling, archivist, Dublin Diocesan Archives; Archivist Sr Carmel Kidd, Sisters of the Little Company of Mary; Edward Hogan, archivist, Society of African Missions, Blackrock, Cork; Roddy Hegarty and staff of the Cardinal Tomás Ó Fiaich Archive, Armagh; Barbara Scally, archivist, Columban Fathers, Navan, County Meath; Marianne Cosgrove, archivist, Mercy Congregation Archives, Herbert Street, Dublin; Betsy Johnson and Deborah Watson of the same congregation working in the United States and Argentina; the Oblate Fathers, Inchicore, Dublin; Sile Ní Chochláin, Legion of Mary; and Vincent Twomey, Divine Word Missionaries. Sr Mary O'Byrne, Dominican Sisters, Cabra, Dublin, has written an account of hers and the sisters' experiences in Buenos Aires during the civilian military dictatorship. Sr Terence O'Keeffe, who was prioress and principal of Santo Domingo College at that time, has died. Sisters Dymphna Tipper and Brigid Fahy were present during that dictatorship. Sr Dymphna confirmed for me a number of important facts about the Rice kidnapping. On hearing the news from Fr Carlos Bustos, she made two phone calls, one to the Irish embassy where she spoke to the Irish ambassador, and the other to the news desk of the *Buenos Aires Herald*.

My thanks to the Irish Christian Brothers in Dublin and in Buenos Aires. Brother John Burke, a former principal in Buenos Aires, arranged for me to consult the Newman College house chronicle. Brothers Tom O'Connell and Seán Hayes were most hospitable to both Ann and myself during our research visits to the college.

I did extensive work in the archives of the Pallottine and Passionist orders in Dublin and in Buenos Aires. Fr Tomás O'Donnell arranged for me to gain access to the rich Pallottine archives in St Patrick's, Belgrano, Buenos Aires. My thanks also to the late Fr José Campion, who worked in Argentina from 1966 to 2003. The former Pallottine archivist in Ireland, Fr Donal McCarthy, has written a draft history of the Pallottines in Argentina to which he gave me digital access. This complemented my findings in the order's archives in Belgrano. Fr McCarthy answered my many queries and sent me a large number of documents, articles and photographs. I am in his debt.

The former archivist at the Passionist monastery of Mount Argus in Dublin, Fr Brian Mulcahy, made files available to me and also supplied material in digital form. His successor, Fr Paul Francis, sourced a collection of photographs which I have included in this volume. My visits to the Passionist archive at Holy Cross in Buenos Aires yielded very good results. In 2010, the late Fr Miguel Egan provided me with a great deal of printed material. He generously gave me his personal copies of two valuable historical works on the Irish in Argentina. After the death of Fr Egan, I revisited the Passionist archive in 2016. The archivist gave me permission to see the personal papers of Fr Federico Richards, the editor of *The Southern Cross* during the 1970s. The historian Mariano Galazzi gave me access to a digital copy of the Holy Cross house chronicle. I had unproductive results in the archive of the archdiocese of Buenos Aires, seeing only a slim file containing a letter from the Irish ambassador together with the contemporary constitution of the Federación de Sociedades Irlandesas de la República Argentina.

I am grateful to the head of the School of History at UCC, Mervyn O'Driscoll; the former head, David Ryan; and to former colleagues Andrew McCarthy, Donal Ó Drisceoil, Katherine McGarry, Gabriel Doherty, Jérôme aan de Wiel, Bozena Cierlik, Damian Bracken and Hiram Morgan. I am indebted to my former colleagues on the Royal Irish Academy and Department of Foreign Affairs project, 'Documents on Irish Foreign Policy': Michael Kennedy, Kate O'Malley, John Gibney, Eunan O'Halpin and the archivists at the Department of Foreign Affairs, Maureen Sweeney and Clare Hanratty. My thanks to Niall Kerney and Barry Whelan for giving me accesss to the Leopold Kerney papers.

The Universidad del Salvador (USAL) has been my academic home in Buenos Aires for over twenty years. The late rector Juan Alejandro Tobias, who died in February 2018, helped build strong academic links between USAL and Ireland, supported by the indefatigable vice rector of research and development, Paula Ortiz, and by the prosecretaria académica, María Verónica Repetti. The Spanish translation of this book has been overseen by a dedicated team at USAL led by Paula Ortíz and Verónica Repetti. Rafael Abuchedid, who was one of the translation team of *Irish Independence: The Argentina Connection* (published in 2016),⁴ did the translation single-handedly of this volume into Spanish with the title *Irlanda y la Argentina del siglo XX* (USAL, Buenos Aires, 2022). Verónica Repetti subedited and oversaw the production of the book, while Mariano Galazzi gave me very useful advice on Chapter 3.

I am grateful to Cork University Press, the publishers of this volume, and to the executive editor Maria O'Donovan and to the publications director Mike Collins. My thanks also to the two anonymous readers and to the copy-editor Aonghus Meaney.

List of Abbreviations

AAA or Triple A	Alianza Anticomunista Argentina (Argentine Anti-Communist Alliance)
ACHA	Cooperativa Ayuda Fraternal de Fortín Olmos (a cooperative for forestry workers)
ACLU	American Civil Liberties Union (US)
ADL	Anti-Defamation League of B'nai B'rith
AI	Amnesty International
AID	Agency for International Development (US)
AMIA	Asociación Mutual Israelita Argentina (Argentine Israelite Mutual Association)
AMPM	Asociación Madres de Plaza de Mayo (Association of Mothers of the Plaza de Mayo) [In 1986 the association split into two groups: Mothers of the Plaza de Mayo – Founding Line; and Mothers of the Plaza de Mayo Association.]
APDH	Asamblea Permanente por los Derechos Humanos (Permanent Assembly for Human Rights)
ARMH	Asociación para la Recuperación de la Memoria Histórica (Association for the Recovery of Historical Memory)
BAH	*Buenos Aires Herald*
CA	Club Atlético (Athletic Club)
CADHU	Comisión Argentina por Derechos Humanos (Argentine Human Rights Commission)
CAR	Confederación Argentina de Religiosos (Confederation of Argentine Male Religious)
CCD	Centros Clandestinos de Detención (Clandestine Detention Centres)
CEA	Conferencia Episcopal Argentina (Argentine Episcopal Conference)
CELAM	Consejo Episcopal Latinoamericano (Latin American Bishops Conference)
CELS	Centro de Estudios Legales y sociales (Centre for Legal and Social Studies)

CFSP	Common Foreign and Security Policy
CGT	Confederación General del Trabajo (General Confederation of Labour)
CIDH	Comisión Interamericana de Derechos Humanos (Inter-American Commission on Human Rights)
CIIR	Catholic Institute for International Relations
COMADRES	Comité de Madres y Familiares de Desaparecidos y Asasinados Políticos de El Salvador (Committee of Mothers and Families of the Disappeared and Victims of Political Assassination)
CONADEP	Comisión Nacional sobre la Desaparición de Personas (National Commission on Disappeared Persons)
CONFER	Conferencia Argentina de Religiosas (Argentine Conference of Women Religious)
CP	Centro Piloto (a 'public relations' initiative to counter 'anti-Argentine' propaganda in Europe and further the political ambitions of Admiral Massera)
DINA	Dirección Nacional de Inteligencia de Chile (Chilean National Intelligence Directorate)
EAAF	Equipo Argentino de Antropología Forense (Argentine Forensic Anthropology Team)
EM	Ejército Montonero (revolutionary guerrilla wing of Peronist movement)
EPC	European Political Cooperation
ERP	Ejército Revolucionario del Pueblo (People's Revolutionary Army)
ESMA	Escuela de Mecánica de la Armada (Navy Mechanical School)
FAR	Fuerzas Armadas Revolucionarias (Revolutionary Armed Forces)
FDDRP	Familias de Detenidos y Desaparecidos por Razones Políticas (Families of those Detained and Disappeared for Political Reasons)
FEDEFAM	Federación Latinoamericana de Asociaciones de Familiares de Detenidos-Desaparecidos (Latin American Federation of Associations for Relatives of the Detained and Disappeared)
FSIRA	Federación de Sociedades Irlandesas de la República de Argentina (Federation of Irish Societies of the Republic of Argentina)

FUNDALATIN	Latin American Foundation of Human Rights and Social Development
GATT	General Agreement on Tariffs and Trade
HIJOS	Hijos y hijas por la Identidad y la Justicia contra el Olvido y el Silencio (Sons and Daughters for Identity and Justice against Silence and not Remembering) – led by the children and grandchildren of the disappeared
IACHR	Inter-American Commission on Human Rights
IAWC	Irish Argentine White Cross
ICA	Irish Catholic Association
ICAED	International Coalition against Enforced Disappearances
ICRC	International Committee of the Red Cross
IEM	Instituto Espacio para la Memoria (Institute for the Preservation of Memory)
IMF	International Monetary Fund
IWC	Irish White Cross
JEC	Juventud Estudiantil Católica (Catholic Student Youth)
JOC	Juventud Obrera Católica (Catholic Young Workers)
JPM	Juventud Peronista Montonera (Montonero Peronist Youth)
JUC	Juventud Universitaria Católica (Catholic University Youth)
LATF	Latin America Trade Forum
LOD	Ley de Obediencia Debida (Due Obedience Law)
MEDH	Movimiento Ecuménico por los Derechos Humanos (Ecumenical Movement for Human Rights)
MSTM	Movimiento de Sacerdotes para el Tercer Mundo (Movement of Priests for the Third World)
MTP	Movimiento Todos por la Patria (All for the Patria Movement)
MVP	Movimiento Villero Peronista (Villero [Slum] Peronist Movement)
NSD	National Security Doctrine
OAS	Organisation of American States
PCA	Partido Comunista de la Argentina (Argentine Communist Party)
PEN	Poder Ejecutivo Nacional (National Executive Power)
PRG	People's Revolutionary Government

PRN	Proceso de Reorganización Nacional (Process of National Reorganisation. The civilian military government gave themselves that title after the 1976 coup d'état.)
PSA	Partido Socialista Argentino (Argentine Socialist Party)
SAC	Societas Apostolatus Catholici (Society of the Catholic Apostolate, or Pallottines)
SADE	Sociedad Argentina de Escritores (Argentina Society of Writers)
SDA	Students for Democratic Action
SERPAJ	Servicio Paz y Justicia (Justice and Peace Service)
SIDE	Servicio de Inteligencia del Estado (State Intelligence Agency)
SMA	Society of African Missions
SOA	School of the Americas (US)
SVD	Divine Word Missionaries
TDM	Teoría de los dos demonios (Theory of the two demons: a 'theory' which saw Argentina torn between two rival forces, the armed forces and the guerrillas. This 'theory' is widely criticised by human rights organisations.)
TFP	Sociedad Argentina de Defensa de la Tradición, Familia y Propiedad (Argentine Society for the Defence of Tradition, Family and Property)
TSC	*The Southern Cross*
UCR	Unión Cívica Radical (Radical Civil Union, wing of Radical Party)
UCRI	Unión Cívica Radical Intransigente (Intransigent Radical Civic Union)
UCRP	Unión Cívica Radical del Pueblo (People's Radical Civic Union)
UNHCR	United Nations High Commissioner for Refugees
WOLA	Washington Office for Latin America

Foreword

The story of the Irish connection with Argentina is an old one, crafted over the past two centuries by the many sons and daughters of Ireland whose aspirations for a different and better life, as they saw it, brought them to Argentinian shores. Here they established what is truly remarkable: the largest Irish community in the non-English-speaking world. Those who emigrated came mostly from the midlands and County Wexford and arrived in Argentina mainly from 1830 to 1930, with the largest wave taking place from 1850 to 1870.

When Irish immigrants first arrived in Argentina, most could not speak the local language, nor did they know the customs of the country to which they came, yet they adapted quickly, became part of the local community, and many had noteworthy achievements despite their unfamiliar surroundings.

They put their talents, their creativity and their hard work at the service of their new homeland, and they brought to it the gifts of Irish music and dance, custom and tradition, history and legend.

They were, in a sense, Ireland's first ambassadors, and today their many descendants are both proud Argentinians and proud Irish. The modern Irish-Argentine community is estimated at 500,000 to one million, the fifth largest Irish community globally.

Official contacts between Ireland and Argentina date back to as long ago as 1921, when the provisional government, presided over by Éamon de Valera, sent Laurence Ginnell as special envoy to Argentina to seek support for Irish independence. Formal diplomatic relations were established in 1947, and a resident mission was established the following year, making the embassy in Buenos Aires one of our oldest resident missions.

Professor Dermot Keogh's new book, *Ireland and Argentina in the Twentieth Century: Diaspora, Diplomacy, Dictatorship, Catholic Mission and the Falklands Crisis*, is another volume from a fine historian, tracing, as it does, these roots of Irish–Argentinian diplomacy, commencing in the age of revolution and famine, with An Gorta Mór being undoubtedly the most significant push factor in the long history of Irish emigration to Argentina.

Keogh examines the development of diplomatic relations from the Irish civil war to after the fall of President Juan Perón in 1962, before proceeding to investigate the function of missionaries and their use of what Keogh refers to as 'soft power' up to Juan Perón's death in 1974 – that is to say, the role played by Irish Catholic missionaries and later Irish-Argentine missionaries in influencing Argentina's society and culture – thus providing a perspective of 'history from below' which complements the work and the world of diplomacy.

This aspect of the book brought to my mind my official visit, as president of Ireland, to Argentina in 2012. Among the many highlights of the trip was an afternoon spent at a former chapel in Buenos Aires, now named Espacio Patrick Rice in honour of a Cork-born missionary who fought for the cause of human rights and who played a role in the global movement against state terror.

This book of Professor Keogh's – one of the first studies of Ireland and Latin America, with particular reference to Argentina and Irish settlement in that country covering the nineteenth and twentieth centuries – does not shy away from difficult subject matter. Between 1930 and 1976, the armed forces overthrew six governments in Argentina, and the country alternated periods of democracy (1912–30, 1946–55 and 1973–6) with periods of restricted democracy and military rule.

The depiction of a country divided, military dictatorship, repression, and the dark and disturbing phenomenon of the disappeared, including the torture and disappearance of figures such as Fr Patrick Rice and Fátima Cabrera, is well-expounded.

Keogh has unearthed some fascinating historical documents, such as Ambassador Walshe's letter to Dublin on 24 November 1982, which provides a snapshot of a local political world of military rule fast becoming more and more surreal as the major opposition group *Multipartidaria* instigated a mounting challenge to the status quo. In a detailed report covering topics such as Argentine history, politics and society, Walshe stated bluntly, 'This is Kafka in the sun.'

Professor Keogh signals the turning point in Ireland's diplomatic relationship with Argentina, with the denunciation of human rights abuses in Argentina in the late 1970s. The role of Irish-Argentines in the Falklands/ Malvinas war is discussed, as is Ireland's (and Italy's) break with the then-EEC's unified stance on sanctions against Argentina, a significant diplomatic event that almost 'derailed Anglo-Irish relations'.

Keogh concludes with a look to the future as democratic reforms take place following the country's democratic crisis of 2001–2 that resulted from the preceding 'Argentine Great Depression', as the country faces up to the difficult journey of peace and justice, as well as ethical and restored memory and historicity.

There is a profound connection and shared history between Ireland and Latin America, having experienced protracted colonisation, repression and a lengthy struggle for political and economic independence. The role of many Irish in the struggle for independence from Spanish imperialism is well-documented, arriving at the time when empires were declining and the impulse for national independence was emerging.

Some of those Irish and their descendants have been immortalised in the history books of Latin America as key players in the struggle for independence – men such as Admiral William Brown, the father of the Argentine navy, and General Bernardo O'Higgins, liberator of Chile. These are historic figures of whose achievements we, in Ireland, are justifiably proud, and who represent the best of Irishness and the profound contribution of the Irish to the crafting of modern Latin America, a contribution that happily continues and is exemplified in the life and work of such great humanitarians as the late Sally O'Neill-Sanchez.

The Irish–Argentinian story is one that has not received the widespread recognition it deserves. This book is a long overdue and highly informative, fascinating and indeed entertaining read that successfully addresses an important gap in the literature on the Irish diaspora and diplomatic relations in Latin America. Professor Keogh has placed all of those interested in this important connection in his debt.

MICHAEL D. HIGGINS
President of Ireland
7 August 2020

Introduction

Diplomacy is a nomadic profession conducted traditionally beyond the public gaze. Its practitioners are usually career civil servants who advise on the management of 'official relations between the governments of independent states'.[1] Since Sir Ernest Satow compiled that definition in 1917 the world in which this book is set demanded much more from that profession. The modern diplomat has responsibilities which extend beyond inter-state relations as defined in the 1961 Vienna Convention.[2] Since the end of the Second World War multilateral diplomacy has grown in importance, as has the practice of working closely with non-state actors and various non-governmental organisations (NGOs). Today, diplomats are also practitioners of what is termed public diplomacy, facilitating the transnational flow of information and ideas in areas such as education, culture, business and trade.[3]

In his memoirs, the US ambassador William J. Burns stressed that one of the main advantages of serving abroad as a diplomat was 'the chance to see your country through the eyes of others'. After a lifetime in the US diplomatic service, Burns drew the following conclusions about his profession: 'Effective diplomats also embody many qualities, but at their heart is a crucial trinity: judgement, balance and discipline. All three demand a nuanced grasp of history and culture, mastery of foreign languages, hard-nosed facility in negotiations, and the capacity to translate American interests in ways that other governments can see as consistent with their own – or at least in ways that drive home the costs of alternative courses.' Professional diplomats also have an obligation to 'offer their honest judgments, however inconvenient' to policy-makers and government ministers even if, Burns writes, it irritates political leaders with 'their broken-record warnings about potential consequences or pitfalls' which 'can seem terminally prudent'. When diplomacy succeeds, he adds, 'it is usually because of an appreciation of its limits, rather than a passion for stretching beyond them'. Burns writes that 'durable agreements' are rooted in 'mutual self-interest, not one-sided imposition of will'.[4] The value to a state of having a professional diplomatic service has, as Burns indicates with the use of the phrase 'terminally prudent', sometimes gone unappreciated by political leaders bent on immediate action like going to war. Diplomacy, he writes, is a 'tool of first resort' best used to explain policy goals abroad, rooted in candour and transparency and not 'in the tattered robe of untampered exceptionalism'.[5]

Niccolò Machiavelli (1469–1527), the Florentine diplomat, philosopher and historian, did little to burnish the good name of the diplomatic profession in his work *The Prince*, which appeared around 1513. Through the centuries his satirical tract became a vademecum for the power-hungry, earning for its author the undeserved accolade of his very name becoming a byword for intrigue, duplicity and ruthlessness, Sir Henry Wotton claiming in a quip that 'an ambassador is an honest gentleman sent to lie abroad for the good of his country'.[6] Very much of its time, that sixteenth-century witticism is sometimes used mistakenly in a literal way to equate diplomacy with cynicism and raison d'état.[7] That pen picture does not reflect the practice of diplomacy in western democracies as exemplified by William J. Burns, quoted above, and hundreds of other diplomats representing democracies in Ireland, Europe and beyond.

The sudden death of the Argentine ambassador to Ireland, Laura Bernal (64), from COVID-19 on 26 April 2020 deprived the diplomatic profession of one of its leading practitioners. She had a personal wish to be buried in Admiral William Brown's birthplace in Foxford, County Mayo. Arriving in Dublin in 2016, she took up her post 'like a gentle breeze, unassuming and discreet', said the papal nuncio Archbishop Jude Thadeus Okolo in the funeral homily. In his eulogy Peter Hynes, the chief executive of Mayo County Council, reminded the congregation that the service was the 'story of connection across the centuries, a story of friendship which spans the ocean and a story of completion, which started here in Foxford in 1777' with the birth of William Brown, who became a national hero in the wars of independence against Spain and the celebrated founder of the Argentine navy.[8] During her four years in Dublin, Ambassador Bernal strengthened cooperation and stronger educational and inter-cultural exchanges between Ireland and Argentina. She did so without any fuss or ego.

THE IRISH DIPLOMATIC TRADITION

As a background to this volume, it is important to sketch out a brief overview of the evolution of the Irish diplomatic service in its centenary year, 2022. When the Irish Free State was established in 1922, its new diplomatic service was built upon a nucleus of Dáil Éireann diplomats who remained loyal to the new government during the civil war in 1922–3. Choosing to be an exclusively professional service, Irish government policy – with one exception in 1950 – remained consistent.[9] In 1919, at the start of the war of independence, Ireland was, together with the other suppressed nationalities, a David that confronted the Goliath of the British Empire. Ireland won an unprecedented constitutional victory in 1922 as it ceased by agreement to remain an integral part of the Kingdom of Great Britain and Ireland. It enjoyed the status of a British dominion. The original title of Department of Foreign Affairs (a term used by Dáil Éireann between 1919 and 1921) became, in recognition of the primacy of the British Foreign Office, the Department of External Affairs. That name was changed to the Department of Foreign Affairs on 3 March 1971. The Trade portfolio was added on 2 June 2011. It reverted to its old name on 24 September 2020.

In the 1920s and 1930s, Ireland had an uphill battle to have its independent identity and sovereignty recognised internationally, but it overcame that difficulty by becoming an independent voice in world affairs as a member of the British Commonwealth, the League of Nations and later the United Nations after securing membership in 1955. The imperial accretion that the British king had to sign the letters of credence of all heads of Irish legations and of the High Commission in London was also something that caused confusion abroad. That remained the practice until the year before Ireland declared itself a republic in 1949.[10] The first Argentine envoy accredited to Ireland arrived in Dublin in early 1948, carrying with him letters of credence addressed to the president of Ireland, Seán T. O'Kelly. That set a precedent for all future foreign envoys and henceforth the British king or queen ceased to have any role in the diplomatic affairs of the Irish government.

It is sometimes forgotten, however, that Irishmen were still to be found in the British diplomatic and foreign service. David Victor Kelly, who was raised in Ireland, was the junior diplomat in the British mission in Buenos Aires in 1919–20. He returned as ambassador between 1942 and 1946[11] (see Chapters 1 and 2). Sir Cosmo Dugan Patrick Thomas Haskard, an Irishman from west Cork, was the redoubtable governor of the Falklands between 1964 and 1970 and a strong opponent of giving Argentina any role in the governance of those islands. The diplomacy of the Holy See, which has a particular relevance for this volume, posted two Irishmen to Argentina in the 1970s: Patrick Coveney (diocese of Cork) served as first secretary from 1972 until 1976;[12] Kevin Mullen (diocese of Meath) succeeded him as first secretary from 1976 until early 1979. The latter played an important role in denouncing the human rights abuses of the civilian military dictatorship which came to power in March 1976.[13]

The Holy See held a great importance for the young Irish state. The first secretary of the Department of External Affairs, Joseph Walshe, strongly influenced the Irish decision in 1929 to open diplomatic relations with the Vatican at the same time as missions were set up in Paris and Berlin. Walshe, who was secretary between 1922 and 1946, had a strong influence on the formation of the dominant administrative culture of the diplomatic service. Gaining his only diplomatic experience abroad in Paris as a Dáil Éireann diplomat between 1919 and 1921, he was an ultra-Catholic who held strongly to the view that Irish foreign policy should mirror that of the Holy See.[14] When giving instructions to the legation in Vichy France in 1940–1, he directed the Irish envoy Seán Murphy to 'Ask the papal nuncio', so close did he consider the foreign policy interests of Ireland to be to those of the Holy See. When appointed as ambassador to the Holy See in 1946, Walshe became the first diplomat to serve with that rank in the Irish service. He immediately sought to clone Irish foreign policy with that of the Holy See and was unwavering in that approach during his eight years as ambassador in Rome. Contrary to the impression conveyed by the instruction 'Ask the papal nuncio', that rule of thumb was discarded after Walshe's retirement in October 1954. Frank Aiken, the minister for external affairs from 1951 to 1954 and from 1957 to 1969, uncoupled Irish policy at the UN from automatic support for the stance of the Holy See. His successor Patrick Hillery continued that line. The appointment of Garret FitzGerald as foreign minister in 1973 brought about a radical change in Irish–Vatican relations.[15]

In the case of Ireland and Argentina, the papal nuncio is – as in many western countries – the doyen or dean of the diplomatic corps, meaning first in terms of hierarchy.[16] He is both the spokesperson for ambassadors collectively should the occasion ever arise and the official go-between with the foreign ministry. During the civilian military dictatorship between 1976 and 1982, the role of the papal nuncio and that of his staff assumed major importance.

Ireland, as a small power, highly valued its role in multilateral diplomacy. As a neutral during the Second World War – a stance Dublin shared with Argentina – the inter-party government in 1949 refused an invitation to join the North Atlantic Treaty Organisation.[17] A second inter-party government succeeded in joining the United Nations in 1955. Argentina, a founding member of the UN, shared Ireland's anti-imperialist and anti-colonial stance in New York. Buenos Aires came to depend upon an Irish vote to discuss the disputed ownership of the Falkland Islands in an anti-colonial context. That Irish vote was changed in 1976 from support to one of abstention and remained so thereafter.

While Irish heads of mission enjoy considerable freedom of action in their respective embassies, an ambassador is required to implement new policies impartially when a change of government occurs. However, if confronted by an instruction that might have – in her or his view – a damaging impact on the national interest, an ambassador has the option to set out for the minister the advantages and disadvantages of taking the intended course of action. Failing to modify the government's intended course of action, the professional paths remaining to her/him are (1) advocate the policy subject to her/his objections being formally recorded in Iveagh House; (2) request to be reassigned; or (3) resign, the nuclear option. In the Irish diplomatic service, ambassadors have preferred to remain in harness no matter how awkward the situation, the better to seek to modify the damage being done by a rogue policy.[18]

It is also worth noting that Irish governments have rarely recalled an ambassador for consultation as a protest. Since the establishment of the Irish Free State, successive governments have never withdrawn an envoy from an authoritarian or fascist regime. Ireland has maintained unbroken diplomatic relations with states irrespective of the political colouration of the regime in power, be it for example in Franco's Spain,[19] in Salazar's Portugal, in Mussolini's Italy, in Hitler's Germany or during the civilian military dictatorship in Argentina between 1976 and 1983.[20] When confronted by opposition and popular demands to recall an Irish envoy – as occurred in 1937 during the Spanish civil war – Éamon de Valera refused to do so. The Irish envoy remained in Saint-Jean-de-Luz in France.[21] Once the Spanish insurgents became the de facto government, Ireland recognised the new order de jure. In those situations, Irish governments always stressed that diplomatic relations were between states and not governments. The question did not arise during the Cold War, as Ireland did not have diplomatic relations with communist-run states. Ireland exchanged envoys with Moscow in 1973 and with Beijing in 1979.

While the Department of Foreign Affairs did not set out during its early decades to be overwhelmingly male in character, it was no accident that it evolved in that particular way. Put at its simplest, Joseph Walshe had a bias against recruiting women to the service. Virtually none of the women who had played such a vital role in representing Ireland during the war of independence were taken on in 1922. The first competition for cadet/third secretary was held in 1929 and a second in the mid-1930s. None of those recruited were women.[22] The career path after third secretary was first secretary, counsellor, assistant secretary, secretary (or secretary general as it would become known decades later). This last position required the office holder to have served abroad as head of mission and to have had considerable administrative experience.[23]

Finally, a brief note on communications between Buenos Aires and Iveagh House – the headquarters of the Department of Foreign Affairs since 1939. In a time long before mobile phones and social media, Irish diplomats relied on the diplomatic bag to send confidential correspondence to Dublin. When an Irish diplomat feared that the bag might be opened – as was the case during the Peronist period up to 1955 – the practice was to cross over to Uruguay and post confidential reports from there. Irish diplomats, on occasions, also used members of religious orders to carry reports home during military dictatorships. The telephone was used sparingly as it was expensive and not a safe form of communication. During the latter years of the first Perón period, the Irish envoy felt that the legation line was bugged. During the civilian military dictatorship between 1976 and 1983, Irish diplomatic staff operated on the working assumption that there was a tap on the embassy line and that the authorities were eavesdropping on their calls. Cables were sent both in cypher using code dearg (red) and en clair. During the same dictatorship, Irish religious working in Buenos Aires also worked on the assumption that their convent or monastery phones too were being monitored. During the Falklands crisis and war in 1982–3, the Irish embassy used Telex to communicate with Dublin. The staff also made much greater use of the telephone. It was sometimes an advantage for embassy staff to know that the military authorities were listening to the content of a phone conversation with international news media.

IRISH DIPLOMATIC HISTORY AND LATIN AMERICA

While academic work on Irish diplomatic history has grown exponentially since the 1990s, the history of Ireland's relationship with Latin America remains a Cinderella in that expanding field. The turning point in the expansion of writing on Irish diplomatic history occurred in 1986 following the passage that year of the National Archives Act. The then secretary of the Department of Foreign Affairs, Seán Donlon, granted me access to the files of his department in 1987, giving me the opportunity to publish an extensive article on the Irish constitutional revolution[24] and the monograph *Ireland and Europe, 1919– 1948*[25] a year later.[26] The setting up of the Documents on Irish Foreign Policy series in 1997,[27] a project run collaboratively by the Department of Foreign Affairs, the Royal Irish Academy and the National Archives of Ireland under the direction of Michael Kennedy, has resulted in the publication of twelve volumes of selected documents covering the period 1919–61.[28] That project has helped greatly to advance study in that area with the appearance of numerous monographs and articles.[29] With a number of significant omissions,[30] the Cambridge *Dictionary of Irish Biography* chronicles the lives of many of the prominent Irish diplomats, but the number of extended biographies of Irish diplomats remains quite small in 2022.[31]

A new generation of graduates and undergraduates in UCC and in other universities from the 1990s wrote theses based on Irish primary sources. Among those researchers I taught and supervised who pioneered the field of international and diplomatic history were Mervyn O'Driscoll,[32] Paula Wylie,[33] Mark Hull,[34] Maurice Fitzgerald,[35] Aengus Nolan,[36] Micheál Martin,[37] Kevin McCarthy,[38] David Ryan[39] and Robert McNamara.[40] Those scholars, together with many others, wrote on a variety of topics, including church–state relations in Central and Latin America.[41] The expansion of Irish diplomatic history was paralleled in many other universities in Ireland and abroad. Besides those monographs mentioned above, the following scholars – and this is not an exhaustive list – have helped open up the study of Irish diplomatic history during the past twenty-five years: I single out here the work by Kate O'Malley on Ireland and India,[42] Kevin O'Sullivan on Ireland and Africa,[43] Bernadette Whelan[44] and Francis M. Carroll on Ireland and the United States,[45] and Michael Kennedy on Ireland, Anglo-Irish relations, the League of Nations and the UN.[46] Eunan O'Halpin's work on Anglo-Irish relations and on Irish and British intelligence services,[47] Rory Miller's studies on Ireland and the Middle East,[48] and Filipe Ribeiro de Meneses on Ireland and Salazar and on Portuguese Africa[49] must also be included. Added to the list should be the scholarship on Ireland and Australia,[50] New Zealand,[51] and South Africa.[52]

In 2010, Dr Kevin O'Sullivan published a review essay entitled 'Irish Diplomatic History in the Twenty-First Century: After the gold rush'.[53] The title, rather than the text of the article itself, is open to misinterpretation. The pace of the take-up of the newly opened Irish archives differed from history school to history school. The pace at which those new Irish archives were consulted was more of a saunter than a frenetic Klondike 'gold rush'. After nearly thirty years of access to the archives of the Department of Foreign Affairs, Irish diplomatic history has gradually been brought up to a level of professionalism matching the work of scholars internationally. Among the topics covered are Irish relations with countries in Europe, the United States, Canada, Russia, China, South Africa, Australia and New Zealand. Despite the progress made, there is one blinding omission involving some thirty countries.

With few exceptions, Latin America and the Caribbean, as I have said above, remains the Cinderella region of Irish diplomatic and foreign policy studies. In 1991, Peadar Kirby published a pioneering study, *Ireland and Latin*

America: Links and Lessons.[54] In his monograph on the League of Nations, Michael Kennedy provides an overview of Ireland and the Chaco War in the 1930s. He also wrote an article on Dáil Éireann diplomacy in Latin America, 1919–23.[55] Paul Hand wrote a thesis on Irish diplomatic relations with Argentina during the time of Juan Domingo Perón, 1948–55.[56] Barry Whelan's biographical study of Ambassador Leopold Kerney has a welcome section on his mission to Argentina in 1947.[57] In 2016, I published in Spanish *La independencia de Irlanda: La Conexión Argentina*. Owen McGee's *A History of Ireland in International Relations*, published in 2020, is a welcome addition to the growing number of survey volumes on Irish foreign policy. There are sixteen references in his index under South America and four under Argentina.[58] In contrast, almost all surveys of Ireland in the twentieth century, including my own, neglect to refer to Latin America.[59] The collection of scholarly essays in *The Cambridge History of Ireland* (vol. IV) provides little detail on Ireland and Latin America or on the Irish in Argentina.[60]

The elegantly produced and well-researched *Ireland: A Voice among the Nations* is an exception in the existing literature.[61] A carefully crafted synthesis of the history of Irish foreign policy published in 2019 provides more entries on the countries of Latin America than any other historical survey in print. While the index makes no reference to 'Latin America' or 'South America', there are entries for Argentina and for the Falklands (Malvinas) War, for Cuba and the Cuban missile crisis, for Brazil and São Paulo, for Mexico, Chile and Colombia. However, I found no reference to any of the Irish envoys who served in Buenos Aires from the setting up of the legation in 1947–8 to the present day, Argentina being the only Irish mission south of the Rio Grande until 1999.[62]

WRITINGS ON THE IRISH IN NINETEENTH- AND TWENTIETH-CENTURY LATIN AMERICA

While Irish diplomatic and general history makes little reference to Latin America, there has been a flowering of interdisciplinary scholarship over the past two decades on the Irish in the region. The earlier writings focused on the Latin American wars of independence in the early nineteenth century and the role of the Irish in those campaigns – Admiral William (Guillermo) Brown[63] (1777–1857),[64] Daniel Florence O'Leary[65] (1801–54),[66] Gen. Juan MacKenna[67] and John Thomond O'Brien (1786–1861),[68] each of whom played an important role in the struggle which led to the founding of the republics of Argentina,

Venezuela, Bolivia, Colombia, Ecuador, Peru and Panama. Tim Fanning, a member of a new generation of Irish historians, has provided a welcome overview of Ireland and Latin American independence for the latter part of the nineteenth century in *Paisanos*, published in Spanish and English in 2016.[69] He has also written a monograph on John Thomond O'Brien, soldier, bullfighter, adventurer and entrepreneur, who was named Uruguayan consul general to the United Kingdom in 1834, a post he held until his death.[70] His remains were returned to Buenos Aires in 1938, where he received a state funeral and was buried in Recoleta Cemetery.[71]

Many disciplines besides history have contributed to the recent academic work on the Irish in Argentina and Latin America, namely geography, folklore, comparative literature, sociology, anthropology, religious studies and journalism. Dr Margaret Brehony wrote a doctoral thesis in NUIG in 2012 on 'Irish Migration to Cuba, 1835–1845: Empire, Ethnicity, Slavery and "Free Labour".[72] In 2018, Prof. Gabriela McEvoy published *La Experiencia Invisible: Inmigrantes Irlandeses en el Perú*,[73] a pioneering study which might be read in conjunction with the earlier work of Prof. Donald Akenson and President Michael D. Higgins, who wrote on the Irish in Montserrat in the Caribbean.[74] In 1994, the historical geographer Patrick McKenna made an important academic contribution with his MA thesis 'Nineteenth-Century Irish Emigration to, and Settlement in, Argentina'.[75] In 2006, Dr Mary Harris published a survey of Irish historical writings on Latin America. It remains an important point of departure for any scholar working in the area.[76] Regarding the Irish in Argentina, Dr Edmundo Murray, Professor Laura Izarra and Dr Juan José Delaney have enriched our understanding of the area. Together with his online sources, Murray's books on the Irish in Argentina are among the earliest in the field.[77] Professor Laura Izarra is both a pioneer in that historical field and also an authority on modern Irish literature.[78] She was the founding editor in 1999 of the interdisciplinary ABEI – the *Brazilian Journal of Irish Studies*.[79] Dr Juan José Delaney is a novelist, historian and expert on Argentine literature and on Irish Argentina.[80] The late Argentine journalist Andrew Graham-Yooll[81] made an important historical contribution in both his *The Forgotten Colony: A History of the English-speaking Communities in Argentina* and *A State of Fear: Memories of Argentina's Nightmare*.[82] Juan Carlos Korol and Hilda Sábato published a comprehensive study in 1981 of Irish emigration to Argentina. Forty years later, their work remains the model on which to base future studies, the gold standard yet to be superseded.[83] The genealogist Eduardo A. Coghlan has produced a detailed book on Irish family names in Argentina.[84]

Dr Gertrude Cotter's highly original 1989 MA on 'Britain and Perón's Argentina, 1946–1955' alerted me to the richness of this subject.[85] In recent years, a generation of younger scholars have published important new studies, namely María Eugenia Cruset,[86] Helen Kelly, Claire Healy, Sarah O'Brien,[87] Patrick Speight and Sinéad Wall.[88] Sinéad Wall has examined the narratives, written in 1845, 1900 and 1945, of three members of the Irish diaspora community in Argentina.[89] Sarah O'Brien's work opens up a discussion on the place of memory in the reconstruction of identity and the tension between the imagined and the historical. Helen Kelly's monograph is a fine historical study of Irish *Ingleses* in Argentina.[90] Claire Healy wrote an important thesis on migration to Buenos Aires between 1776 and 1890 which she kindly made available to me.[91] Dr Healy has also written on the Chilean refugees who came to Ireland in the 1970s.[92] Patrick Speight, whose work was published in 2019,[93] has written an original and challenging examination of Peronism and the recent history of Irish Argentina.[94]

My study, while drawing on the scholarship listed above, attempts to fill the gap in the study of Irish diplomatic history regarding Irish–Argentine diplomatic relations. Tracing Irish–Argentine relations from the nineteenth to the twenty-first century, this both complements my *La Independencia de Irlanda: La conexión Argentina* and extends the range of study to include all of the twentieth century.[95] This new work is a history of Ireland *and* Argentina intertwined with the complementary theme of the Irish *in* Argentina. Divided into eight chapters, the volume remains first and foremost a diplomatic history – a study of Irish foreign policy in a comparative transnational context. Throughout the nineteenth and early twentieth centuries, British envoys in Buenos Aires had responsibility for taking care of the consular needs of the immigrant Irish, many of whom arrived in the country without means to support themselves. That was particularly the case following the arrival of the *Dresden* in 1889 with over 1,400 Irish aboard. After the 1916 Rising and the posting of the Dáil Éireann envoys Eamonn Bulfin (arrived in May 1919) and Laurence Ginnell (arrived in July 1921), many Irish-Argentines stood in solidarity with those fighting for Irish independence in the 'mother country'. They welcomed the setting up of the Irish Free State and lobbied to establish diplomatic relations between the two countries. I will provide evidence to show that de Valera felt so heavily indebted to Irish-Argentines for their support for the nationalist cause that he gave a commitment in writing in 1935 to open a diplomatic mission in Buenos Aires. That pledge was fulfilled in 1947 when Argentina was chosen for what turned out to be Ireland's sole resident diplomatic mission in Latin America until an embassy was opened in Mexico in 1999. While that diplomatic relationship with Argentina has remained unbroken to the present day, I will argue that the opening of that legation was not part of a foreign policy strategy to develop an Irish presence in Latin America. It remained as something of an outlier – with two exceptions – for successive Irish foreign ministers and senior officials in Iveagh House through the 1950s and 1960s. The exceptions were: (1) church burnings in 1955 and the fall of Juan Domingo Perón, and (2) at the UN where, between 1957 and 1969, the minister for external affairs Frank Aiken supported resolutions to debate the Falklands/Malvinas in the context of a discourse on colonialism. The minister for foreign affairs Garret FitzGerald changed Ireland's vote from support to abstention in 1976 influenced by the kidnapping, torture and imprisonment of an Irish citizen.

Besides being an analysis of Irish diplomacy, this book has an important interrelated theme which examines the changing role of Irish Catholic male and female missionaries, a number of whose orders have operated in Argentina since the middle of the nineteenth century. This I refer to as 'Irish soft power'. First serving as chaplains and teachers to the immigrant Irish community, members of the Passionist and Pallottine orders, together with Irish Sisters of Mercy and other orders of Irish nuns, set up primary and secondary schools for the education of their countrymen and women. They built schools and churches when establishing their permanent footprint in Argentina. While that missionary focus lasted up to the mid-1960s, a new cohort of post-Vatican II missionaries began to minister to communities, many with no connections whatsoever to Irish Argentina. Opting for a life dedicated to the service of the poor, many Irish male and female missionaries ran the risk of being denounced as 'communists' and 'Marxists', particularly during the civilian military dictatorship in Argentina from 1976 to 1983. I integrate in my analysis throughout the book material found in ecclesiastical diocesan archives and individual religious orders with findings in personal papers and the foreign ministries of Ireland, the Holy See, Britain, Canada, the United States and Argentina. The Irish embassy, staffed by Ambassador Wilfred Lennon and Justin Harman, helped save the life of Patrick Rice in 1976 after he was kidnapped, tortured and imprisoned. The Irish embassy in Buenos Aires became a central part of the foreign policy-making process during the Falklands/Malvinas war in 1982 as did the voice of many Irish-Argentines. The volume ends with an analysis of the fall of the civilian military dictatorship and the opening of four Irish embassies in Latin America (Mexico, Brazil, Chile and Colombia).

The structure of this book is as follows. Divided into eight chapters, the mainly chronological analysis begins with a study of the arrival of the Irish in nineteenth-century Argentina, the role of Irish missionaries, the construction of churches and schools, and hospitals and refuges. Timothy Joseph Horan, who was head of mission in Buenos Aires between 1955 and 1958, wrote an extensive report which I use to frame the first chapter and to reconstruct the history of Irish emigration to Argentina while, at the same time, drawing out the underlying assumptions on which his analysis is based. Entitled 'Imagining Argentina', this chapter traces the settlement there of Irish adventurers, soldiers, shepherds, farm labourers, governesses, engineers, teachers, doctors, nurses, etc. This book identifies the significant contribution made by many Irish-Argentines to their adopted country while simultaneously retaining close political and cultural ties to Ireland. Many Irish-Argentines, following the lead of the writer and journalist William Bulfin, supported the leaders of radical Irish nationalism from the founding of the Gaelic League and Sinn Féin to the 1916 Rising and the political and military revolution between 1919 and 1922 when Eamonn Bulfin, the son of William, served as an Irish envoy. He was responsible for organising demonstrations in response to the death of the lord mayor of Cork, Terence MacSwiney. The mobilisation of Irish-Argentines to provide relief funds for Ireland through a local branch of the Irish White Cross is examined, as is also the failed Irish bond drive organised by the Dáil Éireann envoy Laurence Ginnell. Both Ginnell and Bulfin opposed the treaty. Their respective diplomatic missions, as shown in Chapter 1, ended in disarray and confusion, both returning to Ireland disillusioned by the split in the nationalist movement.

Chapter 2 traces the engagement of Irish-Argentines from 1923 to the end of the 1950s with the 'motherland'. Many succeeded in remaining close to the government of the Irish Free State and to Éamon de Valera, who led the political opposition until his election as president of the Executive Council in early 1932. Mgr Santiago Ussher, who was an admirer of de Valera, led a delegation to Dublin in 1932 to participate in the Eucharistic Congress. Usually depicted by historians as a purely religious event, I argue that it already had a very strong political dimension. De Valera used the occasion to thank Ussher and other clergy from different parts of the world for their support during the war of independence and when he was in the political wilderness after the civil war. Many clergy supported the foundation of Fianna Fáil in 1926 and de Valera's decision to bring his supporters into the Dáil in 1927. When the Argentine delegation arrived in Dublin in 1932, de Valera met Ussher and his party, inviting them to all the public events. The Argentines also had a meeting with

Sinéad Bean de Valera, Seán T. O'Kelly and the secretary of the Department of External Affairs Joseph Walshe. The lord mayor of Dublin, Alfie Byrne, gave them a civic reception. This chapter continues with a reconstruction of Irish participation in the Eucharistic Congress in Buenos Aires in 1934. Ussher was among those Irish-Argentines who hosted the Irish delegation of bishops and priests. As in Dublin in 1932, there was a political dimension to the Eucharistic Congress in Buenos Aires. Ussher and other leading Irish-Argentines lobbied the Irish delegates to encourage de Valera to open diplomatic relations with Argentina. This book establishes that the outcome was that de Valera gave Ussher a written commitment in 1935 that Ireland would open a legation with Argentina when opportune to do so. Those plans reached a successful outcome in 1947–8. With an Irish diplomat, Matthew Murphy, resident in Buenos Aires throughout the period when Juan Domingo Perón was in power, Dublin received detailed reports hostile in nature to the Argentine government. The chapter concludes with the overthrow of Perón. Irish clergy and Irish-Argentines, in the main, welcomed the setting up of the military dictatorship which followed.

Chapter 3 examines the impact of the Cuban revolution on the politics of Latin America and the impetus it gave to nascent radical movements in many countries in the region, including Argentina where, by the end of the 1960s, two guerrilla bands posed a serious challenge to a series of military dictatorships. Irish diplomats tracked the rise and fall of democracy from 1966 up to the return of Juan Domingo Perón in 1973. Early in the 1960s, Ireland and Argentina raised the status of their respective missions to that of embassy. This chapter traces the foundation of the Federation of Irish-Argentine Societies and the sending of a delegation to Dublin to attend the fiftieth anniversary commemorations of the 1916 Easter Rising while, at the same time, Irish-Argentines at home participated in ceremonies on 9 July 1966 to mark the 150th anniversary of Argentine independence. This chapter also traces the work of the chargé Bernard Davenport and his analysis of the enduring strength of Peronism in anticipation of Perón's return to Argentina. He also provided Iveagh House with an analysis of the Chilean coup in December 1973 and its impact on Latin America. A friend of the new minister for foreign affairs, Garret FitzGerald, Davenport received praise from both him and the secretary of his department for the quality of his political and economic reporting. This chapter also analyses the arrival of new Irish Catholic male and female missionaries to Argentina who had a very different pastoral outlook from the previous generation.

Chapter 4 reviews the work of the Irish ambassador Wilfred Lennon in 1974 during Perón's years in power, his death and the chaotic rule of his widow, Isabel. As the civil war within Peronism became more violent, I provide a case study tracing the early life of Fátima Cabrera, her work with Fr Carlos Mugica in Villa 31, his friendliness with her family and her attendance at his funeral. This excursion into composing a history from below reveals the life of a militant Peronist and that of her partner, their participation in popular protest and the violent repression of such protests. This chapter also describes how, in 1975, two Irishmen, Justin Harman and Mgr Kevin Mullen, were posted to Buenos Aires, to serve in the Irish embassy and in the apostolic nunciature respectively. Harman, in the absence of the ambassador, who was in Ireland for over seven months, reported on the civil unrest in the wake of the death of Juan Perón, the disorder within Isabel Perón's fractious government and the civil war between different factions in that movement. The military coup d'état on 24 March 1976 changed the course of Argentine history as the new rulers set out to destroy resistance to the change of government through a concerted campaign of kidnappings, torture in clandestine centres of detention nationwide and systematic extrajudicial killings. Among the worst atrocities, only three months after the takeover, was the murder of five Pallottines, three priests and two seminarians, on 4 July 1976, in their Belgrano monastery. As two of the priests were Irish-Argentines and the third had studied in Ireland, the reaction to the killings within the local Irish community and in Mercedes in the camp is examined in detail.

Chapter 5 focuses on the work of Patrick Rice in the wake of the Pallottine massacre. Together with one of his confrères, Rice went to La Rioja to investigate the death of his friend Bishop Enrique Angelelli, who died on 4 August 1976 when his truck was forced off the road. Rice, following his inquiries and concluding that Angelelli had been murdered, published his report clandestinely in Argentina. A copy was smuggled out to London where it was published by the Catholic Institute for International Relations (CIIR). The armed forces had identified Rice as a person of interest two years before. When the authorities identified him as one of the authors of the report, he was put on their most wanted list. On 11 October 1976, he was kidnapped by police together with a catechist, Fátima Cabrera. This chapter chronicles their sufferings, beatings, sleep deprivation, waterboarding and electric shock with the *picana* or cattle prod. It reconstructs the efforts mounted by Justin Harman and Wilfred Lennon to locate Rice as they conducted an international media campaign to increase the pressure on the Argentine government to ensure that he was not murdered. The authorities, as a consequence of the international public exposure, were forced to admit that the priest was in their custody and the ambassador and third secretary were allowed to see him in central police headquarters. Imprisoned until early December 1976, he was deported to London. Cabrera remained in jail until January 1979. She was placed, when released, under house arrest until the fall of the dictatorship in 1983.

Chapter 6 is divided into two parts. Part one examines the human rights work of Mgr Kevin Mullen, first secretary at the papal nunciature in Buenos Aires, and his efforts to hold the military to account for the disappearances and torture and the assassinations. This section also traces the founding of the Mothers of the Plaza de Mayo, and the increase in the number of disappearances, among them members of the Little Brothers of Charles de Foucauld, Professor Emilio Mignone's daughter Mónica, two Jesuit priests, two French nuns, and leading members of the Mothers of the Plaza de Mayo, and the jailing of the journalists Jacobo Timerman and the editor of the *Buenos Aires Herald*, Robert Cox. Against the background of mass disappearances and jailings in Argentina, the second part of the chapter documents Rice's campaign to persuade the Irish government to grant a visa to Fátima Cabrera. With what was described in the first part of this chapter in mind, the narrative reconstructs the division within the Department of Foreign Affairs over whether or not she should be granted a visa. The Political Division, together with the support of two foreign ministers, were in favour of granting a visa. There was opposition to that recommendation from the consular section and from the Department of Justice. This chapter concludes with an analysis of a contradiction in Irish government policy towards Argentina under dictatorship. The Department of Industry and Commerce granted an Irish company a licence to export armoured personnel carriers to the federal police. A company representative visited Buenos Aires in 1978 to hold discussions with members of the armed forces. The delegate visited the Irish embassy on two occasions. This study found no evidence to suggest that those sales went through, but the possibility of such a sale had serious professional consequences for the first secretary at the nunciature, Kevin Mullen. At a social event, senior members of the military attempted to humiliate him by pointing out that, while he always spoke about attacks on human rights in Argentina, the Irish government was allegedly helping the Argentine military to learn the latest techniques in counterinsurgency. I found no evidence to substantiate that claim. It was a sinister attempt to intimidate Mullen in the wake of the abduction and murder of an Argentine woman diplomat. The final section of this chapter reviews Rice's lobbying in Washington DC to expose what was happening in Argentina and his confrontations with the staff of the Argentine embassy and with Admiral Massera himself – a central figure in the politics of repression in the country.

Chapter 7 analyses the strength of Argentine nationalism and the place of the Falklands/Malvinas in that ideology. It reviews Irish-Argentine support for the historical claim to sovereignty over those islands – support which was made explicit following the Argentine occupation of the Falklands/Malvinas on 2 April 1982. This was a critical moment in the history of the Irish embassy in Buenos Aires as it sought to advise the government on the depth of nationalist feeling among Irish-Argentines, many joining in the call for the 'return' of the islands. They failed to understand how, throughout April 1982, an Irish government could, as a member of the Security Council, support the 'anti-Argentine' UN Resolution 502 together with EEC-imposed sanctions. Not stopping at expressing mere outrage to the local embassy, Irish-Argentines lobbied the Irish government directly, encouraging it to change its perceived pro-British stance on the conflict in the South Atlantic. With the Irish foreign policy volte face towards the conflict in early May, Dublin called for an immediate meeting of the Security Council and, in the middle of the month, withdrew from EEC sanctions. Many Irish-Argentines and the Argentine government were delighted with that radical 'change' in policy, interpreting it mistakenly as an endorsement of a pro-Argentine position. The Argentine government also took the view that Ireland was a supporter of its occupation of the islands – a view with which the Irish ambassador did not agree but chose to maintain silence. That mistaken perception advantaged Irish economic interests and opened the door to the expansion of Irish exports in the country. This analysis sets the crisis within the overarching context of Anglo-Irish relations. It details Dublin's engagement in the deliberations over sanctions renewal in the EEC and, as a member of the Security Council, its role at the UN.

Chapter 8 examines the surreal atmosphere in Buenos Aires at the end of the civilian military government in late 1982–3 characterised in part by the delusional and self-induced amnesia of the hardline Admiral Massera, who sought to reinvent himself as the new Perón with an ambition to win a presidential election. The chapter outlines the transition to democracy and the struggle for restorative justice, concluding with an examination of the reasons for the growing importance for Ireland of Latin America in the twenty-first century with the opening of new embassies in Brazil, Chile and Colombia.

While the ground covered in this monograph is wide-ranging, I have not included an analysis of the role in Latin America played by Irish Protestants.

I enthusiastically encourage other academics to explore this important area, together with the study of the roles played by the Society of Friends and Jehovah's Witnesses.[96] I am also reminded of the yawning gap in the scholarship on the history of Irish women in Argentina from the period of settlement in the nineteenth century to the end of the twentieth century. The tragic case of Camila O'Gorman, who was executed with her partner by the dictator Juan Manuel de Rosas in 1848, is quite well documented.[97] In neighbouring Paraguay, the life and times of Eliza Lynch is the subject of historical studies, works of fiction and a film.[98] Susan Wilkinson and Carolina Barry have done pioneering work on women in medicine in Argentina.[99] The genderised view of history may be changing, but not fast enough, in my opinion. The field is open to study the role of women teachers, governesses, nurses, nuns, farmers, domestics, doctors and other professionals. When reviewing the role of women in the Irish diplomatic service, it took many decades before the glass ceiling was cracked if not finally broken. Today women have served as ambassadors in Paris, Washington, and the UN, while Jacqueline O'Halloran was the first woman to be appointed to the diplomatic staff of the Irish embassy in Buenos Aires. She served there as third secretary between July 1987 and July 1991 and returned as ambassador on 1 June 2018. Paula Slattery set a precedent when she became the first woman ambassador to Argentina. She served between January 2000 and August 2004. Philomena Murnaghan held the position as ambassador between October 2006 and August 2010.

Finally, while working during my academic career of over forty years on various topics in diplomatic history, I acknowledge the major influence of two academics on my career: firstly, Joseph Lee gave me my first academic post in 1980 and we worked together closely for over twenty years until he took up a position in 2002 as director of Glucksman House, New York University. Secondly, the late Walter LaFeber, Cornell University, gave me great encouragement to tackle difficult subjects which became a series of books.

In my personal experience, the following diplomats were, during my professional life, exemplars of best practice of Irish diplomacy with whom I had contact during the writing of this book: ambassadors Art Agnew, Ted Barrington, Frank Cogan, Bernard Davenport, Seán Donlon, Thelma Doran, Noel Dorr, Justin Harman, Michael Lillis, Philip McDonagh, James McIntyre, Patrick McKernan, Colm Ó Floinn, Jackie O'Halloran, Philomena Murnaghan, Kenneth Thompson and Paula Slattery.

CHAPTER ONE

Imagining Argentina and the Origins of Irish Diplomacy in an Age of Revolution

The immigrants seemed to be losing some of their misery as they moved in the soft morning air and stared at the beautiful countryside ... 'Here,' he said, 'we shall work our own land, care for our own animals, and eat bread made from our own wheat.'[1]

On 22 July 1958, the Irish chargé d'affaires to Argentina, Timothy Joseph Horan,[2] was at work in the Irish legation office on the fourth floor of Avenida Santa Fe 782 in Buenos Aires putting the final touches to a twenty-one-page report entitled 'The Irish in Argentina'.[3] The only Irish diplomat posted south of Washington DC and San Francisco, he felt he was writing in less-than-ideal working conditions.[4] Horan was eager to share with his superiors in Iveagh House (headquarters of the Department of External Affairs) and with the minister for external affairs, Frank Aiken, the professional drawbacks of having 'no colleague with whom to discuss and check the opinions' in his report. He added that, as Matthew Murphy had opened the legation only in 1947,[5] there was 'no fund of accumulated knowledge on which he could draw' and 'each new arrival here must, so to speak, make his own way and learn to see things for himself, without the benefit of tutoring from a colleague who has been here longer than himself'.[6] Isolating another professional shortcoming of his situation, he highlighted that his report was based almost exclusively on his personal observations of Irish-Argentines who lived in the federal capital and in the surrounding camp – an abbreviation for the Spanish *campo* or countryside to be found in the Irish-Argentine sociolect.[7] Horan was conscious that he was living in both a new and a vast country. Argentina, together with the other new republics in Latin America, had come into existence in the early decades of the nineteenth century.[8] After the revolutionary generation had driven out the Spanish crown and defeated invading British armies, it became ultimately a unitary state 1,400 kilometres wide with a coastline of 4,989 kilometres, covering a total area of 2,766,890 square kilometres. This did not include the Falkland Islands, which were under British control since 1833. The island of Ireland is 280 kilometres at its widest and 486 kilometres at its longest, occupying 84,431 square kilometres. Limited as his experience and travels might have been in the country,[9] Horan proved to be an acerbic and self-confident observer: 'One may disagree with them [his views] but they are based on my interpretation of the facts as I see them,' he told senior management in Iveagh House.[10]

In the following fifty years, no other Irish diplomat attempted to cover in a single report so extensive a survey of Argentine history and of the arrival and settlement of the Irish in that country.[11] Horan's description of state-building echoed what the sociologist Zygmunt Bauman has termed 'the etiological myth deeply entrenched in the self-consciousness of our Western society' and rooted in 'the morally elevating story of humanity emerging from pre-social barbarity'.[12] While Horan deconstructed many myths in his analysis of the stories of origin, he did not question the state policy of enforced land 'enclosures' throughout the nineteenth century. The *caudillo* (military strongman) Juan Manuel Rosas led the way from 1829 to 1852 during his authoritarian reign. Horan noted that the later government campaigns of conquest began in 1877 for control of '*the desert* as the inhospitable and uncharted interior was called'.[13] Led by the minister for war and navy, Julio Argentino Roca Paz, he extended the 'frontiers' in the south, building forts and a fortified ditch or *zanja* of 374 kilometres. Arthur Pageitt Greene, an Irish doctor working around Mercedes, made reference in his memoir to 'unfortunate Indians', revealing a humanistic side to his character which was not widely shared by his contemporaries. He was also honest enough to state that while he was alive to the recent bloody history of the conquest of the interior of the country, he was also buying confiscated Indian land.[14] Roca Paz continued that conquest when he served as president of Argentina from 1880 to 1886. Horan judged that the campaign of conquest and settlement with immigrants from Europe had been 'completely successful'.[15]

His main sources supporting that thesis and for tracing the history of the Irish in Argentina were two books: Thomas Murray's *The Story of the Irish in Argentina* (1919) and Mgr Santiago Ussher's tome on the life of the Irish Dominican missionary Fr Anthony Dominic Fahy.[16] Published in Spanish in 1951 and brought out shortly afterwards in an English edition, Ussher wrote that in the 1840s the diocese of Buenos Aires contained the city of that name together with 'all the unexplored territory generally known as the Pampa and Patagonia, down to the southern extreme of the continent including the Malvinas or Falkland Islands'. That territory, he wrote, was divided into two parts, 'one occupied by the Christians, the other by the Indians'[17] of the Mapuche, Guarani, Qom, Chané, Huarpe, Wichí communities.[18] Ussher explained further: 'The Christians had occupied only a narrow strip running from the Atlantic up along the south-western banks of River Plate and River Paraná. The remainder was still the domain of the aboriginal Patagonian tribes, who fiercely resisted the encroachments of the advancing Europeans ... Such civilisation as there was was to be found in the cities and towns and a small area round about them.'[19] Ussher also noted that there was a line of forts between the two territories 'to defend the white population and their property from the frequent raids of the roving savages'. He gave as examples the following forts – 'Guardia del Monte, Guardia de Luján, Fortín de Areco and Salto, now Monte, Mercedes, Carmen and Salto'[20] – all towns in or around which the Irish would settle.

Influenced perhaps by the doctrine of manifest destiny and the romantic myths of 'winning' the West while posted to the US,[21] Horan, echoing the official Argentine narrative for seizing territory, wrote in his report: 'The interior was inhabited by tribes of Indians, primitives, warlike and completely savage. These Indians continued to be a menace to the settlers of the new state through more than half the nineteenth century, and since they proved completely recalcitrant to all civilising influences, the Argentine Government decided to *liquidate* them.'[22] Ussher and Horan held a common position on one of the great debates in nineteenth-century Argentine politics, literature and the arts – the Argentine republic had, by the end of the nineteenth century, journeyed from Spanish colonial and Indian barbarism to civilisation.

Horan, had he searched, would have had a wide range of sources to draw upon on that theme, including Esteban Echeverría's poem 'La Cautiva', which was published in 1837. This concerned the escape of a white couple, Brián and María, from a band of Mapuche. The poem opens with a portrayal of the barbarism of the Indians, engaging in an orgy of celebrations as they fight to determine who among them will have the privilege of taking the decapitated heads of white men from their lances and placing them into a large cooking pot.

> They carry human heads,
> Whose inflamed eyes
> Still breathe fury.[23]

1.1 Detail from Ángel della Valle's *La Vuelta del Malón* (*The Return of the Raiding Party*)

In 1845, Domingo Faustino Sarmiento published *Facundo o Civilización y Barbarie en las Pampas Argentinas*, a dystopian novel on the theme of barbarism defeating a receding civilisation.[24] In 1880, the Uruguayan artist Juan Manuel Blanes (1830–1901) painted *La Cautiva*, in which he portrayed a male Indian captor in his village looking down at a kneeling white woman naked from the waist up. Another of his works presents 'the captive' woman weeping and undone as she is freed by her captors. A third painting in the series shows her 'disgraced' and 'fallen', at a locked door pleading for readmission to her former home.[25] Such archetypal white fears were also vividly portrayed in Ángel della Valle's painting *The Return of the Raiding Party* or *La Vuelta del Malón*, which hangs in the Museo Nacional de Bellas Artes in Buenos Artes.[26] A tribal leader on horseback holds a semi-naked, half-faint white woman, amid a group of half-crazed Indians carrying two severed heads along with sacred vestments and other booty taken from a sacked estancia and chapel which has been left in flames in the background of the painting. Members of the raiding party triumphantly wave a crucifix, a monstrance, a chalice and a thurible. This painting depicted such a terrifying scene on a grand scale. It was put on display in Buenos Aires in 1892 and sent to the World's Fair in Chicago that year.

These paintings are the visual expression of the official orthodoxy that the indigenous Indians were 'primitives, warlike and completely savage'. The corollary of that view was that Horan believed that European immigrants provided Argentina with 'a far superior type of person to the semi-barbarous nomad, more Indian than Latin, who then dwelt on the Argentine plains, and what contact the first Irish had with him (indigenous) must not have encouraged closer association'.[27] Horan may have been influenced by Frederick Turner's thesis of the frontier, first articulated in the US in 1893.[28] It argued that the 'tide of empire moved forward [in the US] to win a continent from a raw and hostile wilderness'. Out of that constant expansion westwards demanding constant readjustment from the pioneers came the indefinable 'Americanisation'.[29] The Irish envoy's view of 'how very new this country is' breezily swept to one side centuries of Latin American history before and after the Spanish conquest; for Horan, 'history' began with independence and with the Europeanisation of Argentina based on the successful expansion of the country's immigrant policy.[30] Compared to his favourable evaluation of industrious European immigrants, Horan was critical of both indigenous culture and the mythical nomadic gaucho who, like the Indians, stood between Argentina and 'modernisation'. Neither José Hernández's *Martín Fierro*[31] (1872) nor Ricardo Güiraldes' *Don Segundo Sombra* (1926) changed Horan's mind about the gaucho's unreliability: 'Though as a class the gaucho is disappearing, he is still there and he still makes a bad employee. His temperament is not suited to regular work.'[32] That view was also shared by the writer William Bulfin, who claimed that the gaucho was '*not* the Argentine equivalent of the cowboy of Wyoming and Montana ... He was merely the typical inhabitant of the Argentine plains, of mixed Spanish and Indian blood' who would 'work for nobody'.[33] By the end of the nineteenth century, the Indian and the gaucho had been removed from the path of the all-conquering 'modernising' forces in Argentina – centralised government, military conquest, economic liberalism and progress based on the industry of immigrants from Europe and elsewhere.

Between 1820 and 1932, some 6.5 million European immigrants arrived in Argentina, while 32.5 million landed in the United States.[34] Argentine immigration policy, particularly from the 1870s, had a distinct preference for migrants from Europe over those from neighbouring countries in Latin America. Under President Miguel Juárez Celman (in office 1886–90) immigration from Europe increased from 51,503 in 1882 to 155,632 in 1888 and 260,909 by 1889.[35] Between 1870, when the population of the country was below two million, and 1914, two and a half million arrived and more than half of those settled in the countryside. Horan provided a different set of figures for immigration. He reported that the Argentine population rose from 3 to 7.8 million, of which one-third was foreign-born, according to the censuses of 1895 and 1914. Some 40 per cent of the increased population was of Italian immigrant stock, followed by Spanish, French, Russian and Turks. The last of these included all of the Ottoman Empire.[36] By 1914, 50 per cent of those living in the federal capital of Buenos Aires were foreign-born, according to Alistair Hennessy.[37] Among the five million living in the same city in 1958, some forty languages were spoken, according to Horan.[38]

Map 1 Provinces of Argentina, and railway lines. *Inset:* Towns mainly in the pampas near which the Irish farmed. Based on information in Santiago Ussher's book *Los Capellanes Irlandeses, en la Colectividad Hiberno-Argentina durante el Siglo XIX*. (I am grateful to Dr Michael Murphy, School of Geography, UCC, for making this map.)

The advent of railways in the second half of the nineteenth century, radiating out from Buenos Aires, went hand in hand with the arrival of more European migrants – more than 100,000 a year between 1904 and 1914.[39] Of the total mileage of railways in the republic in 1914, approximately 65 per cent (22,000 km) were in the pampas, providing a transport infrastructure for new industry and agriculture.[40] The railways, substantially funded, built and owned by British investors, stimulated colonisation. By 1914, the British had become the dominant commercial and financial presence in the country, exercising influence over national governments and helping to form national economic policies. By the end of the First World War, it had become customary to describe Argentina as part of Britain's 'informal empire' and even as 'the sixth dominion'.[41]

THE IRISH IN NINETEENTH-CENTURY ARGENTINA

Irish men and women formed part of that caravan of humanity from nineteenth-century Europe to Argentina and other destinations – Scotland, Wales, England, Canada, the United States, South Africa, Australia, New Zealand, etc.[42]

While the overwhelming majority of the Irish who emigrated in the nineteenth century went to Britain and its empire and the United States, the writer Thomas Murray has left a general view of the arrival of Irish in Argentina. He estimated that they numbered about 2,500 in 1832.[43] By 1844, Ussher, Horan's other major source for his report, wrote that the number of Irish in Argentina had increased to 3,500[44] – a figure he may also have taken from Murray.[45] British residents were estimated at between 5,000 and 6,000: 'Perhaps it is not unreasonable to assume nearly half of those were Irish,' Horan noted.[46] The historian and sociologist Edmundo Murray calculates that from the 1830s onwards between 30,000 and 50,000 Irish came to Argentina, of whom about 50 per cent either returned to Ireland or went on to the United States. Many of those who stayed died in the waves of epidemics sweeping the city.[47] Hilda Sábato and Juan Carlos Korol's study is of enduring scholarly value as is also the MA thesis of Patrick McKenna.[48] The greatest impediment to providing accurate statistics on emigration from Ireland to Argentina lies in the undifferentiated usage of the word *Ingleses* by Spanish speakers to describe the English, Scottish, Welsh or Irish, a subject Helen Kelly has explored in her pioneering study.[49] Viewing mid- to late nineteenth-century Irish immigration to Argentina through the prism of post-independence Ireland, it may be a mistake to overdraw the national distinctiveness of the identity of those who arrived up to the 1880s. Being known as *Ingleses* in a booming economy, substantially funded by British capital, was a flag of convenience which helped the Irish to find work in railway construction as engineers, administrators, labourers, etc. and later in running the rail services which opened up the country so well endowed with natural resources and fertile land.

Exploiting that dual identity of being both Irish and British was useful in getting work in British-owned slaughter and salting houses. Irish women found service with British families in the camp and in the cities. Memories of the Famine in the 1840s and a resurgence of Irish nationalism at the end of the nineteenth century reframed the Irish immigrants' interpretation of the recent history of the Irish in Argentina, sharpening the focus and homogenising diverse experiences. The first two decades of the twentieth century saw the rise of revolutionary Irish nationalism and a corresponding shift in the way many Irish-Argentine immigrants interpreted that past, which was sharpened with the establishment of the Irish state in 1922. Benedict Anderson writes in that context: 'All profound changes in consciousness, by their very nature, bring with them characteristic amnesias. Out of such oblivion, in specific historical circumstances, spring narratives.'[50]

In crafting Irish-Argentine stories of origin, the Irish Catholic Church missionary narrative is the one most frequently followed in the early literature pioneered by Ussher and others. The available archives and printed sources provide a rich resource by which to explore the history of an increasing number of 'souls' requiring pastoral care in the region of the River Plate. An Irish Dominican, Fr Edmund Burke, had ministered in Buenos Aires until his death in 1828. The archbishop of Dublin, Daniel Murray, sent the Jesuit Fr Patrick Moran as a replacement that same year.[51] In a letter dated 22 February 1829, he told the archbishop that the Argentines were 'partial to us' and 'this is the Country for the Irish farmer to emigrate to ... the most productive soil in the world, the best harvest and a people who will show themselves more friendly to Irishmen than to any other nation'.[52] Moran's tenure was cut short by his death on 24 April 1831. Fr Patrick O'Gorman was sent as his replacement later that year to minister to a community grown to about 1,500 Irish Catholics. But for two years, between 1835 and 1837, when he was assisted by Fr Michael McCartan, he was alone tending to a congregation that doubled by the early 1840s due to the rise in immigration. The president of the Irish Catholic Society, James Kiernan, wrote in 1843 to the archbishop of Dublin, Daniel Murray, requesting that another chaplain be sent to take care of the urgent pastoral needs of the growing number of Irish who were arriving in the country.

1.2 Fr Anthony Dominic Fahy OP, chief chaplain and organiser of the Irish in nineteenth-century Argentina

Fr Anthony Dominic Fahy from Galway was chosen for the task. Born in 1805 in Loughrea, he joined the Dominicans and studied in Ireland and in Rome. After ordination in 1831, he worked in Ohio between 1834 and 1836 before returning to take up a position in his home town and then in Kilkenny.[53] Arriving in Buenos Aires on 11 January 1844, he settled into his work and for more than twenty years ministered to the Irish.

An Irish Protestant businessman, Thomas Armstrong, gave his lifelong friend an apartment rent-free at the north-west corner of Reconquista and Bartolomé Mitre. Fahy had a vast territory to cover.[54] Writing to his superiors in Rome twelve years after he arrived, he reported that he had to travel the interior of the province (pampas) every six months, 'which is larger than the

1.3 Monument to
Fr Fahy, Recoleta
Cemetery,
Buenos Aires

whole of England'.[55] In size, it was some 647,497 square kilometres. Jorge Luis
Borges wrote that pampas 'was a word for the far away', which the gauchos took
to mean the open land 'on the other side of the frontier travelled by Indian
tribes'.[56] Kathleen Nevin captured its visual impact on her as a new arrival in
the country: 'At a twist in the dusty road we left the last few houses [of Buenos
Aires] behind us; and as far as I can remember the road never turned again, but
lay flat across flat fields for mile after mile, with neither bank nor hedge to right
or to left of it. That was the "camp"'[57] – the word the Irish used for the pampas.
It is partially thanks to Santiago Ussher's biography that Fahy's pioneering work
became so widely known internationally. He quoted William Bulfin on the
priest's early days as a missionary: 'God be with the old times when Father Fahy

started from Buenos Aires on horseback to visit his scattered flock. From forty to sixty miles a day, he often galloped over the camp, changing horses here and there as opportunity offered. Many a night he slept on his *recao* [riding gear] rolled in his poncho, with the thatched roof of a hut over his head and at times nothing but the starry sky of the pampas.'[58] Fr John Cullen, who was brought by Fahy as a chaplain in 1856, described him as an 'indefatigable, energetic, self-sacrificing priest' who frequently visited the Irish in the camp to say mass and dispense the sacraments – baptising, confirming, marrying and giving the last rites. He also observed that many of the Irish visited by Fahy did not possess independent or average means 'compared with the majority who are employed either as herds on sheep farms or as workers in the *saladeros* or salting houses for curing hides for exportation'.[59] When his elderly helper Fr O'Gorman died on 3 March 1847, Fahy was left alone to minister to increasing numbers of Irish who arrived, in the words of poet Eavan Boland,

> In the worst hour of the worst season
> of the worst year of a whole people [...][60]

According to the historian Joseph Lee, emigrants fled after the Famine 'from an Ireland of intense, often indeed brutal, social change as many landlords hastened to evict smallholders to make way for more profitable livestock exports to the British market'.[61] Over one million people died and some two million emigrated between 1846 and 1855.[62] In the words of the historian Kerby Miller, for most Irish who went to the USA, 'emigration remained forced banishment – demanding political redress and the emigrants' continued fealty to sorrowing Mother Ireland'.[63] In contrast, the Irish Catholics settling in Buenos Aires and the hinterland did not have to confront the religious bigotry of the US nativists.[64] But there is evidence that the bitterness of forceful banishment during the Famine lasted for many generations among the Irish who came in those dark years to Argentina.[65] There was also a feeling of abandonment: 'We were too poor to go [back] and what would Ireland do with us. Nobody ever came to visit our family either from the homeland,' an elderly woman said to Fr Tomás O'Donnell in 2019 in San Antonio de Areco – a town where the majority of the population was once of Irish descent.

Fahy's reaction to the news of famine revealed the great generosity of many of the immigrants who had arrived during previous years. He organised a collection to alleviate the suffering of those most affected by the disastrous failure of the potato crop in Ireland. On 22 May 1847, he published more than 300 names of those who had subscribed and the amount given by each one.

1.4 & 1.5 Admiral William Brown, commemorative stamps

(A small number of donors preferred to remain anonymous.) Fahy sent the handsome sum of £441-1-10 to the central relief committee in Dublin. Murray described that list as the first roll of honour of the Irish in Argentina.[66]

Admiral William Brown, the founder of the Argentine navy, left for Ireland with his daughter in July 1847 on what was to be his final journey home. He arrived in October and travelled, with his daughter, to his native Foxford, County Mayo. An eyewitness to the hardship of the people in the west of Ireland during the worst year of the Famine, unfortunately he left no record of his reaction to the tragedy. Fahy attended at his bedside when he died on 3 March 1857 in Buenos Aires. His legacy as a hero of the wars of independence remains one of the strongest historical links between Ireland and Argentina, likely to endure for centuries to come.

The pastoral and material needs of Irish immigrants obliged Fahy to become a jack-of-all-trades, which he described to his superiors thus: 'I am consul, post office master, judge, pastor, interpreter and provider of work for those people.' Ussher added that he was also their 'secretary, lawyer, banker and guarantor for their banking transactions'.[67] Fahy opened a bank to help Irish immigrants save their earnings and also to borrow in order to purchase land. His hospital provided care for immigrants fleeing the Famine. It continued to function in Calle Tucumán for many years. Fahy had the faculties of a vicar general, which gave him both freedom and status. He was responsible for bringing the Irish Sisters of Mercy to Buenos Aires in 1856; Mother Mary Evangelista Fitzpatrick arrived on 24 February with seven other sisters. Fahy put them in charge of his hospital for Irish immigrants. Within a short time, they had also set up schools and homes for girls. The order remained in the country for twenty-four years before being forced out by political unrest and anticlericalism. They returned to the country ten years later and their mission continues to this day.

With the rising numbers of Irish coming during and after the Famine, Fahy could not hope to take care personally of the chaplaincy work needed to cover such a large area. Thanks to a large donation, he provided scholarships for students in All Hallows Seminary, Dublin, to train for the Argentine mission. His foresight brought twelve priests to Buenos Aires in the 1860s, among them brothers Michael and John Leahy, Michael Connolly, James Curran, Edmund Flannery, Felix O'Callaghan, Samuel O'Reilly, William Walsh and Patrick Lynch.[68] Fahy divided up the mission territory. Each new chaplain was assigned an area to cover which was vast by Irish standards. Usually, he had a house in a country town with a small church where he said mass once a month. On the remaining three Sundays, the chaplain travelled on horseback or by sulky to say mass in other rural churches or in chapels on estancias.[69]

Patrick Edward Joseph Dillon, who was ordained at All Hallows in 1863, would take over the leadership of the Irish chaplaincy after Fahy's death in 1871. He arrived in Buenos Aires in late 1863 and in 1864 and 1865, he served as a chaplain in Cañuelas. At the end of 1865, Fahy sent him to the Falklands, where there was a significant community of Irish Catholics, many working as shepherds to save money to buy land in Uruguay and Argentina. Although the islands were under British jurisdiction since 1833, the Catholic inhabitants were under the ecclesiastical jurisdiction of the archbishopric of Buenos Aires. Over

1.6 Canon Patrick Dillon, successor to Fr Fahy in 1871 as chief chaplain to the Irish until his death in 1889

1,500 kilometres from Buenos Aires, Fahy never had the time to visit those islands but he had the responsibility to ensure that an Irish chaplain was posted there. Towards the end of the century, a chapel, Stella Maris, was erected in the capital, Port Stanley. Before the end of the century, pastoral responsibility for the islands passed out of the hands of Irish chaplains to the Marists.

Reviewing the profile of the Irish in Argentina during the Fahy years, many had fled the Famine tempted by the prospect of acquiring land and settling in a country that had already provided earlier Irish immigrants with a good living. That was the push and pull factor which saw the number of new arrivals increase in 1847 and peak in 1865.[70] They came mainly from Meath, Westmeath, Longford, Roscommon, Galway, Mayo, Wexford, Carlow and Offaly. The journey was long and arduous. They took ship in Dublin, Cobh or Wexford and then sailed from Liverpool and other English ports for Buenos Aires. Under sail, the journey could take from six weeks to three months. (A voyage lasting six months was recorded.) The majority of the Irish travelled steerage.[71] In the early 1870s, Barbara Peart, an Irishwoman who was a first-class passenger to Buenos Aires, left a vivid description of the abominable conditions poor people endured on board those sailing ships: 'They were huddled like cattle in their dark, dismal quarters and most of them were still being horribly sick. At meal times they held out tin mugs and plates for food and water without troubling to get to their feet.' She begged the captain to allow her to take some of the children on deck for air and exercise 'but he would not permit it'.[72] Sarah Elliff (née Flynn), according to Edmundo Murray, left Liverpool in June and arrived in Buenos Aires after six months at sea. There were 600 passengers on board, thirty dying during the journey.[73] Arriving in Buenos Aires, passengers often faced a period of quarantine aboard ship.[74] The names in their passports were often wrongly transcribed by port officials. Immigrants also faced a few days in an overcrowded state-run reception centre called a hotel. Aware of the uncertainties and dangers facing newly arrived immigrants, Fahy set about building the social infrastructure which provided for the medical, educational, economic and spiritual needs of his growing flock. He had a preference for sending many of the Irish to the countryside to take up posts that he had found for them. There, the earlier generations of Irish immigrants confronted the rigid social hierarchy that existed. It mirrored the stratification between farmer and farm labourer found at home. One Irish estanciero told Horan that his father and grandfather had brought farm labourers out 'by the shipload'[75] as did other estancieros, amongst them the following:[76] Duggan,[77] Cavanagh, Garrahan,[78] Ham, Murphy,[79] Morgan and Nelson.[80] Eduardo Casey, once the richest of all of the estancieros, visited Ireland for the first time around 1873. He had a subscription to the *Freeman's Journal*, gave political donations to Charles Stewart Parnell, and employed large numbers of Irish on his estancias. (He went to London and probably Ireland in 1891.) Curamalán was comprised of 280,000 hectares or 692,000 acres. Within its limits, there were five towns, four railway stations, 20,000 horses, 50,000 head of cattle and 300,000 sheep.[81] Casey lost everything due to bad investments in Uruguay and died reportedly by suicide in 1906.[82]

1.7 Eduardo Casey, estanciero and at one time the wealthiest man in Argentina

Pádraic (Patrick) MacManus, a native Irish speaker and radical republican, came to Argentina in the 1880s after spending eight years in the US navy. Born in Mountcharles, Donegal, in 1864, he first worked as a teacher and later became a successful estanciero and a prominent figure in the Irish-Argentine community.[83]

Those self-made men ran their farms in a hard and unsentimental way, reflecting the values as outlined by Michael D. Higgins that they had brought with them from Ireland.[84] According to Horan, what the newly arrived farm

1.8 Four Irish farmers drinking maté in the 1860s. (Museográfico Provincial Enrique Udaondo, Luján, provincia de Buenos Aires; courtesy of Archivio General de la Nación)

labourers faced was 'something like a feudal society composed of ... owners of very vast tracts of land indeed, so vast that land is measured not in acres and not in hectares but in square leagues'.[85] 'One can be quite sure,' the Irish envoy wrote, 'that the great bulk of those [labourers] were destined to be the hewers of wood and drawers of water.'[86] It was 'one of history's little ironies', he added, 'that our emigrants came to Argentina to assist in building up a system and a class, the creation of which in Ireland had led to their own emigration'.[87] Identifying social snobbery and class divisions on Irish-owned estancias, he wrote: 'While the wealthy industrialist may on occasions dine with his white-collared employees, I think it is not untrue to say that the landed aristocrat will not sit down to eat with his farm labourer, will not, as I have heard it put, "share salt" with him.'[88] Once the labourers paid off the price of their sea passage and other debts to the estanciero, they were free to become 'knock-abouts', as William Bulfin termed them, travelling in search of casual labour from one estancia to another.[89]

Many chose, however, to work on the same estancia in the hope of building up a nest egg and becoming a *puestero*, with a patch of land they could farm for themselves and their families while still of course working for a landlord

– a prospect they could never have entertained in Famine-stricken and post-Famine Ireland. Fr John Cullen, an Irish chaplain, explained the system:

> ... every estancia contains a certain number of leagues, a shepherd instead
> of wages has an interest given him in the flock – the owner provides him
> a hut, sheep-pens, etc., the flock will be 1,500 – if seasons be good – in
> three years or at the most four, the flock is expected to double (3,000) the
> shepherd is allowed one-third of the increase of the wool sold and of the
> sheepskin and tallow. Thus in three or four years he ought to be owner
> of 500 sheep, rent land for himself, and add to his share by purchase or
> otherwise.[90]

There was also the further prospect of ascending the estancia social ladder and becoming a *capataz* (foreman) and *mayordomo* (farm manager). Many Irish women who came to Argentina worked as domestics in the houses of established Irish or English families. A privileged few were recruited in Ireland to work as governesses for families in the city or on an estancia. As an alternative to farm work, educated Irish men put their skills to good use finding employment as administrative staff with railway companies, slaughter houses, export companies, etc. William Ussher arrived in Buenos Aires in 1863. An educated man and a native Irish speaker, he was born in 1838 in Turvin, near Athenry, County Galway. He lived through the Famine as a boy and was an eyewitness to terrible suffering as tens of thousands died while the British government, for the most part, stood idly by. The trauma of witnessing so much suffering left him with an animus towards the British which he passed on to his son, Santiago. Soon after his arrival, he met Anne Walsh from Horseleap, County Westmeath, who had arrived in 1859 to join her two married sisters, Catherine Walsh Murray and Eliza Walsh Gannon. Fr Fahy, who also came from Galway, married the couple (22 January 1867) and remained their close friend until his death.

Argentina brought the Ussher family the psychological and financial security they were unlikely to have found in post-Famine Ireland. William and Anne built a secure life which enabled them to bring up and educate their ten children,[91] three of whom became nuns and two of whom were ordained to the priesthood. Santiago, the Fahy biographer, was born in San Antonio de Giles on 11 November 1867. A priest of the archdiocese of Buenos Aires, he became a leader of the Irish community and its historian. He died on 11 March 1960.[92]

Fahy, after a productive missionary life, died in Buenos Aires on 20 February 1871. Having assisted the aged Dominican in his latter years, Dillon became his successor and head of the Irish chaplains. Sr Evangelista, the superior of the Sisters of Mercy in Buenos Aires, wrote of Dillon to archbishop of Dublin, Cardinal Paul Cullen, in 1877 that since his arrival over eight years before, 'he has greatly improved in every way. He is not generally liked, but all must acknowledge he is peaceable and charitable. He does, I think, all the good that, with his disposition, he possibly can'.[93] That qualified approval was written after he had set up *The Southern Cross* (*TSC*), which published its first issue on 16 January 1875 and appeared weekly on Fridays for well over a hundred years, hardly missing an issue. Elegiac and nostalgic in tone when reporting on Ireland, it was a Catholic nationalist rival to the well-established *Standard*[94] founded in 1861 by Dubliners Michael and Edward Mulhall.[95] Very much at home in the world of empire nationalism, the latter supported the Irish Parliamentary Party and the constitutional nationalist movement.[96] *TSC*, in contrast, remained more in tune with developments in the political, literary, cultural and sporting revival at the turn of the century under the dynamic editorship of William Bulfin, who joined the staff of the paper as a reporter in the late 1880s, became its owner in the mid-1890s and remained as editor until 1909.

A long-running anti-clerical campaign in Buenos Aires peaked in 1875 after the archbishop handed over the running of the church and school of San Salvador to the Jesuits. An angry mob demonstrated outside the cathedral and later, on 28 February, attacked and burned down the school. The nearby convent of the Sisters of Mercy was also threatened: 'Indeed our escape that day might be justly called miraculous,' wrote Mother Evangelista to Cardinal Cullen in 1877, noting that 'twice here they have tried to pass a bill, suppressing Religious orders that make perpetual vows – they have failed – but I know the bad are determined to work it out in the end and if they succeed, the first they [will deal] with will be the Jesuits – the second ourselves'. She also told him that there was a strong animus even among the Irish which prevented them sending their children to their convent school: 'But if we have not work, we have suffering', she commented, adding that the chief good they could do was 'with the poor Irish servant girls in our House of Mercy'.[97] But the violent political climate and attack on their school forced Sr Evangelista to withdraw with twenty-four nuns from the country, taking up an invitation to set up a school in Adelaide, Australia. They were replaced for a decade by the Irish Missionary Sisters of the Sacred Heart. The Sisters of Mercy returned in the 1890s and played a central role in the education of girls, the running of an orphanage and other duties. Having left the area of formal education in the late 1970s, they continue to minister in Argentina to this day.

Dillon, who died in 1889, had less than two decades to stamp his leadership style on the Irish community. In 1880, he became the first Irishman to win a seat in Congress. He founded the Irish Catholic Association (ICA) in 1883 – an influential philanthropic organisation which continues to perform very important work supporting Catholic education and other projects.[98] Dillon actively supported the ambitious immigration policies of President Miguel Ángel Celman (in office 1886–90).[99] In the early 1880s, he went on a mission to Ireland to explore whether Irish people were prepared to emigrate to Argentina. His report to the president was positive, and supportive of a scheme to bring more Irish to the country. By the end of the 1880s, John O'Meara and John S. Dillon (the monsignor's brother) were named as Argentine government agents in Ireland and they advertised 'free' passage to Argentina in 1888. Seen as a money-making operation, it was opposed by Irish bishops, other prominent Irish clergy and almost all Irish leaders of the Irish in Argentina. Nevertheless, nearly 1,500 Irish men, women and children set sail from Cobh at the end of January 1889 on the steamship the *Dresden*, for Southampton en route to Montevideo and Buenos Aires. They arrived at their destination on 14 February. Horan wrote in his report: 'These [immigrants] had been rounded up and induced by the specious promises of two agents of the Argentine Government with Irish names to try their fortunes under the Southern Cross.' But the ship's passenger list revealed that almost none of those on board had any farming background and were unlikely to be able to survive in the Argentine countryside.[100] Canon Dillon, who was in poor health, returned to Dublin, where he died in 1889 and was buried in Glasnevin Cemetery. The *Dresden* escapade ended in disaster for most of the Irish aboard.[101] Unable to employ many of the new arrivals, the Irish-Argentine community had to provide support for the women and children. A large number went south by train to join a new colony at Naposta, Bahía Blanca. It failed within a year and the Irish returned peso-less to Buenos Aires, where they were assisted in finding temporary lodgings by the British envoy and by the Argentine government. While a small number of that group were given work on estancias or employed as domestics, a group of adults, leaving their children in the care of families and religious in Buenos Aires, went to the north to help found another colony. But as Horan noted in his report, 'the great bulk of them went to swell the ranks of the poor in the southern districts of the City and Province of Buenos Aires', living on 'the wrong side of the tracks' in *conventillos* (tenements)[102] in La Boca.[103] In large measure, it was thanks to the charitable work of the Ladies of St Joseph, made up of the wives and widows of estancieros, that funding was provided to take care of the *Dresden* orphans in institutions, a number of which would be converted into important schools for Irish boys and girls.

After his death, Dillon's pastoral leadership of the Irish Catholic community fell to the collective governance of three religious orders with a strong Irish-born female and male membership: the Congregation of the Passion of Jesus Christ (Passionists), the Pallottines, and the Sisters of Mercy, who returned to Buenos Aires in 1890. The archbishop of Buenos Aires, Federico Aneiros, petitioned the Holy See in 1879 to send clergy to the Argentine mission. The papacy requested the Passionists to start a mission there to help take care of the 28,000 Irish who lived scattered over 22,840 square kilometres.[104] Fr Martin Byrne, the first to arrive, in April 1879, established his base in Calle Alsina 380, near San Rocque church. Within a short period, he had set up a school for boys, the Confraternity of the Holy Family, a choir, a society to teach catechism to children and a charitable organisation to provide relief for the poor.[105] Frs Clement Finnegan and Fideles Kent Stone arrived in 1880,[106] setting up a new community in Calle Alsina. On 6 January 1883, the order opened a temporary tin chapel in Calle Estados Unidos. Thanks to the generosity of their Irish parishioners, the foundation stone was laid on 4 March 1890 for a permanent structure, which was completed and consecrated on 11 March 1897. Designed by the architect E.A. Merry (another source says it was John Sutton) and modelled on the English-Gothic style of the fourteenth century, it had a handsomely carved pulpit (donated by Margaret Mooney de Morgan from San Antonio de Areco), a beautiful pipe organ, carved statues and stained-glass windows portraying St Patrick and other Irish saints.[107] It remained the jewel in the crown of Irish-Argentine Catholics throughout much of the twentieth century. In 1884, the Passionists were invited by the elderly Fr Largo Miguel Leahy to work in his area of Salto Argentino. Following his death that year, the local bishop put the order in charge of Carmen de Areco, Salto and Rojas. In the same year, a team of Passionist preachers gave a memorable retreat at McGuire's chapel, Capitán Sarmiento, so named because the land on which it was built was donated by the estanciero Tomás McGuire. The Irish living in the area successfully petitioned the bishop to allow the order to take charge of pastoral needs in that extensive area. The estancieros Eduardo Casey, Patricio Farrell and Tomás McGuire donated a very large plot of land to the order in 1888. Adjacent to a railway station, the site was ideal for the building of a church and a minor seminary.[108] Fr Victor Carolan, the driving force behind the ambitious venture, laid the foundation stone for the 'monastery' in 1888. It was completed in 1893. In 1896, Patricio Farrell offered to build a church on the site in memory of his three-year-old son. The church, an imposing Gothic structure, was consecrated in May 1898 and dedicated to St Patrick.[109] Carolan, who saw the project to the end, died on 30 November 1898 and was buried before the main altar.[110]

The Passionists continued through the twentieth century to play an important pastoral role in the lives of Irish-Argentine Catholics and new Argentines.

In *You'll Never Go Back*, Kathleen Nevin has left an arresting description of a mission or retreat – similar to the one given in 1884 – by two newly arrived Passionist priests in the presence of the diocesan chaplain, Fr Slattery: 'We reached the *galpón*, a long zinc-covered shed. It was dark inside, but the dimness was soothing after the glare.' An altar had been set up with flowers, and 'long planks on boxes took the place of benches'. Two Passionist priests were hearing confessions, one hearing the women in the sala and the men under the paraiso tree behind the kitchen. A woman waiting her turn for confession with Fr Augustine told the author: 'An' as I said before, this Passionist Father knows what yer at before the words are out of yer mouth, an' that's a great help to a woman.' The following morning, the men awoke. They had either slept in the sheds or 'perhaps under the sky like the gaucho*s*, and now they were standing under the paraisos the way they do in the chapel-yard at Home [in Mullingar]. The men were tall, weather-beaten and muscular. The women were redcheeked and good natured looking. Long tables had been prepared with white table cloths.' The food was prepared 'so that the people wouldn't have to wait for their breakfasts after Mass and the long fast for Communion'. There were three 'native' babies for christening. The two Passionists were hearing confessions again, 'as more people had driven over in the morning; then Mass began'. When she heard the words being read in English, Nevin cried softly, thinking of her father at home in Ireland. One of the Passionists gave a short instruction before Communion 'and it was very beautiful to see everyone approaching the altar'. Breakfast followed the mass. Fr Slattery, showing his disappointment, said in a loud voice: '"It's the first 'station' I ever gave without a wedding to wind up. Two, three and four, is what I'm used to. What's the matter with the women of this *partido* at all, at all!" "Maybe it's the men, Father," I heard a quiet voice say.'[111] That female voice is one of the few heard – as yet – questioning clerical authority in the history of the Irish in Argentina. Further research will unquestionably reveal the independent-mindedness of many Irish-Argentine women thrust into having to meet the challenges of living in a frontier society.

In the mid-1880s, the Societas Apostolatus Catholici (SAC) sent priests to Argentina. Better known as the Pallottines, or Palotinos in Spanish, they founded a mission in Mercedes about 100 kilometres from Buenos Aires with

1.9 Fr Patrick O'Grady, Pallottine, celebrated Irish missionary in nineteenth- and early twentieth-century Mercedes, Argentina

the objective of providing education and pastoral care for a large number of Irish-Argentines living in that area.[112] In 1887, Fr Bernardo Feeney opened St Patrick's school for boys in Mercedes. Fr Patricio O'Grady, who was ordained in 1888, arrived in Buenos Aires in March 1889 and took over as rector in Mercedes a year later. In 1892, he oversaw the building of new school premises. He was local superior of the Pallottines from 1896 to 1909 in Argentina, Uruguay and Chile. An Irish Pallottine province, including both Argentina and Chile, was formed in 1909. The order opened a seminary in Thurles, County Tipperary, that same year to prepare candidates for missionary work in Latin

America. O'Grady was provincial rector from 1909 to 1911. He became one of the most influential priests of his generation in Argentina, being responsible also for building churches at Rivas, Las Saladas and San Jacinto. He served as parish priest of Suipacha and Capilla del Señor. O'Grady played an active role in the Irish Catholic Association and was outspoken in the press on church matters and Irish politics.[113] He travelled to Europe in 1896, 1903 and 1909 to attend general chapters of the order. His final visit to Ireland was in 1920 at the height of the 'Troubles'. During his lifetime, Pallottines were often referred to as 'Fr O'Grady's priests'.[114] He died on 22 July 1922 and is buried in Mercedes. His nephew Tomás also joined the Pallottines and ministered in Argentina from 1894 until his death in 1940. Fr Thomas Dunleavy opened a new parish in 1929 in a temporary church in Belgrano, a suburb of Buenos Aires where many Irish lived. Replaced by a permanent structure, St Patrick's became a thriving parish with a Pallottine school.[115] The Pallottines later ran St Patrick's parish and school in Belgrano.[116]

The Sisters of Mercy returned to Buenos Aires in 1890 at the invitation of the archbishop of Buenos Aires. Led by Mother Baptist MacDonnell, there were six Irish, Argentine and Australian sisters. They set up Mater Misericordiae school in 1897 on a site at 24 de Noviembre and Estados Unidos. Thanks to generous benefactors, the sisters set up two schools in San Antonio de Areco. The Irish Catholic Association bought a very large site in Flores with the generous help of the estanciero Thomas Duggan.[117] An ornate, castellated school was built and named after a patron saint of Ireland, Santa Brígida or St Bridget's. A large chapel was added ten years later. The Missionary Sisters of the Sacred Heart were chosen to run the boarding school. Opened on 19 March 1899, it was to provide education for the children of Irish-Argentine families and for the orphans of the families of the *Dresden*. The girls ranged in age from four to twenty. Of the original staff of ten nuns, six were Irish. Due to friction within the Irish-Argentine community, the Sisters of Mercy took over the school in 1902 and ran it until the late 1970s. They also set up the San José residence for working girls in Buenos Aires in 1910. St Mary's for girls was opened in San Antonio de Areco on 16 March 1901 and Clonmacnoise for boys on 22 March 1922. The congregation opened Santa Ana school in Rawson on 19 April 1928 and Santa Ethnea in Bella Vista in 1931.

In 1895, the Daughters of St Joseph funded the opening of an orphanage in Capilla del Señor for seventy boys between ages five and ten. Called the Fahy Institute, it was taken over two years later by the Brothers of the Order of Saint Joseph. It moved to Moreno in 1929 when the Pallottines had the responsibility for running the school.[118] It became the main secondary school

1.10 Tin church, Holy Cross, erected by the Passionist order in the 1880s

for the education of Irish boys in the 1930s and 1940s. The Daughters of Charity continued to run an elementary school at Capilla del Señor for boys going on to the Fahy Institute.

Two other congregations of Irish sisters also came to work in Argentina. On 13 May 1913, four sisters of the Little Company of Mary (Blue Sisters) – Mother M. Columba Kealy and Sisters Philomena Haslem, Raphael McCarthy and Rita Carroll – arrived in San Antonio de Areco to run the Maria Clara Morgan Hospital and remained there until it closed in 1956. The order moved to Buenos Aires and set up a new hospital in the Barrio Norte. The Michael Ham Memorial School, endowed by the estanciero Michael Ham, opened on 6 March 1926. Two Irish Passionist Sisters, Sisters Scholastica and Aquinas, were founder members of the teaching staff. The Ladies of St Joseph, a charitable organisation, provided money for the founding and the running of the Fahy Institute. They also underwrote the opening of an orphanage for Irish Catholic girls known as the Keating Institute, adjacent to Holy Cross, which was taken over by Irish Dominican Sisters in the 1960s.[119]

By the end of the nineteenth century, Irish male and female religious and diocesan clergy had built a strong pastoral support system for the immigrants who settled in different parts of Argentina. Holy Cross in Buenos Aires, St Paul minor seminary and church in Capitán Sarmiento, the ground-breaking for the

1.11 Permanent church named Holy Cross opened in the 1890s

Basilica at Lujan in 1890 (completed 1936) and churches in Rosario, Venado Tuerto and in the towns of the camp were tangible signs of both the devotion and prosperity of Irish Catholics. That was paralleled by the evolution of a network of schools run by Irish male and female religious.

In that culture of worship and education, Irish-Argentines forged a common identity which made them comfortable in the country of their adoption.

1.12 Known to Irish Argentines as 'el Monastery', St Paul's church and minor seminary were built by Irish Passionists under the direction of Fr Victor Carolan. The seminary was completed in 1892 and the church was opened in 1898.

Many of the Irish who settled there had left before Cardinal Paul Cullen, the archbishop of Dublin between 1852 and 1878, had helped implement ultramontane reforms resulting in the centralisation of Catholicism. During the archbishop's lifetime, he helped Romanise the leadership of the Irish episcopacy in line with the teachings of Vatican Council I (8 December 1869 to 6 December 1870).[120] His zeal for tighter clerical control was reinforced by invitations offered to religious orders from the continent, such as the Holy Ghost Fathers and Redemptorists, to set up in Ireland. The members of flourishing Irish male and female religious orders[121] greatly reinforced the Catholic educational revolution in the latter half of the nineteenth century. Cullen left his raddle mark on the Irish church, which the historian Emmet Larkin called the 'devotional revolution'.[122]

But how resistant were Irish Catholics in Argentina to the dominance of a reformed Catholicism? Unlike in post-Famine Ireland with its plentiful supply of nuns, brothers and clergy, the vast distances in Argentina meant that immigrants lived in a missionary country. Contact with clergy for the Irish in rural areas was virtually an annual event. Towns with a resident priest and a religious-run school could more easily function as a parish. The most intense catechesis took place in the Irish schools. However, the identity of Irish-Argentines was formed by synergies between the two cultures. While

1.13 & 1.14 Santa Brígida school for girls opened in the late 1890s (old photo and contemporary), with a bust of Fr Fahy in the foreground.

in nineteenth- and early twentieth-century Ireland, the hierarchy and clergy fulminated against 'company keeping' and foreign dances, Irish-Argentines lived in the country where both the milonga and tango were popular dances from the 1880s. The *pulperías* (grocery stores which also sold alcohol, as was once the case in public houses in Ireland) were outside the jurisdiction and control of the clergy. Many of the Irish diocesan clergy and religious, enculturated in Argentine customs and ways, may have become more tolerant of the earthiness of local customs and less puritanical and Victorian in outlook. That hypothesis remains to be explored.

WILLIAM BULFIN, THE GAELIC LEAGUE AND IRISH ARGENTINA

While writing his long report in 1958, Horan was constrained by the paucity of material at his disposal covering the turn of the century and the decades immediately following. However, he could learn of the local reaction to the Irish sporting, linguistic, cultural and political revival from Fr Santiago Ussher, who was, since the late 1890s, both an actor in and eyewitness to events in Irish circles in Buenos Aires. In the years leading up to Irish independence in 1921, he was a presence on many local committees working to provide support and solidarity with Sinn Féin and Dáil Éireann. While credit for the strengthening of the relationship between Buenos Aires and Dublin cannot be ascribed to any single individual, William Bulfin and his son Éamonn in distinctive ways were also pre-eminent in the forging of deep and lasting bonds between both republics. William Bulfin, journalist, newspaper proprietor, author and political activist, helped, between the late 1880s and his death in 1910, to spread the philosophy of 'Irish Ireland' and progressive nationalist ideals among Irish-Argentines. As owner and editor of *The Southern Cross* from the mid-1890s, he had a platform which he could use to strengthen the ties between 'the motherland' and Argentina. His skills as a journalist and as a writer were put to good use on a weekly basis. *TSC* became a cultural and political bridge between Argentina and the changing world of culture and politics in Ireland.

Born in 1863 in Derrinlough, Birr, County Offaly, Bulfin arrived in Argentina as a young man in 1884–5. Thanks to a family connection, he found work as a ranch hand or *chacarero* on the estancia owned by an Irishman, John Dowling. During his time working there, he was promoted to *capataz* (foreman) and later to *mayordomo* (farm manager). Bulfin met Annie O'Rourke, who worked as a governess on the same estancia. Being a Westmeath woman, they had much in common, and their relationship endured separation when he abandoned that 'gaucho life' in the late 1880s for a job on *The Southern Cross* in Buenos Aires.

They married around 1890, settled in Buenos Aires and had a son, Éamonn, in 1892 followed by four daughters, Catalina (Kid), Mary, Aileen and Anita. Bulfin excelled as a reporter and feature writer and by the mid-1890s he was the proprietor and editor of *TSC*, a post he held until 1909 when he returned to settle in Ireland.

1.15 & 1.16 William Bulfin and Annie Bulfin

1.17 The four Bulfin daughters (from left): Catalina (Kid), Mary, Aileen and Anita

From masthead (dating from Dillon's time) to layout and content, the paper was influenced by Celtic typography and by the philosophy of the Gaelic revival of the late nineteenth century. Bulfin's weekly column appeared under the pseudonym Che Buono, a pen-name allegedly resulting from a printer's typographical error when setting the Latin *cui bono* (who stands to gain) in one of his articles. 'Che' is a sobriquet in Argentina meaning 'fellow' or 'guy', hence 'Che' Guevara, and '*buono*' in Italian means 'good'. Bulfin adopted that felicitous typo as his pseudonym and gained a large readership throughout the pampas and beyond. As Che Buono, his articles were awaited with anticipation in the remotest Irish homes in the camp for nearly two decades.[123] Proof of their popularity was the publication of his *Tales of the Pampas* in 1900 – a collection of short stories which had appeared earlier in *TSC* and were based loosely on his years working in the camp.[124]

Bulfin helped build a bridge for his readers between their remote past in Ireland and their present as immigrants and Argentine citizens – a process the US novelist Toni Morrison has called 'rememoration'.[125] He demonstrated weekly in his paper and in his books *Tales of the Pampas* and *Rambles in Eirinn* (published in 1907) that he understood the hidden hinterland of his readers. He recognised that the experience in Ireland of many of those who had come to Argentina had been overshadowed by poverty, famine, trauma and displacement. Bulfin helped his immigrant readers through his writing to 'rememorate' shards of past times when their homes in Ireland were once happy places, and argued that they could be happy again as Argentine citizens free from the coercive reach of imperialist British rule. He wanted them to participate actively in shaping the future of their newly adopted country using the freedom they had under the Argentine constitution to do so. Bulfin converted his newspaper into a platform for the writings and the ideas of the founder of the Gaelic League, Douglas Hyde, and the founder of Sinn Féin, Arthur Griffith. He admired the radical politics of Michael Davitt, who he unsuccessfully invited to Argentina in the early 1900s. An enthusiastic supporter of the Gaelic League, which was founded on 31 July 1893,[126] he became a friend of Hyde, who sought to foster the revival of the Irish language in a non-political way.[127] Bulfin was a founder member of the branch of the league which held its inaugural meeting in Buenos Aires on 14 May 1899. The superior of the Passionists, Fr Eugene Ryan, who was born in New York of Irish parents, provided a room for the meeting at Holy Cross monastery.[128] Many people in attendance had to travel for hours to reach the capital. For example, P(eter) Dinneen, a native speaker, arrived after the meeting had ended[129] but in sufficient time to hand over donations, ten pesos from himself, and five pesos each from his five friends. Pádraic MacManus, an estanciero, contrarian and Bulfin's brother-in-law,[130] was a founder-member, as was another large landowner, David Suffern.[131] The well-attended inaugural meeting elected J.E. O'Curry, the son of the Irish philologist Eugene, as president. Patrick S.H. Conway was elected vice-president and David Suffern treasurer. M.F. Breen was elected secretary and Pádraic MacManus as pro-secretary.[132] William Ussher, a native speaker,[133] was present.[134] Fr Santiago (James), his son, was also in attendance. He was recently ordained and had been appointed an ecclesiastical notary of the diocese of La Plata. Called upon to speak, he received a standing ovation for his few well-chosen words: 'My parents are Irish. I am Argentine by birth, and my first allegiance and love go naturally to my mother land, but in this movement and in all Irish movements I hope humbly that I am as Irish in spirit as I should be.'[135] Writing about the launch, Bulfin said: 'The road now is onward – work, organise, persevere. No *bombo* [hype], no shearing of the goats. Tangible results are what must be sought, and not any brand of empty notoriety.'[136] By June 1899, members had contributed £40 towards helping the Dublin headquarters pay administrative costs and £10 was donated for an Oireachtas prize.[137] On 14 November 1899, Bulfin reproduced a letter in Irish in *TSC* from the executive of the Gaelic League, signed by J.J. O'Kelly, thanking the branch and the paper for their 'great and difficult labours'.[138] At Christmas 1899, the Argentine branch sent a further donation of £100.[139] In 1902, both Bulfin and David Suffern were nominated as delegates to attend in Dublin the Oireachtas of the Gaelic League.[140] There, the visitors were received with great warmth and fanfare. On 5 September, leading league figures held a special dinner in Barry's Hotel in Dublin to honour both men. While Douglas Hyde sent his regrets, Eoin (John) MacNeill chaired the proceedings. Welcoming the Argentines in Irish, he said: 'and Argentina (*Tír an Airgid* – land of silver) is not a misnomer because it is from there that money came to us when we needed it. When we needed help it was you below in Argentina who stood by us. When there was no respect for us here, we got help from *The Southern Cross*, and thanks be to God we have the editor of that newspaper among us tonight and we are here to welcome him'.[141] Patrick Pearse, in his short speech, also referred to *TSC*: 'No newspaper in Ireland did as much for the Irish language as *The Southern Cross*. No newspaper in Ireland can come near it.'[142] During his stay in Ireland, Bulfin was in demand as a speaker at Gaelic League events around the country. He renewed his friendship with Douglas Hyde, with Arthur Griffith of Sinn Féin and with other leading nationalists, including Michael Davitt, who granted him an interview.

Bulfin had personal reasons for returning to Ireland in 1902. While he was going to return to Buenos Aires, he sought to settle his wife, Annie and their five children at the family farm in Derrinlough, Birr, County Offaly. Their four girls were sent to La Sainte Union, in Banagher, County Offaly. Éamonn, an only son, first went to the Dominican College, in Newbridge, County Kildare, and then to St Enda's in 1908 – a school established by the educationalist, barrister, playwright, journalist, Gaelic Leaguer and revolutionary Patrick Pearse.[143] Bulfin admired Pearse and both men had become good friends.

Between June 1902 and January 1903, Bulfin completed a 3,000-mile tour of Ireland on a bicycle manufactured by the Pierce Foundry of Wexford, a factory which exported ploughs to the Irish in Argentina. Descriptions of his cycling travels were serialised in Arthur Griffith's *United Irishman* and later published by M.H. Gill in 1907 in a handsome volume entitled *Rambles in Eirinn*. In strong demand internationally, the volume was reprinted in 1907 and was in its fifth edition by 1920.[144] Written by an Irish immigrant, Bulfin's elegiac text had a particularly strong appeal for the Irish who were spread throughout the world. Writing from his Irish-Ireland perspective, Bulfin described the topography, folklore and history of the countryside and of the local towns, which might be read by immigrants who had never returned to their native country. But interlaced in the nostalgic descriptions of home and place was a subtle incitement to its readers to oppose British rule and to support the movement for national independence.

Bulfin returned to Buenos Aires in 1903 and not until 1909 did he make the final decision to settle in Ireland. Partly because of the success of *Rambles in Eirinn*, which had won him international recognition, prominent nationalist leaders in Dublin urged him to return permanently in order to place his journalistic talents at the service of the national cause. Literally commuting between Buenos Aires and Dublin in the years in between, his friendship deepened with both Douglas Hyde and Arthur Griffith and he became a strong supporter of the Sinn Féin party, which the latter had founded in 1905. Bulfin persuaded friends in Buenos Aires to buy shares in Griffith's paper, the *United Irishman*, which collapsed in 1906, and in the new paper, *Sinn Féin*, which appeared the following year. When he returned in 1909, he was encouraged to apply for a professorship in Spanish at University College Dublin (UCD). There was also a suggestion that he should take over from Pearse the editorship of the Gaelic League paper *An Claidheamh Soluis* (Sword of Light). Taking up speaking obligations all over the country, Bulfin tried to help Griffith resolve his financial situation after he had launched *Sinn Féin* as a daily in August. He travelled steerage to the United States in high winter with a like-minded idealist and personal friend, Michael Joseph O'Rahilly (The O'Rahilly). The fundraising trip was a failure and on 1 January 1910 they returned empty-handed. The newspaper collapsed later in the year.[145] Bulfin, a man of great physical strength and energy, disregarded his doctor's advice and went hunting while suffering from influenza. He developed pneumonia and died on 1 February. He was forty-six. His death was widely mourned in Ireland. In Buenos Aires *TSC* carried a full-page obituary bordered in black.[146] His death deprived Ireland of one of its most talented journalists and radical nationalists of that generation. It is mere counterfactual speculation to dwell upon what might have been his future role during the Irish revolution between 1916 and 1922.

EAMONN BULFIN, FIRST IRISH ENVOY TO ARGENTINA

Bulfin's only son Éamonn carried on the family's radical tradition, not with the pen but with the sword, as a soldier during the 1916 Rising in the garrison of the General Post Office (GPO) in Dublin. In 1919, he became a most reluctant diplomat to Argentina. His education and formation during his school and university days set him on the road of revolutionary nationalism. Eamonn Bulfin was the second pupil to be enrolled in 1908 by his parents in Patrick Pearse's new school, St Enda's (Scoil Éanna). He became a close friend of the headmaster and of his brother Willie, their two sisters Margaret and Mary Brigid, and their mother Margaret. Upon completing his schooling, he continued to board there while attending UCD. As an accomplished athlete and sportsman, he was the first to win inter-varsity medals for both hurling and football – the Fitzgibbon and Sigerson cups.[147] His studies and sporting career ran in parallel with his engagement in revolutionary politics and military drilling. He held the rank of lieutenant in the 4th battalion of E Company in the Dublin brigade of the Irish Volunteers under his commanding officer, Patrick Pearse. He was also a member of the oath-bound Irish Republican Brotherhood (IRB) – the secret organisation responsible for planning the Easter Rising in 1916.[148] He commanded E Company on the roof of the GPO (Prince's St North side) from Easter Monday until the end of the week when ordered to retreat with the rest of the garrison before the surrender to the British. While occupying their position on the roof, Willie Pearse gave Bulfin the honour of raising an Irish flag over their corner of the GPO.[149] Taken prisoner after the surrender on 29 April, Bulfin was in jail under sentence of death as fourteen leaders of the revolution were executed between 3 and 12 May, including Patrick and Willie Pearse.[150] Bulfin escaped the firing squad partially due to the intervention of his mother, Annie, who petitioned for his life, claiming that her son was an Argentine citizen. She went to see the Argentine consul in Dublin, explaining that her son had been born in Buenos Aires in 1892 and had returned to live in Ireland in 1902. The consul agreed to support her claim that Eamonn was an Argentine citizen, and told her that, when her son was released, he should present himself at the consulate, where he would be given his first Argentine passport.[151]

The successor to William Bulfin as editor of *TSC*, Gerald Foley, did what he could to allow his readers to follow the course of the Irish insurrection. The fate of Eamonn Bulfin was of great interest to many of his readers. The paper reported that Bulfin had been arrested on the 29th and had been sentenced to death by a court martial. When his sentence was commuted, he was transported with hundreds of other revolutionaries in unwashed cattle ships to an internment camp in Frongoch, Wales, where he developed a close friendship with Michael Collins, who became one of the most important revolutionary leaders between 1919 and 1922. As part of a mass release, Bulfin was freed just before Christmas 1916. He collected his Argentine passport in early 1917 – a retrospective granting of citizenship to him – and continued his active role in the Irish Volunteers and Sinn Féin, a movement which had grown exponentially after the 1916 Rising to form a popular front in Irish nationalist politics.[152] Bulfin became vice commandant of the Birr battalion, Offaly brigade. Michael Collins put him in charge of the Volunteers during the East Cavan by-election campaign. Voting took place on 20 June 1918 and Bulfin's father's close friend Arthur Griffith took the seat. However, on 17 May Bulfin had been one of hundreds of Sinn Féin activists arrested when the British allegedly discovered a 'German plot' to invade Ireland. On this occasion, he was imprisoned with his uncle Frank in Durham. Among the others jailed at the time were Éamon de Valera, who was sent to Lincoln gaol, and William T. Cosgrave, Arthur Griffith, Terence MacSwiney (elected lord mayor of Cork on 12 August 1920) and Constance Markievicz. The first general election since 1910 took place on 14 December 1918. Sinn Féin's representation jumped from seven to seventy-three seats when the results were announced on 28 December. The Irish Parliamentary Party had dropped from sixty-eight seats to six. The Unionists moved from nineteen to twenty-six. Only twenty-seven of the Sinn Féin deputies were not in jail and, therefore, free to take their seats in the secessionist Dáil Éireann on 21 January 1919 in the Mansion House, Dublin. About thirty-five deputies were described as '*fé ghlas ag Gallaibh*' ('imprisoned by the foreigners'), among them Éamon de Valera.

When standing orders were approved, the Dáil passed a short provisional constitution, a democratic programme and a message to the free nations of the world.[153] The new Irish government's strategy was to convey to the outside world a position of democratic normalcy in a country where British rule was depicted as being 'irrelevant' and redundant. The Irish Republican Army (IRA), using urban and rural guerrilla tactics,[154] were met by a bloody British counter-insurgency campaign.[155] While Dáil Éireann ministries – Finance, Justice, Local Government, etc. – sought to run a government from clandestine locations in Dublin,[156] the minister for foreign affairs George Noble Plunkett (22 January 1919 – 26 August 1921)[157] was responsible for overseeing a network of 'envoys' representing the new 'state' abroad.[158] After de Valera escaped from Lincoln Prison on 3 February 1919, he spent his time coordinating the running of government. That included making decisions about the deployment of a network of diplomats in Britain, Europe, the US, Canada, Latin America, Australia and South Africa. He signed the credentials of those the government appointed. Travelling under an assumed name on 1 June, de Valera was smuggled into the US, where he remained as president of Dáil Éireann (and president of the Irish Republic) to lobby President Woodrow Wilson to recognise the Irish state, to raise funds, source supplies of arms and mobilise public opinion through addressing a series of mass rallies from coast to coast. His large team of co-workers included Harry Boland, Liam Mellows, Robert Brennan, James O'Meara and Laurence Ginnell. John Devoy, the veteran Fenian and editor of the *Gaelic American*, was his ally for much of his eighteen-month stay in the US. As a leading figure in Clann na Gael and Friends of Irish Freedom, he put both organisations at the disposal of de Valera, which made his trips to Boston, Chicago, etc. popular triumphs. As in other countries, de Valera relied strongly on the support of Catholic clergy and Irish members of the US hierarchy to get his message across.[159] Throwing his weight behind an Irish bond drive, he raised nearly $5 million for the Irish cause.[160] But while his mission was a major financial, publicity and propaganda success, de Valera left division in his wake. He broke with Devoy and founded the American Association for the Recognition of the Irish Republic. His success stopped far short of gaining recognition for the new state from the government of the United States.

Before leaving for the US in June 1919, de Valera and the cabinet filled the position of Irish envoy to Latin America. Eamonn Bulfin, still in Durham jail in the early months of 1919, was given compassionate parole in March to visit his sick mother before the British deported him to Argentina.[161] Having decided to surrender his parole and go 'on the run', he went to see Michael Collins, who told him that de Valera and Dáil Éireann had appointed him as

1.18 Eamonn Bulfin, Dáil Éireann's first diplomat to Argentina, 1919–22

Irish envoy to Argentina and that he should return to Durham jail to await deportation. As part of his new mission, Collins told him that as an envoy he had a dual function: to arrange for the distribution of propaganda for all of Latin America; and to buy guns and ammunition and have it shipped to Ireland. Returning to Birr, he handed himself in to the British authorities and was transported to Liverpool to await deportation to Buenos Aires. De

1.19 Eamonn Bulfin's Argentine national service book. He was discharged from the Argentine navy on 13 January 1920.

Valera signed his letters of credence in Spanish, English and Irish. Pearse's sister Margaret was sent to visit him in Liverpool with his letters of credence, cash and instructions from de Valera.

The latter told him that he would be the 'representative of the [Irish] government in Argentina'. The salary attached to the position was £500 per annum 'to cover all expenses, office and personnel, attendant on the appointment'. De Valera confessed that it was 'impossible in the present circumstances to do more than give you a general outline of what is to be done'. But he could give Bulfin no guarantee 'as to the length of time during which we will be able to retain the services of our foreign representatives as this will depend upon the developments which may take place'.[162] The British authorities allowed him to keep the letters of instruction brought by Margaret Pearse but it is probable that they confiscated the cash to cover the cost of his deportation. Bulfin claimed when applying for a pension in 1955 that he never received the £500 a year due to him.[163]

On 13 May 1919, Bulfin was escorted to the SS *Deseado* and deported to Argentina. Arriving in Buenos Aires, he was met by the editor of *The Southern Cross*, Gerald Foley, Mgr Santiago Ussher and others.[164] His sister Anita, who had been sent by her mother to Buenos Aires in 1918 in order to restore her failing health, was also there to greet him. But before he could begin his duties as a Dáil Éireann envoy, the authorities informed him that he was obliged to do military service as an Argentine citizen. Not even the influence of his late father's well-connected friends could prevent him from being drafted into the Argentine navy. Bulfin, tall, strong and athletic, was first employed as a stoker sailing up and down the coast and later as a ship's cook. After a number of months, an appeal for his discharge, based on the fact that he was the only son of a widow, was successful. He re-entered civilian life on 13 January 1920 and thus began his delayed career as a diplomat in Buenos Aires.[165]

BRITISH DIPLOMACY IN BUENOS AIRES

Paradoxically, Bulfin's opposite number in the British mission in Buenos Aires had Irish roots on both his father and mother's side. Sir David Kelly, who would serve as the British ambassador to Argentina between 1942 and 1946, first served as a young diplomat in Buenos Aires from 1919 to 1921.[166] As his name suggests, he was of Anglo-Irish stock. Born in Adelaide, his father came from Derry and belonged to the 'Protestant Anglo-Irish "Garrison"'. His mother, of German background, was born in County Wicklow, the daughter of a Church of Ireland clergyman who was also professor of French and German at Queen's University Belfast. After his father died, Kelly lived in Ireland from the age of three to six years. The family then moved to London. He went to Magdalen College, Oxford, served as an officer in the First World War, and after the armistice he joined the diplomatic service.[167] In Buenos Aires, his minister, Sir Reginald Tower, was a bachelor who resided in the Plaza Hotel for the duration of his mission and was a big hit with the smart society of the aristocratic Jockey Club. He ran the British legation with one career diplomatic secretary and a locally recruited archivist who was also a private secretary and translator. Due to the First World War, a military and naval attaché, a commercial diplomatic secretary and two clerks were added to the legation staff. Tower, who entered the services of the Foreign Office during Victoria's reign, claimed to have been the first English diplomat to have used a typewriter, breaking with the tradition of hand-writing reports with fourteen lines to a page which might be read by Queen Victoria.[168]

Kelly replaced Eugen 'Millars' Millington-Drake as diplomatic secretary. Both first met at Magdalen College, Oxford. The latter was made British attaché to St Petersburg in 1912 and was transferred to Buenos Aires in 1915. Before leaving for a new posting in 1919 at the Paris Peace Conference, he tutored Kelly on local diplomatic mores and introduced him to the families who owned the great palaces of Buenos Aires. He also sponsored Kelly for membership of the Jockey Club and for the even more exclusive Círculo de Armas, where he distinguished himself as a fencer in an institution boasting no fewer than four fencing masters.[169]

Away from such hauteur, the British colony, composed of professionals, business people, etc., lived comfortably on the outskirts of Buenos Aires in the English neighbourhoods in Temperley, Olivos, Martínez, Banfield, Adreogué, Lomos de Zamora, Belgrano 'R', Wilde, Acassurso, San Isidro and Hurlingham. Kelly noted that 'the garden city of Hurlingham ... with its admirable organized country club, complete with facilities for polo, cricket, tennis, squash, golf, swimming and riding, was in 1919 still an almost exclusively British settlement', as was the Buenos Aires Lawn Tennis Club and the Córdoba Athletic Club.[170] The economic and political power in 1919 in Argentina of 'British banking, railway, waterworks, gas, docks, the ocean cable telegraph, electricity, tramways, telephones and finally wireless [interests]'[171] was formidable.

Tower and his legation staff were very much part of an 'old school' diplomacy which remained close to the Argentine 'plutocracy'. When the Radical Party leader Hipólito Yrigoyen assumed the office of president of Argentina in 1916, Tower visited him for a protocolary visit during the course of which he was injudicious enough to remind Yrigoyen of what he described as the established precedent that a new Argentine president traditionally consulted the British government before forming his cabinet. 'That is a custom the ambassador must terminate', was the tart reply Tower received.[172] This exchange may be more anecdote than historical fact, but it serves to illustrate the asymmetry of the relationship between London and Buenos Aires. It also serves to emphasise the president's strong republican views and his respect for the right to self-determination. His domestic policy would show the hundreds of thousands of immigrants who had arrived during the previous forty years that they were respected and esteemed as Argentine citizens. Yrigoyen's government would raise living standards, regulate working hours, improve factory working conditions and introduce compulsory pensions and universal access to public education. The economy experienced unprecedented growth between 1917 and 1922 but at a cost of high inflation and growing disquiet among the estancieros, industrialists and merchants. Moreover, Yrigoyen's foreign policy of neutrality during the latter part of the First World War was perceived by the British as being pro-German. Thus, the British government was seen to side with the plutocrats or oligarchs, who were the sworn enemies of Yrigoyen. Confident that the old order would soon be restored, Kelly viewed the president as a 'demagogue' who was idolised by those who had an 'instinct for a popular dictator' and who groped 'blindly and instinctively for some personal leader – a *caudillo* in the South American tradition – with a mystical rather than a rational appeal'.[173] When Tower was leaving his posting in 1919, the Jockey Club threw him a party attended by several hundred people. Kelly, who was present, made another observation in his memoir that 'the principal function of the banquet' was 'a political demonstration against Yrigoyen'.[174] Replaced by Sir Ronald Macleay in the southern summer of 1919, this practitioner of the 'old diplomacy' continued to run the business of the legation at its usual leisurely pace.[175] Hardly in the door, Macleay and his wife set out for Mar del Plata for holidays lasting from December 1919 to February 1920, having left on his desk blank sheets of despatch papers containing only his signature. Kelly had complete discretion to compose and send reports under the signature of the minister.[176] By early 1920, however, British diplomats in Buenos Aires would be confronted by widespread opposition to their country's human rights abuses in Ireland.

THE DEATH OF THE LORD MAYOR OF CORK: THE VOICE OF THE PAMPAS

Unable to communicate with Dublin while sailing along the Argentine coast, Bulfin's superiors back home had no idea why their responsible and reliable envoy had 'gone dark' and was uncontactable. His first report, dated 26 January 1920, was delivered on 19 March to headquarters in Dublin. Diarmuid Ó hÉigeartaigh, the clerk of the First Dáil and secretary to the cabinet, responded on 3 April acknowledging that Dublin knew he had been taken up for military service 'and that you were finding it difficult to obtain exemption. We are glad to hear that you have now succeeded'.[177] Both men knew each other from their time together as internees after the 1916 Rising and from before as activists in the Gaelic League, the IRB and the Irish Volunteers. Bringing his friend up to date, Ó hÉigeartaigh told him that there had been 'nothing but a continued round of suppressions and proclamations ... police and military murders, arrests, raids and deportations' since he left Ireland. He was also told: '... we own Ireland' and that 'the British hold is only maintained by virtue of one hundred thousand soldiers and ten thousand police'. Dublin was confident that Bulfin would 'accomplish a good deal' in his post.[178] Responding to a query, Ó hÉigeartaigh confirmed that he had not yet heard from Bulfin's uncle by marriage Pádraic MacManus, whom headquarters knew to be a difficult personality and a divisive figure in Irish Argentina. Thanks to Bulfin, he would 'be in a position to deal with any [correspondence] that may come'.[179] The Irish

envoy quickly became aware that the Irish-Argentine community was divided
long before the Irish war of independence. The row dated back to conflict in
the Irish Catholic Association which began in 1900 over the newly opened
Santa Brígida school. The row smouldered on a decade later, as is evident in the
columns of MacManus' magazine *Fianna*, published between 1910 and 1912.[180]
While the details of the disputes were forgotten by 1920, the sense of grievance
and personality clashes remained active. Dublin knew that MacManus was
prominent in La Liga Republicana Irlandesa, which held public meetings
and made collections on behalf of the victims of British violence in Ireland.[181]
Bulfin, with no resources at his disposal but with the help of his sister Anita,
relied on the support of the Comité Argentino pro-Libertad de Irlanda (the
Argentine Committee for the Freedom of Ireland), their slogan being: *Por la
libertad; por la democracia; por la independencia.* The group was a combination
of prominent Argentines and Irish-Argentines who supported the governing
Unión Cívica Radical (UCR) Party.

While the British Foreign Office knew that President Yrigoyen and
his government were beholden to British capital investment in Argentina,
it was also known that leading members of the Radical Party trailed their
coats on the Irish question. The UCR counted on Irish votes, and some of
its more prominent members actively and publicly supported the cause of
Irish independence. The minister for agriculture, Carlos P. Goyena, actively
campaigned for Irish independence and spoke at public events in favour of
that cause.[182] Bulfin's father's circle of friends, besides helping to rescue him
early from military service, stood by him as he set up his campaign of action.
Unable to afford to rent an office for the legation, Gerald Foley, the editor of
TSC, who had just bought out the Bulfin family ownership of the paper with
a consortium of interested parties, gave the envoy office space in its premises
from where he could run operations. That also gave Bulfin and his sister Anita
the opportunity to place pro-Irish articles in the weekly paper. As *TSC* had
its own printing press, it could be used to turn out fliers and posters exposing
British atrocities in Ireland.

Before leaving Ireland, Collins gave Bulfin a secret order to send back arms
to Ireland. He got help from the Ballasty family in Mercedes to procure some
weapons. Writing to the Military Pensions Board on 10 December 1935, he
said: 'I purchased arms, which I sent to Ireland via Liverpool, my activity in
this connexion was limited by the financial resources at my disposal. I may
mention here that I had to borrow sums of money for the purchase of arms
which I refunded personally. I'm still out of pocket to the extent of over
£100.'[183] Gun-running, however, did not take up that much of the envoy's time.

In his negotiations with leading Irish-Argentines, Bulfin found that blood was often thicker than water: the Irish-Argentine railway mogul John Nelson, the Irish-Argentine businessman James E. Bowen and the Irish-Argentine estanciero William Morgan were among the wealthiest of the Irish-Argentines who supported Ireland's struggle for independence. Bulfin was also strongly supported by Irish chaplains working in the pampas, Frs Richard Gearty in San Antonio de Areco, Edmund Flannery in San Pedro and Juan M. Sheehy in Rosario. He had the backing of Fr Patrick O'Grady in Mercedes, and other Irish Pallottines. The Passionist priests in the capital and countryside were very sympathetic. Fr Fidelis Fowler stood out in that regard. His clerical support gave him access to most of the Irish-Argentine Catholics in the camp.

Bulfin's strongest and most successful propaganda campaign centred around the tragic case of Terence MacSwiney, the playwright, poet, pamphleteer, journalist and politician. Without ever firing a shot, that leading member of the Irish Volunteers was arrested in Cork after the 1916 Rising and imprisoned until December in Reading and Wakefield jails. In February 1917, he was held again, imprisoned in camps in Shrewsbury and Bromyard. Released in June 1917, he married, and was arrested again in November for wearing an Irish Volunteer uniform. He went on hunger strike for three days before being released. Elected a TD in 1918, he remained active in politics. When the lord mayor of Cork, Tomás MacCurtain, was murdered by British crown forces on 20 March 1920, MacSwiney was chosen to succeed him. Four days later he was arrested for being in possession of 'seditious articles and documents' and sentenced on the 16th of April to two years in Brixton jail, where he immediately went on a hunger strike which lasted for seventy-four days. It ended with his death on 25 October 1920.

The British government had a well-structured propaganda network in Latin America and was confident that it was sufficiently robust to counter growing anti-British sentiment in the region. Charles Grant Duff, a senior civil servant in London, noted on 21 September 1920 that anti-British information, with its origins in New York and in other parts of the US, continued to grow in 'all the South American Republics'. Unfazed by that development, he observed that the principal newspapers of the Argentine republic were 'systematically supplied by us with news and information on the Irish question'. London, he minuted, sent out cables bi-weekly to provide British missions with 'contradictory statements to any untruths which may appear in the South American Press'. He concluded optimistically that while 'at present a propagandist's Utopia, I think that both in quality and quantity we are more than holding our own [in Latin America]'.[184]

With the help of Irish-Argentine societies and individuals, Irish missionaries, chaplains and nuns, Bulfin helped mount demonstrations in Buenos Aires and

1.20 & 1.21 Medal struck by Irish Argentines to commemorate the death of the lord mayor of Cork, Terence MacSwiney, in October 1921. The reverse side reproduces his words: 'It is not those who can inflict the most but those who can endure the most who will conquer.' This medal was presented by Eduardo Clancy, San Antonio de Areco, to the lord mayor of Cork in 2017. It had been given to a member of Clancy's family in 1920 in gratitude for his donation to an Irish victim relief fund.

in the towns of the camp to rally support for the dying lord mayor. He also found that strong support also came from members of the Radical Party and organisations representing groups of immigrants from Europe and elsewhere. On 26 and 27 September 1920, crowds gathered in the spacious grounds of the Passionist monastery of St Paul's, Capitán Sarmiento, to celebrate the jubilee of the opening of the house. They also gathered to give thanks for the beatification in Rome on 23 May of the archbishop of Armagh, Blessed Oliver Plunkett, who had been hanged, drawn and quartered at Tyburn on 1 July 1681 for remaining loyal to his Catholic faith. Irish and Argentine flags flew over the monastery grounds. The rector, Fr Fidelis Fowler, blessed 'a beautiful, silken Sinn Féin flag' made by Irish nuns. At mass in the large church adjoining the monastery, Fr Santiago Ussher said in his sermon: 'Let us hope, then, that Ireland at long last, her struggle ended, her shackles broken, free and independent, be recognized among the free nations of the earth.' The Irish national anthem – the Soldier's Song – was sung at the end of the final concert and touched 'a respondent note in all hearts', commented *TSC*.[185]

On 10 October, two weeks before MacSwiney's death, La Liga Republicana Irlandesa and the Comité Argentina pro Libertad de Irlanda combined to call a meeting of their respective members to set up a joint special commission to organise appropriate homage to the dying lord mayor.[186] Prayers were said for him in chapels in the camp and in Buenos Aires. MacSwiney died on 25 October in Brixton Prison. He was forty-one. His coffin was placed in Southwark Cathedral in London, where thousands filed past to pay their respects. After the requiem mass the following day, Archbishop Daniel Mannix and over three hundred clergy walked behind the remains, followed by a huge procession. Huge crowds gathered in Cork to receive the remains, which came from Dublin. Before being buried in St Finbarr's cemetery, his cortège brought Cork city to a standstill.

In Buenos Aires, Irish Catholics gathered at Holy Cross on 29 October for a requiem mass celebrated by Mgr Ussher, who was also joined by Fr Juan Morgan Sheehy from Rosario and Thomas O'Grady from Capilla del Señor. Many people came from Córdoba and from Santa Fe, from Salta, and from the different towns in the camp to commemorate the death of the lord mayor.[187] The following day, Saturday 30th, there was another mass, at the Basilica of St Francis in Buenos Aires, attended by many of the most distinguished personalities in the country: politicians, military officers, diplomats, high civil servants, clergy and many deputies and senators.[188] On the same weekend and in the weeks following, requiem masses were said for the deceased lord mayor before large congregations in Mercedes, Rojas, Salto, Rosario, Carmen de Areco, Arrecifes, Junín, Capitán Sarmiento, Venado Tuerto, Pergamino, Navarro, General Pinto and Córdoba.[189] The Comité Argentina organised a protest meeting in the Teatro Nuevo at which the minister for agriculture, Carlos Goyena, was present. That group claimed that it had distributed 10,000 leaflets in Buenos Aires on 2 November 1920, and later made a second leaflet drop with messages from leading figures in support of Irish independence. A paper, *La Voz de la Justicia*, was published in Pergamino in support of the deceased lord mayor. The Comité Argentina also struck a commemorative medal in silver and bronze in his honour.[190]

Such nationalist activities had begun to disturb the equilibrium of the British envoy extraordinary and minister plenipotentiary Ronald Macleay, who reported on 4 November 1920 that, following the death of 'MacSweeney [*sic*], a number of Requiem Masses have been held in Buenos Aires with the approval of the Archbishop of Buenos Aires, and have been attended by the local Irish community, including the wealthier section who do not usually care to identify themselves, openly at least, with "Sinn Féin" activities'.[191] Macleay said that since his arrival in late 1919, he had followed the efforts of the 'extreme Irish elements' to rouse Argentine opinion on the Irish question 'in a sense hostile to

His Majesty's Government, by posters, pamphlets, and participation in popular Argentine demonstrations'. He thought the Argentine press had kept its readers very well informed as regards Irish developments and 'its editorial comments have always been carefully worded so as to avoid giving offence to His Majesty's Government, and no attempt seems to me to have been made to select or in any way discriminate in the publication of news on these subjects'. He regarded the attitude of the Argentine government as being 'equally impartial'. On hearing of plans for a public protest in the streets to be led by the Irish republican flags, the British envoy 'was able to cause private representations to be made to the Chief of Police, suggesting the danger of a disturbance to the public order, which were effectively acted upon'. The police took appropriate action and Macleay was satisfied that 'this [Sinn Féin] propaganda has, on the whole, fallen flat as regards the mass of Argentines, who do not in any case seem to feel very strongly about anything not materially affecting their own interests'.[192]

In the last few weeks of 1920, the bad news from Ireland grew exponentially. On 21 November, Michael Collins sent an IRA squad to assassinate undercover British intelligence officers. Fifteen died in the attacks, nine of them British army officers. As a reprisal, British forces entered Croke Park GAA sports grounds later that day during a football match between Dublin and Tipperary, and opened fire indiscriminately upon the players and on about 5,000 spectators. Six were shot dead – including the player Michael Hogan – and five others later died of their wounds. A second footballer was seriously wounded but survived. Later that Sunday night, three nationalist prisoners were murdered in crown custody in Dublin, shot 'while trying to escape'. In Cork, on the night of 11/12 December, British forces deliberately burnt down the city centre, destroying forty business premises, 300 residential properties, the Carnegie library and the city hall. Many were left homeless. Two thousand jobs were lost and the cost of the damage was estimated at the time at over three million pounds.[193] About the time of those terrible events, the Argentine minister for foreign affairs, Honorio Pueyrredón, went to Geneva for meetings of the League of Nations. He visited London, where he was presented to the king of England and had meetings with senior British ministers. It is probable that the British, among other pressing issues, briefed the Argentine minister on the Irish situation and urged him to keep the Argentine government from taking sides in the conflict.[194]

Bulfin was first and foremost a soldier and quickly tired of his role as envoy. He told Michael Collins in a letter on 17 March 1921: 'Every time I see the papers and read of the boys [the IRA] I get a kind of crazy … I want to be back with them and I am going.'[195] Apart from that reference, Bulfin wrote without complaint that he was glad finally to be receiving regular news bulletins from Dublin together with copies of the *Irish Bulletin*. He was raising funds to have the material translated and distributed in Latin America. He stressed that work had to be done well or nobody would take 'the least notice, except to smile pityingly and pass on'. He told Collins to keep in mind that 'Argentina is pre-eminently a country where people are judged by their clothes (they are the best dressed people in the world), a country where the value of things is largely estimated by the "splash" they make'. Bulfin was disappointed not to get an answer from the United States about, I assume, sending further personnel to Buenos Aires. He did not think that they would look favourably upon the suggestion as 'the Yanks are inclined to regard all South Americans as so many Indians'. Bulfin had lived in hope that he would get help from the US, 'but I feel certain that it is vain to expect anything, they have too many troubles of their own'.[196] He also spoke of the serious divisions within Irish Argentina and that he was unable to control the factions. He was particularly critical of the fact that 'money is being collected here just now for the White Cross, but the clergy are in control, so that there is no chance of sequestering any for our purposes. Incidentally this collection is rottenly organized with the result that not a third of the money which could be got will be collected. Both parties are running a collection. Fine is it not. Impossible to try and get things done rightly ... but things are not rosy among our people out here'.[197] The perils of writing in wartime were well illustrated when the British intercepted Bulfin's typed letter. He was unguarded enough to give his change of address to Nevin's grocery store, the family home of Kathleen Nevin, the author of *You'll Never Go Back*, at Bartolomé Mitre 520, Buenos Aires.[198] The translation of the Irish names caused difficulties in London. A.F. Hemmings of the Irish Office wrote on 12 July 1921 to the Foreign Office: 'I have ascertained that the signature in Erse to the document addressed to Michael Collins is that of E. Bulfin, Sinn Fein representative in the Argentine'.[199]

The Irish White Cross (IWC) already referred to by Bulfin was a non-political and non-partisan body set up in Dublin on 1 February 1921 by the Quaker businessman James G. Douglas. Cardinal Michael Logue was president and the lord mayor of Dublin, Larry O'Neill, was its chairman. Arthur Griffith, Michael Collins and Thomas Johnson (Labour Party leader) were among the trustees. Its general council was comprised of two Catholic archbishops; two bishops of the Church of Ireland; the chief rabbi; an ex-president of the Methodist Conference and by leading members of the Society of Friends. The violence in Ireland had left about 25,000 families or 100,000 in need.[200] The main function of the IWC was to distribute funds raised by the American

Committee for Relief in Ireland and other money sent from abroad together with donations made in Ireland. The Irish Argentine White Cross (IAWC), a branch committed to raising donations, was set up in Buenos Aires in March 1921. Ussher became its president. The provincial of the Pallottines, Fr Patrick O'Grady, was its treasurer and the remainder of the committee was made up of other Pallottines and Passionists.[201] With the weekly help of *TSC*, a public appeal met with great generosity. The names and amounts donated were published weekly in the paper together with a running balance of the overall amount subscribed. There was controversy when an editorial in the English-language paper *The Standard* (edited by Dubliners Michael and Edward Mulhall) suggested that 'only the distressed of the Sinn Fein persuasion would have any participation therein'.[202] Ussher published a detailed refutation on 14 June in the *Buenos Aires Herald*. That controversy, if anything, spurred people on to give more. Some £400 was sent to Cardinal Logue. He acknowledged receipt in a letter to Fr O'Grady on 15 July 1921: 'Hitherto most of the money [mainly from the US] has been sent through me which involves an amount of correspondence which is very heavy for a man in his eighty-first year.'[203] That did not deter the IAWC. When Ussher closed the fund in January 1922, it had sent Logue, in three drafts, 52,041 pesos amounting to £4,210-14s.[204] That was an enormous sum – much of it coming from the *centavos* or pennies of very poor Irish-Argentines.

Between December 1920 and July 1921, two major events occurred which changed the direction of Anglo-Irish relations. The British government passed the Government of Ireland Bill on 23 December 1920, which came into force in May 1921. It created two bicameral parliaments, the northern parliament for the six north-eastern counties and the southern parliament for the remaining twenty-six counties. Elections were held on 24 May. In Northern Ireland, out of fifty-two seats, unionists won forty, moderate nationalists won six and Sinn Féin took six. Sir James Craig became prime minister. King George V opened the parliament on 22 June 1922. Sinn Féin took 124 out of 128 seats for the Dublin parliament and, refusing to recognise the Government of Ireland Act, brought into being the second Dáil.[205] The declaration of a truce on 11 July between the prime minister, Lloyd George, and the president of Dáil Éireann, Éamon de Valera, was the second key event in Ireland that year.[206] Britain's draconian military tactics, whatever about gaining victories in the field, were losing the international propaganda war.[207]

Fr Patrick O'Grady, the provincial of the Pallottines and deputy treasurer of the Irish Argentine White Cross, arrived in Dublin on the day the truce was declared and the fighting ceased. Writing to Ussher on 18 July, he said:

The streets were crowded with people – men, women and children – and continued so during the night. The greatest order was observed, while the police were conspicuous for their absence. I hope we shall have true peace, national and honourable. The people are very quiet and say very little; the priests, except you get one of them alone, are rather reticent because they wish to be careful with regard to what they say and in a special manner the Archbishop of Cashel in public says very little. They have had awful times here; very few would wish to pass a winter as the last one. The Sinn Fein Army is very well trained and is prepared to fight for five years more but I believe all wish peace, especially the older people, some of whom do not sympathise with the Sinn Feiners. But I am convinced these are very few, particularly now, as the Sinn Feiners are the winners.[208]

LAURENCE GINNELL, IRELAND'S SECOND ENVOY IN ARGENTINA

A month before the truce, the Irish under-secretary of foreign affairs, Robert Brennan, highlighted to Dáil Éireann on 6 June 1921 the 'great encouragement' Bulfin felt for the future support that might be expected for the (Irish) republican cause from within government in Buenos Aires: 'In the opinion of Mr Bulfin the President of the Argentine is favourably disposed towards the Irish Republican Cause, and if the United States Government recognised the Irish Republic he (Mr. Bulfin) feels sure that the Argentine Government would do likewise.' Brennan reported that Bulfin remained concerned that a ten-year-old split in the Irish community continued to work against consolidating the full power of the Irish there. He highlighted the envoy's plan to publish a regular bulletin about what was happening in Ireland.[209]

The president of Dáil Éireann, Éamon de Valera, issued a message on 14 June 1921 which may have been sent to the presidents of Latin American republics: 'Remembering their own struggle which they sustained in the past to conquer their national liberty these peoples cannot refuse their sympathy to us in the similar struggle which we are sustaining at this moment and they will join with us in offering prayers to Heaven that we may be granted an equally successful issue.'[210] Shortly after the issuing of that statement, Laurence Ginnell, *teachta dála* (TD) for Westmeath,[211] was sent to Argentina. Born in 1852, he was a lawyer, an author, a polemicist and a social agitator. An independent-minded nationalist MP between 1906 and 1918, he had been expelled from the Irish Parliamentary Party in 1909 and thereafter sat as an independent nationalist in Westminster. Ginnell was the most outspoken of all Irish MPs following the executions in 1916 and was ejected from the House of Commons for his fiery contribution. He was elected a Sinn Féin TD in 1919. He spent the following two years in the US as part of de Valera's staff.

A thorn in the side of the British authorities as a social agitator and land reformer since the 1880s, Ginnell had the distinct advantage when posted to Buenos Aires of being from Delvin, County Westmeath, a county from which many had emigrated and gone to the pampas. Irish immigrants there remembered him to have been the leader of the ranch war between 1906 and 1909 which encouraged cattle-driving (removing livestock from disputed land) to draw attention to the power of ranchers and graziers and to the social inequalities in the Irish countryside. His reputation as a social agitator in that regard may not have endeared him to leading Irish estancieros.[212] *TSC* recorded his exploits over the years in some detail. De Valera signed his credentials as an accredited member of the Irish diplomatic service to the governments and peoples of South America. The hope was that he would have the opportunity to present them to President Yrigoyen, or to the foreign minister, Honorio Pueyrredón. He also had instructions to present his credentials personally to the presidents of Chile, Brazil and Bolivia at a later date. Refusing to use a British passport, he acquired travel documents for both himself and his wife Alice from the US consulate in New York and they were viséd by the Argentine consulate. There was a large gathering of their friends on the quayside when the couple sailed on 3 July 1921. While they were on the high seas, a truce was declared on 11 July in Ireland. De Valera began a correspondence with the British prime minister, David Lloyd George, in July.[213] The Anglo-Irish Treaty was signed on 6 December 1921.[214] Both events, the truce and the signing of the treaty, bookmarked the Ginnell mission. Arriving in Buenos Aires on 25 July 1921, the couple were met by Eamonn Bulfin, Mgr Ussher and Gerald Foley, the editor of *TSC*. Wearing a silk black top hat and sporting his familiar white beard, Ginnell's patrician appearance resembled more a member of the local Jockey Club than that of a dangerous revolutionary. Although sixty-nine and in poor health, he showed great enthusiasm for his new assignment. In his first press conference, Ginnell said that he had come as a special envoy of the Irish republican government on an official mission to the countries of South America. He showed his credentials – in English, French and Irish[215] – to an Associated Press journalist. The British envoy, Macleay, relayed the substance of his comments to London. While unwilling to comment on the details of the talks between de Valera and Lloyd George, Ginnell was reported as saying that he was not 'optimistic as to their outcome, as the English and Irish points of view were entirely distinct. For England the question resolved itself into keeping Ireland in the Empire, for the Irish it was a question of complete

Government of the Irish Republic.

To all to whom These Presents come, Greeting:

In VIRTUE of the authority vested in me by Dáil Éireann
I hereby appoint *Honourable Laurence Ginnell TD*
of *City of Dublin, Ireland*
at *the behest of the Minister of Foreign Affairs*
as *Special Envoy* — from the elected Government of the Irish Republic
to *The Governments and Peoples of South America*
with all the privileges and authorities of right appertaining to that office.

In Witness whereof I hereunto subscribe my name as President of Dáil Éireann.

Done in the City of Dublin this *31st day of May*
in the Year of our Lord 19*21.*

Éamon de Valera.

1.22 Letter of credence for Dáil Éireann envoy Laurence Ginnell posting him to 'the Governments and Peoples of South America' and signed by Éamon de Valera on 31 May 1921

and absolute freedom'.[216] Anxious to gauge the foreign minister Honorio Pueyrredón's reaction to Ginnell's arrival, Macleay arranged a meeting for the 27th and was surprised to be told that the minister knew nothing of Ginnell's arrival in the country. But he was assured that Argentina would act correctly in the matter, Pueyrredón reminding him that President Yrigoyen had not replied to de Valera's telegram mentioned above. After that discussion, the British envoy commented to London:

> I expect that the Argentine Government will be considerably embarrassed by Mr Ginnell's arrival and specially by his avowed intention to make Buenos Aires his headquarters and I do not think that we need fear that he will receive any official support and encouragement, but I am apprehensive that with the assistance of the numerous and wealthy disloyal Irish element here and their support he may get unofficially into touch with the President and other influential persons in his entourage who I suspect of sympathising with the Irish cause and thus giving us trouble especially if peace negotiations break down.[217]

Outlining further concerns of a graver nature, Macleay reported on 6 August: 'Prior to Ginnell's departure the Argentine Government were (? in favour of)

1.23 Laurence and Alice Ginnell (in back seat) driving through Mercedes on a visit to the Irish Pallottines in September 1921

his admission into the Argentine. This was agreed by two countries in view of the possibility of Ireland being granted her independence as a result of conferences now proceeding in London. In the event of the establishment of Irish independence, the United States of America would be the first country to recognise it and the Argentine would follow.' He added that Ginnell had been granted full powers to arrange diplomatic and commercial treaties with the latter.[218]

Not wasting any time, Ginnell sent an official request to Pueyrredón on 5 August for permission to present his credentials to President Yrigoyen. The *Freeman's Journal* reported that should his request be granted, he intended to ask the president to recognise the 'Irish Republic' and added that, 'in the meantime, it is understood that Señor Pueyrredón is consulting Mr. MacLeay [*sic*], the British minister, on the subject'.[219] Ginnell delivered a speech in Spanish at his hotel to a delegation from the Comité Argentino pro Libertad de Irlanda. Afterwards, they escorted him to the cathedral, where he laid a wreath at the tomb of General San Martín with an inscription in Spanish which read: 'To General San Martín, Commander of the Army of Freedom in which was formed the Irish Legion. From the Government and people of Ireland.' Ginnell's speech, published in full in *TSC*, annoyed Macleay, who reported on 18 August that the paper 'has always been pronouncedly anti-English and disloyal'.[220] Macleay was dismissive of the wreath-laying: 'This performance excited but little interest outside the Irish elements and was scarcely noticed in the press.' However, he was deeply upset by the reception afforded to Ginnell on 12 August 1921 at the ceremonies to mark the anniversary of the defeat in 1806 of the English invasion of Buenos Aires. Two days before the ceremonies, Macleay met Pueyrredón at his weekly reception for diplomats and explained how he had been upset by the content of articles in the government-orientated *La Época*. But it was not a government event. The celebrations were organised by an unofficial committee. Macleay read in that paper that various Irish clubs had been invited, and concluded that the organisers intended to give Ginnell a prominent place among the official guests at the ceremony 'and generally to make the celebration of the anniversary the occasion for an anti-English demonstration'. The minister assured the British envoy that 'there was absolutely no trace of ill feeling or hostility' towards Britain in the celebration of the *Reconquista* or reconquest of Buenos Aires. The minister said he would check with the organising committee to ensure that nothing untoward would happen.[221] It was customary for the British embassy to receive an invitation to attend the annual event. The convention was that the British envoy remained absent. On the day in question, the president of Argentina, cabinet ministers and representatives of the armed forces, together with the Spanish ambassador, attended a Te Deum in the Church of Santo Domingo. After the event, Macleay was informed that Ginnell, upon entering, bowed to President Yrigoyen, who returned the salutation. The Irish flag was the only foreign flag in the church. After the ceremony, Macleay was told that Ginnell[222] had been received by the president of the organising committee, Señor Ibarra Pedernera, and by members of the 'Irish Club'. He was conducted to the place reserved for distinguished guests, including the heads of the armed forces. Macleay credited Pueyrredón with ensuring that none of the government speeches made any reference to Ireland, adding optimistically that the 'mass of educated Argentine opinion, excluding, of course, the Irish-Argentine element and people under German or other hostile influences', realised that the British government 'could not agree to the existence of an independent Irish Republic'. Macleay wished he could say the same for the Argentine government and for President Yrigoyen 'as under his extremely personal and autocratic methods the Ministers are merely the subservient instruments of his will who have no initiative and little or no voice in the conduct of affairs'. In his view, the president was motivated by the desire to win the votes of the Irish community, 'the majority of whom are Argentine by the lex soli and who in many cases have amassed sufficient wealth and influence to constitute a factor of considerable moment in a Presidential election'. In such circumstances, Macleay concluded that he would not be surprised if 'the so called Special Envoy of the Irish Republic does not succeed in obtaining a private audience with His Excellency, if possible, not through the Diplomatic channel'.[223] Macleay told London that leading Irish-Argentines on 17 August 1921 had held an official reception for the Ginnells. This occasion was not so easily dismissed, as leading Irish-Argentine estancieros, industrialists and railway moguls were behind the occasion: John Nelson, Daniel Morgan, Patricio Dowling, Mgr James Ussher, Charlie Duggan, Tom Moore, M.Z. O'Farrell, John Duggan, Edward Maguire, Dr Thomas Gahan, Eugene Moore, Patricio Cole and J.E. Bowen. Macleay was told that 'Mr Ginnell was solemnly introduced as the honourable Lawrence [*sic*] Ginnell, Special Ambassador of the Irish Republic'.[224]

While Ginnell's request to meet the president was turned down, he was granted a private meeting on 19 August 1921 with Pueyrredón.[225] The following morning, *La Prensa* reported that while the conversation was of a very cordial character, the foreign minister had made clear that the meeting was a courtesy call, purely private, and had no official status. The same day, Macleay sent an alarmist report to London:

> I learned from my secret source that a man named E. Bulfin who is leader of disaffected Irish element here and is said to be future Consul of Irish republic, conveyed yesterday the following confidence in all seriousness to an Irish sympathizer ... [that the Sinn Féiners are] determined to obtain the absolute independence of Ireland even if this necessitates a declaration of war on England for which they are well prepared. They are already in a position to obtain transport of troops from England by means

of secret agents in London and Liverpool, who will burn and destroy to that end. Bulfin also affirms that they will have the assistance of two secret submarines and other hidden means of destruction. They can also count on munitions of war from United States and they are expecting arrival of two aeroplanes from that country by contraband means, such having been already utilized for receptions of war materials.[226]

Blindsided by only having heard from a journalist of the meeting between the Irish envoy and Pueyrredón, Macleay gave details on 21 August to the British Foreign Office of what he knew about the encounter – Ginnell had shown his credentials to Pueyrredón, who refused to accept them. The British envoy concluded that the Argentine government's attitude 'has been distinctly unfriendly to His Majesty's Government because they must have been aware … of objects of his mission'. Macleay again attributed responsibility for the meeting to the president (Yrigoyen) because of his desire to win the votes of the Irish-Argentine community at the presidential elections in 1922.[227]

While awaiting instructions from London, Macleay met Pueyrredón in the Foreign Office on 24 August during his weekly reception for ambassadors. Speaking in a private and personal capacity, Macleay expressed his surprise to him not only that Ginnell should have been received at the ministry but that the minister should have considered it necessary to see him at all, knowing as he did the objects and nature of the latter's mission. Pueyrredón insisted he had made it clear to the Irish envoy that their meeting was of a purely private character. He added that Ginnell, nevertheless, claiming to speak on behalf of four million Irish people who were demanding complete independence, had asked the minister to arrange an audience with the president in order that he might present his credentials and obtain the Argentine government's recognition of the Irish republic. Pueyrredón told Macleay that he had refused to do so. Ginnell, he said, then asked if the Argentine government would allow him to float a loan in Buenos Aires in support of the Irish republic. Pueyrredón replied in the negative. He promised to show Macleay his written answers to Ginnell on another occasion.[228] The following day, 25 August, the Foreign Office instructed Macleay to advise the Argentine government of 'our extreme surprise that Mr Ginnell should have been received, whether officially or privately, by the Minister of Foreign Affairs, when he has broadcast that he entered the Argentine without a passport as special envoy of the Irish Republic, a state which has no existence, Ireland being an integral part of the United Kingdom within the British Empire'.[229] Macleay conveyed that message to Pueyrredón.

Ginnell, undaunted by the outcome of his meeting at the foreign ministry, carried on as if he was now accredited as an Irish envoy. He opened Irish legation offices in the fashionable Galería Güemes and employed a translator/secretary. Bulfin's sister Anita helped with the administration and with writing reports for distribution on British violence in Ireland. She also acted as sub-editor for texts in both English and Spanish. Ginnell's wife Alice acted as her husband's personal administrator. She took care of his diary, the bookings for speaking engagements, and his extensive travel schedule to the towns in the camp. Alice was rather overbearing at first and that caused friction with the Bulfins, but, despite personal lingering tensions between the two women, all efforts were focused on improving the reach of Irish propaganda in Latin America. Ginnell and Eamonn Bulfin developed a good working relationship.

Ginnell used proven propaganda tactics imported from his previous campaigns in Ireland. When the British prime minister, Lloyd George, made a threatening statement regarding the use of mass arrests in Ireland, Ginnell briefed the local press claiming that Britain planned to use severities 'far exceeding anything ever witnessed in Western Europe'. When *La Prensa* published the British prime minister's own words, the Irish envoy cut out the report, headed it 'What England offers to Ireland: submission or destruction', and issued it as a poster which was stuck up around the city.[230] By way of background, Bulfin noted that a Mr MacConastair[231] helped get the poster out and added, 'It was with some difficulty the municipality agreed to put up the poster, which was put up all over the city, sent to provincial centres, and put up there.'[232] The poster, a copy of which is in the British National Archives, was headed: 'Hurrah! For Liberty! Fé Inglesa!' (Extrapolating from a Press Association statement, Ginnell declared that the British intended to put an end once and for all to Sinn Féin agitation and, in capitals, wrote that the Irish were going to be arrested en masse: *'SIN ORDER DE JUEZ Y SE REANUDEN LAS ENCARCELACIONES SIN SOMETER A LOS DETENIDOS A JUICIO'* ('Without an order of the court they resume the jailings without taking the detained before a judge'). The British envoy heard from the Argentine foreign minister, about 19 September 1921, that the police had received orders to remove offensive manifestos from the walls of the city and that the 'so-called diplomatic mission of Irish republic had been warned by Chief of Police against issue of any further similar publications'. The address at the bottom of the document was Galería Güemes,[233] the location of the Irish legation offices.[234] In an overview of the work of his mission in March 1923, Ginnell wrote: 'While it was on the walls, the British Minister was silly enough to denounce the poster in a public speech. This made everybody read it, opened

¡¡Viva la REPÚBLICA ARGENTINA!!
¡¡Viva la REPÚBLICA IRLANDESA!!

A los hombres libres:
A los amantes de la libertad, del derecho y la justicia:

Hacen ocho siglos que el pueblo de IRLANDA gime bajo el yugo extranjero; y hacen ocho siglos, tambien que ese Pueblo lucha con heroismo sin igual, para conseguir la ansiada libertad de otrora.

IRLANDA, de distinta raza, de distintas costumbres, de distintos idealismo, de distinta religión y de distinto idioma que la Gran Bretaña, en una palabra; completamente separada de Inglaterra, no solo por los mares, sinó tambien por los mas intimos caracteres, capaces de definir una nacionalidad independiente; esa IRLANDA tiene derecho a su libertad, y a figurar en el concierto de los pueblos dueños de sus destinos.

Y sinembargo Inglaterra por tradicionales egoismos y propias conveniencias mercenarias se niega a oir la voz de la Justicia, ahogando en sangre sus legitimas reivindicaciones y acallando en las cárceles las voces de sus hijos mas ilustres!! La poblacion de esa desdichada Isla, de 8.175.000 en 1841, ha quedado reducida a 4.374.000

1.24 Poster displayed around Buenos Aires, *Irlanda Libre*

1.25 Laurence Ginnell, Fr Sheehy and the Irish of Venado Tuerto at a banquet in honour of the Irish envoy in August 1921

up correspondence in the Press, which the Argentine Committee dealt with; and my poster was copied into a number of papers as interesting news. Thus the whole country was prepared for my propaganda.'[235]

However, Ginnell's immediate task was to launch an Irish bond drive and he set about trying to locate a specialist printer who would take on the job. The envoy had high expectations for the campaign. In the US, Ginnell had witnessed the success of the two de Valera-led bond campaigns. By December 1921, the total raised was $5,746,360, or $74,964,360 in current value.[236] The newly arrived Irish envoy was in a far less advantageous position than his counterparts in the US. Moreover, he had – in a much poorer economic climate – to counter the efforts of the British envoy to sabotage the bond drive in Argentina. On 3 September 1921, Macleay reported that Ginnell had called on a local printer, who was 'strongly pro-British in sentiment', to get an estimate for 36,800 bond certificates in various denominations from 10 up to 10,000 pesos. Reluctant to leave the specimens with the printer, the latter 'was able to take a photograph of the specimens which he has submitted to me in strictest confidence'. Macleay told London that the printer later quoted 'a prohibitive price' so that he would not get the order.[237] However, another printer took the order, which had to be ready by early October. Meanwhile, Macleay was powerless to prevent Ginnell and Bulfin being feted by enthusiastic crowds in Mercedes, San Antonio de Areco, Capitán Sarmiento, Venado Tuerto, Rosario, etc. Wherever they went in the camp, they were greeted as the first representatives in Argentina of an independent Irish government and a sister republic. There were speeches, dinners, dances, parades and pageants in each of those towns. While both men were doing a tour of the camp, Patrick J. Little[238] arrived in Buenos Aires, sent by Dublin to help establish a newsletter and to improve the Sinn Féin publicity network throughout Latin America.[239] Previously, he had been in South Africa helping to improve the Irish news network there. He applied for a visa in Cape Town to go on a pleasure trip to Uruguay, Chile, Brazil, the US, France and England. Little's arrival highlighted a dilemma for the local British envoy; Macleay told London that he had no instruction to refuse visas to 'notorious Sinn Feiners', the passport office, with his approval, had informed Little that on his return to Argentina from Uruguay in three weeks his passport would be immediately viséd for a journey to Chile. The British feared that both Little and Ginnell would soon go to Santiago to extend the Sinn Féin propaganda network. For example, *La Nación* announced in Santiago on 17 September 1921 that Ginnell was due to arrive in the country as 'Ambassador of the Irish Republican Parliament' to Chile. It spoke about 'services which the Irish have rendered to World History' and warmly favoured the idea of an 'Independent and Triumphant Ireland'. The British ambassador to Chile, Vaughan, noted that the article was written in such a way as to convey to the Chileans that Ireland 'is nothing less than a sovereign state'. Ginnell was described as an ambassador 'without ceremony' and the paper assured him of a 'warm welcome in this country'.[240] London instructed Vaughan to tell the Chilean government that if Ginnell applied for 'any audience he must be presented by me [Vaughan] as he is a British subject or else not be received'.[241] He brought the matter up with the Chilean foreign minister, Ernesto Barros Jarpa, on 21 September, reminding him that 'any such request emanating from a British subject should be made through me'. The minister assured Vaughan that that course would be followed but – recalling what had happened in Buenos Aires – indicated that 'Mr. Ginnell might possibly ask for a private interview'. The British ambassador replied that 'the same considerations held whether the interview was made private or official'.[242] As things turned out, Ginnell never made it to Chile; the imminent launch of the Irish bonds that month in Buenos Aires made his travel there impossible at that time. That did not prevent him making further plans. He was in touch with a Bolivian deputy of Irish extraction, giving him to understand that he planned to go to La Paz in mid-October.[243]

Behind the scenes, Macleay continued with his efforts to stymie the bond drive. On 30 September 1921, he reported that he had discussed it with Pueyrredón who knew about the matter but did not attach much importance to it as Ginnell was only able to dispose of the bonds privately, stressing that the bonds could not be sold publicly. The foreign minister described Ginnell's visit to Buenos Aires as having been 'a complete fiasco'. In conclusion, Macleay reassuringly told London that the bond drive did not need to be taken seriously and that there was nobody outside the Irish community foolish enough to acquire them as an investment or even as a speculation.[244] But with the help of Little, Ginnell remained confident that the bond sale would be a success. In March 1922, he wrote in summary to Dublin that 'with infinite trouble and patient perseverance', he had managed to get 'an excellent set of Trustees to act ... and they have proved most reasonable and just men'.[245] Robert Brennan, the deputy Irish foreign minister, wrote to Bulfin on 7 October that the government had decided to back the drive and that £1,000 had been cabled to cover expenses. On 1 October, *La Prensa*, ignoring a threat from Harrods to pull its advertising, carried an Irish bond drive advertisement. *La Nación* refused to do so. *TSC*, on 7 October 1921, reported that the bonds were going on sale and, in the weeks that followed, carried a half-page advertisement for the scheme in successive issues.[246]

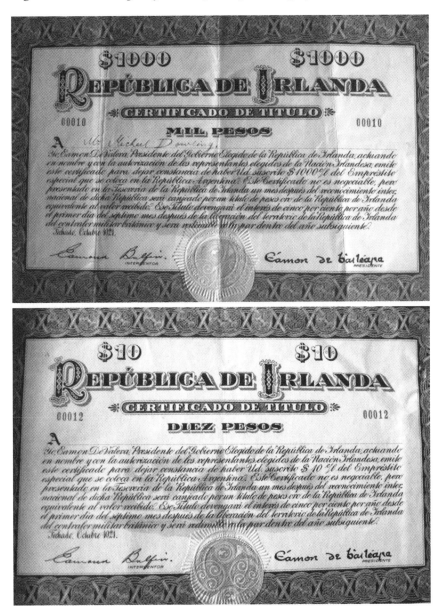

1.26 & 1.27 Irish Republican bonds offered for sale by Laurence Ginnell at the end of 1921. Note how the signatures in Irish of Éamon de Valera on the bonds and on Ginnell's letter of credence (Fig. 1.22) differ.

The British envoy did all within his power to subvert the Irish bond launch. On 8 October, Macleay wrote to Pueyrredón highlighting the reference in the advertisements to a claim that money from the sale of the bonds was to be deposited in the Banco de la Nación Argentina. The British envoy was disappointed to find that the Argentine authorities were not prepared to ban the bond advertisements. However, Macleay was not unduly worried as he felt Argentine public opinion had rapidly lost the little interest it ever placed in the Irish envoy's 'person or his cause'. As proof, he cited that on 5 October only forty of one hundred invited guests had shown up for a banquet in Ginnell's honour.[247]

Macleay's scepticism was well founded but not for the reasons he stated. In truth, Irish-Argentines were, at that point, suffering from donor fatigue. Generous public contributions to the Argentine Irish White Cross appeal ran in parallel with the bond drive. Bulfin and Little recorded that, at a meeting of the trustees on 19 October, 'every possible obstacle' had been put forward to stop a formal public launch from going ahead. Ignoring the concerns expressed by a number of trustees, Ginnell hired the Teatro Coliseo for the night of 29 October, one of the largest and most prestigious venues in the city.[248] All was not well among leading Irish-Argentines. On the morning of the event, Dowling, Moore and Nelson called to the Irish legation informing Ginnell that they did not want to sit on the platform that evening. They had taken exception to the wording on a poster advertising the event. Refusing to act as chairman on the night, John Nelson complained that the poster was 'socialist propaganda'. The elderly and well-liked Irish chaplain Fr Edmund Flannery from San Pedro had paid for a box in the theatre. He returned his tickets at the very last minute without even a 'thank you'. He, too, was put off by 'our big poster', stating that it was 'socialist propaganda' and that 'he could not be associated with it'.[249] Despite the dissent in the ranks, the meeting was well attended and the crowd was well behaved. Patrick J. Little took the chair and towards the end of proceedings proposed the formation of a new Irish organisation. The members of one Irish group 'said that, if a new organisation was formed, it would be a challenge to them, and that it was up to everyone to join their organisation'.[250] Undaunted by the criticism, Ginnell went ahead with the bond sale and also with his plans to form a single organisation to represent all Irish-Argentines. He also requested parish priests to celebrate a requiem mass on the feast of All Souls – 2 November – for 'the dead who died for Ireland'. Some sixty-five positive replies were received from parishes in Buenos Aires and in the camp. Fr Ephraim O'Connell gave a sermon at Holy Cross which, according to Bulfin, 'ought to have some effect on the weak-kneed'. Little, who went to San Antonio de Areco where he stayed with the Blue Sisters, reported that at a requiem mass in that parish the church was draped in purple, with the following written on a banner over the sanctuary: '*A las víctimas de la tyranníra inglesa*' ('To the victims of English tyranny').[251]

Ginnell convoked on 29 November 1921 what he called the first convention of Irish people and their descendants ever held in Latin America. Some fifty delegates attended the meeting, held in the Irish Girls Home in Salgado run by the Irish Sisters of Mercy. On this occasion, William Morgan took the chair. A standing committee was appointed. The following delegates were selected to represent Argentina at the Irish Race Convention in Paris on January 1922: Fr Vincent Logan, Thomas Gahan, Dr and Mrs Walsh, and James Bowen. Leading by example, Morgan bought a 500 pesos Irish loan bond at the event. While the organisers considered the meeting to have been a success,[252] the new organisation did not succeed in unifying the existing Irish organisation. However, Little, as he was about to leave Buenos Aires, reported on 4 December 1921 that 'things are much better'. His primary responsibility had been to improve the news output from Buenos Aires to other countries in Latin America. He found that Anita Bulfin had 'the right ideas and something of the family gift for clear writing'. With her help, he gradually got the *Irish Bulletin* 'on its feet so that my assistance is no longer necessary'. She was, he said, 'the most reliable and active worker'. Little reported that he hoped, before departing the country, to publish a newspaper in Spanish and to draft the constitution for the new organisation that had been formed in late November.[253]

Ginnell, who had thrown himself into the work from the time of his arrival in July, was beginning to have serious health problems, Bulfin noting in early December that his colleague was 'not at all well'. Besides his underlying medical condition, he was overworked and the strain was beginning to have an impact on his already fragile health. His wife Alice accompanied him to San Antonio de Areco, where the Blue Sisters nursed him in the Maria Clara Morgan Hospital. The news from Ireland did nothing to help him improve; on 6 December, articles of agreement for a treaty between Great Britain and Ireland were signed at 2.15 a.m. by Michael Collins, Arthur Griffith, Robert Barton, Éamonn Duggan and George Gavan Duffy.[254] Late on the 7th, Bulfin phoned Ginnell to say that 'Ireland was to be the "Free State of Ireland"' and that 'the oath of allegiance was to be to the Free State of Ireland and to King George'.[255] Alice Ginnell and Anita Bulfin, together with the three Dáil Éireann envoys Ginnell, Bulfin and Little, rejected the treaty outright. They quickly made their views public, causing *La Nación* to describe the members of the Irish legation in Buenos Aires as 'agitators'. Jokingly, Little suggested to Bulfin that as he was a soldier he should follow the Argentine practice and challenge the editor to a duel with sabres, 'but Éamonn did not think that was in his official instructions'.[256] On 8 December, de Valera publicly stated that he could not recommend acceptance of the treaty, but on 14 December the cabinet decided by four votes to three to recommend the treaty to the Dáil. On the evening of 8 December the Irish legation held a farewell dinner for Little. After the singing of a 'rebel song', either Anita Bulfin or Alice Ginnell said, 'We can give up singing those songs, now', to which Little quipped that if that was the way 'the women of Ireland feel about the Treaty, it would not be much of a success'.[257] On 9 December, John Nelson called to the Irish mission office to say that he had sent his telegram of congratulation to Lloyd George before he saw the terms, but that now he wished to withdraw it, and that he did not agree to his name being put to the cablegram, sent by Santiago O'Farrell (president of a railway company) to Lloyd George and de Valera, and that he would repudiate it in the following day's papers. While Little departed on 10 December for Ireland, Ginnell went to Capitán Sarmiento on the 11th to present prizes to the boys at the Passionist school of St Paul's. In his speech at the prize-giving ceremony he pledged his support for de Valera and added that he had every confidence in the man who had guided Ireland's destiny for the past years. There were two powers in the world, he said, the power of light and the power of darkness, and he left his audience with the question: which of the two would prevail?[258]

Between 14 and 22 December, Dáil Éireann debated the treaty. Ginnell cabled Éamon de Valera, 'I vote against ratification', and instructed him to so inform the parliamentary session. The debate resumed in public session on 3 January and after fractious exchanges, the vote on the 7th was sixty-four in favour to fifty-seven against, with three abstentions. De Valera resigned as president of Dáil Éireann. Standing again, he was defeated by Arthur Griffith, who by sixty votes to fifty-eight assumed the role. On 14 January, while the Dáil was adjourned, the provisional government was established with Michael Collins as chairman of the cabinet and Griffith as president of the Dáil. In the forlorn hope of showing that national unity had not yet been lost, the cabinet decided that eight delegates would represent the country in Paris, from 22 to 28 January, at the Irish Race Convention.[259] In a gesture of goodwill, Éamon de Valera, now as leader of the opposition, was invited to choose four delegates. He picked himself, Countess Markievicz, Mary MacSwiney and Harry Boland. The government nominees were Prof. Eoin MacNeill, Prof. Michael Hayes (Ceann Comhairle [Speaker]), Diarmuid Coffey and Laurence O'Neill (lord mayor of Dublin). De Valera travelled disguised as a priest on a doctored passport. He was accompanied by Seán MacBride, the son of Major John MacBride and Maud Gonne. Joined by Seán T. O'Kelly, he remained the centre of international press attention and he was cheered by seminarians when he visited the Irish College with other delegates. It proved impossible during the plenary sessions of the convention to conceal the political divisions caused by the treaty split.[260] Instead of being the launching pad to showcase a united 'Irish race', Paris revealed the brittleness of Irish unity, presaging the danger of civil unrest.[261] The Argentine delegation, however, remained outwardly united, being represented by Fr Vincent Logan, Thomas Gahan, Dr and Mrs Walsh and James Bowen. Little said all were selected because they were travelling anyway to Europe. He described Gahan as being 'oldish – very good and religious, extremely rich, not very republican, but well intentioned – one of the founders of Jockey Club in B.A., a palatial place. He is therefore one of the very pillars of respectability and conservatism'. Dr and Mrs Walsh were 'charming and quiet – oldish'; she was president of the ladies committee which fundraised for the Keating Institute, a school for orphaned girls. They travelled back with him to Europe on the same boat. Little said that she was 'a real Sinn Feiner. He is only partly so'. Fr Vincent Logan was 'a good man but with a poor political and national record'. He had been appointed because he was resident in Paris. Bowen, according to Little, had been a friend of William Bulfin's[262] 'but he wobbled on politics in the old days. Now he is alright and full of enthusiasm'.[263] Bowen made a lively contribution to proceedings, telling delegates that his motto was *Hechos y no palabras* (Deeds not words). He felt that there were many talkers in Ireland who did nothing. Irishmen abroad, he said, should advance the 'buy Irish' campaign and should drink and sell Irish whiskey instead of Scotch. He presented a silk Argentine flag, made by the Sisters of Mercy, to the Irish foreign minister, George Gavan Duffy. Bowen, besides giving a lecture on Irishmen who contributed to the making of modern Latin America,[264] also announced the setting up of a scholarship in Spanish at the National University of Ireland 'in order to develop closer bonds between Ireland and Argentina.'[265]

Far away from Paris, in the camp, Ginnell faced the implosion of his diplomatic mission. Despite growing support for the settlement among many Irish-Argentines, he published a long statement in *TSC* on 20 January comprehensively explaining his reasons for rejection, ending with a declaration often repeated in Ireland in the months ahead: 'A treaty reached under duress is invalid ... England has never kept faith with Ireland', a reference to Lloyd George's ultimatum on 6 December of either signing or facing the consequence of an immediate resumption of war. In his valedictory report from Buenos Aires on 3 March 1922, Ginnell requested: 'Please read the next sentence [of his report], as it is written, as a simple statement of fact, without a shadow of bitterness. Once it became known that the treaty had been signed, no Irish republican Bond could be sold; and once Dáil Éireann had adopted the treaty the Republic was universally regarded as at an end.' It had become Ginnell's duty 'to close up and leave the country as soon as possible'.[266] Broken in health and in spirit, on 27 January Ginnell returned in the heat of a southern mid-summer to Buenos Aires from San Antonio de Areco. He had called a final meeting of the trustees of the Irish Bond Campaign. As many people had left for holidays, the meeting failed to reach a quorum and it was rescheduled for 3 February. The meeting went ahead on the latter date. Ginnell informed those present that twenty people had subscribed 19,155 pesos, which had been lodged in the bank to the credit of the trustees. The expenditure incurred in setting up the loan was 11,280 pesos for printing costs, etc. William Morgan, a major subscriber, strongly disagreed with the majority view that those administrative expenses be paid out of the capital sum. Subscribers were given the option of receiving a cheque if their bonds were returned before 5 March or they could donate the subscribed sum to the new Irish organisation launched on 29 November. That was agreed. The bond drive, according to Ginnell, was 'prematurely stopped by events unforeseen and beyond our control'.[267] The Irish legation in Buenos Aires wound down all activities in February. The only staff, an administrator/translator, was paid off. Bulfin was instructed to dispose of the office furniture. Ginnell received instructions in early March from the minister for foreign affairs, George Gavan Duffy, stating that representatives abroad 'will still represent the Republic, but ... their position will be somewhat different' as they were instructed to abstain from propaganda, either for or against the treaty, 'until the people, at a general election, had decided whether they would accept it, or not'. The minister wanted the legation to be left intact so that Ireland would be ready to resume her former position if Britain broke the treaty. Requested by Dublin to make an official visit to Chile on his return journey to Ireland, Ginnell was not minded to do so. He was – despite his declining health – anxious to make a speedy return to the maelstrom of Irish politics.[268]

Some weeks later, he arrived back to an Ireland on the brink of civil war. In a last-ditch effort to keep the two sides away from the use of violence, Éamon de Valera and Arthur Griffith decided to field an agreed list of candidates for the general election on 16 June 1922. This became known as the 'pact' election. Back in Ireland, Ginnell spent time in hospital in Limerick being nursed by the Blue Sisters, the order who had taken such good care of him in San Antonio de Areco. De Valera appointed him to a twelve-person anti-treaty advisory body. Despite his failing health, he stood and was returned as an anti-treaty candidate for Longford–Westmeath. The supporters of the Anglo-Irish settlement won a majority at the polls. Armed clashes turned into civil war on 28 June in Dublin.

1.28 Laurence Ginnell and his wife Alice celebrate St Patrick's Day at their farewell dinner in Venado Tuerto, 1922

The republican garrison in the Four Courts was bombarded by Michael Collins and members of the Free State army. On 12 August 1922, Arthur Griffith, the close friend of the late William Bulfin, had a heart attack and died.[269] Michael Collins was killed in an ambush in west Cork on 22 August 1922. On 9 September Ginnell was escorted from the Dáil after refusing to sign the roll while seeking clarification as to whether he was in Dáil Éireann or a partitioned parliament.[270]

Ginnell did not live to see the end of hostilities. De Valera sent him to the United States as his personal envoy. There he encountered the same acrimony and divisions as he had experienced at home. Under great personal strain, his health further deteriorated and he died alone in a hotel room in Washington DC on 17 April 1923. He was seventy-one.[271] *The Southern Cross*, in an editorial, recorded that his name continued to be remembered with great affection and warmth by many Irish-Argentines.[272] William T. Cosgrave, who had taken over as president of the Executive Council, secured a military victory for the government. Hostilities ended in Ireland on 30 May 1923.

De Valera, who had evaded capture during the fighting, led his anti-treaty followers – many of them in jail – against the government in a general election held on 27 August 1923. Arrested while campaigning on 15 August in Ennis,

County Clare,[273] he still managed from his jail cell to top the poll. His anti-treatyite party won forty-four seats but lost the election. Upon his release a year later, he led an abstentionist Sinn Féin party until he broke with that organisation in 1925 and founded Fianna Fáil in 1926. Entering the Dáil in 1927 with members of his new party, he was leader of the opposition until coming to power in 1932.

As for Eamonn Bulfin, he returned to Ireland in early 1922 and refused to support either side in the civil war. Despite being in difficult financial circumstances, he turned down a commission to become an officer in the Irish army. He worked in the unpopular job of rates collector for a short time and then, until his retirement, as an old age pensions officer. Apart from his lifelong involvement in sporting organisations and occasional participation in commemorations of the revolutionary period, he lived quietly on the family farm, at Derrinlough House, Birr, County Offaly. He died on Christmas Eve 1968.[274]

Timothy Joseph Horan, whose 1958 report is referred to frequently throughout this chapter, was only ten years old when the Irish civil war began in 1922. Growing up as a teenager in the 1920s and as a student at UCC in the 1930s, he could not avoid becoming acutely aware of the legacy of bitterness left by the violence between former comrades. In 1938 he joined the Department of External Affairs, so named because Ireland had become a British dominion in 1922. Civil war 'sentences memory to extinction', wrote the poet Czesław Miłosz.[275] Horan is unlikely to have heard anything during his training as a diplomat about the generous financial contributions sent by Irish Argentines during the war of independence to support the victims of British violence. That chapter in Irish history became part of the forgotten if not hidden early history of what was once proudly called the Department of Foreign Affairs. Irish foreign policy, restructured during the civil war, had a new beginning. Having stood by the revolution, Irish Catholic nationalists in Argentina hoped that that record would be a platform on which to build closer and more enduring future links with an independent 'mother country'. Éamon de Valera – out of power until 1932 – did not forget the support and solidarity that had come from the pampas.

CHAPTER TWO

Building Diplomatic Relations from the Irish Civil War to the Fall of Juan Domingo Perón

The Irish Free State, confronting the task of rebuilding from the ruins of civil war, had very limited resources after 1923 to expand its diplomatic service. The economic, political and diplomatic interests of the state dictated that scarce national resources be directed towards establishing diplomatic missions in London (8 January 1923), the League of Nations (10 September 1923) and Washington (7 October 1924).[1] Throughout the 1920s and early 1930s, Ireland played an active, constructive role at British Commonwealth conferences, helping to further the autonomy of the constituent states. A significant expansion of the Irish diplomatic service took place in 1929, with resident missions being established on 29 June at the Holy See and on 19 October in Paris and Berlin.[2]

Without resident diplomatic missions at that time in Australia or Canada, it would have been far-fetched for William T. Cosgrave's Cumann na nGaedheal government to justify the opening of a legation in Buenos Aires. Moreover, Irish emigration to Argentina slowed significantly in the first decade of the twentieth century and to a trickle from the 1920s to the 1940s, when there was a significant shift in the social status of new arrivals. Professional people on contract, doctors, railway engineers, teachers, and employees of banks and business firms replaced the earlier flow of farm labourers and the passengers of the *Dresden*.[3] According to Timothy Joseph Horan, census returns revealed that 2,024 Irish reached Argentina between 1925 and 1946. Accounting for 426 departures, net immigration was 1,598. That figure would also have included the arrivals and departures of male and female religious.

Table 2.1 Timothy Joseph Horan's summary of Argentine census returns charting the arrival and departure of Irish people between 1925 and 1946

Census Years	Arrivals	Departures	Balance
1925–30	938	259	679
1931–40	1,006	157	849
1941–6	80	10	70
TOTAL:	2,024	426	1,598

Many of the Irish who had arrived earlier continued to live in the camp and attend schools run by Irish-born Pallottines, Passionists and the Sisters of Mercy. Irish Passionist Sisters arrived in 1926 to teach at and administer the newly established Michael Ham Memorial School. In the decades that followed, a number of their past pupils set up their own schools and language centres. The next significant development in Irish-Argentine education would be the arrival of the Irish Christian Brothers and the foundation of Newman College in 1948.

The leading Irish newspaper, *TSC*, changed ownership in 1919 when the Bulfin family sold it to a consortium led by Gerald Foley, who had been editor since 1909. The Pallottines, the Passionists and the Irish Catholic Association were the other shareholders. When he died on 20 April 1927, his brother Frank,[4] a long-time employee of the paper, took over as editor for two years.[5] He was replaced in 1929 by Fr Miguel Quinn, who became the first Argentine-born editor of the paper. He held that position until his death on 4 April 1938.[6] Its editorial line and content was always loyally Catholic and was a defender of the foreign policies of the Holy See. A number of the older Irish recalled their excitement at its weekly arrival in the camp.[7] It covered local events and activities in the smaller towns dotted around the pampas, and of course recorded the great historical events and milestones in the history of the community. While it admired the new Irish Free State government led by William T. Cosgrave and his Cumann na nGaedheal party, it never lost its admiration or respect for Éamon de Valera and did not fear the prospect of his coming to power. *The Standard*,[8] the other Irish paper, combined in its editorial line support for a Catholic ethos with loyalty to the British Empire. That included support for the Irish Free State's dominion status and membership of the Commonwealth. In Irish politics, it supported the Cosgrave government while remaining fearful of de Valera.

Meanwhile, *TSC* was the paper of record for most Irish-Argentine Catholic families, covering local events in the camp and the great events, including

2.1 Irish pilgrimage train in Buenos Aires en route to the basilica of Luján with '*Viva de Valera*' written on a banner on the front of the engine, 16 March 1924. (Éamon de Valera papers, courtesy of UCD Archives)

2.2 Annual retreat given by Passionists, Venado Tuerto

2.3 Irish wedding, Venado Tuerto, in the early 1920s

comprehensive coverage of annual St Patrick's Day celebrations throughout the country. When the feast day of the patron saint of Ireland fell on a Sunday, it was the local tradition for the community to go on pilgrimage to the Basilica of Our Lady of Luján. That had been practice in 1901, 1907, 1912 and 1918. In 1924, between 12,000 and 20,000 took part – a far larger number than on previous occasions.[9] From Saturday through early Sunday morning, special trains, crowded with pilgrims, many of them fasting since midnight, arrived from Buenos Aires and other parts of the country. Notwithstanding that it was a train from Buenos Aires belonging to an English company, it carried a banner on the front of the engine, flanked by the Irish and Argentine flags, with '*Viva de Valera*' written across it. The Passionist Fr Victor O'Carolan, a strong admirer of 'the chief'[10] as de Valera was popularly known, organised the patriotic demonstration. At Luján, the crowds of pilgrims heard different bands play 'God Save Ireland', 'St Patrick's Day', 'Let Erin Remember', 'The Wearing of the Green', 'O'Donnell Abú' and 'The Soldier's Song' (adopted on 12 July 1926 as the Irish national anthem). *TSC* wrote in an editorial: 'Luján was "a little bit of Ireland" last Sunday and the Irish-Argentine people may feel justly proud of the success of their pilgrimage. It was a wonderful manifestation of faith, and of love of Ireland, and there was not a single discordant note to mar the harmony of the day.'[11]

Moving forward to the weeks of the Irish general election in February 1932, *TSC*, unlike *The Standard* and the *Buenos Aires Herald*, did not regard de Valera's radical programme as 'in any sense alarming'. It argued that the constitutional changes he outlined could be brought about peacefully and democratically. Those plans included the abolition of the office of governor general, the removal of the oath of allegiance, and the excising from the Free State constitution of any mention of the British king. He also planned to halt the payment of land annuities to the British exchequer. Much to the annoyance of *The Standard* and the British government, de Valera and his Fianna Fáil party, with the support of the Labour Party, formed a minority government in early March 1932. The following year, in January, de Valera called a snap election and won an overall majority. In a statesmanlike manner, *TSC* both welcomed de Valera's victory and had kind words for his predecessor: 'Whatever the judgment history will pass upon Mr. Cosgrave, he will be remembered as a Catholic ruler, who on many occasions gave proof of the religious spirit in which he took his government duties.'[12] The paper rejoiced that de Valera, although busy taking up his new governmental duties as president of the Executive Council and minister for external affairs, had honoured Irish-Argentines by sending a telegram of congratulations[13] to the Pallottine

2.4a Hurling team, Mercedes, 1924

2.4b St Patrick's hurling team, Mercedes, 1929

2.5 Raising the bell into place in the tower, St Patrick's church, Mercedes

2.6 St Patrick's church, Mercedes, 1931/2

2.7 Chandelier, St Patrick's church, Mercedes

2.8 Mgr James M. Ussher, historian and leader of the Irish-Argentine community from the early twentieth century to his death in 1960

2.9a The Ussher family, with portraits of their parents on the wall behind the group. Seated centre Mgr Santiago Ussher beside his brother, a Salesian, and, behind, three sisters who are nuns.

2.9b Ussher/Kelly/Leaden families; Canon Santiago Ussher is in front row (middle). Back row (centre, with Roman collars): Guillermo and Alfredo Leaden. Alfredo joined the Pallottines and was murdered on 4 July 1976 in St Patrick's, Belgrano, together with four of his confrères. Guillermo joined the Salesian order. On 28 May 1975 he was appointed titular bishop of Theudalis and auxiliary bishop of Buenos Aires.

community in Mercedes to mark the solemn opening of St Patrick's church – the largest Irish church in Latin America. Fr Thomas Leahy had raised the funds for that ambitious project.[14] Inaugurated on St Patrick's Day 1932, about 2,000 people travelled fasting from Buenos Aires (100 km), from Chacabuco (about 120 km) and from other surrounding towns in the camp in order to receive holy communion at ten o'clock mass. The papal nuncio, Filippo Cortesi, and the bishop of La Plata, Francisco Alberti, were in attendance. The celebrant, Mgr Santiago Ussher, told the large congregation in his sermon that he rejected the accusation that the Irish community was regarded as being too Irish with 'our traditions, and schools, and chapels, and chaplains ... [they] certainly are not ashamed of our forefathers nor of the manly race from which we spring. Esteem and respect for our ancestors and pride of race are very praiseworthy virtues, which cannot in any way render us less patriotic Argentines'.[15] Echoing Ussher's words, *TSC* wrote: 'Let us remain Irish-Argentine by standing for all that [the] word "Irish-Argentine" signifies.'[16]

IRELAND AND ARGENTINA: A BLENDING OF RELIGION, POLITICS AND
DIPLOMACY, 1932–5

News of de Valera's electoral victory and formation of a new government overlapped with preparations in Buenos Aires to send a delegation to attend the 31st Eucharistic Congress in Dublin between 22 and 26 June – 1932 also being the 1,500th anniversary of St Patrick's arrival in Ireland. Mgr Santiago Ussher chaired an organising committee.[17] Frs Richard Gearty, Benedict O'Connor and Juan Santos Gaynor prepared a text in English and Spanish on the influence of the Irish clergy on the spread in Argentina of devotion to the Blessed Eucharist.[18] Gearty was given the responsibility of commissioning the making of Irish and Argentine flags to be carried by the pilgrims.[19] The travel costs of the delegates were subsidised by the Argentine hierarchy, the Irish Catholic Association, the Hurling Club and the Irish Club.[20] On 22 May, Ussher and the delegation (ten priests, two nuns and fifteen lay people)[21] were among about fifty guests who attended a farewell lunch at the London Hotel.[22] Fr Gearty, a priest of the Elphin diocese, had spent thirty-one years in Argentina. Two Irish Sisters of Mercy, Margaret Mary Galway and Cecilia Nugent, were chosen to represent their congregation, a well-merited distinction as they had spent a combined thirty-six years dedicated to education of girls in Buenos Aires.[23] *TSC* described the group travelling as 'the first Irish-Argentine delegation ever sent to the Old Land'.[24] A large crowd gathered to see the pilgrims off on the 25th. On the third deck, an orchestra played a selection of

Irish airs continually, among them 'O'Donnell Abú'. According to *TSC*, it was a tearful departure, 'but when shortly before the moment of sailing they struck up "Come Back to Erin" several of those on the quayside who had been born in Ireland and who were not going back made a hurried exit ... feeling they would need a handkerchief with which to dry their tears if they tarried any longer'.[25]

After almost three weeks travelling, the delegation arrived in Dublin on 14 June. The Argentine consul, Sr Don Juan B. de Lemoine, was present to greet them, accompanied by their relatives and by Mgr T.H. Cummins, the parish priest of Roscommon town;[26] Canon Ambrose Blaine, the president of St Nathy's College at Ballaghadereen; and Fr Denis Gildea, a curate from Charlestown. The clergy in the welcoming party had either worked in or visited Argentina on fundraising missions. The Argentine consul made arrangements for the delegation to meet President de Valera; the lord mayor of Dublin, Alfie Byrne; the papal nuncio, Paschal Robinson; and the archbishop of Dublin, Edward Byrne.[27] On 16 June, Alfie Byrne received the group in his ceremonial robes in the Mansion House and agreed wholeheartedly to the invitation to become an honorary member of the Argentine delegation.[28] De Valera received the delegation that afternoon. In his remarks, Ussher told the president of the Executive Council that the pilgrims had come 'from far-away Argentina' to represent the Catholic people of that country. While he said the delegation took no sides in the internal political questions over which patriotic Irishmen had different opinions, he proclaimed: 'We maintain the right of Ireland, all Ireland, one and indivisible, to be universally recognised as a sovereign independent nation, co-equal with the other sovereign independent nations of the world.' He knew that those were also de Valera's ideals as they were the 'ideals and aspirations of our scattered race in the four quarters of the earth'. De Valera described the Argentine republic in his reply as 'a land where the representative of the Irish Republic, the late Laurence Ginnell, received such a cordial welcome and generous support'. Smiling, he said that his only fear was that the children of Irish exiles might fail to find the Ireland of their dreams, for, based on his experience in the United States, emigrants were accustomed to think of Ireland more as a paradise than as a country.[29] De Valera, at the end of the reception, gave instructions to Joseph Walshe, secretary of the Department of External Affairs, to ensure that the Argentine delegation was invited to the government reception for the papal legate to be held at Dublin Castle.[30] Afterwards, the delegation went to meet the vice president, Seán T. O'Kelly, and later the papal nuncio, Paschal Robinson, at his residence in the Phoenix Park. Before leaving the Phoenix Park they went to view the main altar erected for the congress.[31] The Argentine consul, Juan B. de Lemoine, reported to Buenos Aires that the delegation, despite in his view not having been led by 'a person of high ecclesiastical office' (meaning only a mere monsignor) like all the other foreign delegations at the congress, was the recipient of special distinctions: 'Thus Mr De [*sic*] Valera made an exception in a week filled with official functions to meet [them] during which there were exchanges of friendship and cordiality.'[32]

While the Eucharistic Congress may be viewed narrowly as an occasion of triumphant Catholic nationalism, it was for de Valera as minister for external affairs an unparalleled opportunity to have a series of bilateral meetings in which he could express his personal gratitude to those who supported Ireland during the revolutionary period and beyond. That was certainly the case for Argentina. De Valera also availed of the large number of visitors for the congress to meet opinion-formers and ecclesiastical leaders from all over the world – Irish men and women who had ascended to high office in the Catholic Church, a transnational organisation which would continue in his view to defend Irish interests globally. But those men and women who had returned to Dublin for the Eucharistic Congress were part of what I have termed global Irish 'soft power'. While lack of resources prevented any dramatic expansion of the diplomatic service in the 1930s, Catholic nuns and clergy, together with Irish members of other faiths, extended the country's international reach among the elites of those countries in which they operated, often educating future leaders and senior members of independent post-colonial administrations. Within the Catholic Church, Irish men and women served as leaders of their respective transnational congregations. Irish priests took up senior roles in the hierarchy of different countries and a number served in the diplomatic service of the Holy See. Historians who treat the Eucharistic Congress as a purely religious event fail to understand its international political significance for de Valera – a leader of government and a foreign minister who had ambitious plans for Ireland on the world stage.

Returning to the Irish-Argentine delegation, the pilgrims laid a wreath on 17 June at the tomb of the patriot dead in Glasnevin. Ussher, in a graveside oration, spoke about the 'sacred ground' on which they stood, by the grave of Pádraig Pearse, where they laid a wreath at 'the tomb of one of the noblest of them all'. The inscription on the wreath, in both Spanish and English, said: '*Los peregrinos Argentinos-Irlandeses, a los muertos que dieron su vida por Irlanda*' ('From the Irish-Argentine pilgrims in homage to the dead who gave their lives for Irish freedom'). The pilgrims knelt and prayed as the prayers for the dead were recited in Spanish.[33] They also laid wreaths at the tomb of Archbishop Daniel Murray (1823–52), who had been responsible for sending Fr Fahy and other Irish chaplains to Argentina.[34] Once the Irish papers had reported their visit to Glasnevin, according to *The Southern Cross*, 'every heart in Dublin has warmed towards the Irish exiles from the pampas'.[35] After mass on Sunday the 19th some members of the delegation travelled to Bodenstown to join a crowd of 15,000 who took part in the annual Wolfe Tone commemoration ceremonies, among them the Pallottine Mgr Michael Walsh from St Patrick's, Mercedes.[36]

On 20 June, the delegation participated in the festivities to greet the papal legate, Cardinal Lorenzo Lauri. Later they watched six Irish Air Corps biplanes fly over the city in a cruciform formation. The following day the delegation was among the 14,000 people who attended a garden party in Blackrock College, and later that evening they joined 4,000 guests at a state dinner in Dublin Castle. *TSC's* correspondent commented that 'the order, the culture, the perfect organisation, the distinguished guests, the Cardinal by whose side stood the Chief of the Gaelic Race today, are something worth beholding, and if you add to this the fact that we were standing 'neath a roof that for generations had sheltered the most unscrupulous of Rome's and Ireland's enemies, men who mocked at our heroes, stabbed at the heart of our motherland, and laughed and sneered and boasted that the conquest of Ireland was completed – there is food for reflection and for rejoicing here'.[37]

The congress was formally opened by Cardinal Lauri on Wednesday, 22 June with mass at the Pro-Cathedral. There was exposition of the blessed sacrament in every church in Dublin, concluding with benediction and followed by the illumination of the city from dusk to dawn. On 23 June, 250,000 men attended mass in the Phoenix Park, and 200,000 women the following evening. Members of the Argentine delegation were also present on 22 and 23 June at the National University of Ireland at Earlsfort Terrace to hear Fr Manuel Guillade give a paper on 'Eucharistic Life in Uruguay' and Fr O'Connor read a paper in Spanish on the history of Irish Catholic Action in Argentina. Fr Gearty, speaking on the work of Irish missionaries on the plain of the River Plate, said there was no need to apply a test to the faith of the Irish in Argentina: 'Enough for him is it to see them, coming weary leagues on Sunday after Sunday, to attend the Sacrifice of the Mass; to see them, frequent communicants, approach the Sacrament of the Altar; to catechize their children, instructed from earliest infancy by their parents in the teachings of their faith; to witness their holy lives and to be present at their edifying deaths.'[38]

On Sunday, 26 June the congress concluded with solemn pontifical mass for over a million in the Phoenix Park during which Count John McCormack sang 'Panis Angelicus' and a choir of over 500 men and boys accompanied him under the direction of Vincent O'Brien. At a farewell dinner for the Argentines on the 27th, the *Irish Press* reported that Ussher told the gathering that the delegation had felt quite at home in the land of their forefathers. At the end of the night, considerable enthusiasm was displayed following the playing of 'The Soldier's Song' and the Argentine national anthem.[39] Ussher, Gearty, Michael Walsh and Patrick Rattigan were received on 28 June by Mrs Sinéad de Valera in her home.[40] Commenting on the hospitality shown to the delegation, *TSC* wrote in an editorial that 'Ireland never forgets her exiled children, nor their descendants'.[41]

While most of the members of the delegation then left for the continent or to stay with relatives, a small group travelled on 4 July to Delvin, County Westmeath, to honour the memory of Laurence Ginnell, who had served as a Dáil Éireann envoy in Argentina in 1921–2. After a short ceremony, Ussher placed the Irish and the Argentine flags on the grave. Later, they visited his widow, Alice, at Kilbride.[42] The delegation then travelled to Roscommon town at the invitation of the parish priest, Canon Cummins, who had been on a successful fundraising mission in Argentina early in the century for the building of the Sacred Heart parish church which was opened in 1903. They were greeted at the railway station by a large crowd waving Argentine flags. The delegation placed the Argentine coat of arms in the church to the right of the high altar. Sra Margarita M. de Morgan of San Antonio de Areco had donated the funds for the tabernacle, above which there is a golden heart with her name inscribed upon it.[43] That evening, the delegation attended a concert at the local girls' school run by the Sisters of Mercy. That was followed by a 'sumptuous banquet' in the town hall, the festivities ending with the singing of the Irish and Argentine national anthems. The Argentine visitors returned by train to Dublin and, after a formal farewell dinner in the capital, set out for their nearly three-week journey home.[44] On their return to Buenos Aires, an 'at home' was arranged in Ussher's honour in the Phoenix Hotel.[45] While participation in the Eucharistic Congress reinforced the links between Buenos Aires and Ireland, I have found no evidence that Ussher raised the question of setting up diplomatic relations between the two countries when speaking with de Valera, Seán T. O'Kelly or Joseph Walshe. But, given the importance of such a diplomatic link for Irish-Argentines, it would have been unusual for him not to have availed of the opportunity to do so.

In October 1934, the 32nd Eucharistic Congress was held in Buenos Aires.[46] This event served as another occasion to build even stronger links with Ireland. As part of the elaborate preparations, Ussher was appointed president of the Irish-Argentine section, which set out to give Irish-Argentines a prominent role in the international event. A sum of 17,612.50 pesos was donated by the community to cover the cost of Irish involvement.[47] Ussher, in a special ceremony, blessed the papal, Argentine and St Patrick flags to be carried in the procession.[48] The Irish held an open-air mass in Plaza San Martín on 23 September to prepare for the opening of the congress. The three flags flew at the foot of the altar.[49] Describing Argentina as 'a Catholic Nation',[50] the editor of *TSC* published on 5 October a sixty-page supplement on the history of the Irish community in Argentina. There were articles on the history of Irish Argentina and on the role of the different male and female religious orders in the development of Catholic education in the country. There were photographs of the estancias of the leading Irish ranch-owners. It was a profile of a confident, prosperous and strongly patriotic Catholic community.[51] Demand for the supplement was so great, it had to go into an immediate reprint.

Fr John Hayes,[52] the founder in 1931 of Muintir na Tíre (People of the Countryside), was invited by the Pallottines to come to Argentina for three months to travel around their parishes preaching and preparing people for the Eucharistic Congress.[53] Lecturing on 'Erin, the Tear and the Smile in Thine Eye', Hayes said: 'Religion is deep in the Irish nature and it accounts a good deal for why the smile has survived. When all the world is taken from us we can bank on the next.'[54] Writing to Ussher from St Patrick's, Belgrano, on 25 August, Hayes said: '... I arrived here last night from Mercedes. I seem to be on the road all the time but I am getting to really love this country. The great pastures, the mighty herds and flocks, the rich produce and the homely people are all fast gripping me'. The best compliment he could pay Irish-Argentines was 'to say he wanted to stay on'.[55]

On 9 October 1934, a large delegation from Ireland, led by Archbishop Thomas Gilmartin of Tuam and the bishop of Ardagh and Clonmacnois James Joseph McNamee, arrived in Buenos Aires to attend the ceremonies.[56] A number of Irishmen who were bishops in dioceses abroad also attended, among them the Spanish-speaking archbishop of Manila, Michael O'Doherty,[57] and the bishop of Nottingham, John McNulty.[58] Bishop McNamee[59] left a series of diary entries, including one describing his arrival in Buenos Aires on 9 October: 'Landed at Buenos Aires in a tempestuous "pampero" of wind. Provided for in Dr. Gahan's beautiful house, 2048 Canning'.[60] *The Southern Cross* provided a vivid account of the active role played by Irish-Argentines in the ceremonies. The Irish pilgrims and Irish-Argentines filled the Teatro Avenida to hear addresses delivered by the local and visiting clergy and by prominent laymen. The speakers included Mgr Lyons, representing Cardinal Joseph MacRory, Ussher, Fr Richard Gearty[61] and Jack Nelson. Archbishop Gilmartin gave a lecture on the 'Celts in Argentina'. In the beautiful Teatro Colón, about

600 children, representing all the Irish schools in the vicinity of Buenos Aires and the countryside, gave a gala performance.

Summing up some of the events, Bishop McNamee recorded in his diary: 'Saturday, 13 October: Present at Admiral Brown celebrations at 11 o'c. Great demonstration. President of Republic there and Ministers of State: speeches: band played St. Patrick's Day. Irish meeting at 3 o'c. Spoke there for about half an hour. Then to Luján to visit the famous shrine. [The bishop's host, Dr Thomas Gahan, accompanied them.] Banquet to Irish prelates in the Jockey Club [Buenos Aires]: Spoke to toast.'[62]

On the third day of the congress, a solemn pontifical high mass was said in Palermo Park. Bishop McNamee recorded in his diary on 14 October: 'The great day of the Congress. Assisted at [cardinal secretary of state, Eugenio Pacelli][63] Legate's Mass and sermon at 11 o'c'.[64] Among the highlights was the singing of '*Ecce Sacerdos Magnus*' by about 80,000 voices.[65] Pope Pius XI broadcast live to the huge congregation during the mass. Archbishop Gilmartin and Bishop McNamee led the large Irish delegation. There was a particularly warm welcome for the bishop-elect of Catamarca, Carlos Francisco Hanlon, the first Irish priest to be appointed to an Argentine diocese. After the mass, the different national delegations carried their respective flags through the streets of Buenos Aires. The Argentine, Irish and papal flags were carried by the Irish delegation.[66] The Irish bishops and Fr John Hayes were present, together with the Sisters of Mercy and a full muster of the Passionist and Pallottine orders. Bishop McNamee recorded: 'Assisted at great procession in the afternoon 3–6 o'c. A wonderful success.'[67]

On Monday the 15th, the Pacific Railway laid on a luxury train to take Bishop McNamee and his fellow Irish bishops on a trip to the San Marcos estancia, where they were met by Nelson and all the Irish families from the San Patricio district. McNamee spent a great deal of time talking to the people and finding out where their parents and grandparents had come from in Ireland. A sumptuous banquet was prepared for the visitors. In the afternoon, the special train took them to Hurlingham. They also went by car to Moreno to visit the Fahy Institute, where the visitors were given a rousing welcome by the teachers and pupils. Fr Canning addressed the boys, saying that 'it was the first time since the Irish people began to settle in this country that an Irish school in the camp had the honour of a visit from an Irish bishop'. McNamee then spoke to the boys, telling them how impressed he was by them and by the school. The party returned by car and train to Buenos Aires.[68] Bishop McNamee's diary entry for the 16th is as follows: 'Off by early train to S[an] Antonio [de Areco] where I had a great reception. Addressed meeting.'[69]

Rounding off over a week of celebration, Fr Hayes spoke on the radio of his wish to unite 'more closely the Irish here and those of the mother country'. Such unity, he thought, would benefit both communities: 'In our hour of need Argentina threw open her gates to our exiles.' The two Eucharistic Congresses, he said, had brought both countries closer by 'golden links of Faith'. He bade farewell to his friends and to 'you the noblest of nations, Argentina Queen of the South'.[70] Hayes, on his voyage to Ireland, chaperoned a fifteen-year-old Argentine boy who was on his way to the Pallottine novitiate in Kickham Street, Thurles; Alfredo Leaden was, wrote Hayes to his uncle, Santiago Ussher, on 10 April 1935, a 'grand boy, strong and happy'.[71] The boy in question became a priest and was one of the five Pallottines murdered on 4 July 1976 by the Argentine military[72] (see Chapter 4). On 28 October 1934, Ussher wrote appreciatively about Hayes to the archbishop of Cashel, J.M. Harty: 'He has been untiring since his arrival ... in a word, he has done an amount of good and he has endeared himself to us all. His meritorious work and the very welcome visit of the representatives of the Irish Episcopate ... mark a new era in the history of our Irish Argentine Community, revive Irish ideals and strengthen the links that bind us with the people of our race in Ireland.'[73]

The reciprocal visits of both delegations in 1932 and 1934 had strengthened the friendship between the two countries, out of which grew a common wish to give practical expression to that deepened bond. On 2 November 1934, Ussher wrote to de Valera suggesting that 'some official representative of the Irish Government be stationed permanently in this country'.[74] It was no coincidence that on the same day – 2 November – *TSC* stated in an editorial:

> Since the establishment of the Irish Free State we have often advocated in these columns the desirability of a Representative of that State in Argentina. We are very glad to see that Father John M. Hayes, who has spent some fruitful months in Argentina, returns to Ireland as a firm advocate of this proposal. An Irish Representative in Argentina would be a distinct advantage in many ways. It is true that the vast majority of the members of the Irish-Argentine Community in this country are Argentine citizens; but we would all welcome with very great satisfaction a Representative of the land of our Fathers. Moreover, we think that an Irish Consul in Buenos Aires would be conducive to much good for the Irish State itself. We have pointed out on several occasions that there are the foundations of a brisk trade between Argentina and Ireland, and that by acting promptly, priceless opportunities would not be lost.[75]

Reinforcing that point, Hayes carried a message from the president of Argentina, General Pedro Justo: 'I have learned to admire their [Irish-Argentines] independent character, their strong attachment to duty, the austerity of their lives as the strong characteristics of their race. Interpreting the goodwill of the Argentine nation, I express good wishes for the continued success of Ireland and for the happiness of her people.'[76] Hayes sent the letter to the Department of External Affairs, together with a strong endorsement in support of the opening of diplomatic relations. When speaking to a meeting of Muintir na Tíre in Roscrea Abbey in early December 1934, he made public the recommendation that the Irish government should be represented by a consul in Buenos Aires. Ireland, he said, was represented in countries with a much smaller Irish population than lived in Argentina.[77]

The representations had a positive result. On 18 February 1935, Joseph Walshe, the secretary of the Department of External Affairs, replied to Ussher's letter of 2 November[78] saying that 'the President feels that the time has indeed come for the appointment of an official Irish representative in the Argentine. He feels that it would be a definite step towards the establishment of close and friendly relations as well as of an equitable balance in our trade exchanges. There are, however, very many immediately urgent demands on personnel and administration which have to be met before the Argentine post is established and the President hopes you will understand that a little time must still elapse before the final step is taken'.[79] Hayes, possibly unaware of the Walshe letter, wrote to Ussher on 15 April 1935: 'Would you kindly tell Tim [Leaden] that de Valera is considering the representation. I gave him Tim's name. It will take time but is being considered favourably.'[80]

In the context of the opening of new missions to further Irish foreign policy priorities in the second half of the 1930s, Argentina remained very far down the list. Legations were opened in Belgium on 7 September 1932, in Spain on 3 September 1935, in Italy on 30 April 1938 and in Canada on 18 August 1939. Despite de Valera's personal links with, and appreciation of, what Irish-Argentines had done to support him, his pressing foreign policy concerns lay elsewhere. As minister for external affairs, his new programme provided for continuity and acted as a catalyst for radical change.[81] By the time he signed a new Anglo-Irish agreement in 1938 he had been embroiled in a six-year economic war with London. But during that short period he had also carried through a constitutional revolution which radically changed the relationship between Dublin and London.[82] The office of governor general was abolished, as were appeals to the Privy Council. The Executive Authority (External Relations) Act in 1936 radically diminished the role of the British king.

ROINN GNOTHAI COIGRICHE
DEPARTMENT OF EXTERNAL AFFAIRS

BAILE ÁTHA CLIATH
DUBLIN

18th February 1935

Right Reverend Monsignor,

I am instructed by the President, Minister for
External Affairs, to reply to your letter of 2nd November
last and to express regret for the long delay in replying.

The President appreciates very much your kind
references to the delegates from Ireland and to the good
results achieved by their presence amongst the people of
our race in the Argentine. The President feels that the
time has indeed come for the appointment of an official
Irish representative in the Argentine. He feels that it
would be a definite step towards the establishment of
close and friendly relations as well as of an equitable
balance in our trade exchanges.

There are, however, very many immediately urgent
demands on personnel and administration which have to be
met before the Argentine post is established and the
President hopes you will understand that a little time
must still elapse before the final step is taken.

I beg to remain, Right Reverend Monsignor, with
great respect and esteem

Yours faithfully,

J.P. Walshe

Secretary,
Department of External Affairs.

Right Reverend Monsignor James Ussher,
Rivadavia 437,
BUENOS AIRES.

2.10 Letter from the secretary of the Department of External Affairs Joseph Walshe to
Santiago Ussher, 18 February 1935, promising, on behalf of President Éamon de Valera, that
Ireland would open diplomatic relations with Argentina but with the caveat that 'you will
understand that a little time must still elapse before the final step is taken'.

De Valera won approval for a new constitution in a plebiscite on 1 July 1937.[83] Through membership of the League of Nations, de Valera continued the Irish Free State's active role in collective international security. From the outset, he became what Patrick Keatinge has termed 'one of the League's uncomfortable consciences'.[84] As president of the League Council from September 1932 to January 1933, he was not slow to lecture his colleagues on the need for reform of the international system. His was a strong voice in defence of collective security and he called for radical action during the Abyssinian crisis of 1935–6[85] and the Spanish civil war between 1936 and 1939.[86]

Although Latin America was not at the top de Valera's foreign policy priorities during those early years in power, league membership directly exposed both the minister and the Department of External Affairs to the complexities of conflict resolution in Latin America.[87] At the time, Peru and Colombia were in dispute over control of the border town of Leticia. Seán Lester, the Irish diplomat who was posted to the League of Nations between 1930 and 1933, played a central role as head of the conciliation committee regarding that dispute.[88] He was also involved through the League of Nations with helping to find a peaceful solution to the war between Paraguay and Bolivia, which began in 1928, over the ownership of 259,000 square kilometres in the Gran Chaco region. This area was rumoured to have rich oil fields awaiting discovery. After a loss of roughly 100,000 lives, a ceasefire was finally reached on 12 June 1935. A peace accord was signed in Buenos Aires on 21 July 1938. The dispute was finally and formally resolved only on 28 April 2009, when both Paraguay and Bolivia signed a treaty in Buenos Aires.[89]

By the outbreak of the Second World War, de Valera had lost all confidence in the League of Nations. He declared Irish neutrality at the outbreak of hostilities and held that position throughout the conflict.[90] He remained in office until 1948, winning six consecutive general elections between 1932 and 1944. In those years, he opened two more diplomatic missions – in Switzerland on 10 October 1940 and in Portugal on 26 February 1942. At the outbreak of the Second World War,[91] Argentina joined the US and the Latin American republics in asserting neutrality. Following the attack on Pearl Harbor on 7 December 1941, the inter-American conference in Rio de Janeiro expressed solidarity with the United States. Argentina equivocated. Within a month, Chile and Argentina remained the only two Latin American countries not to have broken off diplomatic relations with the Axis powers. A military coup on 4 June 1943 removed the conservative Argentine president Ramón Castillo and replaced him with a provisional president, Gen. Arturo Rawson.[92] Deposed after three days in power by a United Officers' Group, he was replaced by

General Pedro Pablo Ramírez.[93] Juan Domingo Perón, a career army officer who had taught in the Superior War School and served as a military attaché in Chile and in Italy from 1936 to 1941, served as head of the Department of Labour. His political star was on the rise. The Argentine government, on 26 January 1944, succumbed to pressure from Washington and severed diplomatic relations with Berlin, Rome and Japan. The country entered the war on the side of the Allies in March 1945. Yet, Washington continued to accuse Argentina for the remainder of the war of Nazi and fascist sympathies and of providing a haven to escaping war criminals after hostilities had ended.

Apart from occasional contact during the war between Irish and Argentine representatives at the Holy See and other missions, the links between the two countries were peripheral. There was an exception in 1942–3 when the Spanish Foreign Office brought forward Plan D, a quixotic peace initiative seeking to unite Catholic powers in an effort to broker peace under the leadership of General Francisco Franco. The plan was still-born.[94] There was very limited reportage on Argentine political affairs in the Irish papers during the war and very little contact or trade between 1939 and 1945. Irish film-goers in 1942 were, however, treated to Maureen O'Hara in *They Met in Argentina*. Occasional reports in the press noted the arrival of luxury goods from Argentina: 'More muscatels have arrived from Argentina in very good condition', a wholesaler told the *Irish Press* on 15 November 1943. On 10 December 1945, readers saw the exciting news that 'Argentina is the place that has been sending us those silk stockings, the expensive ones that the drapers are not afraid to put in the windows'. Unable to travel to Europe, Irish-Argentines were not entirely cut off from the 'motherland' as *TSC* continued to appear weekly bringing news from 'home' under the editorship from 1938 to 1959 of the Pallottine Fr Juan Santos Gaynor.[95]

As the war drew to a close, the question of opening diplomatic relations with Argentina was reactivated in both Buenos Aires and Dublin. Raúl A. Laurel represented Argentina in Dublin throughout the latter part of the 1930s and continued reporting to the Argentine embassy in London until after the Second World War.[96] Sources in both Buenos Aires and London, however, believed it was time to upgrade to a legation. The case for an exchange of envoys was greatly enhanced when General Edelmiro Farrell, whose grandfather came from County Longford, became president on 24 February 1944, a position he held until 4 June 1945.[97] The Argentine ambassador in London, Miguel Ángel Cárcano, wrote to the Minister for Foreign Affairs, César Ameghino, on 25 April 1945 recommending the appointment of an envoy in Dublin based on the findings of one of his staff who had made a recent trip there, concluding that

Ireland favoured the strengthening of diplomatic, economic and commercial relations with Argentina. The report further revealed that Ireland had bought maize and wheat from Argentina and was a potential market for other Argentine products. Cárcano stressed the advantage of maintaining, from a social and political standpoint, constant contact with Dublin. That was even more the case at that time given Argentina's diplomatic and economic problems with the United Kingdom, he said, concluding that, while he supported the proposed opening of a consulate in Dublin, he felt that diplomatic relations at ministerial level would serve that purpose better. The ambassador sought permission to advance the proposal with the British government.[98]

On 30 April 1945, the political division in the foreign ministry in Buenos Aires supported the establishment of an economic and trade consulate in Dublin. That argument was reinforced by the fact that it was difficult for the Argentine embassy in London to continue to be the representative in Ireland given the state of Anglo-Irish relations and the ambiguous standing of the country in the British Commonwealth. The foreign minister, Juan Atilio Bramuglia, who held that position between June 1946 and November 1949, was advised by the political division in the ministry to establish diplomatic relations with Ireland. The director of consular affairs, Mario Molina Salas, was opposed to the elevation of the Dublin vice-consulate to that of a consulate general. Such a move, he felt, might be interpreted negatively by the British government.[99] The issue remained unresolved and no policy decision was taken in Buenos Aires due to a rapid and radical deterioration in Anglo-Irish relations at the end of the war caused by an uncharacteristically clumsy diplomatic action by de Valera. On 2 May 1945, the taoiseach and the secretary of the Department of External Affairs Joseph Walshe visited the German minister Eduard Hempel at his home in Dublin to express condolences on the death of Adolf Hitler on behalf of the Irish state. Although de Valera explained his action as merely following the protocol on the death of a head of state with which Ireland had diplomatic relations, his visit was wrongly perceived internationally as being an act of solidarity with the Nazi regime. The visit drove Anglo-Irish relations to below freezing point as the prime minister, Winston Churchill, attacked the taoiseach for frolicking to his heart's content during the war with the German and Japanese ambassadors in Dublin while Britain fought for its very existence.[100] On 18 July 1945, the *Irish Press* carried agency reports that 'Herr Hitler may be alive and either in Argentina or the Antarctic'. It quoted the *Chicago Times* reporter in Montevideo: 'I am virtually certain that Hitler and his wife, Eva Braun, the latter dressed in masculine clothes, landed in Argentina [from a submarine] and are on an immense German-owned estate in Patagonia.' The *Irish Press* carried an official Argentine government denial that there was any truth in the rumours.[101] In his book *The Hitler Conspiracies*, Professor Richard Evans has comprehensively debunked those claims. No matter how solid the scholarship, it has not prevented the continuation of the Hitler myth flourishing in twenty-first-century Argentina.[102]

Ambassador Miguel Ángel Cárcano, during the Second World War, enjoyed great respect in British government circles. The Argentine's refusal to leave London during the blitz won him many friends in official circles. Despite the country's neutrality, nearly 4,000 of his fellow countrymen had left to fight for the Allies.[103] In the light of the tensions in Anglo-Irish relations caused by de Valera's ill-judged visit,[104] Cárcano on 25 October 1945 urged the foreign minister to postpone the requested exchange of envoys for a number of months. Buenos Aires took his advice,[105] thus delaying the establishment of diplomatic relations between Ireland and Argentina for a further two years. The de Valera visit to the German minister may also have cost Ireland membership of the United Nations, resulting in a long delay until the country was finally granted admission in 1955. (Argentina joined the UN in 1945.)

The case for an exchange of envoys soon had a new and powerful champion. Juan Domingo Perón won the presidential election on 24 February 1946, helped greatly by the presence, by his side, of the actress Maria Eva Duarte. The couple had married in Junín on 18 October 1945, with the church ceremony taking place in Buenos Aires on 9 December that year. Sworn into office on 4 June 1946 with substantial majorities in both chambers of Congress, he had a free hand to legislate and to negotiate with foreign powers. Perón had assembled a body of doctrine which he called *justicialismo*, an ideology that was nationalist, reformist, personalist, isolationist and authoritarian.[106] The British ambassador, David Kelly, an Irishman who had previously served in Buenos Aires between 1919 and 1920, observed that Perón believed that 'the disinherited masses' were instinctively and unselfconsciously 'longing for a *caudillo*'. Kelly also felt the new president had 'much personal charm', was a 'brilliant improviser' and not 'in the least interested in Nazism or other ideologies'.[107] Perón's policy of autarky inspired the ideas which underpinned a new agreement with the British government. Mirroring de Valera's challenge to British interests in Ireland during the economic war in the 1930s, the pro-government *Irish Press* wrote in an editorial on 19 September 1946, after the signing of a new Anglo-Argentine trade agreement, that 'in the future we shall probably hear fewer references to "dago Republics"'.[108]

In 1946, the Irish mission to the Holy See was raised from a legation to the status of an embassy. The newly appointed ambassador, Joseph Walshe, was very familiar with the background to Irish-Argentine relations having written the letter to Ussher in 1935 quoted earlier in this chapter. He met his Argentine counterpart, Luis S. Castiñeiras,[109] on 12 June 1946 and they discussed the question of exchanging envoys. Reporting to Buenos Aires, the ambassador said that Walshe had spoken to him in very complimentary terms (*en términos muy elogiosos*) about the strong wave of sympathy (*un gran corriente de simpatía*) that existed in Ireland for Argentina. Walshe also had told him that the Irish government was thinking about creating new diplomatic missions in different countries the following year, 'amongst those being Argentina as one of the first'.[110]

On 25 August 1946, the new Argentine ambassador in London, Felipe Aja Espil, reported that Anglo-Irish relations had become 'much less tense and antagonistic' than had been the case in the recent past. He cited the decision of the Irish government to apply for membership of the United Nations as an example of a breakthrough. The ambassador argued that Irish and Argentine membership of the United Nations would prove grounds for mutual cooperation. Apart from that, he noted that Ireland had diplomatic relations with the most important nations in the world. Dublin, he wrote, planned an expansion of its network of legations. It had no diplomatic relations with any Latin American country, but he noted from the files left by his predecessor that Dublin was eager to establish such relations with Argentina. Similar signals had been received, he noted, by the Argentine ambassadors at the Holy See and in Washington DC. He awaited instructions before raising the matter with the Irish high commissioner, John W. Dulanty.[111] In the meantime, de Valera opened legations in Sweden in July 1946 and in Australia in October 1946.[112]

LEOPOLD KERNEY'S MISSION TO BUENOS AIRES

An Irish-Argentine, James B. Sheridan, wrote on 14 January 1947 to his school friend, the Supreme Court judge George Gavan Duffy,[113] pointing out Perón's friendship for Ireland:[114] 'General Perón is a great admirer of the Irish and is anxious to help in any way he can in this emergency.' This letter was carried by hand to Ireland by Dr John Duggan. A former comrade of de Valera's in the war of independence, he had immigrated to Buenos Aires in the 1920s where he worked at the British hospital. He is almost certain to have met de Valera when back in Ireland. Sheridan's letter to Duffy continued:

> Now the object of this letter is to inform you that President Perón is delighted to afford Ireland from 60 to 100,000 tons of wheat at a very

reasonable price, in view of the fact that the USA refused Ireland a quota ... An official authorization from the government of Eire to Mr Duggan would make matters very simple and by the way I venture to suggest that it is high time that Ireland nominated a commercial representative in this country. Please act quickly, as it appears that President Perón may be leaving in the near future for Europe. 'Carpe diem' as old Horace was wont to say and you can do a magnificent spot of work for Ireland and Argentina.[115]

In the early months of 1947, Ireland experienced the harshest weather conditions in living memory. Heavy snow disrupted food supplies and forced the government to reintroduce rationing. A failed harvest in 1946 caused a grain shortage. British coal supplies virtually dried up and snowstorms cut off many parts of the country.[116] The Irish government turned towards Argentina for help to supply wheat, fats and vegetable oil. Driven by the economic necessity of trying to source wheat and maize, de Valera and the minister for industry and commerce, Seán Lemass, approached Leopold Kerney, recently retired as envoy in Spain, to lead a trade mission to Latin America.[117] A memorandum to government on 19 April 1947 stated:

> The Minister for External Affairs [de Valera] has for some time had in mind the desirability of establishing diplomatic relations with the Argentine. Mr. L.H. Kerney's forthcoming mission now provides a suitable opportunity for proposing formally to the Argentine Government an exchange of diplomatic missions between the two countries. It is felt that much might be gained from the development of closer relations with the Argentine, a country in which there is a large number of people of Irish descent. The Argentine has always taken a very independent stand in international affairs and in view of her influence amongst the other Latin American countries, her goodwill could be of considerable benefit to us in the diplomatic sphere. From the commercial point of view, the advantages of direct contact need not be stressed. The minister would accordingly be glad to have the approval in principle of the Government for the establishment of a legation in the Argentine and for the appointment, in due course, of a chargé d'affaires.[118]

While the ostensible reason for the visit was trade, according to the historian Barry Whelan, de Valera instructed Kerney to accelerate the establishment of diplomatic relations between the two countries. The envoy was also given 'precise instructions [by de Valera] to raise the injustice of Partition at every opportunity'.[119] The assistant secretary of the Department of External Affairs, Leo T. McCauley, wrote on 21 April to the taoiseach's office requesting that the question of exchanging envoys with Argentina be put on the agenda for the meeting of government on the 22nd. A further minute read: 'Mentioned informally but sanction not yet sought or obtained.' That was granted a week later, on 28 April, when Maurice Moynihan, secretary of the Department of the Taoiseach and cabinet secretary, confirmed to Iveagh House that the government approved 'in principle, the establishment of a Legation in the Argentine and the appointment, in due course, of a chargé d'affaires'.[120]

Among the many letters of introduction to Chilean, Brazilian, Uruguayan and Argentine ministers, de Valera gave Kerney a note dated 22 April 1947 for the Argentine foreign minister, Juan Atilio Bramuglia, stating that Dublin wanted to establish a diplomatic mission in Buenos Aires 'as a means of strengthening and developing the relations between Ireland and the Argentine Republic'. De Valera added that such a move 'will do much to further their mutual interests'. He wrote that it would also 'be a source of great satisfaction to the Irish people, who, recalling the part played by their forbears in the history of the Argentine Republic, would see in it an expression of the feelings of friendship and sympathy which have for so long existed between our two nations'. He proposed that the first envoy have the rank of chargé d'affaires en titre.[121]

Kerney arrived in Buenos Aires on 27 April ostensibly as head of the Irish Food Mission. He was accompanied by the leading businessman F.P. Hallinan and his wife; by Mr Whitehead, secretary of Grain Importers, Ltd; and by J. Causer, director, and Mr Savage, secretary, Oils and Fats (Ireland) Ltd.[122] They were met by a large delegation of Irish-Argentines, including Mgr Santiago Ussher, the lawyer Dr Joseph Richards, Dr Juan (John) Duggan and members of the Passionist and Pallottine orders. *TSC* devoted a front page to Kerney's message from 'the first official representative of the Irish government since 1919'.[123] He was feted by the Irish community in Buenos Aires and was made an honorary member of the Jockey Club during his stay of over a month. In the course of his visit he saw the minister for the navy and had an interview with Miguel Miranda, president of the Central Bank,[124] arranged by Timoteo Ussher, a brother of the Monseñor Santiago Ussher.

Kerney called at the Foreign Office on 28 April, where he met Sr Bernini of the protocol section, who promised to get him an interview with Bramuglia the following day and requested him to present himself between 5 p.m. and 7 p.m. that evening, only to learn when he arrived that he was attending the minister's bi-weekly meeting with members of the diplomatic corps. Bernini introduced him around and he had short conversations with each envoy. When the minister did not appear, ambassadors started to drift away, including the French envoy, who 'manifested restrained indignation on learning that the Minister had had to leave and that the political undersecretary, Sr Desmaras, would receive those still waiting'.[125] Kerney presented his letters of credence and requested an appointment with the minister as he wished to present to the latter personally a letter from de Valera. He was told that he would receive a call on 5 May to give him a date for his appointment.

On 30 April, Kerney attended a concert in his honour hosted by the Irish community. Some 1,200 people bought tickets for the performance, a thousand of whom were Irish. When asked to speak, Kerney gave greetings from Ireland and stressed that 'they should cling to "Ireland" rather than to "Éire" and told them that the only obstacle in the way of cordial relations between England and Ireland was the continued existence of Partition'. He concluded with 'God save Argentina, God save Ireland'. Kerney remained convinced that his words had been 'completely devoid of anything resembling hatred or passion', but he reported with surprise that the *Buenos Aires Herald* had received many disapproving letters, with one signed 'A disgusted Briton'.[126] As will be seen later, his words had stirred up dormant divisions within the Irish community, between strong Irish nationalists and those who supported Britain during the war.

Kerney was given an appointment for 6 May to meet the Argentine foreign minister; taking his turn in the queue behind the nuncio and the British ambassador, Kerney saw Bramuglia at 7.50 and presented him with the note in English from de Valera concerning an exchange of envoys. The minister read it and said he would consult President Perón, agreeing to meet Kerney after the three days of public holidays from 10 to 12 May, when a nationwide census was being taken up.[127] As Kerney was travelling to Chile during that period, the appointment was set for 26 May. In Santiago on the 14th, Kerney was received by President Gabriel González Videla. He laid a wreath at the statue of Bernardo O'Higgins and later met the foreign minister. While Kerney was out of the country, the Irish delegation travelled on 18 May to Rosario. Returning to Buenos Aires, Kerney led his delegation on visits to Holy Cross, St Patrick's, Mater Misericordiae and Santa Brígida. He later visited Recoleta Cemetery and laid wreaths at the tombs of Fr Dominic Fahy and William Brown.[128] On 25 May, the Pallottines received him warmly in their school and monastery in Mercedes. Kerney was back at the Foreign Office on 26 May where he met Bramuglia, who told him that he had seen the president, that he was 'in agreement' with an exchange of envoys and that the matter was now being

studied by his ministry. Implying a sense of urgency, Kerney replied that he had
received many inquiries about a diplomatic exchange but all he had done was
counsel patience. He was given another appointment to meet Bramuglia on the
30th.[129]

On 28 May, the Irish-Argentine community gave a formal dinner in
honour of Kerney and his delegation in the Plaza Hotel. Before a very large
audience, Kerney delivered a speech on partition from a prepared text. Giving
it as the main reason why Ireland had been neutral during the war, he urged
members of the audience to add their voices for its removal and for the cause
of reunification. He thanked Argentina for helping to supply Ireland with food
during the war. Kerney hinted that their patience over more than two decades
would be rewarded soon by an announcement establishing diplomatic relations
between the two countries. His entire speech was printed in *The Southern Cross*
and excerpts in other papers. He was again personally shocked to learn that his
views had caused offence to a number of prominent Irish-Argentines who had
been sympathetic to the Allies during the war.

Two days later – 30 May – Kerney returned in the early morning to the
foreign ministry. The chief of protocol, Sr Valenti, told him that the question
of exchanging envoys was being studied for precedents (*en estudio para
antecedents*) and he requested that he return on Monday, 2 June. Kerney had
a meeting in another ministry before travelling to Arrecifes, where he was
received by the Irish Passionist Victor O'Carolan. Taken later to the Passionist
school at Capitán Sarmiento, he was greeted by a Scottish piper playing Irish
airs. He noticed 'a copy of the 1916 Proclamation on one of the walls, flanked
by pictures of Terence MacSwiney on one side and Admiral Brown on the
other'. Kerney gave a short talk after lunch in which he stated that 'a legation
would certainly be opened in due course'. There and then 'Fr Victor made up
his mind to send a telegram to President Perón and another to President Seán
T. Ó Ceallaigh urging the desirability of establishing diplomatic relations
between the two countries.'[130] By way of explanation for the priest's enthusiasm,
Kerney noted: 'It has to be remembered that men like Fr Victor O'Carolan,
shut off from the outer Irish world, live largely in the past, and allowances
must be made. I do not know whether I was the only one to feel a cold shiver
down my spine.'[131] Before leaving, he chatted with a prominent Irish-Argentine,
Lizzie Fox, who confessed that she was not up to date with what was happening
in Ireland. She was surprised to learn from Kerney that a British envoy was
resident in Dublin. Fox said she knew that Perón was very friendly to Ireland
and she hoped the envoy would meet him. In fact, she promised to pull a few
strings to try to set up such an appointment.[132]

On 2 June, Kerney had appointments in two government ministries. Afterwards, he laid wreaths at the tomb of San Martín and at the statue of Admiral Brown. Later that evening, he joined the usual queue of ambassadors at the foreign ministry patiently waiting to get the ear of the minister for a few minutes. His irritation with the delays on his previous visits had already been recorded in his report on 26 May: 'It is my own conclusion, however, that the diplomatic corps is treated with scant courtesy, and that this is not due to malevolence.'[133] After a delay of an hour and a quarter, he handed Sr Bernini 'a p.p.c. card for the Minister, regretting that I could not wait any longer; I told him that I did not think I had been guilty of being impatient, but that I thought that, in view of the circumstances, there was a lack of courtesy displayed towards the diplomatic representative of Ireland'. As Kerney was leaving for Dublin on 4 June, he regretted he could not take his leave personally of the minister. If there was any written communication it could be sent to Dublin. He then thanked Bernini for his courtesy and left. He had no further contact with the foreign ministry up to the time of his departure.[134]

In the wake of that 'incident', Kerney held a press conference to summarise the results of his trip. He also distributed the text of his 28 May speech on the partition of Ireland and spoke on the topic again. His big announcement was that diplomatic relations were 'on the road towards being established' and requested people to be patient for a short time longer 'in the knowledge that patience is a virtue which does not go unrewarded'.[135] Mixing with Irish-Argentines afterwards, he realised that news of his 'walkout' had travelled fast within the Irish community. Lizzie Fox reassured him that he had been quite right to leave. While being sad for Argentina, as an Irishwoman she was proud that Kerney had the courage to walk out. Her only regret was that she had arranged for him to be taken to meet Perón directly after his audience with the foreign minister which never took place.[136] On 4 June, Kerney left for Ireland without ever having met President Perón.

While the envoy was travelling home, on 5 June the *Irish Press* reported that Argentina was to ship 250,000 tons of maize to Ireland. Kerney announced at a press conference immediately after he landed in Dublin that an exchange of envoys was likely and that the Argentine-Irish were excited at the prospect of renewing links between the two countries. He confirmed that Ireland would pay cash for the shipment of maize, which cut 'directly across the "goods for goods" policy which M. Miguel Miranda, President of the Argentine Central Bank ... has enforced when dealing with other countries'. That policy had been waived in the Irish case. Overall, he declared his mission to have been a 'definite success'.[137]

However, there was divided opinion in the Irish community in Argentina over the legacy of the Kerney visit. The retired envoy received letters from prominent Irish-Argentines reassuring him that he had been correct to leave the foreign ministry. However, Matthew Murphy, the envoy sent to open the legation in December 1947, reported negatively in March 1948 on Kerney's handling of his final visit to the foreign ministry. His reconstruction was as follows: 'After waiting for a long time ... to see the Foreign Minister, [Kerney] made a loud protest to one of the officials that he was not getting the consideration due to the representative of a Sovereign nation and left in obvious anger.' He added that it was 'not unusual for Ambassadors [from] great powers to be kept waiting for even longer than Mr Kearney [*sic*]'. Murphy surmised that Kerney's failure to see the foreign minister and President Perón 'was due to their dislike of political problems of outside countries being aired on Argentinian soil'.[138] Regarding the envoy's references to Irish neutrality and his hostility to partition, Murphy said he had been informed by members of the Irish-Argentine community that a reception held in honour of Kerney had been 'the first occasion for many years when such a varied group of Irish-Argentines assembled, [and] a number of guests walked out. In the United States, of course, they might have walked out of a similar gathering if Partition was *not* mentioned'. As a consequence of referring too frequently to the partition of Ireland, Murphy had been informed that 'several prominent people who attended the reception for Dr Kearney [*sic*] refused to attend the reception in my [Murphy's] honour after my arrival [in December 1947], because they expected the same sort of address by me; as I did not know who they were I did not miss them'. Murphy surmised that Kerney's failure to see the foreign minister and President Perón 'was due to their dislike of political problems of outside countries being aired on Argentinian soil'.[139] This interpretation of the Kerney visit entered the folklore of Iveagh House.

Timothy Joseph Horan, Murphy's immediate successor in 1955, was also made aware that Kerney had antagonised better-off Irish-Argentines, particularly the Irish estancieros. With the memory of the Second World War fresh in people's minds, Horan reported that the envoy's public utterances had given great offence when, in defending Irish neutrality, he 'laid the blame for Partition on Britain'. Horan explained that 'the upbringing and education of the Irish-Argentines of this class tended to make them more British than Irish. Many of them would have had their secondary schooling in English colleges such as Stonyhurst and Downside and their associates would be English-Argentines of the same social status as themselves'.[140] Horan also reported that there had been 'a good deal of sympathy' among the rest of the Irish community with the Irish government's stance during the war:

> But for Irish-Argentines in general, since for all practical purposes, there is no further immigration from the home country, Ireland tends to be cut off from their consciousness as a living land and to be enshrined as a memory, static in the mid-nineteenth century. When they think of it at all it is in a remote romantic sort of way ... But though they are as a community proud of their Irish descent and feel a strong sentimental attachment to it, they are not interested in its problems. It is too far away for that, both in space and in time.

He said they were aware of partition, 'but for them it holds no interest'.[141]

Notwithstanding those comments by Murphy and Horan that Kerney may have ruffled feathers unnecessarily among Irish-Argentines, Kerney had brought home the bacon by improving trade relations between the two countries and by also moving forward de Valera's plan to open diplomatic relations.

IRISH–ARGENTINE DIPLOMATIC RELATIONS: FINAL NEGOTIATIONS

Matters moved swiftly in Buenos Aires during and after the Kerney visit. With the internal review completed in the foreign ministry, Pascual la Rosa wrote a memorandum on 2 June stating that while his Department of External Relations did not object to the Irish request to open diplomatic relations between Dublin and Buenos Aires, he felt that the matter would be best handled by the respective ambassadors in Washington DC. Foreign Minister Bramuglia sent a telegram on 3 June to the ambassador in Washington, Oscar Ivanissevich, giving him instructions to prepare to exchange notes with the Irish ambassador Seán Nunan. The same day, the latter sent a formal note requesting an exchange of representatives, and Ivanissevich replied to him on 13 June requesting that he advise Dublin that 'my Government shares this desire of the Government of Ireland [to establish diplomatic relations] and accepts the proposal with pleasure'.[142] De Valera told the Dáil on 20 June of the opening of two new diplomatic missions, in Belgium and Argentina: 'Deputies would see, therefore, that it was necessary as our trade relations were expanding to expand also our diplomatic representation.'[143] As a backdrop to the establishment of diplomatic relations between Dublin and Buenos Aires, the *Irish Press* reported on 19 June 1947 that the cruiser *La Argentina*, with a crew of 600 men and 85 cadets, was to pay a five-day visit to Dublin, arriving on 2 July. Entering Dublin Bay, it fired a salute of guns to which an Irish army artillery unit replied. On 7 July 1947, the *Irish Press* reported that the taoiseach, Éamon de Valera, visited the ship together with other ministers, including the minister for posts and telegraphs, Patrick J. Little, who had been a Sinn Féin envoy for a few months in Buenos Aires in autumn 1921.

The Argentine vice-consul in Dublin, Raúl A. Laurel, took advantage of *La Argentina*'s visit to discuss with the assistant secretary of the Department of Foreign Affairs, Con Cremin, further issues regarding diplomatic relations between the two countries. Cremin told him that the move was imminent and also, off the record, that the Irish government appreciated very much that he was accredited to the whole of Ireland. Brazil had a similar arrangement. Reporting on 23 July, Laurel said that Ireland would not establish a vice-consulate or consulate in Buenos Aires that was under the jurisdiction of an Irish consulate general in Santiago, Chile, or Rio de Janeiro. Dublin did not consider it logical, for the same reason, for a foreign consulate recognised by the Irish government and allowed to operate within its jurisdiction to have a subordinate relationship with a consulate general based in another European country.[144] Laurel asked Buenos Aires whether the consulate in Dublin should continue to report to Buenos Aires through the Argentine embassy in London or whether it ought to do so directly in the future. Cremin also raised another contentious topic when he informed Laurel that historically the credentials of Irish diplomats serving abroad were presented to the king of England for his signature by the Irish high commissioner in London. Indirectly, Cremin was raising whether or not the credentials of the first Argentine envoy to Ireland should be addressed to the king of England or to the president of Ireland.[145]

On 29 July 1947, ambassadors Seán Nunan and Oscar Ivanissevich exchanged further correspondence. The former spoke of the bonds of friendship between 'our two peoples by reason of our common religious heritage and the fact that many Irish exiles and their descendants contributed to the building up of the Argentine Republic in many ways'. He also made reference to the fact that both Admiral William Brown and General O'Brien (aide-de-camp to General San Martín) had been born in Ireland. Ivanissevich, in his reply, referred to the spirit of Admiral Brown and said that the Argentine people knew 'the brilliant part that Irish settlers played in the development of our country. They also know that in our struggle for independence we could rely upon the help of the Irish people'.[146] The final preparations for the opening of diplomatic relations were quickly concluded in Dublin and in Buenos Aires. Bramuglia was informed on 25 August 1947 that all relevant documents had been received. On 12 September, President Juan Perón informed Congress of the agreement to set up diplomatic relations between Argentina and Ireland.[147]

The Irish government appointed the Irish consul in San Francisco, Matthew Murphy, as chargé d'affaires en titre in Buenos Aires, a title that remained unchanged until 1964 when ambassadorial status was granted to the post.[148] Joining the British civil service in 1913, Murphy transferred to the Irish Free State, where he worked in the Department of Defence. In 1925, he joined the Department of External Affairs. He spent the greater part of his professional life in the United States, working first at the consulate in New York and then serving from 1928 as first secretary at the Irish legation in Washington. He helped set up consulates in Chicago and Boston before being transferred in 1933 to establish a consulate in San Francisco, where he served until his posting to Argentina in 1947.[149] Married to a German musician, Olinda *née* Baroness von Kap-Herr Proves, the consulate and at other halls in the city became a venue for violin recitals.[150] She continued to give recitals in Buenos Aires.[151]

The opening of an Irish diplomatic mission in Argentina was not the first step of a de Valera strategic plan to set up a network of missions throughout Latin America. It is probable that the secretary of his department, Frederick Boland, and other senior Iveagh House officials would have felt the need was more pressing to extend the diplomatic network in Europe. Argentina was to be the sole Irish mission in the region and remained so until the last decade of the twentieth century. That was de Valera's way of thanking the many Irish-Argentines who supported him during the war of independence and through the civil war and the dark days in the 'wilderness' during the 1920s and after he came to power in 1932. That new mission was integral to one strand of his long-term foreign policy strategy – to link the 'homeland' to a network of resident missions in countries where historically there had been high Irish emigration. The opening in Argentina had come a year after an Irish legation had been opened in Canberra, Australia. De Valera had set up diplomatic relations with Canada in 1940. Irish missions in London and Washington dated from 1923 and 1924 respectively. De Valera felt that he could depend upon support from the diaspora to end partition. Free of office, he went on the road in March that year, touring the United States accompanied by Frank Aiken and his media director, Frank Gallagher. There he drew the same large crowds in New York and travelled 16,000 kilometres in three weeks, visiting Boston, Chicago, Detroit, Los Angeles, Oklahoma, San Francisco and Philadelphia. Focusing on the question of partition, he attacked the British government for dividing Ireland. While he did not include Argentina in his round-the-world crusade, he visited Australia and New Zealand in April 1948 and spoke repeatedly of the cruel injustice of partition. He travelled to India in June, where he lunched with the British governor general, Lord Mountbatten, and had a meeting with the prime minister, Jawaharlal Nehru, who privately indicated his sympathy for the anti-partition stance in Ireland. Between October 1948 and March 1949, de Valera and his party attended anti-partition rallies in the main cities in Britain, drawing large crowds as he had done in the US and in Australia.[152] His tour kept his name in the headlines at home and abroad as he bided his time in the expectation of a swift return to power.

The new Irish government which took office on 18 February 1948 remained in power until 13 June 1951. John A. Costello of Fine Gael joined forces with Labour, National Labour, Clann na Talmhan and Clann na Poblachta to form what became known as the first inter-party government. Seán MacBride, the leader of radical Clann na Poblachta, was made minister for external affairs. This created quite a stir among the senior management in Iveagh House. As a former 'chief of staff' of the IRA in the 1930s, he had broken with that organisation after the referendum in 1937, which voted in a new Irish constitution.[153] But suspicions lingered in the civil service about MacBride's bona fides. A barrister by profession, he successfully defended members of the IRA during the Second World War. Relations between the departmental secretary Frederick Boland and the new minister did not get off to a flying start. On his first day in the office, MacBride asked: 'Mr Boland, give me a list of all the British agents working on your staff.'[154] The new minister's stewardship of foreign policy between 1948 and 1951 was one of continuity and contradictions. Supportive of the movement for European integration, Ireland joined the Council of Europe in 1949. MacBride negotiated the inclusion of Ireland in the Marshall Aid.[155] Ideologically, he was strongly on the side of the West in the Cold War. That was evident in Ireland's stance on the Holy Places and its refusal to give de jure recognition to the state of Israel until 1963.[156] He virtually cloned Irish policy with that of the Holy See during the run-up to the general election in Italy in 1948, when a combination of the Communist and Socialist parties was in a strong position to win power. MacBride directed the Irish ambassador to the Holy See, Joseph Walshe, to facilitate the transmission of financial support from the Irish Catholic Church to the Christian Democratic Party via the Department of External Affairs.[157] He made a personal contribution to the fund and later received letters of gratitude from the Holy See for Ireland's generosity and role in the defeat of the Italian left. In Holy Year 1950, Ireland showed its devotion to the Catholic Church. Crosses were erected on many hilltops throughout the country. The president of Ireland, Seán T. O'Kelly, led a national pilgrimage to Rome. Ireland became a militant member of the western bloc in the Cold War.[158]

Paradoxically, Dublin surprised and disappointed the secretariat of state of the Holy See by making two foreign policy decisions in 1949 which were contradictory of the country's Cold War militancy. MacBride championed Ireland's refusal to turn down the US invitation to join the North Atlantic Treaty Organisation (NATO). The Holy See also found inexplicable the decision to declare a republic and leave the British Commonwealth. Such volatility in foreign policy decision-making prompted the secretary of the department Frederick Boland to say many years later that the taoiseach, John A. Costello, 'had about as much notion of diplomacy as I have of astrology'.[159] That may explain Boland's decision in September 1950 to trade being secretary for the ambassadorship to the Court of St James.[160]

Boland was still in Iveagh House when Irish–Argentine relations made a major leap forward. Although de Valera had secured the commitment to exchange envoys, MacBride was in place to receive the first Argentine envoy to Dublin in July 1948. The minister was married to Catalina (Kid), the daughter of William Bulfin,[161] who had been born in Buenos Aires in the 1890s and returned to Ireland in 1902, where she was educated and later involved in nationalist politics during the war of independence and civil war. In his memoirs, MacBride explained that he approached the Argentine envoy José Fausto Rieffolo Bessone to explain that the Irish government would prefer if his letters of credence were addressed to the president of Ireland and not to the king of England.[162] The Argentine envoy agreed to consult Buenos Aires. His government approved the suggested change and he was issued with letters of credence addressed to the president of Ireland, Seán T. O'Kelly. The Irish cabinet also approved of the change. MacBride discussed the matter, according to his memoirs, with President O'Kelly, who was delighted with the new protocol and it was agreed that he would give a dinner for the ambassador upon his arrival. The official record of the event in the Department of the Taoiseach diverges significantly from the account in MacBride's memoirs, a warning to those who do not give weight to the fallibility of memory. The secretary of the Department of the Taoiseach, Nicholas Nolan, provided a contemporary note on those events which is much more reliable. He wrote on 3 August 1948 that the arrival of the Argentine envoy was the first time since the establishment of the Irish Free State that letters of credence were addressed to the president of Ireland. That was done, he said, without the prior knowledge of the Department of External Affairs. (That contradicts the account in MacBride's memoirs.) Nolan said Iveagh House considered returning the letters to correct the addressee but rejected that course of action. The Argentine letters of credence were addressed to '*El Presidente del Estados Libre de Irlanda*' ('The President of the Irish Free State'). A decision was taken to change the venue for the official reception ceremony from St Patrick's Hall, Dublin Castle, to the ballroom in Iveagh House. The usual mounted escort of army officers was replaced with an escort of military police on motorcycles. With the new procedures in place, MacBride and his wife Kid met José Fausto Rieffolo Bessone in the Shelbourne Hotel on 31 July 1948. He was escorted with motorcycle outriders around to Iveagh House on the other side of St Stephen's Green. He presented his new credentials to the taoiseach, Costello, who in turn handed them to the minister for external affairs and not the secretary of the government, which had previously been the practice.[163] Afterwards, the party arrived at Áras an Uachtaráin, where the president was waiting in the drawing room. MacBride handed the letter of credence to President O'Kelly. He opened the letter and read the contents. He then handed the letter to the taoiseach who, in turn, passed it to secretary of the government, who retained it for filing.[164] The Argentine ambassador and his wife were then presented to President O'Kelly before all sat down to lunch.[165]

Some six months earlier, the new Irish chargé d'affaires, Matthew Murphy, and his wife arrived in Buenos Aires on 17 December 1947 aboard the *Delmar*. Mgr Ussher and members of the Irish community were there to welcome the couple as they disembarked. According to the *Irish Press*, Murphy was also surrounded by high-ranking city and diplomatic officials, who shook his hand when he left the steamer. A member of the Argentine foreign ministry, Adolfo McLoughlin, from Junín, accompanied Murphy to the Plaza Hotel. On 19 December *TSC* published an editorial in both Spanish and English, hailing 'the advent of Ireland's first diplomatic representative to the Argentine Republic ... [Having] long advocated the establishment of diplomatic relations between the two countries ... we have followed with warm sympathy and encouragement the efforts made down the years to bring this event to its fitting consummation. The day is now at hand. Ireland and Argentina are linked in the comity of nations by the action of their respective governments'. The official seal had now been set on a friendship which dated from the birth of 'this Republic', the paper stated: 'There is much of Ireland in Argentina, for the sons and daughters of Bamba [an ancient name for Ireland] gave their blood and toil generously in the foundation and the consolidation of this Republic. These Gaels of the Dispersion, their sons and grandsons have not ever forgotten the Sion of their ancestors, for they have the long memory of their race ... The name of Ireland is a name respected in Argentina.'[166]

The festivities continued in Buenos Aires. *TSC* on 26 December described Murphy's arrival in a front-page editorial as 'a transcendental event'.[167] On 23 December, Irish-Argentines from Mercedes, San Antonio de Areco, Arrecifes, Junín, Pergamino and Capilla del Señor and other towns in the camp attended an official reception at the Plaza Hotel. Murphy spoke appreciatively to the audience of the warmth of the reception that they received from the community, many of whom had travelled long distances to be in attendance. Mgr Ussher, replying on behalf of Irish-Argentines, said that in the history of both nations permanent diplomatic relations were the realisation of 'a long-cherished hope'. At one stroke, he said, the opening of an Irish legation in Buenos Aires had eliminated 'some hazy ideas, quite common in certain quarters, regarding the national status of Ireland'. It proclaimed aloud, he said, that Ireland was a nation, 'not a province of another nation, nor a fraction of any empire; but a sovereign independent nation governed by her own native citizens, standing on an equal footing with this, our Argentine Republic, alongside the other sovereign and independent nations of the world'.[168] Ussher added that what defined 'the Irish-Argentines, nicknamed as the English language Catholic community', was not religion, politics or language, but their Irish ancestry and the nationality of their forefathers. He counted himself among all those who spoke 'a peculiar blend of English, Hiberno-Spanish English, flavoured with the traditional Irish brogue'.[169] There was no contradiction, he said, between being Irish and Argentine: 'We are thoroughly and unconditionally Argentine patriots ... To it we render unswerving loyalty; its flag is our flag; we revere the memory of its great sons; we admire their heroic deeds; and we aspire to imitate them in their Argentine patriotism.'[170] On Christmas day, a large congregation attended mass at Holy Cross. The chargé and his wife were in the place of honour.[171]

Mgr Ussher, on behalf of the reception committee, had sent a telegram in gratitude to President Seán T. O'Kelly: 'Thousands Argentine Gaels rejoice arrival first Irish representative and ... renew vows devotion land their ancestors ...' O'Kelly replied that Ireland 'will never forget what she owes to the devotion of her children overseas and rejoices at the prospect of closer contact with those who have made their home in great republic of Argentina'.[172]

MATTHEW MURPHY AND THE RISE AND FALL OF JUAN DOMINGO
PERÓN

Matthew Murphy brought a wealth of diplomatic experience to his new posting. He was also a secondary school classmate and friend of the taoiseach,

John A. Costello. That personal link must have given him a greater sense of security at a time when the Department of External Affairs was in a state of policy flux. A vigilant minister for external affairs would have determined early in his posting that Murphy was not well suited to meeting the professional challenges of his new mission. On his last posting before retirement, almost all of his professional experience had been in the United States, in San Francisco for the bulk of that time. In setting up the new legation, Murphy had the help for over a year of Thomas (Tommy) Woods, who had been transferred from Madrid because of his experience of working in a Spanish-speaking culture. When the latter was reassigned, his replacement was sent only on a temporary, short-term basis. For most of his posting, Murphy was left to run the mission alone. Despite MacBride's personal interest in Argentina and Costello's friendship with the envoy, Buenos Aires was on the periphery of Irish foreign policy interests. But as the Costello-led government exhibited a deference to the leaders of the Catholic Church in Ireland beyond what de Valera and Fianna Fáil ever displayed in power, Cold War religious issues in Argentina would become a policy priority when church and state clashed in 1954–5. MacBride was one of the most confessionally minded ministers to hold the external affairs portfolio in the history of the state; his desire to please the archbishop of Dublin, John Charles McQuaid, knew no bounds. And he was an admirer of Perón's efforts to establish autarky and foreign policy independence. In March 1948, the British-owned railways – the visible symbol of foreign domination in Argentina – were, in an assertion of national independence, nationalised by Perón. That also appealed to de Valera, now leader of the opposition. But it would not have pleased the more conservative parties in the inter-party government.

Between 1948 and 1951, MacBride did not question Murphy about his one-sided and hostile reporting on Perón and his administration. The Irish envoy never highlighted Perón's popular appeal, based as it was in part on his pledge to liberate the country from the clutches of *oligarcas* (oligarchs), *vendepatrias* (traitors) and *cipayos* (unscrupulous soldiers or mercenaries).[173] Perón's explicit policy to invert the social pyramid of power and wealth is described by political scientists as populism. Jan-Werner Müller identifies three techniques used by charismatic populist leaders to govern: 1) state colonisation; 2) mass clientelism; and 3) harsh treatment, when in government, of the opposition, NGOs and the agents of civil society. The same author argues that 'populists create the homogeneous people in whose name they had been speaking all along'. It follows, therefore, that 'civil society isn't civil society at all, and that what can seem like popular opposition has nothing to do with the proper people'. That leads, according to the same source, to populism in power reinforcing 'another variety of the very exclusion and the usurpation of the state that it most opposes in the reigning establishment it seeks to replace'. While populist leaders are not necessarily demagogic or mendacious, 'their self-presentation *is* based on one big lie; that there is a singular people of which they are the only representatives'.[174] Such characterisation may help explain the gradual alienation of the Catholic Church leadership from Perón in 1955 and the ferocity of the government reaction.

But in the late 1940s and early 1950s, Juan Domingo Perón and his wife Eva, known to the masses as Evita, were the harbingers of a social revolution for the *descamisados* (shirtless ones), or the poorest of the poor. The president's rhetoric, and that of his wife, was revivalist if not at times millennarian. Perón's 'third way' projected the idea of the power of the state placed at the service of the poor. Therefore, social security became universal. Trade unions were formed in every industry. Education was made free. Housing schemes for lower-income families were funded by the state. Workers were guaranteed free medical care. They received paid holiday leave and the state built resorts where they could spend their leave. Pregnant women received three months' paid leave before and after the birth of a child. Under Perón, the state embarked on the building of over forty hydroelectric power plants. The extension of state power and control over commodity exports through the Argentine Institute for Promotion of Exchange (AIPE) brought him into conflict with the estancieros, as did his raising of farm labourers' wages. Eva was virtually sanctified for her role in introducing labour and social reforms.

Perón sought to make Argentina the leader of an anti-Yanqui coalition, independent of and equidistant from both the US and the Soviet Union – the manifestation of his 'third way' in foreign policy. Perón offered like-minded governments the opportunity to remain aloof from the Cold War power blocs. The US, never Perón's friend, had excluded Argentina from the Marshall Plan. Asserting his independence, Perón refused to enter the General Agreement on Tariffs and Trade (GATT) or the International Monetary Fund (IMF). Realpolitik, however, already had obliged Argentina to become in 1945 a founding member of the United Nations (UN), sign the Inter-American Treaty of Reciprocal Assistance, commonly known as the Rio Treaty, in 1947, and then ratify the charter of the Organisation of American States (OAS) in 1948.

As is clear from his reports, Matthew Murphy, from his arrival in Buenos Aires, saw no virtue in the Perón government. He was more sympathetic to the views of members of the ultra-conservative Jockey Club than to the *descamisados* of the *villas*. The Irish envoy frequented that bastion of privilege, as did many other foreign diplomats, where the corps found themselves '*entre gens de bonne compagnie*' ('between people of good company'). Such social contacts only reinforced Murphy's hostility to the Peronist government. For example, when reporting on 5 November 1950, he stressed that the wealthy classes of farmers, property owners, businessmen and most of the middle classes were among those who wanted regime change. They were joined by 'all who believe in democracy and freedom of speech and of the press. To those can be added the Catholic hierarchy', he wrote.[175] He also reported that Argentina under Perón had become a dictatorship: 'We are living in a Police state here and diplomats are generally agreed on this ... it behoves people who do not like the regime not to say so except to friends whom they can trust ... and some believe that the radical and democratic opposition will be liquidated before the 1951 presidential elections'. The Irish chargé claimed that 'all our phones official and private are believed to be tapped. There have been so many accidents to diplomats' cars that we are beginning to sense that the growing public antagonism towards foreigners is being extended to diplomats'. Murphy also reported that there were spies in restaurants, bars, hotels, etc., and that people were being picked up by the police and jailed without charge and that their relatives often spent weeks or even months trying to locate a missing member of a family.[176] He held Eva Perón responsible for the government's growing authoritarianism as she was becoming, he wrote, 'more powerful as time goes on and Congress votes millions for her foundation or social work and there is not any audit of the funds'. There was, he said, a sinister side to her activities: 'Anyone running foul of her loses their job if in the service and many even disappear.'[177]

Murphy also reported a view shared by many of the foreign diplomats in the city – that Eva Perón had 'no use for diplomats and ... [regards] us as swine for not joining in applause of her husband's political speech [earlier in the year]'. Diplomats, as Leopold Kerney had experienced on his visit in 1947, were forced to wait for hours to see officials.[178] They found that the freedom of officials working in the foreign ministry was 'being curtailed to the extent that they can no longer accept invitations from Embassies'. One Argentine diplomat told Murphy that 'he would welcome a transfer even to Moscow'.[179]

In such volatile political circumstances, Murphy witnessed the foundation of a new Irish educational institution in Buenos Aires. As a former student at O'Connell's School in Dublin, the envoy was delighted to see the arrival of a community of Irish Christian Brothers. Invited by the cardinal archbishop of Buenos Aires, through the local superior of the Passionist order, Bros Cornelius O'Reilly and Ignatius Doorley arrived in 1947. Their mission was to open a bilingual Catholic school for boys. Offered the premises of the Sisters of Mercy's former school, Mater Misericordiae, at Avenida Belgrano 1548, Cardinal Newman College was opened on 29 March 1948. The first rector, Br Alphonsus L. Pakenham, had an enrolment of 148 pupils in its first year. The school motto was 'Fight the Good Fight [Timothy 6:12]. Bro. David O'Connor arrived by boat with two other brothers on 27 March 1949.[180] That year the college had seven brothers, eight lay teachers and 200 students. Quickly recognised for its academic excellence, the brothers encouraged the playing of rugby, a tradition which gained the school a strong reputation in that sport. Murphy became very friendly with the brothers and was a regular visitor to the school, which attracted many students from professional backgrounds.

Before Argentina faced a presidential election at the end of 1951, Murphy took his annual home leave in time to enjoy an Irish summer. His friend the taoiseach John A. Costello had lost power on 30 May 1951. Éamon de Valera and the Fianna Fáil party, on 13 June, formed a new government. Frank Aiken, a prominent member of the revolutionary generation, was the new minister for external affairs. Both men, as revealed earlier in this chapter, were well disposed to Perón for permitting grain supplies to be sent to Ireland in 1947 and for facilitating an exchange of envoys between the two countries. They were also admirers of his domestic economic policies, which were very similar to those Fianna Fáil pursued after coming to power in 1932. Perón though was pursuing policies which brought him into conflict with both Britain and the United States as he attempted to establish sovereignty over the Argentine economy.

While at home, Murphy was briefed on the international implications of Ireland's declaration of a republic on 18 April 1949. A departmental minute on 10 August 1951 read: 'I don't know how far we can press our views on the Argentine but the fact that the changes were made by a public decree would I think justify us in asking Mr. Murphy to take the opportunity on his return to Buenos Aires to point out nicely to the Argentinians that we would appreciate a little more advertence to our separate identity.' Iveagh House wanted Ireland to be removed from the British and Commonwealth section in the Argentine foreign ministry. Upon his return to Buenos Aires, Murphy found that he was pushing an open door; Ireland was swiftly transferred to the Western European division, thus making it easier to deal independently with Irish–Argentine relations.[181]

Murphy continued in his posting in Argentina until 1955. During the remainder of his time in Buenos Aires, he was an eyewitness to Perón reaching the zenith of his popularity following the presidential election of 1951, which he won with the support of prominent members of the Catholic Church. Eva

Perón, despite suffering from terminal cancer, remained her husband's strongest electoral asset throughout the campaign, according to Murphy. While her illness prevented her from running for the vice-presidency, she campaigned with great energy throughout the country. Support for Perón in the elections of 11 November 1951 also came from women, who had been enfranchised for the first time at the national level.[182] Irish-Argentines were to be found on both sides of the political divide.[183] Perón's margin of victory in 1946 was 260,000 votes. His majority in 1951 rose dramatically to 2.3 million. The election was more a coronation than a contest.

A few months before the poll, the Catholic hierarchy issued a joint pastoral encouraging the faithful to support Perón's candidature for the presidency and for the election of Peronists to governorships and seats in Congress.[184] Cardinal Santiago Copello, the archbishop of Buenos Aires between 1932 and 1959, was friendly at that point with the Argentine leader. The bishop of Catamarca between 1935 and 1959, Carlos Francisco Hanlon, was an Irish *porteño* Passionist who was unwavering in his support of Perón. (A *porteño* is a person who lives in Buenos Aires.) But within the space of three years, many members of the Catholic hierarchy, clergy, religious, nuns and lay people were alienated from the government. The historian Lila Caimari has set out the complexities and contradictions in Argentine church–state relations during those years – a task that for reasons of space cannot be tackled here.[185] Suffice it to say that the growing support for the establishment of a Christian Democratic party in the country was seen as an act of betrayal in government circles.

Murphy's hostile attitude to the Perón government grew exponentially in 1952. Convinced that government authorities were interfering with the diplomatic bag, he sent a handwritten report to Dublin on 15 January 1952 from Montevideo, Uruguay: 'The re-election of Perón has changed nothing and solved nothing and Argentina according to all signs and reports is facing a serious economic crisis.'[186] His views were as negative as those of Jorge Luis Borges, who referred to the Perón era as 'the years of opprobrium and foolishness'.[187] That writer's visceral opposition to the regime 'stemmed from a belief that he [Perón] was a Nazi', writes Emir Rodríguez Monegal, adding: 'While Borges was wrong about Perón's being a Nazi ... he was not wrong about his Fascism.'[188] While that is a statement which would have been contested by his followers, Murphy reported in like-minded negative fashion on 29 April 1952 that the Argentine opposition was now unable to hold meetings and that freedom of the press and of speech no longer existed: 'You will see from report I got to you by special airmail that the situation here is tense. However, as far as

I am concerned, they can make Alfie Byrne[189] president here if they only effect the change quietly.'[190] Not trusting the post or the diplomatic bag, Murphy took advantage of any Irish priest or nun travelling to Ireland to deliver his reports.

Perón's victory celebrations were eclipsed by reports that Eva was gravely ill, Murphy reporting on 19 February 1952 that she was dying. He had heard that 'some believe that on her demise Perón will resign and possibly leave Argentina and hand over the country to the workers as he so often promised to do'.[191] She defied those rumours by attending Perón's inauguration on 4 June 1952. Murphy, together with other members of the diplomatic corps, found that Congress was 'packed to suffocation' and 'the aisles between the deputies' seats were also thronged and all joined in the singing of party songs and yelled for Perón and Evita, who was referred to as Vice-President'. Perón and his wife arrived to a deafening ovation and it was 'fully 10 minutes before the house could be called to order to enable the President to take the oath of office'.[192]

In the following days, however, it was feared that Eva's death was imminent. Thousands kept vigil around an altar erected at the obelisk on Avenida 9 de Julio in Buenos Aires. They also stood to hear mass in a wintry downpour.[193] Her death, announced on 26 July, provoked scenes of public grief throughout the country.[194] Standing six-deep, people formed queues stretching some fifty blocks on either side of the Ministry of Labour and waited day and night for a turn to see her remains. Murphy reported that no member of the Peronist Party or of the General Confederation of Labour (CGT) was exempt from attending the obsequies: 'The fact that the latter were not allowed to leave the queue and had to wait as long as 15 hours will convey a fair idea of the condition of the thoroughfares.' Diplomats, too, 'had to wait a considerable time before the file of a shrieking public could be halted to enable us to view the remains'.[195] The remains were transferred to Congress, where they lay in an improvised funeral chapel in the main hall. A group of workers carried her coffin out of Congress, placed it on a gun carriage 'guarded, not by military personnel, but by the same workers' and it was taken not to a cemetery for Christian burial, but to the offices of the CGT. A compulsory levy had been imposed on all wages to defray the cost of Eva's mausoleum, 'the cost of which is expected to be staggering'.[196] Murphy reported that her death had sparked rumours in diplomatic circles that the general – aged fifty-seven – had lost his capacity and his will to govern and the diplomat hinted at the possibility of a coup d'état. However, come what may, Murphy reported that he felt safe in his seventh-floor apartment, but being only two years from retirement, he wrote: 'I could have done without such excitement in my old age ...'[197]

IRISH DIPLOMACY, THE CATHOLIC CHURCH AND THE FALL OF PERÓN

Argentina, although distant, loomed large during the last two years of the de Valera government, which lost power on 2 June 1954. There was increased coverage in the Irish national press about growing tensions in Argentine politics and a looming crisis between church and state. On 15 April 1953 bombs exploded during a monster rally at which Perón was the principal speaker. Five were killed and ninety-six wounded. A violent upheaval followed. As a reprisal, the Jockey Club – associated with oligarchs and estancieros and to which Murphy himself was a frequent visitor – was attacked and set alight,[198] destroying a library of 50,000 books together with priceless works of art, including seventeenth-century tapestries and paintings by Velázquez, Goya, Corot and Joaquín Sorolla, and damaging Falguière's statue of 'Diana the Hunter'.[199] Arsonists also burned down the building which housed the Unión Cívica Radical and the Partido Conservador. The library of the Partido Socialista was also torched, with a further loss of thousands of books. Perón outraged his political opponents by nationalising horse racing and the Jockey Club itself.[200] Some 4,000 arrests were made, among them leading members of the Argentine Society of Writers (SADE).[201]

In Ireland, the second inter-party government came to power. John A. Costello was taoiseach for the second time, taking office on 2 June 1954. He remained in government until 20 March 1957. Liam Cosgrave, a member of Fine Gael and son of William T. Cosgrave, became the minister for external affairs. Reflecting the same subservience to the Catholic hierarchy, the new taoiseach and his ministers were disposed to be deferential to the Holy See and to the leaders of the Catholic Church. Parallel to those developments in Irish politics, Argentina witnessed a serious deterioration in church–state relations in the mid-1950s. Catholic lay and ecclesiastical leaders in Buenos Aires had followed the rise of Christian Democracy in Germany, Italy and France in post-war Europe with great interest. It ought not to have been that surprising when a Christian Democratic Party was set up in 1954 in Buenos Aires,[202] accompanied by a strong recruitment drive and by the publication of pamphlets advocating a new political departure in national politics.[203] Murphy confirmed to Dublin on 19 November 1954 that the new party would field a candidate in the presidential election in 1957. Peronism as a national movement was a 'catch-all' party which may be defined as populist and was based on the dubious premise that 'there is a single people of which they are the only representatives'.[204] As the Christian Democratic movement evolved in post-war Europe, the parties formed were broadly based or 'catch-all' parties. The Argentine Christian Democratic Party challenged Peronism at all levels of society, having its own trade unions, youth groups, etc. The journalist and historian Horacio Verbitsky argues that Perón had sound reason to fear the mounting political challenge of the local Catholic Church, which supported the rise of Christian Democracy.[205] Perón used strong language to describe those recruiting for the new party, calling them '*bosta de paloma*' (pigeon excrement).[206]

In a climate of growing anticlericalism and hostility to the Catholic Church, Murphy reported that nuns collecting alms in Buenos Aires were being attacked in the street.[207] He asked himself, together with other diplomats, whether 'Perón is in his right mind'. He reported salacious rumours without providing any evidence that senior girls in the Unión Estudiantes Secundarios (Union of Secondary School Students) had been given the use of the president's *quinta* (estate) at Olivos one weekend towards the end of 1954: 'The President himself however spends a good deal of his time there, and [the] most amazing stories are current in all ranks of society concerning happenings there. These stories are in general reminiscent of the tales of e.g. the Emperor Tiberius in Capri.'[208] Murphy added that those rumours had caused Cardinal Copello 'a good deal of disquietude'.[209] Such rumours might easily have been dismissed by the Peronists as 'black propaganda'.

Responding to the growing hostility to the Catholic Church in government circles, the hierarchy issued a 'sorrowful but emphatic'[210] joint pastoral[211] which was read at all masses on 21 and 28 November 1954. The text said that the church would not limit itself merely to serving before the altar and administering the sacraments.[212] The bishops were determined to defend the right to give religious instruction in schools and not to allow it to be replaced by a government programme of civil instruction. Seeking to avoid outright confrontation, Perón spoke at a monster rally on 29 November 1954 in Luna Park at which he said that the conflict was not with the church but with certain members of the clergy 'who did not know how to do their duty, and their superiors who did not know how to punish them'. Murphy reported on examples of theatrical anticlericalism: 'Forming part of the [Peronist] procession [from the rally] was a truck on which was mounted the figure of a priest hanged in effigy. A similar figure was displayed outside the convent of Our Lady of Mount Carmel ... The crowd waved banners and placards with abusive phrases for the priests, and demanded the suppression of religious tuition in the schools, as well as the adoption of divorce.'[213] Fearing an attack on the cathedral, thousands turned out to attend mass on the weekend of Saturday, 4 December and gathered outside to cheer the cardinal, whose residence and offices were beside the cathedral.

The government faced a further act of defiance on 8 December, the feast of the Immaculate Conception, usually celebrated in Argentina 'with great fervour [and] with outdoor candlelight processions', Murphy wrote. When the federal police refused a permit to allow a public procession and the celebration of mass in the Plaza de Mayo, the cardinal cancelled the event and switched the location of the mass to inside the cathedral.[214] About 200,000 people gathered, many having to remain outside. After the mass, the congregation and those gathered in the plaza 'proceeded slowly through the principal streets of Buenos Aires behind Catholic Action banners while the police stood by and made no effort to interfere'.[215]

These events received wide international coverage[216] and the Irish nationals devoted a great deal of space to report in detail on the church–state clash in Argentina. The *Irish Independent* wrote in an editorial on 11 December that freedom of the press had ceased to exist in Argentina three years before: 'Now it seems that freedom of religion is in danger', and that the clash reminded many people of the struggle between church and state in pre-war Germany: 'It is disquieting to find that such an extreme form of totalitarianism can exist in an American republic' where the vast majority of Argentina's eighteen million people were Catholic.[217] While the Irish public were able to read reports about the godless events in Argentina, Murphy reported on 21 December that Perón's volte face on church–state relations was due to his mistaken belief that he had 'the church in his pocket' after the introduction of compulsory teaching of religion in state schools. The 'projected' Christian Democratic Party, according to Murphy, caused Perón the most uneasiness, coupled with the fact that it 'became increasingly difficult to get the clergy in the provinces to go along with the Peronista party and the CGT'. The president had been annoyed even more by the clergy's role in advising parents not to allow their children to enrol in the Peronist Union of Secondary School Students, proposing instead that they join a rival Catholic organisation. All that Perón had succeeded in doing by his words and actions, Murphy argued, was 'to fill the Churches for all Masses and evening devotions. Formerly the Church congregations were about 70% women, now the men are attending in numbers unknown for many a year'.[218] Murphy concluded that the president was 'either mentally unsound or is afraid of his regime tottering and chose a round with the Church again to create a diversion'.[219]

Murphy may have been on summer holidays when he reported on 30 December 1954 from Montevideo of the growing authoritarianism of the Argentine government, giving the example of a police officer who mounted the stage in a Buenos Aires theatre and arrested an actor performing a satirical sketch about Perón. He (the actor) 'has not been seen or heard of since', he noted.[220] The clash between church and state reached a new level of seriousness when Perón halted the compulsory teaching of religion in state schools and abolished the inspectorate of the Religious Instruction Board. The original Catholic system was replaced by instruction provided by the Eva Perón Foundation.[221] A bill making divorce automatic after a year's separation became law on 14 December,[222] as did the decriminalisation of prostitution.[223] All those developments were reported in the Irish national press with disapproving editorials.

During the second inter-party government, Irish foreign policy was as confessional as it had been between 1948 and 1951. The taoiseach John A. Costello and the minister for external affairs Liam Cosgrave had a similar crisis on their hands as had occurred in Italy in spring 1948. Senior officials in Iveagh House felt the events in Argentina were of sufficient importance to send Murphy's reports to the new ambassador to the Holy See, Cornelius (Con) Cremin. (Joseph Walshe had retired in August 1954 and died in Cairo on 6 February 1955.) Cremin, who was far less excitable than his predecessor, informed Dublin that the Holy See had sent a letter of protest to the Argentine government. In late January 1955, he reported further that the Holy See had been taken completely by surprise by the events in Argentina and that the Curia found them 'entirely inexplicable'. The same Vatican source told the ambassador that the effort to found an opposition party was the cause of the turnaround.[224] Cremin also learned that there was a view in the secretariat of state that the new nuncio, Mario Zanini, was neither experienced nor adept enough to prevent the church–state crisis from escalating and that the situation would not have become so grave had the former nuncio remained in Buenos Aires:[225] Mgr Giuseppe Fietta, who was transferred in early 1953 back to the Holy See, was apparently 'a vigorous and shrewd Nuncio in Buenos Aires and exercised considerable influence with Perón'.[226]

Murphy wrote on 3 February that Zanini was attempting to negotiate a settlement to the crisis. The archbishop of Buenos Aires, Cardinal Copello, was 'prepared to compromise "to save what is left" of the working relationship between church and state'. But the Irish envoy noted that the official church efforts at conciliation were 'greatly deplored by the rank and file of the clergy and by Catholic Action and the laity in general', adding that 'in outlying provinces, the clergy continued to comment indirectly in their sermons on divorce, religion in schools and the reopening of the brothels'. The feeling among many Catholics was that 'it would be better for the Church to make a firm stand now and not to compromise'. Murphy believed that Perón 'was getting nervous' and that he now realised 'he had gone too far'.[227] In the months before the overthrow of Perón in September 1955, Catholics staged twelve major demonstrations in Buenos Aires. Murphy observed that several processions, in defiance of a government ban, had taken place in the outlying suburbs of Buenos Aires 'and were not interfered with' and that the clergy responsible were 'getting away with it for the time being'. Murphy knew a prominent Irish-Argentine lawyer (unidentified) who had written a manifesto for Catholic Action (Acción Católica), the organisation behind the protests and responsible for publishing many pamphlets which had print runs sometimes of over 20,000.[228] Murphy's source was identified as the secretary of the Irish Catholic Association.[229] A manifesto from the same source encouraged Catholics to wear their badges in public on all occasions, bless themselves when passing a church, and to salute a priest openly in the street. The manifesto quoted the lord mayor of Cork Terence MacSwiney's famous words: it is not those who cause suffering but those who suffer most who will be victorious. Ending with 'Hail the Church, Hail our Country, Hail Liberty', the lawyer who was the author of the document urged each Catholic who had a copy to send it to ten people.[230]

In anticipation of a major outbreak of violence, Murphy set down contingency plans to protect Irish citizens resident in the country, many of them priests, nuns and brothers. The government had ruled that all teachers in primary and secondary schools run by religious, if foreign born, had to become Argentine citizens. Murphy noted that half the Irish Christian Brothers could leave the country voluntarily, but the other half, having become Argentine citizens, would be obliged to remain.[231] Reporting that there were also Irish priests in the same position, he asked his superiors: 'I presume I could grant passports to facilitate such persons to get back home if they are allowed to leave.'[232] He awaited coded instruction on those matters. In April, Murphy warned that he had been told by a prominent Irish-Argentine (possibly the lawyer José E. Richards) and two 'militant brothers in the Passionist Order' that the church–state quarrel had gone too far 'to permit of a peaceful solution'. Another unnamed priest had warned him that 'an explosion will come'. Murphy was led to conclude, therefore, that Perón would cause further tension by announcing on 1 May the formal separation of church and state. He noted with a sense of irony that despite the government's recent reduction in the number of feast days, the president would continue to grant a second free day following 1 May, called popularly 'the day of "San Perón"'.[233]

Matters were not long coming to a head. On 6 May, Cardinal Copello celebrated mass in the cathedral to mark the holding of the Eucharistic Congress in Brazil (from 17 to 24 July). He preached to a capacity congregation, with a large crowd assembled outside in the Plaza de Mayo listening through loudspeakers. The *Irish Independent* reported that government authorities tried to drown out the mass, carrying out 'urgent and noisy road repairs' near the cathedral, playing martial music and blowing car horns.[234] Murphy told Dublin that those attending the mass had blocked traffic in the Plaza de Mayo and refused to allow the buses through. Afterwards, mass-goers processed along Calle Florida and into Avenida Corrientes. There were clashes with police in Calle Agüero.[235] On Sunday, 8 May, Cardinal Copello and the hierarchy published a pastoral letter[236] calling on all Catholics to go to their local police stations and demand the release of those detained. The cardinal said he had waited for more than an hour at police headquarters without being able to see the department chief.[237] *L'Osservatore Romano* carried the main headline on 9/10 May: '*Persecuzione in Argentina*' (Persecution [of the Catholic Church] in Argentina), a headline whose sentiments were reproduced in national newspapers in Ireland.[238]

Murphy was presented with an unenviable consular challenge when an Irish-Argentine priest, Fr Michael Fox, was arrested in Alberti, a town about 300 kilometres west of Buenos Aires.[239] Detained for delivering a sermon critical of Perón and for distributing leaflets allegedly of 'a seditious nature', he was lodged in the local jail, where he was, because of his high standing in the community, treated more as a guest than a prisoner. Dozens of friends were allowed to visit him every day. Perón, according to Murphy, had Fox moved to Mercedes, where he was held incommunicado pending trial 'at the pleasure of the president'.[240] Murphy reported that the arrest 'caused consternation amongst the Irish'. Approached by two of Fox's relatives for help, the envoy explained 'that he [Fox] being an Argentine citizen I could not intervene'. In a meeting with Murphy around 12 May, the editor of *TSC*, Juan Santos Gaynor, argued that a plea to the foreign ministry on behalf of Fox might convey to the Argentine government the view that Ireland was concerned about the Catholic Church in Argentina 'and that might ease the situation',[241] a view which Murphy agreed was shared by 'many of the Irish-Argentines who believe that before long, especially if Cardinal Copello is arrested, I shall be instructed to lodge a protest'.[242] However, Murphy replied that 'without specific instructions from my Government I could not take the step he suggested'. While the Irish envoy knew that the priest might be right to assume that, if carried out, his proposal would help, he told him that he might also be very wide of the mark: 'I suppose I could make inquiries on behalf of the relatives in Ireland if requested, but whether I should go as far as Father Gaynor suggests is a matter for higher authorities.' Estimating that there were about forty nuns and priests who were

Irish citizens working in the country, Gaynor also raised a more general point about what the envoy would do if those lives were in danger. Murphy replied that 'if any of them were arrested and that I was advised as to where they were', he 'could make inquiries on their behalf and do all I could to secure that they had proper legal protection and take any other steps which might be possible to secure their release and return to Ireland if necessary'. Murphy sought confirmation from Iveagh House that he had given the correct answer.[243] While awaiting a reply, a bill providing for the separation of church and state became law on 20 May 1955. On 26 May, Murphy reported that many Peronist Party leaders had resigned in protest at the government's anti-church policies but 'there was no publicity permitted about their defection'. He remained convinced that Perón would fight 'to the bitter end but the end may turn out to be more bitter than he expects. Outwardly everything is calm but over the radio from Paraguay and Bolivia this week came reports that Argentina was on the verge of revolution'.[244] In Rome, an official at the Congregation of the Holy Office was quoted by the *Cork Examiner* as saying: 'We cannot yet say whether he [Perón] has fallen into a state of excommunication nor can we deny it.'[245]

Cognisant of just how febrile the situation was in Buenos Aires, Iveagh House in a coded message instructed Murphy to proceed with great caution, underlining that the envoy had only the status of a chargé d'affaires en titre:[246] 'As Father Fox is not holder of Irish passport we feel intervention on lines suggested to you inadvisable at present.'[247] Fox, meanwhile, stood trial in handcuffs and, when sentenced, was stripped of his clerical garb, put into prison clothes and placed in the same quarters as 'undesirable criminals of the lowest type'. He developed pneumonia and was taken to hospital, where he was well treated and was allowed visitors. Sufficiently recovered, he was released on 9 June and allowed to return home.[248]

The *Longford Leader* reported that Bishop Anunciado Serafini celebrated a high mass in Fox's parish church in gratitude for his safe return. That same weekend in the diocese of Meath (where his relatives lived) prayers were offered at all Sunday masses for 'the persecuted Catholics of the Argentine'.[249] The bishop of Galway, Michael Browne, commented that, so soon after the fall of Hitler, he found it amazing that 'Perón should try to imitate his fatal and disastrous brand of tyranny which could bring only ruin to himself and to his people. The Church would not be beaten'.[250] Irish Catholics, having spent many post-war years praying for the church behind the iron curtain, were in 1955 offering novenas for persecuted Catholics in Argentina. In parallel, Irish government policy, although the country was not a member of NATO, remained militantly anti-communist. The first inter-party government between 1948 and 1951 had attached great significance to aligning Irish foreign policy with that of the Holy See. It was a case of déjà vu for the framing of Irish foreign policy during the second inter-party government between 1954 and 1957. Argentina provided yet another example of how that government's foreign policy was at one with the Irish Catholic hierarchy and the Holy See.

That same weekend, 11/12 June, church–state tensions escalated in Argentina. It was the custom for the Corpus Christi procession to take place in Buenos Aires on the Saturday after the feast day. The government, refusing permission to allow the procession to take place on Saturday the 11th, permitted the church to hold the event on Thursday the 9th, the actual feast day itself. Rejecting that offer, the cardinal made a concession to hold the liturgy and the procession on the 11th inside the cathedral.[251] Throughout the week before that important event in the church calendar, militant Catholics did not wish the cardinal to make any concessions. About half a million leaflets were distributed in the capital and surrounding towns in the camp urging the faithful to defy the ban to gather on the 11th in and around the cathedral. Before noon that Saturday the cathedral was filled to capacity, with large crowds filling the square outside. Barricades were erected at the front of the cathedral in anticipation of a government counter-demonstration being held presaging a possible attack on the cathedral. Murphy, who was not present, confirmed that men, fearing that the cathedral might be set alight, took up defensive positions on the steps.[252] 'When the opposing group arrived there was a hand to hand fight in which I am informed several Irish Christian Brothers took part,'[253] he reported. A former Christian Brother confirmed to me that members of the order came prepared to defend the cathedral.[254]

After the mass, part of the congregation, waving white handkerchiefs, processed up the Avenida de Mayo to Congress, where somebody in the procession allegedly painted 'Christ the King' on its walls. Horacio Verbitsky states that '*Muera, Perón*' ('Die, Perón') was daubed on the walls of Congress and that Peronists were angered when Catholic protesters burned the national flag.[255] Provocation or no, government authorities then conducted raids on churches and monasteries in search of incriminating documents. Police occupied the archdiocesan palace and the headquarters of Catholic Action and searched the homes of priests and prominent Catholics. That manoeuvre resulted in many arrests; a dozen friars were held after a raid on the Church of St Francis – once a favourite church of Perón and his late wife. The vicar general and auxiliary bishop of Buenos Aires, Manuel Tato, and the pro-vicar general, Mgr Ramón Nova, were arrested, escorted to Ezeiza airport at 4.30 a.m. and put on a plane for Rome.[256]

At the Holy See, Ambassador Cremin reported on 16 June on the Vatican reaction to the two deportations. Cardinal Angelo Dell'Acqua, he noted, thought it strange that a country would deport its own nationals. Both men discussed the view that Perón had fallen 'strongly under the influence of advisers of doubtful character'. Cremin found the cardinal to be philosophical about the situation and the Irish ambassador did not think the Holy See would promulgate a formal decree of excommunication on Perón as the Code of Canon Law made excommunication automatic for certain actions. But Dell'Acqua, in his discussion with Cremin, had not ruled out the possibility. Cremin further advised Iveagh House that Dell'Acqua was aware that several Irish bishops had individually condemned the actions taken against their fellow bishops in Argentina.[257]

On 15 June 1955, Murphy was alarmed to receive a phone call from an unidentified Dublin-born Passionist priest urging him to protest immediately over the expulsion of the two bishops. The caller did not think that the envoy needed to wait for specific instructions from Ireland. Believing his phones to be tapped by government authorities, Murphy feared that the call might have put the legation and the Passionists in jeopardy. So disturbed was the Irish envoy, he requested the provincial of the order to visit him the following day at the legation.[258] While waiting for his visitor to arrive the next morning, his office and the entire building on Avenida Santa Fé were shaken by heavy explosions coming from the direction of the nearby Casa Rosada. The long-predicted coup d'état appeared to be in train. Murphy informed Iveagh House that the first bombing of the Casa Rosada took place at 12.40 (on the 16th). The rebel planes were marked with a cross inside a large V, standing for *Cristo vence* – or Christ triumphant. Because the fighting appeared to be very close to the legation, he told Dublin: 'I sent the staff home, locked the office and retired to my residence – an apartment on the seventh floor overlooking the River Plate and with a good view of the skyline of Buenos Aires.' There, he felt he was in personal danger as he lived opposite a police station which he learned later had been listed as a target by the coup leaders. He was also an eyewitness to a dog fight over the River Plate between a rebel navy bomber and a fighter plane which was flown by loyal members of the Argentine air force. Murphy reported that Perón was seen running from the Casa Rosada to take refuge in the Ministry of War and that he was supposed 'to have wept copiously fearing all was lost'.[259]

The Christian Brothers, whose monastery and school were very close to the Casa Rosada across the road from the headquarters of the federal police, made the following entry in the Newman Annals: 'There was an attempted revolution by Navy-Marines on June 16, but the Army crushed it by evening. Airplanes dropped bombs on Govt. House and Plaza Mayo and many people were killed. Bullets from a plane attacking the Police headquarters hit our roof, but not much damage was done to it.'[260] Estimates of casualties ranged from 400 to 2,000. The real number of dead may have been lower than 200.[261] The Newman Annals also recorded what happened in the aftermath of the failed coup: 'That night several churches were burned, including the Dominican and Franciscan churches, San Ignacio, etc. The Curia building was burned also. The destruction was very complete in some cases. Fearing attacks, many of the clergy and religious are wearing secular garb and sleeping away from their usual domiciles, soldiers or gendarmes were placed on guard at Churches and religious houses and a "State of siege" proclaimed for the whole country.'[262]

Murphy gathered other accounts from Irish-Argentine eyewitnesses. He reported: 'Most tragic of all was the behaviour of the young men who invaded the churches. From credible sources I have learned that they looted chalices, vestments, candlesticks and danced outside in the street dressed in the vestments. Police and firemen presumably under orders stood by and did not interfere. It does not seem possible that this could happen in a Catholic country but the campaign of hate fostered by the *Peronista* press for a long time has now shown results.'[263] Describing the gloomy atmosphere on the 17th in the capital, Murphy told Dublin:

> Buenos Aires today is like a city of the dead and the sorrow and despair of my Argentine friends is depressing. A few cling to the hope that the Army will convince Perón that he must quit in the interest of the nation. Whatever happens, Argentina has experienced a tragedy from which it will take a very long time to recover. It is hard to believe that what was such a great country could have sunk so low in such a short time. There are of course a large number of fine Argentines but they do not count anymore and have lost whatever control they once had and martial law will be a serious obstacle to their coming back ...[264]

Murphy went to visit the burnt-out shell of San Nicolás de Bari church, which was not far from the legation and was often referred to in the Peronist press as the 'church of the oligarchs'. Later that evening, Murphy heard Perón blame the communists for the spate of church-burning – a claim the Irish envoy attached no credibility to whatsoever. Perón wanted to show his opposition to the plans for the formation of a national Christian Democratic Party following the publication of its manifesto in *La Nación* and the *Buenos Aires Herald*,

Murphy reported, concluding that Perón was personally to blame for the arson and the looting and that the police could have stopped the attacks if ordered to do so. The night of infamy, as it came to be known for many Catholics, was for Murphy 'apparently part of a preconceived plan to be put into action should an effort be made to dislodge [Perón]'.[265] Visiting the foreign ministry, Murphy spoke again to Jorge A. Serrano Redonnet, who did not conceal his distress at the recent events, blaming the CGT for the destruction and arson. He said that the 'gasoline trucks used to burn the churches had been unloaded under the eyes of the police'. Murphy knew from his other sources that heavy lifting equipment had been at hand, as, in one case, an entire altar went missing from a church. He cited eyewitnesses as having seen mock confessions and blessings being conducted in the streets by members of the mob dressed in stolen vestments. Murphy interpreted those reported scenes as examples of 'what incitement of a mob over a prolonged period can achieve'.[266] The Irish envoy was quite fatalistic: 'All in all, the immediate future for Argentina seems very dark' and 'there may be another serious upheaval'.[267]

The events of the 17th, or 'the day of infamy' as it quickly became known to many Catholics, led international news reports.[268] The national press in Ireland devoted front-page headlines to the church-burning and accompanied those reports with condemnatory editorials. The *Irish Independent* wrote of a news blackout in the capital, with the radio playing solemn music only interrupted by recordings of speeches by Perón. It highlighted also the imposition of a state of siege and carried reports of church-burnings and the probable excommunication of Perón as Pope Pius XII met the two expelled Argentine prelates. It also reported that the Vatican had excommunicated anyone associated with the expulsion of the two prelates. The evening papers, the *Herald* and the *Evening Echo*, led with the conflict in Argentina. On 18 June, the *Irish Independent* continued to lead with the plight of the Catholic Church in Argentina, and reported that the bishop of Limerick had called for prayers that justice and peace might prevail in 'that unhappy land'. Its main headline stated that Argentine rebels were still active in the provinces. The *Irish Press*, on the 18th, printed news of the destruction of the archbishop's palace and of church-burnings, believed to have been seven in number. It also reported that Perón had claimed the arson was carried out by 'Reds'. It carried a front-page photograph of Peronists attempting to fly a flag from the window of the cardinal's palace. The caption began with one word: 'INSULT'. By Monday 20th, Irish papers had received much clearer reports on the recent events in Argentina. The consensus was that Perón, who insisted that he was a Catholic, had been weakened by the failed coup d'état, according to a front-page report in the *Irish Press*. It also reported that a police guard had been placed on churches and carried a photograph of a tank driving through the streets to defend the Casa Rosada.[269]

The *Irish Press* reported on 22 June that the Catholic hierarchy, having met in Maynooth the previous day, expressed their deep sympathy with the 'great Catholic nation of Argentina in the grievous trials which it has endured during the last year'. Recalling the many links that bound the two countries, 'we ask our people to offer fervent prayers that God may restore peace, liberty of conscience and the tranquillity of order to the Argentine Republic'. That message was sent to Cardinal Copello.[270] In parishes all over Ireland, prayers were offered throughout the latter part of June and July for the beleaguered church in Argentina. During the annual pilgrimage to the Marian shrine in Knock, County Mayo, mass was offered 'for the suffering Catholics in Argentina'. Fr James Deignan, St Finian's College, Mullingar, told the pilgrims that the Argentine church 'will yet sing a requiem over the evils of to-day'.[271]

Many of the Irish clergy, brothers and nuns working in Buenos Aires were shaken by the bombings and the rioting but all remained unharmed. The Pallottines in Mercedes, however, were less fortunate. Amid reports of mass arrests in the capital, police raided the Pallottine monastery on 17 June and rounded up Frs Jeremiah Joseph Keogh, Mark Mary Kenna, Patrick Whelan and Jim McGrath. Two seminarians, Peter Davern and Aidan Donlon, and an Argentinian priest, Pedro Blet, were also detained.[272] On hearing of the arrests, a parishioner, Jackie Donnelly, phoned Murphy and requested his assistance to secure their immediate release. Then, with the help of his brother Rodrigo and members of the Ballesty, Casaretto-Brennan and Zamittos families, sandbags were placed across the main door of St Patrick's church so that, were Peronists to try to throw Molotov cocktails inside in order to set it alight, parishioners could better defend it from behind the makeshift barricades.[273] The church was left unharmed. The Pallottines who were held by the authorities were refused permission to phone the Irish legation. When Kenna demanded that the captors give them the reason for their arrest, he was told they had been taken into custody for their own protection. Peter Davern, from Ballylanders, County Limerick, recalled that a police officer asked if they required anything for the night. They requested and were given a pack of cards and a bottle of gin. Blet, unnerved by the experience, asked why there were so many guns around, to which McGrath replied: 'You will know by early morning.' Davern settled down to play bridge through the night with Kenna, McGrath and the others. The local Irish made sure that the captives were sent plenty of food. Afterwards, a local Argentine priest remarked: 'You Irish priests must have ice in your veins.'

We were afraid and there were your priests taking it all in their stride and even singing patriotic songs as well.'[274] (Davern and Aidan Donlon were ordained in early September in Mercedes.)[275]

Murphy, on receiving news of the detentions, immediately contacted the foreign ministry and was promised a report on the cases as soon as possible.[276] The captive Pallottines were released on the 18th. On returning to the college, they found 'both police and military [were] all over the ground[s]'. The police warned them for their own safety not to leave the house in clerical garb.[277] On the same day, Serrano Redonnet called to Murphy to give him the news of the freeing of the Irish priests. Expressing his personal regret over the detentions, he explained that 'all felt that their President had gone insane and that the future was dark for them all'. As a member of an aristocratic family, he 'spoke of the old tradition of the army and said that very little could be expected from the Argentine Army today which was officered by immigrants' sons'.[278]

In all Argentine churches on Sunday, 19 June, masses were said for an end to violence throughout the country. Frs Kenna and McGrath travelled later that day to Buenos Aires to meet Murphy, accompanied by their provincial, Fr M. Walsh. For reasons of security, the meeting took place in a private house in Belgrano. Walsh argued that Perón 'was finished and would be out in 36 hours'. McGrath's view was that if that were to happen, 'everyone would have to face the wrath of the CGT members'. If the situation in the country turned violent, he asked what protection the legation would be able to provide to Irish citizens. Murphy replied that 'if the mob ran wild everyone including myself would have to take cover, but I assured him that I would do anything which might be possible through official channels'. Before the three set out to return to Mercedes, Murphy told them that 'all the clergy in Buenos Aires and I believe throughout the country are in civilian clothes'. On Monday, 20 June, Murphy contacted all the religious orders with Irish members in the province of Buenos Aires to check on the safety of their personnel.[279] He was not given clearance from Iveagh House until September to provide passports for three Irish Marist priests and nine Christian Brothers. (All wore lay clothing in their passport photos.)[280] On 25 June, the *Tipperary Star* reported that all Pallottine priests in Argentina were safe and their churches undamaged. The *Sunday Independent*, on the 26th, carried the same report, adding that the Pallottines had charge of seven parishes and a number of boarding day schools.

Latin America became the focus of the Catholic world when the Eucharistic Congress was being held in Rio de Janeiro, Brazil, from 17 to 24 November 1955. Some 300 bishops, twenty cardinals and thousands of priests from all over the region and beyond participated in those ceremonies.[281] The auxiliary bishop of Sydney, Patrick Lyons, and the bishop of Ballarat, James Patrick O'Carroll, both Irishmen, stopped off in Buenos Aires en route to the congress. They had time to visit the burnt-out shells of Santo Domingo and San Francisco, 'most deplorable sites', according to Murphy. They had become places of pilgrimage with a constant stream of people pouring through the different ruins, further inflaming the people against Perón and the CGT. The government took over both sites on 13 July to begin the removal of rubble and detritus.[282] The primate of all Ireland, Cardinal John D'Alton of Armagh, arrived in Rio on the 13th and remained until the 30th. His original plans were to stop off on his return as a guest of the Christian Brothers and the Pallottines in Montevideo and Buenos Aires. D'Alton had applied for a visa in Dublin before setting out on his journey. The papal nuncio in Dublin, Alberto Levame, wrote to the cardinal on 3 July discouraging him from going to Buenos Aires. He raised serious concerns about the unpredictable impact his planned visit could have on the local church: 'It is observed, in fact, that if the Argentine Authority made visitors welcome, this would offer, among other things, an easy pretext for misunderstandings about the reality of the persecution against the Church and the Hierarchy ... there would be a danger that these visits could have different meanings and purposes than the real ones, which would make the position and work of the Argentine bishops and of the pontifical representation in Buenos Aires more delicate and difficult.'[283] On 12 July, while the cardinal was en route, Murphy sent a telegram in cypher stating he had established that the Perón government opposed the Irish cardinal's visit. A contact in the foreign ministry had informed him that his government would refuse the application even if the cardinal held an Irish diplomatic passport, as his visit 'was expected to draw very large crowds because of the strength of the Irish-Argentine community and the fact that our people were very much to the fore in the fight against the anti-Catholic campaign here'.[284] On 14 July, having been made aware of Murphy's views, D'Alton wrote from Brazil to the secretary of the Department of External Affairs, Seán Nunan, to thank the department for its assistance over the visa question and concluded his note with his opinion that Argentina had not reached the end of its ordeal, a view he expressed later in a press release.[285]

On his return, D'Alton stopped for a few days in Montevideo, where he met Uruguayans with names like O'Neill, O'Brien and O'Farrell whose love of Ireland and attachment to the faith, the cardinal said, had never weakened. He was also pleased to see that a new Irish Christian Brothers school there was 'flourishing' with one hundred pupils. The provincial of the Pallottines, M.P. Walsh, wrote to D'Alton on 20 August expressing disappointment that circumstances had impeded his trip. The cardinal replied on 3 September that it was a great disappointment to me not to be able to go to Buenos Aires, but I was advised to cancel my visit in view of the present disturbed conditions. I know it would have been a great pleasure to stay with the Pallottine Fathers, and to meet a number of our Irish exiles. You are going through a very trying ordeal, but, please God, things will soon change for the better. I thoroughly enjoyed my stay in Rio and Montevideo. Give my kind regards to all your colleagues in St. Patrick's [Mercedes]. May God protect you and send you some peace and full freedom.[286]

THE FALL OF PERÓN

In the end, the Perón government fell with barely a whimper. Amid rumours on 2 August that the president might be assassinated, the government declared a state of siege. In the weeks that followed there were daily reports and rumours of an imminent coup d'état. According to the annals of the Christian Brothers, 'On 31 August [1955] President Perón offered to resign the Presidency of the Republic at a monster meeting in Plaza [de] Mayo', but that was turned down by acclamation. He then 'announced severe measures against all disturbers of public peace'[287] and called his followers to arms, declaring chillingly *cinco por uno* (five for one), which was a public pledge to kill five for every Peronist who would fall in the struggle.[288] Despite a general strike by the CGT and defiant efforts to shore up the Peronist government, the annals of the Christian Brothers record: 'The armed forces revolted on Sept. 16, the revolt beginning in Córdoba. Perón took refuge in the Paraguayan Embassy and later went to Paraguay and General Lonardi was installed as Provisional President of Argentina. Great crowds of people manifested their joy at the change of Government.'[289] While the celebrations continued in the wealthier districts of the city, Carlos Mugica, a seminarian from an upper-class professional family, witnessed the despair of *villeros* (people who live in the *villas*, or slums) at the fall of their hero. Walking through the parish to which he was assigned, he saw a graffito chalked on a wall in a side street: 'Without Perón, there is no *patria* or God. Down with the priests [*los cuervos* (ravens)].'[290] Visiting the *conventillos* (tenements), he found that his parishioners held the church responsible for Perón's overthrow. From his background of social privilege, it came as a great shock to him to learn first-hand that night how bereft the *villeros* felt about the outcome of the coup. (The parents of the footballer Diego Maradona [born 1960], who came from the northern province of Corrientes, were among those who felt bereft.) Mugica began to feel 'out of place' and realised that he was 'standing on the wrong side of the road'. He returned home, where his family were celebrating the ousting of Perón. That night was the turning point on his road to Damascus. His commitment remained to the poor and to Perón for the rest of his short life.[291] A younger Argentine generation represented by Mugica became – during 'the absent one's exile' until 1973 in Madrid – committed to the clandestine Peronists in the belief that it was the only force capable of bringing about a social revolution based on hegemonic nationalism and statism.

Murphy's thirty-year career in the diplomatic service drew to a conclusion in the latter part of 1955. The Irish envoy remained on for a few weeks under the new military dictator in order to handle the formalities of recognition of the new government and to await the arrival of his replacement. During his seven years in the country, he failed to grasp the appeal for *villeros* of millennarian Peronism and for the factory workers and the landless labourers. Murphy lived for nearly seven years within the hermetically sealed worlds of the diplomatic corps and the upper echelons of Argentine society. Without any irony, the Irish envoy and many of his diplomatic colleagues reported that the success of the recent military coup was a victory over tyranny and dictatorship. At best, Murphy and other members of the diplomatic corps suffered from 'groupthink'. They failed to test their presuppositions and never ventured to try to understand the mystery and mysticism behind the appeal of Peronist populism. In his passionate and partisan reporting, Murphy provided his superiors in Iveagh House with a view of Argentina which conformed to the unspoken assumptions of the two Costello-led inter-party governments. He reduced Argentine politics to his having to live in a dictatorial regime brought down ultimately by its radical anticlericalism and a violent clash between the state and the Catholic Church.

The taoiseach, John A. Costello, a friend from schooldays, sent Murphy a note thanking him for the 'valuable services' he had given to the state over such a long period and 'wishing [you] many years of happiness in your retirement'. A few days before stepping down, Murphy was promoted to ambassadorial rank, which improved his pension.[292]

IRELAND, THE UN AND MULTILATERAL DIPLOMACY

The inter-party government lost power on 5 March 1957 to Éamon de Valera's Fianna Fáil, which would remain in power for sixteen uninterrupted years. The outgoing Costello government had succeeded in December 1955 in bringing Ireland into the United Nations. That had widened the parameters of Irish foreign policy and set new professional challenges for the officials in Iveagh

House. In July 1956, the minister for external affairs Liam Cosgrave laid out before Dáil Éireann the principles on which future Irish multilateral policies, under the inter-party government, would be based. The first two were defined as fidelity to the UN charter and the adoption of a position of independence where all questions would be strictly judged on merit 'in a just and disinterested way'. The wording of the third principle reflected the importance of religion for the members of the Irish government: 'It must be our constant concern – indeed our moral responsibility – to do whatever we can as a member of the United Nations to preserve the Christian civilisation of which we are a part, and with that end in view to support wherever possible those powers principally responsible for the defence of the free world in their resistance to the spread of Communist power and influence.' Frank Aiken, who would become the new minister for external affairs in the Fianna Fáil government, replied to the speech, telling deputies that while he agreed with the minister's first two principles, he diverged sharply on the third: 'There are sins that are common both to the Communistic and non-Communistic states,' he said, a direct signal of his intention to take Irish foreign policy in a more independent direction should Fianna Fáil get back to power.[293] In contrast to Aiken, Taoiseach Costello told the Dáil on 11 July 1956 that the state's policy 'must be to see that the forces of atheistic communism are repelled and that we do not allow ourselves to become tools to serve communist imperialist initiatives, no matter how carefully they may be camouflaged'.[294]

The Irish government assembled an impressive team of diplomats to staff the permanent representation in New York. Frederick Boland was transferred from London to head the UN delegation. He worked closely with Dr Conor Cruise O'Brien, who had been made head of the newly established UN section in Iveagh house and attended every session of the General Assembly from 1956 to 1960–1.[295] Cosgrave's policies placed Ireland within a group of western camp allies made up of the US, Canada and Western Europe. While still minister, he had to help craft Ireland's response to the Hungarian uprising, which began on 23 October 1956 and which was crushed brutally by the Soviet Union by 11 November. Ireland was one of thirty-seven countries to accept 541 Hungarian refugees for settlement. Parallel with that central European crisis, Israel's unsuccessful invasion of Egypt, supported by France and Britain between 29 October and 7 November 1956, ended in military and foreign policy humiliation for those powers. Through UN membership, Ireland could also exercise an influence over policy towards Latin American countries.

When de Valera and Fianna Fáil returned to power in March 1957 to form a single-party government, Frank Aiken became minister for external affairs and held that post until 2 July 1969. He had also held the same portfolio between 1951 and 1954 in the previous Fianna Fáil government. A veteran of the war of independence and a close friend of de Valera, Aiken was not cowed by the power of the Irish Catholic Church. Unlike his two immediate predecessors, he brought to his ministerial post a scepticism towards Catholic bishops rooted in his experience of having been excommunicated during the Irish civil war. During his time in Iveagh House, Aiken's tenure represented a new and independent phase in Irish foreign policy.[296] Noel Dorr, who joined the diplomatic service in 1960, wrote that Aiken brought 'a new and distinctive approach to Ireland's participation in the General Assembly'. His policy in those early years after 1957, according to the same source, 'still has around it something of a golden afterglow in the memories of many people of a certain age'.[297] Conor Cruise O'Brien described Aiken's leadership as showing 'considerable courage and pertinacity'.[298] Guided by the UN charter and a commitment to the Universal Declaration of Human Rights which had been passed at a meeting in Paris of the General Assembly on 10 December 1948, he rooted his actions in the second Cosgrave principle – independence of action. Taciturn and a man of few words, whom I interviewed on two occasions in 1977, he helped shape a policy in the late 1950s and early 1960s which placed him in conflict with the United States, most notably on the 'China vote', on nuclear disarmament, on the 'roll-back' of Soviet and NATO forces in Europe and on issues raised by the contentious area of decolonisation. In 1957, the US expected Ireland to vote on a motion in the General Assembly 'not to consider' a discussion on the issue of the People's Republic of China being admitted to the UN. Aiken changed Irish policy in favour of *discussion*, in response to which the US representative Henry Cabot Lodge phoned the State Department on 23 September, saying: 'The FM (Foreign Minister) of Ireland is going nuts.' Cardinal Francis Spellman of New York phoned the consulate general in New York: 'Tell Aiken that if he votes for Red China, we'll raise the devil.' Despite mounting pressure from US Catholic prelates and intense political lobbying, Aiken held his nerve. The Irish vote in the 1960s reverted to traditional support for the US position.[299] UN membership had a very beneficial effect on broader Irish–Latin American relations.

Aiken's supportive policies to speed up the process of decolonisation made Ireland a natural ally of those republics which had won their independence (a number with the help of Irish women and men) from Spain and Portugal in the nineteenth century. Argentina took for granted the annual Irish support for a motion in the General Assembly which set ownership of the Falkland/Malvinas Islands in a colonial context. That remained the situation until 1976.

The human rights abuses of the dictatorship in Argentina, which disappeared and tortured an Irish citizen, changed that vote to an abstention.

TIMOTHY JOSEPH HORAN, NEW IRISH ENVOY IN BUENOS AIRES

Far removed from the UN, the new and now main theatre of Irish foreign policy, Timothy Joseph Horan (43) arrived in Buenos Aires in mid-November 1955 to take over as chargé d'affaires. Speaking French, Spanish, Portuguese and Italian,[300] he was hard-working and his professionalism and intellectual curiosity protected him from falling into the mentalité of those who moved only in privileged circles in the capital's Barrio Norte and the Jockey Club. During his time in Buenos Aires, the new envoy never allowed himself to become a prisoner of the groupthink towards national politics so evident in diplomatic circles before the fall of Perón. On 20 January 1956, Horan made his protocollary call on the under-secretary for foreign affairs and worship Eduardo Agustín García, who had spent two and a half years in jail under Perón. Voluble about the former president and his regime, he told Horan that Perón was 'a madman' (*loco*) and a 'born delinquent' (*delincuente nato*) who had brought one of the richest countries in the world to 'economic ruin'.[301] García claimed that the danger had not yet passed as Perón, who was then in Panama, continued to cause the new government a lot of 'headaches' as he threatened to return by the end of the year to Buenos Aires. If that proved to be a reality, the diplomat predicted that 'the streets of Argentina will run with blood' and that 'a million Argentines may die'. García said the new government was taking steps to counter Perón's influence by having him declared persona non grata by all UN member states, thus preventing him from being able to set up permanent residence in any of those states.[302]

A pro-Perón coup d'état broke out in Buenos Aires on 9 June 1956 but it was crushed the following day by its ringleader General Juan José Valle being swiftly and surprisingly sentenced to death. Pleading for clemency, his wife went to the residence in Olivos but failed to meet President Aramburu. '*Lo lamento, el presidente duerme* ['I am sorry. The president is sleeping'],' a servant told her at the door.[303] Valle was executed on 12 June. Colonel Díaz, a co-conspirator, was also executed. A round-up of 'the usual suspects' followed, during which the federal police arrested a group of twelve Peronists, accusing them of having been implicated in the attempt to overthrow the government. Taken to an isolated spot to be executed, five died in the police fusillade but seven made a miraculous escape, a number with bullet wounds, in what became known as the

José León Suárez massacre. Two were rearrested but survived the interrogation and detention, while others took refuge in the Bolivian embassy.[304] The Irish-Argentine writer Rodolfo Walsh made this infamous episode the subject of his book *Operación Masacre*, published in 1957.[305] Adapted for the screen in 1973 by the director and writer Jorge Cedrón, the film of the same name starred one of the survivors of the massacre.

Horan's mission overlapped with President Aramburu's time in office from 13 November 1955 to 1 May 1958. The general put the Peronist revolution into full reverse. On 20 September 1956, Argentina joined the International Monetary Fund (IMF) and the World Bank.[306] The 1949 Peronist constitution was replaced by the original 1853 document.[307] The Peronist Party was dissolved; even the use of Perón's name was banned, as were party insignia and slogans. Pro-government journalists described him as 'the fugitive tyrant'. Many of his loyal followers were jailed. Horan reported that the number of Peronists in jail rose to about 50,000.[308] Thousands of trade union officials lost their jobs and the CGT was subjected to tight government controls.[309] Despite such draconian measures, on 20 August 1957 Horan concluded: 'Perón may be gone, but Peronismo remains.'[310] Peronism adapted well to its new political conditions and it flourished underground, succeeding, either through tactical vote management or abstention, to have a significant influence on the outcome of presidential elections in the 1960s.[311]

Reassigned to Lisbon in 1959, Horan had during his posting placed the legation on a firm footing and establishing very good working relations with the leaders of the Irish-Argentine community.

CHAPTER THREE

Rediscovering Latin America: Irish missionary 'soft power' and Irish diplomacy in Argentina, 1962–74

The 1960s were years of significant economic, social and cultural change in Ireland – a decade in which a strongly traditional and introspective society was forced to confront the challenges of modernity. Fianna Fáil remained in government from 1957 until 1973 under three different taoisigh: Éamon de Valera (1957–9), Seán Lemass (1959–66) and Jack Lynch (1966–73), who became the first to lead that party who was not a member of the revolutionary generation. Éamon de Valera was elected president of Ireland in 1959, a position he held for two terms between 1959 and 1973. Lemass, his chief lieutenant in cabinet for nearly three decades, took over as taoiseach in difficult times. High emigration and a failing economy through the 1950s forced him to think radically about the need to jettison protectionism for a liberal and more open economy, compelling him to make sweeping policy changes in the early 1960s.[1] Recovery was based on attracting inward capital investment from Germany and the United States to build new industries.[2] Throughout his time in office, Lemass depended upon the strong bond of friendship between the White House and Dublin. Therefore, he ensured that Aiken's initiatives at the UN in the 1960s would not jeopardise his working relationship with the US, which was strengthened by the election in 1960 of the Irish-American John F. Kennedy to the presidency. Complementing that policy, Lemass liberalised trade with Britain and began the task of building a new relationship with Northern Ireland. Both countries worked closely together from 1961 to gain membership of the EEC. Lemass himself had taken charge of that important side of Irish foreign policy. He was ably supported by the secretary of the Department of Finance Ken Whitaker and the secretary of external affairs, Con Cremin. Were Ireland to be accepted as a member, it would become the only state in the community not a member of NATO. When Dublin experienced serious pushback from the EEC over the country's status as a permanent neutral, the taoiseach ranked Irish membership so important that he declared what I call the 'Lemass doctrine' in the *New York Times* on 18 July 1962: 'We recognise that a military commitment will be an inevitable consequence of our joining the Common Market and ultimately we would be prepared to yield even the technical label of our neutrality. We are prepared to go into this integrated Europe without any reservations as to how far this will take us in the field of foreign policy and defence.' That unequivocal declaration was published to reassure the US and the EEC that, despite being neutral and outside of the NATO alliance, Ireland was prepared to participate fully in any future European common defence plan. The Irish and British applications were rejected in 1963. The taoiseach's main political ally in cabinet, Jack Lynch, was made the minister for industry and commerce in 1959 and later minister for finance from April 1965 to November 1966. Upon Lemass' retirement, Lynch took on the role of taoiseach on 10 November 1966 as his anointed successor. Pressing on with the campaign to join the EEC, Lynch suffered a setback the following year when the Irish application was again rejected. After the 1969 general election, Lynch dropped Aiken from his position and replaced him with Dr Patrick Hillery. Together, both Lynch and Hillery negotiated Ireland's entry, together with Denmark and Britain, in 1973.[3] No other decision since the end of the Second World War would have such a profound domestic and foreign policy impact for that small island tucked behind another island west of the European continent.

In the 1960s, there was a division of labour in foreign policy management between Aiken and Lemass. The latter directed Ireland's campaign to join the EEC until Lynch took over as taoiseach in 1966. Aiken concentrated his energies through the 1960s on the UN, remaining in New York for long periods to oversee policy, where he continued to exhibit a refreshingly iconoclastic and independent stance, particularly when the US attempted to dragoon him into taking up an orthodox Cold War line. He pressed Ireland to be ambitious in its membership of the UN. In 1960, the head of the Irish delegation, Frederick Boland, was elected president of the General Assembly. He articulated Aiken's policy as being 'a world order based on justice and the rule of law'. That was the 'surest guarantee of peace and security'. Every nation had the right to determine its own destiny, in dignity and freedom, without outside interference or dictation. Those ideals had inspired the men and women whose efforts and sacrifices made possible the measure of freedom we in Ireland now enjoy, he said.[4] Conor Cruise O'Brien, a senior Irish diplomat and coordinator of Irish UN policy, became the representative of the secretary general Dag Hammarskjöld in Katanga, an area seeking independence from the Democratic Republic of the Congo. General Seán McKeown was appointed commander of UN peace keeping forces there.[5] The 'blue helmet' role of the Irish armed forces began between 28 June 1958 and 18 December 1958 as a fifty-strong contingent of the UN observer group in Lebanon (600 officers from twenty-one countries). Between July 1960 and June 1964, an Irish contingent was deployed to the former Belgian Congo as part of the UN peace keeping force there.[6] Ireland lost nine troops in an ambush at Niemba on 8 November 1960. In all, twenty-four Irish troops were killed over the four years, in an operation which began 'over 50 years of unbroken service on UN missions for the Irish defence forces'.[7] On 19 November 1960, tens of thousands thronged the streets of Dublin to pay their respects as the Niemba funeral cortege passed by. It was a solemn moment in the country's history. Notwithstanding those tragedies, peace keeping became a permanent arm of Irish foreign policy.

In the 1960s, Ireland was engaged through the UN and the presence of a large number of Irish Catholic missionaries in different countries on the continent of Africa. Ireland opened its first diplomatic mission in Nigeria in 1960. That new post, together with Irish UN peace keeping deployments, added a new dimension to Irish foreign policy. Moreover, many Irish people were familiar with the activities of the different Irish religious orders in Africa through the reading of Catholic missionary magazines.[8] There were 6,517 Catholic missionaries worldwide in 1965 – nuns, brothers, priests and lay people – of whom 4,122 worked in Africa.[9] For much of the 1960s, the continent of Africa was prominent in the Irish media. Two events in particular dominated the coverage: the anti-apartheid campaign in South Africa and the Nigerian war in Biafra between 1967 and 1970. The Holy Ghost Fathers played a prominent role in helping to fly in food and supplies during the war, thus increasing awareness in Ireland of what was happening in Africa, which led to the setting up of the NGO Concern. In the South African Transvaal, some 250 people were shot by police during a demonstration in Sharpeville. In Ireland, the anti-apartheid movement, led by people like Rev. Terence McCaughey, continued to lead protests up until the collapse of the regime in South Africa. In 1994, an Irish embassy was opened in Pretoria.[10]

IRELAND, THE CUBAN REVOLUTION AND THE MISSILE CRISIS

Latin America did not enjoy the same high profile in Ireland as did Africa during the 1960s. The Irish embassy in Buenos Aires remained the country's sole outpost south of the US border with Mexico. There were a number of personnel changes at the end of the 1950s. Horan had been replaced by Tom Commins,[11] who served only a few months before being transferred to Rome. William Benedict Butler, who had previously been posted to Canberra and the Holy See, was sent to replace him.[12] Arriving in Buenos Aires in 1960, his time of service coincided with part of the presidency of Arturo Frondizi, which ran from 1958 to 29 March 1962. The general opening up of Irish society in that decade created a popular political interest in the unfolding events in Latin America, the Bay of Pigs invasion in Cuba in 1961, the Cuban missile crisis in 1962 and the death of Che Guevara Lynch in Bolivia in 1967. In Argentina, Frondizi tried to stimulate the economy through huge infrastructural investment and by remaining close to the United States. At the same time, he maintained diplomatic relations with Havana. Butler, during his brief mission, reported on local reaction to the aftermath of Fidel Castro's military victory in Cuba on 1 January 1959 and on that regime's wish to export its radical ideas to the Andean countries and turning that region into a new Sierra Maestra or cradle of Latin American revolution.[13] The new US president, John F. Kennedy, who assumed office on 20 January 1961, had sanctioned a clandestine attack by 1,400 rebel anti-Castroites on the island of Cuba. His decision was based on a plan drawn up by his predecessor to land those forces at the Bay of Pigs and make their way inland. This turned out to be a military and foreign policy disaster.[14] Gauging reaction in the southern hemisphere, Butler reported on 24 April: 'The failure of the anti-Castrist invasion of Cuba has created a general feeling of depression amongst ordinary members of the public here. In the few days the fighting lasted, small noisy demonstrations were held in Buenos Aires by elements of the left sympathetic to Castro.' Resolutions condemning US imperialism and blaming the US government for the invasion were passed, 'but neither of the main political parties made any pronouncement'. In the aftermath, Butler reported that President Frondizi had avoided taking sides out of respect for the principle of non-intervention in the internal affairs of a sovereign state. But he did appeal to Havana to stop the execution of prisoners taken captive after the fall of the dictator Fulgencio Batista, who had controlled Cuban politics since the 1930s and had fled the country on 1 January 1959.[15]

Shaken by the Bay of Pigs fiasco, on 10 August 1961 President Kennedy launched in Uruguay the Alliance for Progress programme – a plan to speed up the economic development of the countries of the Southern Cone. Butler detected that there was a growing awareness on the part of the United States 'of the need to treat her fellow American countries south of the border as equal partners'. New thinking in Washington seemed to accept that the political life of most Latin American countries was at the mercy of internal economic factors. There was an awareness also that when the most depressed elements of the region became aware of their own miserable state and compared it with Cuba, the situation was fast 'becoming explosive'.[16] On 16 August 1961, Butler noted that the Cuban revolution had been received with acclaim in the hemisphere, that 'the unfortunate Cuban incident' had shaken 'some of the faith' in the Kennedy administration and that 'a further feeling of disappointment grew'.[17] Butler, who had given short but distinguished service in Buenos Aires, did not live to see his predictions about radical unrest in Latin America become a reality in the restless 1960s. He died suddenly on 3 November 1961 in Buenos Aires.[18] His body was returned to Ireland and his funeral took place on 20 November in Newman University Church. He was buried in Dean's Grange Cemetery, Dublin.[19]

Ireland's presence at the UN brought Aiken into contact with Latin American diplomats who shared his anti-imperialist stance, his opposition to neocolonialism and his radical ideas on nonproliferation. As a member of the Irish revolutionary generation, he had high regard for the Irish in Argentina. Since 1959, the minister supported the proposal to upgrade the missions in Argentina and Portugal to embassy status. It was argued at that time both in Dublin and Buenos Aires that 'to continue to describe our Heads of Mission in the two capitals concerned as chargé d'affaires deprived them of the consideration automatically tended to heads of mission carrying more clearly defined and more generally known titles'. He pointed out to the cabinet that the Argentine envoy in Dublin had been called minister plenipotentiary ever since the mission had been set up in 1948 and that, on numerous occasions, his government 'had expressed the hope that Ireland would reciprocate fully by the appointment of Minister Plenipotentiary in Argentina'.[20] The wheels of bureaucracy moved slowly and that proposal took a number of years to be put into practice.

Meanwhile, Michael Leo Skentelbery was appointed chargé d'affaires to Argentina on 27 February 1962.[21] He served longer than any other Irish envoy in Argentina – eleven consecutive years – most of which he spent working without the assistance of a diplomatic colleague. Born in Cork and educated at the Christian Brothers North Monastery school, he was a classmate and lifelong friend of the future taoiseach Jack Lynch. Both were among the best pupils in a class of nearly forty students, which included Tadhg Carey, a future president of University College Cork (UCC).[22] Skentelbery won a scholarship to UCC, graduating in the late 1930s. He enjoyed a certain cachet in Iveagh House among his peers for allegedly having beaten the historian and noted literary critic Dr Conor Cruise O'Brien into second position in the entrance examination for the post of third secretary.[23]

He was not long in Buenos Aires when the bipolar world system faced a stand-off over efforts by the Soviet Union to place nuclear warheads in Cuba. Ireland was ten months into a one-year term on the Security Council (having shared with Liberia) when the crisis broke on 16 October and continued until the 28th. The taoiseach Seán Lemass was in Bonn lobbying for Irish membership of the EEC at the time. He immediately expressed support for the US. Although not in NATO, that did not mean, he said, that Ireland should be regarded as neutral. Over and over again, he emphasised that Ireland was on the side of the western democracies. Frank Aiken, speaking in the Security Council on 24 October, supported the taoiseach's view but was more nuanced and contextual in his evaluation of the situation. He said he understood Cuban vulnerability, given the Bay of Pigs invasion, and its need to secure its frontiers, but he found it difficult to understand why Havana would allow itself to become 'a spearhead in a nuclear conflict' and why the Soviet government, given the existing state of tension, would take a step 'which has the effect of upsetting the existing delicate balance of world security'. While the Irish position was clear-cut, Aiken's concern for the security of the Cuban government included his sympathy for an island nation adjacent to a superpower. President Kennedy and Premier Khrushchev narrowly averted disaster in the end and matters were settled through concessions from both sides – Moscow removed the missiles and nuclear warheads in return for the secret withdrawal of US missiles from Turkey. Lemass agreed with a US request on 1 November 1962 to allow planes landing at Shannon to be searched for arms shipments while flying between the Czech Republic and Havana.[24] President Kennedy celebrated his Irish origins and appreciation for Ireland's support during the missile crisis by spending what he described as 'the best four days of his life' on an official visit in June 1963, merely five months before his assassination in Dallas.

With very little publicity, in contrast, another descendant of Irish immigrants made two private stopover visits to Ireland in the first half of the 1960s. Che Guevara Lynch, an Irish-Argentine doctor and one of the most prominent leaders of the Cuban revolution, had not identified with his Irish heritage in his youth.[25] Neither was he ever reconciled to the idea of a non-violent path to development and political stability in Latin America. As a representative of the Havana government at the inaugural meeting of the Alliance for Progress at Punta del Este, Uruguay, in August 1961, Guevara voiced Cuba's hostility to the alliance idea and predicted that it would fail.[26] During a pause in the conference, Guevara flew by private plane to Buenos Aires to visit an elderly aunt and to have a meeting with President Frondizi, which greatly angered the military hierarchy.[27] But Guevara's real interest was in fomenting revolution in Africa and in Latin America. When en route from New York to Algeria in 1964, he made a brief visit to Dublin. He returned again on 13 March 1965, when his flight from Prague to Havana stopped overnight in Shannon, County Clare. A local journalist, Arthur Quinlan, interviewed him. Talking briefly of his Irish heritage, he said he was the first child of Ernesto Guevara Lynch, whose mother Ana Isabel Lynch was the daughter of immigrants from County Galway who had arrived in Argentina around the time of the Famine. After the interview, Guevara went to Hanratty's Hotel in Limerick, got quite drunk and returned to the airport 'festooned in shamrock' as it was coming up to St Patrick's Day.[28] That was his last visit to Ireland. He abandoned his position in the Cuban government, choosing instead to lead a guerrilla band in Bolivia. His objective was to overthrow the local regime and foment revolution in other cone countries. Guevara saw that as the only model of action which would defeat the rise of military dictatorships supported, as he saw it, by the counter-insurgency policies of the United States. In Central America and the Caribbean, there were coups d'état in El Salvador (1960 and 1961), Guatemala (1954 and 1963), Honduras (1963), the Dominican Republic (1963) and Panama (1968). There were also military takeovers in the cone countries – in Argentina in 1962 and from 1966 until 1973; in Ecuador in 1961 and 1963; in Peru in 1962 and 1968; in Bolivia in 1964; and in Brazil in 1964 and 1969. Guevara did not live to witness many of those changes. On 9 October 1967, he was captured by members of the CIA and Bolivian government forces and executed without due process. He was thirty-nine. To mark the fiftieth anniversary of his death in 2017, An Post, the Irish national postal service, issued a one-euro stamp using the image by the Irish artist Jim FitzPatrick showing a long-haired, bearded revolutionary silhouetted against a red background.[29] The stamp received mixed reviews among Irish-Argentines.[30] Purely of symbolic importance, it did not reflect any radical shift in Irish government policy towards Latin America.

IRISH MISSION UPGRADE TO EMBASSY AND THE FOUNDATION
OF THE FEDERATION OF IRISH SOCIETIES OF THE REPUBLIC OF
ARGENTINA (FSIRA)

Two years after his arrival, Skentelbery was given an upgrade in his diplomatic status. The Argentine government had repeated on 1 February 1964 its request for 'the reciprocal election to Embassy status of the Argentine Legation in Dublin, and the Irish legation in Buenos Aires'. In response, Aiken sent a memorandum to government in support, pointing out that such a decision would not involve any 'increase of any kind in emoluments, allowances or otherwise, and would not affect the relative seniority of officers at home or abroad of the same grade'. Heaven forbid! The government approved the change on the 4th, the agréments were received on 13 March in both capitals and finally the respective missions were raised to embassy status.[31]

Traditionally, the Irish embassy had great difficulty liaising with a far-flung Irish-Argentine community. Broken into different societies, many of which were centred in Buenos Aires but also scattered in the camp, it was an impossible task for a single Irish diplomat to liaise with all elements satisfactorily. The founding of an umbrella organisation would allow the communities and associations to speak as one voice. Much credit rests with one of Skentelbery's predecessors, Horan, for planting the seed of an idea which inspired others to act.[32] In his farewell speech five years earlier, Horan repeated the criticism made by the president of the Irish Catholic Association (ICA), José E. Richards, that many Irish-Argentine organisations existed in hermetically sealed compartments. Horan suggested that all the existing organisations might cooperate more closely, the better to benefit their common interests.[33] Under Horan's promptings and those of his successor, William Benedict Butler, the Irish Catholic Association convened a meeting on 1 September 1961 in the Colegio de la Santa Unión at Calle Esmeralda 739 which brought together representatives of most of the Irish societies and institutions throughout the country.[34] Besides the ICA and its branch in Rosario, there were delegates from the Hurling Club, the Irish Argentine Hospital Benevolent Fund, the Ladies of St Joseph's Society, the Holy Cross Altar Society and St Patrick's Society of the River Plate. There were also representatives from the past pupils of the Fahy, Santa Brígida, Mater Misericordiae, Keating, Clonmacnoise school, the Passionists, Pallottines and Sisters of Mercy. Finally, delegates were sent by the Cross and Shamrock Association and the Irish societies of Pergamino, Santa Lucía, Salta, Córdoba, San Antonio de Areco and San Andrés de Giles. The *sociedades* Raza Irlandesa de Arrecifes and Junín joined later, as did groups from Monte and Venado Tuerto.[35]

Richards, in his opening address as acting chairman, stressed that the proposed new association would strengthen the collective voice of Irish Argentina. The majority of their forefathers may have arrived with nothing, he said, but they brought something more precious than material goods – their great faith in God. While their new country gave them the opportunity to better themselves materially, he said that Argentina was in need of the fine character and qualities of those Irish immigrants who had come to those shores from a more ancient land.[36] The Federación de Sociedades Irlandesas de la República de Argentina (Federation of Irish Societies of the Republic of Argentina or FSIRA) was formed. The executive committee (*el consejo directorio*) had about fifteen members and met monthly.[37] The general assembly (*asamblea general ordinaria*) met usually towards the end of each year.[38] Richards, among others, led the federation through its formative years and the membership continued to grow up to the early 1970s.

REDEFINING IRISH ARGENTINA AT A TIME OF SLOW IMMIGRATION

As emigration from Ireland had virtually stopped by the 1960s, the founding of the federation came at a timely juncture in the evolution of the Irish communities in that country, helping to bring greater focus and cohesion to the collective activities of the diffuse communities. It fostered unity of purpose and action and was also the umbrella body through which the different societies could speak with a single voice, as was the case during the Falklands/ Malvinas war in 1982 (see Chapter 7). Prof. Juan José Delaney argues that in the 1960s and early 1970s the power of assimilation was sufficiently strong that the trend towards integration into the wider Argentine society could not be reversed.[39] According to Prof. Delaney, the pull for greater assimilation was found at that time primarily among artists and writers. The poet, novelist, musician and playwright María Elena Walsh (1930–2011) was a good example of an assimilated Irish-Argentine. The daughter of a railway employee of Irish descent and an Argentine mother of Spanish origin, she became a public celebrity through her artistic work, stories for children, poetry, songs, musical performances, plays and novels. In particular, she composed a number of songs which were anti-military dictatorship, such as '*Como la Cigarra*' ('Like the Cicada'), '*Oración a la Justicia*' ('Prayer to Justice') and '*El País del Nomeacuerdo*' ('In the Country of No Memory'), which was used as the theme song for the film *Official Story* (1985).[40] Her fellow writer Rodolfo Walsh (no relation) had been a pupil in the Fahy Institute but failed to identify with the Irish part of his heritage. Yet a book of his short stories, *Los Irlandeses*, is based on his experiences at that school.[41] María Elena Walsh, in contrast, did not share that conflict over her identity; her Irishness blended into her work as a *juglaresa* (juggler) of words and melodies that entertained and educated generations of children in Latin America.

There is now a strong argument to replace the 'classic assimilationist model' with a more pluralist model. That would better include those of Irish stock who no longer defined themselves in religious or ethnic terms.[42] Prescinding from that debate over methodology, the federation succeeded where another attempt had failed in 1921. The federation endured, and endures still in 2022, having become the Irish embassy's point of contact with the wider community and having acted as spokesperson for the constituent societies during times of crisis, the Falklands/Malvinas war in 1982 being a good example.[43]

IRISH-ARGENTINE DELEGATION VISITS IRELAND FOR FIFTIETH ANNIVERSARY OF 1916 RISING

In 1966 Argentina celebrated the 150th anniversary of the declaration of its independence and Ireland commemorated the fiftieth anniversary of the 1916 Rising, in which the serving president of Ireland Éamon de Valera had taken a leading part. That year provided many occasions when Irish-Argentines could give voice to their complementary dual allegiances. President Arturo Umberto Illia invited Ambassador Skentelbery and José Richards to call on him at the Casa Rosada to mark the two commemorations. Both were very impressed by Illia's knowledge of Irish history. Richards told him that he was on his way to Dublin to present a bust of José San Martín to the Irish government and to participate in the Easter Rising commemoration ceremonies.[44] To commemorate the 1916 Rising, Cardinal Copella celebrated mass in the cathedral assisted by Irish priests from the Passionist and Pallottine monasteries and by Irish chaplains working in the camp. According to *TSC*, the cathedral was 'barely sufficient to hold the large congregation of Irish and Irish-Argentines and friends'. In his sermon, the Irish-Argentine Pallottine Fr Kevin O'Neill said that Ireland too had its Good Friday and it was no accident that the resurrection of the Irish people coincided with that of Our Lord (on Easter Monday 1916). Through the centuries, he said, Irish nationalists had fallen back on holy mother church to keep the faith and love of fatherland alive, referring to the holy and edifying way in which the condemned 1916 leaders prepared for their deaths. He paid tribute to those martyrs whom Pope Benedict XV referred to as 'ever faithful'.[45] José Richards and his wife were seen off at the airport by their twelve children[46] and his brother, the Passionist priest Federico.[47] The Richards, together with the federation treasurer William Howlin and his wife,[48] arrived in Shannon on 8 April. Fr M.S. Fox, an uncle of Howlin, was also part of the official delegation. 'One of the ceremonies which we will never forget,' wrote José Richards, 'was the initial parade on Easter Sunday [10 April], when we marched down O'Connell St. bearing the

Argentine flag, the symbol of freedom which in the uncertain times [of] our war of independence had been defended courageously by so many Irishmen.'[49] On 11 April, the delegation attended the opening ceremony of the Garden of Remembrance. They laid a wreath on 14 April at Arbour Hill in honour of the 'leaders of the 1916 Rising and all those who died for the freedom of Ireland'. In Iveagh House, Richards presented the taoiseach Seán Lemass with the bust of General José de San Martín bearing the inscription: 'The Argentinians of Irish descent present to the Irish nation this bust of General José de San Martín, the liberator of the land which afforded such generous hospitality to their forefathers on the occasion of the 150th anniversary of the Declaration of Independence and the 50th anniversary of the Easter Rising.' The minister for external affairs, Frank Aiken, and the minister for defence, Michael Hilliard, were in attendance, together with 150 guests, many with Argentine connections, including members of the Dominican, Passionist, Pallottine and Mercy orders. Richards[50] said that it was most appropriate to present the bust in 1966 as it was a year of dual commemorations and because many Irishmen in Latin America had fought for independence from Spain – Bernardo O'Higgins, William Brown, Juan MacKenna, John Devereux, Daniel Florence O'Leary, Francis Burdett O'Connor and John Thomond O'Brien.[51] He said the Argentine republic 'extended such generous and unbroken hospitality to the dead generations of Irish men and women who made their homes there'. Irish exiles reciprocated the spirit in which they were received and exercised in the country of their adoption an influence out of proportion to their numbers, spilling their blood on the waters of the River Plate or on other battlefields in the cause of Argentine liberty. Richards added that, in answer to an ancestral call, Irish settlers gravitated 'towards the then wild and Indian-infested "pampas", where they built "estancias", founded townships and were the first to introduce cattle-breeding'. Richards said neither time nor distance could dim a love of their motherland in the hearts of the Irish settlers. They had never failed to respond to Irish causes from the time of Catholic Emancipation in 1829 down to the aid they gave to the republican cause in the years following 1916. 'To paraphrase the words of John Boyle O'Reilly, both our countries have wronged no race, have robbed no land and have never oppressed the weak. No country is, therefore, worthier than the Irish nation to receive this bust of General San Martín,' Richards concluded.[52]

On 18 April, the delegation, now joined by Raúl Kelly from Buenos Aires, met President de Valera for nearly an hour at Áras an Uachtaráin.[53] De Valera spoke warmly to them about Argentina and 'expressed his pleasure at the fact that Irish-Argentines were not regarded by their countrymen as "hyphenated

Argentines".[54] He acknowledged that Irish-Argentines had earned their place of honour in both the celebrations of the fiftieth anniversary of the 1916 Rising and the 150th anniversary of Argentine independence. If anyone knew details of the close links between Argentina and Ireland, it was de Valera. He had sent Eamonn Bulfin to Buenos Aires in 1919 as an envoy and Laurence Ginnell in 1921. As president of the Executive Council in 1932, he had welcomed Mgr Santiago Ussher and his party, who had come to attend the Eucharistic Congress. In 1935, de Valera, on the promptings of Ussher, had taken a decision to open an Irish legation in Buenos Aires – a promise delivered on in 1947. The visit in 1966 was the first such occasion when Mgr Ussher had not been present. He had died on 23 March 1962. No single Argentine citizen had done more through his writings and his participation on various committees over fifty years to build bonds of friendship between the two countries.

Richards' visit had a practical outcome of benefit to the Irish embassy in Buenos Aires. His discreet lobbying for the appointment of a second diplomat to be sent to Argentina met with success. Daniel Hanafin was sent as a third secretary in May 1968, serving until September 1970, when he left the diplomatic service for the private sector. Even then, two diplomats were hardly adequate to cover the countries to which the Irish embassy in Buenos Aires was accredited. Between the 1960s and the 1980s, successive Irish governments failed to see the cultural and economic advantages of being more directly represented throughout Latin America. That ignored the economic advantages to be derived from an expanded diplomatic presence in the region. Moreover, Ireland's growing interest in the 1960s in Latin America was reflected in the Catholic Church and other Christian churches, in the political parties, among university students and the trade union movement.

IRISH 'SOFT POWER': CATHOLIC PRIESTS, NUNS, BROTHERS AND LAY MISSIONARIES IN ARGENTINA IN THE 1960S AND 1970S

In 1960, the Vatican set up a programme, Papal Volunteers in Latin America, in which over a thousand US citizens participated in the following decade. Pope John XXIII called in August 1961 for the Catholic Church in the US to send 10 per cent of its personnel to South America. A few thousand responded to that call, coinciding with President Kennedy's establishment of the Peace Corps to supply skilled young people to take up jobs in Latin America. Fear of Marxism was partly the motivation behind both the Peace Corps and Kennedy's Alliance for Progress. US Catholic missionaries numbered 981 in 1960 in South America. In 1968, there were 2,445, representing over 50 per cent of the total US missionaries overseas.[55] Though the Irish Catholic missionary engagement in Latin America in the 1960s and 1970s was influenced by papal appeals for volunteers, there was another force at work. Pope John XXIII summoned the Second Vatican Council on 11 October 1962. During the course of the early sessions, the pope was strongly influenced by members of the Latin American delegation. The archbishop of Recife, Brazil, Dom Hélder Câmara, had spoken eloquently and persuasively of a 'church of the poor',[56] a theme found later in the writings of his compatriot, the theologian Leonardo Boff, and the Peruvian Gustavo Gutiérrez. From 23 September 1963, Pope Paul VI carried forward the work of the council until its closure on 1 December 1965. The council documents on mission, *Gaudium et Spes* and *Ad Gentes*, came as a disappointment for many in Latin America who, like Câmara, sought radical social engagement. Brazil had become a military dictatorship in 1964 and the place of the Catholic Church was, for prelates like Câmara, to stand in opposition to repression. Released on 26 March 1967, Pope Paul VI's encyclical *On the Development of Peoples* encouraged those churchmen and women in Latin America who favoured the development of a pastoral theme of solidarity with the oppressed. The Latin American Bishops Conference (CELAM), meeting in 1967 in Medellin, Colombia, accepted documents, rooted in the schema of an indigenous theology of liberation, which laid a strong emphasis on social justice and on a preferential option for the poor.[57]

In a decade when seminaries and convent novitiates were filled to capacity, at their peak in 1965, papal social teaching placed a new emphasis in Ireland on extending missionary activity in Latin America. Paul VI said on 21 October 1970, unambiguously, that 'torture, that is to say cruel and inhuman methods by which the police extract confessions from the lips of prisoners, is to be explicitly condemned'.[58] That shift in papal social teaching also found support within Irish universities in the 1960s. In UCD, Pax Romana changed its name to Logos in 1967 and actively promoted debate on reform of the Catholic Church and its role in what was then called the Third World. John Feeney, a lay student leader, edited the short-lived magazine *Grille*. In Britain, *Slant*, which ceased publication after thirty issues in 1970, was also influential.[59] However, that lively debate among Catholic students was of secondary importance to the parallel stream of social engagement generated in UCD by Students for Democratic Action (SDA). Student radicalism in UCD peaked in a ferment that led to what was called the gentle revolution – a student revolt made up of different strands calling for better facilities in the university and wider social reform.[60] In the 1970s and 1980s, Irish national newspapers began to take a more active interest in covering events in Latin America, most notably the

Irish Press and *The Irish Times*. The weekly magazine *Hibernia* also followed the fate of those living under the proliferation of military dictatorships in Latin America.[61] Catholic magazines like *Doctrine & Life*, *Studies: An Irish Quarterly Review* and the Maynooth-edited *The Furrow* carried articles and book reviews on Latin American themes. *Radharc*, a Catholic TV documentary maker founded in 1962, reinforced a growing popular awareness of social injustice in Latin America in the 1970s. Fr Joe Dunn,[62] who founded the company, broadcast his films on RTÉ between 1962 and 1996 – fifty of those were on Central America, Latin America, Mexico and the Caribbean.[63] The titles he produced on Argentina were filmed on one visit in 1979: *The Gaucho Irish*; *Mercy on the Move* (on the Mercy Sisters in Argentina); *Round-up at Suncho Corral*; *The Church and Human Rights*; *Not by Men Alone* (on Dominicans in Argentina); and *Who is for Liberation?*[64] The NGO Concern was set up in 1968 with a focus mainly on Africa in its early years. Trócaire, a development organisation founded in 1973 by the Irish Catholic hierarchy, helped focus attention on human rights issues in Latin America. Brian McKeown, the first director, led a programme which developed public awareness in schools on themes of development and structural injustice. When human rights specialist Sally O'Neill joined that organisation in 1978 as head of programmes, her expertise on Latin America brought Trócaire into even closer contact with the roots of social injustice in Central and Latin America. Her work highlighted the challenges and the dangers facing church workers defending basic civil and human rights through its projects and fieldwork.[65] Michael D. Higgins, a student at NUI Galway in the 1960s, completed a master's degree in sociology at Indiana University in Bloomington and returned to Ireland to lecture in Galway. His lifelong interest in Latin America developed in the 1960s and grew when he was a Labour Party senator in 1973 and later a TD. He worked closely with Sally O'Neill on various Latin American projects. As president of Ireland, Higgins has retained his strong interest in the region, as reflected in his three state visits there. He played a prominent role in the formation of solidarity groups relating to Cuba, Chile, Nicaragua, El Salvador, Guatemala and Argentina.

The expansion of the Irish Catholic mission in Latin America dates from the early 1960s. In 1960, Pope John XXIII wrote to the Irish bishops requesting that they allow diocesan priests to assist the Columban Fathers in Latin America. The diocesan and missionary orders, after receiving many new vocations, were in a position to deploy personnel in significant numbers in that region. The Irish Missionary Union, founded in 1970, sought to promote and to provide leadership support for Irish missionary activity in the different parts of the world.[66] Compiled by Peadar Kirby, the following snapshot is a chronology of the deployment of Irish personnel in Latin America: the Cork (diocesan) mission to Peru was founded in 1966 and continued until it closed in 2000; the Redemptorists and Kiltegan Fathers went to Brazil in 1960 and 1963 respectively; Dominican priests and nuns went to Argentina in the mid-1960s; the Holy Ghost Fathers went to Brazil in 1967; and the Franciscans went to Chile and El Salvador in 1968. In 1990, 63 per cent of the 4,498 Irish Catholic male and female missionaries worked in Africa and 22 per cent in Asia and Oceania. Some 14.5 per cent worked in twenty-four Caribbean and Latin America countries, having risen from 585 in 1965 to 655 in 1990. In 1990, Argentina had 54 Irish missionaries working there, compared to 195 in Brazil, 108 in Peru, 62 in Trinidad, 61 in Chile, 38 in Ecuador, 22 in Venezuela, 15 in Mexico, 15 in Grenada, 13 in El Salvador, 12 in Paraguay and smaller numbers in other countries.[67]

More than thirty lay members of the Legion of Mary worked in Latin America between the 1950s and the 1990s, usually serving for three years. Alfie Lambe, who died in 1959, was among the most prominent. Jerry O'Sullivan, who worked in Venezuela between 1963 and 1970, remained on in that country and spent the remainder of his working life as secretary to the local national conference of bishops.[68] The Irish Christian Brothers, who ran Newman College in Argentina, had a community of roughly ten Irish in the 1960s and 1970s. (The order also ran a school in Montevideo.)

The Sisters of Mercy, who had arrived in Argentina in the mid-1850s, were the longest-serving Irish teaching order in the country. That order had, mirroring the Pallottines and the Passionists, a number of Argentine-born sisters who taught in their schools. They had a school for boys, Clonmacnoise, in San Antonio de Areco. The sisters continued to teach at Santa Brígida until the late 1970s, handing over the running of the school on 31 December 1979 to the French order, Congregación de Santa Marta de Perigueux. Free from having to run such a large school, members of the Sisters of Mercy worked in the *villas* around Buenos Aires. The Irish Passionist Sisters taught in the Michael Ham Memorial School from 1926 and continued to work there until the early 1990s. Sr Patricia, who was head of the school, was the last Irish member of the order to teach there. She left Argentina in 1994.

The Passionist and Pallottine missions continued in the 1960s and 1970s to send out priests from Ireland to Argentina to supplement the local Irish-Argentines and Argentines in their ranks. When the history of both orders is written, it will reveal the dynamism of the debate which took place within each congregation over the best way to bear witness and provide pastoral leadership, particularly during a time of dictatorship. However, the Catholic mission in Argentina was also attracting commitments from other religious orders in Ireland. The Columban Fathers, originally called the Maynooth Mission to China, was founded in 1916 by Frs Edward J. Galvin and John Blowick. The order had first gone to Argentina in 1920 when Fr John Conway was sent to raise funds for the society. He found the local Irish community divided and factionalised and that the locals considered ministry to Irish communities abroad more important than work in China. His fundraising efforts did not meet with great success, in part because Conway was never provided with a formal letter of introduction from the Holy See, which would have given him standing in the eyes of the local hierarchy. In reality, his mission failed because he was trying to raise funds at a time when he was in competition with popular efforts to send money to Ireland for the victims of British violence. Disillusioned after two years, he appointed the Sisters of Mercy as agents for the order's *The Far East* magazine and left the country. The Columbans did not return to Buenos Aires until 1951,[69] when the Passionist Fathers asked them to take up the chaplaincy of the Apostleship of the Sea in Buenos Aires. In 1952, Fr John McFadden arrived to minister to Catholic sailors in the port of Buenos Aires. He would meet them on their ships in the mornings and say mass and organise socials and dances in the apostolate building in the evenings. Throughout the 1950s, McFadden was assisted by other priests on a short-term basis. The Columbans unanimously decided in December 1962 to withdraw from the apostleship, terminating their involvement the following year.[70] Their main fields of pastoral work in Latin America in the 1960s and 1970s were in Peru and Chile.

Irish Dominican priests arrived to set up a mission in northern Argentina in 1965 in Parroquia San Roque, Departamento La Paz, and in Recreo in Catamarca. A group of four priests, led by the prior in Galway, Damian Byrne, began the work. He was joined by Fr Flannan Hynes, then the bursar in Tallaght. Both had studied Spanish at the Centro de Información y Documentación in Cuernavaca run by the radical thinker Monseñor Ivan Illich and were much influenced by his writings and ideas. Frs Tim Cathal Manley and John Kieran O'Shea joined them later, as did Patrick Walshe. Damian Byrne was appointed parish priest of San Roque parish, living in the parochial house with Frs Hynes and Manley. The latter was appointed second rector of the recently opened secondary school Colegio Inmaculada Conception. Fr John O'Shea went to teach catechetics at an institute in the city of Catamarca and lived with the Dominican bishop Dr Pedro Torres Farias.[71] The Irish Dominicans also took over the parishes of San Augustín, Paraná, Bovril, El Cerrito and Hasenkamp in rural Entre Ríos. Damian Byrne served as master of the Dominican Order between 1983 and 1992.

In the 1960s, Irish Dominican Sisters were also encouraged to respond to appeals to engage in educational and pastoral work in Argentina.[72] The Keating Institute was to be the focus of their first effort. Supported by the Ladies of St Joseph, the Daughters of Charity had run the Keating Institute from its beginning in 1919. Having evolved from an institution for orphan girls of Irish origin, by the 1960s it was also a secondary school for girls which recruited pupils from all sectors of the community. When the order withdrew from teaching there in 1966, Mrs Marcia Duggan, a philanthropist and member of the Ladies of St Joseph, pressed for a replacement order from Ireland. The Irish Dominican priests working in Argentina were enthusiastic about such a commitment. In response to encouragement from their provincial, Fr Louis Coffey, three sisters from Galway arrived on 1 March 1967 in Buenos Aires to take soundings from local ecclesiastics and educators. They were helped greatly by the Marist, Fr Septimio Walsh. Having visited the Dominican fathers in the north of Argentina, they returned to Galway and reported on their findings. The community there voted by a majority of one to undertake the mission, with the result that Sisters Catherine de Ricci O'Connor, Evangelist Dundon and Margaret Kirby were chosen to go to Buenos Aires. They arrived on 12 February 1968 and settled into their new home at the school, receiving support from the Sisters of Mercy, the Christian Brothers and other Irish institutions in the federal capital. The school was renamed Colegio Santo Domingo. With a number of boarders and 120 day-students, between ages four and sixteen, the running of the school proved challenging but the venture was a success.

All the Dominican Sisters in Ireland voted on 29 June 1970 to amalgamate and from then on became subject to the prioress general in Cabra, Dublin. Sr Brigid Fahy was sent out to join the teaching staff, followed by Sr Veronica Rafferty. During the turbulent 1970s, other Irish sisters joined the staff.[73] Brother Septimio Walsh gave the sisters critical advice – that in the event their lives might be in danger or the lives of others, they were first to phone the Irish embassy and then the *Buenos Aires Herald*, where its widely respected and fearless editor, Robert Cox, would publish details of the crisis.[74]

The Society of African Missions (SMA) sent four Irish priests in 1965 to work in Cosquín, Córdoba.[75] Fr Tony Gill transferred to the diocese of La Rioja in 1970 and worked there for nearly six years with Bishop Enrique Angelelli. He was imprisoned and expelled from the country in December 1975.[76] An Irish Jesuit and a number of Salesians and Marists were assigned duties in Argentina at one time or another. Seamus Kelly SJ, who died in December 2019, did pastoral work in Paraguay and northern Argentina between 1979 and 1980. He taught scripture in the Colegio Máximo de San José, in Buenos Aires, living in the same community as the provincial of the Jesuits, Fr Jorge Bergoglio, later Pope Francis I.[77]

FR PATRICK RICE AND THE LITTLE BROTHERS OF CHARLES DE FOUCAULD

The Divine Word Missionaries (SVD) had a strong presence in Argentina. They had a seminary on the outskirts of Buenos Aires and ran a school, Colegio Guadalupe, in Palermo, Buenos Aires. In addition, they ran three other educational centres in Pilar, Rafael Calzada and Posadas. The Irish province sent a small number of priests to Latin America, one working in Paraguay. In the mid-1960s, it sent five seminarians to study theology in Buenos Aires. After their ordination, Tony Coote worked in Mexico and Neil Doogan worked in Ecuador and later Nicaragua.[78] Patrick Rice, another member of that order, was assigned to work in Argentina after being ordained in Maynooth in 1970. Born in 1945 in Strawhall, Fermoy, County Cork, he came from a family of seven, one girl and six boys. On his mother's side, he was related to Thomas Kent, who was court-martialled and executed in Cork on 9 May 1916 after a gunfight at their farmhouse in Castlelyons with members of the Royal Irish Constabulary. Rice attended the local Christian Brothers school, joined the SVD after his Leaving Certificate in 1963, and studied theology at Maynooth. He read widely on politics and the Catholic Church in Latin America and was drawn to the writings of Ivan Illich, being particularly struck by his article 'The Seamy Side of Charity', which was published in the Jesuit magazine *America* in 1967.[79] He followed with great interest Illich's work in Cuernavaca, Mexico. Rice's last years in Maynooth coincided with the rise of the civil rights movement in Northern Ireland and, while he was radicalised by those events, he never espoused or supported the use of violence or the so-called 'armed struggle', either in Ireland or in Latin America.

Between 1970 and 1972, he was an assistant professor in the Philosophy department and chaplain at the Agronomy and Veterinary Science Schools (FAVE) at the Catholic University of Santa Fe, in Esperanza, province of Santa Fe.[80] He was immediately struck by the radical differences between Irish and Argentine Catholicism. Both countries had a well-organised church, served by a large number of clergy, nuns and brothers. In 1970, the church in Argentina had 2,534 diocesan and 2,867 order priests. There were 1,701 brothers and 13,488 sisters.

The Conferencia Episcopal de Argentina (Argentine Episcopal Conference) had been founded in 1959. There were fourteen ecclesiastical provinces, each headed by an archbishop and subdivided into forty-eight dioceses. Rice learned that male and female religious were represented by two different organisations. They were later united to form the Conferencia Argentina de Religiosas y Religiosos (Conference of Argentine Male and Female Religious). He quickly became aware of the profound divisions within the Argentine bishops' conference. His personal theological formation oriented him towards the small block of bishops in the Argentine hierarchy who were most outspoken on the question of human rights, including Jaime de Nevares, diocese of Neuquén; Jorge Novak, diocese of Quilmes; Miguel Hesayne, diocese of Viedma; Jorge Kemerer, diocese of Posadas; and Enrique Angelelli, diocese of La Rioja. Rice was shocked by the intimate relationship between the Catholic Church and the state in Argentina. He told me of his negative reaction when he first saw the Argentine national flag and the papal flag on display in churches. (The Irish flag rarely made an appearance in an Irish Catholic church except on state occasions.) He was alarmed by what he perceived were the strong links between members of the hierarchy and the armed forces, best exemplified for him by the cohort of army chaplains, which numbered about 200 in the mid-1970s. Each held the rank of officer, wore military uniform, drew an officer's salary and enjoyed promotion prospects and pension rights. They lived in officers' quarters and ate in the officers' mess. The military chaplains said mass and administered the sacraments to their military parishioners. They were under the independent jurisdiction of the *vicario castrense de las fuerzas armadas de la República Argentina* (military bishop to the Argentine armed forces).[81] That arrangement came into existence on 28 June 1957 when the Holy See set up a non-territorial diocese presided over by a vicar.[82] Between 1959 and 1975, that position was held by the cardinal archbishop of Buenos Aires, Antonio Caggiano. He was succeeded by the archbishop of Paraná, Adolfo Servando Tortolo, who held the position between July 1975 and March 1982.[83] The Salesian and auxiliary bishop of Buenos Aires, Fr Victorio Bonamín, was appointed pro-vicar in 1975[84] and was second in command to Tortolo.[85]

Rice shared the views of Emilio Mignone, a former Peronist minister, academic and lawyer, that many priests who became military chaplains 'tended to be those who were attracted to an easy life with a good income and few obligations ... and had often had problems of a moral nature in their own dioceses'.[86] José Comblin makes the more general point that army chaplains throughout Latin America were exposed to the doctrine of the national security state, which held in the 1970s that subversives – supported by anti-Catholic, international, secular forces linked to revolutionary Marxism, communism, freemasonry and Jewish world conspiracies – were destroying Argentina from within.[87] Rice would not have dissented from Comblin's view. While the two sources quoted above are critical of the military vicariate, an academic study of the history of military chaplains during times of military dictatorship in Argentina is long overdue. However, Rice's subsequent experiences in Argentina in 1976 only reinforced his hostility to the close links in that country between the Catholic Church and the military.

Moved by the level of violence in the country in the early 1970s, Rice became involved in the Movimiento de Sacerdotes para el Tercer Mundo (MSTM) (Socially Active Movement of Priests for the Third World).[88] He gave me a copy of a pamphlet in 1973 entitled '*Tercer Mundo y Compromiso Cristiano*' ('Third World and Christian Commitment')[89] which he said had helped him reinterpret what work he wished to undertake in Argentina.[90] The Italian liberation theologian Arturo Paoli[91] was the leader of the Little Brothers of Charles de Foucauld in Latin America. He worked in nearby Fortín Olmos, having been sent there in 1960 to establish the first foundation of the order in Latin America. Paoli was to be greatly admired. Born in Lucca in 1912, he graduated from the University of Pisa. He was ordained in 1940 and during the Second World War he was active in the resistance and saved many Jews from being captured by the Germans. A friend of Giovanni Montini, later Pope Paul VI, he was invited by him to help organise Catholic Action in Rome. Instead of settling for a career in the Eternal City, he chose to join the Little Brothers of Charles de Foucauld – a religious movement founded by the French army officer-turned-hermit who was murdered in 1916 at Tamanrasset, southern Algeria.[92] In 1960, Paoli was sent to Argentina, where he worked in Fortín Olmos, in the province of Santa Fe, among poor forestry workers who were being exploited by a large corporation, La Forestal. A Belgian, Fr Esteban de Querini, who was a member of the Little Brothers, joined him, as did a Frenchman, Fr Marcelo Laffage. An Italian, Fr Mario Grippo, joined later.[93] The Little Brothers, all of whom were worker priests holding down full-time jobs, eventually built a community house at the wood weighing-in box beside the railway line used to transport the logs. They set up a chapel in the same location, which remained as the parish church until the building of a new church in 1980. In 1968, Paoli and his confrères set up a cooperative for forestry workers (Cooperativa Ayuda Fraternal de Fortín Olmos, abbreviated to ACHA). They expanded the cooperative's activities to brick-making and to running a carpentry shop and a market garden. However, their efforts to unionise the workers met with violent resistance accompanied by death threats.

Rice went for short visits to the Little Brothers in Fortín Olmos in 1971 and, after cutting his ties with the SVD, began to live there permanently in 1972–3. The Uruguayan Salesian theologian Mauricio Silva was among the first of the new recruits that he got to know. Rice said that his work with the Little Brothers formed part of the pastoral and social programme of the diocese of Reconquista.[94] He first worked on horticultural and other youth training projects. His main job was to help unionise forestry workers. He drove the ACHA pick-up truck, taking the union leaders and members to meetings in different places. That was a dangerous assignment, as the landowners and the police viewed the union as being run by subversives.[95] Rice also travelled frequently by motorcycle. On one occasion, he had a serious accident while visiting a remote forest area. The Little Brothers worked in an atmosphere of great tension and intimidation. At the end of 1971, because of the persistent death threats being received by Paoli, he was persuaded by his confrères to leave Fortín Olmos and Fr Grippo took over his responsibilities. (On 28 November 2007 the governor of the province of Santa Fe renamed Provincial Route no. 40 between Reconquista and Fortín Olmos in honour of Paoli for his pastoral and social contribution to the region.)

The bishop of La Rioja, Enrique Angelelli, invited Paoli to set up a community house in his ecclesiastical jurisdiction. One of the first to permit the MSTM to hold a conference in 1968 in his diocese,[96] the bishop received Paoli and Julio Sajuero with open arms, bringing them himself in a pick-up truck to Suriyaco, Departamento San Blas de los Sauces, a 'wild and beautiful' place about 170 kilometres from La Rioja. They set up the new community and novitiate in an abandoned mill. Fr Mauricio Silva completed his novitiate there, as did Rice and the Argentine priest Juan José 'Chiche' Kratzer. All novices held down a manual job in the area. Angelelli formed a deep friendship with Paoli and his confrères. He visited them frequently and participated in religious services and retreats. He also presided at the profession of final vows for the new members of the order.[97] Paoli, however, had made enemies in La Rioja. After his name appeared at the top of a second death list, Rice and others persuaded him to leave the country. He first went to Caracas, Venezuela, and later settled in Brazil. In 1975, the Little Brothers were forced to leave Fortín Olmos and to leave Suriyaco a short time thereafter.[98]

Rice followed Mauricio Silva to Buenos Aires, where they were joined by Silva's brother, Jesús. Fr Carlos Bustos, a Capuchin from Córdoba who wished to join the Little Brothers, was a postulant (entry position) in the order. He invited Rice in 1974 to work with him in Villa Soldati in Buenos Aires, an area with 10,000 residents situated near the city dump on the road to Ezeiza airport. All members of the Little Brothers were worker priests. While the Silva brothers worked as road sweepers, Rice got a job as a joiner or carpenter on building sites in Buenos Aires. Fr Kratzer, who worked as a labourer on the railways, joined Rice in Villa Soldati in August 1975. Bustos worked as a taxi driver. As worker priests, their relationship with the Argentine hierarchy was fraught at best, and they were regarded as 'subversives' by the police and military authorities.

IRISH FOREIGN POLICY IN A CHANGING WORLD ORDER

Ambassador Skentelbery enjoyed a close working relationship with many Irish missionaries. He was a popular ambassador in the Irish community, and he grew to like his posting greatly. While there were those who held the post of Irish ambassador who wished to be reposted as swiftly as possible, Skentelbery was quite content to make Argentina his last posting before retirement around 1972. While on home leave, he read in the national press on 12 May 1967 the government announcement that the ambassador to Spain (since 1962), Timothy Joseph Horan, was to be posted to Argentina to replace him.[99] As the government had taken the decision and it had been published in the press, almost everyone would regard that as a fait accompli. However, Skentelbery requested and was granted a private meeting with his friend and former classmate from the North Monastery, the taoiseach Jack Lynch.[100] The government decision was reversed. That was unlikely to have been a case of *post hoc, ergo propter hoc* (i.e. the fallacy of arguing that one event happened after another; it happened because of it). Defying all odds, Skentelbery remained in Buenos Aires until 1972, retiring from the diplomatic corps in November the following year.[101]

The Irish ambassador could have found a more tranquil posting to pass away his final years in the diplomatic service. From the middle of the 1960s, he reported on a country under a succession of military dictatorships. The commander-in-chief of the army, General Juan Carlos Onganía, overthrew the civilian president Arturo Umberto Illia in a coup on 29 June 1966, remaining in office until 8 June 1970. In a country with a strong democratic tradition, the suspension of civil liberties and the use of state violence were accompanied by a continuation of the ban on the Peronist Party to operate as a legal entity. Onganía's time in office was stained by severe repression. Police violently broke up a sit-in by students and staff in the University of Buenos Aires on 29 July

1966 in what became known as *la noche de los bastones largos* (the night of the long batons). There was widespread unrest in many cities, the best known being the civil uprising in Córdoba (*el Cordobazo*) at the end of May 1969.

While many citizens wished for a rapid return to constitutional rule, a minority of the younger generation chose the path of urban and rural guerrilla warfare, involving the use of what they termed 'revolutionary violence'. The Montoneros, or Movimiento Peronista Montonero (MPM) (Peronist Montonero Movement), were formed by Perón after he had been exiled in 1955. But while the authoritarian general had successfully used the ballot box to secure power, the leadership of the new movement, calling itself the Montoneros, sought by use of arms to first destabilise the state and then take it over. Led by Mario Firmenich and Carlos Gustavo Ramus, their chosen methods included armed attacks on police stations and military barracks, assassinations, bombings, kidnapping of industrialists for ransom, etc.[102] The Trotskyite Ejército Revolucionario del Pueblo (ERP) (People's Revolutionary Army) was a rival guerrilla group. Led by Mario Roberto Santucho, it deployed similar tactics and had the same political objective.[103] In one of its most notorious operations – code-named Operation Pindapoy or Aramburazo – the guerrillas on 29 May 1970 kidnapped the former President, Pedro Eugenio Aramburu, who had led the coup which deposed Perón in 1955. They held him responsible for spiriting Eva Perón's body out of the country in 1956 and for ordering (in June 1956) Operación Masacre, in which nine Peronists were shot in cold blood by the authorities.[104] The Montoneros 'tried' Aramburu on 1 June 1970, found him 'guilty' and shot him.[105]

Reporting on the assassination, Ambassador Skentelbery noted that the late president's political solution for Argentina 'pointed to the same long-drawn-out term of office and organization as the Franco regime in Spain'. He concluded that the killing was 'a detonating factor' in the nation's politics.[106] A number of historians have argued that once the decision has been made to use firearms, the use of violence becomes self-justifying.[107] Seamus Heaney in *The Cure at Troy* captures that idea in one verse:

> The innocent in gaols
> Beat on their bars together.
> A hunger-striker's father
> Stands in the graveyard dumb.
> The police widow in veils
> Faints at the funeral home.

>History says, *Don't hope*
>*On this side of the grave.*
>But then, once in a lifetime
>The longed-for tidal wave
>Of justice can rise up,
>And hope and history rhyme.[108]

But in Argentina, as in Northern Ireland, 'the flesh-smell of hatred', to quote a line from Eavan Boland, would stalk both Argentina and Ireland before 'hope and history' finally had an opportunity to rhyme.[109]

Skentelbery, in his reports, looked with foreboding on the likely negative impact for Latin America of the outcome of the US presidential election in 1969. Taking over the White House on 20 January 1969, Richard Nixon and his national security adviser Dr Henry Kissinger[110] became the architects of the new policy of *détente* with the Soviet Union. While pursuing the escalation of the war in South Asia, they sought to normalise relations with the People's Republic of China. On 27 January 1973 the Paris Peace Accord was signed, ending the war in Vietnam. In that new global geopolitical configuration, Nixon and Kissinger viewed Argentina and the other Latin American countries as inherently unstable and a significant security risk.[111] Kissinger saw the region as politically volatile and susceptible to the siren call of revolutionary populism fomented by aid and logistical support from Cuba, the Soviet Union and China.[112] On 3 February 1972, Skentelbery entitled his report 'US–Latin American Relationships at their Nadir'. He argued that Washington was 'under the influence of a native of a country that was the prime exponent of the doctrines of *realpolitik* and *machtpolitik*, an admirer of Otto von Bismarck and Prince Metternich – Henry Kissinger, who thinks only in crudely realistic terms of power'. He thought that the US would, as part of its new global strategy, seek to 'reconcile herself with China and treat Russia as super-power to super-power'. The White House's policy in the southern hemisphere, he reported, was designed to have an understanding with one nation or two, Brazil and Mexico, and not bother about the rest 'of the Banana Republics and unstable democracies and dictatorships'. Skentelbery concluded: 'If Soviet submarines carrying atomic war-heads are sailing in the Caribbean, what does it matter what is happening in Chile? For in the zodiac of the seventies Power is in the ascendant ... In this world of giants L[atin]A[merica] can do little by herself.'[113]

By the early 1970s there were military dictatorships in Uruguay, Paraguay, Argentina, Bolivia, Ecuador, Brazil and, with the exception of Costa Rica and

Belize, all the countries of Central America. Argentina, the country of second greatest importance in the region to the United States after Brazil, provided Nixon and Kissinger with a volatile geostrategic security problem. While the Kennedy and Johnson administrations combatted the rise of the left in Latin America in the 1960s by using the interlocking strategy of the Alliance for Progress[114] and support for the military, Nixon and Kissinger applied the doctrines of realpolitik and machtpolitik in support of the 'restoration of order' achievable in the region through US-supported counter-insurgency campaigns.

Skentelbery had an entirely different perspective, retaining great faith in a democratic future for Argentina and for the region. In his report on 3 February 1972, he argued that the southern hemisphere was

> perhaps humanity's best hope for the future. Latin America is the only one of the world's great subdivisions where the human being is still entirely human, where *es la persona que cuenta* [diplomat's own emphasis. The phrase means: 'it is the person who really counts'] where no one (except Cuba) has nuclear weapons or is ever thinking of developing them, where the great fund of precept and experience and custom that has been created in the Christian West to reconcile man with God and with the requirements of a civilized condition is still wholly relevant. The S.A. continent may prove someday to be the last repository and custodian of human Christian values that men in the European motherlands have thrown away. Indeed, it may well prove to be the last hope on earth.[115]

Skentelbery's final leap of faith before quitting his post and retiring, oddly enough, was shared by the incoming minister for foreign affairs in 1973, Dr Garret FitzGerald.

A CHANGE OF GOVERNMENT AND NEW HOPE FOR IRISH MEMBERSHIP OF THE EEC

In contrast to the preoccupations of the superpowers, the central focus of Irish foreign policy during the first three years of the 1970s concentrated on successfully negotiating membership of the European Economic Community (EEC) and the management of Anglo-Irish relations. That first major diplomatic initiative was carried on against a backdrop of the collapse of the government in Northern Ireland. The rule of the unionists there fell asunder as nationalists marched to secure equal rights and 'one man, one vote' in local elections. Paradoxically, while Anglo-Irish relations reached their nadir over the bloody events in Northern Ireland, both the Dublin and London governments cooperated closely in their combined efforts to join the EEC. President Charles de Gaulle, who had twice obstructed Britain's entry, in 1963 and 1967, retired from the presidency of France in 1969, thereby easing the path towards the enlargement of the EEC. The taoiseach, Jack Lynch (1966–73), and the minister for external affairs, Patrick Hillery, secured that objective in January 1973.[116] Together with Denmark and Britain, Ireland became an EEC member and was now an equal partner with each of the other eight member states. Membership placed Irish foreign policy in a new and more favourable global context, as it did Anglo-Irish relations. Ireland was part of an EEC bloc, giving it access to pooled community-wide foreign policy intelligence and a voice in discussions which led to European Political Cooperation (EPC), which became, after 1993, the Common Foreign and Security Policy (CFSP).

After sixteen years in power, the Fianna Fáil party was defeated in a general election on 28 February 1973. A Fine Gael–Labour Party coalition took office on 14 March. The taoiseach was Liam Cosgrave (FG), a former minister for external affairs in the inter-party government between 1954 and 1957. Dr Garret FitzGerald was appointed minister for foreign affairs. He was a university lecturer, an economist and a journalist. His four years in office were seen in retrospect as a 'golden era' for the department. FitzGerald enjoyed a very good working relationship with the secretary, Hugh McCann (1963–74), and with his successor, Paul Keating (1974–7). During FitzGerald's time in Iveagh House, the department went through a major restructuring, hiring more young staff, reviewing internal structures and making organisational changes. New missions were opened in Luxembourg and Japan in 1973 and in the Soviet Union in 1974,[117] the presence of the latter keeping Garda Special Branch and Irish Military Intelligence (G2) very alert over the decades.[118]

FitzGerald worked actively in the EEC to establish more equitable relations between the first and the third world. While Ireland held the presidency between January and June 1975, making FitzGerald the chairperson of the Council of Foreign Ministers, he signed, in February, the Lomé 1 Convention, a trade and aid agreement between the nine member states and seventy-one African, Caribbean and Pacific (ACP) countries.[119] Ireland also signed the International Convention on Civil and Political Rights and the Convention on Economic, Social and Cultural Rights. As Ireland depended greatly upon inward investment from the United States, FitzGerald might have been expected to be cautious in expressing his differences with Washington. He observed in his autobiography that 'many European countries tended to be less than frank in their communications with the US government, owing to fear of offending such an important ally'.[120] But when he met Henry Kissinger in Washington in October 1975, he pointed out that the Irish ambassador had not withdrawn[121] from Madrid following the executions on 27 September of five Basques convicted of killing policemen.[122] He explained that such a move would be counter-productive, as the ambassador's inevitable return after a brief absence would be presented as a victory by the Franco regime.[123] Kissinger asked FitzGerald: 'Why should the execution of "convicted cop-killers" be turned into a moral issue?' Europeans were living in the past as far as Spain was concerned, with 'their mythic memories of the civil war as a struggle of democracy against fascism', he said. FitzGerald replied that however much the United States might see European attitudes towards Spain as based on myth arising from the Spanish civil war, 'the emotions behind these attitudes were a political fact the United States had to reckon with'. When the conversation ended, FitzGerald, on taking his leave, heard Kissinger 'mutter to himself as he turned away: "A myth, if widely believed, is a reality to be reckoned [with]"'.[124] Unlike Kissinger and his machtpolitik, FitzGerald welcomed the overthrow of the dictatorship in Portugal on 25 April 1974 and the subsequent collapse of its African empire. (Although out of office, he would welcome the return of democracy to Spain in the late 1970s following the death of Franco.) He was supportive of the progressive social teaching of the papacy which set out the principles of social justice on which more equitable structures could be built in the South American republics. FitzGerald and his wife Joan were avid readers of modern Catholic theology and both were very sympathetic to the radical social engagement of Catholic clergy and nuns working in different parts of the developing world in defence of human rights.

ARGENTINA, DEMOCRACY AND THE RETURN OF PERÓN

The embassy in Argentina was a direct beneficiary of the FitzGerald years in Iveagh House. He was both personally interested in Latin America and was a personal friend of the diplomat then serving in Buenos Aires; Bernard Davenport, an economist, had been sent there in July 1971 as third secretary. He overlapped for a year with Skentelbery. In November 1972, he was appointed chargé d'affaires ad interim and he ran the embassy with the assistance of an Irish-Argentine administrator, Corina Flynn, until he was reassigned and a new ambassador sent out in early 1974. The exceptional quality of his despatches won him a written commendation from the secretary of the Department of Foreign Affairs, Hugh McCann; they were, he wrote on 16 February 1973, 'among the best we received from any source' and gave Iveagh House 'an excellent picture of the tensions and problems of political life in the Argentine'.[125] Noting that Davenport did not mention officials or individuals by name in his despatches, he surmised that that might be the practice of the embassy in Buenos Aires 'because of the danger of mail for the Department falling into unauthorised hands'.[126] He instructed Davenport to mark all his reports 'confidential' in future,[127] thus ensuring they went to the secretary's office in the first instance and from there would be circulated automatically to the three assistant secretaries. 'In that way, your splendid reports will receive the widest possible diffusion in the Department, and at the highest level,' McCann wrote.[128]

Between 1965 and 1968, FitzGerald had been Davenport's boss when they worked at the Economist Intelligence Unit in Dublin.[129] Upon taking office, he requested to see the confidential reports for that year from the Irish embassy in Buenos Aires. The minister wrote to Davenport on 30 April 1973: 'We resume, in somewhat different circumstances, a previous relationship.' Explaining that he had called a meeting in Dublin of all serving ambassadors to review Irish policy,[130] he apologised because the occasion 'didn't permit of your return to participate in it' as unfortunately that would have raised 'all kinds of issues about other people of similar rank'. In conclusion FitzGerald wrote that he had read 'with the greatest of interest your reports since the beginning of this year – I haven't had time to delve back beyond that! They are extremely good and I note that I am not the only person to think so! ... Keep it up'.[131] Working with FitzGerald and McCann, Davenport knew he had a minister for foreign affairs and a secretary in Iveagh House who were interested both in the quality and the analytical strength of his political and economic commentaries.[132] With a wide range of good contacts in journalism and politics stretching beyond the confined world of the diplomatic corps, he was well-informed about Argentine public affairs. Both he and his wife Fiamma enjoyed Argentine poetry and literature and their home was often visited by leading popular singers in the style of the famous Uruguayan poet and guitarist Alfredo Zitarrosa. Moreover, as a new EEC member, Ireland's diplomatic hand in Buenos Aires had been strengthened thanks to the initiation of a system of regular meetings of community ambassadors and also set meetings at the level of third secretary. Davenport attended the first meeting of ambassadors, which took place over lunch on 15 January 1973. He reported that when the diplomats present spoke about Argentine elections the conversation was prefaced by 'if they take place'. The unanimous opinion of the group was that the Radical Party or the Peronists would win but that it might require a run-off election to determine the final outcome.[133]

The Argentine military had permitted the Peronists to take part in the elections. Perón, who Davenport reported remained 'the real power', approved Héctor Cámpora as his presidential candidate, a person whose 'obedience to Perón was legendary'.[134] He advised against excessive optimism regarding the outcome of the presidential elections on 11 March 1973 as the military had 'little intention of forsaking politics entirely and handing over complete power to the civilians'. Concluding his analysis, Davenport said that the military 'are to be the arbitrators of the post-election political process' and that any future government would be able to take whatever decisions it wished 'provided the soldiers first approve'.[135] As the Peronists were likely to win the election, he filed a report explaining the background to 'the greatest mass movement in Argentine history', which a military elite had ousted in 1955 and driven underground, motivated less by 'a desire for reconciliation than by a thirst for revenge'. With a series of imprisonments, exiles and even executions, the military 'signalled that the master was back in power and that the servant had better return to his proper place'.[136] That unelected minority, Davenport stated, had 'dominated Argentine political life from behind the scenes, proscribing Peronism at election times and violently overthrowing every elected government which sought a reconciliation with Perón'.[137] On the eve of a possible return of Perón to Buenos Aires in 1973, Davenport judged that Cámpora and his party were likely to win the election. He provided Iveagh House with an overview of the movement, which he judged was 'reformist rather than revolutionary', vague on policy, self-consciously nationalist and its primary goal being reconciling the social classes. He argued that the essence of the movement lay in its 'absolute dedication to the leader' and in the 'passionate belief in his commitment to social justice for the underdog – a belief not without some foundation in historical events'.[138] There was an unshakeable belief that Perón would somehow 'restore the glorious ten years of working-class prosperity and high consumption, between 1945 and 1955 when the despised servant first emerged from his quarters and arrogantly displayed his newly acquired rights, not always mindful that in doing so he sometimes infringed on those of his former master'. Other essential features of Peronism were, he wrote, 'a ritual of sentimental devotion to the memory of Evita', a 'commemoration of its martyrs executed after 1955' and 'a defiant celebration of the feast days which recall the movement's triumphs'.[139] Davenport drew a distinction between historical Peronism and the contemporary movement, which was more conservative and showed much greater respect for the strength and opinions of its opponents. It had become essentially a centre party which draws support from the entire range of the Argentine political spectrum. This latter quality reflects Peronism's almost magical ability to appear as all things to most, if not all, men. Thus, as each group excludes from its memory what it finds unpalatable, Peronism is: to the poor and the workers, prosperity and high consumption; to the businessman, the large profits resulting from a protected home market; to the middle-class, anti-communism; and to the nationalist, anti-imperialism.[140]

Cámpora won without a run-off and Peronists did very well in the contests for governor, the senate and chamber of deputies. The Irish envoy and his diplomatic colleagues attended the installation ceremonies on 25 May where 'more than half a million people had gathered in the square facing government house to celebrate the occasion and except for one isolated minor riot the day passed off almost without incident'. (A few cars belonging to diplomats [including Davenport's] were damaged when caught in a crossfire of rocks and missiles between rioters and the police.)[141] Cámpora spoke for two and a half hours in which he announced an amnesty for political prisoners: 'Of special interest to the Irish community in Argentina was Dr. Cámpora's pledge that there will be no state monopoly of education, and of interest to all Argentines was his promise that there will be no curtailment on freedom of expression.'[142] But Davenport advised that Cámpora was merely a caretaker president:

> Perón is to be the Mao of Argentina with Cámpora as his Chou En Lai ... It is somewhat paradoxical that even his worst enemies are now looking forward to Perón's return to Argentina in the hope that he will stamp out the guerrilla problem and impose total unity on the various factions [of his movement] ... Perhaps the worst thing which could happen to Argentina, and the one prospect Argentines most fear, is that Perón should die. Only Perón holds the various factions of his movement together and his removal from the scene at an early stage without first appointing an acceptable successor capable of assuming Perón's mantle would almost certainly result in chaos.[143]

Davenport's prediction proved only too accurate.

Perón flew to Buenos Aires on 20 June 1973. The day had been declared a public holiday and the government had provided free transport from anywhere in the country to the capital. About a million had gathered around Ezeiza airport to welcome the returning *caudillo*. Davenport remained at his office but maintained contact through the day with a number of prominent journalists.[144] For security reasons, Perón's plane was diverted to another airport as fighting and shooting had broken out among the different factions of the movement. In the ensuing violence, it was reported that 400 died and over 1,000 were injured. Davenport reported that Perón (77) in the weeks that followed was 'remarkably reminiscent of Gaullism in 1958, down to the last detail of the reluctant statesman poised in the wings awaiting the call to save Argentines from themselves'.[145] Frail and in poor health, Perón suffered a heart attack on 28 June.[146] Speculation centred around who he would choose to run as vice-president as it was probable that that person would be his successor. Isabel Martínez de Perón, his third wife, who had no record of holding political office, was chosen.[147] Cámpora duly resigned the presidency on 6 July,[148] and the Peróns won a landslide victory on 23 September. Davenport reported the following day that there had been no sign of any plan for economic recovery during the previous five months of Peronism: 'Given Perón's expertise in the art of dragon killing all these reactions are, of course, according to a plan but the leader himself does run the risk of bearing a growing resemblance to Don Quijote unless he can soon provide evidence that he can successfully tackle the country's basic problem and more specifically what Paul Samuelson in his speech at the Nobel Prize Winning ceremony described as "The Argentine Stagnation Miracle"'.[149] The envoy's expectation was that the country would slide into chaos.

On 12 October 1973, Perón, after an absence of eighteen years, formed his third administration. On inauguration day, the Montoneros carried banners stating their loyalty: 'Today Perón is Argentina. He is Sovereignty. He is Fatherland.' But Davenport's sources told him that the revolutionary left of the party would have no place in the new administration. His sources also told him that the president had 'given the nod for a purge of left-wing elements in his Justicialista Movement which is now taking its predictable violent course', adding: 'This purge is now in full swing and amidst a fusillade of bullets, assassinations, kidnappings, beatings, charges and counter-charges, left-wingers are being weeded out from both the party and the administration.'[150] In a speech on 8 November, the political scientist Richard Gillespie wrote that Perón 'likened the so-called "infiltrators" [Montoneros] to "germs" which were "contaminating" the Movement'.[151] Recalled to work at headquarters, Davenport, in his final report on 31 December 1973, noted that no deviation from 'Peronist orthodoxy' by the youth movement was tolerated and that several of its leaders had been 'assassinated while others have been kidnapped and beaten'.[152] Davenport speculated that the savagery with which the civil war was being fought in the youth movement had been heightened 'by the delicate state of Perón's health which in the short period since he came to power has caused him to be absent from his official duties on several occasions'. He predicted that the struggle would intensify during 'the days ahead when Perón will no longer be around'. While there was no obvious or agreed successor to Perón, Davenport noted that there were indications that 'it is certainly not Isabelita'.[153] Reflecting on the general situation in Argentina, he forecast that 'Argentine political stability therefore currently remains rather perilously balanced on the knife edge of Perón's health and his death in the near future would almost certainly plunge the country into an orgy of violence'. He concluded: 'Already the recent upsurge in kidnappings and other terrorist-inspired violence shows that the country's guerrillas are getting restless and all the indications are that 1974 will be another hot year in Argentina's political history.'[154] That proved to be the case.

COUP D'ÉTAT IN CHILE

Before leaving Buenos Aires in early 1974, Davenport also reported on an event which sent shockwaves through the region – the overthrow on 11 September 1973 of Salvador Allende's Popular Unity government by General Augusto Pinochet. While the US national security adviser Kissinger was once credited with having said that a communist Chile would be a dagger pointed at the heart of Tierra del Fuego, such whimsy did not characterise Washington's covert policy of destabilisation which had been implemented soon after Allende had won the presidential election on 4 November 1970. Following the successful CIA-supported coup, Kissinger justified the intervention, saying that 'if Chile had followed the Cuban pattern, communist ideology would in time have been supported by Soviet forces and Soviet arms in the southern core of the South American continent'.[155] Davenport's analysis – two days after the coup – diverged completely from Kissinger's machtpolitik thesis. He told Iveagh House that the strategy of the 'plotters' had been to 'provoke Allende into violating the Constitution and thus to provide an excuse for staging the coup'. The ousted president's rigid adherence to the constitution, he wrote, finally forced the military to abandon all pretence at legality and the coup was 'ultimately staged as the pretext of rescuing Chile from "the yoke of Marxism"'.[156] It was 'no mere non-political attempt by the military to restore order in a confused and deteriorating situation. On the contrary, both the composition and pronouncements of the ruling junta give the new authorities a strong right-wing flavour. Already Congress has been dissolved and reports reaching Buenos Aires indicate that a witch hunt has now begun for supporters of the Allende administration'. He was convinced that 'a massive repression' was certain to follow the seizure of power. Analysing the geopolitical implications for the region, he said that the coup had 'brought a shocked response in the few remaining Latin American democracies, not least in Argentina', which found itself 'surrounded by five right-wing military dictatorships – Chile, Bolivia, Paraguay, Brazil and Uruguay'. He believed that Allende's 'fall and subsequent suicide has already caused serious bloodshed and could, at the worst, eventually lead to civil war. For the rest of the continent the tragic implication of the coup may be acceptance of the guerrilla thesis that in Latin America, at least, reform through the normal democratic process is impossible'.[157]

On 31 December and with fresh press and diplomatic analysis to hand, Davenport reported that the coup had 'ushered in a reign of terror on a scale hitherto unknown in South America. At least 7,000 people have died although the figure may be as high as 30,000 and still the terror continues – the object being apparently to crush all opposition totally and thus to avoid any resistance which might, in the extreme case, lead to a civil war'. He concluded that neither the Allende government nor the opposition could escape from a share of responsibility for the situation which prompted the coup. But he did not think that Allende would ever have been allowed to complete his term of office: 'A bleak outlook of terror and counter-terror coupled with economic deprivations seems to be Chile's lot, at least for the foreseeable future.'[158]

There was strong international condemnation of the Pinochet regime's flagrant violations of human rights in the months that followed.[159] FitzGerald had, together with other EEC ministers, condemned the coup, the mass arrests and illegal detentions and killings. A number of EEC countries withdrew their ambassadors in protest. However, diplomatic staff in most of the EEC embassies gave sanctuary to hundreds fleeing the dictatorship. Besides the Chileans being sought by the authorities, at the time of the coup there were between 12,000 and 15,000 very vulnerable political refugees from all over Latin America in the country. The French ambassador Pierre de Menthon and his wife Françoise, together with the other staff, saved countless lives.[160] The Swedish ambassador Harald Edelstam rescued hundreds before being declared persona non grata, in December 1973, and forced to leave the country.[161] Italian embassy staff also succeeded in providing sanctuary for hundreds. Roberto Toscano, the second secretary, was in charge of the Italian embassy and consulate in the absence of the ambassador, and his humanitarian efforts were assisted by Damiano Spinola and Emilio Barbarani. The Italian vice-consul in Buenos Aires, Enrico Calami, was seconded to Santiago to help manage the refugee crisis. Calami found on arrival that there were 410 refugees, of whom 50 were children. With the support of other Italian diplomats, Calami helped get many out within a few weeks. The remainder were housed in the Italian embassy for over a year. In all, Italian diplomats saved about 750 Chileans during those years of repression.[162]

Solidarity groups, Amnesty International and religious bodies petitioned the Irish government to admit Chilean political refugees. Brian McKeown, the head of Trócaire, worked closely with the cardinal archbishop of Santiago, Raúl Silva Henríquez, and his ecumenical Committee of Cooperation for Peace in Chile – after 1 January 1976 renamed the Vicariate of Solidarity.[163] McKeown brought leading Chilean churchmen from that organisation to Dublin to take part in public meetings and to brief the government on the violation of human rights by the Pinochet government. FitzGerald and the political division of the department of foreign affairs were strongly in favour of allowing victims of torture and their families to receive asylum in Ireland. However, the Department of Justice took a traditional stance against such a liberal notion. That, at least, had the virtue of being consistent with the position the department had held since the 1930s – particularly in relation to the admission of Jewish refugees.[164] The minister for justice, Patrick Cooney, argued against admission on the grounds that Ireland was not as 'cosmopolitan' as other Western European countries, and that 'the absorption of even a limited number of foreigners of this kind could prove extremely difficult'. The minister cited the example of Hungarian refugees who had come to Ireland after their revolution in 1956; they had, in his view, 'failed to settle down' and 're-emigrated to other countries'. According to the historian Claire Healy, 'the most significant reason for the minister's reluctance, however, was revealed in the same letter where Cooney stated that most or all of the group were refugees because they were Marxists, and that a significant proportion were "activists"'. He feared that they would engage in political agitation and 'they will not change their outlook on arrival in this country'. The minister suggested 'that such left-wing activists would pose a far greater problem for Ireland than for other Western European countries because of the existence in Ireland of 'a relatively large and well-organised subversive group towards whom such persons could be expected to gravitate'. The minister also noted that some of the refugees were from other Latin American countries and had taken refuge in Chile because it had a communist president. He proposed that a screening programme be set up in order to vet any refugees from Chile who came into the country. In the end, the Irish government agreed to admit twelve families. By 1977, there were twenty-three heads of families living in Ireland and a total of ninety-four Chileans.[165]

DAVENPORT LEAVES BUENOS AIRES

The Chilean coup, which took place three months before the twenty-fifth anniversary of the UN's Universal Declaration of Human Rights, was a watershed in Ireland's relations with Latin America. In the Oireachtas, political parties had developed a specialist expertise on Latin America. Irish missionaries working in Santiago provided eyewitness accounts of what was happening under the dictatorship. A modernising Department of Foreign Affairs under FitzGerald began to develop a greater professional knowledge of the region at headquarters. That complemented the specialist skill of the Irish mission to Washington, the UN and the EEC. Thanks to FitzGerald and his senior staff, the Irish embassy in Buenos Aires was no longer seen as being an outlier.

The affection in which Bernard Davenport, his wife Fiamma Alfami and their three children were held by Irish-Argentines was reflected in the large attendance at the farewell reception for the family on 27 December 1973. Dr José E. Richards, speaking on behalf of the community, was warm in his praise of the envoy and his wife. Presenting him with an illustrated copy of the epic poem *Martín Fierro*, Richards hoped the volume would continue to keep vivid in his mind the image of the pampas of infinite horizons 'where our ancestors lived, dreamed and struggled, and in whose maternal lap rest the mortal remains of many of them awaiting the day of final judgment'. 'Visibly emotional', according to *TSC*, Davenport said: 'I feel very much in sympathy with the Latin mentality and this is why I can sincerely say that I greatly enjoyed my time in Argentina.' He was not saying *adiós*, or goodbye, but only an *hasta luego*, until the next time.[166] Bernard Davenport had formed a deep bond with the people of Argentina and he came to love the music and literature of that country. He admired the songs of the Uruguayan Alfredo Zitarrosa, associated with the music of the gauchos and Fernando Ezequiel Solanas' film *Los Hijos de Fierro* (1972) – an uncompromising Peronist view of the country's history between 1955 and the early 1970s. It was no surprise to many Irish-Argentines when Davenport returned as ambassador in August 1989.[167] He later served as ambassador to the Holy See. Retiring in 2004, he died on 11 June 2018 in Florence. An *Irish Times* obituary deservedly and accurately described him as being 'one of the most respected Irish diplomats of his generation'.[168]

CHAPTER FOUR

Irish Diplomats Witness Military Dictatorship, Repression and Disappearances: A divided Argentina and 'history from below'

James Wilfred (Wilfie) Lennon took up his post as Irish ambassador to Argentina in early 1974, serving there until his retirement on 17 January 1977.[1] Davenport met him and his wife Kitty at Ezeiza airport and checked them into a hotel. The following day, Davenport flew with his family to Dublin as he was urgently required to start a new job in Iveagh House.[2] Although a former ambassador to Spain, Lennon had no expertise on Argentina or on the region to which he had been assigned.[3] Buenos Aires had not been his first choice, and during his time there he petitioned Iveagh House repeatedly but unsuccessfully to be reassigned to Geneva.[4] Nevertheless, he brought to his new posting the experience of a lifelong career in diplomacy having served (besides Spain) in Paris, Lisbon and The Hague. When called upon to handle a number of very difficult matters during his three years in Argentina, he rose to the challenge with aplomb.

No believer in long reports of the Davenport style, Lennon, in contrast, spent two years laconically describing the internecine strife in the government of Juan Domingo Perón and later of that of his wife, Isabel. The legacy of bitterness left by the violent clashes between the factions of the fissile Peronist movement did not abate in the short time left in office to the *caudillo*. In rapidly deteriorating health, Perón only managed to regain a tenuous hold on the reins of government. The minister for social welfare, José López Rega, associated closely with 'the absent one' throughout his exile, was the dominant figure in government. Known as *el brujo* (the sorcerer), he was the *éminence grise* who allegedly ran a state within the state. The return of Perón, despite ongoing civil unrest and violence, raised popular expectations among his poorest followers, who had romantic memories of those halcyon days in the late '40s and early '50s. That euphoria, however, was soon tempered by disappointment and disillusionment while his many enemies gloated and some encouraged the 'men on horseback' to seize power. Under Perón's short-lived second coming, the country entered into a period of factionalism, mafia-style murders and incipient civil war.

HISTORY FROM BELOW: PERSPECTIVES FROM THE *VILLAS*

The experience of Fátima Cabrera may help explain the paradoxes and contradictions of living under Perón and later under military dictatorships. Her family were Peronists of the first wave, orthodox and certainly not of the post-modernist pick-and-mix variety. Cabrera was born in the northern city of Tucumán on 13 May 1957,[5] the eldest of five children (three sisters and a brother). Her mother, Doña Blanca, separated from her husband, moved south with her family in 1966 as part of a network migration, joining her own mother, Rosa, and her brothers.[6] The extended Cabrera family lived together in Villa 31 behind the Retiro train station and near the Stella Maris chapel and the Paulina de Mallinckrodt school which the young Fátima attended.

Fr Carlos Mugica, a champion of the *villeros*, was attached to that parish. Born in 1930, his father, Adolfo, was a civil engineer and a founder of the Conservative Party. He held high office in the municipality of Buenos Aires and was minister for foreign affairs and worship between 28 April and 29 August 1961. His mother came from one of the country's biggest landowning families. Ordained a diocesan priest in 1959, he had, during his studies in the seminary, begun to work in the *conventillos* or tenements around the very poor Constitución district in Buenos Aires. Shortly after his ordination, he worked in the Chaco in 1960 with the archbishop of Reconquista, Juan José Iriarte. While there he met and became friends with Arturo Paoli, the leader of the Little Brothers of Charles de Foucauld. Mugica served as private secretary to Cardinal Caggiano of Buenos Aires. He was appointed secretary of Juventud Universitaria Católica (JUC) (Young Catholic University Students) and professor of theology at the Universidad del Salvador. During the course of his youth work, he became friends with Carlos Ramus, Mario Eduardo Firmenich and Fernando Abal Medina, all of whom took up the highest leadership roles in the Montonero guerrilla organisation. Combining teaching in university with pastoral work in slum parishes, his weekly homily was broadcast on radio. He would smile when his poor parishioners called him the 'Pope of

Latin America'.[7] Working in Villa 31, he first met Fátima Cabrera, who, at thirteen, became a catechist attending his mass on Sundays. After mass, the priest was a frequent visitor, with his friends, including Lucía Cullen, who was disappeared on 22 June 1976 at aged thirty, to the open house kept by Cabrera's grandmother, Rosa Lobos de Uñate. Mugica enjoyed eating her empanadas and Cullen liked Cabrera's grandfather Custodio to sing for her the popular waltz 'La Pulpera de Santa Lucía'.[8] Mugica had another reason for visiting the Cabrera household: he was a football enthusiast and a follower of Racing Club de Avellaneda. Fátima had three uncles who worked in the port – two of whom had been professional footballers, Horacio Uñate with Atlético de Tucumán and Racing Club in the 1960s and Rubén with Atlético de Tucumán about 1963. All of them played football with the children in the *barrio* (shanty town).

Mugica took a group of students in 1966 to work in Tartagal, in the north of the province of Salta, and to the Chaco to meet Arturo Paoli and his community. Mugica went to Bolivia in 1967, carrying letters from an Argentine bishop and the family of Che Guevara, in an unsuccessful effort to retrieve his remains and return them for burial in Rosario. He studied in France in 1967 during which time he visited Perón in Madrid and later accompanied him on a ten-day trip to Cuba. He was in Paris during the student revolution in 1968 and had discussions with many of its leaders. Upon his return, he joined the Movimiento de Sacerdotes para el Tercer Mundo (MSTM). He had also helped found Curas Villeros, which united priests working in poor neighbourhoods. In 1970, his brother built a clinic and a church for him in a new parish in Barrio Comunicaciones, Villa 31, which he called Christ the Worker.

As a catechist, Cabrera worked under the direction of an ex-nun, Zulema Facciola. She also had a great deal of contact with Mugica, as did the well-known *villero* leader José Valenzuela, and the lawyer Héctor Sobel. Because of his strong social engagement in Villa 31, Mugica was rarely out of difficulties with his episcopal superiors and he was frequently censored. He was also the object of campaigns of vilification and death threats from the extreme right. He was absent when his parents' home was bombed in 1971. In 1973, Mugica declined an invitation from the Peronist presidential candidate Héctor Cámpora to stand for Congress. For a very short time, he took an unpaid position in the Ministry of Social Welfare, run by López Rega, but resigned because of irreconcilable differences.

Cabrera, now sixteen, continued her work as one of Mugica's catechists. About that time, 1973, she met Alberto 'Galleta' Alfaro, a leader of the Movimiento Villero Peronista (MVP).[9] He was, like herself, an emigrant from the north having come in 1968 from the Chaco.[10] He left school early and worked as a truck driver and as a stevedore. He became widely known in Villa 31 and was greatly respected both as a leader in community politics and as a member of Juventud Peronista. Alfaro's father was disappeared in Buenos Aires in October 1973. Mugica wrote a letter denouncing that crime, which Cabrera delivered to newspaper offices and to one of the national television stations, Canal 7. Participating in October 1973 in Santa Fe in a national meeting of the Peronist leaders in the slums (*villas*) (Congreso del Movimiento Villero Peronista), he also attended the same congress with Cabrera a year later in Córdoba. Cabrera, Alfaro and the residents of the Eva Perón Zone of Villa 31 took part on 25 March 1974 in a march to the Plaza de Mayo in opposition to the government's policy of clearing Villa 31 and other areas. Carrying placards reading '*Casas sin trampas*' ('Houses without any tricks'), they sang the national anthem as the police blocked their way and opened fire with rubber bullets and tear gas, killing one youth, Alberto Chejolán. Alberto Alfaro was arrested, together with the brother of the deceased, though they were freed a few days later. Cabrera remembers Mugica displaying his public anger and frustration at the shooting.[11]

Because of death threats from the Triple A (anti-communist alliance), the priest was forced to leave Villa 31 for a while. He found time to write a mass for the Third World which was to be recorded by RCA Victor – the words of which were not received well by his bishop. Unfortunately, the script for the mass has not survived.[12] He was in his parents' house on 9 May 1974 when the maid answered the phone to an anonymous caller: 'Tell Mugica that we are going to kill him,' a voice said. Without hesitation, she passed the call to him. The voice repeated the threat: 'We have killed a number of people from the *villas*. Now it's your turn.' Using strong language, Mugica shouted an obscenity and put down the phone. Two days later, on the 11th, he spent the day reading, then at 4 p.m. played football with his friends in Villa 31 and at 7 p.m. said mass in San Francisco Solano, in Mataderos. Afterwards, he talked to members of the congregation and left to catch up with his friends who were outside. No sooner had he walked out than he heard someone call out his name. Turning, he saw a man take a machine gun (Marietta) from beneath his coat and shoot him at point-blank range. He had only time to shout in anger at the assailant. Ricardo Capelli, a friend, was also shot in the attack. Friends rushed Mugica and Capelli to hospital by car. The priest died on the operating table; Capelli survived. Cabrera joined the procession of about 10,000 mourners at his funeral. She wrote later: '*Allí sentimos que se nos fue una parte de cado uno*' ('There we felt that we had each lost a part of ourselves').[13] Nobody was ever convicted for the murder.[14]

Amid great national political uncertainties, Mugica's death made him another daily statistic in the vicious cycle of violence that was gripping the country. Cabrera felt his loss keenly but she continued her political work with Alfaro.[15] Both were held by the police in August 1974 because of their involvement in a dispute over the enforced movement of a number of inhabitants of Villa 31 to another area. Released on the 22nd after spending a few days in jail, undeterred they continued their work together. Now a couple, Alfaro and Cabrera were allocated a flat by the government in Edificio 6, Piso 5, Depto D in Barrio Saldías. Cabrera, by her late teens, had been highly politicised and radicalised. She was an activist in the *villero* movement while working as a catechist in the parish of the late Fr Mugica.[16] She received a further, terrible blow in December 1974 when her partner was involved in a rail accident resulting in his having both his legs amputated below the knees. Cabrera helped him during his recovery while she also lived partially with her mother and brothers and sisters in Villa Soldadi. Alfaro suffered persistent intimidation at the hands of the armed forces. His apartment was frequently raided and the milk kiosk which he ran was repeatedly attacked and destroyed. Following the military coup in March 1976, Alfaro was disappeared on 6 July 1977. After his remains had been finally recovered from a clandestine grave in 2002, he was buried in the cemetery of San Martín.[17] Cabrera and Fr Patrick Rice were disappeared together on 11 October 1976 and their story is related in Chapter 5.

THE DEATH OF JUAN DOMINGO PERÓN

The remaining hopes of maintaining unity within the Argentine government were dashed in mid-June 1974 when rumours swept Buenos Aires that Perón was dying. Concern grew when he failed to make an appearance either in person or on television on 20 June, the country's Día de la Bandera (National Flag Day).[18] A pre-recorded speech was broadcast on television on 21 June, giving solid grounds for the speculation, according to Ambassador Lennon, that he was close to death.[19] On 29 June, Radio Uruguay announced that he had died. Lennon reported that he would not 'be surprised if the rumours ... are proved correct – perhaps even before this report reaches Headquarters'. On 1 July, Lennon wrote that the 'later days of June apart from the President's illness, were uneventful – just the usual quota of kidnappings, bombings and shootings (one, a gun battle outside the USA Embassy, was not reported in the daily press: the number of "common criminals" as distinct from "politicos" shot by the police since 1 January now exceeds 500)'. The following was added to his report: 'Above was prepared before noon on 1st July. At 2.15 p.m. it was announced that the President had died', and that, prior to the announcement, María Estela Martínez de Perón, popularly known as Isabelita, had been appointed president ad interim.[20]

News of Perón's death was reported in Ireland and internationally on 2 July 1974.[21] In Dublin, the Argentine ambassador notified the Department of Foreign Affairs that he had arranged a requiem mass to be said at 11 a.m. in the Sacred Heart Church, Donnybrook. An official in the Department of the Taoiseach wrote on 2 July: 'Foreign Affairs think that the Taoiseach and members of the Gov. should attend or be represented also the President.'[22] Iveagh House replied stating that a message of condolence ought to be sent to Buenos Aires and a possible 'half-masting of flags'. The following day, after 12.30 p.m. flags were flown at half-mast on all government buildings in the capital.[23] A book of condolence was opened on 4 July at the Argentine ambassador's residence. 'Taoiseach called to sign book of condolence personally today, 4.7.74', according to a minute in the Department of the Taoiseach.[24] The book, now in the foreign ministry archive in Buenos Aires, was also signed by members of the Irish defence forces and by prominent people in Irish public life. A brief discussion took place over whether or not the president of Ireland, Erskine Childers, should represent the country at the funeral, concluding with the decision: 'Government will be represented at the funeral by the Irish Representative at Buenos Aires.' President Childers wrote to Señora Perón: 'I have learned with deep regret of the death of your husband and predecessor as President of the Argentine Republic. Please accept, Madame, my most profound sympathy and that of the people of Ireland in your personal bereavement and in the grievous loss to the people of Argentina of this distinguished and respected statesman.'[25]

Meanwhile, Lennon, on 2 July, together with the other heads of mission, attended the mass in the cathedral in Buenos Aires: 'Apart from a complete breakdown of the arrangements for actually entering the church, it was a free-for-all, everything was most impressive and the huge crowd outside chanting "Perón, Perón" was visibly affected.' Immediately after mass, Perón's body was removed to Congress, where it lay in state until Wednesday, 3 July. The queues awaiting admission were miles long even though hundreds of thousands had already paid their respects. The government was obliged to delay the funeral a further day to accommodate the huge numbers of mourners still waiting in the streets to file past the body.[26]

Lennon provided a vivid account of the 'foreboding' atmosphere in the city on the day of the funeral. He approached the Congress building, where the body was still, on a dark wet winter morning through empty streets (all ordinary traffic was banned) lined on both sides by army and navy personnel in full combat equipment standing shoulder to shoulder ... Outside Congress itself security precautions were extremely heavy – again thousands of fully armed troops with armoured vehicles and police everywhere. In Congress itself the coffin was in the Senate Chamber, a large semi-circular room with seats for about 500, all of which were occupied by Senators, members of Parliament and other supporters of the regime. The Diplomatic Corps were crowded in a small space behind and to one side of the Speaker's chair where we stood until about 10.15 a.m. listening to speeches (twelve in all) by representatives of the Senate, Chamber of Deputies, Trade Unions, and politicians, including one from the opposition.

Lennon added that the body was then taken amid tearful scenes along the route to the presidential residence in Olivos 'where it reposed in a chapel crypt while plans were made to have it placed on permanent display'.[27]

The funeral over, speculation in diplomatic circles immediately turned to the subject of who would wield power under the new *presidenta*. Lennon reported that according to local sources President Isabel Perón and López Rega had 'a Damon and Pythias relationship'[28] and 'for years a Diarmuid and Gráinne one'.[29] The ambassador noted that the most unpopular López Rega held the strongest portfolio (social welfare) in the cabinet. Without Juan Perón, the ambassador believed that

> the Government will soldier on for some months but that probable attempts by López Rega to dominate the new President will lead to greater friction within the ranks and that ultimately it will fall. Mrs. Perón may well then leave Argentina which would necessitate elections. The extreme left can count on about one third support but divisions between the centrists and rightists could make them relatively more important and disruption of political life which would follow would inevitably lead to a return of military rule.[30]

Lennon explained that the Peronist movement was at war with itself. While Perón was alive, the left-wing guerrillas, the Montoneros, 'claimed to be his loyal followers, but when Mrs Perón took over they denounced her as a usurper'. A recent decision by the Montoneros to resume hostilities was, he reported, 'a declaration of war against the Government and their leader has called upon all those "in the middle" to get out of the line of fire'.[31]

Writing on 9 September 1974, Lennon surmised that the only hope for the survival of Mrs Perón was that she should drop López Rega 'and rely upon the armed forces. It is believed that she is capable of this'.[32] A state of siege was declared as the economy deteriorated rapidly and inflation was rampant.[33] Lennon wrote on 4 October 1974 that an 'anti-communist murder squad – calling itself the Anti-Communist Alliance or Triple A – had emerged[34] and had gone on a killing spree'.[35] A week later, he wrote that a Peronist white guard (anti-Soviet counter-revolutionaries) was acting as an agent of state terror, targeting leaders of civil society. The Triple A, he concluded, was 'in fact sponsored by the Government as a means of ridding itself of powerful and dangerous opponents it cannot reach otherwise'.[36] Surprising many diplomats, the regime staggered on until 24 March 1976[37] but without López Rega, who had clung on until he was forced to resign on 11 July 1975 and appointed ambassador to Spain. He died on 9 June 1989 having spent the last ten years of his life as a fugitive fleeing from Spain to Switzerland and 'on the run' from the justice system in Argentina.

AMBASSADOR LENNON, JUSTIN HARMAN AND THE EMBERS OF PERONISM

Ambassador Lennon spent his first ten months in Buenos Aires running the mission as the sole Irish diplomat with the help of able local staff. Deriving support from his fellow EEC ambassadors, those contacts were codified when the heads of state and of government met in Paris on 9 and 10 December 1974, and took a major step towards strengthening the coordination of common foreign policy management. This process became known as European Political Cooperation (EPC). Besides sharing information and scheduling meetings of the political directors in the respective foreign ministries, EEC ambassadors and counsellors held monthly meetings at the two levels in the capitals where the nine had diplomatic representation. Ambassadors took turns to host their EEC counterparts in each other's embassies or residences.

Justin Harman took up his first overseas posting as third secretary on 14 November 1975 in Buenos Aires.[38] A 23-year-old Dubliner, he had a good knowledge of Spanish and an enthusiasm for the professional challenges facing him.[39] He found it very useful to attend the monthly meetings with the counsellors of the other eight EEC countries. Meeting in the elegant El Club Círculo Italiano, at Libertad 1264, he received a crash course in the politics and economics of Argentina. Minutes of each meeting were circulated to the respective embassies and to Brussels. Overall, both tiers of consultation involving EEC diplomats in Buenos Aires – at ambassadorial and at counsellor levels – proved immensely helpful to a small Irish embassy. Reviewing the Canadian and US archives, it is possible to contrast the level of detailed reporting with the comparable Irish files. While diligent and professional, the two Irish diplomats in Buenos Aires did not have the high-level access to the senior ranks of government enjoyed by the nunciature and the US embassy.

However, being a large power with a large staff was not the only thing that mattered when discussing the importance of a diplomatic mission. It was commonly held in Buenos Aires at the time that the doyen of the diplomatic corps, the papal nuncio Archbishop Pio Laghi, was the best informed of all the diplomats in the city.[40] Serving between 27 April 1974 and 10 December 1980, he tracked events from the privileged position of having open access to all shades of opinion and rank. Archbishop Patrick Coveney,[41] an Irishman who worked in his early diplomatic career between 1972 and April 1976 at the nunciature, confirmed to me that Laghi, irrespective of who might be in power, never failed to retain contacts in government and in the armed forces at the highest levels. Coveney admired the professionalism and the diplomatic skills of the nuncio.[42] The Canadian ambassador, Alfred Pike Bissonnet, considered Laghi 'to be one of the best-informed and knowledgeable members of the diplomatic corps with respect to local affairs'.[43] Bissonnet also reported that the nuncio told him in March 1975 he was aware that 'in certain high places within the government' plans were afoot to establish 'an Argentine Orthodox Church'.[44] That fear underlay the nuncio's difficult relationship with Isabel Perón and her all-powerful minister, López Rega. Another source of tension, according to the same source, was Laghi's refusal to make episcopal appointments sympathetic to the Peronists.[45] In opposition to the express wishes of the government, for example, Laghi in March 1975 recommended the appointment of the coadjutor bishop of Buenos Aires, Juan Carlos Aramburu, as successor to Cardinal Caggiano. Installed on 22 April 1975, he was made a cardinal on 24 May 1976.[46] The Canadian ambassador reported that the nuncio had repeatedly articulated in 1975 and early 1976 the opposition of the Holy See to the threat of a coup d'état. That made him most unpopular in high military circles both during the Isabel Perón government and later during the civilian military dictatorship.

Characteristically *romagnolo* (haughty and shrewd) in manner, Laghi was highly intelligent and quick on the uptake but somewhat superior and stand-offish. He may not have been liked but he was respected. The US ambassador, Robert Hill, was close to the nuncio but not sufficiently partisan to be uncritical of his actions on occasions. Most diplomats were conscious that the Isabel Perón government was on its last legs. On 3 November 1975, Hill told the Canadian and Australian ambassadors, Bissonnet and Hugh Dunn respectively, that 'several reports suggested that the President was so emotionally unstable as to be virtually mad'. Nevertheless, he said she remained determined to stay in office, adding: 'She had expressed that determination in a phrase of shocking vulgarity, which Hill quoted when speaking to the Interior Minister [Ángel Federico] Robledo last week.'[47] But he declined to include the expression in his report. Amid rumours that the government wanted him to be recalled, Laghi hosted a dinner for two army officers before he left for Rome, at which he learned that the armed forces were eager to replace the president but were in a dilemma as to how it should be accomplished. According to the Canadian ambassador, 'the military used the analogy of a cork stuck in a bottle neck – do you get it out by pushing it down or pulling it out? Speaking from his Church position, the nuncio said he had persuaded the armed forces to let the Church handle the few priests who were considered to be actively supporting subversives rather than having the armed forces take direct action against the individuals'.[48] Laghi travelled to Rome in late November 1975 to brief his superiors in the secretariat of state at the Holy See. While there, he is understood to have received further instructions to oppose a coup d'état. Upon returning to Buenos Aires, he invited many senior members of the armed forces to visit him at the nunciature, on Avenida Alvear 1605, Barrio Norte.[49] Laghi, who had been criticised for his contact with the leading members of the armed forces before and after the coup, had Admiral Emilio Eduardo Massera (the commander-in-chief of the navy and later named a member of the junta after the coup) as a frequent visitor to the nunciature. Claudio Uriarte, Massera's unofficial biographer, confirmed that the nuncio played tennis with the admiral on Saturday mornings in the residence of the German ambassador.[50] But Uriarte noted that the relationship remained strictly formal, and correct titles were used on every occasion: *Su Excelencia* and *Señor Almirante.*[51] Horacio Verbitsky casts a very cold eye on Laghi's role in his multi-volume history of the Catholic Church in Argentina.[52] When he died in Rome on 10 January 2009, Laghi took with him to the grave his hidden history of his years in Argentina. Fortunately many of his observations and judgements are recorded in his reports lodged at the Vatican, which are alas as yet unavailable to researchers.[53] However, some related material, as will be seen later, has been made available by Pope Francis I.

In the months leading up to the coup d'état in March 1976, prices increased by 556.3 per cent, with a rise to 800 per cent anticipated for the following year.[54] On 17 November 1975, Lennon wrote presciently that despite the

4.1 Justin Harman, third secretary Irish embassy, on right, with the heads of the Argentine armed forces at a commemoration for Admiral William Brown, 3 March 1976

'dissatisfaction being expressed generally with the lack of government by the President or her Cabinet and her efforts to suppress the allegations of corruption in high places ... the possibility of an open military takeover has in my opinion receded – until at least mid-March next'.[55] Within a few weeks of Harman's arrival, Ambassador Lennon and his wife Kitty returned to Dublin on leave. In January, he had surgery followed by a long recuperation during which time he again requested unsuccessfully to be posted to Geneva. Lennon did not return to his post in Buenos Aires until mid-July 1976. Because of the length of the ambassador's stay in Ireland, Harman was given the title chargé d'affaires ad interim, making him temporary head of mission in the absence of his superior. By mid-January 1976, he was convinced that it was only a matter of time before the armed forces left their barracks and took control of the country: 'Essentially whether the hard line faction within the Armed Forces gains the upper hand will depend to a great extent on the Government's behaviour up until the elections in October.' His conclusion was that if the ultra-rightists won out, '*the events in Chile in 1973 could very well look tame in comparison*'.[56]

Harman, who was present on the podium on 3 March 1976 at the elaborate annual ceremony to mark the anniversary of the death of Admiral Brown (the Foxford-born founder of the Argentine navy), reported on the 8th that the naval chief of staff, Admiral Emilio Massera, had given 'a long and vivid description of Brown's austere life-style' which 'was seen as a reflection on the rampant corruption of present-day Argentina'. Harman singled out the unusual presence for the occasion of all three heads of the armed forces as being 'obviously a demonstration of unity'.[57]

What Harman was not in a position to know was that Massera would tell Ambassador Hill on 16 March that it was 'no secret that the military might have to step into the political vacuum very soon. They did not want to do so but at this point choices seem to be between military intervention and total chaos leading to destruction of the Argentine State'. The admiral also said that 'the military were fully aware of the need to avoid human rights problems should they have to take power' and that 'military intervention if it comes will not follow the lines of the Pinochet takeover in Chile'. Rather, he added, they would try to proceed within the law and with full respect for human rights. They had no intention of resorting to vigilante-type activities, taking extra-legal reprisals or taking action against uninvolved civilians'. Hill noted that Massera was 'very correct throughout the conversation ... all his comments [were] in the conditional tense'. Furthermore, the US ambassador emphasised that the admiral was speaking about 'hypothetical possibilities'.[58] As proximate events would show, Massera was part of the inner circle that planned a military takeover which would show no respect for human rights.

Pio Laghi had a succession of military visitors in the days leading up to the overthrow of the government. Archbishop Patrick Coveney confirmed to me that the nuncio and senior staff at the nunciature had knowledge of the planned coup days before it took place.[59] The British chargé d'affaires, John Shakespeare, thought that a coup was inevitable and among his colleagues at the mission there were those who considered it necessary. The British Foreign Office thought that 'no one could possibly run Argentina worse than the Peronist regime'. Shakespeare wrote a few days before the coup: 'Despite the reluctance of the military leaders to take this step, the consequences of the Peronist regime's three years in office were so dire that some such action became essential.'[60]

The US embassy reported on 22 March that large-scale troop movements had begun at noon.[61] The following day, a leading Argentine newspaper, *La Razón*, published the headline '*Todo Está Dicho*' ('All Has Been Said').[62] That evening – Tuesday – the president took a helicopter from her residence in Olivos to the Casa Rosada, where she presided over what turned out to be the final meeting of her cabinet. In the nearby Ministry of Defence at Paseo Colón 250, the 'new cabinet' of the armed forces was putting in place final preparations for the scheduled takeover. Meanwhile, public attention was elsewhere; River Plate and Deportivo Portuguesa (Venezuela) began their game at 10 p.m. in the Copa Libertadores international club competition being broadcast on TV Channel 7. A 2-1 victory for River Plate brought the celebrating fans onto the streets about midnight.[63] About the same time as the soccer festivities, shortly after midnight on 24 March, Señora Perón boarded a helicopter at the Casa Rosada to take her back to the presidential *quinta* (estate) in Olivos. The flight was diverted for 'technical reasons' to Jorge Newbery airport (known as Aereoparque) in the city, where she was detained. 'Are they going to shoot me? ['*Me Fusilarán?*']', she asked General Villarreal, who was in charge of her arrest.[64] She was flown to El Messidor, a small castle surrounded by gardens, near Lake Nahuel Huapi, Villa la Angostura, province of Neuquén. (Five years later, in July 1981, she was freed from her house arrest and sent into exile in Spain.) When Argentines woke on 24 March, Wednesday, they found that the country was under the control of the armed forces.

Harman, having anticipated in his recent reports that there might be a coup, learned from radio that overnight the military were in control. The TV and radio stations had been seized and were playing martial and patriotic music. The headline in *La Nación* on the 24th read: 'The Armed Forces Assume Power; President Detained'. Setting out early through semi-deserted streets, Harman arrived at the embassy by taxi without incident: 'All was eerily quiet. I was met by infantry troops who were at the front door of the building on Avenida Santa Fe which housed our embassy and the Colombian Embassy and Consulate.'[65] Because of a news blackout, Harman found it difficult to assemble the facts of what had been happening overnight. He sent a cable asking for policy guidelines on the issue of granting asylum to people who presented themselves at either the embassy or the ambassador's residence: 'so far appears unlikely asylum question will arise', he cabled, as both the embassy and residence had been surrounded by troops to prevent a 'refugee situation occurring'. Harman also flagged in the same cable the urgency of receiving instructions regarding recognition of the new regime, which would arise immediately. That morning, in the absence of Lennon, he attended an emergency meeting of EEC ambassadors and learned from his colleagues there via telegram that the 'junta was forced to move due possibility severe reaction right wing among military in face country's immediate crisis'. The meeting agreed that the military were in control of the country and that 'delays in acknowledgment [of the new regime] could weaken position of present moderate military leadership. Strength of right wing among military still unclear. Because of this I recommend acknowledgement soonest. Grateful learn whether any communication received Argentine embassy in Dublin. Generally situation calm and controlled'.[66] Harman, together with other heads of mission, had received a formal note from the foreign ministry outlining the reasons for the military takeover and 'requesting recognition of junta as government'. Harman commented that 'we would of course coordinate with community missions. At present position is each mission when it receives instructions will inform colleagues' and there was a possibility that 'a further meeting of ambassadors might take place to coordinate time of acknowledgement'.[67] No instructions arrived before he left the office that evening.

Harman, travelling by taxi, recalled that that night 'there was a broadcast on TV and radio of a soccer match',[68] a friendly international between Poland and Argentina in Silesian Park, Chorzów.[69] Many of the team played with mixed emotions after hearing news of the coup. Argentina won 2-1 on a snow-covered pitch before a crowd of 60,000.[70] On instructions from Iveagh House, Harman was living in the ambassador's apartment on the first floor of Alejandro María de Aguado 2881, C1425, Palermo Chico, currently the chancery of the embassy of Saudi Arabia. When he arrived, Harman found that the street was in complete darkness:

> As I started walking along the centre, I was challenged by voices which seemed to come from behind the trees lining the street. I stopped and shouted out who I was and where I wanted to go. Following what seemed an age (it was probably only a few moments) I was allowed to advance slowly along the street and eventually permitted inside the front gate. There was silence, broken by occasional sounds of what seemed like gunfire, although nowhere in the immediate vicinity. The overall effort to maintain 'normality' was a priority and seemed quite successful.[71]

The *Guardian* reported on 25 March that 'except for the occasional soldier and army vehicle, and the fact that the streets are more empty than usual, there is little outward evidence of the coup. Factories in the industrial areas around Buenos Aires are working normally'.[72] The same morning, *La Nación* devoted its front page to the fast-moving events of the previous day, the main headline announcing that three generals had taken control of the government. Another read: 'Parliament dissolved; Supreme Court removed; political and trade union activities prohibited; and a president will be appointed in due course.' In a few words, the paper succinctly told its readers that the armed forces had taken control of the national congress on the 24th, dissolved the national legislature and dismissed the Supreme Court. The Comisión de Asesoramiento Legal

(CAL) replaced the dissolved congress. All nine members were military men, three from each branch of the armed forces. They met in rooms in the former Senate and retained the services of many civil servants. A military junta was established, a triumvirate representing the three branches of the armed forces. General Jorge Rafael Videla became de facto president of Argentina and headed the junta and, when chosen, the civilian military government. He ruled with the help of his myrmidons until 29 March 1981, when he relinquished power to a military comrade. Under the Proceso de Reorganización Nacional (Process of National Reorganisation), the new government set out to reorganise the state institutions and to create the conditions for an 'authentic democracy' – based on a foundation of Christian morality which protected national security and eradicated subversion root and branch, rebuilding both the education system and good relations between employers, trade unions and the state. Argentina would take its place in the Western Christian world based on the promise to eradicate bad government, corruption and subversion.[73] Almost all of the most important positions went to military men but the civilian José Alfredo Martínez de Hoz was the exception; a devotee of the free market and the philosophy of neoliberalism, he held the Ministry of Finance from 1976 until 1981. Within a few days, the military had appointed another few civilians to ministerial positions; hence I call it a civilian military government, or dictatorship, in the text. (I have deliberately avoided using the term *guerra sucia* [dirty war] throughout the book as it lends legitimacy to the claim of the military that the takeover was to prevent civil war in Argentina.)

While Harman awaited instructions on the issues of recognition and asylum, Jeremy Craig, political division, discussed the coup with the assistant secretary, Noel Dorr. On the 26th, the Argentine ambassador visited Iveagh House and handed in a copy of the same text already delivered to Harman in Buenos Aires. The third secretary's instructions echoed those sent since the 1930s to many other Irish envoys abroad: 'Our general position on recognition of states explained to him and acknowledgement will issue from here in due course.'[74] Harman was also told that the Minister, Garret FitzGerald, had agreed to grant early recognition provided 'we are satisfied this is in accordance with practice in any previous similar case' and on the assumption that 'embassy did likewise in previous coup in 1955. Timing of acknowledgement and whether to await Nine co-ordination is matter for your discretion. While coordination is desirable you might feel at same time further delay unwise'. Harman was also told that 'the British wished to recognise the new regime and the matter was to be discussed by the EEC political directors. The Netherlands had given instructions on recognition to its ambassador in Buenos Aires'.[75] Iveagh House sent a cable on 26 March to the EEC political directors stating: 'Ireland's general practice is to recognise states rather than governments. Accordingly, the question of a formal act of recognition on our part of the new Argentine Government does not arise.' The EEC partners were further told that the Irish embassy in Argentina, which had maintained contact with the embassies of its partners there, 'has now been instructed that it may acknowledge the note received from the Argentine foreign ministry informing the embassy of the change of government and, if possible, to co-ordinate the time of this acknowledgement with the other embassies of the nine'.[76] Ireland and the other EEC countries quickly acknowledged the continuity in diplomatic relations with the Argentine state. Surprisingly, the Labour government in Britain was among the first to do so. Within two days of the coup, the British chargé d'affaires, John Shakespeare, communicated his government's recognition. Unlike Chile, 'no sanctions were imposed: there was no arms embargo, export credit was not cut, and trade and investment were encouraged', according to the historian Grace Livingstone.[77]

By 30 March 1976, Harman had accumulated sufficient information on the history of recent coups in Argentina to file a comprehensive report. It was, he explained, the 'seventh direct military intervention in Government in Argentina so far this century', which had 'finally put an end to what was undoubtedly one of the most agonizing and traumatic periods in the country's recent history'. He observed that an 'efficient, well planned and, as far as was known, bloodless coup' had been carried out 'in an atmosphere of complete calm among the general population, and a junta formed composed of the three branches of the armed forces'. Harman added that 'meticulous' organisation had, within a few hours of having assumed power, ensured that caretaker ministers had been appointed, the military governors for the provinces had been named, the union and employer organisations had been taken over and their funds frozen, the majority of the most prominent supporters of Mrs Perón's administration had been arrested and the embassies in Buenos Aires had been approached as to recognition of the junta. To avoid 'a Pinochet-type reputation', he reported that the new civilian military government had decided not to cut off international communications, resulting in the permission to transmit a 'vital international football match'. Censorship had been lifted after twenty-four hours. All combined to give an 'image of moderation'. As the national press was hostile to the Isabel Perón regime, the junta knew it 'would not be facing a hostile press'. Harman thought, based on the available evidence, that the new junta had behaved in marked contrast to previous dictatorships by stating that it would not take action against 'specific social groups' – meaning the Peronists. But he cautioned that it would be necessary to wait for some time to see whether that was in fact the policy.[78]

Harman described another aspect of the coup as showing an absence of 'emotional rhetoric appealing to the national sentiment of the population'. The military communiqués used 'the most austere of language'. There had been no attempt as yet to break up national institutions. The political parties had merely been suspended and representatives of the junta had been placed as heads of the universities. A decision had been made not to close the Congress building, and to retain the expert staff to help a newly established legislative advisory council. In 1966, the coup d'état led by Gen. Juan Carlos Onganía set out to establish a new political and social order. His military regime was not a temporary corrective before handing back power to the political parties. In contrast, his takeover had been followed by 'extraordinary measures against the political parties, universities, etc' and, Harman noted, 'in summary the strategy of the military has seen a profound change from previous coups, and particularly when compared to those of 1955 and 1966'. He argued that the military leadership 'was firmly within the school of thought of ex-President Lanusse, who led the way back to constitutional rule in 1973, and who was convinced of the necessity for the Armed Forces to remain outside the political arena'. Harman recorded that there had been frantic efforts by the Peronists on the night before the coup to find an agreement to promise the military unlimited concessions and seats in cabinet provided Mrs Perón remained in power, but, in the face of 'a real danger of total anarchy', the military had acted.[79]

Harman, who had earlier in the report hypothesised that what had emerged in Buenos Aires was not 'a Pinochet-type regime', qualified his appraisal of the new regime by saying that there would 'obviously remain an element of disquiet, until the names of all those arrested had been made public' and the military were 'seen to act as effectively against the right-wing terrorist groups which have operated in the country over the past 15 months as against those of the left'. He noted that General Videla, both commander-in-chief and a member of the junta, had promised a return to constitutional rule within less than three years. Harman was sceptical of that claim, stressing that the guerrilla movement in the country was 'one of the largest and probably the best organized in Latin America'. Having realised their objective of provoking a coup, he said, the guerrilla leadership 'will undoubtedly try and lead the military into a policy of repression in order to gain support among the general population'.[80]

If journalism is a first draft of history, diplomatic reporting also falls into the same category. Harman prudently warned Dublin that, irrespective of what had happened following the previous six military interventions in Argentine politics, historical parallels were not necessarily a reliable guide to what would transpire in the aftermath of 24 March 1976.[81]

Unlike Harman's cautious and nuanced report, US ambassador Hill told Washington on 29 March that the coup was 'the best executed and most civilized coup in Argentine history'. He concluded: 'Argentina's best interests, and ours, lie in the success of the moderate govt. now led by General [Jorge Rafael] Videla.'[82] He was convinced that the seizure of power could 'now definitely be judged as moderate in character'. For the time being, Hill thought that Videla was 'strong enough to keep the hardliners in check and impose a moderate approach'.[83] Hill ought not to be judged too harshly. Jorge Luis Borges, the doyen of Argentine writers, had lunch with General Videla after the coup d'état and thanked him 'for what he had done for the *patria*, having saved it from chaos, from the abject state we were in, and, above all, from idiocy'. He said that Argentina had 'a government of soldiers, of gentlemen, of decent people'. Later, Borges, as did many other Argentines and foreign observers, had a change of view of the civilian military government when the regime displayed its true nature. But, given his detestation of Peronism, Borges remained equivocal.[84] The editor of the *Buenos Aires Herald*, Robert Cox, who was later arrested and imprisoned, was also mistaken in his first impressions of the nature of the new regime. A seasoned observer, he was at that time positive in his reaction, thinking that the civilian military government would bring stability to the country.[85] The provincial delegate of the Pallottines, Alfredo Leaden,[86] who was stationed at St Patrick's, Belgrano, Buenos Aires, wrote to his superior on 17 April 1976: 'Since the military took over things have changed somewhat; the people look happier; there is a feeling of greater hope and that things will get better. Of course, we are in for a lean period and violence is by no means over. However, we have to thank the Lord that we haven't had a Chile-style revolution. Many people are being arrested amongst them some priests, but on the whole it has been a pacific changeover. Let's hope it keeps that way.'[87] It did not. Tragically, Leaden and four other Pallottines were, on 4 July 1976, assassinated by the forces of the 'moderately led' civilian military government. By May 1976, US ambassador Robert Hill felt compelled to protest to the Argentine government about the human rights abuses perpetrated by the dictatorship.[88]

STATE TERROR, KIDNAPPINGS, DISAPPEARANCES AND REPRESSION

Despite the religious rhetoric and professions of adherence to Christian principles, the new civilian military dictatorship quickly demonstrated that it borrowed more from the Chilean armed forces when tackling the task of 'restoring order' than it did from the New Testament or the other lofty religious vocabulary which characterised their early statements. The Argentine coup and aftermath were more violent, bloody and ruthless than those of the existing military regimes in neighbouring Uruguay, Chile and Brazil. An Amnesty International (AI) report published in March 1977 outlined the repressive legal apparatus introduced since the military takeover, stating: 'The military junta is now the supreme organ of the state and has taken upon itself extraordinary powers.' The divisions between legislature, executive and judiciary – the separation of powers – ceased to exist. The new executive exercised judicial functions. A state of siege, under Security Act 20.840, had been declared, prescribing severe prison terms for any person attempting to alter the social peace of the nation, or caught distributing literature or emblems of 'subversive organisations'.[89] Decree 21.264 changed a breach of the peace from being a minor offence, punishable by a fine or thirty days' confinement, into a major federal crime which carried a penalty of eight years in prison. The AI report noted also that the armed forces had been authorised to use firearms when a person was caught in the act and refused to heed a first warning. Law 21.272 imposed the death penalty for anyone causing serious injury or death to military personnel or police. The age of criminal responsibility was reduced to sixteen years – the age at which a prisoner could be executed. Under law 21.322, some forty-eight organisations were banned, as were all 'political acts' that related to a political party. Law 21.338 introduced the death penalty by firing squad within forty-eight hours of the sentence being pronounced. The same law made the penalties for 'illicit association' more severe. Law 21.460 allowed the police or armed forces to arrest anyone on suspicion alone when investigating a crime of subversion. It also provided that a confession from a prisoner might be used in evidence against him/her, in violation of Article 14 of the United Nations Universal Declaration of Human Rights.[90] Press censorship had become draconian. Under Communiqué 19, publication was forbidden of all news items concerning terrorist activity, subversion, abductions or the discovery of bodies. That decree also extended to comment on or reference to those subjects, including the death of members of the armed or security forces or on kidnappings and disappearances.[91]

The final clause of Article 23 of the constitution granted a citizen the right to petition to be allowed to leave the country, but, on 29 March 1976, Decree 21.338 annulled that right of option. The AI report concluded: 'In short, the new government, by taking upon itself the power to regulate the Right of Option of prisoners held at the disposal of the Executive Power, and by placing all trials of crimes of subversion under the jurisdiction of military courts which are themselves directly responsible to the President of the Republic, is violating the Constitution, which firmly states in Article 95 that "under no circumstances can the President of the Nation pass sentence or exercise judicial functions".'[92] This paragraph is particularly relevant when dealing in the following chapters with the cases of Fr Patrick Rice and Fátima Cabrera.

The civilian military government, under those draconian laws, immediately set about rounding up members of the professions, the trade unions, the Catholic Church, the Jewish community, the Protestant communities and Latin American political refugees who had come to Argentina to escape the very dangers they now confronted anew. Some 25,000 had arrived there between 1972 and 1976, mainly from Uruguay, Chile and Bolivia. Mr Jegler of the United Nations High Commissioner for Refugees (UNHCR) visited Buenos Aires and briefed Harman on his findings: about 14,000 refugees had been registered with UNHCR; about 4,000 of those had been resettled outside Argentina. The UNHCR had 10,000 cases, not including dependants, on its books. Less than 2,000 had received work permits. Political refugees were very vulnerable in the new circumstances. On 20 May 1976, Harman alerted Dublin to the increased danger in which those refugees were living. He noted that there was increased diplomatic activity between the dictatorships in Chile, Brazil, Bolivia, Uruguay and Paraguay. He concluded that those contacts were 'an indication of an increasing solidarity among these countries' which would become more evident at future meetings of the Organisation of American States (OAS). Operating a campaign of transnational repression, that consortium of dictators implemented what became known as Operation Condor.[93] In another report, on 26 May 1976, he gave details of the murder of two Uruguayan senators in Buenos Aires[94] and the abduction of twenty-four Chilean refugees. He wrote that it had been the work of 'right-wing terrorist groups' and he confirmed an escalation in the killing of political refugees.[95] Fr Patrick Rice, working in Villa Soldati, went to the site where the bodies had been left – the municipal rubbish dump – and administered the last rites. On 1 June 1976, Juan José Torres, a former left-wing president of Bolivia, was kidnapped and assassinated in Buenos Aires; his tortured body was found a day later. Videla refused him a public funeral. His wife took his remains to Mexico for burial.[96] Harman concluded that 'the continuing spate of political murders, and particularly those which are being carried out in an apparently unrestricted manner by the right-wing terrorist groups, all provide an indication of the growing loss of control over the situation by the Junta, and by President Videla himself in particular'.[97]

Videla and his associates had not lost control of his subordinates in the armed forces. The 'cleansing' of society was a long time in the planning. Detailed lists had been drawn up of citizens targeted to be disappeared, interrogated under torture and, in many cases, 'executed' without due process.[98] The kidnap or snatch units were called 'task forces'. The army ran Task Forces 1 and 2 and the Navy Task Force 3. The air force was in charge of Task Force 4 and the State Intelligence Agency (SIDE) ran Task Force 5. Rear Admiral Rubén Jacinto Chamorro and Captain Carlos Acosta Ambone led Task Unit 3.3.2, or Unidad de Tareas 3.3.2. It was based in the Escuela Superior de Mecánica de la Armada (Navy Mechanical School, ESMA), a very large site on Avenida Libertador in Barrio Nuñez. The detainees were housed in the basement, the attic or loft and on the third floor of the Casino de Oficiales. An estimated 5,000 people were 'disappeared' from that complex.[99] Today it has been renamed as the Espacio Memoria y Derechos Humanos ex-Esma (Space for Memory and for the Promotion and Defence of Human Rights).[100]

There was a 'healthy' competition between the different task forces as they vied with each other to prove which of them was the most 'efficient', ruthless and patriotic. Working in groups of five or six, a 'snatch squad' often drove a Ford Falcon without number plates. Receiving prior warning of 'an operation', the local police would helpfully seal off the area around the targeted address, sometimes blocking streets and cutting off electricity to ensure there would be no interruptions. The military unit would gain entry to a home at gunpoint, identify the target/s, handcuff, blindfold and hood them and take them to an awaiting car or truck. It was quite common for the kidnappers to steal objects of value from an apartment. A single captive was usually stuffed into the boot of a waiting Ford Falcon. An operation was timed to last under five minutes. The *chupados* (literally, those who had been sucked up) were driven to clandestine torture centres directly or via police headquarters.

During the time of the civilian military dictatorship, there were thought to be over 340 Centros Clandestinos de Detención (CCD). Later there were estimated to be between 320 and 520[101] dotted throughout Argentina.[102] By 1984, that figure had been revised upwards to over 700, and might even be higher given further information that has since come to light.[103] Members of a task force rotated the different duties of kidnapping, interrogation, torture and

murder, the better to ensure complicity and mutual silence.[104] No member of
the Argentine armed forces – save one exception – has ever given details of his
official role in enforced disappearances, the running of clandestine detention
centres or the killing of the detained-disappeared (*detenidos-desaparecidos*).
Adolfo Scilingo, a retired naval officer who was serving a thirty-year jail sentence
for his crimes, gave an extensive interview in 1993 to Horacio Verbitsky on
which he based his book *Confessions of an Argentine Dirty Warrior*, published
in 1996.[105] Scilingo admitted to going on 'the flights', a term used to describe
the practice during the civilian military dictatorship of throwing drugged
prisoners out of aeroplanes at night over the River Plate. Scilingo and other
officers would check nightly on coming to work at the ESMA to see whether
they were assigned to go on a 'flight' during their shift. Prisoners were told that
they were being transferred to the south of Argentina. A navy doctor gave them
a 'vaccination' which turned out to be a heavy sedation. Loaded on to covered
green navy lorries, they made the short journey to the nearby military airport,
where the same officers carried the barely conscious prisoners to a navy Skyvan
for the 'flight'.[106] Scilingo or his other fellow officers rostered for the flight then
dumped the prisoners out of the plane at high altitude and to certain death
in the River Plate. Disturbed and feeling guilty, Scilingo consulted a navy
chaplain, a member of the military vicariate,[107] who provided him with the
following 'Christian explanation' for what he had just done: '... telling me that
it was a Christian death, because they didn't suffer, because it wasn't traumatic,
that they had to be eliminated, that war was war and even the Bible provided
for eliminating the weeds from the wheat field'.[108]

THE CIVILIAN MILITARY GOVERNMENT TARGETS CATHOLIC PRIESTS,
NUNS, CATECHISTS AND MEMBERS OF OTHER RELIGIONS

Besides Argentine political activists and foreign refugees, the civilian military
government also targeted so-called subversives who were members of the
Catholic Church. Emilio Mignone, a lawyer and a former Peronist minister
for education, was the founder president of a public university, the University
of Luján, and held that position at the time of the military coup in March
1976.[109] When soldiers invaded his campus on the day of the coup, he evaded
arrest and went into hiding. All universities were placed under direct military
control. Deprived of his job, he resumed his ordinary life, living with his
wife and children in their apartment at Avenida Santa Fe 2949. His second
child, Mónica, twenty-four, worked as an educational psychologist at a local

hospital and as a teaching assistant in her father's university. She also worked as a catechist with three of her friends and two Jesuit priests, Orlando Yorio and Francisco (Franz) Jálics, in Villa Belén, Bajo Flores. On 14 May 1976, at 5 a.m., five men stood outside Mignone's apartment, banging on the door and demanding entry.[110] 'This is the Argentine army. We've come for Mónica Mignone,' they yelled. At first, Mignone thought that he was going to be the one arrested. He opened the door. 'Show me your identification,' he asked as a machine gun was waved in his face.[111] Four of the raiding party held his family at gunpoint in the kitchen while the officer in charge went into Mónica's bedroom, ordering her to put on her clothes. Unnoticed, she managed to slip her address book to her sister as she dressed. Mignone asked if they were from the intelligence service. They claimed in reply that they were from the First Patricios, a regiment of the first army corps based in Palermo. More likely, they were a navy unit, working out of the ESMA.[112] The officer told Mignone that they wanted to question his daughter about another person. She was being taken to Palermo barracks. The family was assured that Mónica would return home in about two hours. Her mother gave her the pesos to pay the taxi fare home. The entire operation was over within four minutes. Mignone last saw his daughter as her abductors put her into the narrow lift outside the apartment. Immediately afterwards, he rushed downstairs to follow the captors' car but the air had been let out of all four of his car's tyres. Mignone and one of his sons then hurried to the apartments of Mónica's friends to warn them but they were too late. That same morning, a catechist working in the *villa* with Mónica had also been disappeared. Beatriz Carbonell was taken away with her husband, as was a pregnant María Marta Vázquez Ocampo and her husband. María Ester Lorusso had been seized in her apartment at 3 a.m. the same night as Mónica's abduction. Another of her friends was picked up the following day. All were lifted between 13 and 14 May, all the daughters of well-placed and influential people: an ex-government minister, a military officer, a diplomat and a church worker. None survived.[113]

When Mignone discovered that his daughter's friends had also been taken, he went to the Palermo barracks, where they denied any knowledge of his daughter's whereabouts. He then went to his local police station to register her abduction. There were no witnesses to the disappearance of Mónica, not even the guards at the home of a general who lived next door. They were conveniently 'not on duty' that night.[114] He then made a distressing round of calls on the nuncio, the archbishop of Buenos Aires, etc., without receiving any help or hope. He told me he was convinced his daughter had been taken to the ESMA, interrogated, tortured, drugged and then put on 'a flight' and dumped out alive over the River Plate.[115] Mignone, who lectured at University College Cork in 1989 and with whom I maintained a friendship, died in 1998 without anyone ever being charged before the courts with Mónica's murder.

After the abduction of the four catechists, the two Jesuit priests, Yorio and Jálics, refused to obey their provincial and superior, Fr Jorge Mario Bergoglio (now Pope Francis I), who was reported to have instructed them to leave the *villa*. A group of fifty marines 'disappeared' both men on 23 May as they celebrated mass in the *villa*. Horacio Verbitsky, who investigated their disappearance,[116] is highly critical of Fr Bergoglio for the manner in which he allegedly acted. The two priests were held in the ESMA, left tied up and hooded for three days. Fr Bergoglio made strenuous efforts to have them freed. He went to see Admiral Massera in his office and tried unsuccessfully to demand their release. Instead, both were 'transferred' to a CCD or clandestine detention centre in a house about fifty kilometres from Buenos Aires. While they were hooded and handcuffed, with their legs bound together, they were tortured and interrogated; they were not murdered. On 23 October 1976, five months after their kidnapping, they were taken by helicopter and set free in a swamp area near Cañuelas. Fr Jálics was later reconciled to his former provincial: 'It is thus wrong to claim that our capture was initiated by Fr Bergoglio,' he said.[117] Fr Yorio wrote an account of his ordeal in 1977. Having worked for the remainder of his life in the diocese of Quilmes, he died in 2000 unreconciled to the former Jesuit provincial. His sister Graciela continued to campaign for the holding of a full investigation of Fr Yorio's case.[118]

The above is merely a sliver of the state of terror that existed in Argentina at the time, where nobody was safe from becoming a *desaparecido*. Catholic Church activists were merely one vulnerable group but the same could be said for the activists in other Christian churches: Episcopalians, Methodists, Presbyterians and Jehovah's Witnesses. Anti-Semitism was an integral part of the culture of repression also and many Jews were disappeared between 1976 and 1982. The repression took a great toll on actors, artists and musicians, on the professions, on trade unionists and on ordinary men and women critical of the regime. Nobody, but nobody, could consider themselves safe from arbitrary detention, interrogation under torture, long-term imprisonment or disappearance.

History moved swiftly in the weeks following the coup. The civilian military dictatorship wanted to 'get the job done'. While they did not have official support from the US government for their actions, there were powerful voices in Washington 'understanding' of their position. In Santiago, Chile, on 6 June 1976, the US secretary of state, Dr Henry Kissinger, told the Argentine minister for foreign affairs, Vice Admiral César Augusto Guzzetti: 'Look, our basic attitude is that we would like you to succeed. I have an old-fashioned view that friends ought to be supported. What is not understood in the United States is that you have a civil war ... We want a stable situation. We won't cause you unnecessary difficulties. If you can finish before Congress gets back, the better.'[119] Ambassador Hill, shocked when he received news of those comments, made a formal protest to his superiors in the State Department and received a supportive message that US policy remained unchanged and that Kissinger's words did not represent the official stance of the US government.[120]

When confronted by accusations of repression, the strategy of the Argentine government was to deny that there was any such thing going on in their country. Guzzetti denied to a reporter at the UN in August 1976 that there was any such thing as 'subversion or terrorism by the right' in Argentina. He argued, using the language of biology, that his country was a social body contaminated with an illness which had formed antibodies.[121] The antibodies could not be considered the same as the germ, he explained: 'As the Government controls and destroys the guerrilla, the action of the antibodies is going to disappear ... This is just the natural reaction of a sick body.'[122] Such language dehumanised Argentine citizens, turning them into *subversivos*, with violence the necessary state-administered 'antibiotic' to eliminate the 'germs' and heal a 'sick society'.[123]

JUSTIN HARMAN, IRISH DIPLOMACY AND ATTACKS ON IRISH-ARGENTINE RELIGIOUS

Harman welcomed another Irish diplomat to Buenos Aires – Mgr Kevin Mullen, a priest from County Meath, who took over from the departing Mgr Coveney as second-in-command at the nunciature on 23 May 1976.[124] Ordained in 1964, he joined the diplomatic service of the Holy See in 1969.[125] Having served in Rome, Bangkok and Bangladesh, he was posted to Damascus in 1973, remaining through the Yom Kippur war and the beginnings in 1976 of Syria's intervention in the Lebanese civil war. Those postings prepared him well for the role he would be called upon to play in Buenos Aires.[126] Federico Richards wished Mullen, in *TSC* on 25 June, 'a happy stay amongst us and the greatest success in fulfilling his delicate mission'. The adjective 'delicate' was apposite. Mgr Austin Mullen told me that his brother had prepared well for the challenges he would face in Buenos Aires. Being deeply committed to the cause of human rights, he added that his brother was ever willing to help those who were oppressed. 'Kevin had a good relationship with Pio Laghi' and he

4.2 Formerly of the diocese of Meath, Mgr Kevin Mullen, first secretary, apostolic nunciature, Buenos Aires, 1976–9, talking to journalists through the railings of the nunciature.

always heard him refer to the nuncio 'in a friendly way' and 'seemingly had good communications with him',[127] Austin Mullen said. Shortly after Kevin's arrival a woman 'journalist' came to the nunciature ostensibly to interview him. He knew instantaneously that the military had sent her to try to snare him in a 'honey trap'.[128] That tawdry plan failed, as would efforts later to intimidate him into silence. Robert Cox, the editor of the *Buenos Aires Herald*, became his close friend.[129] Both Cox and his wife, Maud Daverio,[130] invited Kevin frequently to their home, which was very near the nunciature. They came to admire him greatly for his tenacity and courage when helping the relatives of the disappeared who came to him for assistance in tracing their loved ones. During the two and a half years he served in Buenos Aires, he badgered the authorities constantly to find out whether the missing were alive or dead. High-ranking members of the military and the federal police rewarded him with the unenviable nickname: Monseñor Rojo (the Red Monsignor).[131] According to many contemporaries, he ought to be named as one of the righteous for the courage he frequently displayed in his daily work (see Chapter 6).

When Mullen first arrived in Buenos Aires, the prevailing view in diplomatic circles was that Videla was a moderate who blocked the efforts of the far right in the armed forces from replacing him with a hawk. So all-pervasive was that erroneous view that Mullen, too, fell in temporarily with that line of thinking. Justin Harman, who became friends with Mullen, reported on 25 June: 'While it is certain that President Videla is personally opposed to the use of such methods [state terror], he is apparently powerless to stop them' because 'hard-liners' were determined to take 'a tougher stance' against both 'the subversives and the various left-wing political activists'. While 'dissatisfaction with his [Videla's] moderate approach clearly does exist', he noted, '... there is as yet no firm indication that his position is in danger'. Harman concluded that 'individual military participation' was suspected 'in the activities of such groups as the Triple A'. There had been public surprise that the activities of the Triple A had not stopped after the coup, he reported, but that was explained away because 'it never in fact existed as a fully-fledged organisation with Head Quarters, etc., but rather is composed of individual groups who take "private action" against "leftists", and then simply ascribe it to the organisation'.[132] But there was overwhelming evidence at that point that the armed forces and the police played an integral role in the campaign of disappearances. Reporting on the 26th, Harman told Dublin:

> ... the most frightening aspects of the current situation are the indications that active members of the Armed Forces are participating in these right-wing terrorist groups. The cases of the Uruguayans, that of Torres and those of the 24 Chilean refugees all have certain characteristics in common which point clearly in this direction. The incident concerning the refugees is a case in point. 40 armed men arrived at the hotels in trucks, identified themselves as members of the security forces and took them away. The fact that this occurred close to the city centre and not very far from a police station all lead one to the conclusion that individual units of the armed forces are taking matters into their own hands.[133]

EEC counsellors, including Harman, had, at a recent meeting, accepted those conclusions as fact. He reported those views to Iveagh House.[134]

During the early months of the civilian military dictatorship, the activities of the two religious communities traditionally associated with the chaplaincy to the Irish community had come to the notice of the military authorities. Both the Passionists and the Pallottines were committed to pastoral work in the federal capital and in the camp. They gave annual retreats and taught in the schools run by their respective orders. By 1976, many members of the orders working there were Irish-Argentine or Argentines descended from other immigrant groups. While Holy Cross was historically the spiritual home for many lay Irish-Argentines living in the federal capital, the radical pastoral message was delivered by members of the order in sermons and in their writings at that time. The content of the once conservative *TSC* changed radically under the editorship of the Passionist priest Federico Richards. The letters columns of the newspaper provided regular evidence of the displeasure of a number of Irish-Argentines regarding the editorial policy of Richards, who fearlessly each week presented a critical commentary on what was happening in the country. His editorials and his column, *'Desde el Mangrullo'* ('From the Watchtower'), exhibited a firm resistance to the human rights abuses perpetrated by the civilian military dictatorship. At different times, Richards was persona non grata with his religious superiors, with the conference of bishops, with the Federation of Irish-Argentine Societies and with the government on account of his multiple weekly fulminations – described by Horacio Verbitsky as 'thunderous' editorials in which 'without a silencer' he constantly denounced 'the state's violation of the human rights of its citizens.'[135]

The Holy Cross monastery complex had become a centre of resistance to the government's Proceso de Reorganización Nacional. It occupied the entire block or Manzana Santa Cruz, in Barrio San Cristóbal, between calles Estados Unidos, Urquiza, 24 de Noviembre and Carlos Calvo. It housed the church and the monastery, as well as a number of institutions devoted to education and pastoral formation. Fr Bernardo Hughes was the parish priest. He ran a very active parish in line with the teachings of CELAM. Hughes[136] was replaced in May 1976 by Mateo Perdía, a close friend of the Nobel laureate Adolfo Pérez Esquivel. Eugenio Delaney became parish priest in the middle of 1977. Christian base communities (CBCs) were established in the parish. The *Revista Santa Cruz*, first issued 20 June 1976, was widely respected. Frs Carlos O'Leary and Jorge Stanfield were also active. The Holy Cross monastery had become a place of sanctuary in the mid-1970s for Chilean and other refugees from Latin American dictatorships. The order's Casa Nazaret, at Calle Carlos Calvo 3121, was a centre of prayer, reflection and solidarity where Frs Eugenio Delaney,[137] Bernardo Hughes, Mateo Perdía and Federico Richards worked. The Passionists also helped found the Movimiento Ecuménico (MEDH) (Ecumenical Movement for Human Rights), la Asamblea Permanente por los Derechos Humanos (APDH) (Permanent Assembly for Human Rights) and a Centre for Justice and Peace. A French nun, Alice Domon, who was deeply involved in the work of those organisations was murdered in December 1977. Three Irish Dominican Sisters, Terence O'Keeffe (superior), Dymphna Tipper and Brigid Fahy, taught in the Colegio Santo Domingo, formerly the

Keating Institute, across the road from the monastery. During the years of the dictatorship, priests, nuns and refugees living in that large complex experienced a climate of constant menace. On 24 August 1976, a bomb was placed at the front door of Casa Nazaret.[138] When it exploded, part of the front door was blown in and the windows shattered in the building and in the nearby school.[139] Graffiti on the monastery walls read '*Viva Videla*' and '*Fuera Curas Comunistas*' ('Communist Priests Out').[140] Surprisingly, no Passionist priest was murdered between 1976 and 1983. Tragically, that was not the case for the Pallottine order, five members being murdered by the armed forces.

The Pallottines ran a school and the parish of St Patrick's, in Belgrano. This had become a fashionable upper-middle-class suburb in Buenos Aires where a number of senior military personnel lived with their families locked behind security railings in English-style houses. Videla had a home a few blocks from the church and often attended mass there on Sundays with his wife, Alicia Hartridge.[141] The military governor of Neuquén, Gen. Martínez Waldner, lived near the church and his home was guarded round the clock, together with that of Videla and at least one Supreme Court judge who also lived nearby. The provincial delegate or superior of the Pallottines in Argentina, Alfredo (Alfie) Leaden, was based in St Patrick's. His brother Guillermo, a Marist, was an auxiliary bishop of Buenos Aires. Leaden, the superior of an all-Argentine community in the Belgrano house, was universally admired and respected. He had great personal charm and strength of character and was never found wanting in courage or determination. Alfredo Leaden's leadership was tested severely in the early months of the dictatorship. His commitment to the service of others ultimately cost him his life. John Mannion, who became parish priest of St Patrick's in the middle of July 1976, said: 'The first weapon that was fired at our martyrs were the rumours from this parish community.'[142] He referred to a whispering campaign that the Pallottine community was made up of *zurdos* (left-wingers) and *subversivos*.

Alfredo (Alfie) Kelly, the parish priest in St Patrick's, oversaw the management of the parish school. Besides, he was director of studies, in charge of religious formation for the small number of seminarians attached to the house. Born in Suipacha in 1933, his parents, Lisa (Casey) and Johnny, were farmers. (Harman would marry Carmen Casey. Lisa was a sister of Tomás Casey, Carmen's grandfather.) Alfredo attended secondary school at a Pallottine college and then joined the order in Rawson. He studied in Rome, and, visiting Ireland for summer holidays in 1954 and 1955, stayed with the Power family in Midleton and with Fr Tony Stakelum's family in Tipperary.[143] Kelly had been heavily influenced by the ideas of a German Pallottine, Fr Joseph Kentenich,

4.3, 4.4 & 4.5 The three Pallottine priests (clockwise from top left), Alfredo Leaden, Alfredo Kelly and Peter Duffau, murdered on 4 July 1976 with two seminarians, Salvador Barbeito and Emilio Barletti, by persons unknown in St Patrick's, Belgrano

who was a courageous public witness against Nazism, surviving three years in Dachau. He founded the Schoenstatt Apostolic Movement in 1914 in Germany and established branches in Chile and Argentina. Attracted by Kentenich's teaching, Kelly went to Chile as a young priest to learn more about his ideas.[144] A courageous and dedicated priest, he was a victim during the last weeks of his life of mendacious rumours that he was left-wing and there was also a further falsehood circulating that he was even linked to the Montoneros.[145] Juan José Delaney, the Irish-Argentine writer, who lived with his aunt and uncle near the monastery during this period, told me that he used to go frequently to Sunday mass with his Jewish friend, the painter Andrés Waissman, to hear the outspoken Kelly preach.[146]

Fr Pedro Duffau, a third community member, had no Irish family roots but he had studied in Thurles between 1927 and 1930. A former principal of the parish school, he was a curate of a conservative bent who frequently clashed with Kelly.[147]

Salvador Barbeito and Emilio Barletti, a seminarian and a postulant, also lived in the house together with another student. The former had taken first vows. Barletti, born in San Antonio de Areco on 22 November 1952, was undecided about his future in religious life. Patrick Rice told Verbitsky that Barletti had shared a meal with the Little Brothers in La Boca at which Frs Gazzarri, Bustos and Silva were also present. Barletti, who was active in Cristianos para la Liberación (Christians for Liberation), spoke to them about his inner struggles and that he was thinking of leaving the Pallottines.[148] On 4 July, all five were murdered. The sequence of events is as follows. The Montoneros planted a bomb on Friday, 2 July, in the dining room of the Coordinación Federal, the central federal police headquarters. The blast, timed to go off at lunchtime, was reported to have killed twenty-two policemen and one civilian and injured sixty. The following day, the minister of the interior, Gen. Albano Harguindeguy, held an emergency meeting with senior police officers to formulate a response. That morning, the bodies of three women and five men were found shot dead in a parking lot in San Telmo. The bodies of six youths were also found at Villa Lugano, in southern Buenos Aires. Sanctioned or otherwise, the death squads continued their work that Saturday evening, 3 July.

Meanwhile, the provincial of the Pallottines, Fr Alfredo Leaden, became anxious about the deteriorating situation in Buenos Aires. He decided to forego an invitation to attend the installation that weekend of Alfredo Mario Espósito Castro as bishop in the new diocese of Zárate-Campana. He chose instead to remain with his confrères in the monastery in Belgrano, who continued with their normal duties. Fr Duffau celebrated a nuptial mass in a church in another part of the city. Originally intending to remain overnight at the wedding festivities, he changed his mind and returned to Belgrano later that night. Kelly had supper that Saturday evening with Leaden and later went to visit Abel Tapino, whose home was a few blocks from the monastery.[149] He had appointed the latter to act as a mediator in a management dispute enveloping their parish school which also involved Fr Duffau.[150] Kelly spoke freely about the circumstances in which the Pallottines then lived – the tapping of the monastery's phone, the growing number of recurring threats and a deteriorating atmosphere in the parish resulting from the denunciations by conservative residents of the order's alleged pastoral philosophy.[151] Kelly, the parish priest for three years in St Patrick's parish, had been targeted for personal attack. A letter calling for his dismissal was allegedly in circulation and had been signed by an unknown number of parishioners. 'If anything might happen to me, the signatories of that letter are going to have to repent [of their actions],' he commented.[152] Kelly said goodnight to his friends and walked the short distance back to the monastery. Salvador Barbeito and Emilio Barletti had gone to the cinema in the city centre with a third seminarian that evening. The latter went to stay with his parents while the other two took a bus back to the monastery.

Fr Patrick Rice, who was living underground and alone in a safe house in Soldati, recalled that a death squad had gone first that Saturday night to the Capuchin monastery where Fr Bustos used to stay sometimes. By good fortune he was out. The same unmarked car proceeded to the parish of Nuestra Señora del Carmen, in Villa Urquiza, where the postulant of the Little Brothers Fr Pablo Gazzarri was living. He, too, was out.[153] That same car later drove to Belgrano. Two youths returning home early on the morning of Sunday the 4th stopped off in the house of a friend about a quarter of a block from St Patrick's church and monastery. As the policeman guarding the nearby home of Gen. Martínez Waldner talked to the youths, a black Peugeot pulled up and the driver signalled to the policeman to come over to the car. The youths overheard him ordering the policeman: '*Si escuchas cohetazos no salgas, que van a reventar una casa de zurdos*' ('If you hear loud shots don't come out as we are going to bust up the house of leftists'). Suspicious of what was likely to happen, one youth, the son of a senior army officer, called the local police station to report the presence of the suspicious car.[154] He had to identify himself for the policeman before his call was taken seriously. A police car was despatched to Calle Estomba and approached the occupants of the Peugeot. Its driver was overheard saying abruptly: 'We are on an assignment. Get out of here!'[155] Later, a neighbour saw heavily armed men get out of the car, ring the community's doorbell and gain entry to the monastery.[156]

On Sunday morning, Rolando Savino, the parish organist, arrived about 7.30 a.m. at the church to serve the 8 o'clock mass. He was surprised to find a church worker, Señora Celia Harper, standing outside a locked monastery. Ringing the bell and knocking brought no response. Savino found a half-open skylight in a side patio and climbed into the monastery and opened the door from the inside. Savino then made the grim discovery of the five bodies lying on the carpet in the community room in pools of blood. Leaden, Kelly, Duffau, Barbeito and Barletti had been shot in the head at close quarters. It was confirmed later that they had been beaten, tortured and violated. Written on one of the doors were the following words: '*Por los camaradas dinamitados en Seguridad Federal – Venceremos – Viva la Patria*' ('For our dynamited comrades in Federal Police Headquarters – we will win – long live the homeland'). Written on the floor was the following: '*Estos zurdos murieron por ser adoctrinadores de mentes vírgenes y son MSTM*' ('These left wingers died because they were indoctrinators of innocent minds and were members of Movimiento de Sacerdotes para el Tercer Mundo').[157]

On hearing the terrible news, Harman went immediately to Belgrano to express his condolences on behalf of the ambassador to the members of the Pallottine community who had arrived from Mercedes, San Antonio de Areco and other towns in the camp. The federal police chief, General Arturo Corbetta, and the second in command of the first army corps, General Jorge Olivera Róvere, visited the scene to begin an 'investigation' of the capital crimes. The official investigators did not observe even the basics of good police work and unsurprisingly nobody was ever charged for those crimes.[158] That remains the case in 2022. As the news of the massacre spread, a crowd gathered outside the locked church, shock, grief and disbelief showing on the faces of parishioners, relatives and friends. Just after midday, Monsignor Guillermo Leaden, the brother of Alfredo and an auxiliary bishop of Buenos Aires, said mass in a convent a block away. When the church was finally opened that afternoon, two priests led the congregation in the rosary and other prayers. The bodies of the murdered priests and seminarians were placed in open coffins in front of the main altar. A mass was said at 4 p.m. Later, hundreds filed past the bodies until well after midnight, among them Justin Harman, who cabled on 5 July:

> Deeply regret to inform you of tragic assassination over weekend of three prominent Argentine-born members of Irish Pallottine Fathers

... Fr Leaden was superior of Pallottines here but Argentine region of order is actually under Irish Province. While all three priests were of Irish descent none were in possession Irish passports. However, all three had many contacts and friends in Ireland having studied for some years in a seminary Thurles ... assassinations apparently politically motivated. Grateful inform Ambassador Lennon and indicate condolences expressed on his behalf.[159]

Iveagh House phoned Ambassador Lennon at his home in Dublin to inform him of what had happened. A minute on the file noted that he had been aware of the tragedy from the media reports. Lennon had last been at his post in Buenos Aires in November 1975. There is little doubt that his prompt return to Argentina after the massacre was consequent to Dr FitzGerald giving him a clear and unambiguous instruction to resume his post.[160]

Harman attended the funeral mass on 5 July, concelebrated by about two hundred priests of whom thirty-five were from the Pallottine order. The congregation overflowed into the street outside the main door and around the corner in front of the monastery. Bishop Guillermo Leaden presided. The attendees included Cardinal Juan Carlos Aramburu, the primate of Argentina, and the minister for foreign affairs and public worship, Admiral César Augusto Guzzetti. The papal nuncio, Pio Laghi, was accompanied by Mgr Kevin Mullen. The congregation included Kelly's mother Elisa Casey, his three brothers Dickie, Jack and Clement, and his sisters Gerty and Mary.[161] The Leadens were also represented by another brother, Patrick, and three sisters. Fr Duffau's sister, a nun, was present. Salvador Barbeito's parents and his sister were in attendance as were Emilio Barletti's mother Natta and his brother Gastón. Fr Kevin O'Neill, a Pallottine, gave a short homily on the theme of peace, pardon, faith and hope. 'Come back to Erin' was one of a number of Irish airs played on the organ during the mass.[162] So large was the congregation that priests had to go into the streets outside to distribute communion.[163]

The Conferencia Argentina de Religiosas (Argentine Conference of Women Religious) and the Confederación Argentina de Religiosos (Argentine Confederation of Male Religious) read a joint statement before the end of the mass. After the final blessing, the five coffins, followed by a large line of mourners, were taken in procession along Calle Estomba and the adjoining streets. The cortège left for Mercedes, stopping en route at Castelar, where Fr Duffau had founded a parish. Arriving in Mercedes, Videla's birthplace and home town, another huge crowd gathered to receive the cortège inside and around St Patrick's church.[164] A large number of priests concelebrated requiem

4.6 Bodies of the five Pallottines lying in state before the altar in St Patrick's, Belgrano

mass at 10 a.m. on Tuesday the 6th. Thousands of friends and parishioners lined the streets as the coffins of the three priests were driven to the local graveyard a few kilometres outside the town. They were buried in the Pallottines' plot in the presence of surviving parents, brothers and sisters, relatives, confrères and church dignitaries.[165]

The official reaction of the church hierarchy came on the Wednesday. Cardinal Aramburu sent a letter of protest on behalf of the Argentine Episcopal Conference to General Videla and his government.[166] One of the most fearless journalists in Buenos Aires, Robert Cox, the editor of the *Buenos Aires Herald*, asked the leading question on 5 July: *Cui bono* ('Who benefits?'). He informed his readers in the same editorial that fifty people had been killed over the previous four days, with the usual official justification being given 'that the victim is of this or that political persuasion'. With 'every unsolved murder, our society dies a little because there is no justice in vengeance', he wrote, urging that it was necessary to identify the criminals 'behind every act of terrorism and bring them to justice so that we may see exactly in which dark corners danger lurks'.[167] Fr Richards was equally blunt in his *TSC* editorial on 9 July, asking pointedly: 'May we know who is managing and arming the delinquents who are kidnapping, torturing and murdering?' As an illegal, clandestine war was being waged in the country, he wondered why the military and the police were unable to arrest and prosecute members of the Triple A. He noted that 'ethical citizens' found such impunity 'completely inexplicable'.[168]

Consternación y horror ante la masacre sacerdotal

Miles de fieles tributan su homenaje

En esta hora inaudita que vive l Argentina, se escribió esta se-iana un sangriento capítulo que r tiene precedentes en toda la storia del país: la despiadada iasacre de toda una Comunidad ligiosa, sin distinción de edad o ndición.

Para la Comunidad argentino undesa esta dolorosa tragedia se ribetes de una desgracia per-al, porque las víctimas de es-nueva locura subversiva han s los Padres Palotinos, colum-deade hace casi un siglo de stras comunidades y familias. s población despertó el domin-son la inconcebible noticia del

P. ALFREDO LEADEN
R.I.P.

de una conocida y respe-nilla de nuestra Comu-ontaba 57 años. Orde-i unos 35 años, había cur-estudios en Thurles, Ir-Juego en Roma. Sirvió en as comunidades palotinas i, Mercedes y San Anto-eco. Una de las figuras guidas de su Orden ocu-ilmente el cargo de Su-or de la Vice Provincia '. Palotinos. Hombre de rtud, caballero en la to-i de la palabra, era ama-s feligreses y amigos.

Cerca de doscientos sacerdotes y una multitud de fieles rodean los féretros en la Misa exequial

frío e inhumano asesinato de los PP. Alfredo Leaden, Alfredo Kelly, Pedro Duffau y los seminaristas de la Congregación Salvador Barbeito y José Emilio Barletti, miembros de la Comunidad religiosa sita en la iglesia de San Patricio, en Belgrano.

LOS HECHOS

De todas las fuentes posibles hemos podido recoger que el brutal asalto a la parroquia de San Patricio se produjo en la madrugada del domingo 4, probablemente hacia las 3 de la mañana, cuando ya algunos de los religiosos estaban entregados al reposo y otros a punto de hacerlo, luego de regresar. No habiendo testigos, se presupone que los asesi-

nos hayan tocado el timbre, y penetrado dentro al ser contestada la llamada. Qué pasó luego, sólo Dios y los monstruos lo saben, pero al llegar los feligreses para la primera Misa a las ocho y ver cerradas las puertas del templo y nadie contestar a las llamadas a la casa parroquial, un joven, luego de violentar una ventana hizo el terrible descubrimiento: el cadáver de los tres sacerdotes y dos seminaristas, acribillados a balazos.

Sobre la puerta de una de las habitaciones estaba escrita la leyenda: "por nuestros hermanos policías dinamitados" y sobre una alfombra roja, otra que leía: "a los que pervierten las mentes de los jóvenes". Se comprobó asimismo que se había realizado una re-

quisa de la casa especialment libros, papeles y hasta casset Se abría para todo el pa interrogante de quiénes seria autores de la masacre y c sus motivaciones.

VELATORIO DE LOS RES

La horrible noticia corrió damente por la ciudad y una titud continua, comenzó a e sar a los fieles que acudí templo de San Patricio, ani de compartir el dolor de lo Palotinos, de manifestar su sión y su repudio y ofrece oraciones por los religiosos ficados. Este desfile duró to domingo hasta pasada la me che, permaneciendo los fiel

(Continúa en la página 2)

4.7 Front page of *The Southern Cross* on 9 July 1976 reporting the reaction to the murders

Bishop Guillermo Leaden, brother of the murdered Alfredo, celebrated mass on Sunday, 11 July in St Patrick's, Belgrano, before another overflowing congregation. The superior of the Pallottines, Andrés Kessler, was present as were Kevin O'Neill, the provincial, Patrick Dwyer and John Mannion. In a short homily, Leaden said the murdered priests had set a beautiful lesson in their lives and that their deaths had all the features of martyrdom, adding: 'They have wanted to shut those voices up [of the assassinated] but their voices

4.8 Editorial in *The Southern Cross* on 9 July condemning the massacre

are even stronger from their graves. Nothing or nobody may shut up the voice of the Church.'[169] Leaden asked everyone to listen to 'that voice which is not going to be silenced by any human forces'.[170] When I met Bishop Leaden in 2016, he repeated to me over and over again: 'They murdered my brother. They murdered my brother.'[171]

There was a consensus at the time in ambassadorial circles that the killings had been carried out by agents of the state. The Canadian ambassador, A.P. Bissonnet, reported on 17 July that his US counterpart, Hill, had concluded that 'it was right wing police job and that some of priests had been involved in minor way in third world activities' but he had dismissed an 'earlier police statement to effect that priests had been sheltering Montonero leader [Mario], Firmenich' as 'fabricated, deliberately misleading and false'. Concluding his report, the Canadian envoy wrote: 'there is no doubt but that Argentina today is in hands of jackboot govt. with shades of fascism and Nazism evident'.[172] Attending a meeting of EEC political counsellors towards the end of July 1976, Harman reported that there was agreement that some members of the security forces had been 'involved in that [Pallottine] affair, most likely motivated by a desire for reprisal following the bombing a few days previously of the central police head-quarters in which some 20 people died. It was also the view of the meeting that all five had been shot in order to avoid the identification of the perpetrators'.[173] Thirty-six years later from his prison cell, Videla still could not bring himself to issue an apology for the murder of the Pallottines, saying merely that it was '*un acto de torpeza tremenda*', or 'a tremendous blunder'.[174] Thousands – many Irish-Argentines – had disregarded their personal safety at the time and had defiantly turned out to attend the various liturgies for the murdered religious. Each occasion was an act of defiance, which uncovered delicate shards of hope in the interstices between repression and resistance.

CHAPTER FIVE

Irish Diplomacy and the Disappearance, Torture and Illegal Detention of Fr Patrick Rice and Fátima Cabrera

Hundreds of bodies were thrown over the mountains, lakes and sea of Chile. Perhaps a dream dreamed there were some flowers, there were some breakers, an ocean, raising them up out of their tombs in the landscapes. No. They are dead. The non-existent flowers were already spoken. The non-existent mourning was already said.[1]

Ambassador Lennon returned to Buenos Aires from Ireland in late July 1976 to find that much had changed in the eight months that he had been away. Asking an unidentified anti-Peronist 'leading light' if things had altered in his absence, he was told: 'Yes – for the worse.' His informant predicted that the junta 'which is on the whole, liberal, may be displaced by a stronger rightwing faction and a situation like Chile develop'. But he was hopeful however that 'a Chilean position may be averted' based on the perceived popular support for General Videla and for the Minister for Economics, José Alfredo Martínez de Hoz,[2] which would allow them to use even stronger measures against left-wing terrorism. In point of fact, the Argentine situation already shared a number of the characteristics of Pinochet's post-coup Chile and worse was to follow. A recurring theme in Lennon's reports in the weeks ahead was the danger of a coup within the coup. 'All visible signs seem to indicate', he wrote on 19 August, that Videla could still be unseated by the hardliners – 'something which, if it happens, could see Argentina following the Chilean lead. Terrorism both by Government and opposing forces is on the increase. Although, as usual, the press reports only a small part of the actual kidnappings and killings, scarcely a day passes with less than five to ten deaths being reported and it is significant how many of these consist of "terrorists killed while trying to escape". He quoted an air force source confirming that 'the number of deaths runs into hundreds each week and bodies are cremated – no records being kept'. The general impression was that the honeymoon was over and that matters could deteriorate rapidly, he reported, adding: 'It is not considered safe to walk out-of-doors after dark even in the top diplomatic residential areas of Palermo Chico – where the official residence is. The disappearance of two Cuban Embassy staff[3] has not inspired confidence in the Corps, particularly in the "Socialist" bloc and security has become one of the main topics of conversation at diplomatic receptions.'[4]

While Lennon and his fellow diplomats felt unsafe in one of the most fashionable suburbs of Buenos Aires, the lawyers, teachers, doctors, priests, nuns and catechists who worked in the *villas* and in remote towns in the pampas were exposed to being spirited away at night by government forces or kidnapped in broad daylight on a street crowded with helpless eyewitnesses or the complicit, whose mentality was summarised in the expression *algo habrán hecho*, meaning 'they must have done something' (to be disappeared). Since the Pallottine massacre on 4 July, Catholic Church workers and those of other religions had reason to fear arbitrary detention, torture and disappearance. Raúl Eduardo Rodríguez and Carlos Antonio Di Pietro, two Assumptionist seminarians and friends of the Little Brothers, were disappeared in San Miguel, province of Buenos Aires, on the same day the Pallottines were killed.[5] The Mafia-style 'executions' of the five Pallottines and the campaign of state-sponsored terrorism drove a number of religious to go underground, fearing for their lives. For example, Rice and his confrères were worker priests living in *villas*. That was sufficient in itself to place them under suspicion. As they had full-time jobs by day, they were visible to the authorities. He frequently visited his cousin, Sr Terence O'Keeffe, a Dominican nun who worked in Colegio Santo Domingo with Sisters Dymphna Tipper and Brigid Fahy. Rice often said mass there, shared a meal with the sisters and sometimes ran classes for catechists. His mother used the convent address to send him letters.[6] Rice got used to changing his route to work every day and moving his place of residence frequently in order to avoid capture.[7] Fr Mauricio Silva was the only one of the Little Brothers who refused to go underground. He lived openly in Calle Malabia in the Palermo Hollywood district. He went to work as a road-sweeper at the same time every day, where he covered the same block of streets. Two young lay members of the Little Brothers, Carmen and Lorenzo, lived with him. They had fled San Miguel after the disappearance of the two

Assumptionists.[8] The fact that Carlos Bustos and Pablo Gazzarri were founder members of the recently formed Peronist Cristianos para la Liberación was another reason why they were persons of interest for the authorities. Rice described it as 'a movement seeking to act as the nucleus for the reconstruction of the progressive sectors of the church to replace the defunct Movimiento de Sacerdotes para el Tercer Mundo (MSTM)'.[9] The military authorities saw it in a very different light. Beyond the scope of this book, Cristianos para la Liberación is a subject for further research.

A month to the day after the murders at St Patrick's, there was another assassination which captured international headlines. The bishop of La Rioja, Enrique Angelelli, a close friend of Rice and the Little Brothers, had lived for many years with the knowledge that his name appeared frequently at the top of death lists. Known by his enemies as 'Satan-elli', he faced opposition from the local military and from the ultra-conservative Sociedad Argentina de Defensa de la Tradición, Familia y Propiedad (TFP) over his progressive pastoral policies. Many of his priests worked under the same sense of menace. In February 1976, the vicar general of the diocese, Esteban Inestal, and the parish priest of Olta,[10] Eduardo Ruiz, a Capuchin, were arrested. The commander of the air force base in Chamical Lázaro Aguirre accused Bishop Angelelli of being mixed up in politics because of the content of a homily he had delivered. Religious ceremonies at the base were suspended. Fr Águedo Puchetta was arrested in Chamical. An Irish SMA priest, Tony Gill, was imprisoned for a short time and was released following a strong intervention by Angelelli.[11] On 18 July, the cadavers of Frs Gabriel Longueville and Carlos de Dios Murias, together with the layman Wenceslao Pedernera, were found near Chamical – blindfolded and with their hands tied execution-style behind their backs. All three had been tortured and then murdered. The bishop had known de Dios Murias since he had joined the Franciscans as a boy in Córdoba. Rice also knew the murdered priest very well. He had been a frequent visitor to the Little Brothers in Suriyaco and Rice often drove him back to his parish.[12] Longueville, born in France in 1932, came to work in Argentina in 1969. He worked with de Dios Murias in the parish of El Salvador, in El Chamical.[13] Pedernera, married with three children, was an organiser of the Rural Catholic Movement.

In view of the heightened danger to Angelelli's life following the three murders, his fellow workers tried to persuade the bishop not to drive to Chamical to preside at the funerals. Nevertheless, he went, said the funeral mass and attended the burials. The bishop used his time there also to investigate the circumstances surrounding the murders, receiving documentary evidence which implicated named members of the military in the killings. He set out

5.1 Fr Patrick Rice, Little Brother of Charles de Foucauld, at a press conference in London, March 1977

with his driver, Fr Arturo Pinto, to return to La Rioja on 4 August but was murdered in a staged accident at Punta de los Llanos on Route 38. Pinto, left for dead on the road by his attackers, survived and later bore witness to the fact that their vehicle had been rammed and forced off the road.[14] In his testimony at several trials, the priest repeated that an old truck which he had seen earlier on their journey had come up from behind, passed them out at speed and then cut across the front of their vehicle, forcing them off the road. Pinto, who was badly injured, said in evidence that he was knocked unconscious as the vehicle rolled over. It is possible that Angelelli may have regained consciousness before his attackers delivered the coup de grâce – a blow to the head. His corpse was then dragged by the assailants into the middle of the road. The killing of the five Pallottines, Bishop Angelelli, his priests and the layman, had a Machiavellian purpose – it sent the macabre message that nobody was beyond the reach of the death squads.

The Little Brothers received the news of their friend's death with great shock and personal sadness. None believed the official reports that his death was the result of a freak road accident. His driver had survived and he was an eyewitness to what had actually happened up to the time he was rendered unconscious. It was decided at a community meeting of the Little Brothers that Rice and Carlos Bustos would travel to La Rioja to investigate the bishop's cause of death and publish their findings. Fr Gazzarri was asked to remain in Buenos

Aires to prepare reports on the assassination of Fr Carlos Mugica and on the massacre of the five Pallottines. Rice and Bustos made the 1,155 kilometre bus journey to La Rioja during a 'state of siege'. While stopping to change bus lines in Córdoba, soldiers subjected them to an intensive interrogation and search of their bags. They were allowed to continue their journey. Upon arrival in La Rioja, they visited the bishop's house and were invited to share a meal with the community. Rice recalled the sorrow of the priests and nuns at the sight of the bishop's vacant chair.

They were thorough in their investigations. Bustos' fellow Capuchins who worked in the area, Frs Antonio Puigjané and Eduardo Ruiz, helped greatly with inquiries.[15] After travelling to interview people in Chamical, Rice and Bustos completed their work and returned to Buenos Aires convinced beyond all reasonable doubt that the bishop had been murdered. They compiled a report with the help of Gazzarri which was entitled '*Informe sobre la violencia contra la Iglesia de las comunidades parroquiales de Capital Federal y el Gran Buenos Aires*' ('Report on violence against the Church in the parish communities of the Federal Capital and of greater Buenos Aires'). Rice typed the text. It was signed by '*grupos parroquiales de Buenos Aires*' ('parish groups of Buenos Aires').[16] Reproduced on a mimeograph machine, copies were clandestinely circulated by hand in the city and in the camp. No copy of the original Spanish version, to my knowledge, has survived. It is probable that a copy may be found in the files of the Ministry of the Interior. Rice told me that the authorities had identified him as being one of the authors of the report. He also told me he had learned from a reliable source many years later that the minister of the interior, Gen. Albano Harguindeguy, had been infuriated when he read the report. A government document showed that the authorities had regarded Rice for three years as being a person of interest.[17] The circulation of the report placed him in a higher category of danger and at risk of imminent 'arrest'. Rice made his personal position more perilous when he translated the text into English and had it smuggled out to London, where it was published in mimeograph format in October by the Catholic Institute for International Relations (CIIR) entitled 'Death and Violence in Argentina'.[18]

On 3 August, the day before the Angelelli murder, a priest from the diocese of Connecticut and a missionary of Our Lady of La Salette, Fr James Weeks, was arrested in Córdoba, together with five seminarians (four Argentines and one Chilean). Weeks was refused access to a US consular officer on the grounds that he was being accused of subversion and was being held incommunicado.[19] But news of his detention leaked and the US embassy formally protested on 9 August and again on 12 August demanding his immediate release. Consular access was granted on 16 August and Weeks was released the following day. Arriving back in the United States, the priest denounced his captors and exposed the fact that five seminarians of his order had been imprisoned and tortured. Fr Weeks, whose experiences are the subject of a study by Fr Gustavo Morello,[20] remained a strong critic of the Argentine government and would later work for the release of Rice.[21]

Justice remained decades away for Angelelli and the two priests and the layman who had died within weeks of each other. The official military investigation at the time found that Angelelli had been killed in a highway accident. In a democratic Argentina over thirty years later, a judge found in November 2011 that the death of the bishop was 'a planned and premeditated act'.[22] The trial revealed that Angelelli had in his possession, at the time of his murder, documents which implicated the interior minister Harguindeguy in certain crimes. The then commander of the third army corps, Luciano Benjamín Menéndez, was found to have been implicated in the assassination. Other high-ranking officers in the La Rioja region were also indicted. The judgment convicted fourteen members of the military, including Videla, for the crime of murder. Justice was finally rendered to Bishop Angelelli.[23] Three years later, in a case brought by Fr Esteban Pinto, Menéndez, who was then eighty-seven, was found guilty of ordering the murder of Angelelli. Retired commodore Luis Estella was also found guilty in the case. Both were sentenced to life in prison. Menendez was already serving a life sentence for his previous conviction in seven human rights abuses. The Argentine-born Pope Francis I ordered the release of two letters from the archives of the Holy See that Angelelli had written to Rome shortly before his death denouncing the military's involvement in murder and disappearances. The letters were read out in court.[24] Pope Francis I approved the decree on 8 June 2018 that Angelelli, the two priests, Carlos Murias and Gabriel Longueville, and the layman, Wenceslao Pedernera, were martyrs.[25] The beatifications of the four took place in La Rioja on 27 April 2019, during which Cardinal Giovanni Angelo Becciu said the four men were killed 'because of their active efforts to promote Christian justice'.[26]

Going back now to August 1976, Fátima Cabrera, who worked with Fr Carlos Bustos, experienced what it was like to live during the repression in Villa Soldati in Buenos Aires. She recalled for me her personal experience as a catechist and as an active member of the proscribed Peronist Youth Movement. As in Nazi-occupied Europe during the Second World War, activists put up posters clandestinely at night and painted anti-government graffiti on *barrio* walls. Leaflets were distributed when safe to do so. Cabrera told me also that she and her friends made an effigy of Videla and displayed it in a place in the *villa* where it could be seen by people on their way to work. But there was a price to be paid for such acts of resistance, defiance and protest. Nobody was immune from being *chupado*, or sucked up, by the death squads. Her friends Negrito Martínez and his partner Silvia – seven months pregnant – were disappeared on 20 August 1976. Earlier two other friends, Nelly and her partner Guillermo, were taken and later dumped from a car on the street, having been tortured and badly beaten. The nearby city rubbish dump continued to be used by the death squads during the time of the civilian military dictatorship to dispose of the bodies of their victims.

Ambassador Lennon during August 1976 reported to Dublin on the escalation in state-sponsored violence in the capital. On 3 September, he wrote that 'the wave of criticism of the [Catholic] Church now apparently prevalent in all Latin-American countries seems to be extending in Argentina', where one leading general defended the actions of his government, claiming that 'it was not criticism of the Church but of specific clergy who "sympathized"! with the subversives'. Lennon also noted that, in parallel, there was 'a growing wave of anti-Semitism' and that 'Jewish shops and synagogues have been shot up and bombed'.[27] Mgr Mullen reported from the nunciature in greater detail than Lennon on the rising death toll. The Holy See, angered by the flagrant breaches of human rights, kept Pope Paul VI informed about the deteriorating situation. When the new Argentine ambassador to the Holy See presented his credentials on 27 September 1976, the pope departed from protocol to issue a reprimand to the Argentine government, saying: '... as common Father, we cannot but participate intensely in the anguish of those who have been dismayed by the recent episodes which have cost the loss of precious human lives, including those of various ecclesiastics. These facts took place in circumstances which are still awaiting an adequate explanation. At the same time we deeply deplore this increase in blind violence'.[28] When opened, the foreign ministry archives in Buenos Aires ought to reveal whether the statement had any impact on government policy.

But it did not deter the Argentine military from searching in early October for Patrick Rice and his confrères. During the first week of the month, the police detained John Cleary, then an Irish Pallottine priest, when he left the monastery at St Patrick's to collect a prescription in a nearby pharmacy. Fearing for his confrère's safety, Fr Kevin O'Neill had followed him to the shop. There, he found Cleary surrounded by four men demanding to see his identity card, which he had inadvertently left behind in the monastery. O'Neill offered to return to get it and two of the men went with him. The remaining two stayed to guard Cleary. When O'Neill returned with the document, the four in unison accused Cleary of drug trafficking and insisted that he accompany them to the police station. There he underwent a rough interrogation. O'Neill phoned for help to the office of the archdiocese and the Irish embassy. Following an intervention by Ambassador Lennon, Cleary was released. A short time later, a police source told Fr Juan Mannion, PP of St Patrick's, that the episode had been a case of mistaken identity. The police had a tip-off that Patrick Rice was in the monastery. Mistaken for Rice, Cleary had been picked up in error.[29]

Argentines had a public holiday on Monday, 11 October, celebrating what was then called Columbus Day or Día de la Raza. While the embassy was closed, Ambassador Lennon reported to Dublin that evening about two recent unsuccessful attempts on the life of President Videla. The second failed attempt was the work of a sniper: 'I have heard it suggested that only the Army could have mounted these attempts,' he wrote.[30] Back in Villa Soldati that same evening, Bustos, who was required elsewhere in the parish, asked both Rice and Cabrera to run the weekly meeting of the Movimiento Villero Peronista.[31] It was illegal for more than three people to meet together. But in defiance of the law of assembly, about eight people, using assumed names, met in the home of a member of the *comisión del barrio* (neighbourhood commission).[32] At that time, Rice had met Cabrera only a few times and he did not know her real name. He only found out later as they were being kidnapped. At the meeting, one of those in attendance gave Cabrera a packet of *obleas*, or self-adhesive leaflets, printed by the Confederación General del Trabajo de la República Argentina – CGT de la Resistencia, for short. The fliers were to be distributed to other activists.[33]

Cabrera waited to meet Rice at the door after the meeting and asked to speak with him. She wanted his help to get medication for her younger sister, who had been suffering from depression after being violated by a policeman. Rice, because of the danger of a woman walking alone at night, offered to accompany her to her home, saying that they could chat on the way.[34] It was about 8 p.m. and completely dark. (There were no street lights.) They had to pass through an area at Calle Mariano Acosta,[35] where a man jumped out of a van parked in the shadows near Avenida Cruz, shouting: 'Stop or I'll shoot.' Rice recalled: 'We didn't know what to do. He seemed very nervous. He fired a shot into the ground. He pointed his gun at us and asked for our documents.'[36] Rice, in another account, said that he fired another shot in the air when they gave him their documents.[37] Another man carrying a gun came around the corner: 'They bundled the two of us into the back of the van. At no time did they identify themselves.'[38] Both were taken the short distance to Comisaría 36 (Police Station 36), in Villa Soldati. It was unusual for the victims of enforced disappearances to be taken to a local police station because of the risk that they might be recognised by locals.[39] Both were well known in the area and news quickly got out that they were being detained there. Rice and Cabrera were hooded and put into separate rooms. Cabrera was punched repeatedly in the stomach while being questioned. At the same time, in another room, Rice was handcuffed and 'my shirt was pulled up over my head and face. They asked my name and where I lived. I identified myself as a priest. I was then beaten up'.[40] Later, while seated on a chair, he was beaten about the head, face and testicles. Whistling and making noise to cover up his shouts, his interrogators stamped on his bare feet. Taken to a cell, other men came later to tell him that he was being handed over to the military.[41] They said coldly: '*Los romanos fueron muy civilizados con los primeros cristianos comparado con lo que te va a pasar a vos*' ('The Romans were very civilised towards the early Christians compared with what's going to happen to you').[42] At one point in his interrogation, Rice had been told that 'some 30 soldiers had just arrived from Tucumán, and that they are going to have fun with the Cabrera girl'. He was roughed up again, and at about 11 p.m. he was taken outside, where two men in civilian clothes joined the original abductors: 'So they took me out, still with a hood over my head and put me in the boot of a [Ford Falcon] car. Since I am a big man, they had something of a problem in getting me in. I heard Cabrera crying in the back seat but we arrived very quickly.'[43] Cabrera could hear the struggle to stuff Rice into the boot of the car. On the journey, she was seated between what she believed were two military officers, who ordered her to keep her head looking down and they questioned her as they drove to an unknown destination. One of the men asked her if she could swim: 'Better if you can't,' he added, meaning that she would likely wind up at the bottom of the river. The car made a number of very abrupt turns, in order, Rice felt, to disguise the location of their next place of detention. When the car stopped, Rice was taken inside the clandestine detention centre. Cabrera, left in the car alone with one of the men, had to fight him off as he attempted to assault her. Taken inside the building, she recalled, though hooded, catching a glimpse of a uniformed soldier giving maté to the men who had been in the car with her, confirming her suspicions that they were all officers in the armed forces. As he stood in handcuffs, Rice recalled his hood was removed 'and replaced by a yellow canvas hood with strings round the neck'. The man making the switch said to me: 'Don't look at me. If you look at me, you're a goner.'[44] Hearing traffic moving close by, Rice got the impression that their new place of detention was a building between two highways. Cabrera told me that only a few years before Rice died on 7 July 2010, they found out they had been taken to Garage Azopardo, Calle Moreno

1417, which at the time was allegedly being used by the Mantenimiento de Automotores de la Superintendencia de Seguridad Federal (Car Maintenance Section at the Superintendence of National Security [belonging to the Federal Police Department]).[45] Rice and Cabrera, when visiting their former clandestine detention centre, or Centro Clandestino de Detención (CCD), decades later, found that the interior of the building had been altered in order to disguise its original use.[46] W.H. Auden captured the mundanity of evil in his poem 'Musée des Beaux Arts':

> About suffering they were never wrong,
> The old Masters: how well they understood
> Its human position: how it takes place
> While someone else is eating or opening a window or just walking dully
>   along.[47]

While most Argentines strolled 'dully along' in ignorance and innocence past that CCD, Rice and Cabrera together with other disappeared people were being interrogated under torture. From shortly after their arrival at nearly midnight on the 11th and all day on the 12th, both were 'interrogated' separately and without a break while very loud music drowned out their screams. Repeatedly accused of having collaborated with 'terrorists', Rice's interrogators demanded he give the names of people in the *villa* who were involved with subversive groups. Despite being constantly beaten and punched, he denied any such involvement, telling his torturers over and over again that he was a priest who did manual work by day on a construction project between Avenida La Plata and Estados Unidos, and by night he administered the sacraments and did pastoral work in the *villa*. He wrote later: 'By this time I was in a bad state.' Forced to lie on the floor, he was handcuffed behind his back and beaten all over his body with the butt of a pistol: 'I had lived in Argentina for six years and knew about the torturers and what to expect. I was then submitted to water torture. My nose was held and water was poured in my mouth. You swallow a lot of water and it has a drowning effect. My interrogators told me that they belonged to the Triple A.' The beatings and the drenching continued at three- or four-hour intervals through Tuesday, 12 October while his feet were chained to the wall of his cell. The screams of other prisoners were worse than his own suffering, he recalled, adding that, as he was taken to another room from his cell later that night, 'I knew that electric shock treatment was coming'. Removing his hood, they replaced it with a blindfold and strapped him to a bed in wet clothes. So forceful was the electric shock that he involuntarily broke his restraints and landed on the floor. As he lay there, he became aware that Fátima Cabrera was in the same room being tortured. Her torture had gone on all day long too, he said.[48]

Over thirty years later, Cabrera wrote: '*Ellos, los militares, eran los dueños de la vida*', meaning that 'those, the military, were the masters over life [and death]'.[49] Stripped naked, her interrogators used a sandbag to beat her all over her body. They applied electric shock with a cattle prod (*picana*), which they sometimes put in her mouth to prevent her from screaming. Cabrera wrote that her torturers taunted her and the other women prisoners that they would not be able to have children after what they were being put through.[50] She said that 'they tortured us all night. When we asked to go to the toilet, we were taken but then tortured with greater intensity. Finally, we did not ask to go to the toilet'.[51] She told me in 2019: 'After a night of being tortured, I was forced to walk the length of the building to an office where an army officer ordered me to remove my hood. I was very weak and disorientated. Forcing me to look at him was his way of letting me know that he was able to do whatever he wished with me. He said: "*Yo ya estoy jugado y vos de acá no salís*" ("I have already played my hand. You will never get out of this place [alive]").' Putting a statement in front of her, he ordered her to sign it. If she did so, he said, the interrogation (torture) would end. When she read the document, Cabrera immediately realised that she was admitting to being a member of a subversive organisation if she signed. She flatly denied that allegation and refused to sign. So sure was the official that she would not live, he allowed her to see him. She was sure he was a military officer. Calling out to one of her torturers, he gave the order: '*Ésta está todavía entera, llévala y denle más*' ('This one is still unbroken. Take her away and give her more [torture]').

Rice was in the same room when Cabrera was brought in on a chair and placed near where he was being tortured. The beatings she received were so severe, she lost all track of time. There were moments, she recalled, when she had the sensation that she was no longer alive. She prayed to die when she felt she could take no more. Rice was told that, while he was strong and capable of resisting the electric shock, because of him 'they were going to destroy Fátima'.[52] They were both tortured in the same room and at the same time. At one point, Cabrera heard one of the torturers say excitedly, '*El cura canta*', meaning that they had broken him and that the priest was 'singing'. When an English translator arrived, he discovered that Rice was praying for his captors and torturers in Latin and in Irish.[53] The torture continued for both of them. When he heard Cabrera screaming again, Rice attempted in desperation to lift his hood off. His torturers started to choke him and he lost consciousness.

When Rice came round, he heard the torturers urgently calling for a doctor as Cabrera had stopped breathing and they could not revive her.[54] (A severe asthmatic, she had had no medication since being 'lifted'.) A woman doctor arrived and succeeded in bringing her round. She prescribed medicine for the 'patient' and ordered one of the torturers to rush to the nearby Faculty of Medicine in the university to fulfil the prescription. In the perverse netherworld of that secret torture chamber, perhaps the doctor remembered why she first studied medicine as she brought Cabrera back from the brink of death.[55] But as she drifted in and out of consciousness, Cabrera heard one of the torturers say that the prisoner had to be saved because the United Nations were asking about her. Later, she also overheard another of her captors being told on the phone that senior officers were enquiring about herself and Rice.[56]

Writing about his experience decades later, Rice said:

> I never thought very seriously that one day I was going to be taken. Even up to today I find it hard to believe that here are human beings, so depraved and perverse, that they can torture other completely defenceless human beings. Now I know that it is the case that the human being has the unique capacity for brutality and evil. Although I had a terrible experience, I have to confess at the same time one can find the presence of God in the middle of such pain and uncertainty. During that time I never felt truly defeated and I believe, with Fátima imprisoned beside me, we shared something very profound with our brothers and friends who are no longer alive.[57]

Rice quoted the words of the murdered archbishop of San Salvador, Saint Oscar Romero: 'If they kill me, I will be resurrected in the struggle of the people.' He also quoted Tertullian in the same essay: 'The blood of martyrs is the seed of Christians.'[58]

On 3 December 2018, some forty years later, I sat beside Cabrera in a courtroom in Tribunales de Comodoro Py, Buenos Aires, at the beginning of the trial of the former intelligence officer Raúl Antonio Guglielminetti and five federal policemen accused of violating her human rights and those of over a hundred others during the civil military dictatorship.[59] The instant Guglielminetti walked into the courtroom in handcuffs, Cabrera recognised him as the man who had sent her back for more torture when she refused to sign a confession. Justin Harman appeared as a witness at a later session of the trial on 9 May 2019.[60] Guglielminetti eventually received a sentence of life imprisonment to accompany the other sentences he was already serving.

A RACE AGAINST TIME: DIPLOMATIC REACTION TO THE ENFORCED
DISAPPEARANCE AND KIDNAPPING OF AN IRISH CITIZEN

The Irish embassy learned quickly about Rice's abduction as the news travelled swiftly through a network of parishioners, colleagues and friends. It is probable that he was recognised by locals at the police station in Villa Soldati. Fr Juan José 'Chiche' Kratzer, a member of the Little Brothers, phoned the ambassador's residence on the night of the kidnapping.[61] The following day, he went to the embassy on Avenida Santa Fé to tell Lennon personally all he knew about the disappearance. (The ambassador, see below, reported that the embassy first found out at 4 p.m. on the 12th.)[62] Kratzer also went to the nunciature and to the office of the archbishop to report the kidnapping of Rice and Cabrera. In normal times, he would have gone to a police station to make a denunciation. He did not do so on this occasion out of a well-founded fear that he, too, would be disappeared. Kratzer alerted sympathetic local organisations and phoned the fraternity's headquarters in Belgium to tell them of Rice's disappearance.[63] Prior François Vidil, the congregation leader, made contact with the Rice family in Fermoy. The same day, Vidil phoned Cardinal Aramburu to request him to intervene with the authorities over Rice's abduction. Fr Guido Doglione, representing the fraternity, appealed to Garret FitzGerald, the minister for foreign affairs, in mid-October for help seeking information about the Irish priest's arrest, place of detention, reasons for his detention and his state of health.[64] Bishop Dermot O'Mahony, head of the Irish Commission for Justice and Peace, also contacted the Department of Foreign Affairs, the Argentine embassy in Dublin and the head of the junta in Buenos Aires requesting information about Rice's kidnapping and disappearance.[65]

In a telegram to Iveagh House on 13 October, Ambassador Lennon provided a timeline of the actions of the embassy following confirmation of the disappearance:

> Confirming call re abduction in Buenos Aires suburb of worker priest Patrick Michael Rice (from Curraghmore, Fermoy Co. Cork, passport n. F126126, born 29.9.45) at approximately twenty-one hours on eleventh and reported to us at sixteen hours on twelfth. After having extracted full information from colleagues of priest we made our first representation to foreign ministry [seeking information about Rice's condition, whereabouts and welfare] at twenty-three fifteen hours on twelfth [delivered by Justin Harman] and again on morning and evening of thirteenth. Assurance has been received that machinery now in

motion to locate his whereabouts and secure release. We have advised his colleagues to seek writ of *habeas corpus*. Press here has given full coverage to disappearance and all main news agencies have now contacted embassy for information. We have also enlisted help of nunciature and ministry of interior.[66]

The records of the papal nunciature in Buenos Aires also shed additional light on Rice's abduction. An undated minute in the files, in Italian – probably written on the 13th – recorded a meeting between Justin Harman and, most likely, Kevin Mullen. It stated that four of Rice's priest confrères – two of whom were street cleaners – had been in touch with the Irish embassy. Rather than make a denunciation to the police, the text read in Italian that the priests had instead informed the Irish embassy as they were afraid to present themselves at a police station lest they, too, would be held. The nunciature instructed Harman to advise the priests to get in touch with their bishop. (In this minute, Rice's work was described in Italian as a carpenter [*falegname*].) The minute, probably written by Kevin Mullen, stated that Archbishop Adolfo Tortolo had been informed, as had Mgr Graselli and Padre Gustin. On 13 October, the papal nuncio Pio Laghi reported Rice's disappearance to his superiors at the Holy See. He also sent a note to both the foreign ministry and the minister of the interior, General Albano Harguindeguy, requesting information about the priest who had been kidnapped (*secuestrado*) in the Villa Fátima area close to the main road to Ezeiza airport.[67]

Sr Terence O'Keeffe,[68] a cousin of Rice, was the superior at Santo Domingo College in Buenos Aires.[69] Fr Carlos Bustos called on the afternoon of the 14th to the convent, which is adjacent to Holy Cross monastery and church. In an agitated state, he relayed to Sr Terence, Sr Dymphna Tipper and Sr Brigid Fahy that Rice had been abducted on Monday evening and taken away in an unmarked car. When the sisters asked why he had not come to tell them sooner, he said he was afraid to leave his house out of fear of being kidnapped and disappeared.[70] The sisters immediately implemented the protocol they had prepared to cover such an emergency – to first phone the Irish embassy and then call the *Buenos Aires Herald*. Despite suspecting that the convent phone was tapped, Sr Dymphna placed a call to the Irish embassy at 4.30 p.m. Ambassador Lennon, fearing that his line was tapped, requested that the nuns visit his office the following day as 'the interference' on the line made it impossible to understand what was being said. Sr Dymphna then phoned the *Buenos Aires Herald* at 5 p.m. and reported the priest's disappearance to the news desk. She recalled the kindness of the journalist who took the details of the case. The following day, the 15th, they went to the embassy, where they met Lennon. When they began to relay the news about Rice, the ambassador asked if they spoke Irish. Lennon then suggested that they go for a coffee to a café on the street. Keeping silent even in the lift, the ambassador explained to the sisters the reason for his reticence to talk in his office as they sat in the safety of a café on Avenida Santa Fé. The ambassador told the sisters that he was sure the embassy was bugged but that they could not be overheard in the café and the sisters could speak freely to him about Rice's disappearance.[71]

Parallel to the official contacts, the embassy took more direct routes to discover the whereabouts of the priest. Harman systematically visited city police stations to enquire if they were holding Rice and is also believed to have spent two entire nights, probably the 12th and 13th, waiting in his car outside the headquarters of the federal police to alert the authorities to the fact that the Irish embassy was not leaving anything to chance as the life of an Irish citizen was at stake.[72] Parallel with the approaches to official channels – the Ministry of Foreign Affairs and the Ministry of the Interior – the Irish embassy mounted a local press campaign to bring the glare of international publicity onto the actions of the Argentine authorities. Harman and Lennon recruited sympathetic diplomats from other embassies and members of the Irish and Irish-Argentine communities to use their good offices to discover the priest's whereabouts. Harman briefed the local press during those critical days – 12, 13, 14 and 15 October. Reports appeared in *La Opinión* (13th), the *Buenos Aires Herald* (13th) and *La Razón* (14th).[73] Both Irish diplomats also briefed the four Irish dailies, the *Irish Times*, *Irish Press*, *Irish Independent* and *Cork Examiner*. On 14 October, the *Irish Times* reported on the front page that the Irish embassy had contacted the Argentinian foreign ministry to enlist the aid of the local authorities in tracing Rice's whereabouts. Harman explained: 'No word has been heard of him since', adding: 'We look on this with extreme concern in view of happenings here over the past years.' He reported the ambassador's calls to the foreign ministry, where he was assured that machinery had been set in motion to locate the missing priest. Harman also said that it was understood that local church authorities had also asked the government to investigate the priest's kidnapping.[74]

Harman was the source for the Reuters report in *The Times* (London) on the 14th, which read:

> An Irish priest has been kidnapped by unidentified gunmen here, an Irish Embassy spokesman said today. He is Father Patrick Rice, aged 31, of the Little Brothers of Charles de Foucauld, a French Roman Catholic

mission. The spokesman said that he was abducted on Monday while holding a prayer meeting at a shanty town on the road to Buenos Aires international airport ... Informed sources said the Irish Embassy and church authorities had asked the Argentine Government to investigate the kidnapping, which happened after an appeal by the Pope for an end to what he called 'blind violence' in Argentina.[75]

Also on the 14th, the *Washington Post*, citing Irish embassy sources, carried virtually the same report under the headline: 'Abducted Irish Priest'. A second item in the paper gave further information about Rice's disappearance and again cited Irish embassy sources.[76]

Rice was completely unaware of the international campaign being mounted for his release. However, on Thursday, 14 October, the torture stopped and he noticed that his captors had undergone a serious change of attitude. They made him sit on the side of his bed and, to his great surprise, offered him a cigarette. He told me that he was so weak he was hardly able to inhale the smoke. Identifying himself as an army officer, one of the men in his cell repeatedly accused him of being a subversive. He was not punched or beaten. Rice denied vehemently the accusations levelled against him. Before the officer left to report to his superiors, he told Rice that his denials would only make his situation worse. Later, two officers came to his cell and, according to Rice, took him 'in a very kindly way' to a waiting car. Despite their 'kindness', they made him get into the boot. As they were about to drive away, he heard another voice tell the two men in the car to return Rice's hood as they were in short supply.

Rice was taken to the Superintendencia de la Policía Federal, also known as the Coordinación Federal, 1550 Calle Moreno. Upon arrival, when he had difficulty giving his name because his mouth was swollen from the electric shock, he was punched in the ribs with great force and knocked to the ground. Blindfolded but no longer handcuffed, he was placed in a tiny cell in solitary confinement. That night, he was allowed to shower and for the first time he saw the bruises left by the beatings and torture all over his body. He had cigarette burns on his arms and on the back of his hands. Later, he was given something to eat and reassured that he was now safe. But Rice did not find the assurances that convincing. He knew that Grupo de Tareas 2 (Task Force 2) operated a CCD on the floor below his cell.[77]

Unbeknownst to Rice, on Friday the 15th Cabrera had been transferred to the police headquarters[78] and placed in a cell on the women's corridor not far from where the priest was being held. Although the beatings and the torture had stopped, she was threatened there with being raped on two occasions.[79]

Two days later, they would meet briefly in unusual circumstances. On 14 October, the Irish embassy told Dublin that they had learned from Capitán Seisdedos of the foreign ministry at 9.30 a.m. local time (1.30 p.m. Irish time) 'that Father Rice is now in custody of Federal Police of Buenos Aires'.[80] They added that Seisdedos alleged that when Rice and Cabrera had been taken into custody, the police had identified themselves to the priest. (Both denied that that was the case.) The Interior Ministry had sent that information to the foreign office. Lennon added: 'We are to be provided with further details as to exactly where he is being held, etc. during the course of the day … We will keep you informed of events. Presumably we will be able to visit him shortly. Grateful if family could be made aware of these developments.' When that message arrived in Iveagh House, the following minute was written on it: 'I told PSM [private secretary of minister] who will tell Deputy P. Hegarty who was the family's contact with the Department.'[81] In order to place maximum pressure on the Argentine authorities, Harman briefed the local press on the 14th, telling them that the embassy knew Rice's whereabouts and that an Irish official could soon visit him. He added: 'We have not been informed of the charges against him, but the foreign ministry is being extremely co-operative and they expect to give us further information in the course of the day.'[82] The *Irish Press* on the 15th reported Lennon saying, '… we will keep on to the foreign ministry here until we can see him', adding: 'It is a relief to know that Fr Rice is safe and in good health.'[83] The same day the *Buenos Aires Herald* reported that Rice had been arrested and was being held incommunicado in federal police headquarters.[84]

The nunciature also exerted pressure on the authorities to have Rice released. Pio Laghi wrote on 15 October to the prefect for public affairs (secretariat of state), Cardinal Jean Villot, stating that the nunciature had not failed to make representations to the government authorities on behalf of Rice (*'La quale no ha mancato di compiere doverose gestioni presso la autorità governative'*). He informed Rome that he had received a call that evening from Captain Vascello Allara, under-secretary of foreign affairs, that Rice was being detained in the headquarters of the federal police. The under-secretary of the interior, Colonel Fauret, phoned the nuncio later informing him that the police were 'completing the investigation of the case'. There follows a redacted section in the nuncio's letter, most probably in which Fauret gave the number of priests held and referred to the expulsion to the US of Fr James Weeks (who had been kidnapped in Córdoba, together with five seminarians).[85] On 15/16 October, the Argentine foreign minister, Admiral César Augusto Guzzetti, issued a statement to the effect that Rice was being held on suspicion of involvement in subversive activities.[86] On 17 October, Ambassador Lennon told the *Irish Press* that 'we have no suggestion from the authorities here as to what subversive activity he is accused of'.[87] The embassy was anxious to ensure that Rice was either brought to justice or released: 'As far as we are concerned there is no justification for the authorities' suspicions,' Lennon added.[88]

Pio Laghi was among the first to hear officially of the charges being brought against Rice and Cabrera. The minister of the interior, General Harguindeguy, told him in a letter stamped 27 October 1976 that the authorities had been keeping a file on Rice's activities over a period of four years. He said that the police had come upon both the priest and Cabrera putting up self-adhesive Montonero stickers (*obleas*)[89] on the walls[90] and that Cabrera had a variety of incriminating documents on her when taken into custody.[91] The reason for Rice's arrest was published on 8 August 1978 when the Inter-American Commission on Human Rights pressed the Argentine authorities for the reasons for his detention. The official reply read: 'RICE, Patrick Michael: Deported by Decree 2665 of 27-10-76 under the charge of violation of Law 21.259, which prohibits activities affecting the peace and security of the Nation. The above-named maintained links with elements of the subversive Montoneros band (Case 2450).' The same source stated that Cabrera had been 'detained by order of the National Executive because of her involvement with the subversive Montoneros band, released on parole by Decree N° 3891 of 27-12-77, authorized to travel freely within the Federal Capital, with the Federal Police of Argentina acting as the supervising authority'.[92] When the relevant records of the Argentine embassies in Dublin, London, Washington and the Holy See are opened, together with the files of the Argentine foreign ministry, historians may find further evidence of the importance of the international press campaign in the rescue and recovery of both Cabrera and Rice.

IRISH DIPLOMATS VISIT PATRICK RICE

Cabrera and Rice met on Sunday, 17 October in the federal police headquarters. As it was *Día de los Madres* (Mothers' Day), Cabrera asked the guard if he would open the cells on the women's wing to let Rice lead them in prayer. Although the guard was tough, she said he opened the doors and the women stood in a line in the narrow corridor. The women, when Rice was released from his cell, quickly gathered scraps of bread and polenta which he shaped into the form of a host and made a chalice from silver cigarette paper. He then said a mass which lasted only a few minutes, offering holy communion to those who wished to receive it. When Rice returned to his cell, the male prisoners asked him to perform a similar service for them.[93] With the agreement of the guard, he did so, improvising in the same way.[94] Thirty years later, the details of those events were recalled by Lucy Gómez de Mainer, who was in the same jail with her pregnant daughter, María Magdalena (Malena), and her son, Pablo. Both her children were murdered. Lucy survived.[95] When giving evidence at the trial of Fr Christian von Wernich in 2007,[96] Lucy, who was Jewish, said she remembered meeting an Irish priest in 1976 and attended the service, adding: 'I am not a believer but it was the most moving Mass I ever attended.' All she remembered was that he had been tortured and had left the country. Rice, who was attending the trial, introduced himself during a break. It was a joyful reunion.[97]

A doctor tended to Rice's injuries later that Sunday (17th) and prescribed him a course of antibiotics. Afterwards, he was visited by an army officer who warned him to tell his visitors that he had sustained his cuts and bruises falling down stairs. He also told him that if he did not do so he would be found in a block of concrete at the bottom of a river.[98] However, it was plain for anyone to see that he had cigarette burns on the backs of his hands and up both arms. On Monday, 18 October, his captors ordered him to shave. Rice said that a captor splashed 'perfume' (probably aftershave) on his face. He was then escorted to a room where he was surprised to find Ambassador Lennon and Justin Harman waiting for him. Two officers remained in the room during the interview. Both pretended that they did not understand English but it is certain that they did. Rice felt unable to say anything about his ordeal: 'I was quite disorientated and the ambassador realised that it wasn't in my interests to talk about ill-treatment.'[99] The ambassador asked him in Irish: '*An bhfuil tú droch íde?*' ('Are you being badly treated?')[100] Remembering a few words in Irish, Rice nodded. Noticing the burns on his arms and on the back of his hands, Lennon asked indignantly whether they had been done by cigarettes. Rice replied swiftly they were the least of a person's worries 'in here'.[101] Lennon and Harman reassured him that everything was being done to secure his release and that the embassy would keep in regular contact with him.[102] He was given cigarettes and other personal items. Lennon later informed Iveagh House: 'Visited Fr Rice today. Obvious signs of bad beating up and cigarette burns. Very distraught but had been instructed by police authorities not to mention ill treatment. Requests therefore that we don't refer to it either as fears further ill treatment. He is being held at the disposal of the executive which means indefinitely. We will press as far as possible for trial or expulsion. Latter best hope.'[103] Later that day, Lennon spoke to Philip Molloy of the *Irish Press*: '*An bhfuil Gaeilge agat?*' he

asked, adding, '*Tá a lán rudaí nach féidir liom a rá.*' He described how he and
Harman had met the priest under police supervision in an office at the prison.
Conscious that the embassy phone was tapped, he said to Molloy in English
that he had seen Rice and that he 'seemed nervous'. The ambassador added
that Rice had told Harman and himself that he had never been involved in
subversive activities of any kind and knew nothing about the 'suspicions' under
which he was being detained.[104]

Lennon informed the nuncio of their visit to Rice. An unsigned minute
in the nunciature file said that both diplomats had been 'quite shocked' by
his condition – both physical and psychological ... 'He was badly treated
(more accurate to say tortured) and the condition of his face was notable
and apparently his hands were burned with cigarettes. Psychologically he is
depressed,' the minute noted, adding that when taken to the federal police
station on the 14th, he 'was told not to speak to anybody of how he had been
treated ... He was afraid to tell the ambassador what had happened to him'.
The same minute added the following: 'Apparently he is a rather naïve person'
('*Pare che sia una persona piutosto ingenuo*'). The minute did not attribute that
observation to any named member of the Irish embassy staff. It is more likely
that it was an inference from what Ambassador Lennon had said.[105]

IVEAGH HOUSE CALLS IN THE ARGENTINE AMBASSADOR

The secretary of the Department of Foreign Affairs, Paul Keating, sent Lennon
instructions on the 18th to make robust representations on behalf of the
detained Irish citizen:

> If signs of Fr Rice's beating ... were obvious to your naked eye and if you
> would have been aware of them without complaint by him you should
> make immediate and strong protest to Foreign Office about his condition
> and demand that he be treated properly. Say that since he is in custody we
> hold Argentinian authorities responsible for his wellbeing. You should
> consider if circumstances warrant seeking Foreign Office agreement
> to medical examination by embassy doctor. We await full report on his
> ill treatment and charges on which he is held. Re. question his trial or
> expulsion you should not repeat nor at this stage give any countenance
> to belief he is guilty either to Foreign Office or to journalists. Latter have
> quoted you in Sunday papers here re expulsion.[106]

The nunciature file contains a minute dated 20 October 1976, which stated that the Irish embassy had informed the nuncio that the ambassador's request for an explanation for Rice's injuries from the foreign ministry had produced the answer: 'He resisted when police arrested him.'[107] The nunciature also recorded that the Irish ambassador was going to request Rice's expulsion from the country. Laghi wrote in Italian 'visto' (seen) on the document.[108]

While attending a lunch hosted by the Argentine foreign minister shortly after his visit to see Rice, Lennon described to one senior official the injuries suffered by the priest as if it were 'a medical examination'. The under-secretary at the foreign ministry told him that his understanding was that 'Rice was distributing subversive literature assisted by young girl who was also arrested'.[109] In order to emphasise the importance the Irish government attached to the Argentine state's disappearance, torture and imprisonment without trial of an Irish citizen, Lennon informed that unidentified foreign office official that the Argentinian ambassador in Dublin, Señor José Alberto del Carril, was to be summoned to the Department of Foreign Affairs to answer questions regarding the kidnapping: 'They seemed perturbed and promised immediate investigation requesting meantime that I suspend representations here,' Lennon noted.[110] On 19 October 1976 del Carril came as requested to Iveagh House for what he knew was not going to be a routine visit. FitzGerald had made it clear, as reflected in Keating's instruction above, that del Carril was to be left in no doubt as to the seriousness with which the Irish government took the Argentine state's kidnapping, torture and detention of an Irish citizen. The assistant secretary, Joseph Small, met the ambassador and told him of the minister's concern over the violent way the priest had been treated. He was also informed that 'our own Ambassador in Argentina had visited Father Rice in prison on the previous day and was shocked by Father Rice's appearance' and that it was evident he 'had suffered a considerable degree of ill-treatment'. Small added bluntly that in any circumstances ill-treatment was bad but 'when it was indulged in by the official forces of law and order in a country, as appeared to be the case in this instance, it was unforgivable'.[111] The Irish government, he said, had asked for Rice to be examined by an Irish embassy doctor, adding that del Carril 'would be aware of the revulsion of people in this country if word got out that Father Rice had been badly beaten up by the police ... The Ambassador would also be aware of the special position in which a clergyman is held in the eyes of Irish people'. Small continued: 'That was not to say that if Father Rice had broken the law he should not be tried in the usual way. But in the case in point we were not aware of any charges or any proposal to bring Father Rice to trial. We would in fact welcome full information in that regard.' He reminded the ambassador of the serious damage to Argentina's image abroad if word got out that Father Rice had been subjected to brutality while in official custody.

In that connection, Small cited the recent case of the doctor Sheila Cassidy,[112] a British citizen from an Irish family who had been arrested on 1 November 1975 by the secret police (DINA) in the Irish Columban house in Santiago, Chile.[113] Called there to attend a sick nun, she witnessed the police bursting in and shooting dead the priests' housekeeper. The doctor was taken to a secret detention centre at Villa Grimaldi and tortured on what her tormentors referred to macabrely as the *parilla* (grill or griddle). Repeatedly accused of having given medical assistance to a wounded member of an armed opposition group, an allegation she consistently denied, the torture continued and Cassidy was kept in solitary confinement for three weeks and a further five in detention.[114] She was released on 29 December 1975 and deported to England.[115]

In his reply, Del Carril said he was 'very much alive' to the reputational damage done to his country, as would be his foreign ministry in Buenos Aires. The trouble was, he said, that his ministry had very limited influence with the military and the police: 'The security forces simply were not conscious of the external dimension,' he noted, adding that he had been serving in Chile at the time of the coup against Allende (September 1973) and he had had to work extremely hard to save and repatriate his nationals in that country. On one occasion, he said, he had housed up to 700 citizens in the Argentine embassy.[116] He had found in Santiago that friendly and influential contacts at a high level in the army and the police were much more effective than reliance on the Chilean foreign ministry. Del Carril advised that Lennon should 'not hesitate to use his contacts with the military and the Ministry of Internal Affairs'. He regretted the whole affair and 'laboured under the disadvantage of not having information', adding that 'terrorism was rife in the country and that hundreds of people were being killed including many industrialists'.[117] Small advised del Carril, when concluding the meeting, to convey to his government the serious concerns of the Irish government and 'to use his influence to resolve the matter speedily'. The Argentine ambassador was also advised that with a new Dáil session about to commence there was a possibility that questions would be raised about the Rice case. Small concluded that 'it was in everybody's interest to have the matter dealt with expeditiously and satisfactorily'. Before leaving, the ambassador 'again expressed regret' and said he would do everything he could to resolve matters.[118]

When seeking the release of Rice, the Irish government did not follow the British example in their handling of the Cassidy case. The Foreign Office had been very reluctant to support the permanent withdrawal of the ambassador from Santiago, despite pressure from within the left wing of the Labour Party to do so. The British had already in 1974 cut off arms sales to Pinochet. The foreign secretary, Jim Callaghan, moved cautiously and prudently in crafting his response. He did not act until Cassidy had been released and was safely in Britain. He then made it public that she had been tortured and wrote a letter of protest to the Chilean government which was delivered by Ambassador Reginald Secondé.[119] Immediately afterwards, the ambassador, who was being recalled, took a flight to London. Callaghan then revealed the tough actions he had taken: the letter of protest, the withdrawal of the ambassador and that the Cassidy case was to be raised at the UN.[120] He did not permit Secondé to return to Santiago. With the ambassador recalled, Callaghan refused to sever all diplomatic relations with Chile on the advice of the Foreign Office, and trade between the two countries continued uninterrupted. Before the return of the Conservatives to power in 1979, Britain had given asylum to approximately 3,000 Chilean refugees.[121] Ireland gave asylum to fewer than 300.

AMBASSADOR LENNON CALLED IN TO THE FOREIGN MINISTRY

Once news reached Buenos Aires that del Carril had been summoned to Iveagh House, Lennon was requested to present himself at the Ministry of Foreign Affairs. He went armed with firm instructions from Minister FitzGerald not to mince his words when discussing the Rice case. He was informed by officials that the priest had been 'arrested by off duty policemen while posting notices claiming ERP guerrilla army only legitimate Argentine army'. Regarding the priest's poor physical condition, 'they claim injuries to face caused by resisting arrest and hand injuries result of manual labour'. Lennon remained unpersuaded by that explanation. But when reporting to Dublin, he relayed the following information: 'From information received [at Irish embassy] another Irish priest who knows Rice it would seem quite possible some substance in suggestions of subversion.' The priest who made that allegation was not identified by the ambassador but he regarded that source to have had sufficient credibility to include it in his report.[122]

Ambassador Lennon, who had been campaigning unsuccessfully since his arrival for a different posting, was irritated by the line in Keating's recent instructions which was interpreted as being a reprimand: 'Latter [Irish journalists] have quoted you in Sunday papers here re expulsion'. Lennon replied that he had expressed a personal view in answer to queries made during a phone call from the *Sunday Press* that 'expulsion probable in view precedent

US priest Weeks. I still consider this most probable result and most desirable solution in view present dangerous situation'.[123] Setting to one side the implied criticism from the secretary, both Lennon and Harman continued to brief the international and Irish press about developments in the Rice case. Harman confirmed to the press on 19 October that the ambassador had met foreign ministry officials but said that there were no new developments to report. He said Lennon was trying to gain Rice's release subject to his being expelled from the country.[124] Lennon told the *Irish Press* the same day that the authorities were likely to deport Rice and that that had happened in the case of a US priest (Fr Weeks) who had been seized on 3 July and released on 17 August.[125] At his most recent meeting at the Ministry of Foreign Affairs, Lennon said he had been told that they were still investigating the case and that, as yet, no concrete decision had been made. They would make up their minds within a few days. He would try to see Rice the following day.[126]

On 20 October, Lennon confirmed to the *Irish Press* that he had met the priest on Monday, the 18th. He also said that he or the embassy first secretary would be seeing him again on Thursday, the 21st. He also made it known that he had had two meetings with the foreign ministry over the previous two days: 'I have met the Foreign Minister and embassy representatives, and we are now trying to force some decision by Friday (22nd).' He had learned that Rice was being held on suspicion of distributing subversive literature. They hoped to take him cigarettes and literature and observe his condition and see how he was being held: 'The foreign minister has promised to try to expedite matters, and although this country is in a state of war where anything could happen, we are hopeful that we will hear that he has been released soon. The embassy solicitor had been appointed to represent Fr Rice but he had not been allowed to see him. If charged, he [the solicitor] believed that he would receive permission to visit and consult with his client.'[127] When Harman called at the federal police headquarters on 21 October, he was told that Rice had been transferred to Villa Devoto prison, at Bermúdez, Buenos Aires. The *Irish Times*, quoting an Associated Press (AP) report, confirmed on 22 October that Rice had been transferred from police detention to a penitentiary and that the transfer had prevented, according to the Irish embassy, a scheduled meeting between Harman and Rice.[128] Lennon sent a telegram on the 22nd: 'Transferred to Villa Devoto prison which holds both politicos and common criminals. Arrangements made for visit twenty second. No other developments.' The ambassador reported subsequently that 'with the assistance of the Foreign Ministry, arrangements have been made for a visit on 23rd'. When the chief of protocol at the foreign ministry was informing Lennon of those arrangements, he expressed some annoyance at the action of the Irish Department of Foreign Affairs in summoning Ambassador José Alberto del Carril, 'as I was being kept informed of all developments and presumably keeping Dublin informed'.[129] Lennon also reported that Britain and the US had 'aimed at expulsion [for their citizens] and nuncio considers this best solution if obtainable. Certainly, Rice could not in any circumstances continue to work in Argentina. No charges brought as yet. No limit on period of detention without trial. If expelled may embassy guarantee payment of fare if necessary?'

Iveagh House replied: 'Accept deportation is desirable solution. You must judge well time at which you negotiate this and must not at any point accept proposition that Rice is guilty. You may advance the money for Rice's travel if this is necessary.' On the 25th, Lennon reported that Harman had succeeded in visiting Rice earlier that day: 'Conditions much improved and requested family be informed accordingly. Our observations of ill treatment confirmed but requests you make no allusions to this. Rice requests we aim at expulsion. In meantime we are providing items requested by him. Will visit again end of week. Reporting more details by air mail.'[130] Harman wrote to Joseph Small on 25 October that he had found Rice 'in very good form. He repeated that he was satisfied with general conditions at the prison ... [and] that he was quite optimistic that the case will be resolved quite soon'.[131] He also wrote on the 25th to Rice's parents:

> I found him in much improved form, and we had a lengthy conversation together. He specifically asked me to let you know how he is getting on: he is being held in Villa Devoto prison, and is in a cell with four others. He has no complaints about conditions in the prison and mentioned that he is visited daily by the chaplain. He gave me a list of items he requires, and I am arranging to have them delivered to him. He is still being held 'under suspicion of involvement in subversive activities' but no charges whatsoever have been made against him as yet. We here at the Embassy are doing our utmost to have him either brought to trial, or else released. So far, however, we have no substantive indication of what the Argentine authorities intend to do.

Harman gave Rice a letter from his parents (dated 1 October) which the Irish Dominican nuns had passed on to the embassy. He was allowed to read the letter but not keep it. Harman offered his parents to deliver any letters that they would like to send care of the embassy.[132]

In the United States, Fr Weeks actively campaigned for Rice's release. He was encouraged to do so by Mr Glavin from Albany, New York, a relative of the jailed priest. Weeks called the Irish embassy in Washington stating 'that publicity can be extremely effective in such cases, and was, for example he alleged, in his own case'. Ambassador J.G. Molloy reported that 'naturally I did not comment one way or the other on whether similar publicity would be beneficial in the case of Fr Rice. I assured Fr Weeks that our embassy was doing everything possible to ensure a satisfactory outcome in the matter'.[133] On 29 October, Iveagh House replied to the ambassador: 'question of publicity is a matter for Fr Weeks to decide. Department is satisfied that case is getting sufficient publicity. Officers of embassy have visited Fr Rice twice. His condition is reported to be satisfactory. Embassy is continuing to press for his release in the absence of charges against him. Matter has been raised with Argentinian Foreign Minister and Argentinian Ambassador in Dublin ...'[134]

In late October, Joseph Small phoned Ambassador del Carril to inform him that, as predicted, a number of Cork TDs would raise the Rice case in the Dáil. He asked whether the ambassador had any further information which would be useful to the minister for foreign affairs FitzGerald when answering the questions. Del Carril replied that he had nothing to add to the information already given to the Irish ambassador in Buenos Aires. He phoned later to enquire whether Iveagh House knew the name of the prison in which Fr Rice was being detained. He felt that if he was being held in a particular prison the probability was that he would be brought to trial. Small informed him that 'our latest information was that he had been transferred to a different prison – Villa Devoto – from one he had mentioned'. Del Carril also said that after his visit to Iveagh House 'he had sent a telegram to his home authorities requesting them to mediate in the matter with a view to solving the problem in the most diplomatic way. If it was true that Fr Rice assisted a girl who was a known subversive, he might conceivably be sentenced to one year or six months'. On the other hand, if the charge of involvement in subversive activities was not proved against him, the ambassador said that 'the best and most friendly way of dealing with the matter might be to ask him to leave the country'. When Small expressed mild surprise at that suggestion, the ambassador replied that there was a state of war in his country at present.[135]

PATRICK RICE MOVED TO ANOTHER PRISON

Without prior warning to the Irish embassy, Rice was moved on 28 October 1976 to Unidad 9, La Plata Prison, about sixty kilometres from Buenos Aires. He later explained that he and about a hundred other prisoners were woken up at 4 a.m., handcuffed and herded into the chapel 'as if we were animals', watched over by about fifty guards armed with long batons. When being loaded onto trucks, the prisoners were made to run the gauntlet with blows reigning down on them from all sides. Rice remembered that the atmosphere was very tense as they did not know whether they were being driven away to be murdered in a remote area or being transferred to another prison. He also recalled how a guard in his truck added to that collective state of anxiety by pointing his machine gun at the prisoners as they were being driven close to the river – a favoured place for the military to dispose of bodies. However, an hour later the convoy of trucks arrived at the prison in La Plata. Rice was put into a punishment cell and, the following morning, prison guards entered all the cells holding the newly transferred prisoners and began to beat them up. Then they were ordered to strip naked, permitted to shower and lined up for a haircut. Doctors took detailed notes of their injuries and of the burn marks on their bodies left by cigarette butts and electric shock.[136]

On 30 October, Ambassador Lennon told Iveagh House that Rice was being housed in a 'politicos prison'. Harman, who visited him the previous day, found that he was 'in relatively good form with no complaints about conditions or present treatment' but he was 'naturally apprehensive about his situation' while 'again categorically indicated total innocence'. The *Irish Press* carried the headline on 30 October: "'I'm Innocent," says Fr Rice'. Harman had told the paper that he had spoken to the priest for fifty minutes and that he found him to be in 'reasonably good form'. He was finding it difficult to adjust to prison life. Members of his order were not allowed to see him and the authorities were only allowing direct relatives and consular people to visit him. No charges had been preferred against him. Rice had strongly emphasised his innocence of all charges of subversion, saying he knew nothing whatsoever about subversion, had never had anything to do with it and knew nothing about anyone who had. Harman said that there had been no further clarification of the missionary's legal position and they were trying to ensure that he should be allowed to write to his family. He told the paper he thought that Rice might be deported.[137]

The diplomatic reports might give the impression that Rice's attitude in jail was one of submission and resignation. In fact the opposite was the case.[138] During his time in jail he won the respect of many of his fellow prisoners, among them a future Argentinian foreign minister (November 2005–June 2010), Jorge Enrique Taiana.[139]

By early November, the Irish embassy still awaited clarification from the authorities regarding the charges to be preferred against Rice or any word of his expulsion from the country. Ambassador Lennon reported that his continuing contacts with the foreign ministry 'revealed no indication intentions in his regard'. He hoped the Argentinian ambassador in Dublin 'might express minister's trust that authorities here [in Buenos Aires] will expedite this case particularly in view tradition of friendly ties between our two countries'.[140] On 2 November 1976, Harman wrote to Rice's parents, informing them that 'he has again been moved, is now in fact held in a prison in La Plata, some forty miles from Buenos Aires. He had no complaints about conditions in the prison or about his present treatment, but I must admit that he is, naturally, quite apprehensive as to his situation, since he has not yet been informed what it is intended to do in his case. Similarly, we here in the Embassy have been given no indication by the foreign ministry. However, we are keeping up the pressure and, hopefully, we will hear something soon'. He also told Rice's parents that the superior general of the Little Brothers of Charles de Foucauld had arrived in Buenos Aires and he (Harman) was hoping to be able to arrange for the superior general to see his imprisoned confrère.[141]

In the absence of FitzGerald, who was abroad, the parliamentary secretary, John Kelly, answered questions on 4 November from a number of TDs on the abduction of Rice.[142] He replied that repeated representations at high level had been made by the Irish ambassador in Buenos Aires to have Fr Rice released and that representations had also been made to the Argentinian ambassador in Ireland. To date, he said, the government had not been able to get a statement of what charges, if any, had been brought against the priest. Kelly said FitzGerald was 'disturbed that an Irish citizen should be in prison abroad in such circumstances and continuing efforts are being made to secure Fr Rice's release, or at least to have any judicial proceedings that may be contemplated in his regard concluded as speedily as possible'. He said that the Irish embassy in Buenos Aires would make sure he was properly represented and that everything possible would be done to ensure justice and proper treatment.[143] Kelly followed up his Dáil contribution with an instruction that the embassy in Buenos Aires keep in regular contact with Rice and suggested there ought to be a visit once a week.

On 5 November, the secretary of the department, Paul Keating, instructed the ambassador in Buenos Aires: 'We should be glad if you would arrange this and continue to exert pressure on the appropriate authorities with a view to securing a satisfactory outcome in the matter.' In response, Harman visited the foreign ministry on 8 November, where he saw Captain Seisdedos, who was in charge of the secretary general's office. Expressing his government's dissatisfaction and grave concern at the continuing detention of Rice, he noted that the embassy had not been 'provided with any indication as to official intentions in his regard'. Harman gave a detailed account of public opinion in Ireland to the case and drew his attention to the 'obvious damage being done to Argentina's image abroad'. He also made him aware of the recent debate in the Dáil on the case:

> Seisdedos replied that while he was aware of this situation, his only information was that the investigations into the case were continuing. He then asked me what was Rice's version of the circumstances surrounding his arrest. I replied that he had indicated to me that he was walking along one of the streets in the shanty town in the company of a girl, with whom he was not well acquainted, but who had expressed an interest in teaching catechetics in the area. A man dressed in civilian clothes alighted from a car and ordered them to stop. He then fired two shots in the air, apparently to summon help from some others in the area. Both Rice and the girl were then ordered into the car and taken to a police station in the area. I also mentioned that Rice had indicated to me on a number of occasions that he had never anything to do with putting posters on walls.

Seisdedos, in his reply, 'limited himself to simply saying that his information was that this was not the case'. He claimed that 'certain documents had been found on the girl and that those appeared to indicate some involvement in subversive activities'. Harman asked pointedly whether 'the suspicions in regard to Rice were merely circumstantial, i.e. that he was found in the company of the girl'. Seisdedos 'replied somewhat evasively, which may perhaps be due more to lack of information on his part than to any wish to appear cautious'. Harman then raised with him the question of expulsion: 'He replied that this possibility could perhaps be considered, and suggested that the Embassy submit an Aide-Mémoire outlining the reasons for the request. Once this was received, his Ministry would then make approaches to the Ministry of the Interior. He said, however, that if the evidence indicated that Rice was guilty, then of course there could be no question of expulsion.' Harman agreed to submit the document to the ministry the following day.[144]

Harman made another visit to La Plata and reported on 9 November that Rice had no complaints about conditions, but had said that the jail had 1,200 prisoners and that it was run on very strict lines, 'with extremely heavy punishment in case of any mis-behaviour'. Details from another source revealed that those punishments included days in solitary confinement with cold showers, and that beatings were given for the most trivial of reasons. A second offence brought double the punishment. During his visit, Harman gave

Rice details of his conversation with Seisdedos, and later reported the priest's reaction to Dublin: 'He first reiterated his total innocence as regards any form of subversion, and when I asked him about the girl, he said that his own impression was that she was not connected with the subversive movement.'[145]

On the evening of 8 November, both Lennon and Harman drafted an *aide-mémoire* which read in part: '... given that this Embassy has to-date been without any means of ascertaining the basis of the suspicions on which he is held and taking into account the traditional friendly ties between Ireland and Argentina, it is suggested that the relevant authorities may wish to consider the possibility of providing Rice with the option of leaving the country'. The document then dwelt upon the negative effects which 'this unfortunate episode' has had among the Irish people, in the Irish parliament and on Argentina's image, 'a country which has always been remembered for its generous hospitality to thousands of Irishmen since the dawn of its independence'. The document expressed confidence that the matter would be resolved as soon as possible, 'even shortening the normal procedures in such cases'. The Irish embassy offered its fullest cooperation, 'taking responsibility for Rice's custody until the moment he leaves the country for Ireland, as well as the costs of his return journey'. A Spanish translation of the document was presented on 9 November to the foreign ministry.[146] The *Irish Independent* reported on 11 November that the embassy had asked the Argentinian government to release Rice and allow him to leave the country and that that request had been contained in a note handed in by Justin Harman on Tuesday night, the 9th. There had been no response yet, the paper reported.[147] (The same day, the *Irish Times* carried a similar report, quoting an AP source.) On 13 November, Reuters reported that the Irish government had asked the authorities in Argentina to allow Rice to leave the country.[148] On 16 November, Lennon and Harman visited Rice: 'One still notes,' reported Harman, 'a certain nervousness in his general disposition.' He had no complaints about the conditions in the prison but made a further reference to 'the extremely severe punishment that arises in case of any mis-behaviour'. Both asked him how he was sleeping. He replied that he was sleeping all right but he experienced pain from an injury which he had suffered when he 'was strapped to some form of structure for an entire night, in the course of which he was tortured with electric shocks'. The two diplomats discussed law no. 21449 with him, which held that people detained at the disposition of the executive power had the right to petition to leave the country, ninety days from the date of their arrest. Aware that Rice was unable to say anything of consequence, they nevertheless concluded that he agreed with such an approach. That same day, the embassy took the proposition to the Interior Ministry. Harman also took a copy to the foreign ministry, where reference was made to the embassy's *aide-mémoire* submitted earlier. He learned that the ministry's 'attitude is one of general agreement with its contents' and that the ministry officials 'remained extremely optimistic' that the case might be settled 'any day now'.[149]

The public campaign in Ireland to have Rice released intensified throughout November. On 20 November, fifty students and staff of the Mater Dei Institute of Education in Drumcondra handed a letter in to the Department of Foreign Affairs expressing concern and demanding Rice's release.[150] On 22 November, the provincial of the SVD, Fr Brendan O'Reilly, led a delegation of clerical students and nuns to the Argentine embassy in Dublin to hand in a letter of protest signed by 530 students and staff at St Patrick's, Maynooth. Mgr Tomás Ó Fiaich, the president of that college, headed the list of signatures.[151] On 25 November, O'Reilly sent a telegram to the Irish embassy requesting that Rice be given the news on the next visit that his 'sister has had a baby daughter and both are well'. The minister for foreign affairs, Garret FitzGerald, received a large number of letters from private citizens and public bodies, particularly from Munster, requesting the minister to do all in his power to seek Rice's release. FitzGerald received an official delegation from Fermoy, the priest's home town, on 1 December 1976.

In light of the increase in public protest, on 24 November Iveagh House sent a new instruction to Lennon, which the ambassador read as a criticism of how the embassy was handling the Rice case. Keating wrote:

> (1) In the embassy's dealings with Argentine authorities you should use weight and influence of your own office of ambassador to the full, including high contacts outside foreign ministry if necessary as recommended by ambassador del Carril here. This no reflection on secretary of embassy whose rank automatically limits access. (2) Embassy should convey minimum of information to Irish newspapers and should in future inform press enquirers that this dept. has all information available to embassy. On no account should embassy have given the detailed information which appeared in Irish Independent on 11 November. Neither should it make use of terms quote expulsion or expel unquote in its dealings with press and the local authorities as this implies presumption of guilt. (3) Any major initiatives contemplated by embassy in this case should be cleared in advance by dept. (4) All correspondence between embassy and Rice family in Cork should be routed through Dept. in future, in normal way.[152]

Due to retire in January 1977, Lennon replied with forbearance on 25 November:

> Pressure for release of Rice being brought on all levels including
> presidential. It is extremely doubtful however with whom final decision
> rests. We have had no Dublin press contacts recently. Information given
> to local agencies mainly confined to Rice still in custody and in good
> form. Thing [?] obviously being inflated by agencies without justification.
> In future we shall confine ourselves to saying no developments. As you
> will see from enclosure to minute of ninth, we do not formally mention
> expulsion in writing.[153]

Harman had met Rice again on 24 November. He reported to Joe Small the
following day that he found him 'in very good form'. Adhering to the recent
directive, Harman ended his report: 'As per paragraph D of your C23, I attach
a letter from the embassy giving Mr and Mrs Rice details of my latest visit.
Presumably you will have it dispatched from the Department.' A minute on the
report reads: 'letter released'.[154]

RELEASE AND DEPORTATION

By the end of November, the ambassador and Harman were confident that
Rice would soon be released and allowed to leave the country. In Ireland,
public disquiet had grown in his native Fermoy over the delay in his release.
The parliamentary secretary to the minister for health, Dick Barry, brought the
strength of local feeling to the attention of the government. Despite the icy
conditions, a congregation of over two thousand people which included Rice's
parents and his siblings turned out on 29 November to hear mass celebrated
by the bishop of Cloyne, John Ahern, in St Patrick's church, Fermoy, at 3 p.m.
Following a meeting of the urban district council, a municipal book of protest
was opened for public signature in the town. Signed by 1,500 people, it was
delivered by nine local urban councillors to the Argentine embassy.[155] On 1
December, Small wrote a minute to his colleague, Liam Rigney, on the margin
of a report received from Harman: 'As you know, Amb. Lennon phoned me
at home last night to say that Fr Rice will be released and expelled within a
few days.'[156] The ambassador understood that the relevant documents had been
signed. Small sent a telegram to Lennon later that day:

> Further to our conversation last night about the impending release and
> expulsion of Fr Rice we feel it is important that in your conversation with

Fr Rice before he leaves the country you should sound him out on the following matters; One, Does he acknowledge that the department and embassy did everything possible on his behalf; Two, Does he propose to make any public statements, directly or indirectly about his detention and ill-treatment; Three, If he proposes to publicise his ill-treatment you should confirm to him that it was at his request we refrained from giving any information on this aspect of the matter to anybody including his parents, Dáil Éireann or press. In discussing these matters with him you should refrain from offering him any advice as to how he should proceed as this is essentially a matter for himself possibly in consultation with the superiors of his order.

There were further details about the purchasing of a ticket for Rice from KLM and to make the date of departure transferable in case of a delay. On 3 December, Harman told Small in a phone conversation that he had spoken to Rice about those points, with the following results: '(1) Fr Rice acknowledges that the embassy and Dept. did everything possible on his behalf and he appreciated it; (2) He would be influenced by the advice of his confrères in the matter of publicising his ill-treatment; (3) He confirmed that it was at his request we refrained from publishing his ill-treatment.'[157] On 2 December, the *Irish Times* reported that Rice, having agreed to the conditions being set, was due for release. His mother Amy (64), delighted at the news, told the reporter that it had been a trying time for the family. She felt that the public had done an awful lot of good by their prayers. Rice's father (66) paid tribute to the work of Ambassador Lennon and Justin Harman and to the other staff of the Irish embassy in Buenos Aires: 'Only for the pressure applied by Mr Lennon and by the Irish Government and people, things could have been a lot worse,' he said.[158] He also said that the family had received letters from all over the country and it was very gratifying that people took such an interest and showed so much concern.[159] The *Irish Times* on 4 December quoted Harman as saying that the Argentinian government had signed a decree to deport Fr Rice, as the first step towards his expulsion. It said Rice had told the embassy staff that police had accused him of passing out leftist guerrilla leaflets and literature at prayer meetings. Harman said that Rice had denied that allegation, but he had admitted to knowing people who were doing it.[160] Quoting AP and Reuters sources, the paper reported the same day that Rice had been detained for two months 'on suspicion of being connected with left-wing guerrillas'.[161]

Rice spent his last night in La Plata Jail on 1 December. Before being transferred on the 2nd, his captors, to his astonishment, asked him to write something positive in their 'hospitality' book. With characteristic understatement, he wrote drolly in Spanish: 'I might have been treated better.'[162] A car took him to the railway station and, accompanied by two policemen, he travelled to Buenos Aires where he was transferred to federal police headquarters. He was put in a cell on the ninth floor. (During his earlier stay, he had been housed in a cell on the third floor.) He was given no food during the following twenty-four hours. The following day, the 3rd, two policemen escorted him to Ezeiza airport. Harman was there to ensure that he was treated properly by the authorities and that he got safely on to the plane.[163] (In previous months, a number of intending passengers had been disappeared from within the airport terminal.) Harman gave him cigarettes, thirty letters and a telegram, and clothing to keep him warm as he was going to arrive in winter in Ireland.[164]

On boarding the plane, Rice's passport was confiscated and held by the captain and not returned to him until he had landed twenty-three hours later in London. During stopovers, Rice was obliged to remain on the aircraft. He arrived in England on Saturday evening, 4 December. The first secretary of the Irish embassy in London, Richard O'Brien, met him at Gatwick airport, where Rice answered a few questions for reporters. O'Brien took him to dinner that evening and Rice told him how he had been taken from prison to prison in the boot of an army car, beaten and interrogated for hours on end. He spoke nervously about his personal experience of torture and how he witnessed other prisoners being subjected to electric shock – including a pregnant woman. O'Brien finally succeeded in getting Rice to spend most of their time together talking about his pastoral work in Argentina, his religious formation, his days at Maynooth, his family and how Ireland had changed since his last visit.[165] Ambassador Tadhg O'Sullivan met Rice on Sunday morning, the 5th. That evening, he was taken to the airport. After briefly answering questions from reporters, he said he would speak more fully on his experiences at a press conference in London on 7 December. Rice landed in Cork on a wet, windy, wintry Sunday evening, 5 December, where he was met by his five brothers and his sister. His eldest brother Liam took off his coat and put it over his shoulders before he answered questions for a crowd of journalists. Press reports said that Rice, on arrival, was still wearing the casual clothes, including white plimsolls, given to him in Buenos Aires by the staff of the Irish embassy. Jean Sheridan of the *Irish Press* noted: 'Penniless and without a personal belonging in the world apart from letters and his passport, Fr Patrick Rice arrived safely home in Fermoy last night after eight weeks in Argentinian jails and permanent expulsion from the country where he had served the poor and downtrodden for the past six years.'[166] Donal Musgrave of the *Irish Times* wrote that Rice looked 'gaunt, exhausted and nervous, as if mentally drained'.[167] After standing for photographs with his siblings, he patiently explained the circumstances of his arrest: 'I was walking with another person (a girl who had personal problems and who was suspected of being a subversive) when one of them [a policeman in plain clothes] approached me. He was armed, holding a revolver, and was pointing it at me. I didn't know whether he was a robber or a policeman. He told me to stop or I would be shot.' Accused of being a subversive, Rice denied that was the case or that he had been involved with leftist guerrillas: 'I had always denied it – but it was not a judge who asked the questions,' he remarked. Queried about the use of torture, he told the journalists: 'Ill-treatment is normal under the harsh military regime in Argentina, and I got the usual sort of treatment.' He said that he had been kept in a small compound with eighty prisoners, including ten priests. They heard mass, celebrated by the prison chaplain, every Monday.[168] Asked by Musgrave if he felt that he would come out alive, he said: 'I felt all along that I would come out alive.' He stressed that he had never been charged with any crime. When released from jail, he signed a police declaration saying that there were no grounds for any such charge. Rice expressed great concern for the girl arrested with him, Fátima Cabrera, and a priest of his own congregation who had been 'disappeared'. He then singled out Justin Harman for special praise, explaining that his support 'was really fantastic'. Rice said that both Harman and the Irish ambassador Wilfred Lennon had communicated regularly with him and that, as he was only permitted to write letters to his parents in Spanish, Harman had translated them and sent them to his home in Fermoy. In conclusion, he thanked all the people in Ireland who had helped him. He asked that they continue to pray for the people who were suffering in Argentina: 'I have left an awful lot behind me. Argentina has had six years of deep influence on my life. I am leaving all my friends behind.' He looked forward to spending Christmas with family, which he had not done for thirteen years.[169] He then left the airport with his siblings for an emotional reunion with his mother and father at the family farm in Strawhall, Fermoy.

Rice did not give himself much time to rest. He flew to London at 7.45 p.m. on the 6th to participate in a press conference the following day, organised by the Catholic Institute for International Relations. The *Times* (London) reporter on 8 December described Rice as a boyish thirty-one and that when he had addressed the press after his flight to London he 'spoke haltingly ... and was obviously suffering the effects of the electric shock and water torture to which he was subjected after his abduction'. His abductors, Rice said, belonged to the Anti-Communist Alliance (AAA) or Triple A and they had accused him of 'collaborating with revolutionaries and painting propaganda slogans'. He never had any requests for assistance from guerrillas, he said, and, as far as he knew, he had never been in contact with any of them. But in the context in which he worked, he added, it was impossible to distinguish a guerrilla from any ordinary person.[170] Edmund Townshend in the *Daily Telegraph* quoted Rice as saying that 'at no stage have I co-operated or collaborated with any revolutionary organisation in Argentina. I did not paint any slogans on any walls, as alleged against me. I identify myself completely with the Catholic Church in Argentina, which does not endorse violence but pleads for social justice for all Argentinians'.[171]

The *Irish Times* carried the most complete account of his London press conference, reporting that Rice identified completely with the Catholic Church in not endorsing violence. He said the Catholic Church was the only institution in Argentina which had the confidence of the mass of the people. But he was critical of the 'unfortunate support' given by military chaplains and some members of the hierarchy to the regime.[172] Rice described how he had been hooded and tied to a foam rubber couch before electric current was passed through his hands and feet, his head and his genitals.[173] The *Irish Press* coverage of the press conference detailed how he had been tied down on a couch with his clothes still on. The hood was taken off and his eyes were blindfolded. They put rubber around his hands and feet. He felt the electric current going through his body: 'When they do it to your head, one has the sensation that your body sort of paralyses. It is difficult to sleep for a long time afterwards. One hears the screaming of another person. One sometimes thinks one is dreaming, like in a nightmare.'[174]

Rice repeated that he was fortunate to have had the help and support of the Irish embassy in Buenos Aires. He remained very fearful for the thousands of Argentines who did not have his connections. He also repeated his concern for Fátima Cabrera, who was still in detention, and he promised to work tirelessly for her release and for the freedom of others in Argentina held in illegal and clandestine detention.[175] Concluding, Rice said that the 'Irish government has done everything for me. Perhaps other governments could do a bit more ... My ambassador also did an awful lot. I would like to thank everybody for their efforts to secure my release. I ask that these efforts be directed to the plight of those who are being imprisoned, tortured and killed in Argentina today'.[176] The *Irish Independent*, in response to what Rice had said, wrote an editorial on 8 December: 'Let us not get entangled in South American politics – they mean nothing to most of us. But we ought to be concerned with the outlook of any government which permits, where it does not order, torture to be used on suspects. And for a start we ought to tell the Argentinians what we think of their barbaric methods.' The morning that editorial appeared, the Department of Foreign Affairs emphasised that the Irish embassy in Buenos Aires had taken immediate action as soon as it had learned that Rice was in custody. While Ambassador Lennon knew that the priest had suffered ill-treatment, he could only mention that briefly on his first visit to the priest in prison. Rice had requested the embassy staff not to give publicity to that situation for various reasons, including the desire to not prejudice his own situation in any way. The department had taken up the question of Rice's treatment with the Argentine government in both Dublin and Buenos Aires 'and we are not aware of any further ill treatment after our official protests'. The ambassador had pressed for Rice to be released or charged and brought to trial. Rice had received regular visits from Lennon and Harman.[177]

But hovering around behind the press criticisms was the question of whether the Irish government ought to have withdrawn its ambassador from Buenos Aires. Apart from recalling the Irish ambassador to London for a briefing in the early 1970s over events in Northern Ireland during a phase of great difficulty in Anglo-Irish relations, successive Irish governments since the very foundation of the state had refused to withdraw its envoys from countries undergoing wars, revolutions, military coups or authoritarian rule, as in Nazi Germany and fascist Italy, civil war in Spain from 1936 to 1939 and revolution in Portugal in 1975. Neither did FitzGerald follow the example of other countries[178] when General Francisco Franco's government executed five revolutionary Basque nationalists on 28 September 1975. The ambassadors of Britain, West Germany, East Germany, the Netherlands, Norway, Denmark, Sweden, Italy and Belgium were withdrawn for consultations. The French ambassador had left Spain 'on holidays' before the executions took place.[179] On that occasion, FitzGerald believed that it was inevitable that the recalled ambassadors would have to return to Madrid after a short period at home, thereby serving merely as a propaganda victory for the Spanish dictator.[180]

During FitzGerald's efforts to have Rice released, the political division, as already mentioned, reviewed whether it would be valid to withdraw the Irish ambassador in response to the kidnapping and torture of the priest – a precedent having been set by the British Labour government in the Sheila Cassidy case. Noel Dorr asked his senior staff member Patrick McKernan to find out the current British thinking on the Cassidy precedent. Dr O'Dwyer at the Irish embassy in The Hague informed McKernan that during a recent Latin American working group he met the British delegate, who confirmed that 'the decision to withdraw their ambassador was very much the result of party political pressure and not the advice of [then foreign secretary] James Callaghan's civil servants, who felt it was not in the national interest to take such a drastic step. British delegate felt in the case of Father Rice that we would do better to make a very strong private statement to the Argentine authorities on the issue, a statement which could if necessary be released in the event of a P.Q. [parliamentary question] on the matter'.[181] The withdrawal of Ambassador Lennon was never an option during the time Rice was in prison.

FitzGerald raised the Rice case when he held talks in Moscow on 15 December with the Soviet foreign minister Andrei Gromyko and with President Podgorny, chairman of the Praesidium of the Supreme Soviet. FitzGerald spoke of the ineffectiveness of the UN mechanism on human rights and used Chile as his primary illustration of how UN action could be blocked. He also gave the case of Fr Rice in Argentina as another example of the need for some international form of protection for fundamental rights.[182] FitzGerald, back in Dublin the following day, stoutly defended the actions of his staff when answering questions on the Rice case from the opposition spokesman on foreign affairs Michael O'Kennedy:

> We are not aware that Father Rice suffered any further ill-treatment after our protests. As I indicated in the House on 4 November we also urged most strongly at the highest level that Father Rice should either be released or brought to trial without delay. I am glad to say that our intervention in the case led to Father Rice's release. The Deputy will be aware from the replies I have just given to his previous questions that basic standards of human rights should be upheld in other countries and of my views on the most effective way of achieving this.[183]

He stressed that while the Irish government deplored the violation of human rights wherever it occurred, the breaking off of diplomatic relations was not among the measures which would be taken as a general rule. 'Such a drastic action would not be in the interests of the very people whom they wished to protect,' he said.[184]

Though Ireland traditionally did not recall its ambassadors even in difficult circumstances, there was one episode which might be classified as an exception (or aberration) and a precedent. In November 2011, the Irish government suddenly announced the closure of its embassy to the Holy See because 'it yielded no economic return and that Ireland's interests could be sufficiently represented by a non-resident ambassador'.[185] Ironically, that was at a time of great need, probably the greatest need since that mission was established in 1929. If ever a resident Irish diplomat was called for, it was during the years when the government was seeking to gain information in files held in the Holy See regarding the role of a number of priests and brothers in child sexual abuse cases in Ireland through the decades. The fact that successive Irish governments were frustrated by the Holy See's perceived lack of cooperation was no justification for the closure of the embassy at that critical time.[186]

Paradoxically, Ireland had no ambassador resident in Buenos Aires from shortly after Rice's deportation. Lennon was spending his last few days in Argentina before his retirement. On 5 December, there was a mass in his honour at Holy Cross and a reception at the Colegio Santo Domingo, where he was presented with an engraved image of Our Lady of Luján by the Federation of Irish-Argentine Societies.[187] On his final work day in the Buenos Aires embassy, he wrote a single word in his diary: 'Out'. He and his wife left Argentina on 15 December. In a front-page article in *TSC*, Fr Richards described Ambassador Lennon as 'the epitome of a perfect diplomat', with 'intelligence, learning, dignity, courtesy, generosity, protocol and professional informality, all rounded off with a delightful dose of wit, humour and repartee'. His wife Kitty was described as having been very popular, charming, enchanting and the 'perfect and gifted hostess'.[188] Lennon was sixty when he retired as ambassador with the rank of assistant secretary on 17 January 1977. Harman was again left to hold the fort alone in Buenos Aires for two and a half months until the new ambassador arrived at the end of February.

The expulsion of Rice received little more than a few paragraphs in a few Argentine papers such as the *Buenos Aires Herald* and *La Opinión*. My research is not exhaustive in this area. The editor of *TSC*, Fr Richards, wrote an editorial on 17 December: 'In view of the gravity of the facts that constitute the violation of express norms of our National Constitution and of the Penal Code and given that in the case of the detained Father Rice we believe an error was made, we do not doubt that the competent authority would have initiated the corresponding investigation in order to formulate a categorical disclaimer [denial] in defence of the prestige of our country, especially in Ireland, or otherwise proceed to the punishment of the guilty.'[189] Richards' tongue was firmly in his cheek when he made that latter observation. However, the Argentine authorities in an official notification on 27 December set out the legal basis on which Rice's expulsion was based. Harman sent the translation of the relevant paragraph of the document to Iveagh House on 11 January 1977. One section read as follows: 'In this regard, the Foreign Ministry wishes to state that at no stage was the said individual held under arrest at the disposition

of the National Executive Power, having been expelled from the country under
Decree no. 2665/76 for being in contravention of the terms of Law no 21.259.'[190]
During the entire period of Rice's detention, Harman noted that the embassy
– and the prisoner himself – were under the impression that he was being held
at the disposition of the executive power, under the provisions of the state of
siege. Having discussed the note with one of the embassy lawyers, Harman
concluded that 'it would seem [it] was issued to cover a legal technicality',
explaining as follows: 'Law 21.259 covers the deportation of non-nationals from
the country, and the section which has relevance to the Rice case is Article 1,
sub-section C which indicates that the Executive Power can order the expulsion
of a foreigner when "he has carried out, in the Republic, activities which affect
social peace, national security and public order".' Harman commented that
'this process is entirely extra-judiciary (and thereby, according to our lawyer,
un-constitutional) in that it is the Executive Power which decides if the
foreigner is guilty of such activities, and not the Courts. No appeal is allowed.
Presumably, the note may also be seen as an indication that, notwithstanding
Fr Rice's subsequent declarations of total innocence, he is and will continue to
be regarded officially by the Argentine authorities as being guilty'.[191] Harman's
clear parsing of the document calls to mind the Erasmus adage: *in regione
caecorum rex est luscus* or 'in the country of the blind, the one-eyed man is king'.
In late December and in early 1977, Harman attended meetings with his EEC
political counsellor colleagues. Reporting on 11 January, he outlined how he
had 'described the [Rice] case at a recent meeting of the Political Counsellors
attached to the Embassies of the Nine and the US here, and it was pointed out,
in the experience of most of those present with similar cases, that seven weeks
was a remarkably short period of time [in which to secure Rice's release]'.[192]

The Irish embassy's management of the Rice kidnapping ought to be used
as a case study when training Irish diplomats – the better to prepare them
for future postings when, having to deal with unorthodox consular cases in
authoritarian regimes, the life of an Irish citizen may hang in the balance.

CHAPTER SIX

Ireland and the Denunciation of Human Rights Abuses in Argentina, 1977–9: Mgr Kevin Mullen – 'I just keep coming up against a stone wall'

Political change in the United States in autumn 1976 marked a serious reversal for the civilian military government in Argentina. Sworn in on 20 January 1977 as the thirty-ninth US president, the Democrat Jimmy Carter gave notice in his inaugural address that he was about to make major changes in his country's foreign policy: 'Because we are free, we can never be indifferent to the fate of freedom elsewhere. Our moral sense dictates a clear-cut preference for those societies which share with us an abiding respect for individual human rights.'[1] The composition of his newly formed foreign policy team made for gloomy reading for the military regimes in Latin America which had proliferated during the heyday of Kissinger's era of machtpolitik. Cyrus Vance, a liberal lawyer with previous political experience in the Johnson presidency, was named secretary of state. The civil rights veteran Andrew Young was appointed the US permanent representative at the UN. Patricia (Patt) Derian, a registered nurse and veteran civil rights activist, became director of a small State Department bureau created by Congress the year before to keep the legislature informed about the recipients of US aid and who were committing human rights abuses. Later, she was given the title US coordinator for human rights. In 1978, Derian was made assistant secretary of state for human rights and humanitarian affairs. In gratitude for her work on human rights in Argentina, a Peronist government in 2006 gave her its highest award, the Order of the Liberator General San Martín. She died from an Alzheimer's-related disease on 20 May 2016.[2] Her obituary in the *New York Times* noted that she 'earned a reputation for angering despots as well as career State Department diplomats, many of whom viewed her as well-meaning but unsophisticated'.[3] The Argentine civilian military regime, to which she paid particular attention, swiftly came to regard her with disdain.

On 6 December 1978, the thirtieth anniversary of the passing of the UN Universal Declaration of Human Rights, Carter encapsulated his thinking when asserting that 'human rights are the soul of our foreign policy'.[4] While determined to engineer that radical change in foreign policy, Carter faced continued opposition from the traditionalists in the State Department and from his hawkish national security adviser Zbigniew Brzezinski. Although Latin America was not ranked high on the latter's agenda, he supported a tough policy towards Cuba and any other country in the region in receipt of support from the Soviet Union. US foreign policy traditionalists inadvertently shared the hope of many Latin American military dictators who had entered into a cynical consensus, according to the historian David Sheinin, that the Carter administration 'marked a temporary aberration in US policymaking', and 'if they could handle Carter for the short term, human rights would return in the *longue durée* to a much less significant place in a restored, traditional American foreign policy'.[5] Sheinin also observed that on the other side of the international Cold War divide, the Argentine junta felt almost no pressure on human rights from the Soviet Union and the communist states, including Cuba. The Soviet bloc accepted 'the supposed need for military intervention in Argentina' in the same way as the US had done in March 1976.[6]

In Ireland, the election of a Democrat as US president was warmly received by the public and by the government. The minister for foreign affairs, Garret FitzGerald, was philosophically more at one with Carter than with his Republican predecessors. Besides sharing common values regarding the major geopolitical issues of the day, Dublin traditionally enjoyed stronger support from the Democratic Party than from within Republican ranks on the vital question of ending violence in Northern Ireland. Remaining in office until June 1977, FitzGerald worked particularly hard to secure a Washington-backed breakthrough in that vital area and his determination and that of senior Irish diplomats paid off. In a historic and precedent-setting statement, Carter said on 30 August 1977 that the US had a legitimate interest in seeing that a 'peaceful settlement' was secured there and that he would provide financial assistance to help bring about such an outcome. Reporting in early November, the Irish ambassador to the US, Seán Donlon, confirmed that Carter had been 'the first president to commit his administration on the Northern Ireland issue'.[7] That

White House statement greatly displeased the British government.[8] However, FitzGerald was no longer minister when that diplomatic breakthrough occurred. A general election on 16 June 1977 had returned a Jack Lynch-led Fianna Fáil government to power. FitzGerald was now leader of Fine Gael and of the opposition. In early 1977, Michael O'Kennedy was the new minister for foreign affairs. In Iveagh House, there were staff reassignments following the change in government.[9] In relation to Irish–Argentine relations, the assistant secretary and political director Noel Dorr was central to decision-making in that area and was ably assisted by Pádraic [Patrick] McKernan,[10] Jeremy Craig, Tom Lyons and others.[11]

There were also personnel shifts in Buenos Aires at the US embassy. Raúl Héctor Castro, a Mexican-American who had been governor of Texas between 1975 and 1977, was appointed as the new US ambassador to Argentina. His predecessor, Robert Hill, left his post in May 1977.[12] In addition, the appointment in 1977 of Franklin Allen 'Tex' Harris as political officer with responsibility for human rights was of great importance. He opened the doors of the US embassy to the relatives of victims and human rights advocacy groups seeking to find news of the disappeared. He recorded each case of disappearance, detention and torture. His reporting on human rights abuses, based on interviews with families of the disappeared, created friction with what he termed the 'front office' staff at the embassy. Despite being nearly fired for insubordination as efforts were made to prevent his reporting reaching Washington, he insisted on interviewing the relatives of the disappeared at the embassy. Collecting over two thousand personal accounts of disappearances, he put each case on an index card, which became a full dossier of human rights violations by the Argentine government. His work was recognised in 1993 when the State Department awarded him the coveted Distinguished Honor Award for his reporting between 1977 and 1979 in Argentina.[13] The first secretary at the nunciature, Mgr Kevin Mullen, found Harris to be a kindred spirit. He worked closely throughout his posting with Harris and others working with him. Mullen was not impressed with the narrow policy framework of many European embassies in Buenos Aires which were concerned exclusively with the fate of their citizens and passport-holders.

The Irish embassy in Buenos Aires was without an ambassador between mid-December and the end of February. Justin Harman was again left alone to run the mission until Seán Ó hÉideáin took up his appointment. Ó hÉideáin had joined the diplomatic service in 1949, gaining wide professional experience in London, Chicago, Washington, the Holy See and the United Nations while also doing short relief postings to Buenos Aires in the early 1950s. He also provided relief cover in 1961 following the sudden death of the chargé William Butler.[14] The new Irish ambassador possessed many strengths as a diplomat, being very dedicated and hard-working, and he enjoyed excellent personal relations with the Irish-Argentine community, who held him in the highest esteem. However, his professional conservatism, punctiliousness and rigid administrative style did not best equip him to face the challenges confronting the Irish mission in the extraordinary circumstances of a country in the throes of a brutal and sustained repression. A long-standing reservist in the Irish army,[15] Ó hÉideáin proved to be all too credulous in his dealings with the high command of the Argentine armed forces. Together with many other ambassadors, including the US envoy Hill, he cleaved to the mistaken view that General Videla represented the moderate wing of the armed forces and that he was a bulwark against a 'hardline' faction waiting in the wings to stage a coup within the coup. Despite abundant evidence to the contrary, he never wavered from that pro-Videla view for the duration of his posting. Coinciding with Ó hÉideáin's arrival in Buenos Aires, on 1 March Amnesty International published a damning report finding the civilian military government responsible for a campaign of disappearances and the running of a nationwide network of clandestine detention centres in which systematic torture was carried out, followed, in many cases, by extra-judicial killings. The investigations had been conducted between 6 and 15 November 1976.[16] The report included names of the disappeared[17] and featured evidence provided by Patrick Rice and many other victims and eyewitnesses to human rights abuses in Argentina.[18] Its overall conclusion was that there was 'overwhelming evidence that many innocent citizens have been imprisoned without trial, have been tortured and have been killed. The actions taken against subversives have therefore been self-defeating: in order to restore security, an atmosphere of terror has been established; in order to counter illegal violence, legal safeguards have been removed and violent illegalities condoned'. It added that 'no one can rely on legal protection, and in view of the practice of the security forces, no one is safe from abduction and torture'.[19] Amnesty asked the Argentine government to publish a list of all its prisoners and the report invited the UN to send a mission to investigate the state of human rights in the country.[20]

In response, the Argentine foreign minister briefed the Irish ambassador, together with other envoys, strongly calling into question the credibility of the report and claiming that the findings were based on hearsay and on slanted information received from subversives. But having had an Irish citizen kidnapped, tortured and jailed without charge for over two months at the end of 1976, the new Irish ambassador found the official government response to be lame and unconvincing.[21] However, Ó hÉideáin did not interpret his instructions upon arrival in Buenos Aires as giving him a brief to intervene on behalf of jailed Irish-Argentines unless they were in possession of an Irish passport. As he interpreted it, the ambassador's job was to maintain a good working relationship with the civilian military government and to advance Irish economic, cultural and historical links between the two countries. As we will see, in his handling of the Fátima Cabrera case, Ó hÉideáin provided many arguments to Iveagh House as to why she should not be given a visa to live in Ireland. As Ireland had diplomatic relations with Argentina, he perceived his role to be to retain a good working relationship with the regime. Although Ó hÉideáin and the first secretary at the apostolic nunciature, Mgr Kevin Mullen, became good friends during their time in Buenos Aires, they differed radically in their respective interpretations of the role of the diplomat during the civilian military dictatorship. Mullen sought to save lives and to hold the government to account over disappearances. He received the families of those who had been taken away and confronted the military with carefully composed lists of names to determine whether those held in the many clandestine detention centres were dead or alive. The editor of the *Buenos Aires Herald*, Robert Cox, recalled that senior members of the armed forces and the federal police quickly bestowed on Mullen the unenviable moniker 'monseñor rojo' or 'red monsignor'.[22] Ó hÉideáin, soon after his arrival, witnessed Mullen excoriate the government in public. The occasion was less than two weeks before the first anniversary of the coup d'état and a few days before the feast of St Patrick. Together with Harman, the ambassador attended mass at Holy Cross on Sunday, 13 March 1977. A large congregation was present to celebrate St Patrick's Day, among them Frs Kevin O'Neill (Pallottine), Ricardo O'Farrell (SJ), Patricio J. Geoghegan (Salesian) and Passionists Juan Langan, Eugenio Delaney, Dionisio Doyle, Esteban Quaine, Heriberto Dolan, Ambrosio Geoghegan, Cristóbal Gibson and Gregorio Miles. Mullen gave the homily in Spanish.[23] Preaching on the life and Christian witness of St Patrick, Mgr Mullen had in mind the five Pallottines who had been murdered on 4 July 1976 and the many thousands of others who were victims of state violence – teachers, lawyers, academics, journalists, artists, actors, catechists, etc. He began with a reflection on the life of St Patrick in an historical context and then posed the question: what would the saint think of contemporary Ireland and the military conflict in Northern Ireland? While using the trope of talking about modern Ireland, he was in reality critiquing contemporary Argentina.

If I may use the Spanish phrase, on that occasion Mullen *puso el dedo en la llaga* – put his finger into the wound – when he recalled the work of St Patrick,

6.1 Mgr Kevin Mullen (left) with the papal nuncio Pio Laghi and on his left three Christian Brothers from Newman College, Buenos Aires, Seán Hayes, David O'Connor and John Burke (principal)

who had sought to convert a pagan society 'which had primitive and savage customs', as there were people in that ancient society who had disappeared others and killed with ease and sold people as slaves. St Patrick, kidnapped as a boy from his home in Wales by an Irish raiding party, was once among the disappeared. Returning to Ireland many years later as a bishop, Mullen said, Patrick 'preached the gospel with its strong ethical code that taught the ideas of a God of love, that human life was sacred and that kidnapping was a sin'. What would St Patrick think if, 1,500 years later, he revisited Ireland and enquired about the influence of Christian values, the belief in God in that society and whether a sense of justice and respect for one's neighbour was evident? Answering his own question, Mullen said that St Patrick would condemn the actions of the Irish Republican Army, terrorists who planted bombs among innocent people who had nothing to do with them or with their cause. If St Patrick could also visit the European Court of Human Rights, he said, the saint would be shocked to hear that the armed forces in Northern Ireland had admitted to the use of repressive measures in order to stop the guerrillas, which included torture.[24] He said St Patrick, in his letter to Coroticus, condemned in the clearest language those who kidnapped, robbed and killed. As those writings demonstrated, Mullen said, the threat to society came not only from the use of violence but from the silence of those who were confronted by rape (*violación*). He said the celebration of St Patrick's life should not be confined to a single day a year which evoked the memory of an honest but uneducated man, explaining the Trinity with a shamrock and casting snakes out of Ireland. St Patrick, he said, 'is not a lifeless mummy, a bell to ring, or a flag to hoist once a year' but that his call was the call of Christ – a call to action in the midst of a cruel and violent world. Patrick knew that peace was not merely the absence of violence, but the reign of justice and of Christian love.[25]

The organ played traditional Irish airs which were sung throughout the service, ending with the rousing hymn 'Faith of Our Fathers', the words of which read in part:

> Our fathers, chained in prisons dark,
> Were still in heart and conscience free;
> How sweet would be their children's fate,
> If they, like them, could die for thee.
> ... Faith of our Fathers, living still
> In spite of dungeon, fire, and sword;[26]

Those fiery sentiments condemning British colonial violence and intolerance in Ireland through the centuries had a particular resonance for a congregation living under a dictatorship. Using an Irish historical trope throughout his sermon, who in the congregation would not have known that Mullen was speaking in metaphor about the abuse of human rights in Argentina! *TSC* reported his words in full.[27] Unfortunately, I have been unable to find the relevant report by Ó hÉideáin, though it is certain that he did comment on it at the time as he wrote in January 1979: 'Vide my report dated 15 April 1977, pages 2–3 re his St Patrick's Day sermon.'[28] On the day the sermon was delivered, 13 March, Ó hÉideáin reported that a US State Department document showed that 'vigilante squads operated with apparent immunity and used torture to extract information and that current and previous Argentine administrations had looked the other way'.[29] In conversation around 23 March with the commander-in-chief of the air force, Brigadier General Orlando Ramón Agosti, Ó hÉideáin was told that 'the violence of subversives, amounting to a state of war, had to be countered and defeated by governmental armed forces' and that the job of 'pacifying' the country had not yet been completed. The Irish ambassador concluded that there was no prospect of a softening of government policy on 'subversion'.[30]

The daily kidnappings and street shoot-outs continued. The distinguished Irish-Argentine writer Rodolfo Walsh was among those to die that month. On the first anniversary of the coup, 25 March, he left his hiding place to distribute copies of an 'open letter to the military junta' (*'carta abierta de un escritor a la junta militar'*) in postboxes around the city. That was a ruse to prevent the authorities from seizing all the copies in a single batch.[31] Continuing to work as a press officer for the Montoneros, in the weeks before his death Walsh had tried to persuade the guerrilla leadership to abandon the armed struggle in favour of political action. He lost both the ideological argument and his life, dying that day in a firefight in the street with members of the armed forces. He was fifty.[32] The artist León Ferrari created a glass wall monument with lines from that last letter in the grounds of the ex-ESMA – a building now called the Space for Memory and Human Rights. The monument to Walsh was unveiled in a ceremony on 25 March 2012.[33]

The US assistant secretary of state for human rights and humanitarian affairs, Patricia (Patt) Derian, visited Buenos Aires in March 1977 to see for herself what was happening in the country.[34] For the duration of her visit, she noticed that three cars always followed her limousine. When she complained to one of her US embassy bodyguards about such ostentatious 'security', he informed her that she was being watched by the three branches of the armed forces, each one not trusting the other to guarantee her safety. She also told me that a 'human fly' had climbed up several storeys on the outside of her hotel to search her room.[35] Derian met the leading members of the military and engaged in robust exchanges. By the end of her brief stay, she collected over five thousand denunciations and presented them to the government. She met the papal nuncio Pio Laghi,[36] who said that Argentina was '100 metres beneath the water' when the military took over in 1975, the result of the influence of Perón 'in and out of office' who had 'dominated and distorted the political scene for thirty years'. The nuncio used her to send a warning to Washington to move cautiously when dealing with the Argentine government. Videla and other military leaders were 'good men at heart', he said.[37] Singling out Videla, he said he was 'a good Catholic' and 'a man deeply aware of and concerned over the personal religious implications of his responsibilities'.[38] Laghi warned Derian that 'the moderate elements in the government around Videla might be weakened and that hardline generals would take power [with] their own coup'.[39]

When she asked the nuncio for his views on the persecution of the Argentine Catholic Church, he rejected 'her inference that the Church as such was under attack'. From among the 5,500 priests and 11,000 nuns in the country, he said that there were twelve priests in detention, seven of whom were non-Argentine. Several of those in custody, Laghi added, had been detained by the previous government up to two and a half years ago. The church had been pressing for resolution of their cases. Laghi said that about seven of the priests had admitted their involvement in, or association with, subversion, 'one had hidden arms for the guerrillas and two had been captured 'with arms in hand leading an assault on a police station'. In the case of the imprisoned foreign clergy, Laghi was hopeful that it would be possible 'to secure their expulsion from Argentina after trial'. He concluded: 'But aside from these cases and isolated episodes such as those involving Father [Patrick] Rice and Father [James] Weeks, it could not be said that the Church was subject to special persecution by the government.'[40] The nuncio also denied to Derian 'that Jews were subject to persecution'. He acknowledged that individual anti-Semitic military or police officers might have exhibited their bias 'when dealing with a subversive suspect who also happened to be Jewish, but felt that in the broader sense there was no anti-semitism in Argentina'.[41] A few years later, Laghi said, when posted to Washington DC: 'Perhaps I wasn't a hero but I was no accomplice.'[42]

Derian may never have known that Mgr Kevin Mullen's role at the nunciature mirrored that of 'Tex' Harris at the US embassy. She refused to meet Laghi again even after he became apostolic delegate to the US in 1980 and pro-nuncio in 1984.

Robert Cox, whose courage during those years of dictatorship has been chronicled in a documentary made in 2018,[43] worked closely with Mullen between 1976 and early 1979. He wrote in his memoirs that the first secretary at the nunciature 'worked in the shadow' of Laghi, who 'played an ambiguous role'.[44] Cox drew this word picture of Mullen: 'He was short in stature but lion hearted. He ignored death threats and shrugged off efforts designed to intimidate him. The threats included a suitcase bomb left outside the mansion that housed Vatican diplomats. The bomb failed to go off.'[45] Cox also wrote: 'I reported as much as I could in the [*Buenos Aires*] *Herald* without endangering more lives. He [Mullen] was drawing up lists of the missing and asking the military where they were. When would they be put on trial if believed to be guilty, or freed if innocent?'[46] Cox further noted: 'Kevin heard so many sad stories', and he 'continued to compile lists of names and badgered the generals with them'.[47] Again and again, Mullen repeated to Cox in frustration: 'I just keep coming up against a stone wall.'[48]

As stated earlier, Mullen worked closely with like-minded officials in the US embassy throughout his posting. In a meeting on 2 December 1977 with the US political counsellor William H. Hallman, he explained his view that the Argentine government was 'deeply suspicious of any member of the hierarchy who is not 100 per cent behind the government's repression. There is an apparently genuine belief that many priests – and even bishops – are "marxists". This is especially true of priests who have involved themselves in social action programs'. Mullen further observed that he did not detect 'great public outrage in Argentina against the principle of human rights violations, only sadness on the part of affected families'. When trying to find out the fate of many detained and disappeared persons, the nunciature quickly gave up having dealings with Minister Arlia's Foreign Office working group. Mullen said the nunciature preferred to 'deal directly with Minister of Interior Harguindeguy or the first army corps commander Suarez Mason', with whom they had reasonably close working relations. 'Not that they'll give us answers either', Mullen said. 'It's just that we grew tired of fighting it out with Arlia.'[49]

The editor of *TSC*, Federico (Fred) Richards, provided independent proof of Mullen's role in working on behalf of the families of the disappeared. On 13 April 1995, Richards recalled that he had visited the nunciature twice during the dictatorship seeking help to trace the whereabouts of his niece Gloria Kehoe Wilson (23). Having published a book of short stories entitled *Pico de Paloma* in late May 1977,[50] she was kidnapped from her apartment in Belgrano on 13 June, never to be seen alive again by her family. Accompanied by her father Ernesto 'Ernie' Kehoe, Richards met Mullen, who agreed to make immediate enquiries to determine her whereabouts: 'He ... told us that the Vatican Embassy used to periodically, every ten or fifteen days, send a list up to the Ministry of the Interior of people it knew had disappeared, requesting news or information.' On that visit Richards concluded that 'the nunciature staff could tell who was dead and who remained alive by the wording of the reply received from the ministry'.[51]

Overwhelmed by both his personal family loss over the then near certain death of his niece and the widespread loss of life through state violence in the country, Richards wrote an editorial in *TSC* on 24 June 1977 entitled 'Dialogue of the Deaf' ('*Diálogo de Sordos*'): 'The government of the Nation recognises that there are about 2,000 persons "disappeared". Our opinion is that there are a number of zeros missing from that number.' He wrote that people wanted 'to know where their loved ones are, of what are they accused, if they are alive, and if they are not, return the bodies. Is that too much to ask?'[52] On 8 July, in an editorial entitled 'Our Martyrs Live', Richards reminded his readers of the murder of the five Pallottines whose first anniversary fell on July 4th: '... where are the brave executioners of that black night? Why, if they thought they were saving the Homeland and purifying it from vermin, did they not come out and give their names in order to receive the deserved gratitude of the Homeland that they claim so much to serve? Why not preach about that epic [event] involving so much risk and courage? Only silence envelops them and their constituents ... They sought darkness for their crime and that same darkness will continue to be in their lives as a torment, as long as the mercy of God does not save them'. Taunting the murderers and the government, he wrote that the blood of the martyrs of Belgrano, Chamical (Bishop Angelelli, two priests and a layman) and many others would lead to victory; in the words of Martin Luther King, 'We shall overcome, we shall overcome.'[53] Despite his unwavering, consistent and forceful denunciation of human rights abuses in his country, Richards survived the years of civilian military dictatorship.[54] But his single-mindedness was a source of tension between himself and his religious superiors on the one hand and with a number of leaders of the Irish community on the other who had a controlling financial interest in *TSC*.[55]

Meanwhile, Mullen sent crystal clear reports to the secretariat of state in Rome which left no room for ambiguity about what was happening in Argentina. (The opening of the files in the Holy See for the period of the civilian military dictatorship will reveal the importance of Mullen's human rights work and the extent to which he cooperated with the families of the disappeared. That lies in the future.[56]) As a consequence, official Argentine visitors received a frosty reception when visiting the Holy See. At the end of October 1977 Admiral Massera visited Rome and had 'sharp exchanges' with the secretary of state, Cardinal Agostino Casaroli, 'who pointedly asked about the situation of several Catholic priests who had been attacked and detained or disappeared'. Later, Pope Paul VI admonished the admiral at an audience and expressed his 'wish for a speedy return to peace in Argentina'.[57]

Mullen had much to report on resistance to the military dictatorship. The future (1980) Nobel Peace Prize winner, Adolfo Pérez Esquivel, was one of those Christians who raised his voice in public. An architect and writer, he had become a full-time activist for peace and justice in 1974. He had condemned the violence both of the guerrilla groups and the armed forces. He was most closely identified with El Servicio de Paz y Justicia (SERPAJ) (Justice and Peace Service), which had its origins in Pax Romana.[58] His work for peace, though, had led to his jailing in Brazil in 1975 and in Ecuador in 1976 as a result of his outspokenness in the Permanent Assembly of Human Rights, set up in Buenos Aires in 1975, and in the Ecumenical Movement for Human Rights established in 1976. He was also a close friend and strong supporter of Emilio Mignone and his Center for Legal and Social Studies, Centro de Estudios Legales (CELS), established in 1979. In April 1977, Pérez Esquivel was arrested by Argentine police and held without trial for thirteen months, during which time he was tortured. He was released in May 1978 and immediately placed under house arrest for several months.

Members of the Episcopalian Church, Methodists, Lutherans, Presbyterians and Jehovah's Witnesses were also the targets of military repression, as was the very large Jewish community. Within the senior ranks of the Argentine military, there was a view that US Jews were responsible for the persistence and vehemence of President Carter's human rights policy towards their country. During one of Patt Derian's visits to Buenos Aires a senior army officer told her that 'most of the trouble [in Argentina] was caused by Israel because Israel wanted to occupy Patagonia because they were running out of land and there wasn't enough room for all the Jews'. Derian laughed in his face.[59] The infamous anti-Semitic forgery *The Protocols of the Elders of Zion* circulated freely in Argentina during the reign of the civilian military dictatorship, and an anonymously funded printing house disseminated Nazi literature such as *Mein Kampf*.[60] There were strong Jewish voices in Argentina and abroad against state-sponsored anti-Semitism. Rabbi Morton Rosenthal, head of the Latin America section of the Anti-Defamation League of B'nai B'rith (ADL), played a prominent role.[61] In Argentina, Rabbi Marshall Meyer and others were prominent in the resistance to the abuse of human rights. While working in Buenos Aires between 1959 and 1983, Meyer became well known for his weekly anti-dictatorship sermons at the Beth-El synagogue which attracted a wide following, many non-Jews among them.[62]

Many young Jews active in the professions, culture and the arts were among the thousands of disappeared. The founding editor of *La Opinión*, Jacobo Timerman, became one of the most prominent in the community to be taken.[63] (His assistant editor, Enrique Jara, was also disappeared and tortured. He survived to publish a full account of his ordeal.) Derian met Timerman shortly before he was abducted on 15 April 1977. He was tortured while, at the same time, being taunted with anti-Semitic jibes.[64] Robert Cox, his journalistic colleague, wrote trenchantly in the *Buenos Aires Herald* demanding his immediate release only to be arrested himself on 24 April and locked up in the same block as Timerman in federal police headquarters. Cox was as shocked as Rice and Timerman were to find a large swastika painted on an interior wall of the police headquarters: 'There in the antechamber was a huge swastika, emblazoned on the wall by the police themselves. Underneath was the word:

Nazinacionalismo (Nazi-nationalism)'.[65] Taken before a judge after twenty-four hours in custody, Cox was charged with two infractions of press law. Released on bail, he returned to work immediately to write about his imprisonment. A few days later, he went to the Casa Rosada and requested to see Videla. Refused an interview, he told the general's press secretary that the head of the junta should go down to the police headquarters and whitewash over the swastika which had been painted on the wall: 'It is a symbol of mass murder,' Cox said. The press secretary, Capt. Carlos Carpintero, told him as he was leaving: 'Don't expect him to do anything about it.'[66] Timerman was released on 17 April 1978. He was placed under house arrest and forced into exile the following year when his citizenship was revoked. Based on his sojourn in that Buenos Aires jail, he published *Prisoner without a Name, Cell without a Number* in 1981 to international acclaim.[67] He later lived in Israel, Madrid and New York before returning to Argentina on 7 January 1984. He died in Buenos Aires in 1999.[68]

An analysis of the role of the Catholic hierarchy and the Conferencia Episcopal Argentina (CEA) (Argentine Episcopal Conference) lies beyond the scope of this study, as do the parts played by the Conferencia Argentina de Religiosas (CONFER) (Argentine Conference of Women Religious) and the Confederación Argentina de Religiosos (CAR) (Confederation of Argentine Male Religious).[69] Mullen, reviewing CEA activities at the end of 1977, commented that the hierarchy had issued a public statement of concern in May over disappearances, detention without stated charges and long prison terms that included the use of torture. Dissatisfied with the impact the document had on the military, the bishops prepared an aide-mémoire repeating the concerns expressed in the published statement and adding additional concerns about unemployment, grave social inequalities and growing poverty. Mullen held that the hierarchy hoped their change of tactics would yield better results. Three archbishops presented the document to Videla at a lunch on 30 November 1977, a document Mullen described as being more a 'laundry list' of the concerns of individual bishops over incidents in their respective sees. Videla replied to the archbishops that he was aware of the grievances and wished only that he had the power to correct them. That comment was relayed to Mullen by a person who had been present at the lunch. The document was passed on to Admiral Massera and to Brigadier Orlando Agosti. According to Mullen, the bishops did not release it to the public.[70] Esquivel, Mignone and other prominent Catholics, including a small number of bishops, were outspoken, and their resistance came often at a very high personal cost, including loss of life.[71]

MOTHERS OF THE PLAZA DE MAYO

The mothers and grandmothers of the disappeared became the most widely known internationally of those who protested in Argentina during the early months of 1977. Initially, they gathered outside army barracks, police stations, government offices and churches to seek news of the disappeared. According to María Adela Antokoletz, whose brother – a lawyer – was disappeared,[72] families of the missing began to stand in front of the Stella Maris church, near the offices of the military vicariate which was close to the port in Buenos Aires. There Fr Emilio Grasselli (the private secretary of the military vicariate director, Bishop Adolfo Tortolo) allegedly played an ambiguous role while recording their petitions. Instead of helping, Grasselli was alleged to have used those private meetings with grieving families to gather intelligence for the military.[73] Frustrated by feelings of powerlessness, on 30 April 1977 Azuena Villaflor de De Vincenti, one of the leaders of the mothers, suggested that they hold a silent protest at 3.30 p.m. every Thursday in the Plaza de Mayo, which was close to both the cathedral and the Casa Rosada. And so it began. The Madres del Plaza de Mayo emerged.[74] Wearing simple yet distinctive white headscarves on which the names of their missing family members were written, the mothers and grandmothers walked quietly in a circle. Their presence quickly began to attract the attention of the international media and there was little the government could do to stop photos being published worldwide.[75] Fr Eugenio Delaney, the superior of the Passionist Fathers at Holy Cross, provided a room in which the group could meet every Monday at 5 p.m. or when they had need to do so. They received support from Fr Bernardo Hughes and other Passionist priests.[76] At the meetings, the mothers shared information, made lists of the disappeared and arranged for masses to be said in the different *barrios* for the missing.[77] The year (1977) drifted towards a close with little sign of an end to the abductions, the torture or the killings, but nothing could have prepared the mothers for what occurred between 8 and 10 December. Their group had been infiltrated by Captain Alfredo Astiz, an undercover naval officer, who had been posing as the brother of a disappeared person. His exploits earned him the name 'the blond angel of death'.[78] He was responsible for taking twelve in all, including the founding member of the group, Azuena Villaflor. The majority of the those taken were seized after a meeting at Holy Cross on 9 December. During the following days[79] two French nuns, Alice Domon and Léonie Duquet,[80] were seized. They were members of the Soeurs des Missions Etrangères, Notre Dame de la Motte.[81] A US embassy source confirmed that the State Intelligence Agency (SIDE) had carried out the twelve abductions.[82] Taken to ESMA, the detainees were interrogated, tortured, drugged and transported to a nearby airport, loaded onto an aeroplane and dumped while still alive into the River Plate. Sr Léonie Duquet's remains were found in a mass grave in July 2005 in General Lavalle Cemetery, 400 kilometres south of Buenos Aires. She is now buried in the grounds of Holy Cross monastery. The body of Alice Domon has never been located.[83] With the return of democracy, the two nuns had Plaza Hermana Alice Domon y Hermana Léonie Duquet in Buenos Aires named in their honour.[84] Cox and his wife Maud went to Paris in January 1980 to meet Mullen at the nunciature, where he was serving as the first secretary. Speaking about the murder of the nuns, 'he indicated with a gesture that their chests were cut open [and rocks inserted] before they were thrown into the sea [from a plane] in order that their bodies would sink to the bottom of the ocean'. Cox's wife asked Mullen how he knew. 'Confession, Maud,'[85] he replied. 'And let me tell you that all the information I have has been reported to the Vatican.'[86] The French authorities commemorated both nuns, in homage to their courage, by naming a street in Paris' thirteenth arrondissement Rue Alice-Domon-et-Léonie-Duquet.

RICE'S INTERNATIONAL SOLIDARITY CAMPAIGN AND THE FÁTIMA CABRERA CONSULAR CASE

The role of Kevin Mullen, first secretary at the nunciature, served as an example of how his interpretation of the policies of the Holy See required him to confront the military authorities over the growing number of disappearances. EEC embassies, with the exception of the Italian consulate, were slow at first to do the same. But latterly, the German and French embassies in particular offered visas to Argentines who were in danger and they were allowed to leave the country.

The policy debate in Iveagh House or in other relevant departments did not centre around whether or not to allow a few dozen or a few hundred Argentine refugees to find shelter in Ireland. Confronted by the human rights situation in that country, Minister for Foreign Affairs FitzGerald and a number of senior officials in Iveagh House were greatly impacted by the Rice kidnapping, disappearance and torture. They were aware in January 1977 that Rice was at the family farm near Fermoy recovering from a nervous breakdown and was under the care of Prof. Robert Daly, professor of psychiatry at University College Cork.[87] They were also aware that the girl imprisoned and tortured with him was still in danger in prison and that the priest had requested that she be given asylum. The Fátima Cabrera case was discussed intensively throughout

1977 in Iveagh House and between the departments of Foreign Affairs and Justice, where opinion was divided on whether or not to give her asylum. The Irish ambassador in Buenos Aires was opposed to her being given a visa or that the embassy should take any action on her behalf. Support for Rice's request to grant her an Irish visa came from the head of the political division, Noel Dorr, and was endorsed by FitzGerald and by his successor (after July 1977) Michael O'Kennedy. With the first half of this chapter as a backdrop to what was happening in Argentina, there follows a reconstruction of the policy debate on the Cabrera case which ran from 1977 to early 1979.

On 15 January 1977, Rice sent a somewhat confused handwritten letter to the minister thanking everyone 'from the lowest clerk in the building [Iveagh House] to the Irish Ambassador Mr Lennon and his secretary Mr Harman who were so courageous and good to [me]. Few knew the harassment, the long hours lost on sleep, or giving up to visit me, the degrading searches they had to go through with'. He also thanked the chauffeur of the Irish embassy, who had given him his own tie before he boarded the plane in Buenos Aires.[88] Referring to Fátima Cabrera, he said he had learned from other prisoners while in jail that her family still did not know her whereabouts. He believed that the Argentine authorities had taken the view: 'I am innocent and she is guilty.' Rice wrote that his admiration for her grew during his first days in prison, and that she was a person he hardly knew before they were abducted together: 'I think her example of bravery, self-sacrifice and true Christianity is [an] example for me and I think for many Irishmen. She could easily have falsely denounced me yet she did not. 4 times she was put naked on the electric torture rack and stopped screaming because they put an electric point in her mouth. In that state of coma she heard of the embassy's intervention on our behalf so she could at least heave a sigh of relief thanks to the Irish Government and people. She is 21 years of age, is married, of a very poor family, she is the only breadwinner. Her husband was crippled, losing his legs in a train accident some one and a half years ago.'[89]

Rice made a number of factual errors in the text above. Being barely acquainted with Fátima Cabrera, he did not even know her real name at the time of their abduction.[90] Cabrera, who was not yet twenty-one when abducted, was not married. She had had a partner, Alberto Cayetano Alfaro, from whom she had separated by the time of her abduction. Already introduced in Chapter 4, her former partner was a Peronist community leader in Villa 31[91] and was disappeared on 7 July 1977 while Cabrera was still in jail. (His remains were discovered in 2000 in a clandestine grave.)[92] Rice's main purpose in writing to the minister was to persuade him to grant her a visa to live in Ireland, where she could pursue her education. He based his argument on the constitutional right of every Argentine to request that she/he be allowed to go into exile provided they were in possession of a visa from another country. Rice asked FitzGerald to grant her a visa 'and if at all possible proclaim her an Irish citizen which would entitle her to visits from the [Irish] embassy'.[93] He followed up the letter with a visit at the end of January 1977 to Iveagh House accompanied by an unidentified priest friend. They were received by Tom Lyons (political division). Convinced that the Irish embassy would be able to locate her in the Argentine jail system, Rice said that there had to be an official record of her whereabouts, even if she had not been brought to trial. He said Cabrera could request permission to leave Argentina if the Irish government granted her a visa. Lyons replied that the department would be guided by the new ambassador's on-the-spot assessment of the position and of the possibilities available for approaching the authorities: 'I [Lyons] pointed out that Sra Cabrera is not an Irish citizen and has no claim to Irish citizenship so that we could not claim to represent her interests as of right, as we did in the case of Fr Rice himself, but would have to make any approach to the authorities on a basis of "good offices" or some similar argument. Fr Rice seemed to accept this.'[94]

Rice's superiors in the Little Brothers of Charles de Foucauld requested him to travel to Jamaica in early February 1977 to attend a meeting of its Latin American members. He was reunited there with his confrères Juan José 'Chiche' Kratzer and Mauricio Silva. They told him about what had befallen various members of the brothers: Frs Pablo Gazzarri, Carlos Bustos and Kratzer had gone underground, living in an apartment without a bathroom or a kitchen. Silva continued to live in Palermo and work daily as a road sweeper. Marta Garaygochea, a lay member of the order, lived there too. On 27 November 1976, the three priests – Kratzer, Gazzarri and Bustos – changed address and celebrated mass together to mark the fifth anniversary of Gazzarri's ordination. Afterwards, Gazzarri went out, never to be seen again. He was abducted and murdered by agents of the state.[95] That meeting brought home to Rice that the human rights situation in Argentina had got worse since he had been deported in December 1976. He returned to London, where he combined his pastoral work in a home for the terminally ill with participation in the solidarity campaign to highlight what was happening in Argentina. Together with two Little Brothers, he also worked in a centre set up to provide support for political refugees from Latin America. He helped establish the Committee for the Defence of Human Rights in Argentina and worked closely with Amnesty International and the Catholic Institute for International Relations. Rice was called to testify before the United Nations in Geneva on 21 February 1977 as one of a group representing the Argentine Commission for Human

Rights. There, he spoke about his experience under torture: 'You can feel your heart stop beating when they give you the electricity.' While being held in the Coordinación Federal, he said he remembered seeing a swastika painted on the wall: 'Some Jewish prisoners were pale and emaciated,'[96] he observed, adding that 'the attitude of the police towards them had been markedly anti-semitic'.[97] Those observations were independently confirmed by others who had been jailed in Argentina.[98]

Rice wrote to Harman in Buenos Aires on 9 February 1977 requesting a visa for Cabrera and giving the embassy information on how to reach her family. He also provided details of the support system his family had put in place for her when (if) she came to Ireland. She would live with his sister Kathleen Lee at the Pike, Fermoy, and arrangements had been made for her to have English lessons and to complete her secondary education in a local convent school. Her stay in Ireland would cost the state nothing. Rice's family had booked her an airline ticket with KLM, costing $778 or £550, which the embassy could pick up from the airline offices in Buenos Aires.[99] Harman informed Dublin on 28 February 1977 of the contents of the letter. He delayed replying to Rice until he had an opportunity to discuss the letter with Ambassador Ó hÉideáin.[100] On 11 March, Harman reported to Iveagh House that, a few days before writing, he had met 'Chiche' Kratzer at the embassy, who handed him a letter signed by all the Little Brothers present in Jamaica thanking the Irish embassy for getting Rice out of jail and out of the country. Kratzer also gave him news about Cabrera's family. Before being disappeared and jailed, her mother told Kratzer that Fátima had been the only breadwinner in her family, and Kratzer also reported that Cabrera's mother 'seems to include priest workers in blame for her daughter's imprisonment'. He also confirmed that Cabrera was separated from her husband. (The term 'husband' is misleading in this context.)[101] With the information received from Kratzer, the Irish ambassador wrote on 11 March requesting instructions from the minister 'as to whether embassy should try to contact Fátima's family' and whether the embassy should make an informal inquiry about her at the Argentine foreign office.[102] As will emerge later, Ó hÉideáin attached great weight to the report that Cabrera was 'married' and that her mother allegedly blamed worker priests for her imprisonment. While Rice was conscious of the danger of her remaining in jail where she might be murdered, the ambassador appeared to operate *sub specie aeternitatis*. Those fears were reinforced by another blow suffered by Rice's order in April 1977. Fr Carlos Bustos travelled in late March to his native Córdoba to meet the president of the episcopal conference, Cardinal Raúl Primatesta. As a founder member of Cristianos para la Liberación, Bustos urged the cardinal to encourage the Catholic hierarchy to broker a peace between the Montoneros and the armed forces. So hostile to that proposal was the cardinal that Bustos was forced to flee the residence under threat of being denounced to the military authorities. Returning safely to Buenos Aires, Bustos joined his confrères in Calle Malabia to celebrate the liturgy of Holy Week. While returning from the church of Nueva Pompeya on Good Friday, 8 April, Bustos was disappeared and taken to the CCD in Club Atlético, where he was tortured and killed. His body was never recovered. Knowing that he too was wanted by the authorities, Kratzer was smuggled by a nun into the nunciature. There he was provided with diplomatic travel papers and driven on 19 April in the nuncio's car to the airport. He was escorted onto a flight bound for Italy, where he went into exile. He worked as a nurse. Leaving the priesthood, he later married the niece of Arturo Paoli.

Concerned about the safety of the members of his order in Argentina, Fr João Cara, the regional of the Little Brothers for Latin America, arrived on 26 May 1977 in Buenos Aires. He stayed with Mauricio Silva at Calle Malabia, Palermo.[103] Both men visited the nunciature on 6 June, where they met Pio Laghi and Mullen. The nuncio informed them that 'the military government had given a commitment not to "touch" ["*tocar*"] priests or religious anymore'. Laghi advised them to visit Cardinal Aramburu.[104] The following day, Cara presented the cardinal with letters from the congregation of religious accrediting him as the regional of the Little Brothers in Latin America. The cardinal assured both of them that they could leave with the peace of mind (*andar tranquilos*) provided by a general who had landed by helicopter at the last episcopal conference to confirm that the government had nothing against priests or religious and that the authorities were only looking for one priest, '*un tal Chichio* [sic]'. (Cara believed that to be a reference to 'Chiche' Kratzer, who had already left the country.) Cara asked Aramburu to provide Silva with the *celebret* – a formal letter in the name of the cardinal allowing the priest to hear confessions and celebrate mass in dioceses other than his own. The cardinal signed the letter and handed it to Silva. A week later, 14 June, Silva was stopped by armed men while working as a road sweeper, bundled into the boot of an unmarked Ford Falcon and taken to an unidentified CCD in Buenos Aires. He was believed to have had the cardinal's letter in his pocket at the time.[105] The following morning, Cara and Marta Garaygochea went to the nunciature, where they informed Mullen of Silva's disappearance. Slamming his fist on the table, Mullen replied: '*Ay, no! Esto no debe ser. Los militares habían prometido*' ('Oh no! That can't be. The military have promised us'). He agreed to look into the matter immediately. That night four armed members of the federal police called to Calle Malabia, where they searched each room and spent two hours interrogating Cara and Garaygochea separately about Silva's activities.

Cara went on the 16th to the Uruguayan embassy (Silva was an Uruguayan citizen) to report the kidnapping. Afterwards he visited the cardinal, who was out when he called. An unidentified auxiliary bishop told Cara to remain calm, that he (the bishop) had been assured personally that the military no longer tortured anybody. The worst that could happen to Silva, he said, was that he would be given an injection of a truth serum, Pentothal. Cara regarded those remarks as being 'truly idiotic' ('*verdaderamente idiota*'). On the 17th, Cara made a denunciation to the police. He then went to La Plata to visit the auxiliary bishop, Mario Picchi, a friend of Silva's since their time as classmates in the Salesian order: 'But he acted as if he hardly knew him,' according to Cara. Returning on the 18th to the street where Silva had disappeared, Cara and Garaygochea[106] found a neighbour willing to talk. She told them she had witnessed from her apartment window at 8.30 in the morning the occupants of a white Ford Falcon kidnapping Silva.[107]

Speaking on 27 June to Yvonne Thayer of the US embassy, Mullen said that Silva 'could have been taken for assisting Argentines to leave the country'. He added that 'he [Mullen] and others had also tried to help threatened Argentines leave the country, usually via overland routes to neighboring countries'. Mullen commented that the church and the US government were the only two groups championing human rights: 'He expressed disdain,' according to the US minute, 'that European and other countries were only interested insofar as their own citizens were affected.' Mullen said the Catholic hierarchy believed those on the right were trying to provoke confrontations between the church and Videla in order to replace him with hardline elements – a trap the church had no intention of falling into. He added that the Catholic Church would probably refrain from new, public challenges to the government on disappearances and human rights practices 'so as not to jeopardize Videla's hold on the government' as he was seen as preferable to a possible more hardline and brutal right-wing replacement. He repeated that the Catholic Church would continue 'active, personal behind-the-scenes lobbying on human rights cases'.[108]

Cara continued his fruitless search to find Silva. Interviews with the cardinal archbishop of Córdoba, Raúl Francisco Primatesta, and Videla's secretary did not provide any answers. It is believed that Silva was tortured and then murdered in a place unknown. At the time of writing in 2022, his body has not been recovered.[109]

Rice, who respected and looked up to Silva, took the death of his close friend very badly. It also intensified his concern for Cabrera. For as long as she remained in jail, she was in grave danger. While the granting of citizenship to Argentines in such situations may have been a contested issue in foreign ministries around the world, in Ireland the debate was centred on whether or not the government would grant a visa to *one* Argentine citizen costing the state not a single penny to live in the country.

UNWELCOME VISITORS FROM ARGENTINA AND THE LAST PHASE IN THE FÁTIMA CABRERA VISA DEBATE

Reaching a decision on whether or not to grant Fátima Cabrera a visa was interrupted by the general election on 16 June 1977. Before the new Jack Lynch-led Fianna Fáil government took office on 5 July, a high-powered Argentine naval delegation arrived in Dublin to take part in ceremonies on 22 June to mark the bicentenary of the founder of the Argentine navy, William Brown,[110] in his native Foxford, County Mayo. Ambassador Ó hÉideáin stood four-square behind Ireland receiving the high-ranking naval officers without a caveat or reservation. His view was that it was important to maintain normal contacts with any country with which Ireland had diplomatic relations. Noel Dorr, however, the head of the political division and a native of Foxford, was unenthusiastic about the visit. Uppermost in his mind was the fact that the civilian military government had condoned the abduction, torture and wrongful imprisonment of an Irish citizen, as it did in relation to many thousands of its own citizens. However, the objections of the political division did not prevail on this occasion.

Arriving in Dublin on 21 June, the delegation was led by Vice-Admiral Armando Lambruschini, chief of staff of the navy and a classmate and close friend of Admiral Massera.[111] Accompanied by his aide de camp, Lieutenant-Commander Norberto Horacio Dazzi, the party also included Commander Julio Gandolfo and Commander Miguel Guruceaga.[112] On the afternoon of the 21st, President Patrick Hillery received them at Áras an Uachtaráin. The delegation was invited to dinner that evening by the lord mayor of Dublin, Michael Collins. The following day, the Argentines were present in Foxford to take part in the official ceremonies. The Irish navy acted as a guard of honour; the Band of the Western Command provided the music.[113] In a speech, Dazzi described Admiral Brown as 'the greatest hero' of the Argentine navy.[114] Lambruschini unveiled two plaques in honour of Brown and laid a wreath at a monument presented by the Argentine government to the town in 1957.[115]

The presence of the Argentine naval delegation provoked protests. Supported by Amnesty International, Rice published a letter on 23 June: 'There is a question of principle at stake. The admiral should be a very unwelcome visitor and should not have been admitted to the country.' He described the modern Argentine navy as 'one of the cruellest sections' of the armed forces of that country as they worked out of a notorious base at ESMA.[116] Rice wrote to President Hillery on 7 July hoping that he was 'fully aware of the reign of terror that has been unleashed in Argentina by the present Government which the Navy fully supports ... having more than their quota of responsibility for those present crimes'. Rice 'only hoped that in private conversation, the Irish Government has expressed its serious preoccupation for the situation in Argentina to the delegation [that] came'.[117]

The new Fianna Fáil government took power on 5 July 1977. Michael O'Kennedy was, as mentioned above, the new minister for foreign affairs. The visit of the Argentine delegation, very much the ambassador's project, had left a bad taste in the political division where Noel Dorr was in charge. There was no wish to encourage further ceremonial contacts while the dictatorship was in power. Ó hÉideáin, in contrast, interpreted the visit as a great success and reported that in gratitude Rear Admiral Laurio H. Destéfani[118] had offered to present a bust of Admiral Brown to the Irish government: 'I said that this idea sounded very interesting and I would mention the thought to my authorities. Perhaps you would let me have a reaction in principle which I could convey to Admiral Destéfani informally ... I think that I should be instructed to tell Admiral Destéfani informally that if the Argentine authorities decided to make this generous gift it would be welcome.'[119] Destéfani also informed him that there was to be 'a great naval review' around November of the Argentine fleet and that 'a political figure or public personality from Ireland would be a very welcome guest'. Ó hÉideáin mentioned the possible future visit to Dublin of the Argentine training tall ship *Libertad* and that he could 'arrange an interesting forum for a distinguished speaker from Ireland with an Irish-Argentine or other cultural society'.[120] The ambassador encountered sufficient blowback from Iveagh House concerning his amicable relationship with leading members of the Argentine navy that he found it necessary to defend his action, and he did not hold back in a telegram on 6 August: 'As a general comment on taking due notice of the Brown bicentennial I would submit a few points. No country subordinates all its foreign relations to one point. We recognise the Republic of Argentina and the Government of Argentina. Normal relations should be maintained. The give-and-take of official visits do not imply approval of the policy of passing Argentine governments in all respects, or in any respect. On the contrary the maintenance of normal political, economic and social relations gives an opportunity of influencing the present Argentine

Government for the good as seen from Ireland. In that Government there are moderate elements such as President General Videla, working for moderation, in the right direction. President Carter's strong views on human rights in Latin America including Argentina will not prevent the young men of the A.R.A. *Libertad* being received in New York.'[121] Dorr was not sympathetic to that point of view. How the ambassador considered Videla to be a 'moderate' in August 1977 was not based on observable fact. But it was a view still shared by a number of members of the diplomatic corps in Buenos Aires. The very same day as the Jack Lynch-led Fianna Fáil government took office (7 July), the outgoing minister FitzGerald wrote to his successor, Michael O'Kennedy, regarding the unresolved Fátima Cabrera case, which, in the following months, proved to be another policy flashpoint between the ambassador and the political division. In his letter, FitzGerald explained to O'Kennedy that Cabrera was still being held 'at the disposal of the government' in the women's section of Villa Devoto prison. 'Given the particular circumstances of the case,' he continued, 'I would, myself, have been very disposed to permitting her to come here, but this would obviously be a matter for your own decision and that of Gerry Collins [the incoming minister for justice].'[122]

On 9 July, Rice wrote to the new minister warning that recent press reports covering the release of prisoners in Argentina could be very misleading: 'Freedom in Argentina is extremely dangerous. Five of those sent from La Plata Prison had been shot within a few days of their release,' he wrote, and with renewed urgency he petitioned that Cabrera be granted a visa to come to Ireland as soon as possible. He had heard indirectly from the International Committee of the Red Cross (ICRC) that its delegation in Buenos Aires had been in contact with her family. He suggested that the Irish embassy might approach that delegation to relay to Cabrera the offer of an Irish visa. Rice believed that her 'family naturally feel that she may be allowed [to go] free in Argentina but do not sufficiently consider the dangers involved for her life afterwards'. He repeated his view that her family would be well disposed to her leaving the country if they were made aware that the Argentine government would prefer that she be exiled. He wanted the Irish government to act swiftly. Rice pointed to the policies of the British, the Swiss and the Belgian governments in granting visas to Argentine prisoners. He also thought that the Irish government might intervene in the cases of prisoners with Irish connections, such as 'a 50-year-old farmer from Córdoba, [?] McLoughlin, who is imprisoned without charge ... All his people are Irish'.[123]

The new minister was already very familiar with the Rice portfolio. He had raised the case in the Dáil as opposition spokesman on foreign affairs and had been in touch with Rice's parents. As the outgoing minister was in favour of giving Cabrera a visa, Noel Dorr asked his colleague Jeremy Craig to review the Cabrera file and to set out for him the policy options. On 9 July 1977, Craig submitted a detailed handwritten report in which he summarised the previous correspondence involving the consular section in Iveagh House, together with an evaluation of the ambassador's reports. According to Craig, the consular section had taken the view that 'it would be preferable not to engage in any enquiries about Srta. Cabrera or to give Fr Rice the impression that we could do anything on her behalf'. He explained further that the section had been 'influenced partly by Fr Rice's personal condition but primarily by a concern that the Embassy in Buenos Aires should preserve its credibility with the Argentine authorities, and that nothing be done which would reduce its ability to act effectively on behalf of Irish citizens should, as could not be excluded, cases similar to that of Fr Rice arise in future'.[124] Craig himself arrived at the diametrically opposite conclusion:

> Although I fully share the concern of Consular Section, I am inclined to think that representations by us on behalf of **one** Argentine citizen should not have an unduly deleterious effect on relations. The approach could be made on the basis of widespread concern among members of the Irish public who have become acquainted with the case as a result of Fr Rice's account of his detention in Argentina. Although I do not think we should have any exaggerated expectation about the results, I do feel that representations through our Ambassador in BA would be more likely to be effective than through the [Argentine] Ambassador here.

Craig concluded with the further recommendation that a decision in principle should be taken to make an official inquiry as to Cabrera's whereabouts, adding that, as a first step, the embassy should make contact with the family and initiate inquiries about her whereabouts only 'if they had no objection'.[125]

The first part of this chapter described the actions of a murderous regime and the disappearances taking place throughout Argentina. Cabrera, who had never been charged, remained in danger, whether in or out of prison. The Irish ambassador in Buenos Aires did not display any sense of urgency regarding her fate. Dorr read the situation differently and he wanted a decision on whether or not she would be given a visa to come to Ireland. Having consulted the new minister, he asked Tom Lyons to ask the consular section to put a query regarding Cabrera to the Department of Justice. A reply was received on 5 August:

The Department of Justice's attitude which was given to me [Liam Canniffe] by Mr. P. O'Toole is that it is not in favour. He [O'Toole] said that from previous experience, e.g. refugees from Chile and Hungary, these people found life in Ireland very different and difficult to cope with. This even applied to people who already possessed skills before coming here. Integration with the Irish population never fully took place and consequently they were not happy. It was felt that this girl [Cabrera] who would be on her own when coming here would be even more unhappy within a very short space of time and the problems which she would experience after coming here would outweigh the good we should do by admitting her in the first place. She would also be penniless on arrival and [it] would appear that she would have to be maintained by the state.

On reading the reply from the Department of Justice, Dorr wrote in the margins of the document: '[? but Fr Rice has made arrangements for her to stay with his sister. ND]'.[126]

On 18 August, Rice wrote again to the minister reminding him of the dangers of Cabrera continuing to be held in jail.[127] He also sent letters to an official in the consular section (on 5 and 8 September) reconfirming that his family was prepared to support her and that she would live with his sister and go to school locally. He repeated the suggestion that the embassy make an intervention through the chaplain or International Committee of the Red Cross: '*La última que se pierde es la esperanza* [Hope is the last thing to be lost][128] so even though the months have now become a year I still believe something effective can be done.' Unknown to Rice, the political division was pressing for a resolution of her case. Lyons was instructed to write to Ó hÉideáin to point out that, for some time, the department had been under constant pressure to take action in regard to Cabrera. Aware that she was not an Irish citizen and not in any way connected with Ireland, the department wished 'to decide in principle whether an approach should be made to the Department of Justice with a view to securing that Department's agreement to the admission of Ms Cabrera into Ireland'. Before doing so, Lyons was requested to ask for additional information about Cabrera and her family circumstances and to find out if, as Rice believed, the ICRC had been in touch with her family and had access to her in prison. Ó hÉideáin replied on 28 September to what he described as 'Rice's well intentioned and generous proposal'. But the ambassador was not in favour of her being given a visa. In a wide-ranging answer, he made reference to Articles 41 and 42 of the Irish Constitution on the family as a partial reason for that stance: 'In this country are her mother and family including her crippled husband (from whom she was said in March to be separated presumably not just factually by her imprisonment). Her mother was said to blame Fr R. at least indirectly for her daughter's imprisonment and the loss of her much-needed earnings for the family.' Ó hÉideáin surmised that the Argentine authorities might consider it extremely risky to allow Cabrera to join Rice's family as that might strengthen the priest's 'publicity campaign in Ireland and England as a focus for anti-Argentine Government propaganda'. He also opposed making an informal overture to the foreign ministry or to make inquiries through the International Committee of the Red Cross.[129] Ó hÉideáin's preferred course of action was to 'leave matters as they are in the absence of any approach to embassy or ICRC from her family. This might be best in the long run. She would get released eventually and be able to pick up the threads of her life socially and economically in her own milieu, society and country'.[130]

Faced with such prevarication, Iveagh House instructed the ambassador to make contact with the ICRC. He complied, and replied on 8 November that his inquiry found that the Red Cross representative in Buenos Aires was on holidays.[131] Dorr, on receipt of the ambassador's telegram on the 9th, sent a minute to Craig explaining the reasons for urgency in the case: 'The primary reason for action, would, of course, be that we might be able to help someone whom we believe to have been tortured and who is still in prison. But beyond this, I think we may expect a parliamentary Question at some stage and possibly further correspondence from Fr Rice and it would be well to be able to show that we have done what we can in the matter.'[132] Dorr did not think that the arguments in favour of doing nothing were sustainable. Irrespective of the fact that Ireland had no formal standing in the case, he argued that it would be open to the Irish government at some stage to make a private and informal approach to the Argentinian authorities as the case had got considerable publicity in Ireland and because Cabrera had been arrested at the same time as Rice, which reflected very badly on Argentina. Dorr added trenchantly: '... I do not think we need feel too inhibited about such an approach to the Argentinian authorities at least in so far as our relations with Argentina are concerned. After all they appear to have arrested and tortured an Irish citizen, Fr Rice, with no apology at any time; and we have accepted nevertheless an Argentinian delegation here to add a further plaque to the several which have already been erected to the memory of Admiral Brown'. Dorr favoured that the department act fairly quickly,

> or else decide for once and for all that we have good reasons for letting matters rest and try to explain this to Fr Rice. The immediate thing

seems to be to await an early report from the Ambassador in Buenos Aires on his contact with the Red Cross but if this does not work out we may have to consider commending to the Minister that we make an informal approach through the embassy to the Argentine authorities first to express concern and seek information and secondly perhaps to seek her release to come to Ireland. In the meantime, I think we should press Justice further as to whether they would agree to admit her if necessary – since the reasons they gave in response to our earlier approach are quite misplaced.[133]

Ó hÉideáin acted on instructions and, probably around 16 November, met the ICRC local representative, Dr Jenny, who agreed to get information about Cabrera provided the Irish government undertook to make no mention of the Red Cross's involvement. On 21 November, Harman went to the Red Cross offices 'by way of gentle reminder' but he received no news of the inquiries they had made regarding Cabrera.[134] That visit may have been prompted by a stiff minute from Lyons to the ambassador on 21 November setting out the departmental response to his report (dated 28 September). The department had not requested or suggested to Ó hÉideáin that a direct approach be made to Sra Cabrera 'and we of course are aware of the difficulties such an approach would entail'. The departmental position was that the

> International Red Cross, given its humanitarian orientation, should be a suitable channel for establishing contact with her. Such a procedure should enable the Embassy to distance itself to some extent from the contacts and should permit of enquiries being made without giving Sra. Cabrera the impression that (as your message puts it) she is being offered a permit to come to Ireland ... It would be appreciated if the Embassy would approach the local ICRC representative and seek information ... on the basis of which the Department should be in a position to take decision in the matter and instruct Embassy.[135]

While those exchanges were taking place about Cabrera, Ó hÉideáin's diplomatic duties required him to attend a meeting of the heads of mission at the nunciature in early November to discuss arrangements for the hosting of a diplomatic corps dinner for the three members of the junta (Videla, Massera and Agosti) and their wives in the Plaza Hotel. Each ambassador paid 20,000 pesos towards covering the overall cost of the event. In order to make the evening more memorable, the Cuban ambassador offered boxes of cigars for the occasion and the French ambassador offered champagne. Seizing the opportunity to promote an Irish product, Ó hÉideáin would provide three half cases of fifteen-year-old John Jameson – eighteen bottles in total.[136] On the night of the dinner, around 19 November, Videla was detained by 'urgent business' and he was over half an hour late. 'During this unscheduled time of thirsty waiting,' Ó hÉideáin reported, 'there was some anticipatory discussion about the Irish whiskey waiting off-stage.' Upon Videla's arrival, the whiskey was served at the cocktail stage 'and it went down well'. When one ambassador commented that he 'found the whiskey unpalatable because of what he called its burnt taste', Ó hÉideáin retorted that the ambassador in question had not enough practice drinking it. His verdict was that overall 'the guests of honour and the colleagues were appreciative and, in the case of many, enthusiastic'. Besides general bonhomie, the Irish ambassador reported that little of political importance was discussed at the dinner other than – in answer to Ó hÉideáin's question – 'Massera described the Naval review which would be held for Admiral Brown in 1978'.[137] While ambassadors, as part of their professional duties, were obliged to 'sup with the devil' in those dark times in Buenos Aires, it might have been more appropriate for Ambassador Ó hÉideáin to have done so using an even longer spoon.

Among the EEC diplomats serving in Buenos Aires during the time of the dictatorship, there was at least one equivalent of Raoul Wallenberg, the Swedish diplomat who saved thousands of Jews in Nazi-occupied Hungary.[138] That honour fell to Enrico Calamai, the Italian consul in Buenos Aires between 1972 and 1977, who saved at least 300 lives regardless of whether or not they were Italians.[139]

On 8 December, Ó hÉideáin told Dublin of a recent development which might have a bearing on Cabrera's case. Law 21,650, published on 21 September, partially restored the right in the Argentine constitution for a jailed citizen to exercise the option to leave the country when released. The ambassador added that Harman had found out on 30 November at a meeting of EEC consular officials that, since the new law had been published, EEC embassies in Buenos Aires had received some 630 requests for certificates stating that a particular detainee would be accepted in the other country's territory, and that so far thirty-five had been issued. There was also a report around that time that an Irish-Argentine detainee, Juan M. Halvey, had been released.[140] On 14 December, Craig noted that the EEC Latin American group in Brussels had recently established that there were conflicting indications of the willingness of the Argentine authorities to accept inquiries about their citizens from foreign embassies and to release them if visas were obtained. The Federal Republic of

Germany said that they had obtained the release of 200 people in that manner, many of them Argentine citizens. The French told the meeting that they had no success in that respect except in the case of French citizens and double nationals. In the absence of a collective EEC démarche on Argentina, Craig recommended – even if he was not optimistic about its success – that Iveagh House send the proposed visa request for Cabrera to the Department of Justice. The minister, Michael O'Kennedy, wrote a strongly worded request to the minister for justice Gerard Collins on 23 December requesting that Cabrera be given a visa. Collins was told that her release might be secured under Article 23 of the Argentine constitution:

> It was understood by the department [of Foreign Affairs] that a number of our partners in the European community have secured the release of detainees by informing the Argentinian authorities that those persons would be accepted into their countries. The present case must be seen against the background of a declared state of siege in Argentina, and a situation in the last eighteen months in which a large number of persons have been murdered, have disappeared or have been imprisoned without trial. Widespread breaches of human rights, including the use of torture, are known to have occurred.[141]

The minister for foreign affairs recommended that, 'in the light of Father Rice's willingness to arrange that his family will take full responsibility for Fátima Cabrera if she comes to Ireland, she should be admitted to Ireland, if that is her wish'. O'Kennedy's letter concluded that that was the proper course 'given the general background of serious breaches of human rights in Argentina, the response of other countries in particular that of our partners in the Community to this situation and the specific background of Fátima Cabrera's arrest in the company of [an] Irish citizen'. The minister requested the minister for justice to give approval in principle and 'that an undertaking be given by the Embassy in Buenos Aires if this corresponds with Fátima Cabrera's wishes. An early reply would be appreciated'.[142]

In the fortnight ending 23 December, the ICRC saw Cabrera in Villa Devoto prison and reported that 'her health was good'.[143] Ó hÉideáin sent wrong information to Iveagh House on the 24th that she had been among a list of thirty prisoners released from detention to supervised liberty within Argentina. Ten people detained by the government had been given the option to leave Argentina under Article 23 of the national constitution. The minister for foreign affairs wrote to Rice confirming that she had been released. In early

January, Rice visited Iveagh House and was shown the text of Ó hÉideáin's telegram. However, Cabrera was still in jail and officials became alarmed by a report in the French newspaper *Le Monde* on 19 January 1978 that many of the people named by the authorities as having been released prior to Christmas were still in prison and that many political prisoners had been murdered on the pretext that they were trying to escape.

The political division, based on the information received from the embassy, wrote on 25 January 1978 to the Department of Justice that the prisoner had been released before Christmas and 'in those circumstances the approval in principle of your department to the course suggested in this department's minute reference is not sought at present'.[144] On 9 February, Rice published a letter in the *Irish Times* giving the news of Cabrera's release from jail and thanking all those who supported him in the campaign to have her freed. Such publicity prompted Lyons to telegram the ambassador on 17 February: 'It would be a matter of considerable concern to the Minister if it were found that Señora Cabrera were still in detention. It would also give rise to particular difficulties if this were to come to the knowledge of Fr Rice before the Department was aware of it.'

On 3 March, Ó hÉideáin wrote that he had met the ICRC local representative, André Tschiffeli, on 27 February requesting confirmation that Cabrera had been one of those released in the list published on 24 December. After consulting his records, he confirmed that she had in fact been released but on 11 January. The ICRC officer also confirmed that her mother had called in person to inform them of her daughter's release under supervised liberty, meaning that she was obliged to report to the local police station three times a week. The same officer suggested to her mother that she should contact the Irish embassy to advise of her daughter's release. She had not done so. Ó hÉideáin noted: 'Naturally in view of Fátima Cabrera's remaining supervised parole and the possibility that her mother regards the Fr Rice connection as having been responsible for her daughter's involvement it is perhaps not unnatural that she should hesitate to make the contact with the Embassy.' The ambassador wondered 'if an opportunity should not soon be taken by the Department at a suitable senior level to speak to Fr Rice as to the need for prudence now that Mrs. Cabrera is on supervised parole within Argentina. He should be aware that letters from him to the daily newspapers (particularly those under such headings as 'Terror in Argentina') regarding her are bound, at the very least, to draw unnecessary and unwelcome attention to her case and could indeed prejudice her continued security'.[145] There is no record of that suggestion ever having been implemented.

On 7 March 1978, Rice wrote to Iveagh House that he had heard from two friends recently arrived from Argentina that Cabrera was 'under a type of house arrest but apparently quite ill ... There may be something one could do to help through the Red Cross or something'.[146] Suffering from chronic asthma, Cabrera was subjected to house arrest (*libertad vigilada*) for four years, living under the constant threat of being disappeared again. On one occasion, she was questioned in her home by members of the security forces, who also came to her place of work to check on her. That harassment lasted until the fall of the dictatorship in 1983. In all probability, Cabrera was unlikely to have been able to take up an offer to live in Ireland. She was the breadwinner for the family. Her mother was a lone parent with, besides Fátima, three girls and a boy to support. If she believed that Rice and his confrères bore some responsibility for her daughter's detention, she revised that view completely in due course, as I discovered when I had the opportunity to speak extensively to her over a number of years.[147] Cabrera attaches great importance to the role of the Irish embassy and the work done by both Harman and Lennon at the time of their kidnapping. At no time did she ever hold Rice responsible for her imprisonment. On a number of occasions, Cabrera told me that she was certain that Rice had saved her life in two different ways. She remained convinced that she survived because both their names had been published in the international press within a day of their disappearance. Following Rice's release, she felt safer in jail as he was a witness to her torture and imprisonment. While in Villa Devoto, she felt protected by the international coverage her case continued to receive thanks, in part, to Rice's persistence.[148]

In fine, the Cabrera case revealed a major contradiction in Irish foreign policy. Ireland was committed to the defence of human rights and the dignity of the person. As a member of the UN, it was bound by the Universal Declaration of Human Rights. Yet, despite the commitment of two ministers for foreign affairs to grant Cabrera an Irish visa, it did not happen in 1977–8. The Department of Foreign Affairs' file on Cabrera has implications beyond the fate of a single individual. It reveals the vacuum in Irish government policy regarding the admission of Argentine refugees during the years of the civilian military dictatorship. While other EEC countries used Article 23 of the Argentine constitution to open their doors to receive refugees from the dictatorship, Ireland, on the evidence provided above, did not admit a single one at the time of greatest danger. In view of the fact that her three children, as will be explained later, are Irish passport-holders, Fátima Cabrera might be offered in 2022 the visa that she failed to receive over forty years before.

WORLD CUP FEVER AND THE SUPPLYING OF TIMONEY ARMOURED
PERSONNEL CARRIERS TO THE ARGENTINE FEDERAL POLICE

In 1978, football was the first area of contention in Irish foreign policy
regarding Argentina. The second was an effort to export army personnel
carriers (APCs) to the federal police or armed forces in the country. From 1
to 25 June, Argentina hosted the FIFA World Cup. In the run-up to the main
event, its national team played a warm-up game on 19 April against a League
of Ireland side in La Bombonera, the home of the Boca Juniors club. The Irish
team was beaten 3–1. As the Irish national side had not qualified for the World
Cup, only a small number of print and broadcast journalists travelled to cover
the tournament, among them Jimmy Magee of RTÉ and Elgy Gillespie of the
Irish Times. The US ambassador Raúl Héctor Castro reported on 19 June that a
'prophylactic national campaign against the "distorted" Argentine image in the
world press' had been 'front and center' in the national media since April.[149] He
commented also that all the country's problems had been temporarily shelved
'as the nation celebrated the progress of the Argentine national team with
thousands of flag-draped vehicles honking horns throughout the night and
other thousands parading and snake dancing in the street, chanting Ar-gen-
tina'.[150] Admiral Massera allegedly bought off the Montoneros with a payment
of $1.2 million to halt their guerrilla campaign during the competition.[151]
The matches, involving sixteen national sides, were played in Buenos Aires,
Córdoba, Mendoza, Rosario and Mar del Plata. Henry Kissinger attended a
game in Rosario and was General Videla's personal guest at both the semi-final
and the final.[152] Argentina needed to win by four clear goals against an in-form
Peru. Defying the form book, Argentina won 6–0. On 25 June, Argentina and
the Netherlands were 1–1 at full-time in the final. The home side won after
extra time by three goals to one. The Netherlands, as a protest against human
rights abuses in the country, declined afterwards to attend the official banquet.
That gesture was obscured by the euphoria of the mass celebrations throughout
the country.[153] Elgy Gillespie was critical in her reports of the claims being
made by a number of British journalists that the federal capital was now 'one
of the safest big cities in the world'. In response to the hype, she wrote: 'Well, if
you are not one of the priests who disappeared or died in "accidents" (a bishop
included) or one of the few Montoneros left in the country I suppose it is. Petty
thefts and muggings are few compared to Lima or the dreaded Bogotá. It is far
safer than, say, Los Angeles, New York, Naples, Liverpool or O'Connell Street,
Dublin. If your name isn't Father Patrick Rice I suppose it is indeed "one of
the safest cities in the world".'[154] Gillespie had hit the right note, as the staging

of the World Cup had changed nothing of government policy. Ambassador Ó hÉideáin echoed the views of his fellow EEC ambassadors that they had no expectation of a dramatic change of policy. Any hopes of an amnesty had been dashed by the air force junta member Brigadier Orlando Ramón Agosti when he said that the government would not make the same mistake as President Cámpora in May 1973 by letting 'loose a flood of criminals on the country'.[155]

Mgr Kevin Mullen, the first secretary in the papal nunciature, continued as he had begun; the more his relationship with the military deteriorated, the more doggedly he advocated on behalf of the relatives of the disappeared. Besides the upper echelons of the armed forces, only a few very close friends in whom he could confide, such as Robert and Maud Cox, were privy to the danger and atmosphere of menace in which he operated. Most of the Irish community knew him best as a popular priest who was very much in demand to officiate at baptisms, marriages and funerals. He celebrated the nuptial mass for Justin Harman and Carmen Casey in Holy Cross on 4 October 1978. The bride, an artist, photographer and classical musician,[156] was from Cañuelas, province of Buenos Aires.[157] Not long after the wedding, Mullen was ridiculed and belittled by a senior army officer in the presence of other members of the high command. The secretariat of state at the Holy See reassigned Mullen to the nunciature in Paris amid speculation that he was being taken out for his own safety. What brought matters to a head at the end of 1978 may have been a series of events about which he knew absolutely nothing. The Timoney firm at Gibbstown, Navan, County Meath, had designed an armoured personnel carrier (APC)[158] which was built in cooperation with a manufacturing company in Belgium and had been supplied to the Belgian army.[159] In 1978, the firm entered into exploratory discussions to supply the federal police in Argentina with APCs, sometimes referred to as AFC on file in the Department of Foreign Affairs.[160] The firm applied to the Irish government in early 1978 for an export licence. The political division of the Department of Foreign Affairs voiced strong reservations to the minister for industry and commerce, Bobby Molloy, about allowing such exports. On 23 May, Molloy wrote granting permission to export an initial five APCs to Argentina, adding that 'it will be possible to grant further licences permitting shipment of additional quantities if and when required'.[161] Eanna Timoney, a company representative, arrived in Buenos Aires in June 1978 to explore the viability of supplying the vehicles. Ó hÉideáin informed Iveagh House that he was a personal friend of Séamus Timoney, the owner of the company, and that he also knew his wife and family.[162] The ambassador and Justin Harman met Timoney on 28 June and Ó hÉideáin reported that the visitor had already been to army general headquarters earlier that morning and had been 'impressed' by the mechanical expertise and quickness of the military personnel to whom he had spoken. Ó hÉideáin surmised that Timoney was dealing directly with the army but the visitor did not name any of the officers he had met. He told the two diplomats that his firm had an order for five AFCs for the federal police and an assurance of a total order of sixty-five. He regarded that as quite a breakthrough, confirming that the vehicles would be manufactured at Gibbstown. Timoney said he had come personally to Buenos Aires to see what the human rights position was in the country and whether that would justify accepting the order. His army contacts had told him that military operations 'against subversives' had been successful but the guerrilla groups still retained some capability for isolated offensives and nuisance operations like leaflet bombs.[163] In briefing his guest, the ambassador described General Videla as a competent and conscientious moderate who would continue as president after the first of August 1978. But he believed that the educated middle, the workers and the remnants of the political parties were unlikely to remain indefinitely content with no vote, no elections and no representation. For the moment, they were constrained by the memory of the economic chaos preceding the military takeover in March 1976. That would be long remembered and not only by the rich, Ó hÉideáin concluded.[164] Timoney assured both diplomats that his company was not prepared, for human rights reasons, to export to South Africa or Chile. The ambassador responded that Chile was in some ways further advanced on the road to normalisation than Argentina but he was sure that if 'Irish-made armoured personnel carriers were supplied to the police as distinct from the Army (police who sometimes had the custody of detainees and were accused of maltreating them in some instances) then some Irish-Argentines *inter alios* would be shocked'. Ó hÉideáin also told him that there might well be a public reaction in Ireland 'where people were even less used to the idea of the police having armoured personnel carriers in law enforcement'.[165] Ó hÉideáin concluded that 'the final assessment of the human rights position in relation to this order had to take into account possible political repercussions at home', and that that was a matter for the Department of Foreign Affairs in Dublin.[166] The files in Iveagh House do not state whether the company ever supplied APCs to Argentina at that time.

But the visit and the possible supplying of military vehicles to Argentina indirectly had serious repercussions for Mgr Mullen. Scheduled to leave for his new posting in February 1978, he accepted an invitation to mass in November to mark the quincentennial of the birth of Thomas More, and he welcomed the British consul Graham Langford (the British did not have an ambassador in

Buenos Aires between 1975 and 1979), the chairman of the British Legion, the president of the Federation of Irish Societies, representatives of the Anglican community and Spanish-speaking nurses in uniform from the British Hospital. Accompanied by Harman, Ó hÉideáin attended, avoiding what he considered to be a possible embarrassment: 'Flanders poppies were offered around as Armistice Day was near, I took care not to be presented with one to wear.'[167] Mullen, in his sermon, spoke about world peace and described St Thomas More as 'a victim of state totalitarianism'. He quoted papal condemnations of violence against innocent people ranging from the unborn to the imprisoned, irrespective of whether those acts were inflicted by individuals or groups or governments.[168] There is no text of the sermon available but *La Razón* reported that it was about 'the necessity to strive for concord and to keep in mind the self-sacrifice and the struggle of the saint against totalitarianism and in defence of freedom and human dignity'.[169] The contents of that sermon were not missed by the Argentine authorities.

As Mullen was in his last few weeks in the country, Ó hÉideáin on 20 December 1978 gave a formal farewell dinner in his honour. In gratitude, Mullen wrote thanking him for the opportunity to spend a few 'very pleasant hours in the company of the ambassador, friends and colleagues' which had left him with 'a happy memory on the eve of his departure'.[170] Mullen continued to work up to the day he left in early February 1979. He attended an informal meeting at the US embassy on 22 December in which he said to the officials present that a senior army person had told the papal nuncio that the 'armed services had been forced to "take care of" 15,000 persons in its anti-subversion campaign'.[171] That was a significant admission, in Mullen's view.

On 22 January 1979, Ó hÉideáin held a private dinner for Mullen to mark his imminent departure from Buenos Aires. Mullen took the ambassador aside later in the evening, confiding in him that he had been involved in a 'serious incident' with the chief of the federal police, Brigadier General Edmundo René Ojeda.[172] Ó hÉideáin described Ojeda in his subsequent report as 'one of the most powerful officers outside the Military Junta itself'.[173] Mullen said Ojeda had made disparaging remarks about him to his face 'in the hearing of 15 military people and high personalities'.[174] In what the Vatican diplomat described as 'a brusque and jovial manner', he said Ojeda had made 'an argumentative reference' to the fact that 'Ireland was supplying anti-subversive material to Argentina' and added mockingly for the benefit of the other officers:

You [Mullen] are always talking about human rights and going easy
on Marxist subversives in Argentina. But where is Argentina going to
learn about being tough with terrorists? To your country, Ireland; there
are military officers from Argentina in Ireland at present buying anti-
subversive weapons, what the Irish Government has been using against
its terrorists and what is being used against the terrorists in the North
of Ireland. You are being tough with subversives in Ireland and other
countries have to learn from you in practice. Your theories are up in the
air. You are not being consistent in blaming Argentina for taking measures
against the terrorists here who have murdered people.[175]

Mullen replied to Ojeda that 'he knew nothing about any such activities but
that what he had said in no way invalidated anything he had said about a
person's right to life, or the right not to be arbitrarily kidnapped or not to be
tortured. He also told him that there was no analogy between the situation
in Ireland and Argentina'.[176] Ó hÉideáin, in an effort to reassure Mullen, said
he thought that Ojeda's statement was full of non-sequiturs and that any such
sale had nothing to do with the thrust of his arguments on human rights.
Ó hÉideáin reported that 'He [Mullen] assured me that he would not be
deflected' from his work.[177]

Mullen attended a meeting on 8 February, only days before his departure,
at the US embassy with two political officers, Yvonne Thayer and F. Allen
Harris, and the political counsellor William H. Hallman. He presented the
meeting with a confidential memorandum he had written about an episode in
November 1978 in which the first army corps security forces had carried out
a raid on Villa del Parque, Buenos Aires. They had worked from a list of the
names and addresses of young people who, up to a few years before, had been
members of Cristianos para la Liberación, attached to the Casa de la Juventud
(youth centre) and run at that time by Redemptorist Fr Rivas, who had since
left the priesthood.[178] Mullen's memorandum noted: 'This movement has
long been considered by the military authorities as highly subversive.' He also
wrote that his informant said the youths no longer belonged to it. However,
one military officer said that they had come to round up a terrorist cell. The
military first went to the parents in their home 'demanding with threats,
verbal abuse and physical maltreatment (punches and kicks) to know where
a son or a daughter now lived'. They arrested between sixty and seventy youths
'who were invariably manhandled and hooded before being taken away'.
Many of the apartments were ransacked and robbed of their contents by the
military, he wrote, and 'often, what was not stolen was broken'. The military

authorities at first denied any involvement though the youths swept up were numbered among the disappeared. However, the authorities had to admit involvement based on the discovery of an official notice pinned by an officer to one of the apartment doors. Mullen speculated that the captured youths were probably held in the ESMA where they were maltreated and tortured with the *picana* (electric cattle prod) while being questioned mainly about the church and subversion. All but two of the youths had been released between 21 December and some time in January 1979. Mullen wrote also that Cardinal Aramburu had not played an important role in pressing for the release of the Catholic youths. And he informed the US officials that a statement from the bishops' conference on peace in the country had been discussed by a meeting of army officers and that the generals had found the 'low keyed complaint of the continuation of abductions, torture and disappearances' to be 'moderate, balanced and accurate'.[179]

The stand-in editor for Fr Richards, who took a break from his position at *TSC* between April 1978 and May 1979, paid tribute in an editorial to the departing Mullen. Praising his work at the nunciature, he congratulated the diplomat on his promotion but said that the local community would be sorry at the departure of a priest known to all members of the community simply as 'Kevin'. He recalled that Mullen had taken part with spontaneity and generosity in all the festivities and events in the Irish community. The editorial also said that people admired Mullen's open, dignified and warm personality. He was held in high regard for the way he celebrated the Eucharist and performed his other priestly ministry. The editorial also spoke of the deep Christian and human solidarity he displayed when responding to the anguished cries for help from so many victims of the incomprehensible (*incomprensión*) times who felt their rights violated or denied.[180]

Besides Mullen's close friends Robert and Maud Cox, Ambassador Ó hÉideáin too was convinced that Mullen was being withdrawn due to pressure from the Argentine government: 'During his tour of duty here, now drawing to a close, Mullen has spoken pointedly in private and even in public addresses regarding Argentine short-comings on human rights. (*Vide my report dated 15 April 1977, pages 2–3 re his St Patrick's Day sermon.*)[181] While his Columbanus-like outspokenness is not welcomed, he has apparently retained the respect of Argentine officers and officials and their co-operation in his work.'[182] Mullen, the ambassador wrote, had 'spoken out courageously in public sermons on more than one occasion on the subject of human rights, as well as on the private occasions when diplomats of Western Christian countries and others try to influence the decision-making [of] members of the Argentine government to release internees rotting in jail, to stop torture, to stop right-wing kidnappings'.[183] On 30 January 1979, Ó hÉideáin attached the following addendum to his report: 'I gather that he [Mullen] welcomes the change from the point of view of being nearer home as his mother is advanced in years.'[184]

Was Mullen ever in serious danger of being disappeared because of his refusal in public or in private to remain silent? Diplomatic immunity might normally have bestowed upon him the fullest of protection, but that had not prevented two Cuban and two Argentine diplomats from being murdered. The two Cubans were kidnapped on 9 August 1976 in Buenos Aires. They were believed to have been tortured and killed at Automotores Orletti, a CCD in Floresta.[185] On 18 July 1977, the outspoken Argentine ambassador to Venezuela, Héctor Hidalgo Solá, was disappeared and murdered while on a visit home to Buenos Aires.[186] Elena Holmberg, another Argentine diplomat, suffered the same fate.[187] Not even her status as the niece of the former military dictator Alejandro Agustín Lanusse gave her immunity. Holmberg had been posted to Paris and was a cultural attaché at the embassy, which also housed the Centro Piloto, a propaganda unit under the control of Admiral Massera and his navy personnel. She allegedly witnessed the admiral giving the Montonero leader, Mario Firmenich, a large dollar sum in cash to halt guerrilla attacks during the World Cup.[188] A CIA source reported to Washington on 18 January 1979 that Holmberg had discovered while in Paris that Massera had met with the Montoneros '... and that she had forwarded that information to high officials of the Argentine government'.[189] Having returned to Buenos Aires, Holmberg was very outspoken about what she knew.[190] On 20 December 1978, she was kidnapped in daylight by Task Group 3.2.2 near her apartment in the centre of the city as she was on her way to meet a group of French journalists. Her body was found on 11 January 1979 some 30 kilometres north of Buenos Aires in the River Luján.[191] At the time of the murder, Mullen was still in the country. He left soon afterwards.

In December 1979, Robert and Maud Cox were finally forced to leave Argentina with their young family. The victim of many death threats since the coup in 1976, Cox, who had a short spell in jail in 1977, felt forced to leave to protect his family when Maud narrowly escaped being disappeared as she crossed the road in front of their apartment on Avenida Alvear.[192] When he heard that they had left the country, Mullen wrote to Cox from Paris:

> You are one of the very few who raised a voice in the name of humanity and civilization at an awfully agonizing moment in history, and I remember that. I would grieve really, if you could not go back to a country

you patently love and have loyally defended in the best sense in which a nation is defended – by standing for the basic rights of its people. I think of you often and pray that you, Maud and the children are reasonably happy. I would be as sad as you would be frustrated to think that you were condemned to a nomadic life.[193]

The Cox family relocated to the United States, where Robert worked on a newspaper in South Carolina. He later returned to Argentina to testify against many of those responsible for the disappearances, the torture and the killings. In 2010, he was made 'an illustrious Citizen of the Autonomous City of Buenos Aires'. That same year the British government honoured him with an OBE.[194]

Mullen, after an unhappy posting in Paris, was sent in January 1982 to the nunciature in Havana – a hardship post where he was subject to very strict government surveillance. His brother, Mgr Austin Mullen, visited him in summer 1982: 'I witnessed some of the strain and stress that Kevin experienced. I remember him saying that he had to go out for a swim in the ocean with the papal nuncio, Giulio Einaudi, in order to be able to talk in confidence without being overheard.'[195] Hermana Maria Fe Rodríguez López, who worked in the nunciature for over twenty years, recalled in 2018:

> I worked closely with Mons. Kevin Mullen from the time of his arrival in Cuba from France in early 1982 until his very premature death on 14 September 1983. In this period, I developed a deep friendship with him ... I witnessed the impact on him of the very challenging conditions in Havana at the time, notably the tense relationship between the Church and the Cuban authorities, and the pressures that this placed on him. I came to appreciate the deep faith of Mons. Kevin, his sense of principle and attachment to the truth, and his dedication to the cause of justice. In his time in Havana, he was revered by so many within the Catholic Church in Cuba.[196]

Mullen liaised with an underground seminary and tried to supply it with books and equipment. Einaudi took extended leave in 1983 and the running of the nunciature fell entirely on Mullen's shoulders during those three months. Due to take leave in summer 1983, he wrote to the rector of the Irish College, Mgr John Hanley, on 31 August, asking him to reserve a room for him on 17/18 September. He had plans to travel to Rome after he accompanied the Meath diocesan pilgrimage to Lourdes. On the night of Einaudi's return to Havana on 13 September, he held a dinner party. Mullen declined to attend as he was not feeling well. He was found collapsed early the next morning and was rushed to hospital, but did not survive. 'Kevin died in Havana 14/9/1983,' Mgr Hanley noted[197]

Mgr Austin Mullen wrote: 'He telephoned me a couple of days previous to his death. He was leaving for Lourdes to join the Meath pilgrimage and be with our mother & two of our sisters. They were members of the pilgrimage. I had the sad duty of going to Havana to accompany his body back to Ireland for the funeral Mass in Mullingar and burial at our home cemetery.'[198] Hermana Maria Fe recalled: 'His sudden death came as a painful shock to his colleagues but also to the members of the Church with whom he had close contact. I saw him both as a much-valued colleague but also as a brother. His death greatly distressed me. I was so overjoyed to meet his brother Jerome in Santiago de Compostela in September 2018 to recount to the family of Mons Kevin the person whom I grew to know in Havana, and the memories I have kept to this day of an extraordinary individual. May he rest in peace.'[199]

Since Kevin Mullen's untimely death in 1983, his two surviving siblings, Austin and Jerome, had unsuccessfully sought a formal explanation from the Holy See concerning the circumstances of his death, and also the withdrawal of the falsehood that their brother was an alcoholic. Thirty-six years later, on 25 June 2019, Archbishop Jan Pawlowski wrote on behalf of the secretariat of state: 'After an exhaustive investigation over these last few months, I can confirm the findings communicated to you in previous correspondence that concern both the natural causes of his death and the medical treatment he received. With regard to the hurtful suggestion that he suffered from alcoholism; this is not borne out by the review carried out. On the contrary, your brother was an example to those around him and it is more than unfortunate that such an insinuation was made to the family, and which disrespects the memory of this fine priest.'[200]

RICE AND INTERNATIONAL SOLIDARITY IN THE LATE 1970S

Had Rice been allowed to remain in Argentina, his subsequent vocal opposition to the regime would never have received international attention. Expelled from the country where he had worked for six years, he was free to participate in solidarity campaigns in Europe and the United States. Restored to full health, he moved in early 1978 to Washington DC. He worked with Héctor Timerman (son of the journalist Jacobo) to secure Jacobo's release on 17 April 1978.[201] Rice also lobbied on Capitol Hill with Senator Edward (Teddy) Kennedy and members of Congress – Christopher Dodd, Gus Yatron, Benjamin Stanley Rosenthal, Henry Arnold Waxman and Gladys Noon Spellman.

In parallel with his solidarity work, Rice had taken a case in mid-1977 with the Inter-American Commission on Human Rights, an organ of the Organisation of American States (OAS). Both accused the Argentine government of enforced disappearance, torture and illegal imprisonment.[202] On 7 December 1977, the commission sent details of the denunciation to the Argentine government, receiving a terse reply on 9 January 1978. Rice, receiving the relevant parts of that correspondence on 9 April, returned to the commission a detailed account of his kidnapping. He gave testimony before the 44th session of the Inter-American Commission in June during which he handed over additional documentation. On 9 June, the OAS requested a response from the Argentine government to the specific allegations. Rejecting the government's reply on 8 August, the OAS, following its General Assembly in La Paz, Bolivia, upheld the charges on 18 November that both Rice and Cabrera had been illegally detained by agents of the Argentine government in violation of the right to life, liberty and personal security, the right to a fair trial and the right to protection against arbitrary detention.[203] Rice was present at the assembly from 22 to 31 October.[204]

In Washington, Rice was a founder member of the Coalition of Christians concerned for Justice in Argentina. He based himself at Tabor House – a Christian community established in 1973 which was heavily engaged in helping Latin American refugees to find asylum in the US. Scott Wright became a close friend and fellow campaigner, together with the late Fr Peter Hinde (Carmelite) and Betty Campbell (Sister of Mercy).[205] They planned to hold a demonstration on El Día de la Revolución, 25 May 1979, a public holiday in Argentina commemorating the setting up of the first junta in 1810 and the rejection of Spanish dominion. It was the custom in Washington DC to hold a special mass every year on the 25th in St Matthew's Cathedral to commemorate that act of defiance which led to Argentine independence in 1816. The Argentine ambassador to the US between 1976 and 1981,[206] Jorge Antonio Aja Espil, was to attend the annual event together with the Argentine embassy's other diplomatic staff, the military attachés and their families.[207] Rice and Peter Hinde went in May 1979 to see the dean of the cathedral, Mgr W. Louis Quinn, to ask to have the mass cancelled. They also met with Fr Seán Patrick O'Malley, a Capuchin who worked as the episcopal vicar for the Hispanic, Portuguese and Haitian communities of the archdiocese of Washington. In previous years, O'Malley celebrated the same mass and was scheduled to do so again on 25 May 1979. Made the archbishop of Boston in

2003 and a cardinal in 2006, Seán Patrick O'Malley knew personally about the extent of the human rights abuses in Argentina. As a Capuchin he was aware that members of his order such as Fr Carlos Bustos, who had been disappeared on 8 April 1977, and Fr Antonio Puigjané had worked closely with the murdered Bishop Angelelli. Fr Hinde, too, had visited Argentina three times and had experienced personally the terror under which people lived. Hinde, who went with Rice to the cathedral, told me: 'I said to both men [O'Malley and Quinn] it would be sacrilegious to use this very public holy Mass to let the Argentine diplomatic community pretend that all was well with church and State in their country.' He argued that the authorities should not allow the mass to proceed. According to Hinde, O'Malley was adamant that he would say the mass. He had prepared a strong sermon which he was anxious to deliver. The rector, Quinn, was unyielding in his decision to hold the mass.[208] Hinde, Rice and other members of Tabor House, having failed to have the mass cancelled, made preparations to hold a peaceful demonstration on the day of the service. Flyers were printed for distribution on the street outside the cathedral. Brown cloth hoods were made with a prison number printed across the front of each one. The protesters also made a large banner which read: 'First, go and make peace with your brothers.' Colman McCarthy covered the event for the *Washington Post*. He wrote that the cathedral had been filled with Argentine diplomats and military officers in splendid white uniforms. Of Ambassador Espil's place of honour in the front pew, McCarthy commented: 'Tyranny doesn't look so bad when it kneels in a holy place and is given respectability by so grand a tribunal as the Archdiocese of Washington.'[209] Hinde, who was one of the worshippers in the cathedral, recalled that about 140 officials and families were present when Rice, dressed in a Roman collar and black clerical suit, stood at the lectern to the side of the main altar. Citing the Gospel text, 'Before you bring your gifts to the altar, reconcile with your offended brother' (Matthew 5.23–4), he quickly introduced himself and hurriedly described how he had been disappeared, tortured and imprisoned. Before he could go into any further details, his microphone was cut off. When he raised his voice to be heard, the organ boomed out, drowning his words. Rice descended the altar steps and, walking towards the ambassador and the other diplomats and officers, he offered to be reconciled to them. At that point, the rector of the cathedral intervened, requesting Rice to leave. As Rice was escorted down the main aisle and out onto the street, three hooded women protesters stood in front of the congregation holding the twelve-foot banner.[210] An Argentine, probably a security officer, seated in the front pew got up and snatched the hood off the middle protester with such force that he took away a tuft of her hair.[211] Another woman protester said to him: 'Now here, do what you do in Argentina!' McCarthy observed: 'The police looked the other way when members of the embassy goon squad punched some of the demonstrators and belligerently yanked cloth hoods from the heads of some of the others.'[212] Police escorted the remaining protesters out of the cathedral.

At that point Fr O'Malley came out of the sacristy and started the mass. Fr Hinde, who remained behind in the congregation, sent word to the protesters to come inside to participate in the mass and to hear the sermon. The celebrant read the Gospel from the pulpit and started to read his carefully crafted and well-balanced homily. He touched a raw nerve among those who sat in the front pews when he quoted from CELAM documents. Before O'Malley had completed the homily, an embassy official and his family walked out, followed immediately by the rest. A single military officer remained to hear the end of the sermon: '*Decidí darle la otra mejilla* ['I decided to turn the other cheek'],' he said afterwards.[213] As O'Malley began the offertory, the ambassador, the official embassy party and military attachés returned. Five women wearing white headscarves, in the style of the Madres de la Plaza de Mayo, stood among the congregation and participated in the prayers of the faithful. When the mass was over, Hinde and Sr Betty Campbell went to the sacristy to thank O'Malley for his sermon. But he was 'miffed at our protest action' and told them: 'If you hadn't done that [protest] they would have listened and learned.' Decades later, O'Malley gave Rice a copy of the sermon, which Rice then published as part of a collection of essays that he edited.[214]

After mass outside the cathedral, embassy staff complained that a religious event had been turned into a political protest. One Argentine officer said that 'priests have no place in politics. He [O'Malley] should have given a sermon on another subject, like the love of God.'[215] Rice was surrounded by angry Argentines, one uniformed officer saying to him: 'You are not a priest. You are a Jew. Where did you buy your collar? How much do they pay you? Dear priest, where did you study? You have your geography mixed up, you studied in Cuba.' Rice attempted to explain to him that he had worked in Argentina for six years, only to receive the reply: 'You were in prison with the terrorists. That's what you studied.' Pointing his right index finger at him, forming the shape of a gun, the officer said menacingly: 'When you return to Argentina, we'll send you to heaven.'[216] McCarthy quoted Rice: 'In Argentina few people have much hope in the church because they see it lined up with the government ... Anyone who tried to help or organize the poor, or has ideas the military object to, is branded a subversive. Anything goes – death or torture – to stop him.'[217] In that context, McCarthy wrote that the archdiocese of Washington would have been better to bar 'these tyrants in the first place'. He concluded optimistically: 'Word is likely to get back to the Argentine prison camps that at least two priests [Rice and O'Malley] in Washington dared confront the fake piety of the junta.'[218]

Rice was later involved in a protest against Admiral Massera when the Argentine visited Washington DC in the summer of 1979. He had stepped down from the junta and civilian military government in September 1978, having the self-deluded notion that he might become, as the new Perón, the next elected president of Argentina.[219] Massera had accepted an invitation from the Centre for Strategic Studies at Georgetown University to give a lecture in early June 1979, and Rice told me that he had joined the audience in the university with another priest he did not identify. As the proceedings were about to get underway, Rice interrupted the speaker, accusing him of being personally responsible for enforced disappearances, torture and murder.[220] Unable to continue, Massera felt obliged to leave the hall.[221] After Rice and the other priest had been escorted outside, Massera returned to continue his talk, in the course of which he accused the aristocratic minister for finance Martínez de Hoz of bringing the country's industry to a state of bankruptcy.[222] The admiral still harboured such presidential fantasies in late 1982 after the defeat in the Falklands/Malvinas war.[223]

Rice was sent by his order in late 1979 to work in a shanty town (*barrio*) east of Caracas, Venezuela. He was unable to return to Argentina. But he kept in touch with his friends still inside the country. From Caracas, he watched as the civilian military government in Buenos Aires occupied the Falklands/Malvinas on 2 April 1982 and lost a war against Britain in the South Atlantic.

CHAPTER SEVEN

Irish Foreign Policy, Irish-Argentines and War in the Falklands/Malvinas

Nowhere was the seismic shift in US foreign policy in the early 1980s felt more immediately and dramatically than in the Caribbean and in Central and Latin America. On 20 January 1981, Jimmy Carter was replaced by the right-wing Republican Ronald Reagan, who served two terms that witnessed the rapid dissolution of the Soviet empire, presaging allegedly the 'end of history'.[1] The Reagan doctrine was solemnly proclaimed in his State of the Union address on 6 February 1985: 'We must not break faith with those who are risking their lives – on every continent from Afghanistan to Nicaragua – to defy Soviet-supported aggression and secure rights which have been ours from birth.'[2] That new-found US determination to roll back the global influence of the Soviet Union was complemented and reinforced by political changes on the other side of the Atlantic: Margaret Thatcher, who shared Reagan's global vision, became the prime minister of Great Britain and Northern Ireland on 4 May 1979 and remained in that position until 28 November 1990. A third change in world leadership preceded both Thatcher and Reagan's arrival in power. On 16 October 1978, the Polish cardinal Karol Jósef Wojtyla was elected Pope John Paul II, replacing John Paul I who died after only thirty-three days in office. The pontificate of John Paul II, lasting until his death in 2005, has been credited with being the catalyst for a peaceful revolution in his native Poland and elsewhere throughout the communist bloc countries.

However, in Latin America, the new pope, notwithstanding his popular and populist approach, tended to appeal to more traditional Catholics. He was critical of the writings of many liberation theologians and many of the social ideas of the Conference of Latin American Bishops. At the opening of the

CELAM meeting in Puebla, Mexico, on 28 January 1979, he warned against the '"re-readings" of the Gospel' which were 'the result of theoretical speculation rather than authentic meditation on the word of God and a true commitment to the Gospel'.[3] Jeane J. Kirkpatrick, a conservative Catholic professor of government at Georgetown University, was of a like mind to the new pontiff. In her article 'Dictatorship and Double Standards', which was published in November 1979, she set out the framework for what became President Reagan's approach to Latin America. Her ideas first gained traction with Reagan's transition team and later with the president himself. She argued in her article that Washington should support 'friendly authoritarian' rather than Marxist 'totalitarian' regimes in the southern hemisphere.[4] Between February 1981 and 1985, she served as the first female US ambassador to the United Nations.[5] Translating her ideas into practice meant recommencing the supply of *matériel de guerre* to the civilian military dictatorship in Argentina – perceived as being a necessary bulwark against communist subversion in the region. According to the British ambassador in Washington, Nicholas Henderson, Kirkpatrick was 'pro-Argentinian'[6] out of concern that the country was in danger of being driven into the arms of the Soviet bear.

A large number of Reagan emissaries visited Buenos Aires from February 1981 onwards, including Kirkpatrick and ambassador-at-large General Vernon Walters. The US army chief of staff, General Edward C. Meyer, was there between 5 and 11 March 1981, together with two admirals and the commander of the Air Force Command and Staff School. The US Congress, in May 1981, approved the lifting of the ban on aid to Argentina and supported loans from the Inter-American Development Bank. General Roberto Viola, who succeeded Videla as president on 29 March 1981, made a commitment in Washington to share the burden of the defence of human freedom in any way he could, particularly in Central America. Before leaving office, Videla himself visited Washington and met the secretary of state, Alexander Haig, the secretary of defence, Casper Weinberger, and the vice president, George Bush. President Reagan told him he understood that firm action needed to be taken to curb the terrorist violence in Argentina.[7]

Reversing Carter's policies in Central America, Reagan tried to topple the Sandinista government in Nicaragua which came to power in July 1979. In El Salvador, he supported a civilian military government that ruled through repression and extra-judicial killings.[8] On 24 March 1980, the archbishop of San Salvador, (now Saint) Oscar Romero, was shot dead while saying mass in the oratory of a cancer hospital. During his funeral in the cathedral in San Salvador on the 30th, over thirty people were killed as the military opened fire on the congregation, who were attending mass in the open air. (Working as a freelance journalist, I was present in the cathedral on that occasion, as was the bishop of Galway, Éamonn Casey, and Irish Franciscan and Poor Clare nuns.)[9]

With the support of Latin American countries like Argentina, the United States sought to reassert its hegemony in Central America and the Caribbean, striving unsuccessfully to oust a Marxist government in Cuba. Nicaragua, at that time with a government more heterodox in its formation, was branded as a pro-Soviet revolutionary outlier. The little island of Grenada, which had gained its independence from Britain in 1974, witnessed the rise of the New Jewel Movement which came to power on 13 March 1979 in a bloodless coup d'état. The new premier, Maurice Bishop, proclaimed a Marxist People's Revolutionary Government (PRG), but after a power struggle in the party he was overthrown on 13 October 1983 by the deputy prime minister, Bernard Cord. Bishop and three members of his cabinet were executed by the insurgents. On the 23rd, US forces took control of the island and ousted the revolutionary regime.

Popular interest in Central and Latin America accelerated in Ireland during the time of the Reagan presidency. Solidarity groups highlighted the human rights abuses in the individual countries. Irish political parties, through their international affiliations, were also a strong source of support and solidarity. There was cross-party support in the Oireachtas for policies critical of the US policy. Michael D. Higgins took a leading role in exposing human rights abuses in Central America, Chile and Argentina. (In 1982, he was denied entry to El Salvador and held at gunpoint before being put on a plane to Nicaragua – though he was later allowed to enter El Salvador to carry out his investigations.)[10] Higgins criticised US policies during Reagan's four-day visit to Ireland in early June 1984. On 19 May, people were invited to sign a national petition opposing US foreign policy in Central America. In anticipation of President Reagan's arrival, on 27 May about a thousand demonstrators marched in Dublin. Led by a group of nuns, they carried a coffin inscribed with the names of three US nuns who had been killed in El Salvador four years before.[11] They handed in the petition, signed by 20,000 people, to the Department of Foreign Affairs.[12] Some twenty-seven organisations, including the Irish Anti-Apartheid Movement, the Irish Campaign for Nuclear Disarmament, the Irish Friends of Palestine, the Irish Sovereignty Movement, Pax Romana, the Union of Students in Ireland, the Irish El Salvador Support Committee, and the Irish Nicaragua Support Group, combined to organise a campaign of protest. Members of the coalition involved in the protest included Senator Michael D. Higgins, Dr Noël Browne, Seán MacBride, and the artist Robert Ballagh.[13] The primate of All Ireland, Cardinal Tomás Ó Fiaich, refused an invitation to the state dinner, as did the archbishop of Dublin, Dermot Ryan.[14] There was strong public opposition to the decision of the National University of Ireland to confer on President Reagan an honorary doctorate of laws, but the ceremony went ahead and the degree was conferred at NUI Galway. Members of the academic staff at St Patrick's College, Maynooth, passed a resolution disassociating themselves from the decision. The archbishop of Tuam, Joseph Cunnane, declined to attend the ceremony, as did Bishop Joseph Cassidy of Clonfert, as they had scheduled confirmation ceremonies. The bishop of Galway, Éamonn Casey, who was the most outspoken of all the bishops against the visit, pointedly refused to attend any of the ceremonies in Galway relating to the presidential visit. However, Reagan's visit overall was festive, the popular welcome was warm, the honorary doctorate was conferred and the protests respectfully conducted.

TURMOIL IN IRISH POLITICS AND ANGLO-IRISH RELATIONS, 1979–82

In the early 1980s, Ireland became more focused on events in Latin America than at any other time in the history of the state. The Falklands/Malvinas war in 1982 touched upon the most important aspects of Irish foreign policy – Anglo-Irish relations, inter-EEC relations, Irish–US relations, Irish UN policy and bilateral Irish–Argentine relations. Those events took place against the backdrop of unprecedented domestic turmoil in Irish politics. Charles Haughey, a controversial figure since his sacking as minister for finance in 1970, succeeded his great rival, Jack Lynch, as leader of Fianna Fáil and as taoiseach in December 1979. Although the manner in which he took over the leadership of the Fianna Fáil party was controversial, he began his time as taoiseach quite promisingly, adopting a statesmanlike pose at his first Anglo-Irish summit in May 1980. But Prime Minister Margaret Thatcher, who had come to power in May 1979, soon developed a strong dislike for him. Just over six months later, on 8 December 1980, their second Anglo-Irish summit ended amicably but Mrs Thatcher took exception to the way in which she felt Haughey had later oversold the joint communiqué to his followers.[15] The British prime minister's angry public reaction had, according to the Irish diplomat Noel Dorr, 'a chilling effect on what had started as a very positive relationship'.[16] The senior British civil servant David Goodall commented in his memoirs: 'Not for the first time Haughey showed his propensity to go for short-term political gain, thereby sacrificing the possibility of long-term progress on a critically important issue.'[17] According to another well-placed British diplomat,

H.A.J. Staples, a 'love/hate' relationship[18] developed which had time and cause to fester. Firstly, Haughey was very badly damaged politically by Thatcher's inflexible handling of two hunger strike campaigns in 1980 and 1981 by jailed Irish Republican Army members during which ten prisoners ultimately died. Haughey, in the wake of those deaths, fought and lost a general election on 11 June 1981. FitzGerald led a Fine Gael–Labour coalition but it too fell after another snap election on 18 February 1982. Returning to power, Haughey led a minority Fianna Fáil government for 279 days, characterised by a series of domestic scandals, economic crises, and a major deterioration in the situation in Northern Ireland. The retired Irish diplomat Dr Conor Cruise O'Brien, playing multiple roles as public intellectual, historian, politician and journalist, described that time in Irish politics as **G**rotesque, **U**nbelievable, **B**izarre and **U**nprecedented or GUBU – an acronym that stuck.[19] Rightly or wrongly, Haughey blamed Thatcher for his many domestic political misfortunes and that clouded his judgement in 1982 during the Falklands/Malvinas crisis and war in the South Atlantic.

Prior to his return to power in early 1982, Haughey's relationship with senior officials in the Department of Foreign Affairs might be described as tetchy. There had been frequent references in the press about his jousts with Seán Donlon, the Irish ambassador to Washington between 1978 and 1981.[20] Tension arose over Donlon's highly successful implementation of the innovative and long overdue strategy to build a bipartisan coalition in the US Congress to monitor affairs in Northern Ireland. Donlon returned to Dublin in 1981 to become secretary of the Department of Foreign Affairs. His professional skills, and those of his senior colleagues, were rigorously put to the test during the Falklands/Malvinas war. Noel Dorr and Patrick McKernan were, with Donlon, the leading actors in the drama about to unfold. Dorr became permanent representative – or ambassador – to the United Nations in September 1980. It was a particularly challenging time to take up such an appointment. On 20 October 1980, Ireland had won a seat on the Security Council, the term to begin on 1 January 1981. McKernan replaced Dorr as head of the political division; his responsibilities as political director included meeting routinely with his EEC counterparts and advising the minister for foreign affairs on related policy matters. Given the volatility of Irish politics in those years, the minister changed multiple times between 1979 and 1982. For the purpose of clarity, the sequence was as follows: Michael O'Kennedy, Fianna Fáil (5 July 1977–11 December 1979), Brian Lenihan, Fianna Fáil (12 December 1979–30 June 1981); John Kelly, Fine Gael, acting minister (30 June 1981–21 October 1981), James Dooge, Fine Gael (21 October 1981–9 March 1982),

Gerard Collins, Fianna Fáil (9 March 1982–14 December 1982), and Peter Barry, Fine Gael (14 December 1982–10 March 1987).

IRISH FOREIGN POLICY TOWARDS ARGENTINA

Argentina, for the first time since diplomatic relations were established in 1947, moved centre stage in Irish foreign policy concerns in the weeks leading up to and during the seventy-four-day Falklands/Malvinas war (April–June 1982). The war also led to what was arguably the most serious crisis in modern Anglo-Irish relations since the early 1940s, when de Valera refused to give Winston Churchill access to three ports, returned to the Irish government in 1938, for the use of the British navy. After the sinking of the *Belgrano* (see below), Haughey withdrew support for EEC sanctions against Argentina and called for an immediate meeting of the UN Security Council to prepare a resolution to end hostilities. The senior British civil servant David Goodall wrote in his memoir: 'Thatcher was furious at what she regarded as a stab in the back from her nearest neighbour.'[21] If it had any rationale, according to Goodall, it was that 'Mr Haughey had chosen to act once again on the principle that England's difficulty was Ireland's opportunity'. While President Mitterrand of France stood with Thatcher throughout the war, she never understood why Haughey could act in what she saw as a purely vindictive and gratuitous manner that threatened Ireland's vital national interests with her most important trading partner.[22] Since 1982, neither London nor Dublin has ever acknowledged publicly the damage done to Irish economic interests during the Falklands/Malvinas war. Being a man of destiny with a keen interest in securing his place in history, Haughey raised Ireland's profile in Latin America and in May 1982 made the country the toast of the civilian military dictatorship in Argentina. The Irish embassy in Buenos Aires had, since it opened in 1947–8, remained – with two exceptions – on the periphery of traditional Irish foreign policy interests – those exceptions being the threat to Irish citizens during Perón's final year in power in 1955 and the disappearance of Fr Patrick Rice in October 1976 and the diplomatic struggle to get him released.

Ireland was fortunate to have two very capable diplomats assigned to Argentina when war broke out in April 1982. There had been a change of Irish ambassadors in Buenos Aires in late 1981, with Seán Ó hÉideáin departing in September. Liked and respected by Irish-Argentines, highly professional and conscientious to a fault, Ó hÉideáin sustained a friendly working relationship with the civilian military dictatorship throughout his period of service. Irrespective of who was in government, his view had been that Ireland's formal relations with the Argentine state required him to advance his country's interests in an undifferentiated manner, be it in trade, commerce, or cultural or commemorative events. Patrick Walshe (39), who took up the post of ambassador in November, was of a very different stripe to his immediate predecessor. Joining the service in 1964, he served in Chicago, at the EEC and in Paris; he was appointed ambassador to Argentina on 7 August 1981. Because 'the postal service is unreliable and political climate unstable', he was permitted to bring his letters of credence with him when, on 9 November, he left with his wife Dymphna for Buenos Aires.[23] Walshe was a member of a new generation of Irish diplomats unbounded by the conservative, confessional constraints of many of his older colleagues. He was independent-minded and his reporting style was succinct and direct. While he got on well with the Irish-Argentine community, there were those who did not admire what they perceived as his hauteur and his patrician style.

Colin Wrafter, his diplomatic colleague, had arrived in Buenos Aires in March 1980 on his first foreign posting. He overlapped with Ó hÉideáin for a year and a half. Both Wrafter and Walshe were quick to ascertain the danger posed to peace in the South Atlantic by the upcoming 150th anniversary of Britain's occupation of the Falklands/Malvinas since 1833. *Las Malvinas son Argentinas* (The Falklands are Argentine) was a slogan frequently chanted at patriotic gatherings throughout the country. Taking control of those islands formed a central plank of the Argentine nationalist canon. *Las Malvinas son Argentinas* was not a shibboleth for the Argentine civilian military government. Neither was winning 'back' sovereign control of the islands an aspiration. By 1982, it was the government's primary strategic military objective.

Wrafter, speaking at his retirement reception in 2016, said: 'I compiled [in 1981] a list of the Embassy's objectives, the first was monitoring the situation in relation to the Falklands/Malvinas Islands. A year later Argentina launched its invasion that resulted in a considerable loss of life, demonstrating that failures of diplomacy can have awful consequences.'[24] South Georgia and the South Sandwich Islands, some 1,500 kilometres from Port Stanley, the capital of the Falklands, were also part of the disputed territory.[25] However, Iveagh House had received accurate reports over three decades on how perfervid Argentines really were about regaining control of those islands. The territory in question lies 12,578 kilometres from Portsmouth, England, and 783 kilometres from Río Gallegos, Argentina. There were fewer than twenty Irish passport-holders working there when conflict broke out.

The British government based its right to the Falklands/Malvinas on continuous occupation (prescription) since 1833.[26] Argentina established its case for rightful ownership on the principle of *uti possidetis* (succession of states, in this case, from the Spanish crown).[27] Claiming that Britain had taken the islands by force, successive governments in Buenos Aires asserted their right to ownership de jure and de facto and that claim was sustained through the decades, making official protests to Britain in 1833, 1841, 1849, 1884, 1888, 1908, 1927, 1933, 1946 and every year following.[28] Given that in 1908, Britain had annexed South Georgia, South Sandwich, South Orkney and the South Shetland Islands, the Argentines also counter-claimed for South Orkney in 1925, South Georgia in 1927 and the South Sandwich Islands in 1948.

In the 1960s, Miguel Fitzgerald, an Irish-Argentine aviator, made two bold gestures to assert his country's claim to ownership of the islands.[29] Ambassador Skentelbery reported on 10 September 1964 that the pilot, noted for accomplishing a non-stop flight from New York to Buenos Aires (6–8 April 1962), flew on 8 September without authorisation from Río Gallegos to Port Stanley, capital of the Falkland Islands.[30] The timing of his flight was prompted by an upcoming vote on decolonisation in the United Nations during which the Falklands/Malvinas case was to be discussed.[31] Fitzgerald said that he had thought about such a trip for 'fifteen years or thereabouts, but I always seemed to be awaiting a favourable opportunity – you know how the years pass. And now that the question of the Argentine territory (and I wish to emphasise the qualification of "Argentine") has risen for the first time to the level of international discussion and so to world opinion in the UN, I hesitated no longer'.[32] *TSC*'s headline over the interview read: 'At Home with the Fitzgeralds' and described him as being 'the most talked of man in Argentina for the past ten days'. The interviewer also noted that the pilot had 'a great patriotic sentiment and a great admiration for Argentina's national heroes'.[33] Fitzgerald told *TSC* that he was a member of no political party and, 'because of the faith of his parents and the traditions of Ireland', he was a practising Catholic. His flight had been 'inspired purely by my feelings as an Argentine'. Fitzgerald described his arrival in Port Stanley thus: 'I suddenly appeared out of the sky from nowhere. When I landed, I gave the proclamation [asserting Argentina's sovereignty over the island] to the first one who approached me, running. I spoke to him in English: "Will you please give this to your governor."' After that meeting, Fitzgerald placed an Argentine flag in an upright position 'by working it through the strands of a barbed wire fence'. Having enough fuel for the return trip, 'I left immediately, he said'.[34]

The British chargé d'affaires in Buenos Aires lodged a complaint with the Argentine government about the unwanted landing, as did the British permanent representative at the UN. In contrast, the official Argentine response was – according to Ambassador Skentelbery – that, while the pilot may have been technically at fault for not seeking the normal official permission to land at Port Stanley, 'his action showed the depth of feeling of the Argentine people about this matter and [it] expresses their determination to obtain sovereignty over the territory'.[35] The Argentine government had good cause to be pleased with Ireland's policy stance at the UN in the 1960s on the Falklands/Malvinas issue. Under the Fianna Fáil minister for external affairs Frank Aiken, Dublin took a favourable view of the Argentine claim to sovereignty. Ireland, having joined the United Nations on 14 December 1955, was in favour of UN Resolution 1514 (adopted 14 December 1960) calling for an end to colonisation worldwide.[36] In 1964, the British government placed a petition before the UN in which the inhabitants of the islands expressed their firm wish to remain British. In 1965, Aiken instructed his officials to vote for UN Resolution 2065 (adopted on 16 December 1965), calling in the preamble for the accomplishment of 'the cherished aim of bringing to an end everywhere colonisation in all its forms, one of which covers the case of the Falkland Islands'.[37] The resolution urged both governments to proceed with negotiations with a view to finding a peaceful solution to the problem.[38] Ireland, in its contribution in the General Assembly, drew an analogy between the Falklands and the territorial integrity of Ireland. Discussion within the Irish delegation preceding the vote had been divided over whether to support the motion. Those opposed felt at the time that the Northern Ireland analogy was not valid as there was little evidence to show a historical link between the Falklands/ Malvinas and Britain prior to the British occupation of the islands in 1833. There was also doubt as to whether the dispute might properly be considered a colonial issue. But Aiken felt at the time that it was unrealistic for the British to retain sovereignty over 'widely-scattered outposts of little strategic or other value'.[39] Afterwards, on 21 January 1966, the Argentine embassy thanked Aiken for Irish support, adding that news of the Irish stance had been received 'with the warmest enthusiasm both in official circles and by the people of Argentina', given the tremendous importance of the Argentine aspiration to bring about 'the reintegration of the Malvinas Islands to our country'.[40]

Sir Cosmo Dugal Patrick Thomas Haskard, the governor of the islands from 1964 to 1970, was an Irishman and a stout defender of the rights of the islanders to remain British.[41] After Fitzgerald's first landing in 1964, an Argentine magazine published the governor's photograph above the caption '*El último gobernador inglés*' ('The last English governor'). Haskard had other ideas. Ambassador Skentelbery reported on 28 March 1966 on local press speculation that Anglo-Argentine talks were about to cede the islands to

Buenos Aires. Harold Wilson's Labour government saw the South Atlantic as one of the areas where Britain ought to divest itself of the few remaining parts of the old empire and silence forever the debate in the UN General Assembly about 'British colonialism'. According to *The Times*, it was 'his [Haskard's] intervention – some would say insubordination – that prevented the British government ceding the islands to Argentina in the late 1960s'.[42] Haskard was a very popular and energetic administrator and, during his time there, he visited almost every farm on the islands on horseback. He also made an annual visit to South Georgia. His energy helped boost the sheep industry and revive arts and crafts fairs, and he was instrumental in having the scuttled Brunel steamship *Great Britain* raised and towed back to Bristol in 1970, where it is now a tourist attraction. But he is best remembered for his sterling defence of retaining British sovereign rights over the islands. Haskard pressed home to his superiors the dangers of an Argentine takeover when an eighteen-strong Peronist group hijacked an Aerolíneas Argentinas passenger plane on 28 September 1966 en route to Río Gallegos with six crew and forty-three passengers aboard and forced the pilots to fly to Port Stanley. The stunt was timed to take place during a visit by the duke of Edinburgh to Buenos Aires.[43] The plane landed on the racecourse and a protester read a proclamation declaring that the inhabitants of the Falklands/Malvinas were now Argentines. Surrounded by the small British garrison, they surrendered to the local Catholic priests after thirty-six hours.[44]

Haskard took very seriously what policy-makers in London dismissed as mere pantomime. Fearing a real invasion, he successfully requested the deployment on a permanent basis of a small group of marines to the islands. In his remaining years as governor, he continued to fight a rearguard action with his superiors in the Foreign and Commonwealth Office to prevent the secession of the Falklands to Argentina. He discussed the future of the islands on 31 May 1967 in London with an official at the Commonwealth Office, warning that it was better to announce a long-term policy of withdrawal than to be forced out by Argentina. But he saw little chance of the islanders wishing to live under the Argentines. Haskard was ordered not to reveal the details of his discussions in London with the islands' Executive Council. The foreign secretary, George Brown, had a conversation on 21 September 1967 with the Argentine foreign minister, Costa Méndez, at the Plaza Hotel in New York. According to the official minute, Brown said he wished to assure his Argentine counterpart that the British had no desire to retain sovereignty over the islands 'and were prepared to cede this to Argentina always provided that we had been able to satisfy ourselves that the interests of the Islanders had been met'. Costa Méndez replied that the islands were 'his most important problem'.

The big question for him was how to woo the islanders. He thought that they might 'wish to go to New Zealand or exchange their land for land in South Argentina'. Another proposal was to allow Argentina to purchase the Falkland Islands Company (FIC). Founded in 1851, it received a royal charter in 1852 and became the biggest landowner and employer on the islands. The British crown granted the company the right to tame wild cattle, build the farming of sheep and establish a general store which provided a postal service within the islands and between the islands, the Latin American mainland and Europe. The company prospered and by the end of the nineteenth century it had increased its sheep herds from 35,000 to 150,000. The meeting agreed to continue the talks at the official level.[45]

When details of that discussion reached the inhabitants of the islands their response was one of incomprehension and fury. In a long letter on 21 October 1967, Haskard told the Foreign and Commonwealth Office that 'the whole future of the colony is now at stake'. He added that on the Falklands

> we are largely ignorant of Argentina and all things Argentine. We know as much about Argentina as the inhabitants of the Shetlands know about Poland. We have a strong emotional feeling for the Queen, the flag (flying every day over Stanley) and the national anthem (sung vigorously once a week in the Cathedral and played last thing at night over the wireless). Our links, sentimental and economic, bind us firmly to England. Argentina, seen through Falkland eyes, is unknown, foreign, aloof, disdainful, corrupt, feared; a place where taxation is high and the standard of the public service low.

Perhaps a change of heart is not possible, he thought, but 'the price of wool and the drift of population may in the long run decide the issue'.[46] He went to Britain again in 1968 and had an angry meeting with Foreign Secretary Brown. Under a 'gagging order' when he returned to Port Stanley in February, he had received permission only to tell his council after swearing them to secrecy. (For entirely unrelated reasons, Brown resigned as foreign secretary on 15 March 1968.) News leaked out and islanders quickly knew exactly what was afoot. A number wrote a letter of protest to *The Times*. In London, a Falkland Islands Emergency Committee was formed to act as a lobby group, mounting a strong and sustained campaign to influence parliament to halt any handover or lease-back of the islands.[47]

Despite Haskard's vigorous objections, the cabinet took a decision to proceed in September 1968 with a two-track strategy to (1) sign a memorandum of understanding with the Argentines about a transfer of sovereignty by a date still to be specified; and (2) simultaneously issue a statement explaining how sovereignty would not be transferred unless the change was acceptable to the islanders. Believing that such a strategy would destroy any prospect of settlement, Haskard requested that a minister be sent on a visit to Port Stanley. Noting his objections, the British cabinet nevertheless voted to continue its policy as it was feared that, without a memorandum of understanding, Argentina would 'not agree to reopen communications with the islands, an essential first step in the normalisation of relations'. Lord Chalfont, a junior foreign minister, was sent to the islands in November to mollify the islanders. His Foreign Office brief advised him that Britain could no longer defend the islands effectively 'except by a force ridiculously large in relation to the population and resources'.[48] Upon landing in Port Stanley, he was greeted by demonstrators waving Union Jacks and with placards reading 'Chalfont go home'. The reception he received indoors was even more hostile from islanders he imperiously considered to be of a 'paternalistic, almost feudal character'. During the minister's visit, Miguel Fitzgerald made a second flight to Port Stanley, damaging his larger plane while attempting a landing on the road. Haskard had it stripped of its wings and humiliatingly returned by ship, via Montevideo, to Buenos Aires. Returning to London, Chalfont reported that the government should prepare for the transfer of sovereignty, partly because Britain could not offer any defence against an Argentine attack on the islands. But he had been persuaded that the memorandum of agreement which the British were on the point of signing with Argentina should not take place at that time.[49]

His visit coincided with speculation in the British press that a transfer of sovereignty was about to take place. The public reaction in Britain was so hostile that the government issued a denial on 16 December 1969 in the House of Commons. Haskard received some satisfaction when Michael Stewart, who served as foreign secretary from March 1968 until 1970, pledged that the islands would never be transferred to Argentina without the consent of the islanders, reflecting what Skentelbery reported on 23 April 1968 as being 'a significant, one might almost say epochal, advance from the deadlock in which the problem has stagnated for generations'.[50] The Labour government had not resolved the fate of the islanders when it was replaced by the Conservatives in June 1970.

Retiring in 1970, Haskard returned to live in the family home in west Cork but always remained in close contact with the islanders. He received their weekly paper, *Penguin News*, and served as vice president of the Falkland Islands Association. He told the BBC in 1972: 'I didn't feel it was my job to sell the islanders down the river because, of course, I had become very involved in the country.'[51] On his one hundredth birthday in November 2016, the islanders presented him with a painting of Government House in Port Stanley. He died on 21 February 2017, aged 100, at his home in Tragariff, Bantry, west Cork. As a mark of respect, flags were flown at half-mast across the islands in the South Atlantic.[52] Haskard's struggle to frustrate any attempt by a British government to hand the islands over to Argentina was carried on in the 1970s by his immediate successors, Sir Ernest Lewis, Sir Neville Arthur French and Sir James Roland.

When Labour came back to power in February 1974, discussions on the islands continued without any resolution. Buenos Aires raised the Malvinas question at the UN General Assembly in late 1975, stating that it would 'not fail to assert its rights in the form which it deemed most appropriate'. The position of the British government was that London would not agree to negotiate the transfer of sovereignty without the concurrence of the islanders, which was not forthcoming.[53]

Reporting from Buenos Aires on 23 January 1976, the third secretary in the Irish embassy, Justin Harman, told Dublin that the popularity of the Peronist government was explained both by the sterile political situation in the country but also by 'the utter misunderstanding by Britain of the strength of national feeling here on the islands'. Emphasising that point, he wrote: 'This present "contretemps" in relations between the two countries has shown above all else the seeming inability on Britain's part to recognise the importance attached (to the islands) in Argentine public opinion.' That view was supported by an editorial in the *Buenos Aires Herald* on 6 January 1976 which said: 'The issue of the islands is one on which the nation is unified.'[54] The Argentine ambassador to Britain, who had returned to Buenos Aires, was ordered on 13 January 1976 not to return to London, while the British government was advised that its ambassador in Buenos Aires should be withdrawn. He left for London on the 19th for 'consultations'. Although the issue was used by different political factions in Argentina to gain popularity, Harman concluded that it 'in no way detracts from the importance which is attached to the issue by public opinion'.[55]

Underlying the strength of feeling on the issue reported by Harman, an Argentine destroyer fired several warning shots in early February 1976 across the bow of a British research vessel south of the disputed islands, threatening to fire shells into its hull if it did not heave-to. Fortunately, the ship docked safely and without any casualties.[56] Argentine telecommunication workers, in early March 1976, cut links with the islands when Falkland Islands radio asked Buenos Aires not to address messages to the 'Malvinas'. A retired Argentine

general, Benjamín Rattenbach, was reported in the press as saying that
Argentina had been on the verge of taking the islands in 1945 upon learning
that the British were thinking of ceding the archipelago to the United States.
When the general taught in the war college in 1942, he said that he was asked
to study plans for a possible invasion. His conclusion was that it would be easy
to take the islands but hard to hold them.[57] Harman reported that the Irish
embassy had been invited by the Argentine government on 12 March 1976 to
attend the 'first national congress for the restoration of the Malvinas' as part of
a plan to counter a British position paper submitted on 3 March 1976 to the
UN[58] and unite all the different organisations in the country pressing for the
islands' restoration. The Irish embassy declined the invitation.[59] The Argentine
government lobbied Ireland in September to support UN Resolution 31/49 on
the Falklands/Malvinas.[60] Although Argentina had gained full support for its
sovereignty claim from the Non-Aligned Conference of Foreign Ministers in
August 1975, recent events caused Dublin to change its position. Ireland and
the other EEC member states were expected to support the British. Argentina,
in the wake of the coup, was a pariah among the democratic nations. Moreover,
at the time of the discussions on the vote, the Argentine government had
disappeared, tortured and was holding an Irish citizen in prison without any
charge being preferred. When the Argentine ambassador, José Alberto del
Carril, met the political director, Noel Dorr, on 3 November 1976, Dorr told
him that 'while I was not aware in detail of the past history of the issue at the
UN, I thought we would wish to balance, in such cases, our general anti-colonial
position against the fact that we were partners in the Nine with the United
Kingdom'. In the follow-up discussions in Iveagh House, Dorr argued on 12
November that Ireland ought to change its position from support of the UN
resolution to abstention. Arguing that the wording of the resolution was likely
to be tougher than before, he felt that the issue was not really a colonial one,
though the Argentines had succeeded in having it considered in that context.
He believed that Ireland should not vote against an EEC partner whose 'basic
wish is to disengage'. That view was accepted by his colleagues, one pointing
out that 'an abstention or negative vote might also act as a warning sign to the
Argentine authorities of our current disquiet about the state of human rights
in their country'.[61] Minister for Foreign Affairs FitzGerald, conscious of the
abysmal human rights record of Argentina and the torturing of Patrick Rice,
agreed with Dorr's recommendation to change the original position of support
to one of abstention.[62] The resolution was passed on 16 November 1976 in the
UN with ninety-four in favour, Britain against, and thirty-two abstentions –
including Ireland and the eight other members of the EEC.[63]

When Margaret Thatcher became prime minister on 4 May 1979, she did little in her early months in power to reassure the 1,800-strong Falkland islanders that their future rested securely within the British orbit. At best, the Thatcher government was agnostic about their future. A British ambassador, Anthony Williams, was sent to Buenos Aires in February 1980, the first to serve at that rank since Argentina had asked in 1975 for the recall of his predecessor. During the Peronist governments of Juan Domingo and Isabel, Anglo-Argentine relations were at a low ebb. Argentina had recalled its ambassador in London in 1975 for 'consultations'. The British envoy, Sir Derrick Ashe, returned to London after protests in early 1976 from the government in Buenos Aires. Two chargés d'affaires, John Shakespeare and Hugh Carless, had kept the British mission open in the interim. While there was continuity in policy with the outgoing Labour government, Thatcher set out to improve trade relations with Argentina. The new British ambassador wrote soon after his arrival in 1980 that the civilian military government had become 'more nannyish than oppressive'. He encouraged an intensification of trade, including *matériel de guerre* such as bomber planes.[64] On 29 March 2012, Shakespeare wrote an article in the *New Statesman* in which he said: 'We [the British] unwittingly encompassed our own destruction by trying to sell the very weapons most capable of it [Argentine military intervention].' Lord Carrington, the foreign secretary until 5 April 1982, continued to explore a lease-back solution to the question of the governance of the islands. Had there not been a war, that might have led to a Hong Kong-style solution for the Falklands/Malvinas.[65] When the Foreign Office minister Nicholas Ridley made a goodwill visit to Port Stanley in November 1980, the islanders gave him a hostile reception, defiantly singing 'Rule Britannia' as he was departing. On 2 December, his report proposing a 'lend lease' solution was rejected by the House of Commons, and the Falkland Islands Council voted it down on 7 January 1981. Reassurances from the British foreign secretary Lord Carrington that the islands would remain British for as long as there was a majority of Falklanders in favour of that position did nothing to dissipate anxieties in Port Stanley. A further cause for concern was that none of the islanders were automatically entitled to British citizenship.[66]

According to the historian Lawrence Freedman,[67] the Foreign Office in 1981 was left 'pursuing an increasingly fragile middle ground, desperately trying to avoid a major crisis with Argentina but with an increasingly weak hand to play'.[68] A decision by the secretary for defence, John Nott, to decommission the ice patrol ship *HMS Endurance* – Britain's only naval presence in the South Atlantic – was evidence of the policy confusion in London.[69] Nick

Barker, captain of the ship since 1980, argued trenchantly with his superiors that the planned scrapping would encourage Argentine aggression. Lord Buxton, one of the captain's friends in London, told the prime minister in a letter on 21 July 1981 that the British electorate would not 'take kindly to the international humiliation which could well be possible if the Argentines see there is nothing to hinder their bullying of the Falklanders'. Thatcher replied on 19 August that the withdrawal of *Endurance* from service 'would not impair our ability to maintain the operational effectiveness' of the garrison of Royal Marines on the island: 'We are in no doubt about the legitimacy of our sovereignty over the Falkland Islands and we are determined to ensure that the Islands' territorial integrity is preserved'.[70] Critical of the role played by the British ambassador Anthony Williams and for being 'far from in touch with activities of the Argentine government',[71] Barker repeatedly warned London of the warlike intentions of Buenos Aires, as did Sir Rex Hunt, governor of the islands between 1980 and 1985. In blunt naval language, the captain despaired of 'incompetent diplomats, bloody-minded mandarins and lying Argentines. The Ambassador and Whitehall making "tut tut" noises is not impressing the Argentines'.[72] Accusing the British embassy staff in Buenos Aires of a 'symphony of errors', Barker felt that the ambassador's 'words carried with them such a weight of credibility' that they contributed 'to the exclusion perhaps of reports made by [Governor] Rex Hunt'.[73] (The *Endurance* remained under sentence of being scrapped but the war in the South Atlantic gave it a stay of execution.) The warnings were plain for everyone to see in London. Even the much criticised British ambassador, Anthony Williams, warned his superiors on 2 October 1981 against Micawberism, a policy based on the forlorn hope that something will turn up. He considered it deceptive for London to convey the impression that a natural convergence of views between the islanders and the Argentines would evolve. He concluded that rather than 'live a lie it would be better to be frank with the Argentines and take the consequences'.[74]

While Britain grappled with its 'end of empire' problems, hawkish military elements in Argentina read the signs of indecision and dither in London as a lack of resolve to remain in the South Atlantic. Had not British governments made significant concessions to anti-colonial movements, most notably with the formation of India and Pakistan in 1947?[75] The Irish Free State declared itself a republic in 1949 and left the British Commonwealth without incurring any sanction. The Suez Canal debacle in 1956 demonstrated the weakness of the British in the post-war world. Sudan gained its independence in 1956 and a procession of African colonies followed in the 1960s. Searching around

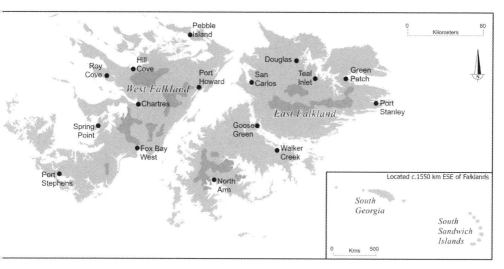

MAP 2. The Falkland Islands. (I am grateful to Dr Michael Murphy, School of Geography, UCC, for making this map.)

for international examples on which to find justification for an invasion, the Argentine armed forces were aware of India's forcible ejection in 1961 of the Portuguese from Goa, which the latter had held since 1510. Morocco, engaging in an act of annexation, seized possession of Western Sahara in 1975 and got away with it. In 1976, there was another example of 'might is right' when Australia ceded independence to the eastern half of Papua New Guinea. Indonesia seized Portuguese East Timor in 1975 from the revolutionary government in Lisbon under an anti-colonial pretext. After twenty-five years of struggle in which over 100,000 people died in conflict-related violence, a referendum resulted in an overwhelming vote for independence.[76] After a further two and a half years, helped by the presence of a United Nations international peace keeping force, East Timor became independent on 20 May 2002.[77] Southern Rhodesia became the independent republic of Zimbabwe on 18 April 1980 and Britain also granted Belize independence on 21 September 1981. By 1997, when the city-state of Hong Kong reverted to China, fifty-four former British territories in the Commonwealth had been shed. The once great British Empire had been reduced to fourteen scattered islands in the Caribbean, South Pacific and South Atlantic.

OPERACIÓN AZUL/ROSARIO: ARGENTINE INTERVENTION IN THE FALKLANDS/MALVINAS

A majority of Latin American countries at the UN in the late 1970s and early 1980s considered the British presence in the Falklands/Malvinas to be an illegal occupation dating from an era of 'gunboat diplomacy'. In Argentina, irredentism bound conflicting sectors of a divided society together under the slogan *Las Malvinas son Argentinas*. Nationalism and patriotism cauterised deep political wounds, bringing the most unlikely rivals together behind that slogan. A change of personnel in the military junta in 1981 strengthened the argument that an opportunity should not be missed by the Argentine government to seize control of the Falklands/Malvinas islands. General Roberto Eduardo Viola, who had become president on 29 March 1981, was replaced on 10 December that year by the commander of the army, General Leopoldo Fortunato Galtieri. He was joined in the junta by the head of the navy, Admiral Jorge Anaya, together with the head of the air force, General Lami Dozo. Nicanor Costa Méndez was reappointed minister for foreign affairs. Galtieri was not opposed to planning for a military occupation of the islands. After all, force and the threat of force had earlier secured a satisfactory outcome in the Beagle Channel dispute with Chile. The year 1983 marked 150 years of continuous British control of the Malvinas. In an act of defiance, Galtieri jumped the gun, declaring 1982 the 'Year of the Malvinas'. While preparing for war, the Argentine foreign minister Costa Méndez threatened to break off talks with the British and take whatever course of action was in the interest of his country.

On 19 March 1982, a party of Argentine scrap metal merchants, led by Constantino Davidoff, landed at Leith Harbour on the island of South Georgia claiming to have a licence to dismantle a derelict whaling station owned by a Scottish company. The tiny island, about 169 kilometres by 29 kilometres, was virtually uninhabitable except for penguins, seals and a small British Antarctic Survey team. On 24 March, the Argentine government published news of the presence of workers on the island. The Argentine flag was reportedly flown over the island for the first time. In Port Stanley, Governor Rex Hunt, believing that the salvage operation was cover for an Argentine invasion to be staged imminently, sent the *HMS Endurance*, captained by Nick Barker, to reclaim the island for Britain, a journey of 1,556 kilometres.[78] When it arrived, the twenty-two marines aboard landed to monitor the activities of the Argentine scrap workers. The head of the British delegation at the UN, Sir Anthony Parsons, raised informally on 31 March the unauthorised presence of the Argentines on

South Georgia. The Irish representative on the Security Council, Noel Dorr, saw what had happened in the South Atlantic as 'a small cloud on the horizon' compared with crises in Nicaragua and the Middle East.[79] Within a matter of days that 'small cloud' enveloped the UN and the threat of war grew between Britain and Argentina.

On 30 March, the civilian military government had to respond to a challenge from about 40,000 workers converging in columns on the Plaza de Mayo from different parts of the city to protest against the national economic crisis under banners which read: *Paz, Pan y Trabajo* (Peace, Bread and Work). Surrounded by assault vehicles and a cordon of police, the workers in the plaza were the victims of excessive force for over six hours as efforts were made to disperse them.[80] However, within a few days, the grave industrial and political crisis in the country took second place to a call for unity when *Operación Azul/Rosario* was launched. At 4.30 a.m. local time on 2 April the first Argentine troops landed by helicopter five kilometres from Port Stanley. A main force of 1,000 landed two hours later. The British garrison of thirty marines, supported by the islanders' auxiliary forces, put up a stiff resistance. Four Argentines died and two were wounded in the action. However, at 9.30 a.m., Governor Rex Hunt was forced to halt hostilities; Argentine forces had control of Port Stanley. (A planned Argentine landing on South Georgia on 2 April was delayed until the following day. The handful of British marines on the island only stopped fighting when confronted by overwhelming odds.)[81]

Despite the repeated warnings from Governor Hunt, the invasion took the British prime minister by surprise. Her secretary for defence, John Nott, was vacillating and indecisive. When Thatcher asked one of her admirals whether sending a task force was a practical plan, he replied yes and preparations got under way. On 2 April, Lord Carrington made that decision public. He resigned the following day over what he called the 'humiliating affront' of Argentina's seizure of the islands; three junior ministers did the same.[82] Sir Francis Pym became the new foreign secretary. On 5 April, a fleet of over a hundred ships set out for the South Atlantic provisioned for the nearly three-week journey of 13,000 kilometres and with sufficient supplies to fight a war. The aircraft carriers *HMS Hermes* and *HMS Invincible* were part of the flotilla scheduled to arrive in the South Atlantic to face the prospect of fighting a winter war. The British government froze Argentine assets, estimated to have been $1.5 billion, and imposed an arms embargo and a general ban on Argentine imports.[83] Thatcher broke off diplomatic relations with Argentina on 3 April. It would be ten years before a British ambassador returned to that post in Buenos Aires. David Joy, an ex-counsellor at the British embassy, became head of a British interest section under the Swiss flag. Although there was no British ambassador in Buenos Aires, the embassy building remained open throughout the war and beyond.[84] Australia, New Zealand and Canada also withdrew their ambassadors.[85] The Argentine embassy in London came under the Brazilian flag and remained so until diplomatic relations were formally restored in 1990.

UN SECURITY COUNCIL RESOLUTION 502 AND IRISH-ARGENTINE REACTION

Britain moved swiftly at the UN to win international support for its stance. On 2 April, the British permanent representative Sir Anthony Parsons spoke to Security Council members in public session. Describing the Argentine action as a blatant violation of the United Nations charter and of international law, he said the council faced an emergency and it must act at once. Argentina was in breach of Article 2(3) of the UN Charter which stated that 'All members of the UN shall settle their international disputes by peaceful means in such manner that international peace and security and justice are not endangered.'[86] While the Argentine representative Eduardo Roca asked for time to clarify the situation, Parsons sought an emergency Security Council meeting to convene within twenty-four hours.[87] The Irish permanent representative, Noel Dorr, spoke on the duty to uphold the rule of law in international relations, making clear that Ireland's concern was not with the merits of the dispute. The British delegation prepared the text of a motion calling for an immediate cessation of hostilities between Argentina and the United Kingdom and the complete withdrawal of Argentine forces. The motion also urged both governments to seek a diplomatic solution to the conflict and to refrain from further military action in the region. Parsons knew that the outcome of the vote on the 3rd was unpredictable: 'As I recall, we concluded that we would probably secure seven or eight votes, with luck we would get nine, with unbelievable luck we might achieve the maximum of ten.'[88] Britain was counting on the votes of fellow EEC members who were on the Security Council. The Irish delegation led by Noel Dorr discussed its options later that day. There were two choices: support the resolution or abstain. The latter choice would be consistent with the earlier vote on the Falklands in 1976. But in 1982 the situation was very different. Dorr, after much deliberation, recommended to Dublin that Ireland should vote in favour of the British motion. That view was supported – having consulted with Foreign Minister Gerard Collins – by the secretary of the Department of Foreign Affairs, Seán Donlon. That same day, the foreign ministers of the ten member states of the European Community had issued a text strongly condemning the Argentine action, calling on Buenos Aires to withdraw its forces and adhere to the appeal of the UN Security Council to refrain from the use of force and to continue the search for a diplomatic solution. The following morning, Saturday, 3 April, the early news bulletin on Ireland's national radio, RTÉ, carried a report wrongly underlining 'Ireland's support for the UK'. As Minister Collins was away in his Limerick constituency for the weekend, the taoiseach, Charles Haughey, took a central role in making the final policy decision. Donlon, speaking to him on the phone, got the impression that Haughey 'had been a bit grumpy about the way in which my speech had been covered in that morning's news reports at home'. The taoiseach gave the secretary instructions in three parts: 1) If Ireland had to vote for the resolution, it should do so; 2) If Ireland could avoid voting for it, it should do so; and 3) if it were possible to find a situation where the motion was not voted on and Ireland did not have to vote, that would be 'even better'. At the end of the conversation, Donlon told Dorr: 'If we have to vote for the resolution as it stands, we have clearance to do so.'[89]

During a very tense meeting of the Security Council, Dorr left the room six or seven times to phone Donlon to check if there were any further instructions. Phoning the taoiseach again, Donlon was told to pass on the following instruction: Dorr was to stress in the Security Council that Ireland was not taking sides on the merits of the dispute and was upholding the authority of the Security Council and did not want to see either side use force. Returning to the meeting, Dorr drafted a text on the basis of those instructions and went out again to telephone Donlon. Having read the text over to him, he received word back a short time later that the taoiseach had approved it but his preference was to leave the Irish seat vacant during the vote if possible. After Dorr explained that that was not possible, he was told that the taoiseach agreed that Ireland should vote in favour of the resolution. Dorr did so, making the vote ten in favour of Resolution 502 (one more than was needed for it to pass), four abstentions and one against.[90] The outcome placed Anglo-Irish relations at the UN on a cordial footing. Parsons, the British representative, may never have fully appreciated the behind-the-scenes diplomatic and political drama which had unfolded in Dublin nor that the decision had been so closely run. The hope was that war might be averted.

However, Britain and Argentina were on a war footing. The British flotilla was sailing towards the South Atlantic. Britain announced on 8 April that from the 11th it would sink any Argentine ship that came within 200 miles of the

Falkland Islands. In response to the British threat, Argentina announced on the 8th that it had created a 200-mile defence zone off its shores and around the Falkland Islands. On the same day, Gen. Mario Benjamín Menéndez was appointed governor of the Falkland, South Georgia and South Sandwich Islands. According to the Irish diplomat Colin Wrafter, the Argentine flag was to be seen flying everywhere in Buenos Aires after the taking of the islands. It was hanging from apartments and houses and flying on taxis and on public transport. Radio stations played patriotic music and English-speaking popular music disappeared from the airwaves. English speakers were careful not to be heard speaking that language in public.[91] Many Irish-Argentines supported their government's military action. In their upbringing and in their schooling, Argentines were conditioned to see the Malvinas as an integral part of the national territory. The Christian Brothers Newman College annals had the following entry for 2/3 April:

> Today was a historic day for Argentina. In the early hours of the morning the Argentine Armed Forces invaded and captured Las Islas Malvinas. Before classes commenced all the secondary boys assembled in the main hall for the singing of the National Anthem. Prof. Gonzalez spoke on the significance and importance of the invasion. A half day was given to allow the boys to attend the celebrations in Plaza de Mayo. It was decided to ask for police protection as the vast majority of people who are not closely connected with the college think that Newman is an English College.[92]

Other Irish schools, including St Brendan's, St Bridget's and Santo Domingo, were in an equally vulnerable position, and the fear felt by teachers in Irish schools in the capital and in the camp was well founded. In the weeks leading up to the outbreak of war, there was anxiety over whether the government might act against Irish schools and Irish citizens working in those institutions. There was also a concern that the monuments to Admiral William Brown and Fr Anthony Fahy in public spaces might be vandalised. The authorities in St Bridget's took no chances, covering the bust of Fahy outside the main door of the college.[93] (Two Irish monuments, as will be seen later, were damaged, probably in the mistaken belief that they were British.) Living with the fear of being mistaken for British and liable to be attacked in the street was a far cry from a few weeks before when the Irish-Argentine community celebrated St Patrick's Day with the usual enthusiasm and public spectacle. On 12 March, Ambassador Walshe was the guest of honour at a banquet for 100 people organised by the Federation of Irish-Argentine Societies. In his address, Walshe said he was 'acutely conscious that this is the greatest non-English-speaking Irish community abroad' and he encouraged them to come to Ireland: 'Don't let Yankees command the trade routes to Ireland, to the homeland,' he said.[94] Coverage of St Patrick's Day celebrations filled the editions of *TSC* on 19 and 26 March.

However, Ireland's support for UN Resolution 502 turned that mood of celebration in the wider Irish-Argentine community into one of surprise, hurt and incomprehension. As the representative of the Irish government, Walshe became a *persona non grata* for many in the Irish community. Usually invited to community events, he suddenly found that he was being dis-invited. Dr Jorge M. Hamos, representing the Monte municipality, wrote on 14 April that it would be 'inopportune' for a representative of the Irish embassy to attend their local celebrations to unveil a statue of Admiral Guillermo Brown.[95] Oscar E. Villani Wynne and three others wrote on 17 April withdrawing the same invitation because of their opposition to Ireland's stance at the UN, which was at variance with the history of that country's anti-colonial past. His presence was not appropriate as they were mourning their Argentine dead following the taking of the islands.[96] Further dis-invitations followed. The principal of Newman College, Br John Burke, who took over that post in 1978, wrote to the ambassador on 19 April withdrawing the invitation for him to be the guest of honour on 23 April at the annual school prize-giving ceremony. While 'he did not think anything unpleasant would happen', Br Burke said, 'it would be embarrassing all round if the school was to maintain the invitation'.[97] The entry in the Newman annals for those days reads: 'The Irish Ambassador had been invited to present the prizes but because of the Irish vote in the United Nations Security Council it was thought better that he should not attend.'[98] That cancellation reflected the nervousness of the 100 Irish passport-holders like Br Burke living in Buenos Aires at the time. In that 'fog of war', irredentists might misguidedly attack Irish colleges like Newman, St Brendan's, Michael Ham, Santa Brígida and other English-speaking schools in the capital and in the camp. Br Burke recalled for me the anxiety among the community of Christian Brothers about future Argentine government policy towards the college. In that climate of uncertainty, there was also a danger that Irish passport-holders might be expelled from the country. Paradoxically, a number of the brothers in the community were very supportive of the actions of the Argentine government in occupying the islands. The taoiseach, Charles Haughey, a former pupil of the Christian Brothers in Dublin, was the recipient of correspondence from one or two members of the community.[99] Anxious for the safety of his staff and pupils, Br Burke was relieved to receive an assurance from the Argentine government that it would not interfere with the running of his school. The authorities also agreed to assign a policeman to guard the school round the clock.[100] That protection was withdrawn on 3 September 1982.[101]

Asked to explain urgently the official position of the government in Buenos Aires on the South Atlantic crisis, Ambassador Walshe told Iveagh House that that was difficult to accomplish in a single telex. His view was that the perceived foot-dragging by London in the diplomatic talks on the islands had led to frustration on the Argentine side: 'They [Argentine government] argue that, after seventeen years of fruitless talks since 1965 following reluctant British agreement at that time to open talks as result of pressure of international opinion particularly in UN, nothing has happened.' Walshe recalled that when General Galtieri's new government had come to power before Christmas (1981), he had instructed his foreign minister, Costa Méndez, to press Britain 'for regular, systematic schedule of talks with view to reaching outcome within measurable period of time. They say Britain promised to reply within month but did not do so'.[102]

Walshe also reported that the South Atlantic occupations had been greeted with patriotic euphoria by a wide section of the community. On 5 April, he noted that 1983 marked the 150th anniversary of the British occupation of the islands and that that 'emotive date would have posed great patriotic challenge to whatever Govt was in power in run-up that date'. The ambassador thought that while it would be simplistic to say that the Argentine military intervention had been merely a 'calculated external distraction from internal economic and social troubles, nevertheless the fact remains that intervention occurred only a few days after police brutality put down protest against present govt. economic policies'.[103] When in contact with the foreign ministry during the days following the seizure of the islands, the ambassador had expressed his concern for the safety of up to twelve Irish people who were on the islands, among them two teachers from Dublin, Shay Mahoney and his wife Jean.[104] He requested that the Argentine authorities take responsibility for their safety.[105] Walshe repeatedly emphasised in his reports the high degree of popular support for the Argentine government's actions. He illustrated this by referring to the editorials in the *Buenos Aires Herald* of 3 and 4 April: 'This paper, as you know, is liberal with well-known reputation during "dirty war" here. The editorials, taken together, are significant; showing that liberal, pro-human rights, Anglo opinion here basically shares national consensus on the islands and would deplore any British military reaction to Argentine action.'[106] Reporting on 7 April, the ambassador questioned the accuracy of British media reports that the 'Argentines are so chastened by British reaction that they are reconsidering [the occupation]'. He conceded it was true that the initial mood 'of carefree jubilation had passed' but that the popular solidarity with the government action 'was apparently undiminished'. In that highly charged patriotic atmosphere, the Irish ambassador said that there was very little opportunity for questioning Argentine rights to the islands in private and none in public. He noted that all the technically illegal political parties were vociferously in support of the regime's action. There was also a general feeling of concern locally among the public that '"that madwoman" [Thatcher] might actually do something really foolish'. At the same time, Walshe concluded there was a feeling of incredulity in official circles that 'Britain would indulge near the end of the 20th century in Victorian gunboat imperialism'. Commenting on the official EEC reaction and the probable imposition of economic sanctions, he argued that they might well be desirable and 'impossible for Ireland to avoid going along with them'. But he warned Dublin that sanctions might prove to be counter-productive in Argentina as they would only hurt the economy, but 'not disastrously'. The Irish ambassador was convinced that such sanctions were unlikely 'to impress military dictatorship whose prestige heavily invested in island exercise'. He concluded that the overall effect of sanctions would likely be to create a feeling of persecution 'by ex-colonial European powers ganging up with colonial Britain against colonised Argentina'. He warned further that the proposed EEC action 'could encourage lurch to Soviets, already largest trading partner'.[107] Based on a conversation with a highly placed source close to the junta, the ambassador reported on 8 April that Argentina knew that it could not defeat the British fleet in battle 'but [his source] estimates that, given Argentine's dug in positions on islands, Britain would have to accept at least three times and perhaps five times Argentine level of casualties to gain victory'.[108]

In the early weeks of April 1982, Walshe's mailbag bulged with letters of protest from Irish-Argentines. Many were incredulous and uncomprehending of the Irish stance at the UN. They could not understand how an Irish government would support a country that had occupied Ireland for 800 years and turn its back on Argentina, which had given refuge and a home to Irish immigrants in the nineteenth century.[109] (This file, of all the files of the Department of Foreign Affairs I have read over forty years, has had the most documents withheld or redacted.) Víctor H. Pereyra Murray, in a letter published in *La Prensa* on 6 April, speculated as to how Admiral Guillermo Brown would have felt, standing on the bridge of his frigate *Hercules*, seeing 'his beloved Ireland backs the English assaulter and that she prevents the Argentine people from recovering part of the territory for which he fought and which he defended courageously against Colonial pretension'. Murray felt defrauded and cheated, never expecting such a stance from Ireland – the land of 'courageous and liberty loving people'.[110] Describing himself as a descendant of the Irish with the blood of the Slevins, Lorans, Dohertys and Kearneys running through his Celtic veins, Dr Carlos Alberto Giacobone wrote hoping that Argentina in the future could count on the Irish – a country that had held out for 800 years against English imperialism.[111] Ricardo Gómez Kenny and Roberto S. Ryan, writing from Rosario on 8 April, regretted that the Irish government did not respect the legitimate rights of the Argentine republic to the 'islas Malvinas, Georgias y Sandwich del Sur'. They doubted that the Irish policy was in line with the sympathies of the Irish public and that it 'contradicted the principles of liberty and sovereignty for which the Irish had fought for centuries against the very same British oppressor and did not take into account Argentina's generous hospitality to the legions of Irish who had been forced in the nineteenth century to leave their homeland and given there peace, a roof, work and food'.[112] Guillermo R. McCann wrote on 11 April asking whether the nobility of the Irish lineage had fallen so low among Old Ireland's present authorities (as to take such a policy line). He speculated as to whether the 'functionaries' responsible for taking the decision were 'renegades'.[113] Patricio Garrahan commented in a letter on 10 April that, if Argentine blood were spilt in the islands and the sea of the South Atlantic, 'part of that blood will be without any doubt that of the descendants of the Irish who will give their lives, as their ancestors did on many occasions in the past – fighting for what they believe in and consider just'.[114]

Fr Richards, the editor of *TSC*, wrote of his profound disappointment as someone who was as proud an Irish nationalist as he was an Argentine patriot. He came from an Irish republican family which had two members 'out' in the rising of 1798. His thesis and that of many Irish-Argentines was simple if not reductionist – how could Ireland side with the traditional enemy against a country trying to right the wrongs wrought by British imperialism? On 9 April, the main *TSC* headline read: '*!Las Malvinas Argentinas en Dominio ya Inmortal!*' ('Argentina's Malvinas already under Immortal Rule'). This is a line from the patriotic anthem 'La Marcha de las Malvinas', which was written in 1940 by the poet Carlos Obligado with music composed by José Tieri. The words are universally known and sung at demonstrations when asserting Argentina's sovereignty of the islands.

The Southern Cross article referred to above said that 2 April 1982 would become part of the great history of the Argentine *patria*. One of the greatest national objectives had been achieved that day – the 'recuperation of the

Islas Malvinas, an integral part of the nation, which was occupied by Britain's unjust action and use of force, extending their territories by cannon shot and by devastating the natural rights of the inhabitants of vast and different nations [*pueblos*]'. The taking of the islands in 1833 was described as an act of 'transparent piracy' and that the nation since then had felt the 'inconsolable stinging' of that wound in its 'body and honour'. Another front-page article quoted an unnamed member of the Irish embassy in London who allegedly said 'well done' to an Argentine envoy on hearing about their action in the South Atlantic and to which the editor added the line: '*Gracias, desconocido discípulo de Wolfe Tone y Pearse*' ('Thank you, unknown disciple of Wolfe Tone and Pearse').[115] The same issue also carried a photograph of Miguel Fitzgerald, who, the paper said, displayed the courage and *quijotismo* (quixotic or idealistic vision) of the Irish race during his two flights to Port Stanley in 1964 and 1968.[116] *TSC* argued in an editorial on 9 April that both the British and the Argentine sides in the conflict had been urged by the UN General Assembly to find a peaceful solution in 1966, 1977, 1979 and 1981: 'We can truly and proudly say that Argentina faithfully complied with the admonition of the United Nations in trying to overcome the obstacles that the British Government put in her way, trying as well to offer the best living conditions to the inhabitants of the island ... Great Britain's answer to Argentina's attitude was cynically to accept everything and not to yield anything.'[117]

Argentine sovereignty over the islands was a tenet of national faith. That was reflected in the statements of many organisations representing different immigrant communities. The Confederation of Italian Institutions in Argentina (FEDITALIA), with 500 affiliated associations, published its support for the same irredentist views.[118] The board of directors (*consejo directivo*)[119] of the Federation of Irish-Argentine Societies[120] passed a resolution on 6 April condemning the Irish government decision to vote for Resolution 502. President John J. Scanlan, Vice President Santiago M. Quaine and another leading member, Carlos Brady, were given the task to draft a strongly worded letter to the ambassador which the board also released to the press.[121] It appeared on the front page of *TSC* on 16 April under the heading: '*La Federación ante la Actidud Irlandesa*' ('The Irish Federation against Irish Government Policy').[122] The letter said in summary that the sons of Ireland who arrived in Argentina had left behind in their own country a repressive (British) colonialism, death and persecution and that the ease with which the Irish vote (at the Security Council) purported to help Great Britain over the '*islas Malvinas*' could not be forgotten. The letter queried whether the Irish government had forgotten the executions of Wolfe Tone and Robert Emmet, and the Fenians of 1867, and

Pádraig Pearse and the patriots of 1916. The text declared: (1) that the federation supported without qualification the historical but long-delayed decision of the Argentine government (to reclaim the islands by force); and (2) that it deeply deplored the helpful attitude of the Irish government to Great Britain at the UN in open contradiction of its past struggle for liberty against unjust British domination and its present-day claim to sovereignty over a part of Ireland.[123]

Ambassador Walshe, in an effort to set the federation's statement in its local context, reported that Scanlan had admitted to him in private 'that he knew it was Argentina which was out of step with international community but statement had to be made to protect interests of Irish-Argentines here living under dictatorship ... as explained above however hard reality here is that Irish-Argentines are not in position publicly endorse anything less than total endorsement by Ireland of Argentine position'.[124] Walshe, in a telex on 9 April, emphasised the raw patriotic feelings of many Irish-Argentines. He explained that there was a 'strange simplistic belief throughout the country and supported by minority ethnic communities' that the 'Malvinas, were, are, and will be, Argentine'. That was 'partly result of genuine anti-colonial feeling and partly of massive, demagogic quasi-totalitarian manipulation of opinion by many administrations over many years' and that Argentines were 'living in climate of black and white, right or wrong, for us or against us, national sentiment'. While he noted that 'some of the letters written to papers by individual Irish-Argentines are genuine expressions of spontaneous feelings: other utterances, including statement issued by the Federation of Irish-Argentine Societies, are partly spontaneous indignation, partly calculated exercise in self-protective colouration'.[125]

THE EEC, IRELAND AND THE FALKLANDS/MALVINAS CRISIS

Margaret Thatcher, in parallel with her military preparations for war in the South Atlantic, requested the taoiseach and other EEC heads of governments to support economic sanctions on all Argentine imports together with a prohibition on exports. The prime minister also pursued her claim for a substantial rebate on the annual British contribution to the EEC budget. Instead of giving immediate support to the London request for sanctions, an Irish government meeting recorded the 'informal decision'[126] that it would not begin to consider the British request for sanctions until other issues were out of the way – a reference to the intransigent British refusal to accept the new European Community farm package until Thatcher had received a settlement for her claims to a rebate on London's 'over-payment' to the community budget. However, the EEC Commission on 7 April condemned 'the armed intervention of Argentina against a British territory linked to the Community, an intervention committed in violation of international law and the rights of the inhabitants of the Falkland Islands'. The commission made an urgent appeal to Argentina to implement Resolution 502. The statement also expressed the hope that the Organisation of American States (OAS) would join with the United States in order to ensure, 'by diplomatic means, that a solution based on law prevails'. On 8 April, the political director in the Department of Foreign Affairs, Patrick McKernan, had attended a meeting of political directors in Brussels which deferred taking a decision on sanctions as Ireland, together with the Danes, the Dutch and the Italians, had yet to clarify their respective national positions on the crisis in the South Atlantic. But on Good Friday, the 9th, consensus emerged among the EEC member states in favour of measures which would mean a loss annually of $2 billion to Argentina – about a quarter of the country's foreign currency earnings.[127] Irish exports to Argentina in 1980–1 were £9.5 million. In compensation, those sanctions would mean that banning Argentine beef and leather in EEC markets would result potentially in a greater market share of those products for Ireland and other countries.

The agreed EEC text and draft communiqués were sent back to the capitals for approval. McKernan, who strongly recommended support for the sanctions option, awaited the final decision of the taoiseach. As the Easter weekend had started, Seán Donlon in Iveagh House had difficulty making contact by phone with Haughey. The taoiseach had already retired to his private island home off the County Kerry coast. Once contact was finally made – in this time before mobile phones – he secured Haughey's verbal approval of the *relevé de conclusions* (statement of conclusions), and also that of the foreign minister Gerard Collins, who was in his Limerick constituency. The decision to impose sanctions for a month – beginning on 17 April – was published, as was the agreement to reconvene in a month to decide whether to renew, ease or extend the measure.

The president of the Federation of Irish-Argentine Societies, John J. Scanlan, was on a private visit to Ireland that same weekend. Interviewed on RTÉ radio on 11 April, he warned that the imposition of sanctions would 'seriously affect diplomatic relations between the Irish-Argentinian community and the Argentine one'. He emphasised that the Irish in Argentina might very well be – if the boycott went ahead – 'lumped together with the British in the Argentine mind and so suffer reprisals'. These could be against Irish institutions like schools and hospitals, though he did not think there was any immediate danger of that happening. Scanlan said that Argentines could not understand how Ireland could vote with England, whom they saw as Ireland's enemy too. In the event of war, he said that every Irish-Argentine, including his two sons, would be prepared to take up arms to defend their country.[128] Scanlan's words, as subsequent events demonstrated, had no discernible impact on the Irish decision to support EEC sanctions.

As Irish–Argentine relations plummeted, Anglo-Irish relations went through a brief purple patch. Thatcher sent her thanks to all EEC leaders, and on 16 April Haughey sent her an appreciative reply. The British foreign secretary Sir Francis Pym and his senior officials, at a meeting of the foreign ministers in Auderghem, Belgium, on 20 April, made a particular point of thanking the Irish foreign minister Gerard Collins for Ireland's support at the UN and for EEC sanctions.[129] Collins explained on RTÉ that evening: 'We supported the United Nations Security Council resolution because it's a question of principle, it's an issue of principle and that was the only reason why we supported it.' There could be no bargaining or horse-trading on a question of principle, he said, rejecting any idea that Ireland's traditional policy of neutrality might be affected and that Ireland might be drawn in if it came to war: 'No, our neutrality will not be affected,' he reassured listeners.

In Buenos Aires, the foreign ministry called in each of the EEC ambassadors individually to issue a stern rebuke, warning of Argentina's displeasure over the imposition of EEC sanctions. Walshe was received by Feliz Peña, the economics' undersecretary. He was personally cordial but his message was hostile. Protesting that the proposed embargo on Argentine exports to the eleven member states was a violation of international law and in breach of GATT (General Agreement on Tariffs and Trade) terms, Peña said that the sanctions totally violated 'the norms and practices of international law and was establishing a dangerous precedent which would affect profoundly the future of international economic relations, particularly those of developing countries, with industrialised countries'. The Argentine government, he said, held that the EEC had acted ultra vires over the situation in the South Atlantic, pointing out that the EEC had never acted with such ferocity against the Soviet Union, Poland, Iran or any other country. Peña also said that sanctions would have long-term consequences and that a 'different' Argentina would find it difficult to forget the EEC's action.[130]

Walshe transmitted the details of the rebuke to Dublin, commenting that the impending war had given the civilian military dictatorship a renewed sense of purpose and unified the most incongruous forces in Argentine society. He gave two examples: the Mothers of the Plaza de Mayo carried signs reading

'The Malvinas are Argentine – and So Are the Disappeared' at their weekly protest marches; while Adolfo Perez Esquivel, a former political prisoner and 1980 Nobel Peace Prize winner, spoke out in favour of Argentine sovereignty over the islands and urged a peaceful solution to the crisis.[131] Irate Irish-Argentines sent another salvo of hostile letters and rebuffs to the embassy in Buenos Aires. The *Southern Cross* editorial on 16 April asked people to set aside all political differences in the light of the extremely dangerous situation in which British colonial arrogance had placed them. Fr Richards added that no Argentine could remain on the sidelines: 'The dignity of our men in taking the Malvinas must fill us with pride, for the restraint they have shown.'[132] Walshe also reported that he had been informed by the Argentine government in early April that it had no plans, for the time being at least, to advise Irish citizens in the country to return home. He also received a further assurance from the government regarding the physical safety of Irish citizens in the country. But on 24 April, due to the worsening international situation, the Irish embassy asked the Christian Brothers in Newman, and all Irish citizens teaching in other schools, to complete a form giving their document number, addresses of nearest relatives in Ireland, telephone numbers, etc.[133]

ANGLO-IRISH RELATIONS: A ROCKY PHASE

Taoiseach Charles Haughey's underlying unease over Irish government support for Resolution 502 and for EEC sanctions did not surface in public until the first week in May. On 21 April, the president of the Council of Ministers, Leo Tindemans, told the European Parliament that 'we must now really show that we will stand by the United Kingdom in difficult times and help her with all the means available to the European Community'. Haughey, with his slender Dáil majority, had cause to worry about the dissent on the backbenches of Fianna Fáil. Neil Blaney, MEP, a former member of the party, told the European parliament: '… I, as an Irishman, totally and absolutely disassociate myself from your solidarity effort on behalf of the Falkland Islands and of the efforts of the United Kingdom to re-establish the colonialism imposed on so many places down so many years'. Blaney said the taoiseach should support Argentina 'because of the continued British occupation of the six counties'.[134] Although no longer a member of the parliamentary party, Blaney had considerable influence on the Fianna Fáil backbenches. Síle de Valera, a former Fianna Fáil minister and niece of Éamon de Valera, told the parliament that 'the influence of Britain … has eroded our neutral stance'.[135]

The British navy arrived off South Georgia on 21 April. Delayed by bad weather, British marines landed two days later and on the 26th accepted the surrender of the Argentine naval commander, Alfredo Astiz, who was wanted elsewhere for questioning by Swedish and French authorities over his role in the disappearance of their nationals.[136] Thatcher told Britain to 'rejoice' at the news of the victory. The main story on the front page of *TSC* on 23 April spoke of the 'stupor and painful incomprehension' felt by local Irish-Argentines over the stance of the Irish government. Fr Richards wrote that Dublin had failed to take into account that the British had seized the islands in 1833 and that since then Argentina had tried through diplomatic means to secure their return. In a signed front-page article, the editor adapted the story from the Old Testament that the Argentine David, mocked by a piratical and imperialist adversary, had no option but to confront the British Goliath even without his sling. Richards concluded that more than once a miracle occurs and David knocks Goliath over (*David voltea a Goliat*).[137]

That escalation of the conflict in the South Atlantic made discussions within the EEC more difficult for Ireland. On 22 April, the EEC political directors, meeting in Brussels, discussed a new British request to the presidency to approach third countries to ask them to take steps to see to it that sanctions would not be circumvented. McKernan explained to Collins that the matter would be raised at a meeting of foreign ministers on 26–7 April. After the retaking of South Georgia by the British, McKernan thought that a decision by the eleven member states might be hedged with qualifications that Thatcher would find unhelpful. Pointing out that 'our own long-standing policy is that arms should not be provided to areas of tension', he recommended that Ireland should agree to an informal approach by the EEC presidency to selected third countries provided the remaining nine were willing to do likewise and that the démarche would receive no publicity. In an effort to assuage Dublin, the British ambassador Leonard Figg called on Seán Donlon on 26 April to reassure the Irish government that the South Georgia islands had been taken with only one casualty, an Argentine sailor who had been shot accidentally. The British foreign secretary Francis Pym assured Haughey personally of his government's determination to settle the crisis without further use of force. When the Argentine ambassador called again to Iveagh House on 27 April, Donlon told him that the crisis 'engaged the personal attention of the Taoiseach on a day-to-day basis'. On the one hand there was a long-standing Irish–Argentine tradition of friendly relationships, and on the other the very important Ireland–UK relationship, which was fraught. Donlon stressed to the ambassador that Ireland had not taken a position on the sovereignty issue and that the Irish government was focused solely on the question of the rule of law in international relations and the use of force to resolve a dispute.[138]

McKernan, who was in Luxembourg for the meeting of political directors and foreign ministers, spoke to the taoiseach on the morning of 27 April regarding the proposed approach to third countries in the light of the British recapture of South Georgia. Haughey instructed that it would be better if the EEC presidency did not take any further démarche. McKernan pointed out that Italy and the Netherlands might seek to emphasise in a future statement the need for a negotiated and peaceful settlement in the South Atlantic. The taoiseach agreed that that would be helpful to Ireland.[139] On 28 April, the British embassy informed Dublin that its government was imposing a total exclusion zone, a circle of nearly 200 nautical miles, effective from 11.00 GMT on 30 April: 'Her Majesty's Government would prefer a peaceful settlement but there should be no misapprehension about the British Government's resolve to use force if this proves necessary,' the statement read.[140] On 29 April, the British embassy delivered a note to Iveagh House requesting Irish support for an approach by the EEC to third countries, in particular Israel, to stop the supply of arms to Argentina. (A draft note outlining the Irish position, prepared on 30 April for the British government, was never sent as its contents were overtaken by events.)

Anglo-Irish relations came under strain from two other unrelated sets of events. Firstly, the Haughey government was angered by Thatcher's intransigence over supporting an increase in community farm prices, linking her approval to receiving first a substantial rebate on the annual British contribution to the EEC budget. Secondly, on 18 April a freak accident in the Irish Sea, involving a British nuclear submarine, resulted in the sinking of an Irish trawler, the *Sharelga*, with no loss of life. A part of the submarine had been found tangled in the nets of the submerged trawler.[141] On 1 May, the British ambassador made a formal apology to the Irish government for the accident. But by that time, Haughey had begun to question the wisdom of Ireland's policy on the South Atlantic as a hot war was likely to break out.

The British forces faced major logistical challenges some 13,000 kilometres away in the South Atlantic. The flotilla was operating in high seas and facing worsening weather conditions as winter approached. Besides confronting the opposing army, which had time to fortify its positions, a landing on the islands would have to cope with heavy swells while under enemy fire from fixed, well-dug-in positions and also air attack. Once on land, British forces would have to establish supply lines, land war *matériel* and advance over open terrain. Argentina had a short supply chain of only 600 kilometres to the nearest mainland port, where their navy and air force were able to undergo repairs and take fresh supplies on board. As both the US and the UN pursued two distinct peace initiatives, on 30 April Noel Dorr sent a non-paper (an unofficial paper prepared for discussion) to Dublin with ideas which might help provide a peaceful solution to the crisis,[142] including a plan for a temporary UN administration of the islands. Dwelling on the vexed question of sovereignty, he thought that it might be possible to allow Argentina to buy out the Falkland Islands Company land bank on the islands: 'This would give ownership though not of course sovereignty to Argentina but if used imaginatively in a package deal it could be a helpful card to play.' He said he had planted those ideas 'without direct attribution to ourselves' with an unidentified permanent representative who was meeting the secretary general.[143] Unfortunately, his ideas were overtaken by events.

On the day Dorr submitted his non-paper (30 April), Fr Richards provided his *TSC* readers with a table of British 'pillage' in different parts of the world between 1583 and 1937. Under a front-page banner headline, he wrote: 'Great Britain insults our sovereignty for the fifth time, 1806, 1807, 1833, 1845, 1982'. His editorial, entitled *'Presente, Argentina'*, stated that every citizen was prepared and ready to do her/his duty for the *patria*. He said that Argentine blood, as he was writing, was being 'nobly spilt in defence of the *patria*' in South Georgia. He concluded with the stirring lines: 'At this time, words are superfluous. One only has to be ready for the call of the *Patria*. If at any time the country is in need of support, if we hear your voice calling us, we already know the only answer is "Presente Argentina", no matter whether we are dressed in a military uniform, a suit or soutane.'[144]

On the same day, 30 April, Brendan Moran of the political division in the Department of Foreign Affairs, met with the president of the Irish Argentine Chamber of Commerce, Juan Bryan O'Sullivan, who delivered a document setting out the Argentine position. Representing the Argentine ministries of Economics and Foreign Affairs, his mission was to persuade the Irish government of the ineffectiveness of economic sanctions and to try to get them lifted.[145] While O'Sullivan understood the Irish backing for Resolution 502, he explained that he 'found it difficult to understand how Ireland could agree to take economic sanctions against Argentina', adding that the Haughey government had received a bad press in Buenos Aires, much more than a number of the other European countries. He explained that that was because it was considered in Buenos Aires that Ireland ought to have had a special understanding of Argentine claims to sovereignty over the islands. He said he wanted to take back a message of goodwill from the Irish government. When Moran referred to the

Irish government's concern about the human rights situation in Argentina, O'Sullivan at first denied that any violation of human rights had occurred, but then went on to say that a 'dirty war' had been going on in Argentina for five years: 'Unfortunately things had happened in that time, though he believed most of the allegations of torture, disappearances etc. was the work of leftist propaganda.' But he denied that human rights violations were happening in contemporary Argentina.[146] While O'Sullivan did not get a meeting with the taoiseach, he did have an interview with the minister for industry and commerce, Desmond O'Malley, and also with leaders of Irish industry. On his return to Buenos Aires later in May, he told *TSC* that he had been well received by everybody in Dublin. He had met the captains of Irish industry, including Brian Joyce, the director general of Guinness; Bryan O'Doherty, the director of the Irish Export Board; Liam Connellan, Confederation of Irish Industries, and Frank Carty, the president of the Association of Irish Chambers of Commerce. Besides his interview with the minister for industry and commerce, he said he had also met with senior officials in the Department of Agriculture and with the leader of Fine Gael, Dr Garret FitzGerald, and the leader of the Labour Party, Michael O'Leary. The warm reception he received from all he met in Dublin 'filled him with joy', as he had an opportunity to explain the Argentine position regarding the conflict in the South Atlantic. His central message regarding the lifting of sanctions was well received by everybody, he said.[147] Meanwhile, the Irish ambassador in Britain, Eamonn Kennedy, had warned Dublin on 30 April that the atmosphere in London suggested that there was little basis for achieving a negotiated settlement to the conflict in the South Atlantic and that an armed clash seemed inevitable before the weekend or possibly that day.[148] That same day, the US announced its unconditional support for Britain in the conflict. The British task force was in the 200-mile exclusion zone surrounding the islands. On 1 May 1982, Argentine aircraft attacked the British task force, while RAF Vulcans dropped bombs on the Port Stanley airport and on a small airfield at Goose Green.[149]

IRISH GOVERNMENT RESPONSE TO OUTBREAK OF HOSTILITIES IN SOUTH ATLANTIC

In his memoirs, Ambassador Figg dismissed the minister for foreign affairs Gerard Collins as a 'mere cypher' and said that all 'Haughey wanted [was] to protect his precarious Dáil majority and to be seen as an international statesman'.[150] So great was Haughey's personal antipathy to the Thatcher government and his feelings of victimisation that, in my view, the conflict in the South Atlantic was the *context* rather than the *cause* of the Irish government's foreign policy volte face in early May on the conflict in the South Atlantic. Haughey had privately shown his personal reluctance throughout April 1982 to support Resolution 502 and European Community sanctions against Argentina. Without assessing the hierarchy of Irish foreign policy interests, he allowed his venality to determine Irish policy. Without any vital Irish interest being served by the radical change of policy, Thatcher saw the action, together with the Tory press, as a stab in the back. Figg, writing decades later, conveyed his sense of hurt over the Irish démarche. At 15.57 hours local time on 1 May, following the attacks on Port Stanley and Goose Green by the Royal Navy and air force, the British nuclear-powered submarine *Conqueror* torpedoed and sank the *ARA General Belgrano* as it sailed away from the exclusion zone. Some 362 young Argentine conscripts lost their lives.[151] The Argentine foreign minister, Costa Méndez, described the sinking as 'a treacherous act of armed aggression'.[152]

Haughey, in response to all-out war in the South Atlantic, called an emergency cabinet meeting on Sunday, 2 May. The statement issued afterwards affirmed that the Irish government's policy at the UN and the EEC had been to promote the achievement of a negotiated, honourable settlement to the conflict and that there was still an adequate framework within which a settlement could be achieved if the parties demonstrated the political will to do so. The government offered Ireland's good offices on the Security Council to help find a solution. The statement concluded with a reaffirmation of the country's 'traditional role of neutrality in relation to armed conflicts'. The inclusion of a reference to Irish neutrality was puzzling.

In anticipation of questions from the taoiseach's office regarding the legality of the sinking of the *Belgrano*, Brendan Moran, political division, requested legal opinion on the sinking from the legal section of his department and from the office of the judge advocate general, Irish army. His colleague, Jane Liddy, replied promptly that the British were entitled to use violence to resist the attack on the islands and that the naval bombardment of military targets was justified under the general rule of international law. She added the important caveat: 'Obviously this argument that it amounted more to "anticipatory" self-defence than a necessary measure is rather strained, and may not take account of military realities, but the whole scope and interpretation of Article 2(4), like that of Article 51, is, as you are aware, by no means established and much depends on the good faith of the members of the UN and their ability to cooperate with SECCO [Security Council].'[153] The deputy judge advocate general, Colonel Tadhg O'Shea, was in agreement that the actions taking place in the South Atlantic were governed by the original Argentine aggression against the islands and that the Argentine occupation was illegal. He said Article 51 of the UN Charter provided for the right of the UK to exercise self-defence if an armed attack occurred against it. He added that from a military point of view the Argentine cruiser represented a potential threat to the UK force and, in those circumstances, the commander of the British forces would have been negligent if he had not taken the action that had been taken. The sinking of the *Belgrano* was justified under the rules of war and O'Shea's judgement was that the UK naval commander's duty was to take whatever actions were necessary to preserve the safety of his force.[154]

The tone and tenor of those measured professional responses were not replicated in Irish government circles or in the Irish media. The *Evening Herald* carried the headline 'Boy Sailors Lost – 900 Dead'. The minister for defence, Paddy Power, told over 200 members at a Fianna Fáil meeting in Edenderry, County Offaly, on 3 May: 'We felt that Argentina were the first aggressors. Obviously, Britain themselves are very much the aggressors now.' In the same wide-ranging speech, he attacked the British over the sinking of the *Sharelga*, calling what the British had said about the incident 'blatant lies'.[155] Power added that the Irish government would be announcing a neutral stance immediately because of the new and aggressive attitude by the British.[156] He also stated that only a withdrawal of British troops 'from the little island of ours' would bring peace to Ireland.[157]

Power received a thunderous standing ovation – and according to the journalists present he was also warmly congratulated afterwards by party members.[158] His speech got headlines around the world and was as much a source of comfort to Argentina as it was a slap in the face for Britain. Whatever about the charged feeling on the Fianna Fáil backbenches, in his speech Power had departed very far from government policy. On 4 May, the *Sun* led with the infamous headline 'GOTCHA', with the subheading: 'Our lads sink gunboat and hole cruiser.' (The headline was changed in a later edition to 'Did 1,200 Argies drown?')[159] Haughey summoned Power on the 4th to his office and asked him to withdraw the most offensive line in his speech in reference to the British. He refused to do so, returning to his ministerial office in the Phoenix Park. According to his son, J.J. Power, he 'heard no more about the subject' as 'support for Paddy Power's stance continued to grow, both at home and abroad'.[160]

The same day, 4 May, the cabinet held its regular weekly meeting, where feelings ran high around the table over the sinking of the *Belgrano*. The terse statement issued afterwards announced a radical change in Irish government policy. The fears expressed in the government statement on 2 May, it said, have 'now unfortunately been realized', adding: 'The Government are appalled by the outbreak of what amounts to open war between Argentina and Great Britain in the South Atlantic and at reports that hundreds of lives have already been lost. They see the present situation as a serious threat to world peace.' There followed a few lines in the statement which undercut existing foreign policy as it called for the immediate involvement of the UN 'to secure an end to the present conflict', adding: 'Accordingly, the Irish Government will seek an immediate meeting of the Security Council in order to prepare a new resolution calling for 1) An immediate cessation of hostilities by both British and Argentinian forces, and 2) The negotiation of a diplomatic settlement under the auspices of the United Nations.' Those lines were a slap in the face for the British government, as was the following: 'The Irish Government regard the application of economic sanctions as no longer appropriate and will therefore be seeking the withdrawal of these sanctions by the Community.'[161] That evening, Haughey said on RTÉ that Ireland had been obliged to act in conscience in the circumstances of 'open war out there'. The taoiseach repeated his view that the situation in the South Atlantic was 'threatening world peace' and 'if world peace is threatened that's something which concerns us all ... then we're all involved, all our lives are at stake'.[162]

The British press carried the Irish government statement on 5 May, the same day as papers reported that an Argentine Exocet missile had hit the *HMS Sheffield* with the loss of thirty sailors. There were also reports that a Harrier jump jet had been shot down over Port Stanley with the loss of the pilot. Feelings ran high against the Irish government and that evening in the House of Commons, Julian Amery (Conservative), described the Republic of Ireland's stance towards Britain as a 'stab in the back'. Malcolm Rifkind, a minister of state in the Foreign and Commonwealth Office, replied that a fair number of people in the house would agree with that point of view.[163] On 6 May, an editorial in the *Sun* was even more visceral: 'In a time of trouble, our Irish neighbours brand us as aggressors. We would be more prepared to listen to lectures in political morality from the Republic if it ceased to give sanctuary to the killers of the IRA.' The *Sunday Express* entitled its editorial on 9 May 'Knife in the Back', stating that 'while British servicemen die in the South Atlantic and worried diplomats the world over strive endlessly for a peaceful solution to the crisis, our neighbours over the Irish Sea deliberately and with malice plunge a knife into our backs ... But there will come a time when the problem is resolved and the ships come home. That will be the time to take in the lessons of the crisis. That will be the time to remember the hypocrisy behind Charles Haughey's smile'. That same Irish government statement infuriated Margaret Thatcher. The *Sun's* Westminster team reported on 25 May that a Tory MP who heard Thatcher's private reaction to Haughey's position said, 'She clenched her fists, shook them up and down and declared, "I knew my first instinct about that man was right. I should never have talked to him in the first place."'

HAUGHEY, NOEL DORR AND THE UN

Noel Dorr's compelling account of his professional experiences as head of the Irish Permanent Representation during the crisis in the South Atlantic is an essential resource for any scholar working on this topic.[164] While his detailed narrative in *A Small State at the Top Table* brings the reader close to the corridors of power at the UN, the Iveagh House files record in greater detail that Irish diplomat's energetic, creative and subtle attempts to deal with the challenges he faced when implementing the Irish government's ill-thought-out démarche.[165] Many years after 1982, he wrote: 'I have to admit the statement [4 May] came as a surprise too to us in the Irish delegation. We had not known that the Government intended to issue a statement, nor had we been consulted about the text.'[166] In 1983, Patrick McKernan confirmed to me that as head of the political division of the Department of Foreign Affairs neither he nor his colleagues had been consulted prior to the release of the statement.[167] The five-hour time delay between Dublin and New York meant that the change in Irish government policy was across the international airwaves before Dorr and his small team had time to brief other UN delegates on the Security Council of its potentially explosive contents. Following a phone call with the UN secretary general, Dorr reported to Dublin that Pérez de Cuéllar did not think it helpful to call the Security Council into session that day as it might be damaging to his ongoing diplomatic efforts to broker a cessation of hostilities. As he was waiting for a reply on 5 May from both Britain and Argentina on his peace proposals, he recommended Wednesday afternoon New York time for an emergency meeting of the Security Council: 'I would recommend strongly that we accede to this request,' Dorr wrote, adding that he would submit the formal letter required to request such a meeting: 'If you wish me to use the phrase "immediate meeting" in the letter itself I will of course do so. I would prefer, however, to avoid using the word "immediate" in the letter itself. We are asking immediately for a meeting but we do not need to insist formally that it be an immediate meeting ... Even if you instruct me to use the word "immediate" in the formal letter, however, I could still act as above if you see no objection.' He included the wording of a draft resolution in his message while also informing Dublin that the British representative, Sir Anthony Parsons, had made it crystal clear that his government would 'veto any (repeat any) resolution today'. He would regard the holding of a meeting that very day as freeing the UK from any obligation to consider further the secretary general's proposals, to which they had intended to reply the following day, Wednesday. That did not of course necessarily imply that British reaction would be any better to the peace proposals if the meeting was deferred until later, he reported.[168]

Dorr has yet to receive full credit for his diplomatic deftness at the UN in steering Ireland between the Scylla of Resolution 502 and the Charybdis of Haughey's new-found but ill-defined and ill-thought-out foreign policy radicalism.[169] Dorr's semantic juggling and word play converted the Irish government's call for 'an immediate meeting of the Security Council' into an immediate call for a meeting of the Security Council – a distinction which avoided Ireland becoming involved in a direct confrontation with the British and its more powerful EEC partners. Sir Anthony Parsons wrote many years later that Dorr's 'behaviour during the Falklands was intolerable and I left him in no doubt as to what I thought of him'. His comments were withering, describing the Irish diplomat as being 'his usual sententious self',[170] sententious being defined as given to pompous or aphoristic moralising. With the knowledge of hindsight, the British might have considered themselves fortunate to have had Dorr representing Ireland throughout the crisis. Both Dorr and Donlon have been criticised by a former high-ranking Irish diplomat for not either resigning or requesting to be reassigned when confronted by the Irish government's policy volte face on 4 May.[171] That passionately held and cogently argued position might be counter-balanced by the thesis in this book that both diplomats plied their craft artfully at that critical moment during the Falklands/Malvinas conflict. The rupture in Anglo-Irish relations was temporary rather than lasting due in no small part to the diplomatic skills of both Dorr and Donlon, together with fellow diplomats in the Irish and British services. Few would have predicted in May 1982, with Fleet Street, Thatcher and MPs in the commons speaking about Haughey's volte face as a 'stab in the back', that an Anglo-Irish agreement would be signed in 1985 thanks in no small part to British and Irish diplomats like David Goodall and Michael Lillis respectively.

IRELAND AND ITALY BREAK EEC'S UNIFIED STANCE ON SANCTIONS

In parallel with the drama at the UN, the crisis over the renewal of sanctions against Argentina in the first three weeks of May 1982 might also have derailed Anglo-Irish relations for a decade or more. Despite the sharpness of the alienation in the heat of battle, wiser counsel prevailed. The government statement of 2 May announced Ireland's withdrawal from EEC sanctions. That presented a dilemma for the political director Patrick McKernan, who had recommended that Ireland continue to retain solidarity on the matter with her EEC partners.[172] On the evening of 4 May, Haughey invited McKernan and the secretary of the Department of the Taoiseach, Dermot Nally, to a meeting in his home in Kinsealy, on the outskirts of Dublin.[173] Both men argued that the government's decision to withdraw from EEC sanctions would seriously damage the country's international standing and have the most unforeseen consequences for Anglo-Irish relations, particularly relating to Northern Ireland. McKernan argued that the proposed Irish unilateral démarche could not be explained as a defence of an Irish foreign policy core value or the protection of a vital national interest. Haughey refused to change his mind. Before leaving for Brussels to attend the meeting of political directors, McKernan phoned the taoiseach to ask for his instructions: 'Do the best you can,' the diplomat told me was Haughey's Pythian reply.[174] The EEC consensus for a renewal of sanctions was on the wane. On 22 April, MEPs had voted 203 to 28 in favour but on 12 May the vote in the European Parliament was 137 to 79. At the meeting of political directors in Brussels on 7 May, McKernan stated that Ireland would not renew the sanctions, which were due to expire on 17 May. During the weekend of 8 and 9 May, the Council of Foreign Ministers met in Belgium in what turned out to be 'an extremely acrimonious' and ill-tempered encounter.[175] Renewal of sanctions led the agenda followed by the matter of a reduction in the British budget contribution. British sources 'began to suggest that refusal to renew sanctions, or linkage of sanctions to other issues, might lead Britain to pull out of the EEC'. The meeting was made aware that Britain, while losing ships and lives in the South Atlantic, cooperated with the UN secretary general's efforts to bring about an end to hostilities.[176] The British hoped that the carrot and stick approach would be sufficient to win over the other member states to their point of view. The French favoured linking support for the continuation of sanctions in return for British concessions on farm prices and on its EEC budget. The idea of linkage had arisen in a number of member states during late April and early May. In order to get a budget rebate, Thatcher had been holding up an EEC increase in farm prices.

The meeting was told that Ireland would withdraw from sanctions but that it agreed to continue until the 17th, the date of expiry.[177]

Amid rumours that Ireland might use the veto to block the renewal of sanctions, the foreign ministers met in Brussels and in Luxembourg on 15, 16 and 17 May.[178] The British refused the offer on the table for a reduction in their budget contribution. The Italians took the lead in opposing the renewal of sanctions. That went against the grain for both foreign minister, Emilio Colombo, and prime minister, Giovanni Spadolini. Both wanted to stick with the status quo, but pressure from the Socialist Party leader Bettino Craxi compelled them to act against their best judgement by threatening to bring the government down. In the end, Italy and Ireland invoked the Luxembourg compromise on 17 May to permit their abstention. Both agreed to continue the arms embargo. Ireland also agreed, in the words of Charles Haughey, that 'Ireland and Italy will not allow their countries to be used so as to permit goods imported from Argentina to enter the territory of our other partners'.[179] Further research will determine the accuracy of McKernan's professional view, which he expressed to me in 1983, that in his judgement Italy would have continued to support sanctions if Ireland had done so. He was also convinced that Britain believed that to have been the case, and that had provoked even more intense feelings of hostility in London towards Dublin, as Thatcher failed to understand what vital interest Ireland was protecting by those actions.[180] The ascendant view in the Conservative government was that Haughey had acted vindictively and out of bloody-mindedness. If there was any theoretical basis for his actions, it was the cliché that Britain's weakness was Ireland's opportunity. But opportunity for what?

The British government silently punished Ireland by targeting the country's £1.5 billion annual exports to the United Kingdom. An unofficial and undeclared boycott was imposed.[181] (Irish annual exports to Argentina were £15.5 million.)[182] The *Sun*, in an editorial on 19 May, said that the Irish could not 'resist the chance to make mischief for Britain' and called for a boycott of Irish goods. Press hostility towards Ireland intensified after British forces made landings on the Falklands/Malvinas on 21 May. *HMS Ardent* landed troops off San Carlos Bay in a settlement in the north-western part of the East island. It was sunk the following day with the loss of twenty-two sailors. *HMS Antelope* was abandoned on 24 May after a bomb exploded while being defused. On 25 May, *HMS Coventry* was sunk, killing nineteen sailors. The same day, the *Atlantic Conveyor* was crippled when hit by two Exocets, killing twelve sailors. As British forces fought their way across the islands, the press became more stridently anti-Irish. In his *Sunday Telegraph* column on 23 May, Auberon

Waugh wrote: 'Connoisseurs of Irish logic may welcome Mr Haughey's argument that the ending of sanctions made a military solution less likely. It is tempting to yearn for a return of the Vikings to plunder Ireland's coastal areas and rape her nuns so that we, too, can have an opportunity to declare high-minded neutrality and demand a diplomatic solution.' The same day, John Junor, writing in the *Sunday Express*, said that Haughey was quite entitled to 'stick the knife in Britain's back' if it was in his interest to do so, but there was a price to be paid: 'But since the Irish do regard themselves as foreigners, why don't we treat them as such?' Why should the Irish be given the vote in British parliamentary and local elections, he wondered, and 'why do we allow them to come here, as so many of them do, to live on Social Security? ... If they are so mad keen on Argentina, why don't they go and stick their snouts into the Argentinian trough instead of into ours'. The *Daily Mail*, too, on the 25th, questioned allowing the Irish to continue to live and vote in Britain and, on the same day, the *Daily Express* joined the chorus: 'When the French and Germans are with us, we may well wonder what we think we are doing allowing the Irish to live here, vote here and pick up Social Security payment here when their government is so stubbornly against us.'

As if to rub salt into British wounds, the Football Association of Ireland (FAI), with impeccable timing and consummate diplomacy, sent the Irish national selection on 19 May on a tour of Latin America. Up to a week before the team left, the schedule was to play games against Chile, Brazil and in Buenos Aires against Argentina. When asked by Iveagh House, around 10 May 1982, about the local reaction to the proposed tour, Walshe replied that the team would be given a 'warm and friendly reception' in light of the 'present pro-Irish mood here'. The team visit 'would be likely to be seen as an extension of what is perceived as the Irish Govt's "friendly neutrality" in the current dispute'. The fact that every member of the team played for an English club 'would only enhance their welcome, provided it was clearly understood at popular level on the terraces that they were not "*Ingleses*"'. He thought that the FAI and its Argentine counterpart would be able to get that message across. The ambassador said he would attend the match and hold a reception for the team. He thought that, unless there was a change in Irish policy, the issue of security of the players was more likely to arise in Britain rather than in Argentina.[183] That guarded warning, if passed on to the FAI, went unheeded. Reaction to Ireland playing Argentina in Buenos Aires was one of predictable outrage. A number of Irish players simply refused to go when selected. The Irish manager, Eoin Hand, when he requested the manager of Manchester United, Ron Atkinson, to release players for the tour, was told to 'F... off'. When Hand pressed him for an official response, Atkinson replied, 'F... off. That's my official response.' Newcastle, Arsenal and Brighton were equally unwilling to release players like David O'Leary and John Devine. The FAI felt pressured to call off the scheduled game with Argentina but not the tour of Latin America.[184] The squad, which included Liam Brady, left on 19 May and travelled, via Buenos Aires, to Chile. Many on the Irish team held British passports and thus experienced a long delay while the Argentine authorities checked all the documents. The president of the Irish Federation, John Scanlan, met the team in Ezeiza airport. He told them that he had the good fortune to be in Ireland when the crisis in the South Atlantic broke out. As a resident of over thirty-four years in Argentina, he was in a position to defend the legal position of the country over 'las islas Malvinas'. He said that there were about 300,000 of Irish descent in Argentina and that they supported Argentina's claim to those islands.[185] His words did little to inspire the Irish selection. Chile beat Ireland in Santiago, 1–0. The tour then went from bad to worse. Facing a very strong Brazilian side on 27 May, they were beaten 7–0. On 30 May, in the final match, Ireland played Trinidad and Tobago and lost 2–1.[186] The tour was both a footballing and a diplomatic disaster.

A PLACE OF HONOUR FOR IRELAND IN BUENOS AIRES: OFFICIAL GOVERNMENT REACTION TO IRELAND'S FOREIGN POLICY SHIFT

Argentine's civilian military government in early May responded with great warmth to the Irish government's policy *volte face* on the UN Security Council and on EEC sanctions. The sorely tested faith of Irish-Argentines in the mother country was restored virtually overnight, that is, between 2 and 4 May when the Irish government issued both statements on the conflict in the South Atlantic.[187] Two Irish journalists, Olivia O'Leary of the *Irish Times* and Gerald Barry of RTÉ radio and television, were on hand in Buenos Aires through most of the war to report the story from the Argentine perspective. A number of other journalists, with Irish passports, reported for the BBC and other channels.[188]

TSC failed to publish on 7 May as a consequence of the confusion caused by the outbreak of hostilities.[189] When it reappeared a week later, Fr Richards had completely changed his editorial line on Ireland. In the leading story on the front page, he praised the Irish government for having asked that EEC sanctions be lifted because of what he described as the growing aggression and intransigent politics of British imperialists. The paper also noted that the Irish

7.1 Fr Federico Richards' editorial 'Present, Argentina' on 30 April 1982 declaring the readiness of Argentines to support the government policy on the Malvinas/Falklands

government had sought an immediate meeting of the Security Council and he reproduced the quotation from the Irish minister for defence, Paddy Power, stating that the British were 'the aggressors now'. He described Wednesday, 5 May as one of those 'unforgettable days'. Richards recalled that the Argentine descendants of Irish immigrants had 'lived with an open sore in their souls' for over two weeks because of the earlier position taken by the Irish government at the UN and in the EEC. They found it necessary, for the first time in their experience, to condemn, 'in a stupor and with a great sense of shame', the policy of 'our beloved *Madre Patria*'. Richards wrote that the unalterable Irish-Argentine support for '*la causa nacional de la recuperación de Las Malvinas*' obliged them to raise their voices in bewilderment against the mother country 'of a thousand rebellions' for voting for an imperialist and colonial nation. Quoting the Irish nationalist John Boyle O'Reilly, he wrote that Ireland 'has wronged no race. We have robbed no land. We have never oppressed the weak'.[190]

On 4 May the Irish Christian Brothers recorded in the Newman annals that a 'large number of parents and teachers thanked and congratulated the Brothers on the attitude of the Irish Government'. Br Nicky O'Brien was recorded as having written a letter (of praise) to the taoiseach and (of criticism) to Thatcher.[191] The principal of Newman College, Br John Burke, received a very friendly welcome when he was called to meet Dr Raúl Fonseca at the Ministry of Education. He was told that the ministry wanted all directors of all the Newman-type colleges 'to meet the international press and explain how these colleges can operate in complete freedom within the Argentine Educational system. This is certainly true with regard to Cardinal Newman College', the house annals recorded on 14 May. All the Newman secondary school boys and teachers attended an *Acto Patriótico* on 17 May – Día de la Armada – with forty other schools at the San Isidro racecourse.[192]

The Federation of Irish-Argentine Societies, meeting on 4 May, unanimously agreed to invite the Irish community to a mass on the 13th in the Pallottine church, St Patrick's, to be offered for 'the intention of peace and an end to the great events *en las islas Malvinas*'. Ambassador Walshe acknowledged receipt of the invitation but, citing a prior engagement, he declined to attend. His deputy, Colin Wrafter, represented his ambassador at the mass.[193] Walshe also received an invitation to attend a mass in the Basilica in Luján to be offered for peace and for 'those fallen for the nation'. Santiago Pedro Brady, the organiser, represented the Irish-Argentine communities of Capitán Sarmiento, San Antonio de Areco, San Andrés de Giles, Suipacha, Mercedes and Luján. The ambassador sent his regrets. Frs Fred Richards and Cornelius Ryan (Pallottine) celebrated mass on 15 May before a large congregation of Irish-Argentines.[194] Richards preached about the rights and responsibilities of Argentines living in a state of war, referring to the brave gestures of many Irish at the time of the struggle for their independence. The mass ended with the singing of the Argentine national anthem.[195]

John Scanlan, the president of the Federation of Irish-Argentine Societies, wrote on 6 May to Ambassador Walshe on behalf of the federation: 'It is

7.2 Prominent members of the Irish-Argentine community (from left): E. Doyle and John Scanlan, together with their wives, Justin Harman (third secretary, Irish embassy), Fr Alfie Kelly and G. Ford

only fitting that just as we disagreed with Ireland's first stand on the Malvinas issue, we should now hasten to thank him [Haughey] for his government's reappraisal of the situation.'[196] He requested the ambassador to pass on a letter to the taoiseach from the federation representing 300,000 Argentines; the text acknowledged that they had received 'with unlimited satisfaction the news of Ireland's reappraisal of the crisis in the South Atlantic'. Scanlan continued that the federation, 'proud of their Irish ancestry and heritage', wanted to express its pleasure 'at Ireland's statesmanlike stand' – a position which had won 'also unanimous approval from the Argentine people themselves many of whom have indicated their delight through personal and written messages of congratulations'.[197] In writing to Haughey, Scanlan had the double advantage of being a former Christian Brother and that he had met Haughey in Buenos Aires when he was minister for Finance early in October 1967.[198] His letter was sent to the Department of the Taoiseach via the diplomatic bag. While Scanlan awaited a reply, it is opportune to discuss the reaction of the Argentine government to the Irish government's welcome volte face at the beginning of May 1982 and its withdrawal from sanctions in the middle of May. On 5 May, the minister for foreign affairs, Gerard Collins, made a statement in the Dáil outlining Ireland's new position on the war in the South Atlantic. The embassy in Buenos Aires received a copy of the speech that afternoon. As it was important to deliver the text to the foreign ministry, Colin Wrafter phoned for an appointment for Ambassador Walshe for that evening. Fixed for 6.30 p.m., Walshe expected to hand over the statement to the deputy minister, Enrique Ros. But he was surprised to be taken to see the foreign minister, Nicanor Costa Méndez, who wished 'to thank the Irish Govt. not only for its friendship but more important, "its objectivity"'. Walshe replied that while his only instructions were to hand over the text, he would be glad 'to report to my Govt. any suggestions he [Costa Méndez] might wish to make as to how we might be helpful in the UN context'. The foreign minister replied that he was very interested in 'our proposal but he did not elaborate'. Walshe made a reference to the UN secretary general's 'apparent plans and papers'.[199] In reply, Costa Méndez gave him a *tour d'horizon* of the various peace initiatives being canvassed at that time. He was certain that the US secretary of state Alexander Haig's mission was definitely over and that a well-intentioned Peruvian peace initiative 'had been dictated by Haig'. Costa Méndez was convinced that the US still wanted to be involved in a peace process 'but this was impossible now that the US had taken sides [with Britain]'.[200] He thought that the US had made a great mistake as 'their interests would suffer throughout Latin America'. Referring to his own personal background, he said he was a 'nationalist conservative' like generations of his family before him who had always fought the left; two of his uncles had been foreign ministers and they had struggled to keep Argentina out of the hands of the left. As they had struggled to do so, he considered it 'a bad prospect' that countries like Cuba and Nicaragua had moved closer to Argentina, while the US was going in the opposite direction. He added that it would be difficult for Buenos Aires 'not to return the Cuban and Nicaraguan compliments in the future'. Costa Méndez stressed that his government could not accept that the wishes of the islanders should be the determining factor in any future talks. As the meeting ended, his final words were an offer to see Walshe 'at any time'.[201]

On 11 May, Walshe was called again to the foreign ministry to discuss Ireland's proposed withdrawal from EEC sanctions. Received again by Costa Méndez, the ambassador passed over to him another statement on the Irish position. It would appear that the foreign ministry wished to use the Irish ambassador to pass on a message that Britain did not have to recognise

Argentine sovereignty in order to get negotiations going but that London had to agree to discuss sovereignty in advance. Costa Méndez also said that the recuperation of sovereignty was the Argentine aim and that London 'must be willing to discuss it'. The British would also have to accept 'guidelines' in the negotiations which were basically the *acquis* of the UN resolution. However, Costa Méndez feared that Thatcher 'needed "military satisfaction"', which she had not got. Coming away from the meeting, Walshe concluded that what he had just heard was 'a significant shift of [the Argentine] position though it is expressed in terms of a consistent position'. He told Dublin that he thought that it would be good for the Security Council to meet 'and call for a ceasefire even though Britain was certain to veto it'. Walshe, who met the deputy foreign minister Enrique Ros, as he was leaving the building, was told that an intermediary, representing moderate elements in the British cabinet, had secretly approached a close friend of Admiral Jorge Anaya. A veteran of seventeen years of talks with the British, Ros spoke to Walshe 'with eloquence and fluency' about how deeply he mistrusted the English: 'The picture he paints of hypocritical British use of the arts of diplomacy is all too recognizable', the ambassador commented in a report the following day (12th).[202] TV, radio and the press 'door-stepped' Walshe as he left the foreign ministry in Plaza San Martín. Asked about the details of the meeting with Costa Méndez, he gave very general replies and made his excuses and left. In the following days, the other EEC ambassadors were anxious to know how Ireland had managed to get an interview so swiftly with the foreign minister. One ambassador enquired whether Ireland had broken ranks with the EEC and sent in a third-party note. That was not the case.

The Argentine newspapers on 12 May gave prominent coverage to the changing of the Irish position and to the ambassador's talks at the foreign ministry. *Clarín* carried the headline: 'Ireland Changes Its Position'.[203] *La Nación*, the same day, reported that the ambassador had handed Costa Méndez a document which included a reference to Ireland's call for an immediate meeting of the Security Council. Quoting ministry sources, the news item described the meeting as the most important event of the day and added that Ireland had called for the lifting of EEC sanctions. A few weeks later, Ros expressed to Walshe his government's disappointment over the lack of progress on the Irish initiative at the UN: 'While grateful for our efforts in New York, he was clearly disappointed that our original draft resolution had been diluted.' He said he had the impression that the Irish permanent representative, 'while a man of conscience', had very tight instructions not to provoke a British veto. Ros was 'cynical' about British intentions but he said that Argentina would do its best to work the resolution. They intended to try to 'make the British an offer they won't be able to refuse'.[204]

Summing up his understanding around 20 May of how Ireland was perceived in Buenos Aires, Walshe noted that the 'public perception of our position, generally speaking, is that we have changed sides'. But that had to be set in the context of strict government censorship and control, he said, adding that all the radio and television stations were 'emitting a constant flood of infantile propaganda' and 'in this crude context, nuances of our position tend to become invisible'.[205] But the ambassador reported that Ireland's policy shift had brought with it the possibility of tangible, new economic benefits. He reported that distilleries in Argentina were interested in changing from Britain to Ireland the source of their supply of malt whiskey for further blending. He predicted that there would be 'continuing bitterness against Britain for a long time to come and (if we play our cards right) continuing gratitude to Ireland for its "constructive" approach'.

Costa Méndez told the ambassador in a meeting that 'Argentina will never forget [what Ireland had done]'.[206] Walshe again pointed out that there was an impression in Argentine public opinion 'that we are rather more "pro-Argentine" in this dispute than is the case'. But he felt that 'as long as there are no serious illusions at Government level on this point, I see no reason to fight strenuously against this general impression which is generating goodwill and should generate good business'. Walshe argued further that in the medium and long term 'we should be in a position to take commercial advantage of the special status we have gained here as the first EEC member country to advocate the ending of sanctions'. There was also the possibility, he thought, of 'cashing in on overall Latin American gratitude in other markets on this continent' and he suggested that the Irish government ought to commission a 'discreet but urgent study' of the opportunities for substituting Irish products for British, etc. '... while the glow of goodwill to Ireland and bitterness towards Britain and other countries remain intense'.[207]

While Walshe continued his visits to the foreign ministry, Irish-Argentines continued to heap praise on the Irish government throughout the second half of May 1982. Richards, the editor of *TSC*, congratulated Ireland on 21 May on the front page of the paper for 'being true to her soul' and for returning to the position it had always upheld against all colonialism and imperialism ... '*¡Enhorabuena Irlanda!*' or 'Well done, Ireland'. The editor wrote an article in the same edition entitled 'A Painful Awakening' in which he hoped the conflict in the South Atlantic would open the eyes of the Argentine ruling class and stop once and for all the country 'being the "sepoys" of the great colonies and of the colonial multinationals to which the church has referred so many times as the insatiable bloodsuckers of poorer countries'. He wanted Latin America, together with Argentina, to become the flag bearer of a Christian movement for good in the world.[208] (The same edition also carried photos and a report on the mass in the Basilica de Luján.)

On the 28th, a *TSC* editorial again praised Ireland's stance on the conflict in the South Atlantic, highlighting Dublin's 'treason' as the reason for the marked deterioration in Anglo-Irish relations.[209] An Irish priest, Fr John Healy with the Society of African Missions, wrote in the same edition from his parish in Missiones that he fully supported Ireland's change of policy and concluded: '*Viva la Argentina libre y soberana*' ('Long live a free and sovereign Argentina').[210] *TSC*, a week later, reported the support of Seán MacBride, the Nobel and Lenin Peace Prize winner, as a reason for the revised Irish stance on the crisis. He said the Irish were correct to seek a solution at the UN and that Irish sovereignty and neutrality were anathema for the British.[211] *TSC* on 11 June published an interview with Juan Peña, first secretary of the Argentine embassy in Dublin, in which he relayed that there was strong support throughout Ireland for the Argentine position.

The taoiseach, through his private secretary Seán Aylward, replied directly to Scanlan stating that the government had supported EEC sanctions on the basis that the measures were designed to promote acceptance of Resolution 502 and would help bring about a peaceful solution through diplomatic means. With the outbreak of full-scale hostilities around the islands, the situation had changed, he wrote, and the taoiseach had requested him to point out that Ireland had carefully avoided taking a stance on the merits of the longstanding dispute over the islands. The government, the letter said, would continue to try to bring about a peaceful and an honourable solution.[212] Scanlan replied to Aylward on 10 June:

> By way of curiosity, and if it is not out of place, you may have occasion to ask Mr Haughey in one of your private conversations with him if he remembers me from his visit to Buenos Aires. I interviewed him in Cardinal Newman College for my radio programme, and then he was kind enough to come to my flat for drinks with Ambassador Skentelbery. That is why I feel I am writing not only to a man who is a public figure but to one who is not a stranger to me personally. It just adds a touch of warmth for me which gives me special pleasure in the present circumstances.

On 25 July 1982, Aylward replied: 'He [Haughey] recalls with pleasure his visit to Buenos Aires some years ago and his meeting with you there. The further points which you have made about the Falklands/Malvinas crisis have been noted by him.'[213] *TSC* carried the details of that correspondence, which was perceived locally to be a coup for Scanlan and the federation.[214]

Independently of the Scanlan/Haughey/Aylward correspondence, Scanlan told a meeting of the executive of the federation on 1 June that they had an inescapable obligation to acknowledge publicly the manifest courage shown by Ireland through its supportive votes for Argentina in different international bodies during '*el conflicto de las Malvinas*'. The decision on the nature of that public action was left to be decided at an extraordinary assembly of the federation.[215] Discussing other business, the meeting agreed that on 15 June the *intendente municipal* (municipal mayor) of Buenos Aires, Guillermo Del Cioppo, would unveil a statue of Patrick Pearse in Plaza Irlanda in front of Santa Brígida college. The meeting also agreed that the Irish community should participate individually in the celebrations to greet Pope John Paul II on his arrival on 11 June.[216] There was agreement too on the remaining item of business, that the federation was to help raise funds for the Fondo Patriótico Malvinas Argentinas (Argentine Malvinas Patriotic Fund). Different Irish institutions helped individual fundraisers in the following weeks. On 5 June, at a 'tea' in the Fahy Club, *TSC* reported that a sum of over 9,000 pesos had been collected and deposited in the Banco de la Nación Argentina. The Hurling Club collected over 15,000 pesos for the same fund. Other such gatherings were held and the community donated generously. On 11 June, *TSC* published details of the patriotic appeal. It also highlighted that its readers 'will fully appreciate' that 'Prime Minister Haughey has taken notice of the Irish-Argentine community's position regarding the Malvinas Islands'. The article also confirmed that Scanlan had received that news by letter from the Department of the Taoiseach.[217]

The pope arrived in Argentina on a 32-hour visit on 11 June 1982 during which he celebrated mass at the national shrine at Luján. In Buenos Aires, he said mass before over a million people. The Argentine trip was hastily arranged to counterbalance his visit to Britain, which ended eight days before he landed in Buenos Aires. The papal visit did not have any of the pageantry of other papal visits such as Mexico in 1979 and Brazil in 1980. Vatican spokesmen were clear that he was on a pastoral visit, not a diplomatic one, and that he was not attempting to repeat the role the Holy See was currently playing in helping to resolve the Beagle Channel crisis.[218] Ambassador Walshe reported that even a pontiff noted for his 'muscular Christianity' seemed 'daunted by what he

Irish Press 1931-1995, 24.06.1982, page 5

Thank you, Ireland

O, sons of green Erin lament o'er the time
When religion was war and our country a crime
When man in God's image inverted his plan,
And moulded his God in the image of man.

William Drennan

Those were the times when Irishmen and women collected on the strands of Drennan's Emerald Isle, and, like the Wild Geese, sought abroad what was denied them at home. Some 20,000 Irish emigrants in that vein arrived in Argentina, and, finding a haven of peace in untrammelled surroundings, began to forge their future and contribute to the progress of the young South American republic. Over 300,000 (three hundred thousand) descendants of those victims of British colonialism still look today with tearful pride on the struggles of their ancestors for Irish sovereignty. Their Argentine hearts likewise beat with joy at the recovery of the Malvinas Islands, and all the more so at the thought that Ireland was the first country in Western Europe to withdraw the economic sanctions against Argentina over the crisis in the South Atlantic.

The Malvinas have been part of the Argentine national territory since 1810 by way of inheritance from the Spanish Crown to which they belonged as an integral part of her territory. The Argentine Government rightfully appointed the first governor of the Islands, distributed land and granted fishing concessions. The Argentine population of the Islands prospered under Buenos Aires.

In 1829 a civic and military command was established over the Malvinas with headquarters in Puerto Argentino (Port Stanley) and with Luis Vernet as Governor. The United Kingdom made no reserves about Argentine sovereignty over the islands in a treaty it had signed with Argentina in 1825. Yet on January 3rd, 1833, a British warship took possession of the islands by force. Never since did Argentina cease to reclaim the islands which had been illegally occupied by the British Empire. In 1965 the XX General Assembly of the United Nations accepted this claim by an overwhelming majority and ordered the decolonization of the islands. The Conference of Non-Aligned Countries held in Sri Lanka in 1976 firmly supported Argentina's claim to sovereignty.

Since the United Nations' resolution in 1965, Argentina has contributed handsomely to the welfare of the 1,800 inhabitants of the islands, while England has virtually washed her hands of those same islanders. This contribution which merited the congratulations of the UN consists principally of: (a) a distribution centre of oil and petrol; (b) the construction of an airport; (c) medical attention and transfer if necessary to hospitals on the Argentine mainland; (d) communication once a week for the islanders with the outside world instead of a previous two or three times a year in a boat sailing between the islands and Montevideo.

Finally, for the best part of the last 20 years England deliberately dragged her feet on the negotiations and shouted diatribes against Argentina because she rightfully recovered the Malvinas Islands after 149 years of patient waiting England has now taken them again by force as she did in 1833.

THANK YOU, IRELAND. Argentines without distinction of race or creed will remember your stand for their country.

Federation of Irish-Argentine Societies.

NOTE : The cost of this Open Letter has been defrayed by the contributions of Irish nationals and Argentine nationals of Irish descent all resident in Argentina

7.3 Paid advertisement in the form of a letter from the Federation of Argentine Irish Societies in the *Irish Press* on 24 June 1982, thanking Ireland for its support during the Falklands/Malvinas war.

was up against'. He was 'grim and preoccupied on his visit', the ambassador reported, as 'assorted torturers and numbered-account operators queued up to press the Papal flesh or knelt with obsequious ostentation to kiss the Petrine ring'.[219]

By the time of John Paul II's arrival in Argentina, the war had reached a final phase and a British victory was assured. Papal entreaties for peace fell on deaf ears. At 9 p.m. on 14 June in Port Stanley, General Mario Menéndez ended the fighting – the term 'unconditional surrender' not being used. The blame game began immediately within the Argentine armed forces over the debacle. Retribution was swift: within forty-eight hours of the surrender, General Galtieri was forced to resign as president and commander-in-chief. Retreating into retirement in the Campo de Mayo military complex, he never wavered in his belief that the war could have been won. On 1 July 1982, General Reynaldo Bignone took over as president and served until 10 December 1983. Margaret Thatcher told the House of Commons on 26 October 1982 that the war against Argentina had cost the British exchequer 700 million pounds.[220] Some 25,948 British personnel served in the campaign. In terms of casualties, the war cost the lives of 649 Argentines (almost half in the sinking of the *Belgrano*), over 230 British and three Falkland islanders. About 1,200 Argentines were wounded and more than 10,000 were taken prisoner.[221] Quite how many Irish-Argentines or Irish serving in the British armed forces spilled their blood in the conflict is a subject for further research.[222]

In the wake of that military defeat, on 15 July Irish-Argentines enjoyed a very proud moment which publicly manifested their twin allegiance to Argentina and to Ireland. Ambassador Walshe was present, together with the mayor of the city, Guillermo del Cioppo, and the minister of justice, Lucas Jaime Lennon, for the unveiling of a bust of Patrick Pearse in the Plaza Irlanda, a park in front of the main entrance to Santa Brígida school. There was a large turnout of members of the Irish Federation, the Fahy and Hurling clubs and from the Irish schools in the federal capital and the pampas. Scanlan gave the main address. Ambassador Walshe recited Pearse's poem 'Renunciation', in Irish and in Spanish. The military band played 'La Marcha de las Malvinas' at the conclusion of the proceedings.[223]

In the weeks coming up to that event, the Federation of Irish Societies secured the approval of its general assembly to spend the large sum of 6,300 US dollars which it had raised to pay for an advertisement in three Irish national newspapers to thank the Irish people for their support during the war.[224] Dr Eduardo A. Coghlan and John Scanlan were asked to prepare a text which appeared under the heading 'Thank You, Ireland' in the *Irish Press* (24 June), the *Irish Times* (25th) and the *Irish Independent* (26th). The concluding line of the advertisement in the form of a letter read: 'Argentines without distinction of race or creed will remember your stand for their country' and it pointed out that Ireland 'was the first country in Western Europe to withdraw the economic sanctions against Argentines over the crisis in the South Atlantic' (see Fig. 7.3).[225] *TSC* devoted almost a full page to that advertisement accompanied by an editorial written by Richards entitled 'The lies of Mrs Thatcher'. He wrote that the name of that 'undaunted' (*impertérrita*) lady 'would pass into history in the distinguished company of 'the smooth [Oliver] Cromwell or the no less delicate Lord Castlereagh'.[226] He wrote also that the woman who enjoyed the reputation of being the exponent of the unwavering will of the United Kingdom will be discovered to have had feet of clay when, before the judgment of God, she is called upon to render a final account.[227] While the reputation of Ireland was garlanded in Buenos Aires, in Britain on 26 June the *Sun* implored its readers to boycott Irish butter as a 'reward' for Haughey and the 'treachery' of the Irish government.[228]

Irish-Argentines lost a strong ally when Charles Haughey's minority government was defeated in a general election on 24 November 1982 by a Garret FitzGerald-led Fine Gael–Labour coalition.[229] Appointed taoiseach on 14 December, FitzGerald was far less sympathetic than his predecessor to Argentina's claim to sovereignty over the disputed islands in the South Atlantic. His immediate challenge was to restore Anglo-Irish relations, replacing the megaphone diplomacy of the previous May and June with a staid and long-term strategy in an effort to rebuild trust between Dublin and London. The new minister for foreign affairs, Peter Barry, was of one mind with FitzGerald in hoping to make progress in trying to bring an end to the conflict in Northern Ireland. It was a time, in Anglo-Irish relations, to build bridges. The Falklands/Malvinas quickly receded in importance as a priority in Irish foreign policy. Proof of that was provided on 16 November 1983 when Ireland abstained in a vote on the Malvinas/Falklands in the UN General Assembly.[230] Thus the status quo ante was restored. The new Irish government accepted that ownership of the islands would be determined by a resumption of the talks which had been broken off in 1982. The war had made it impossible to hand the islands over to Argentina. Paradoxically, by seizing the islands by force, the Argentines had ruled out any possibility of getting a Hong Kong-style solution. The British proceeded from the 1980s to convert the Falklands/Malvinas into a fortress.

Lest it be thought that the fears of Irish-Argentines during the Falklands/Malvinas war were not legitimate but rather the product of over-heated imaginations, there were a few serious incidents following the ending of the conflict that illustrate that, in the minds of local xenophobes or criminals, the distinction remained blurred between *Irlandeses* and *Ingleses*. The fact that the Patrick Pearse statue stood in a park opposite Santa Brígida school may be another reason why it might have been mistaken for an English monument. On

14 July 1984, the monument in Plaza Irlanda was vandalised and Patrick Pearse decapitated. The unknown attackers tried unsuccessfully to prize the bronze plaque off the base. While the defacing was interpreted in the Irish community as having a political motive, one must not rule out that the attack was the work of criminals in search of valuable scrap metal. In a signed article on the front page of *TSC* on 29 July 1984, Richards wrote that one theory explaining the attack was that the outrage was the product of the monumental ignorance of a group of ultra-nationalists who, on the occasion of the anniversary of the conflict in the South Atlantic, wanted to show a spirit of violence against what they thought in their supine ignorance to be a British monument. He mentioned that another hypothesis doing the rounds was that the attack was the work of football hooligans (*barra bravos*). He added that the ignorance of the attackers had caused them to insult the memory of one of the most distinguished of the innocent prisoners and victims of British imperialism. Richards asked for a more suitable replacement in stone or bronze funded by both Argentina and Ireland.[231] The mayor of Buenos Aires, Julio Cesar Baguier, expressed his outrage at the attack, which, he said, may have been committed out of ignorance. He made a commitment that the authorities would help financially with the replacement of the monument.[232] Today the restored and much-improved monument continues to stand proudly in Plaza Irlanda.

CHAPTER EIGHT

The Aftermath of Dictatorship, Human Rights and the Evolution of Irish Policy towards Latin America

In the twilight of the dictatorship, Ambassador Walshe wrote to Dublin on 24 November 1982 about a local political world of sclerotic military rule becoming ever more surreal as an emboldened major opposition group, Multipartidaria, mounted an ever-growing challenge to the longevity of a rudderless, floundering regime. In an uncharacteristically detailed report ranging far and wide over centuries of Argentine history, politics and society, the ambassador summed up the political situation epigrammatically: 'This is Kafka in the sun.' He further described the macabre atmosphere in Buenos Aires at the fag-end of the civilian military dictatorship as 'a mixture of Webster and Wodehouse and Dante country'.[1] Illustrating that point, he gave an account of a dinner party which he and Dymphna, his wife, had recently attended in the course of which a fellow guest whispered to Walshe 'that the rich ex-military-man-turned-politician, sitting opposite, was a multiple murderer and retired Arch-torturer'. The ambassador identified that over-vaunting fellow diner as Admiral Emilio Massera. The latter had bombarded Dymphna with details of his self-delusional and fictive plans to become the next president of Argentina; his magic formula for political success, he explained to her, would be to fill the populist gap 'left by the leaderless chaos in the Peronist Party' with 'a kind of parody of Peronism' accompanied by 'a constant reiteration of bombastic vacuities' such as '"the people must have bread" and "I tell the people I know they are human beings"'.[2] Ambassador Walshe, in a mercifully brief exchange that night with Massera, confined himself to pleasantries he described as 'candlesticks and sealing wax', a reference to a verse in Lewis Carroll's nonsense poem 'The Walrus and the Carpenter':

'The time has come,' the Walrus said,
'To talk of many things:
Of shoes – and ships – and sealing wax –
Of cabbages – and kings –
And why the sea is boiling hot –
And whether pigs have wings.'

In other words, Walshe avoided having to listen to a repetition of Massera's phantasmagorical political plans already suffered through by Dymphna. The world of flummery and menace in which Walshe was carrying out his professional duties during those final months of the dictatorship threw up many Mad Hatter moments. Massera's rodomontades did nothing to convince Dymphna or Ambassador Walshe of the admiral's credibility as a possible future president of Argentina. Concluding his report with the prediction that the 'neo-Peronist populist' Massera 'has now almost certainly been stopped in his tracks', he predicted that the admiral's quixotic political ambitions would sink without trace.

Despite the nightmare years of dictatorship, Walshe remained quite buoyant about the future of the country, hoping that Argentina might 'discard its feudal impediments and at last find the modern destiny for which it has so long yearned'.[3] That was achievable, Walshe believed, in a post-dictatorship Argentina where the Peronist Party had become a 'shapeless amoeba of a political movement' since the death of its founder in 1974 and was 'a headless monster' which, at its worst, was a 'vicious, fascistic rabble ... of multiple fractures and fissures'. The Irish ambassador correctly predicted that the country's immediate political future would rest in the hands of the two historical branches of the Radical Party, which, if united, might win over 40 per cent of the vote in any future presidential election.[4] That was what ultimately happened.

But in the meantime, the civilian military government did not go quietly into the night. Following the ignominious defeat in the South Atlantic, that discredited civilian military combination clung on tenaciously to power as the national foreign debt shot up from seven billion to forty billion US dollars and inflation ran at more than 300 per cent, causing a dramatic fall in real wages and a surge in hunger and poverty in the *villas*.

The democratic coalition Multipartidaria, made up of the two Radical Party branches, Peronists, Christian Democrats and many other groups, joined in a general strike called by the CGT on 6 December 1982 which shut down all public transportation and paralysed most industries. A march of resistance was held on UN Human Rights Day, 10 December, to demand the government release the names of the disappeared and the whereabouts of their bodies. On 16 December, the CGT and Peronist Youth took part in a huge 'march for life' in which an estimated 100,000 turned out on Avenida 9 de Julio and one worker lost his life in violent clashes with police. Capitulating to the inevitable, a tottering government agreed to call a presidential election on 30 October 1983. The candidate for the Radical Civic Union (UCR), Raúl Alfonsín, was a lawyer who had opposed the decision to go to war, calling it 'an illegal act by an illegitimate government in a just cause'. He had also condemned the British decision to retake the islands by force, describing it as 'an aggression of the North against the South'.[5] With the slogan *'Ahora, Alfonsín'* ('Now, Alfonsín'), his wing of the Radical Party won the presidency convincingly. His inaugural address on 10 December 1983 uncompromisingly supported his country's claim to sovereignty over the islands, pledging to recover them by peaceful means by using the good offices of the UN.[6]

It is beyond the scope of this book to provide a detailed account of Argentina's successful return to democracy. But what is relevant is the provision of a brief overview of the new government's commitment to reinforce social and political peace and bring about restorative justice and respect for the memory of those who had lost their lives or were victims in the contested recent past. On 15 December 1983, Alfonsín established the Comisión Nacional sobre la Desaparición de Personas or the National Commission on Disappeared Persons (CONADEP). Chaired by the novelist Ernesto Sabato, it produced a 50,000-page report in nine months. A summary of some 500 pages was published for mass circulation under the title *Nunca Más* (Never Again). On 20 September 1984, Alfonsín received a copy of the full report. Parallel to the CONADEP inquiry, the president had issued a decree (158/83) in December 1983 by which he instructed the Supreme Council of the Armed Forces (Consejo Supremo de las Fuerzas Armadas) to judge members of the juntas. Up to that point, the military could only be judged by their own military courts. It quickly became apparent that military omertà had settled for inaction and a code of silence. In February 1984, the military code was changed. Law 23049 permitted the military to be judged under certain circumstances in a civilian court. The National Chamber of Appeals in Criminal and Federal Correction of the Federal Capital (Cámara Nacional de Apelaciones en lo Criminal y Correccional Federal de la Capital Federal) took control under Law 23049 of what became known as 'Juicio a las Juntas'.

In democratic Argentina, the senior officers charged with serious crimes were, unlike their victims, subject to due process. There were no firing squads.

Judith did not slay Holofernes. Argentina did not replicate what had happened in parts of liberated Europe after the Second World War or in Cuba after Castro came to power in 1959. On 22 April 1985, the trial began of nine members of the different juntas, presided over by six judges. Subjecting members of the Argentine military high command to a trial governed by the laws of the state and the constitution was a punishment in itself. Under their orders, the disappeared were subject to extra-judicial punishments, torture and even death. Therefore, being subject to the rule of law, those senior officers underwent during their trial a version of Dante's *contrapasso*, where the punishment of souls in his version of the inferno (hell) resembled or contrasted with their crimes. While due process was never given to the thousands of disappeared, Videla and his associates were obliged to stand trial in public and to accept whatever verdicts were handed down. Some 833 witnesses were called. In his closing argument the chief prosecutor Julio César Strassera said: 'I wish to waive any claim to originality in closing this indictment. I wish to use a phrase that is not my own, because it already belongs to all the Argentine people. Your Honours: *Nunca Más*.' On 9 December 1985, General Jorge Videla and Admiral Emilio Massera were sentenced to life imprisonment for murder, torture and other crimes. They were discharged from the armed forces. The court sentenced two of the remaining accused to long jail sentences. The remaining defendants were acquitted. Due process had been restored in Argentina and that extended to former members of the juntas.

The CONADEP findings formed the backdrop to the trial, having established that 8,961 people had been forcibly disappeared between 1976 and 1983. Due to family fears about coming forward to give testimony to the investigation, the report estimated that the real numbers ranged between 10,000 and 30,000.[7] Rather than being fixated on numbers, the terror of those years is best captured in the conclusions of *Nunca Más*: 'State terrorism' was responsible for the policy of disappearances, torture, secret detention and the clandestine disposal of bodies in unknown sites and that all of those still disappeared people had been killed. The Sabato investigation found that the repressive practices of the armed forces were planned and ordered at the highest level, while the military documentation proving responsibility within the chain of command had been deliberately destroyed under orders.[8] *Nunca Más* also showed that the victims of state violence, a third of whom were women, were from all social classes and many were completely innocent of any involvement in any guerrilla organisation. It also found that about 200 children under fifteen had been kidnapped and that three per cent of those taken were pregnant women. The report also identified the location of over

300 clandestine detention centres (CCDs) used between 1976 and 1981. A few decades later that number was revised upwards to 520, of which 45 were in Buenos Aires.[9]

While the search for a definitive figure of those murdered by the civilian military government continues to be a matter of dispute in some quarters in 2022, human rights groups in Argentina have repeatedly refused to be manoeuvred into a trivialisation of what happened between 1976 and 1983 by entering into a debate over numbers. In August 2021, a street in the ex-ESMA was renamed 'Son 30,000' (They Are 30,000).

Democracy prevailed in Argentina and the courts delivered verdicts in accordance with the law. After 1983, about 1,700 prosecutions were filed against over 500 members of the military and security personnel accused of ordering and carrying out kidnappings, torture, assassinations and other crimes while prosecuting the 'war against subversion'. Carlos Menem led a Peronist government from 10 December 1989 to 1999. He presided over an artificial economic boom as he sold off major state assets to the private sector. Two terrorist attacks on Jewish targets during his time in office revealed vulnerabilities in the state's security system. On 17 March 1992, when Bernard Davenport was serving as Irish ambassador, a suicide bomber attacked the Israeli embassy in Buenos Aires on the corner of Arroyo and Suipacha, resulting in the deaths of thirty people. The blast shattered windows in the nearby Irish embassy but fortunately the ambassador and all staff were on official duty elsewhere in the city because it was St Patrick's Day. On 18 July 1994, the Asociación Mutual Israelita Argentina (AMIA), or Argentine Israelite Mutual Association, was bombed, killing over eighty-five people. During Menem's time in office, little was done to bring to justice those responsible for the disappearances and torture. The labyrinthine process of restorative justice, despite many stops and starts, slowed and faltered.

In the latter part of 1998, Argentina fell into deep recession and the Peronists lost power in December 1999 when the Radical Party's Fernando de la Rúa became president. The economy crashed in 2001, and the phrase *dos mil uno* ('2001') became synonymous with that collapse. De la Rúa was replaced by two presidents who, failing to halt the meltdown of the national economy, had short reigns. The Peronist Néstor Kirchner was elected president in 2003. His wife, Cristina Fernández, succeeded him in 2007 and served until 2015. Néstor Kirchner died on 27 October 2010. During the Kirchner years, the courts found a number of the leaders of the juntas guilty of various crimes. Mortality caught up with the highest echelons of the armed forces. Viola died on 30 September 1994. Admiral Armando Lambruschini, who visited Ireland in

1977, died on 15 August 2004. Massera died on 8 November 2010. Videla died in prison on 17 May 2013. Alfredo Astiz, who had infiltrated the Mothers of the Plaza de Mayo, avoided extradition to France. Tried in Paris *in absentia* in 1990, he was found guilty of the kidnapping of the two French nuns Alicia Domon and Léonie Duquet. In Buenos Aires in October 2011, Astiz was found guilty of torture, murder and forced disappearances for his role in the Holy Cross operation.[10] He showed no signs of repentance, claiming that he was saving his country from the threat of left-wing forces and he dismissed his trial as an act of political vengeance.[11] He continues to serve out a term of life imprisonment in 2022.[12]

Meanwhile, the Argentine courts in 2022 continue to face the labyrinthine task of bringing to justice those charged with crimes going back to the 1970s and early 1980s.

THE EVOLUTION OF IRISH FOREIGN POLICY AND LATIN AMERICA IN THE TWENTY-FIRST CENTURY

It has been evident throughout this book that the Irish state was glacially slow to integrate Mexico, the countries of the Caribbean and those of Central and Latin America into its national diplomatic network. For over fifty years after independence, successive Fianna Fáil and inter-party governments repeatedly underestimated the importance of having a strong diplomatic presence in that vast region. The Irish embassy in Argentina – with a staff of never more than two diplomats – remained the country's sole mission south of Washington DC in the Americas from 1948 until the early 1980s – a region with nineteen Spanish-speaking countries and with a population of 375 million. (That figure rose to thirty-three countries if the Caribbean states were added.[13]) Admittedly, the Irish embassy in Washington DC bore some of the burden of representing the country in Mexico, Central America and the Caribbean. The Irish ambassador in Lisbon was accredited to Brazil. However, the burden of representation throughout the Americas fell unevenly on the Irish mission in Buenos Aires. Traditionally it was accredited to Paraguay, Uruguay, Bolivia, Colombia and Chile.[14] When diplomatic relations were opened with Venezuela in 1980, Caracas was added to that extensive list of accredited missions. How an ambassador and a third secretary were expected to cover such a demanding portfolio of countries defies logic or reason. The reality was that it could not be done other than for the ambassador to visit those capitals for formal talks at the foreign ministries roughly once a year or when need arose.

Reviewing the benefits of having an Irish mission in Buenos Aires, the following ought to be considered:

1. Since the mission was opened in 1947/8, successive generations of Irish diplomats serving in Buenos Aires have retained a very close working relationship with the Irish-Argentine 'diaspora', financially supporting cultural and social events, promoting closer links with Ireland and helping to unify the activities of people so widely dispersed in such a vast country. Since the early 1960s, the different associations and societies formed part of a national federation – an idea first promoted in 1958 by the diplomat Timothy Joseph Horan. That, in turn, has made it much easier to maintain links with the families of Irish-Argentines who originally came from Longford, Westmeath, Meath, Roscommon, Mayo, Wicklow, Carlow and Kilkenny – many widely dispersed in the vast countryside outside Buenos Aires. The Irish embassy has remained very close to those societies. It provided a subsidy for the publication of the centenary review of *The Southern Cross* in 1976. The Irish government also paid for the microfilming of that paper from its foundation in the 1870s up until the 1990s. The embassy helped fund the building of a spacious community hall in the Fahy Club, the beating heart of the Irish community in Buenos Aires. Without the presence of an Irish embassy and the support it has provided since 1948, the Irish-Argentine collective would have found it more difficult to retain its present-day cohesion and unity. However, many of the active members of the Irish-Argentine community are now advanced in years and in need of a new wave of young Irish immigrants to help sustain the collectivity in the coming decades. The challenge remains to persuade those new arrivals to take an interest in the activities of the traditional Irish societies.

2. During the turbulent political history of twentieth-century Argentina, oscillating as it did between democracy and military dictatorship, the Irish diplomatic presence has provided strong consular protection for Irish citizens. During the civil unrest and political upheaval in 1955, an Irish envoy was on hand to intervene on behalf of Irish citizens who had been held under house arrest by the Peronist government. In the light of the prevailing violent anticlericalism that same year, the Irish envoy was authorised to issue new passports to over a dozen Irish priests and brothers – each one photographed in civilian clothing. Thus, those passport-holders were freer to move about Buenos Aires in anticlerical times without fear of being identified as foreign priests and brothers. Otherwise, they would have run the risk of being manhandled in the street and possibly imprisoned.

3. Shifting the academic focus away from the great metropolitan centres of power, this book sheds new light on the workings of the Department of Foreign Affairs in an area of secondary foreign policy importance. It shows how reluctant the department was to devolve responsibility downwards to an ambassador and third secretary in the field. During the civilian military dictatorship between 1976 and 1983, Irish diplomats in Buenos Aires were obliged to trust their own judgement and act swiftly in order to save the life of an Irish citizen. In such a hierarchical structure, the secondary foreign policy importance of the embassy in Buenos Aires was evident in another telling way: given the volatility and complexities of Argentine politics, Iveagh House rarely interrogated the content of confidential reports or questioned the underlying assumptions which sometimes reflected groupthink within diplomatic circles in Buenos Aires. Neither the minister nor senior officials ever questioned the reliability of Matthew Murphy's professional judgement reflected in his undifferentiated and consistent hostility to Perón and to Peronism throughout his posting. An obvious question to pose to Murphy at the time was why, if Perón was so authoritarian, was his movement so loyal to him during his time in power, in exile and upon his return in 1973 to become president? Between 1976 and 1981 during the dictatorship first headed by President Videla, the staff of the Irish embassy reported with unwavering consistency that he was a moderate who kept more radical members of the armed forces out of power. When the question arose about disappearances, the use of torture and the mass violation of citizens' human rights, the answer given in reports from different embassy staff was that Videla was powerless to stop the extremists and that the situation would get much worse if he were to be deposed. Ambassadors Wilfred Lennon and Seán Ó hÉideáin, together with two US ambassadors, the Canadian ambassador, the papal nuncio Pio Laghi and his first secretary Kevin Mullen, held to that unchanging position even when the facts flew in the face of such a hypothesis. Specifically in the case of Ireland, no secretary or assistant secretary ever queried the repetition of such an analysis and asked the simple question: Why, if Videla is in charge, are such human rights abuses so widespread, systematic and carried out under orders from the high command of the Argentine armed forces? In the diplomatic world of Buenos Aires during the dictatorship, was it a case of diplomatic groupthink because the alternative was too frightening to contemplate?

4. While the Irish embassy in Buenos Aires was treated until 1973 as if it were on the periphery of Irish foreign policy interests, the country's membership of the UN, together with the radical policies of the minister

for external affairs, Frank Aiken, brought Ireland support from a bloc of Latin American countries for its championing of anti-imperialism and decolonisation. On 14 December 1960, Resolution 1514(XV) declared that all peoples had the right to self-determination and that any attempt at the partial or total disruption of the national unity of a country was incompatible with the principles of the UN charter. As Third World membership of the UN grew in the 1960s, that issue remained one of great contention. For example, Argentina was very grateful for the support given by Ireland to an intermittent motion which set the sovereignty of the Falklands/Malvinas within an anti-colonial context. Support for that motion ended abruptly in 1976 when Ireland changed its vote from support to one of abstention and sustained that position afterwards.

5. When Éamon de Valera was elected president of Ireland in 1959 and Seán Lemass replaced him as taoiseach, the short period of Ireland's radicalism at the UN drew to an end. Frank Aiken's maverick foreign policy initiatives between 1956 and 1959, which profoundly annoyed the US, were a thing of the past. The country's overriding foreign policy objective throughout the 1960s was two-fold: (a) to achieve membership of the EEC with US support and (b) to build up inward investment from the US and continental Europe to help in the transition from protectionism to free trade and to provide the economic conditions for Ireland to become a full member of the EEC. Lemass, therefore, led Ireland into an ever-closer relationship with the United States between 1959 and 1966, supporting Washington during the Cuban missile crisis. Jack Lynch, who succeeded Lemass in 1966, maintained continuity with the foreign policies of his predecessor and intensified Ireland's efforts to join the EEC. Winning the general election in 1969, Lynch's decision to appoint Dr Patrick Hillery as minister for external affairs signified that he wanted his most talented colleague in Iveagh House to advance Ireland's application for membership of the EEC and to help manage Anglo-Irish relations at a time of unprecedented and escalating violence in Northern Ireland. Dropped from the cabinet, Aiken could only watch from the backbenches as the last vestiges of his unilateralism and foreign policy radicalism became little more than a distant memory. He retired from public life in 1973. By compartmentalising the deteriorating situation in the North, both Britain and Ireland cooperated closely as EEC membership talks intensified. In January 1973, Ireland, together with Britain and Denmark, joined the EEC. That was the most transformative development since independence in 1922 for the Irish economy, agriculture, society and education.

6. Victory for a Fine Gael/Labour coalition in early 1973 had great significance for Ireland's policy towards Latin America. A former minister for external affairs between 1954 and 1957, Liam Cosgrave, became taoiseach. He appointed Dr Garret FitzGerald as minister to his old portfolio, now called foreign affairs. Quickly realising that Ireland was very much out of step with many of the other EEC member states which had large embassy networks, FitzGerald opened an Irish mission to the Soviet Union in 1974 and did the preliminary work which led to the setting up of an embassy in the People's Republic of China in 1979. The Lynch government had set up an embassy in Japan in 1973. FitzGerald's arrival in Iveagh House both coincided with, and was responsible for, a broadening of the Irish foreign policy perspective to include Latin America. Although he did not open a new embassy in Latin America, he had a strong personal interest in the affairs of the region. His former work colleague in the Economist Intelligence Unit in Dublin, Bernard Davenport, was chargé in Buenos Aires. FitzGerald read his report with admiration and encouraged him to continue sending high-grade analysis to Iveagh House. Davenport was posted back to headquarters in early 1974 but not before he had an opportunity to report on the tragic events in Chile.

7. On 11 September 1973, General Augusto Pinochet seized power in a coup d'état ushering in a period of protracted repression in Chile. There was a strong Irish missionary presence in the country and news of human rights abuses came back to Ireland through media and personal contacts. The presence of Irish Catholic missionaries working throughout Latin America was an important method of communicating with the region, where Irish priests, nuns, brothers and lay workers were eyewitnesses to human rights abuses and disappearances. Modern communication brought a new sense of immediacy to what was happening in Chile and other countries under authoritarian rule. In Ireland, newly formed solidarity groups lobbied for the admission of political refugees. FitzGerald, with a long-standing interest in Catholic theology and mission, helped negotiate the admission of over 200 Chileans.

8. When the Argentine civilian military government kidnapped, tortured and, without a charge, imprisoned an Irish citizen in late 1976, the importance of having an embassy in Buenos Aires was reinforced. The prompt action by Ambassador Wilfred Lennon and the third secretary Justin Harman in October of that year helped save the life of Fr Patrick Rice. Disappeared on the 13th, both diplomats moved swiftly to report his disappearance to the foreign ministry, launch a local press campaign to advertise the kidnapping

and enlist the support of diplomats in other embassies to work with the nunciature and church authorities to locate his whereabouts. The two Irish diplomats also worked through the Irish international diplomatic network to build a media campaign to help identify his whereabouts, ensure that he was kept alive and negotiate his freedom and deportation from the country. Those strategies combined to force the Argentine authorities to admit that he was in custody and to allow him to be seen by the two Irish diplomats, where they confirmed for themselves that he had been repeatedly beaten, had cigarette burns on his hands and arms, was subjected to electric shock torture and had suffered repeated assaults and beatings. The press campaign mounted by the embassy, together with their hounding of the Argentine authorities, saved Rice's life and also saved Fátima Cabrera, the catechist disappeared with him. Released in early December 1976, Rice was forced to leave the country.

9. The related Fátima Cabrera case revealed that FitzGerald and his successor Michael O'Kennedy – prompted by Rice and senior officials in the political division of Foreign Affairs – took a strong interest in the welfare of the young woman, who was in jail from October 1976 until January 1978 and then placed under house arrest until the fall of the civilian military dictatorship in 1983. The administrative struggle to secure an Irish visa for Cabrera revealed a sclerosis at the heart of the decision-making process because of divided views within the Department of Foreign Affairs, a clash between the Irish ambassador in Buenos Aires and the political division in Iveagh House, and the opposition of the Department of Justice to the idea of granting a visa to one Argentine. At a time when other EEC countries were offering visas to many who were not citizens in order to save their lives, a bureaucratic wrangle continued throughout the entirety of 1977 to determine whether or not Cabrera ought to be offered a visa – and that despite the fact that two ministers approved of doing so. The Rice family had bought her an airline ticket and guaranteed that she would live with Rice's sister without costing a single 'penny' to the Irish state. While Cabrera did not receive the offer of an Irish visa, the debate in Irish diplomatic circles generated by her case serves to illustrate the absence of a more general consideration of the wider need to allow Argentines under threat to be offered asylum in Ireland. When preparing newly recruited diplomats for what they might face in the field, the Rice/Cabrera files ought to serve as a blueprint to illustrate what to do and what not to do.[15]

10. Nowhere was the importance of the Irish embassy in Buenos Aires demonstrated more clearly than during the Falklands/Malvinas war. This

was an international crisis in which all the moving parts of Irish foreign policy were involved. At a critical juncture in the crisis and the war, Ireland was a member of the UN Security Council. Contiguously, Ireland was a member of the EEC. In terms of Ireland's vital interests, Anglo-Irish relations were of daily importance because Britain was Ireland's largest export market while the bloody conflict in Northern Ireland throughout the 1970s complicated that relationship. For the first time in the history of the diplomatic mission, Buenos Aires became a central focus for the country's foreign policy in April/May/June 1982. The Falklands/Malvinas war created conditions for a perfect storm in Anglo-Irish relations exacerbated by an uncharacteristic volatility in the decision-making process in Dublin. Ambassador Patrick Walshe, who served in Buenos Aires at the time, together with the third secretary, Colin Wrafter, dealt with a hurt and disillusioned Irish-Argentine community, many of whom were uncomprehending of Ireland's stance on the UN Security Council in support of Resolution 502 in early April and of its voting for EEC sanctions later that month. The mobilisation of the Irish-Argentine community in favour of their country's right to sovereignty over the Falklands greatly complicated the Irish government's conjoined Anglo-Irish, Irish EU and Irish UN policy processes. When Ireland reversed those policies in the first week of May 1982, brickbats from Irish-Argentines were replaced by bouquets in the form of letters of gratitude, including correspondence from the Federation of Irish-Argentine Societies to the taoiseach, Charles Haughey. Ambassador Walshe, having been received coolly by the Argentine foreign ministry in April, was welcomed with great warmth and appreciation in early May. The Argentine foreign minister Nicanor Costa Méndez received Walshe in the second week of May 1982 to thank the Irish ambassador personally for the decision taken in Dublin to break ranks with other EEC countries. Argentina would never forget Ireland's stance, he told Walshe on that occasion. But while it was bouquets in Buenos Aires, there were brickbats in London, incomprehension in Brussels and confusion at the UN. Charles Haughey's handling of the Falklands crisis did lasting damage to Anglo-Irish relations and earned him the mistrust of Margaret Thatcher and senior British officials.

11. Based on Ireland's bruising experience in New York in early May 1982, there are those who argue that small powers ought not to take a seat on the UN Security Council as it exposes the country needlessly to the risk of having to take up positions inimical to its national interests and liable to antagonise any one of the five permanent members of that body –

China, France, Russian Federation, the United States and Britain. Among those who oppose Irish participation, their real concern is the potential collateral damage such as was done to Anglo-Irish relations during the Falklands war. However, such a view is held in ignorance of Irish foreign policy since 1919 or 1922, where successive governments maximised their position in multilateral organisations such as the British Commonwealth, the International Labour Organisation, the League of Nations in the 1920s and 1930s, the Council of Europe in 1949, the UN since 1955 and the EEC after 1973. The challenge of lobbying for support to win a seat on the Security Council is an exercise in network-building and it has proved to be a productive use of senior diplomats' time, supported sometimes by recently retired colleagues. A small power like Ireland does not carry the burdens of having vital geopolitical and geostrategic interests to defend or the residue of empire. Ireland enjoys the freedom to instruct its diplomats to act as honest brokers when holding a seat on the Security Council, as it does for the third time in 2020–2. Gaining a seat at the 'top table' or on the Security Council provides Ireland with the opportunity to use its best diplomats to deploy their skills to address events often at a time of major international crisis such as Afghanistan in the wake of US withdrawal in 2021 or the Russian threat to Ukraine in 2022.

12. Charles Haughey did not convert the sunburst of importance for the Irish embassy in Buenos Aires into an immediate commitment to open new missions in Latin America. His term in office in 1982 lasted only from March to December. When he was next in office, between 1987 and 1992, the country faced a major economic crisis and the government had limited resources available to extend its network of embassies abroad. However, contrasting the increase in Irish diplomatic activity in Africa and Latin America from the 1960s, the former assumed far greater importance than Latin America. A mission was opened in Egypt in 1975, in Lesotho (development co-operation office) in 1978, in Kenya and Tanzania (development co-operation office) in 1979, Zambia (development cooperation office) in 1980, in Ethiopia, Uganda and South Africa in 1994, in Mozambique in 1996 and Sudan (development co-operation office) in 1999. Other residential diplomatic missions outside Europe established between the late 1970s and 1990s were China (1979), Iraq (1986), Republic of South Korea (1989), Malaysia (1995), Israel (1996) and Turkey (1998).

13. Irrespective of which combination of parties formed an Irish government in the 1980s, progress remained painfully slow in broadening the diplomatic network in Latin America. While Ireland and Mexico

established diplomatic relations on 10 January 1974, the Irish ambassador in Washington was still accredited to Mexico in 1977. In 1992, Mexico sent a resident ambassador to Dublin. Art Agnew, a former Irish ambassador to Argentina, opened a new embassy in Mexico in 1999. He served in that post until 2005. But even with the opening of a second embassy, the tasks facing Irish diplomats in Latin America at the turn of the century remained immense. The Irish embassies in Mexico and Argentina had responsibility for covering thirteen of the nineteen Spanish-speaking countries in the region.[16] The Irish embassy in Mexico was also accredited to El Salvador, Nicaragua, Costa Rica, Cuba, Venezuela, Colombia and Peru. That gave Mexico the highest number of accreditations (8) of any Irish embassy in the world.[17] (The Irish army, between December 1989 and January 1999, was part of the United Nations observer group in Central America. The army was part of the UN observer mission in El Salvador between January 1992 and May 1994. Between January 1992 and May 1994, the Irish army also participated in the UN mission in Haiti.) With the ceding of responsibility for Colombia to the embassy in Mexico, the Irish embassy in Argentina was accredited to only four other countries – Chile, Paraguay, Uruguay and Bolivia. The Irish embassy in Washington DC had ten diplomats in 2018 in addition to six consulates general in the United States employing another ten diplomats – New York, Boston, Chicago, San Francisco, Atlanta and Austin. By way of contrast, five Irish diplomats in Mexico and Argentina in 1999 covered thirteen of the nineteen Spanish-speaking countries in the region.

14. In the latter decades of the twentieth century, a number of prominent Latin American countries with resident envoys in Dublin lobbied the Irish government to set up reciprocal diplomatic missions. Diplomatic relations had been established with Brazil in 1975 on a non-resident basis. Historically, the Irish ambassador in Lisbon was accredited to that country. In view of the colonial relationship between the two countries, that was not an ideal solution. In 1992, Brazil opened an embassy in Dublin and an Irish embassy was finally set up in Brasilia in October 2001. A consulate general was opened in São Paulo in 2014.

15. As a member of the EU since 1973, Ireland has enjoyed the advantage of working collaboratively with diplomats from the fellow member states through the protocols of European political cooperation. The regular meetings of EU ambassadors in Mexico City and Buenos Aires,[18] together with meetings of first secretaries, provided useful information-sharing exercises. Ireland has participated in the 1990s in the EU's structured

political dialogue with the South American Rio Group and the Central American San José Group. There have been ongoing discussions between the EU and Mercosur (Argentina, Brazil, Paraguay and Uruguay) together with the signing of bilateral accords, for example with Mexico, which came into force in 2002. The Madrid summit in 2003 between EU and Latin American and Caribbean (LAC) countries laid a solid foundation for cooperation. The Irish presidencies of the EU over the past seventeen years have helped broaden Ireland's stance in the region. That was the case when Ireland chaired the third EU–LAC summit in Mexico in May 2004. By 2019, the country was much better placed to deepen her diplomatic, cultural and economic ties with the LAC countries. The launching on 10 April 2014 of the Latin America Trade Forum (LATF), by the Irish Exporters Association, brought greater cohesion to Irish export campaigns in the region, while Education Ireland has expanded the range of cooperation and exchanges between universities in the LAC region.[19]

16. The organogram of the Department of Foreign Affairs and Trade reflects the growing importance of Latin America in the diplomatic, political, cultural, educational, economic and trade areas. The Latin American unit is situated within the Ireland, United Kingdom and Americas division. It has horizontal links to the Political (including human rights), European and Development Cooperation divisions.[20] In 2019, the minister for foreign affairs and trade, Simon Coveney, published *Global Ireland: Ireland's global footprint to 2025*.[21] In that document, he stressed the importance of Latin America and the Caribbean with thirty-three countries and a population of some 650 million people. In 2016, the total two-way goods trade between Ireland, Latin America and the Caribbean was 3.25 billion euro. The Irish foreign minister also announced the strengthening of the embassy and agency presence in Mexico. He spoke of plans to expand the Irish presence in Brazil and to open new embassies elsewhere in Latin America, the Caribbean and Central America. Irish embassies opened in Santiago, Chile, in 2018[22] and in Bogotá, Colombia, in 2019. The number of Irish diplomats has now risen to roughly ten for all of Spanish-speaking Latin America. Mercosur, comprising Argentina, Brazil, Paraguay, Uruguay and Venezuela (the latter suspended since December 2016) and seven associate members, is a trading block of great importance for Ireland and the other member states of the European Union. A political agreement was signed on 28 June 2019 between the two entities for a comprehensive trade agreement which covers an area with a combined population of 780 million. The then commissioner for agriculture and rural development,

Phil Hogan, called the agreement 'fair and balanced' with opportunities to benefit both sides.

17. Finally, as the Irish diplomatic presence in Latin America has both grown and become more diverse, the number of Irish women diplomats serving there has grown significantly in recent years. In 1985, Ms Jackie O'Halloran was the first woman to be appointed as a third secretary to Buenos Aires – and therefore to Latin America. She served there until 1991. In 2022, she was the serving ambassador in Argentina. She was preceded in that post by Paula Slattery between 2000 and 2004 and by Philomena Murnaghan from 2006 to 2010. Sharon Lennon was third secretary in Buenos Aires from 2013 to 2014 before moving in 2014 to open an Irish consulate in São Paulo. Sonja Hyland became ambassador to Mexico in 2013 and served until 2017. Alison Milton became the first resident Irish ambassador to Colombia in January 2019.

A DECLINING IRISH CATHOLIC MISSIONARY PRESENCE IN ARGENTINA

As the Irish diplomatic footprint grew in Latin America at the beginning of the twenty-first century, the Irish Catholic missionary presence in the region had shrunk significantly between the 1960s and 2022. Historically, that movement played multiple roles in Argentina from the nineteenth to the mid-twentieth century. Irish women and men religious, together with Irish diocesan priests, looked after the pastoral, educational and health needs of Irish-Argentines. Those generations of religious left strong evidence of their presence in the ecclesiastical material culture of the country – the imposing churches of Holy Cross, St Patrick's Belgrano, St Patrick's Mercedes, St Patrick's Rosario, the cathedral church in Venado Tuerto, Santa Fe, San Pablo, Capilla del Señor and the neogothic Basilica of Our Lady in Luján. Those same missionaries also built schools: Mater Misericordiae, Santa Brígida, Michael Ham, Fahy Institute, San Pablo, the Keating Institute/Colegio de Santo Domingo, Clonmacnoise, San Antonio de Areco, San Patricio, Mercedes, and San Patricio, Belgrano.

By 2022, the Irish missionary presence in Argentina had declined to a point where there are only a handful of Irish priests, nuns and brothers working in that country. The Pallottines are, with one exception, made up today of Argentine priests and others from Brazil and other Latin American countries. Fr Tom O'Donnell from Limerick, who came to Argentina in 1976 a few weeks after the Pallottine massacre, continues his missionary work in Mercedes. The Passionist Province, which includes Argentina, Uruguay and Brazil, remains active and vibrant in 2022, but the last Irish-born priest, Frank Murray, died in

2020. Irish Dominican priests, who worked in Corrientes from the 1960s, left that mission. One Irish Dominican priest works in Montevideo. There are two Christian Brothers, Tom O'Connell and Seán Hayes, living in retirement in Buenos Aires. One other Christian Brother is active in the city. The Irish Sisters of Mercy, who first arrived in Argentina in 1856, continue to have a strong presence in the country working in the *villas* around Buenos Aires. They no longer work in the large schools they founded in the nineteenth and twentieth centuries. The Irish Dominican Sisters, who came in the 1960s, closed their Argentine mission in 2020.

Overall, the traditional centres of worship for the Irish and for Irish-Argentines in Buenos Aires are today churches frequented by Argentines and by new immigrants. While the Irish iconography remains in stained-glass windows and in the statues, parishioners do not relate to the material culture characterised by another moment in history in which they have not shared. Holy Cross, built with the mites of the poor Irish in the nineteenth century, is now the centre of a vibrant parish reflecting the demographic of modern Argentina. That is not so much the case in the two Pallottine churches in Belgrano and Mercedes, which continue to be attended by a fast-ageing Irish-Argentine congregation.

The majority of the post-Vatican II generation of Irish missionaries did not serve the traditional Irish-Argentine communities. Priests, nuns and brothers, together with those working for the Catholic NGO Trócaire, worked in the *villas* in Buenos Aires and in other cities throughout the country. Now, in 2022, though radically diminished in numbers, those that remain in Argentina continue both to evangelise and to play the 'informal' role of representatives of Ireland, which has a strong commitment to social justice and the defence of human rights. Irish religious 'soft power' – now supported by lay missionaries and development aid workers – continues to be of importance in the forging of Ireland's humanitarian international reputation. Although the gap between the Catholic Church and the Irish state has widened and the unhealthy closeness of the first fifty years has been ruptured, a broad common ground remains between both parties when each seeks to defend human rights globally. Irish missionaries and Catholic NGOs strive to defend human rights, promote the fight against poverty, pandemics and economic underdevelopment while at the same time fighting to avoid the catastrophe of 'ecocide'.

Irish Catholic religious women and men have set down deep roots in Argentina; where many gave a lifetime of service as teachers, catechists, social workers and parish priests. The remarkable history of successive generations of Irish missionaries there deserves to be told in full. Many made national contributions in their respective fields. I will illustrate the richness of their contribution by focusing on the work of Patrick Rice – one of a number of Irish priests and ex-priests who made it their life's work to seek justice for the disappeared and for the families of the disappeared in Argentina, Latin America and in other parts of the world – including the Balkans, Sri Lanka, the Philippines and Rwanda. Rice, who died in 2010, was prominent in the campaigns to bring restorative justice to the victims of repressive regimes in Latin America and latterly in a wider international context. As he has been an integral part of the narrative of this volume, it is valuable to trace his work during the final thirty years of his life. Transferred at the end of 1979 by the Little Brothers of Charles de Foucauld from Washington to Caracas, Venezuela, he was in contact with Argentine exiles across Latin America in his capacity as a member of the Latin American Foundation of Human Rights and Social Development (FUNDALATIN). He also combined his parish work in a *villa* (called a *barrio* in Venezuela) with the promotion of human rights training within the pastoral structures of the local archdiocese. While travelling around Latin America in the early 1980s, he was repeatedly struck by the need to establish an international organisation to represent the families of the disappeared in the region. Rice estimated there were 88,671 disappearances in Latin America between 1970 and 1990.[23]

Two human rights groups funded a conference in Costa Rica in January 1981 attended by different associations representing the disappeared throughout Latin America. Rice and Betty Campbell, a Sister of Mercy,[24] also attended. The conference agreed to find the funds to run what soon became the Latin American Federation of Associations for Relatives of the Detained and Disappeared (FEDEFAM).[25] Setting himself up in an office in Caracas with a borrowed typewriter, Rice became its executive secretary, supported by a volunteer administrator. A founding member of the Mothers of the Plaza de Mayo, Élida Galletti, became its first president.[26] FEDEFAM held a conference in Caracas at the end of 1981. Progress was swift and branches were set up in many countries in Latin America. A plan emerged to hold an annual conference in different countries. Rice accepted the Spanish government's human rights award in 1982 on behalf of FEDEFAM. During the following years, he helped coordinate conferences in Peru (1982 and 1989), Mexico (1983), Argentina (1984), Uruguay (1985), El Salvador (1987) and Colombia (1988). Because of a decade of solidarity work, Rice became better known in Latin America, Africa, Asia and at the United Nations than in his native Ireland. His work also took him to the UN in Geneva. The UN General Assembly passed a resolution on enforced disappearances on 20 December 1978, and a working group was set up in 1980. Rice went to Geneva every year to lobby the Human Rights Commission and to encourage more rapid progress. In 1983, the FEDEFAM delegation were very disappointed at the lack of progress and the fact that the UN report had omitted the appendices of the oral testimony of the relatives of the disappeared which they had supplied. However, it had acknowledged that the working group had submitted 1,377 names to the Argentine permanent representative, Gabriel Martinez. Returning in February 1984, the FEDEFAM delegation of six, of which Rice was the only male, expressed again their disappointment with the progress being made by the working group and unfurled a banner before the Human Rights Commission. Requesting the assistant secretary general, Kurt Herndl, to act within three months on the information supplied by FEDEFAM, Rice and the delegation left the UN building and went on hunger strike in a nearby church. Three months later, FEDEFAM cut off communications with the UN working group.[27]

Rice had tried unsuccessfully since the return of democracy to Argentina to get a visa to re-enter the country. Having been deported in 1976, he remained on a list of undesirables. However, the Argentine embassy in Mexico in May 1984 issued him a visa to return to help prepare for a FEDEFAM conference that September in Buenos Aires. Rice was relieved to learn that Fátima Cabrera was alive and living in Villa Soldati with her mother, brother and two sisters.[28] He had not seen or spoken to Cabrera since 17 October 1976 during their brief meeting as prisoners in the federal police headquarters. He was reunited with her family and she agreed to keep in touch with him by letter. They corresponded extensively over the following months and during that time the nature of the relationship changed: 'After many letters over a few months, we discovered that our lives ought to be together. That was a very sudden change for me,' she told me. Before returning to Buenos Aires in the latter part of 1984 for the FEDEFAM conference, Rice had decided to dedicate his life to the promotion of human rights and to leave the priesthood. In those altered circumstances, they met during Rice's short time in the city and took the decision to become a couple. Rice left for a ten-city speaking tour of the US organised by the Robert F. Kennedy (RFK) Memorial Foundation, and he acted as a translator for Alicia Emelina Panameño de García (died 2010),[29] a founder of the Comité de Madres y Familiares de Desaparecidos y Asesinados Políticos de El Salvador (COMADRES), when she was presented with the first RFK Human Rights Award.[30] Four empty chairs were placed on the podium to represent the Salvadoran mothers who had been denied access to the US.[31]

Rice returned to Buenos Aires in late December 1984. Fátima Cabrera told me that she had at first been completely opposed to becoming his partner.[32]

8.1 Patrick and Fátima Cabrera on their wedding day, Caracas, 1985

Cabrera's mother, Doña Blanca, was not best pleased to learn that she had fallen in love with a soon-to-be former priest. She did not stand in her daughter's way, telling her that when the relationship failed in a few months she could come back to Buenos Aires and resume her life there. Cabrera wrote: 'I was moving from the horror, the silence over many years and the death of my sister,[33] to a life in Venezuela.' Together with Jesús Silva and Elena González who ran a refuge centre for children for a few decades in Caracas,[34] they built an extended family in Venezuela and kept an open house. As a rebuke to the taunts of her torturers in December 1976 that she would never be able to become pregnant, the couple decided to start a family immediately: 'Life was further affirmed with the births of Carlitos, our son [1985], then Amy [1987] and Blanca Libertad [in Buenos Aires] in 1989. It wasn't easy. But with small steps, we were reconstructing a new life, in hope,' she wrote.[35]

Rice represented FEDEFAM in New York in 1988 when the UN Economic and Social Council NGO committee gave that organisation consultative status.[36] The Cabrera–Rice family moved to Buenos Aires later that year, where

Fátima could continue her work in adult literacy. They first lived in Monte Grande, a city in the suburbs of Buenos Aires. Their second daughter, Blanca Libertad, was born on 20 November 1989. Later, Cabrera and Rice bought a house near Estación Constitución which became a centre for the activities of the Little Brothers of Charles de Foucauld and a refuge for many passing through the city. Rice got a job with the Ecumenical Movement for Human Rights and in 1992 became their national coordinator. He travelled widely in Latin America and continued to make an annual visit to Geneva to attend the UN Commission on Human Rights, where he lobbied for a convention on the rights of the child. The UN General Assembly unanimously adopted that convention on 20 November 1989 and it came into force on 2 September 1990. Rice renewed his active association with FEDEFAM in 1999 and was nominated as a senior adviser to the executive committee. His new work took him to Sri Lanka, Benin, Croatia and Kosovo. In 2002, the Irish diplomatic mission in Geneva nominated him as the Western Group's candidate for membership of the UN Working Group on Enforced and Involuntary Disappearances. In that capacity, he contributed to winning approval in 2005 for an international instrument against enforced disappearances. The UN General Assembly adopted on 20 December 2006 the International Convention for the Protection of All Persons from Enforced Disappearances. It was opened for signatures on 6 February 2007.

In acknowledgement of a lifetime of service to the international human rights movement, Rice was conferred in 2008 with an honorary doctorate at University College Cork.

He was appointed in early 2010 as the international coordinator of the International Coalition against Enforced Disappearances (ICAED) (Coalición Internacional contra la Desaparición Forzada). In fulfilment of those duties, he made two trips to Europe and the United States in 2010, one early in the year and the second in June/July. Rice died suddenly on 7 July in Miami airport while returning home. His funeral service, held in Holy Cross Church, Buenos Aires, lasted three days as many parishioners from Fortín Olmos, where he had worked in the early 1970s, travelled by bus to be present. Large numbers came from Villa Soldati, where he worked as a priest for over two years. The Mothers of the Plaza de Mayo left their white scarves on his coffin as a mark of respect. Serving and former government ministers came to pay their respects, including the former foreign minister, Jorge Taiana, with whom Rice had been in prison in La Plata in 1976. There was also a large group representing a number of international human rights and religious organisations. Rice did not live to see the UN Convention on Enforced Disappearances come into force on 23

8.2 On the occasion of receiving an honorary doctorate from University College Cork in summer 2008: Patrick Rice (*centre*) with Fátima Cabrera and his daughter Blanca. Dermot Keogh (*on left*) and Ann Keogh (*on right*).

December 2010 but he died knowing its implementation was inevitable. He is buried in the English cemetery at La Chacarita in Buenos Aires.[37]

In autumn 2010, the Argentinian government under the Peronist president Cristina Fernández de Kirchner, honoured six leaders of different churches and faiths for their courage and bravery during and after the period of civilian military dictatorship.[38] Two of the recipients were the retired bishops of the Methodist Church, Aldo Manuel Etchegoyen[39] and Federico José Pagura.[40] Rabbi Bernardo Javier Plaunick was also a recipient, as were the Catholic priests Raúl Troncoso[41] and Elías Musse.[42] The sixth recipient was Patrick Rice. The families, friends and representatives of the human rights community in Argentina gathered on 25 November at the foreign ministry, Palacio San Martín, to hear a government minister pay homage to the six men who had refused to bend the knee to the dictatorship or to look the other way as heinous violations of human rights were being perpetrated in the name of 'Christian civilisation'. All six recipients had been kidnapped, illegally imprisoned and tortured by officials of the state and held in secret places of detention in Buenos Aires and elsewhere in the country. Recalling a dark phase in the history of Argentina, the citation stated that all six were being honoured 'for their commitment to social justice and the defence of human rights, on the occasion of the XXIX anniversary of the UN Declaration on the Elimination of all Forms of Intolerance and of Discrimination Based on Religion or Belief'.[43] The secretary for religions, Ambassador Guillermo R. Oliveri, representing the Ministry of Foreign Affairs, spoke of the courage and the tenacity of each person being honoured. Each recipient spoke briefly in turn about their experiences, their hopes and their continued commitment to the struggle for the achievement of universal respect for human rights.[44] Rice was represented by his three children, Carlos, Amy and Blanca, and his wife Fátima Cabrera, who spoke about her husband's deeply held convictions as a Christian and as a human rights activist.[45]

On 7 December 2010 another ceremony in Buenos Aires paid Rice a further tribute. The Escuela de Mecánica de la Armada (ESMA) had been repurposed to house a new institution – Ex-Esma: Espacio para la Memoria y para la Promoción y Defensa de los Derechos Humanos (Ex-Esma: Space for Remembrance and for the Promotion and Defence of Human Rights). Created in 2004 to preserve the memory of the victims of the dictatorship and to promote human rights, the seventeen-hectare site includes the national memorial archive, a cultural centre, the Malvinas museum and a former chapel now called Espacio Patrick Rice.[46] *Pagina 12* reported: 'It had long since ceased to be a chapel. That was where the chaplains of the Argentinian armed forces had once blessed the members of the military death squads. Patrick Rice had proposed the conversion of the chapel into a place of dialogue between religions. He died earlier this year but his children, Amy and Carlos, continue to advance his unfinished plans.'[47] The elderly Uruguayan priest Jesús Silva attended the ceremony. His brother Mauricio[48] had been disappeared in 1977 and may have spent his final days in the ESMA. Thirty years after the dictatorship, Hannah Arendt's phrase 'the banality of evil' aptly describes the atmosphere of the former ESMA even to this day.[49] The secretary for religions, Dr Guillermo Oliveri, joined the large crowd, as did the minister for human rights Dr Eduardo Luis Duhalde. Daniel Schiavi and Haroldo Conti represented the Space for Memory and for the Promotion of Human Rights. Luis Duhalde said he had known Rice since 1979 and their paths had crossed many times in the intervening thirty years. He regarded him as a tireless worker who stood in

8.3 The president of Ireland, Michael D. Higgins, visiting the Espacio Patrick Rice in 2012, in what used to be the officers' chapel in what is now called the ex-ESMA or former naval academy. Fátima Cabrera is speaking (between the president and a mother of the Plaza de Mayo) and in front are Amy and Blanca Cabrera Rice.

solidarity with those who fought to defend human rights. Rice was, he added, a militant with *patas de bronze* (bronze feet), in other words a man who stood his ground and refused to yield an inch while he worked for the defence of human rights. The minister hoped that Rice's name would be incorporated into the historical memory of all Argentines. The president of the Mothers of the Plaza de Mayo (Linea Fundadora), Marta Vázquez, recalled meeting him first in Costa Rica in 1981: 'I don't want to neglect to point out the long road that he travelled lobbying at the UN for the ratification of the convention on enforced disappearances which he brought to final success after twenty-two years of struggle.' Rice had accompanied Vázquez on many foreign visits and they had worked very closely together for nearly thirty years. The culmination of a life's work, she said, was about to be realised when the convention would come into effect on 23 December 2010 at the General Assembly of the United Nations.

'We should toast his memory,' she said with force, adding that the Espacio Patrick Rice was now converted from a place of suffering into a little bit of heaven, *un lugar de pequeño cielo*.[50] Fátima Cabrera said that Rice's dream had become a reality and that pain and suffering had now been transformed into joy. The ceremony concluded with a concert by indigenous musicians led by Carmelo Sardinas, professor of Quechua at the University of San Martín. They were joined by Nelly Benitez, the director of the *villa* band 'Los Guardianes de Mugica'. The Espacio Patrick Rice quickly became a venue for the performance of popular and classical music. La Tecnicultura de Música Popular inspired by the Mothers of the Plaza de Mayo (Linea Fundadora) gave concerts there, as did the classical pianist Miguel Ángel Estrella, who is a UNESCO ambassador and was a friend of Rice's from his prison days. Rice's widow Fátima Cabrera and her three children, all members of HIJOS, continue to participate in the struggle for Memory, Truth and Justice.[51]

The connection between the work of Irish missionaries and the advancement of respect for human rights has been recognised by three Irish presidents during their visits to Latin America in 1995, 2004, 2012, 2013 and 2017. Presidents Mary Robinson[52] and Mary McAleese[53] made one visit each in 1995 and 2004 respectively. President Michael D. Higgins has made three extensive visits to the region: Brazil, Argentina and Chile in 2012, Mexico, El Salvador and Costa Rica in 2013 and Peru, Colombia and Cuba in 2017.[54] On those visits, President Higgins has stressed the shared history of Ireland and Latin America, having experienced protracted colonisation, repression and a lengthy struggle for political and economic independence. Speaking in Havana on 16 February 2017, he made reference to the role of many Irish in the struggle for independence from Spanish imperialism:

> Arriving at the time when empires were declining and the impulse for national independence was emerging, some of those Irish and their descendants have been immortalised in the history books of Latin America as key players in the struggle for independence – men such as Admiral William Brown the father of the Argentine Navy, and General Bernardo O'Higgins, Liberator of Chile. They are historic figures of whose achievements we, in Ireland, are justifiably proud, and who represent the profound contribution of the Irish to the crafting of modern Latin America. How moving it always is to know that they are remembered annually at ceremonial services such as graduation services for naval officers in Argentina.[55]

Other leaders of Latin American independence bore Irish names – Guillermo Brown, Don Juan O'Brien and Daniel Florence O'Leary. When President Higgins visited the ex-ESMA in Buenos Aires in 2012, he spoke movingly about Patrick Rice and of those who fought for the cause of human rights during the time of the civilian military dictatorship. Recalling the role Rice played in the global movement against state terror, he said that his legacy would serve as an example for future generations.[56]

It is fitting that President Michael D. Higgins should have the first and last words in this volume. While on an official visit to Argentina in 2012, he visited the Espacio Patrick Rice and later at a reception on 12 October he recalled the courage and the determination of the Irish emigrants who settled in Argentina in the nineteenth century:

> Far from being overawed or defeated by circumstances, the Irish people have been addressing head-on the challenges and difficulties we face. This resilience typifies the attitude of the Irish, both at home and in the countries in which we have made our homes around the world. When Irish immigrants first arrived to Argentina, for example, they could not speak the local language nor did they know the customs of the country to which they came. But they adapted quickly, became part of the local community and many achieved noteworthy success despite their unfamiliar surroundings.[57]

While warmly praising the historical contribution the Irish had made in their adopted country, President Higgins looked towards 'the contribution they will make to its future' and to the deepening of relations between Ireland and the countries of Latin America.[58]

List of Irish Envoys/Ambassadors to Argentina, 1919 to Present, and Argentine Envoys to Ireland

Name	Appointment
Eamonn Bulfin	1919
Laurence Ginnell	1921
Matthew Murphy	1947
Timothy Joseph Horan	1955
Thomas Vincent Commins	1959
William Benedict Butler	1959
Michael Leo Skentelbery	1962

ELEVATED TO EMBASSY STATUS, 1964

Name	Appointment
Michael Leo Skentelbery	1964
Timothy Joseph Horan	1967*
Michael Leo Skentelbery	1967
James Wilfred Lennon	1973
Seán Ó hÉideáin	1977
Patrick Walshe	1981
Bernard Davenport	1989
Art Agnew	1996
Paula Slattery	2000
Kenneth Thompson	2004
Máirtín Ó Fainín	2005
Philomena Murnaghan	2006
James McIntyre	2010
Justin Harman	2014
Jacqueline O'Halloran	2018

* appointment not proceeded with

LIST OF IRISH THIRD SECRETARIES TO ARGENTINA, 1961 TO PRESENT

Name	Appointment
Sean Ó hÉidéain	1961
Daniel Hanafin	1968
Bernard Davenport	1971
Justin Harman	1975
James Carroll	1978
Colin Wrafter	1980
John Redmond	1983
Jacqueline O'Halloran	1987
Brendan Ward	1991
Eamonn Robinson	1994
David Noonan	1995
Jonathan Conlon	1998
David Brooke	2001
Derek Lambe	2004
Andrew Noonan	2009
Jerry O'Donovan	2012
Sharon Lennon	2013
Bobby Smyth	2015
Dermot Fitzpatrick	2016
Louise Ward	2019

SERVING LOCAL STAFF IN 2022

Julia McKenna
Patricia Sgabetti
Yanina Bevilacqua
Héctor Viavattene (driver)

The Argentine diplomatic mission in Ireland was established on 17 April 1948

ARGENTINE REPRESENTATIVES IN IRELAND

Name	Appointment
José Fausto Rieffolo Bessone	1948
Jorge Escalante Posse	1949
Raúl Fernando De Olano	1953
Lorenzo McGovern	1955
Carlos Alberto Fernández	1959

Miriam Cummins served as personal secretary to a succession of Argentine ambassadors to Ireland.

The Argentine consulate was made an embassy on 27 February 1964

Name	Appointment
Luis Santiago Luti	1967
José María Parodi Cantilo	1967
Santos Goñi Demarchi	1967
José del Carril	1974
Eduardo Esteban Pérez Tomás	1977
Federico Diego Erhart del Campo	1982
Juan José Árias Uriburu	1987
Nicolás Adria Sonschein	1989
Juan Manuel Figuerero Antequera	1991
Alberto Eduardo Ham	1993
Víctor Enrique Reauge	1998
Marcelo Eduardo Huergo	2003
Ana C. Pisano (Charge d'Affaires)	2008
María Esther Bondanza	2009
Ana C. Pisano (Charge d'Affaires)	2012
Laura Bernal	2016
Sandra Moira Wilkinson	2020 to present

Glossaries

GLOSSARY OF IRISH-ARGENTINE TERMS (SOCIOLECT)

Porteño vocabulary	Spanish	English
camp	*campo*	countryside
convention	*conventillo*	boarding house
cheena	*china*	young girl
department	*departamento*	flat or apartment
divert	*divertir*	have fun
grip	*gripe*	influenza
knock about	*peón*	migrant farm labourer
mate/matty	*mate*	tea
milics	*milicios*	members of the military
nap	*from napolitano*	Neapolitan (all Italians)
Porteño	*Porteño*	people born in Buenos Aires
pupil	*alumno*	boarder
señalled	*señallar*	marked or branded

I am grateful to Juan José Delaney who compiled this list.
See *What, Che? Integration, adaptation and assimilation of the Irish-Argentine community through its language and literature* (Ediciones Universidad del Salvador, Buenos Aires, 2019).

GLOSSARY OF OTHER SPANISH WORDS USED IN THE TEXT
(translated in english)

calle   street
capataz   person in charge of a few ranch hands
chacarero   small farmer
criollo   people of Spanish descent born in Latin America

encuentro　annual meeting of Irish Federation

estancia　large farm or ranch

galpón　large shed or warehouse on estancia

gaucho　an Argentine term which is inadequately translated as cowboy. A skilled horseman and farm worker. Neither *vaquero* nor *charro* may adequately capture that meaning.

mate　tea

mayordomo　foreman

partido　an administrative and political division of the provinces in Argentina; can also mean a political party

puestero　a farm worker or shepherd who is given charge of a parcel of land with a hut in which to live

pulpería　a general store in town or countryside. Like Irish pubs in old times which sold groceries, clothes, saddlery goods and drink, the latter often being consumed on the premises, sometimes resulting in fights.

quinta　small farm but sometimes means a secondary residence in countryside

In the above list, I used a number of words cited in the glossary given at the back of Edmundo Murray's *Becoming Irlandés: Private narratives of the Irish emigration to Argentina (1844–1912)* (LOLA, Buenos Aires, 2004), pp. 159–60, and Susan Wilkinson (ed.), *Recollections of an Irish-born Doctor in Nineteenth-Century Argentina: Arthur Pageitt Greene (1848–1933)* (The Memoir Club, Dublin, 2015), pp. 157–8.

GLOSSARY OF IRISH TERMS

Bunreacht na hÉireann　Constitution of Ireland (1937)

ceann comhairle　speaker of the Dáil

Conradh na Gaeilge　Gaelic League

Dáil Éireann　lower house of Irish parliament

President of the Executive Council　The title of prime minister between 1922 and 1937

Fianna Fáil　Soldiers of Destiny

Fine Gael　Family of the Irish

gaeltacht　Irish-speaking areas

Oireachtas　houses of parliament

Sinn Féin　Ourselves Alone

Saorstát Éireann　Irish Free State

Seanad Éireann   upper house of Irish parliament
teachta dála   TD or member of Irish parliament
taoiseach   prime minister
taoisigh   prime ministers
tánaiste   deputy prime minister
uachtarán na hÉireann   president of Ireland

LEXICON OF WORDS AND PHRASES USED IN THE TIME OF THE
CIVILIAN MILITARY DICTATORSHIP IN ARGENTINA, 1976–83

asado   Traditional Argentine barbecue. But term used for the burning of the
bodies of prisoners.

capucha   hood

chupado/a from *chupar*   slang for being disappeared (sucked up) by armed
forces

comida de pescado   fish food, a term used by the military who threw prisoners
to their death from planes over the River Plate

desaparecida/o   A term which has its origins in the Nazi doctrine of the Night
and Fog when prisoners were made to disappear without trace and with
no possibility of being tracked by family or friends. During the civilian
military dictatorship between 1976 and 1983, people were *chupado*, hooded
and taken to clandestine detention centres where they were handcuffed,
shackled and later tortured and many were murdered.

guerra sucia (dirty war)   I have not used that phrase in Spanish or in English
other than when it appears in a quotation. Human rights organisations
argue that it was a euphemism employed by the Argentine armed forces
claiming that the country was in a state of civil war and that 'different
methods' were required to preserve Christian values and to secure a victory
over the guerrillas and their supporters.

orga   military slang for *organización* or revolutionary group like the Montonero
guerrillas

parrilla   Argentine traditional grill for cooking an *asado*. Term adapted by
torturers for bed or table on which a victim was strapped down.

picana   a cattle prod used by torturers

Proceso de Reorganización Nacional   The Process of National Reorganisation
was the term used by the civilian military government to describe itself in
1976.

Operación Cóndor   Secret coordinated plan carried out by several South American dictatorships to eliminate left-wing opponents. Beginning in 1968, the dictatorships supplemented the concept of territorial defence with a plan based on ideological frontiers which targeted people based on their political ideas rather than on any crimes committed. This transnational cooperation allowed the intelligence services of different countries to cooperate and to work within all of the countries in the consortium. *Cóndor* specialised in targeted kidnappings followed by interrogation/torture. The disappeared were transferred across borders. In 1976, *Cóndor* set up a squad of assassins who travelled worldwide to eliminate 'targets'. (See work by J. Patrice McSherry, *Predatory State: Operation Cóndor and Covert War in Latin America* (Rowman & Littlefield, New York, 2005)

traslado   Often 'official' language for a prisoner being taken away to be murdered. Prisoners were often told that they had been given their *boleta* or ticket.

submarino   water-boarding

vuelo/s   Flight – but, in context of 1976–82, it meant death flight. Drugged prisoners were loaded onto a plane, flown out over the River Plate, stripped, and dumped into the sea below.

I am grateful to Fátima Cabrera, a torture-survivor, for helping provide an explanation for many of the above macabre words, which debase the currency of language. See also Marguerite Feitlowitz, *A Lexicon of Terror: Argentina and the Legacies of Torture* (Oxford University Press, Oxford, 1998), pp. 51–61.

Notes

(all URLs correct at the time of writing)

Acknowledgements

1 I spent many hours talking to Fátima's mother Doña Blanca who shared her personal experiences with me of living in Tucumán, as did her other children Inés, Adela and Juan.

2 Under the direction of Prof. Nuala Finnigan, University College Cork in 2018 became the institutional home for SILAS within higher education in Ireland. Edward Walsh continues to make a significant contribution to our understanding of the area: http://www.irlandeses. org/.

3 This initiative was taken at the invitation of Ambassador Justin Harman, Dr Paula Ortiz and María Verónica Repetti, in USAL, Buenos Aires, together with Drs Izarra and Delaney. The website for the association is: https://asociaciondeestudiosirlandesesdelsur.wordpress.com/. See also site for related associations: https://asociaciondeestudiosirlandesesdelsur.wordpress. com/page/.

4 Verónica Repetti, pro secretaria Académica de la Escuela, coordinated with Mariano Galazzi the translation of my earlier book, *La Independencia de Irlanda: La Conexión Argentina* [*The Independence of Ireland: The Argentine Connection*] (USAL, Buenos Aires, 2016). The translators were Rafael Abuchedid, Lucía Carretero, Mónica Eleta and Victoria Zimmermann. I have not published this book in English.

Introduction

1 See Sir Ernest Satow, *Guide to Diplomatic Practice* (Longman, London, 1979), volumes 1 and 2, quoted in Iver B. Neumann, *At Home with the Diplomats: Inside a European Foreign Ministry* (Cornell University Press, Ithaca and London, 2012), p. 1.

2 While it is the case that the 1961 convention only recognises the diplomacy of states, the world has expanded greatly, taking into account the role played by transnational corporations, intergovernmental organisations (IGOs), non-governmental organisations (NGOs) and transnational actors like major religions and major religious orders. In the pandemic which began in 2020, for example, the voice of the World Health Organization was very powerful. See Joseph M. Siracusa, *Diplomacy: A Very Short Introduction* (Oxford University Press, Oxford, 2010), p. 1 and p. 106 ff.

3 Siracusa, *Diplomacy*, pp. 4–5.

4 William J. Burns, *The Back Channel: A Memoir of American Diplomacy and the Case for Its Renewal* (Hurst and Co., London, 2019), pp. 388–423.

5 Ibid., p. 419.

6 Satow, op. cit., pp. 168–74, p. 10; Sir Henry Wotton was an English diplomat and politician who sat in the House of Commons in 1614 and 1625. He served as secretary to the earl of Essex in Ireland between April and September 1599. Satow records that Wotton did not

mean that the witticism should have been taken at face value. It was a light-hearted entry in a friend's album.

7 Satow, op. cit., pp. 168–9. There are many quotes which portray the diplomatic profession as being characterised by cynicism, dissimulation and intrigue, a view reinforced by practitioners like the French diplomat Charles Maurice de Talleyrand (1754–1838), who is credited with stating: 'A diplomat who says "yes" means "maybe", a diplomat who says "maybe" means "no", and a diplomat who says "no" is no diplomat.'

8 Ronan McGreevy, 'Argentina's Ambassador to Ireland Buried in Co. Mayo', *Irish Times*, https://www.irishtimes.com/news/ireland/irish-news/covid-19-argentina-s-ambassador-to-ireland-buried-in-co-mayo-1.4254473.

9 The minister for external affairs, Seán MacBride, appointed Josephine McNeill to The Hague, in 1950. She became the first woman to head up an Irish mission abroad. From Fermoy in County Cork, Josephine McNeill was born in 1895. She studied French and German in UCD and was a teacher in Mayo and Tipperary when she joined Cumann na mBan in 1918 and had a distinguished career during the war of independence. She married James McNeill in 1923, a brother of the leader of the Irish Volunteers, Eoin. Her husband served as high commissioner in London and later governor general in Ireland. She was chair of the Irish Countrywomen's Association (ICA) up to 1950. After leaving The Hague in 1955, she was appointed to Stockholm for a year and then was moved to Switzerland. She remained in Berne until her retirement in 1960. See Oliver O'Hanlon, 'Josephine McNeill, an Irish Diplomatic Trailblazer', *Irish Times*, https://www.irishtimes.com/opinion/an-irishman-s-diary-on-josephine-mcneill-an-irish-diplomatic-trailblazer-1.4175388; see also Ann Marie O'Brien, 'A Century of Change: The (In)Visibility of Women in the Irish Foreign Service, 1919–2019', *Irish Studies in International Affairs*, vol. 30, 2019, pp. 73–92, at p. 84, www.jstor.org/stable/10.3318/isia.2019.30.6.

10 Mary MacDiarmada, *Art O'Brien and Irish Nationalism in London, 1900–25* (Four Courts Press, Dublin, 2020), pp. 186–9.

11 David Victor Kelly, *The Ruling Few: or, the Human Background to Diplomacy* (Hollis & Carger, London, 1952); Francis Pakenham was the British envoy extraordinary and minister plenipotentiary to Argentina between 1885 and 1896.

12 I interviewed Archbishop Coveney in Crosshaven, Cork, in 2013. He served as secretary in the apostolic nunciature in Buenos Aires from 1973 to 1976.

13 In the course of my research, I got to know Kevin Mullen's two brothers, Jerome and Mgr Austin Mullen. I very much appreciated their friendship and help.

14 See Dermot Keogh, 'Profile of Joseph Walshe: Secretary of the Department of External Affairs, 1922–1946', *Irish Studies in International Affairs*, vol. 3, no.2, 1990, pp. 59–81; see also Michael Kennedy, '"Nobody Knows and Ever Shall Know from Me That I Have Written It": Joseph Walshe, Éamon de Valera and the Execution of Irish Foreign Policy, 1932–8', *Irish Studies in International Affairs*, vol. 14, 2003, pp. 165–83, https://www.jstor.org/stable/30001970. Aengus Nolan, *Joseph Walshe and the Management of Irish Foreign Policy, 1922–1946: A Study in Diplomatic and Administrative History* (Mercier Press, Cork, 1997).

15 See Dermot Keogh, *Ireland and the Vatican: The Politics and Diplomacy of Church–State Relations* (Cork University Press, Cork, 1995).

16 Pro-nuncio is the name given to a papal ambassador to a country that does not grant the pope's ambassador automatic precedence. Apostolic delegate, another category of papal representation, is appointed to countries that do not have diplomatic relations with the Holy See. He does not have the power to deal with civil governments and his relations are with the national hierarchy. For a background to Vatican diplomacy, see André Dupuy, *La Diplomatie du Saint-Siège après le IIe Concile du Vatican: Le Pontificat de Paul VI 1963–1978* (Téqui,

Paris, no date); Mario Oliveri, *The Representatives: The Real Nature and Function of Papal Legates* (Van Duren, Gerrards Cross, London, 1980); and Thomas J. Reese, *Inside the Vatican* (Harvard University Press, Cambridge, MA, 1996).

17 Ireland refused an invitation to join the North Atlantic Treaty Organisation when it was founded on 4 April 1949. Ireland's request to join the United Nations when it was founded on 24 October 1945 was turned down; it was accepted ten years later on 14 December 1955. Ireland has played an active role in the UN General Assembly and when elected for a two-year term as a member of the Security Council in 1961, 1981, 2001 and 2021.

18 I have been told that one Irish ambassador may have resigned over policy differences. But I have no name nor have I found independent evidence to support that view.

19 Two Basque political activists and three members of the communist revolutionary organisation FRAP were executed in 1975 while General Francisco Franco was in power. With the exception of Ireland, the EEC countries withdrew their ambassadors in protest. At the time, I was in favour of recalling the Irish ambassador and picketed the Spanish embassy and Iberia offices in protest.

20 Dermot Keogh, *Ireland and Europe 1919–1989: A Diplomatic and Political History* (Hibernian University Press, Cork and Dublin, 1990), pp. 67–70; during the Spanish civil war, I describe in those pages how the then minister for external affairs, Éamon de Valera, insisted on maintaining the distinction between state and government.

21 Following the shooting dead of thirteen unarmed civilians by the British army in Derry on 30 January 1972, the Irish government recalled Ambassador Donal O'Sullivan in protest. A chargé, Charles Whelan, remained in London as did other staff members. In 2011, the Holy See recalled the papal nuncio, Giuseppe Leanza, from Dublin for consultation following a speech made by the taoiseach, Enda Kenny, in which he criticised Rome for its failures to deal with clerical child sexual abuse and its further failure to cooperate with the Irish government in the investigation of serious allegations.

22 For the first full-length study of women and the Irish foreign service, see Ann Marie O'Brien, *The Ideal Diplomat? Women and Irish Foreign Affairs, 1946–90* (Four Courts Press, Dublin, 2020).

23 Because Ireland remained a member of the British Commonwealth until 1949, the titles of Irish envoys abroad were high commissioner and also envoy extraordinary and minister plenipotentiary. Outside the British Commonwealth, Ireland raised its legations to the status of embassies in keeping with contemporary practices between states.

24 I am grateful to Mr Seán Donlon, then secretary (now called secretary general) of the Department of Foreign Affairs, for granting me speedy access to Iveagh House files. See Frank Litton (ed.), 'The Irish Constitutional Revolution: An Analysis of the Making of the Constitution', *Administration*, vol. 35, no. 4. 1988, pp. 4–84.

25 Dermot Keogh, *Ireland and Europe, 1919–1948* (Gill & Macmillan, Dublin, 1988), p. 256; published in paperback: *Ireland and Europe 1919–1989* (Hibernian University Press, Cork and Dublin, 1989).

26 Dermot Keogh, *The Vatican, the Bishops and Irish Politics* (Cambridge University Press, Cambridge, 1986); *Twentieth Century Ireland: Nation and State* (Gill & Macmillan, Dublin, 1994) [reissued 2005 with extra chapter covering the period between the 1980s and 2005]; *Ireland and the Vatican: The Politics and Diplomacy of Church and State, 1922–1960* (Cork University Press, Cork, 1995); *Jews in Twentieth Century Ireland: Refugees, Anti-Semitism and the Holocaust* (Cork University Press, Cork, 1998); *Jack Lynch: A Biography* (Gill & Macmillan, Dublin, 2008); *La Independencia de Irlanda*; (with Ann Keogh), *Sir Bertram Windle: The Honan Bequest and the Modernisation of University College Cork, 1904–1919* (Cork University Press, Cork, 2010).

27 I was a member of the editorial team from the time it was established until I decided to step down in 2019.

28 Michael Kennedy, '"Publishing a Secret History": The Documents on Irish Foreign Policy Project', *Irish Studies in International Affairs*, vol. 9, 1998, pp. 103–17; 'Establishing and Operating a Diplomatic Documents Publishing Project', *Irish Studies in International Affairs*, vol. 15, 2004, pp. 191–204, https://www.jstor.org/stable/30002086?refreqid=excelsior%3 A09c19c624b3fda3974409dd9239d359b; '"In Spite of All Impediments": The Early Years of the Irish Diplomatic Service', *History Ireland*, vol. 7, no. 1, 1999, pp. 18–21, https://www. jstor.org/stable/27724635?refreqid=excelsior%3A1997246bcfc7fb48ac52942a6cde8af6; and '"Nobody Knows and Ever Shall Know from Me That I Have Written It"'. See also John Gibney, Michael Kennedy and Kate O'Malley, *Ireland: A Voice among the Nations* (RIA, Dublin, 2019).

29 Ronan Fanning, an original editor of the project, was a forceful advocate in those early decades for the study of diplomatic history. See his 'The United States and Irish Participation in NATO: The Debate of 1950', *Irish Studies in International Affairs*, vol. 1, no. 1, 1979, pp. 39–48; 'Irish Neutrality: An Historical Review', *Irish Studies in International Affairs*, vol. 1, no. 3, 1982, pp. 27–38.

30 There are entries for three Dáil Éireann envoys who served in Argentina between 1919 and 1922. See John Gibney, Eamonn Bulfin; Pauric J. Dempsey, Shaun Boylan, Laurence Ginnell; and Marie Coleman, Patrick John Little. In Michael Kennedy's entry for Thomas Vincent Commins, it is stated: 'Appointed minister to Argentina in May 1959, he spent only a matter of months in Buenos Aires before being appointed ambassador to Italy (1960–62).' There are no entries for Matthew Murphy, Leo T. Skentelbery or Timothy Joseph Horan.

31 Niall Keogh, *Con Cremin* (Mercier Press, Cork and Dublin, 2006); Eugene Broderick, *John Hearne: Architect of the 1937 Constitution of Ireland* (Irish Academic Press, Dublin, 2017); Aengus Nolan, *Joseph Walshe: Irish Foreign Policy 1922–1946* (Mercier Press, Cork and Dublin, 2008); Barry Whelan, *Ireland's Revolutionary Diplomat: A Biography of Leopold Kerney* (Notre Dame University Press, South Bend, 2019); Owen McGee, *A History of Ireland in International Relations* (Irish Academic Press, Newbridge, 2020).

32 Mervyn O'Driscoll, *Ireland, Germany and the Nazis: Politics and Diplomacy, 1919–1939* (Four Courts Press, Dublin, 2004); *Ireland, West Germany and the New Europe 1949–73* (Manchester University Press, Manchester, 2018); and with Dermot Keogh (eds), *Ireland in World War Two: Diplomacy and Survival* (Mercier Press, Cork, 2004); and with Dermot Keogh, *Ireland through European Eyes: Western Europe, the EEC and Ireland, 1945–1973* (Cork University Press, Cork, 2013).

33 Paula L. Wylie, *Ireland and the Cold War: Diplomacy and Recognition, 1949–63* (Irish Academic Press, Dublin, 2006).

34 Mark Hull, *Irish Secrets: German Espionage in Ireland, 1939–45* (Irish Academic Press, Dublin and Portland, 2003).

35 Maurice Fitzgerald, *Protectionism to Liberalisation: Ireland and the EEC, 1957 to 1966* (Ashgate, Aldershot, 2000).

36 Nolan, *Joseph Walshe*.

37 Micheál Martin, *Freedom to Choose: Cork and Party Politics in Ireland 1918–1932* (Collins Press, Cork, 2009).

38 Kevin McCarthy, *Gold, Silver and Green: The Irish Olympic Journey 1896–1924* (Cork University Press, Cork, 2010).

39 David Ryan, *US–Sandinista Diplomatic Relations: Voice of Intolerance* (Macmillan, London and New York, 1995).

40 Robert McNamara, *Britain, Nasser and the Balance of Power in the Middle East, 1952–1967: From the Egyptian Revolution to the Six Day War* (Frank Cass, London and Portland, 2003).

41 In UCC, I supervised many undergraduate and postgraduate theses on Latin America to doctoral level, including the following MAs and MPhils: Gertrude Cotter, 'Britain and Perón's Argentina, 1946–1955' (1989); Geraldine Barry, 'Batista to Castro: Anglo-Cuban Relations in Transition, 1958–1959' (1993); David Ryan (PhD, 1992), 'An Examination of Diplomatic Relations between the United States and Nicaragua during the Reagan Presidencies'; see his monograph, *US–Sandinista Diplomatic Relations: Voice of Intolerance* (Macmillan, London and New York, 1995).

42 Kate O'Malley, *Ireland, India and Empire: Indo-Irish Radical Connections, 1919–1964* (Manchester University Press, Manchester, 2009); Mervyn O'Driscoll, Review of *Ireland, India and Empire: Indo-Irish Radical Connections, 1919–1964*, *Irish Historical Studies*, vol. 36, no. 143, 2009, pp. 465–7, https://www.jstor.org/stable/20720352?refreqid=excelsior%3A 7631eda31b7b8601c17ac5685b6bf9c4; Kate O'Malley, 'The Elephant and Partition: Ireland and India', *History Ireland*, vol. 18, no. 4, 2010, pp. 10–11, https://www.jstor.org/stable/ i27823005; Kate O'Malley, 'Ireland and India: Post-independence Diplomacy', *Irish Studies in International Affairs*, vol. 22, 2011, pp. 145–62, https://www.jstor.org/stable/41413198; Kate O'Malley, 'Learning the Tricks of the Imperial Secession Trade: Irish and Indian Nationalism in the '30s and '40s', *History Ireland*, vol. 18, no. 4, 2010, pp. 32–5, https://www. historyireland.com/20th-century-contemporary-history/politics-learning-the-tricks-of-the-imperial-secession-trade-irish-and-indian-nationalism-in-the-30s-and-40s/; Michael Holmes and Denis Holmes (eds), *Ireland and India: Connections, Comparisons, Contrasts* (Folens, Dublin, 1997); Michael Silvestri, *Ireland and India: Nationalism, Empire and Memory* (Palgrave Macmillan, Basingstoke, 2009); Tadhg Foley et al. (eds), *Ireland and India: Colonies, Culture and Empire* (Irish Academic Press, Dublin, 2006); Eunan O'Halpin (ed.), *MI5 and Ireland 1939–1945* (Irish Academic Press, Dublin, 2003).

43 Kevin O'Sullivan, *Ireland, Africa and the End of Empire: Small State Identity in the Cold War, 1955–75* (Manchester: Manchester University Press, 2012; paperback edn 2014); 'Humanitarian Encounters: Biafra, NGOs and Imaginings of the Third World in Britain and Ireland, 1967–70', in Lasse Heerten and A. Dirk Moses (eds), *Postcolonial Conflict and the Question of Genocide: The Nigeria–Biafra War, 1967–1970* (Abingdon: Routledge, 2017), pp. 259–77; '"The Cause of Nationality is Sacred in ... Africa as in Ireland": Ireland and Sub-Saharan Africa at the United Nations, 1960–75', in Michael Kennedy and Deirdre McMahon (eds), *Obligations and Responsibilities: Ireland at the United Nations 1955–2005* (Dublin: Institute of Public Administration, 2006); 'Between Internationalism and Empire: Ireland, the "Like-Minded" Group, and the Search for a New International Order, 1974–82', *International History Review*, vol. 37, no. 5, 2015, pp. 1083–101; and Michael Holmes et al., *The Poor Relations: Irish Foreign Policy and the Third World* (Trócaire with Gill & Macmillan, Dublin, 1993).

44 Bernadette Whelan, *Ireland and the Marshall Plan, 1947–1957* (Four Courts Press, Dublin, 2000); 'Ireland and the Marshall Plan', *Irish Economic and Social History*, vol. 19, 1992, pp. 49–70. 'The New World and the Old: American Marshall Planners in Ireland, 1947–57', *Irish Studies in International Affairs*, vol. 12, 2001, pp. 179–89, https://www.jstor.org/ stable/30002065; *United States Foreign Policy and Ireland: From Empire to Independence, 1913–1929* (Four Courts Press, Dublin, 2006); *American Government in Ireland, 1790–1913* (Manchester University Press, Manchester, 2016); 'Recognition of the Irish Free State, 1924: The Diplomatic Context to the Appointment of Timothy Smiddy as the First Irish Minister to the US', *Irish Studies in International Affairs*, vol. 26, 2015, pp. 121–5; and *De Valera and Roosevelt: Irish–American Diplomacy in Times of Crisis, 1932–1939* (Cambridge University Press, Cambridge, 2021).

45 Francis M. Carroll, *America and the Making of an Independent Ireland* (New York University Press, New York, 2021).

46 Michael Kennedy, *Ireland and the League of Nations, 1919–46* (Irish Academic Press, Dublin, 1996); with Deirdre McMahon (eds), *Obligations and Responsibilities*; '"If There Is No Other Suitable Candidate": Why Ireland was Elected to the United Nations Security Council in 1961', in Gabriel Robin (director), *8th International Conference of Editors of Diplomatic Documents: About States and UNO* (Peter Lang, Brussels, 2008), pp. 251–62; with Comdt Art Magennis, *Ireland, the United Nations and the Congo* (Four Courts Press, Dublin, 2014); with Till Geiger, *Ireland, Europe and the Marshall Plan* (Four Courts Press, Dublin, 2004); with Kate O'Malley, *Ireland: Sixty Years at the United Nations* (DFAT/RIA, Dublin, 2015).

47 Eunan O'Halpin, *Spying on Ireland: British Intelligence and Irish Neutrality during the Second World War* (Oxford University Press, Oxford, 2008); *Defending Ireland: The Irish State and Its Enemies since 1922* (Oxford University Press, Oxford, 2000).

48 Rory Miller, *Ireland and the Middle East: Trade, Society and Peace* (Irish Academic Press, Dublin, 2007); 'The Look of the Irish: Irish Jews and the Zionist Project, 1900–48, *Jewish Historical Studies*, vol. 43, 2011, pp. 189–211; *Britain, Palestine and Empire: The Mandate Years* (Routledge, New York and London, 2016); *Ireland and the Palestine Question: 1948–2004* (Irish Academic Press, Dublin 2005); 'Frank Aiken, the UN and the Six Day War, June 1967', *Irish Studies in International Affairs*, vol. 14, 2003, pp. 57–73, www.jstor.org/stable/30001964; Marie-Violaine Louvet, *Civil Society, Post-Colonialism and Transnational Solidarity: The Irish and the Middle East Conflict* (Palgrave Macmillan, London, 2016).

49 Filipe Ribeiro de Meneses, 'Investigating Portugal, Salazar and the New State: The Work of the Irish Legation in Lisbon, 1942–1945', *Contemporary European History*, vol. 11, no. 3, August 2002, pp. 391–408; 'Meeting Salazar: Irish Dignitaries and Diplomats in Portugal, 1942–60', *Archivium Hibernicum*, vol. 64, 2011, pp. 323–48.

50 Patrick James O'Farrell, *The Irish in Australia: 1788 to the Present* (Cork University Press, Cork, 2001); *Vanished Kingdoms: Irish in Australia and New Zealand. A Personal Excursion* (New South Wales University Press, Kensington, NSW, 1990); Laurence M. Geary and Andrew McCarthy (eds), *Ireland, Australia and New Zealand: History, Politics and Culture* (Irish Academic Press, Dublin, 2008); Colm Kiernan, *Ireland and Australia* (Angus & Robertson, North Ryde, NSW, 1984); F.B. Smith, *Ireland, England, and Australia: Essays in Honour of Oliver MacDonagh* (Australian National University, Canberra, 1990); Malcolm Campbell, *Ireland's New Worlds: Immigrants, Politics, and Society in the United States and Australia, 1915–1922* (University of Wisconsin Press, Madison, 2008); Jeff Kildea, *Anzacs and Ireland* (UNSW Press and Cork University Press, Sydney and Cork, 2013); Richard Reid, *Not Just Ned: A True History of the Irish in Australia* (National Museum of Australia Press, Canberra, 2011).

51 Peter Kuch and Lisa Marr (eds), *New Zealand's Response to the 1916 Rising* (Cork University Press, Cork, 2020).

52 Donal P. McCracken (ed.), The Irish in Southern Africa, 1795–1910 (Ireland and Southern Africa Project, Durban, 1992); *The Irish Pro-Boers: 1877–1902* (Perskokor, Johannesburg, 1989); 'Imperial Running Dogs or Wild Geese Reporters? Irish Journalists in South Africa', *Historia*, vol. 58, no. 1, 2013, pp. 122–38; *MacBride's Brigade: Irish Commandos in the Anglo-Boer War* (Four Courts Press, Dublin, 1999); Anthony J. Jordan, *Major John MacBride, 1865–1916* (Westport Historical Society, Westport, 1991); Donald H. Akenson, *God's Peoples: Covenant and Land in South Africa, Israel, and Ulster* (Cornell University Press, Ithaca, 1992).

53 Kevin O'Sullivan, 'Irish Diplomatic History in the Twenty-First Century: After the Gold Rush', *Irish Economic and Social History*, vol. 37, no. 5, 2012.

54 Peadar Kirby, *Ireland and Latin America: Links and Lessons* (Trócaire and Gill & Macmillan, Dublin, 1991); *The Church in Latin America: Lessons in Liberation* (Dominican Publications, Dublin, 1981).

55 Kennedy, *Ireland and the League of Nations*, pp. 177, 180–4; '"Mr Blythe, I Think, Hears from Him Occasionally": The Experiences of Irish Diplomats in Latin America, 1919–1923', in Michael Kennedy and Joseph Skelly (eds), *Irish Foreign Policy 1919–1966: From Independence to Internationalism* (Four Courts Press, Dublin, 2000), pp. 44–60.

56 Paul Hand, '"This Is Not a Place for Delicate or Nervous or Impatient Diplomats": The Irish Legation in Perón's Argentina (1948–55)', *Irish Studies in International Affairs*, vol. 16, 2005, pp. 175–92, www.jstor.org/stable/30001941.

57 Whelan, *Ireland's Revolutionary Diplomat*, pp. 231–40.

58 McGee, *A History of Ireland in International Relations*, pp. 355 and 359.

59 The index in my book *Twentieth Century Ireland: Revolution and State Building* (Gill & Macmillan, Dublin, 2005) makes no reference to Latin America and neither does John J. Lee in *Ireland 1912–1985* (Cambridge University Press, Cambridge, 1989) but has a small section on the Falklands/Malvinas crisis and war.

60 Thomas Bartlett (ed.), *The Cambridge History of Ireland: 1880 to the Present* (Cambridge University Press, Cambridge, 2019). There is no reference in the index to either Latin America or South America. There are two references to Argentina, one a reference to the existence of a branch of the Gaelic League in Argentina and a second to its economic performance in the 1920s. There are two references to the Falkland Islands. There is a reference to the sculptor Michael Bulfin, but no reference to either his grandfather, William, or his father, Eamonn. In Daithí Ó Corráin's fine essay on Catholicism in Ireland, he refers to the increase from the 1920s in Irish clerical and religious up to the 1970s 'when they plateaued at about 6,000 spread across Africa, Asia and Latin America' (p. 747). There is one reference (p. 532) to Bishop Eamonn Casey of Galway and his criticism of US policy in 'South America', but no reference to the Irish in Argentina. My remarks are not a criticism of the volume. I wish merely to point to the invisibility of Ireland's relationship with Latin America in much of contemporary Irish historiography. That also holds true for my earlier books.

61 Gibney, Kennedy and O'Malley, *Ireland: A Voice among the Nations*.

62 Eamonn Bulfin and Laurence Ginnell, two Dáil Éireann envoys who served in Argentina between 1919 and 1922, are the only diplomats named in the index who served in the region.

63 His grave is marked by an imposing monument in Recoleta Cemetery. The Instituto Browniano was established on 22 February 1948 to study and keep his name and contribution in the public eye. This foundation was elevated to the status of *Instituto Nacional* on 18 December 1996. His statue was moved from near the Casa Rosada to near Puerto Madero. A statue of Brown, a gift of the Argentine navy, was unveiled in Dublin in 2006 and relocated in 2012 to Sir John Rogerson's Quay. In his birthplace in Foxford, County Mayo, Brown is commemorated in other bronzes. The Argentine navy has named a number of vessels after him. Four football teams proudly bear his name as does a province in greater Buenos Aires and a department in the Chaco. Both the Irish and Argentine governments issued a stamp to mark the centenary of his death in 1957.

64 John de Courcy Ireland, *The Admiral from Mayo: A Life of Almirante William Brown of Foxford, Father of the Argentine Navy* (E. Burke, Dublin, 1995); Thomas Malcomson, 'My Inestimable Friend: An Account of the Life of Rear-Admiral William Brown (1764–1814)', *Mariner's Mirror*, vol. 104, no. 3, 2018, pp. 358–60; and Desmond McCabe, 'William Brown', *Dictionary of Irish Biography*, https://www.dib.ie/biography/brown-william-a1018.

65 In 2010, the Venezuelan government presented a bust of O'Leary which was placed in Fitzgerald's Park, Cork. In 2019, President Michael D. Higgins unveiled a plaque at O'Leary's home in Barrack Street, Cork. Eoin English, 'Plaque to Honour Cork-born Hero of South America', *Irish Examiner*, 11 February 2019.

66 Robert F. McNerney, 'Daniel Florence O'Leary: Soldier, Diplomat, and Historian', *The Americas*, vol 22, no. 3, January 1966, pp. 292–312; Daniel Florencio O'Leary, *Bolívar and the*

War of Independence (University of Texas Press, Austin, 1970); *Memorias del General O'Leary* (Ministerio de Educación, Bogotá, 1952–3); *Escritos Politicos del General O'Leary* (El Ancora Editores, Bogotá, 1981); R.A. Humphreys (ed.), *The Detached Recollections of General D.F. O'Leary 1800–1854* (Athlone Press, London, 1969); *Memorias del General Daniel Florencio O'Leary* (Ministerio de la Defensa, Venezuela, 1981); *Últimos Años de la Vida Pública de Bólivar: Memorias del General O'Leary 1826–1929* (Editorial-América, Madrid, 1916); *Junín y Ayacucho* (Editorial-América, Madrid, 1919) and Angel Crisanti, *El Archibo del Libertador: Indice Collección* (Imprenta Nacional, Caracas, 1956); J.G. Healey, 'Daniel Florence O'Leary', *Cork Historical and Archaeological Society Journal*, vol. 64, 1959, pp. 28–34.

67 John [Juan] Mackenna was born in Clogher, County Tyrone, in 1771. He went to Spain and studied in the Royal School of Mathematics, in Barcelona. He rose in the ranks in the Spanish army. He went to Peru in 1796 and was appointed governor of Osorno, in southern Chile, and later governor of Valparaíso in 1811 in the new republic of Chile. He saw action at the battle of Membrillar in 1814. He died in a duel on 21 November 1814. Raúl Tellez Yañez, *El General Juan MacKenna* (Editorial Francisco de Aguirre, Buenos Aires, 1976). See also Edmundo Murray, 'John Mackenna', in *Dictionary of Irish Latin American Biography*, https://www.irlandeses.org/dilab_mackennaj.htm.

68 Tim Fanning, *Don Juan O'Brien: An Irish Adventurer in Nineteenth-Century South America* (Cork University Press, Cork, 2020); and Patrick M. Geoghegan, 'John Thomond O'Brien', https://www.dib.ie/biography/obrien-john-thomond-a6478.

69 Tim Fanning, *Paisanos: The Forgotten Irish who Changed the Face of Latin America* (Gill Books, Dublin, 2016), and in Spanish translation, *Paisanos: Los Irlandes Olvidados que Cambiaron la Faz de Latinoamerica* (Editorial Sudamericana, Buenos Aires, 2017); see endnotes for Chapter 1 of this volume for further details of publications in this area.

70 See Fanning, *Don Juan O'Brien*, and Geoghegan, 'John Thomond O'Brien'.

71 O'Brien died in Lisbon in 1861 on his way back to Latin America.

72 Margaret Brehony was also the organiser of an influential travelling exhibition, 'The Irish in Latin America'. She researched and wrote the text for the exhibition which was launched by President Michael D. Higgins in 2016 and has since been shown in a number of cities in the region including Havana, Buenos Aires, Mexico City, Santiago and São Paulo. Department of Foreign Affairs and Trade, 'Exhibition – The Irish in Latin America', https://www.dfa.ie/irish-embassy/mexico/news-and-events/2017/irish-latin-america-exhibition/.

73 Gabriela McEvoy, *La Expeniencia Invisible: Inmigrantes Irlandeses en el Perú* (Universidad del Perú, Lima, 2018).

74 Donald Harman Akenson, *'If the Irish Ran the World': Monserrat, 1630–1730* (McGill-Queen's University Press, Kingston, Montreal, Liverpool, 1997); see also *Radharc* film *The Black Irish of Montserrat* (1976) and Michael D. Higgins documentary *The Other Emerald Isle* (1986), https://www.youtube.com/watch?v=bXhqqCBV_6c.

75 NUI, Maynooth, MA thesis, http://mural.maynoothuniversity.ie/325/.

76 Mary Harris, 'Irish Historical Writing on Latin America and on Irish Links with Latin America', in Csaba Lévai (ed.), *Europe and the World in European Historiography* (PLUS, Pisa University Press, Pisa, 2006); Harris, 'Irish Images of Religious Conflict in Mexico in the 1920s', in Mary N. Harris (ed.), *Sights and Insights: Interactive Images of Europe and the Wider World* (PLUS, Pisa University Press, Pisa, 2007).

77 Edmundo Murray, *Devenir Irlandés: Narrativas Íntimas de la Emigración Irlandesa a la Argentina 1844–1912* (Eudeba, Buenos Aires, 2004); see also revised and updated edition in English: *Becoming Irlandés: Private Narratives of the Irish Emigration to Argentina, 1844–1912* (LOLA, Buenos Aires, 2006).

78 See *Narrativas de la Diaspora Irlandesa bajo la Cruz del Sur* (Corregidor, Buenos Aires, 2010); Laura P.Z. Izarra, 'Locations and Identities in Irish Diasporic Narratives', *Hungarian*

Journal of English and American Studies (HJEAS), vol. 10, nos. 1/2, 2004, pp. 341–52, www.jstor.org/stable/41274286. See also endnote 3 in the Acknowledgements.

79 *ABEI: The Brazilian Journal of Irish Studies*, http://revistas.fflch.usp.br/abei.

80 Juan José Delaney, *What, Che? Integration, Adaptation and Assimilation of the Irish-Argentine Community through Its Language and Literature* (doctoral dissertation, 2016; published in 2018 under the same title by USAL, Buenos Aires, 2017).

81 Obituary, Andrew Graham-Yooll, *Guardian*, 18 July 2019, https://www.theguardian.com/world/2019/jul/18/andrew-graham-yooll-obituary.

82 See Graham-Yooll, *The Forgotten Colony: A History of the English-Speaking Communities in Argentina* (Hutchinson, London, 2007) and *State of Fear* (Eland Books, London, 2009); his papers were presented to the Universidad de San Andrés, Buenos Aires, where a run of the paper *The Standard* is kept in the archives.

83 Hilda Sabato and Juan Carlos Korol, *Cómo fue la Inmigración Irlandesa en Argentina* (Editorial Plus Ultra, Buenos Aires, 1981). See also entry under Sabato in Edmundo Murray's online bibliography 'The Irish in Latin America and Iberia' [Argentina 6], https://hcommons.org/deposits/item/hc:30333/ and a translation of the book's final chapter, 'The Camps: Irish Immigration in Argentina', https://www.irlandeses.org/sabato.htm.

84 Eduardo A. Coghlan, *Los Irlandeses en la Argentina: Su Actuación y Descendencia* (no publisher, Buenos Aires, 1987); and 'Orígenes y Evolución de la Colectividad Hiberno-Argentina', *TSC: Numero del Centenario, 1875–1975*; *Andanzas de un Irlandés en el Campo Porteño 1845–1864* (Ediciones Culturales Argentinas, Buenos Aires, 1981); and *El Aporte de los Irlandeses a la Formación de la Nación Argentina* (Buenos Aires, 1982); see also Murray's biographical note, https://www.irlandeses.org/dilab_coghlanea.htm.

85 Gertrude Cotter, 'Britain and Perón's Argentina 1946–1955', MA, University College Cork, 1989.

86 María Eugenia Cruset, *Diplomacia de las Naciones sin Estado y de los Estados sin Nación: Argentina e Irlanda, Una Visión Comparativa* (Editorial Academia Espanola, Buenos Aires, 2011) and *Nacionalismo y Diaspora: Los Casos Vascos e Irlandés en Argentina (1862–1922)* (Ediciones Lauburu, San Sebastian, 2006).

87 Sarah O'Brien, *The Irish in Argentina: Linguistic Diasporas, Narrative and Performance* (Palgrave Macmillan, London, 2017).

88 The bibliographical details of those works are cited in Chapter 1.

89 Sinéad Wall, *Irish Diasporic Narratives in Argentina: A Reconsideration of Home, Identity and Belonging* (Peter Lang, Oxford, 2017).

90 Helen Kelly, *Irish 'Ingleses': The Irish Immigrant Experience in Argentina 1840–1920* (Irish Academic Press, Dublin, 2009).

91 Claire Healy completed a doctorate in 2005 in NUI, Galway, on 'Migration from Ireland to Buenos Aires, 1776–1890'. This outstanding research deserves to be published. I read this work after I had completed my manuscript.

92 Claire Healy, '"Foreigners of this Kind": Chilean Refugees in Ireland, 1973–1990', https://www.irlandeses.org/0610healy1.htm; a researcher with the International Centre for Migration Policy Development (ICMPD), she has written *The Strength to Carry On: Resilience and Vulnerability to Trafficking and Other Abuses among People Travelling along Migration Routes to Europe* (ICMPD, 2019), and *Targeting Vulnerability: The Impact of the Syrian War and Refugee Situation on Trafficking in Persons* (ICMPD, 2016). She is also co-author, with Roberto Forin, of *Trafficking along Migration Routes: Bridging the Gap between Migration, Asylum and Anti-Trafficking* (ICMPD, 2018), and has been working with the Economic Community of West African States (ECOWAS) Commission on anti-trafficking reporting and policy since 2014.

93 Patrick Speight, *Irish-Argentine Identity in an Age of Political Challenge and Change, 1885–1983* (Peter Lang, Oxford, 2019). Timothy Horan is the only Irish diplomat cited in the index. There are references to the two Dáil Éireann diplomats, Eamonn Bulfin and Laurence Ginnell.

94 Speight, *Irish-Argentine Identity*, pp. 187–296.

95 Keogh, *La Independencia de Irlanda*, p. 376.

96 While I have not examined Irish Protestant missionary work in Latin America, I note the important role played by members of the Church of Ireland in the South American Missionary Society (SAMS), founded in Brighton. When its work expanded geographically, it changed its name in 1864 to the South American Missionary Society, working in Paraguay and later in Chile and Bolivia. Greatly expanded, its work continued in 2020, http://anglicanhistory.org/sa/every1915/sams.html. The society was also active in Ireland. See also letter from Henry Mahony, chaplain to the bishop of the Falkland Islands, and Irish secretary of SAMS, *Irish Times*, 13 May 1909. The exclusive Anglican school St George's was founded in 1898, https://www.stgeorges.edu.ar/quilmes/history/.

97 O'Brien, *The Ideal Diplomat?*. The history of Irish women in Latin America was often confined to two historical figures, Eliza Lynch and Camila O'Gorman. The latter was an Argentine socialite, the daughter of a prosperous and prominent family in Buenos Aires, who eloped with a Jesuit priest. Together they set up a school in the north of the country, in Corrientes, were denounced to the Argentina authorities by Fr Michael Gannon, and returned as prisoners to the vicinity of Buenos Aires. The dictator Juan Manuel Rosas ordered their execution. Despite being eight months pregnant, both faced a firing squad on 18 August 1848. She was nineteen and her partner, Ladislao Gutiérrez, was twenty-four (see Appendix). See film *Camila* (Maria Luisa Bemberg, director, 1984).

98 See Ronan Fanning and Michael Lillis, *The Lives of Eliza Lynch: Scandal and Courage* (Gill & Macmillan, Dublin, 2009). She is also the subject of works of fiction: see Lily Tuck, *The News from Paraguay* (HarperCollins, New York, 2004), and Anne Enright, *The Pleasure of Eliza Lynch* (Atlantic Monthly Press, New York, 2002). See an earlier work by William Edmund Barrett, *Woman on Horseback* (Frederick A. Stokes, New York, 1938).

99 See Carolina Barry's work on Cecilia Grierson: 'Argentina's First Female Doctor', https://www.irlandeses.org/0811barry1.htm. The pioneering research of Susan Wilkinson has set a very good example when writing about health, physicians and nurses in the region. See https://www.irlandeses.org/0811wilkinson1.htm.

CHAPTER 1 Imagining Argentina and the Origins of Irish Diplomacy in an Age of Revolution

1 Rabbi speaking about recently arrived Jewish immigrants in the pampas and set in the late nineteenth century, in Alberto Gerchunoff, *The Jewish Gauchos of the Pampas* (University of New Mexico Press, Albuquerque, 1998), p. 43.

2 Horan was born in Cork in 1912. He was educated at University College Cork and entered the Department of External Affairs in 1938 as third secretary; he held the following posts: consul, New York (1942–5); acting head of Consular Section, Department of External Affairs (1945–56); first secretary, Madrid (1946–7); first secretary, Paris (1947–9); counsellor, Department of Foreign Affairs (1949–52); chief of protocol (1952–5); minister to Argentina (1955–9); assistant secretary (1959–60); minister to Switzerland (1960–2); ambassador to Spain (1962–7); ambassador to Sweden (and Finland) (1967–73); permanent representative to the United Nations at Geneva (1973–5). He died in Geneva on 22 March 1975 and is buried in Glasnevin, Dublin. See death notice, *Irish Press*, 24 March 1975; see also https://www.findagrave.com/memorial/40665956/timothy-joseph-horan.

3 When I use the term Irish-Argentines, I refer specifically to the Irish Catholic community in Argentina. There is an urgent need to study members of the wider Irish-Argentine

community who identified more readily with English Catholic or Irish Protestant traditions and who may never have identified with Catholic Irish-Argentines. However, it may also be the case that Irish identity, rather than religious affiliation, might have unified some of those distinctive Irish religious groupings during the Irish war of independence between 1919 and 1921. However, nationalism rather than religion divided the Irish in Argentina after the First World War. Argentine volunteers from English-speaking families joined the British army in both world wars. For a contemporary evocation of life for one Anglo-Irish eyewitness, see Barbara Peart, *Tia Barbarita: Memoirs of Barbara Peart* (Houghton Mifflin Company, New York, 1934). Her name was Barbara O'Loughlin Peart and she was originally from Kilkenny. For an excellent overview of Irish identity in Argentina, see Kelly, *Irish 'Ingleses'*. Unfortunately, I did not read Claire Healy's outstanding doctoral thesis, 'Migration from Ireland to Buenos Aires, 1776–1890', NUI Galway, 2005. Dr Healy, whose work deserves to be published, gave me permission to read her text when I requested access in April 2021.

4   See Horan's 21-page report, 'The Irish in Argentina', NAI/DFA/313/24d, confidential reports, 22 July 1958.

5   There is a strong argument to be made for the case that Matthew Murphy 'reopened' the legation in 1947 as the Dáil Éireann envoy Eamonn Bulfin first set up a diplomatic mission in Buenos Aires in 1919 and a colleague, Laurence Ginnell, arrived to support him in mid-1921.

6   When Horan used the pronoun 'himself', he was a member of an Irish diplomatic service which was almost exclusively male. Ms Jackie O'Halloran was the first woman to be appointed to Buenos Aires as a third secretary from 1985 to 1991 and therefore to Latin America. She was the serving ambassador in 2021.

7   President Michael D. Higgins has written extensively on the Irish emigrant experience, including 'Reflecting on Irish Migrations: Some Issues for the Social Sciences', *American Journal of Irish Studies*, vol. 9, 2012, pp. 139–50. I am hesitant to use the term 'diaspora' without qualification when referring to Irish-Argentines. For a very helpful discussion on the concept of diaspora, see Kevin Kenny, *Diaspora: A Very Short History* (Oxford University Press, Oxford, 2013). I find the use of 'community' also problematical but unavoidable. While the use of that term creates the misleading impression that the Irish in Argentina formed a single entity or community, the reality was more prosaic; there were significant differences in class, while religion was also a dividing factor. In Spanish, the phrase 'Irish-Argentine collective' is used. But that only compounds the conceptual problem. In essence, the Catholic parish structure, Catholic education and Catholic social and sporting organisations helped build links between the Irish in the capital and those living in dispersed towns and country areas in the 'camp'. The Catholic nexus incorporated other Irish living in Córdoba, Mendosa, etc. For a model study on emigration, see David Fitzpatrick, *Oceans of Consolation: Personal Accounts of Irish Migration to Australia* (Cornell University Press, Ithaca and London, 1994).

8   See John Lynch, *The Spanish American Revolutions, 1808–1916* (Norton, New York, 1973), pp. 37–126; Fanning, *Paisanos*, and, by the same author, *Don Juan O'Brien*.

9   After two years in the country, Horan had made a two-day visit to Rosario a year and a half before writing the report but had not been elsewhere other than Buenos Aires and the adjacent towns in the pampas.

10 Horan report, NAI/DFA/313/24d, confidential reports, 22 July 1958; I first read this report in the early 1980s before the departmental archives were opened. I am grateful to Ambassador Ted Barrington for giving me access to a copy.

11 Two diplomats of a later generation wrote less ambitious overviews on democracy and revolution in Latin America. In 1972, Bernard Davenport filed an important overview of democracy in Latin America in the early 1970s. In 1983, Ambassador Patrick Walshe submitted a report on Argentina under the recent military dictatorship together with an idiosyncratic and highly personal view of the reasons explaining violence in the country.

12 Zygmunt Bauman, *Modernity and the Holocaust* (Polity Press, Cambridge, 2017), p. 12.

13 Horan report, NAI/DFA/313/24d. Emphasis in original.

14 Susan Wilkinson (ed.), *Recollections of an Irish-born Doctor in Nineteenth-Century Argentina: Arthur Pageitt Greene (1848–1933)* (The Memoir Club, Tyne and Wear, 2015), p. 107.

15 Ibid.

16 Santiago Ussher, *Father Fahy: A Biography of Anthony Dominic Fahy, OP, Irish Missionary in Argentina, 1805–1871* (Archdiocese of Buenos Aires, Buenos Aires, 1951); and, by the same author, *Los Capellanes Irlandeses, en la Colectividad Hiberno-Argentina durante el Siglo XIX* (n.p., Buenos Aires, 1954); *Las Hermanas de la Misericordia (Irlandesas): Apuntes Históricos sobre sus Cien Años en la Argentina* (n.p., Buenos Aires, 1955); see also *Guía Eclesiástica de la República Argentina* (n.p., Buenos Aires, n.d.).

17 Ussher, *Father Fahy*, p. 39.

18 In 2004, some 600,000 declared themselves to be native Argentines or Argentine Amerindians. In the 2010 census, over 950,000 Argentines opted to describe themselves as Amerindians or first-generation descendants of Amerindians. For a general discussion on different aspects of this area, see: Cesar Bustos-Videla, 'The 1879 Conquest of the Argentine "Desert" and Its Religious Aspects', *The Americas*, vol. 21, no. 1, 1964, pp. 36–57, www.jstor.org/stable/979704; Carolyne Ryan Larson, '"The Ashes of Our Ancestors": Creating Argentina's Indigenous Heritage in the Museo Etnográfico, 1904–1930', *The Americas*, vol. 69, no. 4, 2013, pp. 467–92; Kristine L. Jones, 'Nineteenth Century British Travel Accounts of Argentina', *Ethnohistory*, vol. 33, no. 2, 1986, pp. 195–211, www.jstor.org/stable/481774.

19 Ussher, *Father Fahy*, p. 39.

20 Ibid.

21 See also Julie Schimmel, 'Inventing "the Indian"', in William H. Truettner, *The West as America: Reinterpreting Images of the Frontier* (Smithsonian Institution Press, Washington and London, 1991).

22 Horan report, NAI/DFA/313/24d, confidential reports, 22 July 1958. Horan's emphasis.

23 Christopher Conway, 'Gender Iconoclasm and Aesthetics in Esteban Echeverría's *La Cautiva* and the Captivity Paintings of Juan Manuel Blanes', *Journal of Nineteenth Century Hispanic Cultural Production*, vol. 12, no. 1, http://www.decimononica.org/wp-content/uploads/2015/02/Conway_12.1.pdf.

24 Text of novel, https://bcn.gob.ar/uploads/Facundo_Sarmiento.pdf.

25 Museo Blanes, Montevideo, https://blanes.montevideo.gub.uy/exposiciones/catalogos-del-museo-blanes.

26 The painting was exhibited in 1892 at the World's Columbian Exposition, in Chicago. Both the United States and Argentina had shared founding myths concerning Native Americans or First Nation members. The fact that it was the 400th anniversary of the arrival of Christopher Columbus in the Americas added poignancy to the painting. See Laura Malosetti Costa, 'The Return of the Indian Raid (*La Vuelta del Malón*)', Bellas Artes, Buenos Aires, https://www.bellasartes.gob.ar/en/collection/work/6297/.

27 Horan Report, NAI/DFA/313/24d, confidential reports, 22 July 1958.

28 Frederick Jackson Turner, *The Frontier in American History* (Dover Publications, New York, 1996). Patricia Nelson Limerick has provided an interesting re-examination of the Indian conquest in the United States of America in *The Legacy of Conquest: The Unbroken Past of the American West* (Norton, New York, 1988).

29 J.A. Burkhart, 'The Turner Thesis: A Historian's Controversy', *The Wisconsin Magazine of History*, vol. 31, no. 1, pp. 70–83, http://www.jstor.org/stable/4631887; see also Alistair Hennessy, *The Frontier in Latin American History* (Edward Arnold, London, 1978), pp. 9–27.

30 Horan report, NAI/DFA/313/24d, confidential reports, 22 July 1958.

31 The poem, published in two parts in 1872 and 1879, has appeared in hundreds of editions and inspired two film classics, Leopoldo Torre Nilsson's *Martín Fierro* (1968) and Fernando Solanas' *Los Hijos de Fierro* (1982).

32 Horan report, NAI/DFA/313/24d, confidential reports, 22 July 1958.

33 For a first-hand Irishman's account of the Argentine countryside in the 1880s and 1890s, see William Bulfin, *Tales of the Pampas* (T. Fisher Unwin, London 1902), and in revised edition with an introduction by Juan José Delaney, published by Corregidor, Buenos Aires, 2014, pp. 9–15; Bulfin, who was the editor of *The Southern Cross* from the mid-1890s to 1909 and wrote under the pen name Che Buono, also wrote *Rambles in Eirinn* (Gill, Dublin, 1907).

34 Between 1856 and 1932, 6,405,000 immigrants arrived in Argentina compared with 32,244,000 who went to the United States in the period from 1831 to 1932. The figure for Chile from 1882 to 1932 was 726,000 roughly; Brazil from 1821 to 1932, 4,431,000; and Uruguay 710,000 from 1836 to 1932. See Eduard José Míguez, Preface, p. xiv in Samuel L. Baily and Eduardo José Míguez (eds), *Mass Migration to Modern Latin America* (Scholarly Resources Inc., Delaware, 2003); see also Samuel L. Baily, *Immigrants in the Lands of Promise: Italians in Buenos Aires and New York City, 1870 to 1914* (Cornell University Press, Ithaca and London, 1999).

35 See Fernando Devoto, *Historia de la Inmigración en la Argentina* (Editorial Sudamericana, Buenos Aires, 2009), and Jorge Ochoa de Eguileor and Eduardo Valdés: *¿Dónde Durmieron Nuestros Abuelos? Los Hoteles de Inmigrantes en la Capital Federal* (Fundación Urbe, Buenos Aires, 1991).

36 Report dated 1 May 1956, NAI/DFA 313/24C.

37 Alistair Hennessy, *The Frontier in Latin American History* (Edward Arnold, London, 1978), pp. 90–1.

38 Report dated 1 May 1956, NAI/DFA 313/24C.

39 Figures from Julia Albarracín, *Making Immigrants in Modern Argentina* (University of Notre Dame Press, Notre Dame, IN, 2020), pp. 32–3.

40 Walter S. Tower, 'The Pampa of Argentina', *Geographical Review*, vol. 5, no. 4, 1918, pp. 293–315, www.jstor.org/stable/207422.

41 Alistair Hennessy, 'Argentines, Anglo-Argentines and Others', in Alastair Hennessy and John King, *The Land that England Lost: Argentina and Britain, a Special Relationship* (British Academic Press, London, 1992), p. 11; see also H.S. Ferns, 'Britain's Informal Empire in Argentina, 1806–1914', *Past and Present*, no. 4, November 1953, pp. 60–75.

42 For general works on Irish emigration, see the following: Donald H. Akenson, *An Irish History of Civilization* (McGill-Queen's University Press, Montreal, 2005), vols. I and II; *Ireland, Sweden and the Great European Migration, 1815–1914* (McGill-Queen's University Press, Montreal, 2011); *Small Differences: Irish Catholics and Irish Protestants, 1815–1922: An International Perspective* (McGill-Queen's University Press, 1988); *If the Irish Ran the World: Montserrat, 1630–1730* (McGill-Queen's University Press, Montreal, 1997); *A Mirror to Kathleen's Face: Education in Independent Ireland, 1922–1960* (McGill-Queen's University Press, Montreal, 1975); and *The Irish in Ontario: A Study in Rural History* (McGill-Queen's University Press, Montreal, 1999); Tim Pat Coogan, *Wherever Green is Worn: The Story of the Irish Diaspora* (Hutchinson, London, 2000); Andy Bielenberg, *The Irish Diaspora* (Routledge, London, 2015); Breda Gray, *Women and the Irish Diaspora* (Routledge, London, 2004); Mícheál Ó hAodha, *Narratives of the Occluded Irish Diaspora: Subversive Voices* (Lang, Oxford and Berlin, 2012); Charles Fanning, *New Perspectives on the Irish Diaspora* (Southern Illinois University Press, Carbondale, 2000); Arthur Gribben, *The Great Famine and the Irish Diaspora in America* (University of Massachusetts Press, Amherst, MA, 1999); Lawrence John McCaffrey, *The Irish Catholic Diaspora in America* (Catholic University of

America Press, Washington, 1997); Michael Doorley, *Irish-American Diaspora Nationalism: The Friends of Irish Freedom, 1916–1935* (Four Courts Press, Dublin, 2005).

43 Thomas Murray, *The Story of the Irish in Argentina* (P.J. Kennedy & Sons, New York, 1919). A revised edition was published by Cork University Press in 2011 and by Corregidor, Buenos Aires, 2012. Michael Geraghty and Juan José Delaney re-edited the book. The former, who died in 2016, wrote a masterful introduction. The author, Murray, was born in 1871, in Kilbeggan, County Westmeath. He emigrated with his family in 1897 to the United States. Early in the twentieth century, he went to Buenos Aires. His history of the Irish in Argentina did not appear until 1919 (Geraghty, Introduction, footnote 1, p. 8). Geraghty wrote that the book was objective, written by an 'outsider' from Westmeath, and that many of the events related in the text would not have been told had the book not been known. Geraghty highlights the fact that Murray distinguished those Irish who came to Argentina as immigrants from those who came earlier as soldiers and adventurers. The author also described how the immigrant community broke up into a wealthy minority and an impoverished majority.

44 Ussher, *Father Fahy*, p. 38.

45 Murray, *The Story of the Irish in Argentina*, p. 94.

46 Horan report, NAI/DFA/313/24d, confidential reports, 22 July 1958.

47 Murray, *Becoming Irlandés*, pp. 1–27; Edmundo Murray, 'From Kilrane to the Irish Pampas: The Story of John James Murphy', Society for Irish Latin American Studies, http://www.irlandeses.org/murphy.htm; and Edmundo Murray, 'The Irish Road to Argentina', *History Ireland*, vol. 12, no. 3, autumn 2004, https://www.historyireland.com/18th–19th-century-history/the-irish-road-to-argentina/.

48 Hilda Sabato and Juan Carlos Korol, *Cómo fue la Inmigración Irlandesa en Argentina* (Plus Ultra, Buenos Aires, 1981); and 'Patrick McKenna, Nineteenth Century Irish Emigration to, and Settlement in, Argentina', MA Geography thesis, NUI Maynooth, 1981.

49 Kelly, *Irish 'Ingleses'*; see also the very interesting article by Deborah Jakubs, 'The Anglo-Argentines: Work, Family and Identity, 1860–1914', in Oliver Marshall (ed.), *English-Speaking Communities in Latin America Since Independence* (Palgrave Macmillan, London, 2000), pp. 135–57.

50 Benedict Anderson, *Imagined Communities: Reflections on the Origin and Spread of Nationalism* (Verso, New York and London, 1991), p. 204.

51 The Jesuit historian Fr Aubrey Gwynn had written extensively on earlier Irish missionaries in Latin America. See 'Documents Relating to the Irish in the West Indies', *Studia Hibernica*, no. 4, 1932, pp. 139–286; 'An Irish Settlement on the Amazon', *Proceedings of the Royal Irish Academy*, no. 41C, 1932, pp. 1–54; 'The First Irish Priest in the New World', *Studies: An Irish Quarterly Review*, vol. 21, no. 82, June 1932, pp. 213–28.

52 David Sheehy, 'Dublin diocesan archives: Murray papers (7)', *Archivium Hibernicum*, vol. 42, 1987, p. 59, jstor.org/stable/25487474.

53 Ussher, *Father Fahy*, pp. 13–38.

54 For a chronology of Fr Fahy's life and work, see Edward Walsh, https://www.irlandeses.org/fahychrono.htm.

55 Ussher, *Father Fahy*, p. 47.

56 Jorge Luis Borges, *On Argentina* (Penguin, London, 2010), p. 49. He also wrote on the same page: 'Pampa. Who found the word pampa, that infinite word that is like a sound and its echo? All I know is that it is of Quechuan origin, that its primitive meaning is "that of plain" and that it seems to be spoken syllable by syllable by the pampero, the fierce wind of the pampa.'

57 Kathleen Nevin, *You'll Never Go Back* (Cardinal Press, Maynooth, 1999), p. 55.

58 Ibid., pp. 45–7.
59 See also Edward Walsh, 'The Irish in the Argentine Republic: John Cullen's 1888 Report', *Collectanea Hibernica*, vol. 43, 2001, pp. 239–46, at p. 242.
60 The opening lines of the poem 'Quarantine' by Eavan Boland.
61 Joseph J. Lee, endorsement of this book, 5 April 2021.
62 Liam Kennedy, 'Why One Million Starved: An Open Verdict', *Irish Economic and Social History*, vol. XI, 1984, pp. 101–7; Donal Kerr, *A Nation of Beggars: Priests, People and Politics in Famine Ireland 1846–1852* (Oxford University Press, Oxford, 1994); Cormac Ó Gráda, *Ireland before and after the Famine: Exportations in Economic History 1800–1925* (Manchester University Press, Manchester 1988); and Ó Gráda, *Black 47 and Beyond: The Great Famine in History, Economy and Memory* (Princeton University Press, Princeton, 1995).
63 Kerby Miller, *Emigrants and Exiles: Ireland and the Irish Exodus to North America* (Oxford University Press, Oxford, New York and Toronto, 1985), p. 556.
64 See the following for a study of the Irish in the US: Oscar Handlin, *Boston's Immigrants, 1790–1880: A Study in Acculturation* (Belknap Press, Cambridge, MA, 1991); John J. Lee and Marion Casey (eds), *Making the Irish American: History and Heritage of the Irish in the United States* (New York University Press, New York, 2006); Kevin Kenny, *The American Irish: A History* (Longman, New York, 2000); Lawrence J. McCaffrey, *The Irish Diaspora in the United States* (Indiana University Press, Bloomington and London, 1976); Jay P. Dolan, *The Irish Americans: A History* (Bloomsbury Press, New York, 2008); and Linda Dowling Alameida, *Irish Immigrants in New York City, 1945–1995* (Indiana University Press, Bloomington, 2001).
65 In my conversations with various Irish-Argentines over nearly twenty years, I was struck by the estanciero Mateo Kelly's blank refusal ever to visit Ireland because he mistakenly thought that he would have to pass through England. He remained unforgiving over the role of the British government in not acting to contain the Famine in 1847, the year his grandfather arrived in Buenos Aires fleeing its ravages. He celebrated his one hundredth birthday in 2018 and died in 2021. See article in *TSC*, 28 June 2018.
66 Nevin, *You'll Never Go Back*, pp. 117–21.
67 Santiago Ussher, *Los Capellanes Irlandeses en la Colectividad Hiberno-Argentino* (Buenos Aires, 1954), p. 130.
68 Ibid., pp. 31–55, 81–5. Among the priests to arrive were Thomas Joyce (1850), Edward Kavanagh (1851), Robert McCormack (1855), John Cullen (1856) and Lawrence Kirwan (1856); see also Edward Walsh, 'The Irish in the Argentine Republic: John Cullen's 1888 Report', *Collectanea Hibernica*, vol. 43, 2001, pp. 239–46.
69 Ussher, *Los Capellanes Irlandeses*, pp. 83–5.
70 Murray, *The Story of the Irish in Argentina*, p. 110.
71 Susan Wilkinson provides a moving account of the sailing of *Mimosa* in May 1865 bringing 162 Welsh emigrants (29 children among them) to start a colony to Patagonia. *Mimosa: The Life and Times of the Ship that Sailed to Patagonia* (Y Lolfa Cyf, Talybont, 2015), pp. 152–67.
72 Barbara Peart, *Tia Barbarita: Memoirs of Barbara Peart* (Houghton Mifflin Company, New York, 1934), pp. 50–1.
73 Murray, 'The Irish Road to Argentina'.
74 Ibid.
75 Horan provided a definition of the term 'oligarch' as understood by General Perón and the Peronists. '*Oligarch* is a term popularised by [Juan Domingo] Perón, who was a born orator and most felicitous in his choice of expressions to label persons, groups or situations. By it he meant the aristocracy whose wealth and social position are based largely or at any rate originally on the ownership of land. The ownership of land still carries a social cachet in

Argentina that is not conferred by industry or trade. The estanciero is still at the top of the social scale, even though he too may now be in business also, and the industrial magnate is also a landowner or hopes to become one.' Horan report, NAI/DFA/313/24d, confidential reports, 22 July 1958.

76 In anticipation of the holding of the Eucharistic Congress in Buenos Aires in 1934, *TSC* published a special supplement (5 October) in which they profiled the most prominent Irish landowners in the country, together with photographs of their homes: 'Tres Bonetes', owned by John W. Maguire, was in Lincoln, 300 kilometres from the capital; 'Los Tres Pozos', owned by Thomas Murray, was spread over the *partidos* of Campana, Capilla del Señor, Zárate; 'Santa Isabel', owned by Joseph P. Ryan, was near Arrecifes; 'San Marín', owned by William Murphy, was in Salto Argentino; and 'El Trio' and 'Santa Catalina' were owned by Juan C. Campion. Further names included were: Juan Browne, 'La Choza', in Luján, province of Buenos Aires and in Cañada de Gómez in Santa Fe province; the Morgans from San Antonio de Areco and Giles; the Moores and the Dolans from Lobos; the Mahons from Altamirano; the Allens from San Antonio de Areco; McKeon from Lobos; Ready and Gaynor and the Kellys from Coronel Dorrego; the Hams and the Heffernans from Lincoln in the province of Buenos Aires; and the Healys of 'San Miguel', in General las Heras, north of Buenos Aires. The following landowners lived around Mercedes: James Ballesty, William Balton, Archibald Craig, John Dillon, John Flanagan, James Kavanagh, T. Kearney, Lawrence Kelly, Michael Murray and Patrick Keating. Near Cármen de Areco, John Dowling, who arrived in 1840, held large tracts of land right on the frontier with the Indians and his estancia had been the target of raids.

77 Patrick Kenna, 'An Irishman's Diary', 12 February 2008, *Irish Times*, https://www.irishtimes.com/opinion/an-irishman-s-diary-1.893230.

78 Edmundo Murray, 'The Memoirs of Tom Garrahan', in *Becoming Irlandés*, pp. 115–38.

79 Murray, 'From Kilrane to the Irish Pampas'.

80 Martín Parola, 'Estancieros Irlandeses', *The Southern Cross, 1875–2000: 125 Years Providing News for the Irish-Argentine Community* (special anniversary edition 2000), p. 15.

81 Interview with Eduardo Casey, see 'Irishmen in Argentina: Their Views on the Irish Split', *Freeman's Journal*, 13 March 1891.

82 Roberto E. Landaburu, *Eduardo Casey, Vida y Obra* (Fondo Editorial Mutual Venado Tuerto, 1995), and *Irlandeses en la Pampa Gringa: Curas y Ovejeros* (Corrigidor, Buenos Aires, 2006), pp. 22–8. See also 'Eduardo Casey, Soñador de Embresas', *Revista de Instituciones, Ideas y Mercados*, no. 58, May 2013, pp. 101–18, http://www.eseade.edu.ar/wp-content/uploads/2016/07/62.-Newland-Casey.pdf.

83 The details in this profile are taken from Edward Walsh, *Fr Anthony Fahy OP*, a poem of 1919 by Patrick MacManus and a comment about the death of Fr Fahy in 1871, in *Society for Irish Latin American Studies*, (January–February 2005), http://www.irlandeses.org/walsho2.htm. See also Michael Fahy, 'Fr Anthony Fahy of Loughrea: Irish Missionary in Argentina', *Society for Irish Latin American Studies*, https://www.irlandeses.org/fahyloughrea.htm; Fr Fahy continues to be remembered in Buenos Aires today as the guiding light of the Irish Catholic community in the nineteenth century. A cross commemorating him is to be found in Recoleta Cemetery, twenty yards from the main entrance. The Fahy Club is a centre in Buenos Aires for gatherings of the community, for dinners, dancing and cultural events. Today, the Instituto Fahy is to be found in Moreno, having begun life as an orphanage in Calle Cochabamba, Buenos Aires. It changed its use in the 1930s to that of a school run by the Irish Pallottines. The writer Rodolfo Walsh is among its most famous alumni. There are two streets named after Fr Fahy, one in Capilla del Señor and the other in La Reja, partido de Moreno. The name MacManus also appears as McManus. As he signed his name in his journal MacManus, I have kept that form in the text.

84 See Michael D. Higgins, 'Liam O'Flaherty and Peadar O'Donnell: Images of Rural Community', *The Crane Bag*, vol. 9, no. 1, 1985, pp. 41–8; Michael D. Higgins and John P. Gibbons, 'Shopkeepers-Graziers and Land Agitation in Ireland, 1895–1900', in P.J. Drudy (ed.), *Ireland: Land, Politics and People* (Cambridge University Press, Cambridge, 1983), pp. 93–118; Michael D. Higgins, *Renewing the Republic* (Liberties Press, Dublin, 2012). See also James S. Donnelly Jr, *The Land and the People of Nineteenth-Century Cork: The Rural Economy and the Land Question* (Routledge & Kegan Paul, London, 1987); Terence Dooley, *The Land and the People: The Land Question in Independent Ireland* (UCD Press, Dublin, 2004); Paul Bew, *Land and the National Question in Ireland, 1858–82* (Humanities Press, Atlantic Highlands, NJ, 1979).

85 Horan report, NAI/DFA/313/24d, confidential reports, 22 July 1958. One square league is equal to 30.87 square kilometres.

86 The phrase 'hewers of wood and drawers of water' is a biblical allusion to Joshua 9.21 and in the context used here means those who do menial work.

87 Ibid. The diplomat did not have the advantage of being able to read Tim Fanning's *Paisanos*, see pp. 164–5, 206–7, 219–20 and 224–9.

88 Horan report, NAI/DFA/313/24d, confidential reports, 22 July 1958.

89 The term 'knock-about' for a casual labourer was used by William Bulfin in his writings. I heard the term used in Mercedes in 2016, when Mr Kelly, the brother of the Pallottine priest murdered by the military on 4 July 1976 in St Patrick's, Belgrano, admonished me not to forget the 'knock-abouts' when I was writing about the Irish in Argentina.

90 Edward Walsh, 'The Irish in the Argentine Republic: John Cullen's 1888 Report', *Collectanea Hibernica*, vol. 43, 2001, p. 242.

91 William was representative of what was believed to have been a relatively small number of native Irish speakers in Argentina in the last decade of the nineteenth century. William Ussher lived in Chivilcoy, Giles, Carmen de Areco, Baradero, Pavón and Buenos Aires. He died on 20 January 1907. In an obituary in *The Southern Cross*, Gerald Foley wrote that Ussher spoke Irish in his youth, 'and even in his mature years, notwithstanding his long want of practice, he could speak and read the language. He was an ardent Gaelic Leaguer and had a passionate love of Ireland'. See obituary, *TSC*, 25 January 1907.

92 Besides his work as a priest and community leader, Santiago M. Ussher became the historian of Catholic Irish Argentina. See *Padre Fahy: Biografía de Antonio Domingo Fahy, OP, Misioneiro Irlandés en la Argentina* (Buenos Aires, 1952); *Las Hermanas de la Misericordia (Irlandesas)* (n.p., Buenos Aires, 1955); *Los Capellanes Irlandeses en la Colectividad Hiberno-Argentina durante el Siglo XIX* (D. Francisco A. Colombo, Buenos Aires, 1954); *Cien Años de Acción Católica en la Argentina* (Tall. Gráf. Domingo E. Taladriz, Buenos Aires, 1957); and *María Benita Arias: Fundadora del Instituto de las Siervas de Jesús sacramentado* (Propagador Cristiano, Buenos Aires, 1938). The Fahy biography was published in English. For a short biography see Julián Garcés, 'Monseñor Santiago M. Ussher', *Revista de Historia América*, no. 50, December 1960, p. 506, https://www.jstor.org/stable/20138339?sid=primo&seq=1#meta data_info_tab_contents.

93 Ibid.

94 Mariano Galazzi, *Los Irlandeses en Sudamérica* (Elaleph, Buenos Aires, 2009), pp. 7–11.

95 The *Standard* archive is in the Universidad de San Andrés, Buenos Aires. Marion Mulhall, a sister of the two editors, wrote a number of books, including *Between the Amazon and Andes: or, Ten Years of a Lady's Travels in the Pampas, Gran Chaco, Paraguay and Matto Grosso* (E. Stanford, London, 1881); and *Beginnings or Glimpses of Vanished Civilizations* (Longmans, Green & Co., London, 1909).

96 A parallel study of both papers needs to be undertaken. David Rock, in the outstanding book *The British in Argentina*, quotes *The Standard* throughout as a rich repository for his coverage of the history of the British in Argentina, see pp. 121–2. While dwelling on the strength and diversity of Irish nationalist sentiment in Argentina at the turn of the century, there were Irish immigrants – yet to be quantified and identified – who remained an active part of what may be termed Britain's informal empire. There were those who worked for British companies and who built the railways and tramways and had jobs in the meat-packing industry and in offices in Buenos Aires. Their loyalty was to Ireland and to empire, that is, to Ireland *within* the British empire. Their political loyalties may have been far more resilient and resistant to the blandishments of Irish nationalism than the pages of the *Southern Cross* indicate. The other Irish paper, *The Standard*, was much more circumspect about the rise of radical nationalism. But many of the Irish – by no means all – who came to Buenos Aires over many decades in the nineteenth century arrived with a hostile attitude towards the British government.

97 Sr Evangelista Fitzpatrick to Cardinal Paul Cullen, dated simply 1877, 329/4/vi/2, Cullen papers, DAA, Clonliffe College, Dublin.

98 Patricia María Gaudino Farrell, *La Asociación Católica Irlandesa y los Irlandeses en la Argentina* (Asociación Católica Irlandesa, Buenos Aires, 2009), pp. 40–80.

99 See Baily, *Immigrants in the Lands of Promise*, pp. 47–91; Fernando J. Devoto, 'A History of Spanish and Italian Migration to the South Atlantic Region of the Americas', in Baily an Míguez (eds), *Mass Migration to Modern Latin America*, pp. 29–50; Devoto, *Historia de la Inmigración en la Argentina*, Chapter V; Ochoa de Eguileor and Valdés, *¿Dónde Durmieron Nuestros Abuelos?* pp. 1–50.

100 Horan report, NAI/DFA/313/24d, confidential reports, 22 July 1958.

101 I have covered the *Dresden* episode in *La Independencia de Irlanda*, pp. 29–68.

102 For a profile of a *conventillo* in Buenos Aires in the 1880s, see Che Buono [William Bulfin], '*Apuntes Porteños: El Conventillo*', in Keogh, *La Independencia de Irlanda*, pp. 370–6.

103 Horan report, NAI/DFA/313/24d, confidential reports, 22 July 1958.

104 'Los Pasionistas', *TSC: Numero del Centenario, 1875–1975*, p. 74.

105 Ussher, *Los Capellanes Irlandeses,* pp. 97–9.

106 Susana Taurozzi, *Los Pasionistas en Argentina y Uruguay: 100 Años de Historia* (Misioneros Pasionistas, Buenos Aires, 2006), pp. 23–140; by same author, 'Las Misiones en las Estancias Irlandesas', *Todo Historia,* no. 471, October 2006, pp. 32–8.

107 See Passionist historical archives, 'The Passionist Mission in Argentina', https://passionistarchives.org/publications/passionist-heritage-newsletter/the-passionist-mission-in-argentina/.

108 See María José Roger, 'The Children of the Diaspora: Irish Schools and Educators in Argentina, 1850–1950', *Society for Irish Latin American Studies*, http://www.irlandeses.org/education.htm#pallotines.

109 Ussher, *Los Capellanes Irlandeses*, pp. 99–100.

110 Passionist historical archives, https://passionistarchives.org/explore-our-history/international-passionist-history/argentina/; see also https://www.flickr.com/photos/buenosairesmiprovincia/29608140118.

111 Nevin, *You'll Never Go Back*, pp. 188–99.

112 Kevin O'Neill, *Apuntes Históricos Palotinos* (Editora Palloti, Buenos Aires, 1995). The order also worked in Uruguay, Brazil and Chile. See also María José Roger, 'Irish-Argentine Schools 1850–1950', *Society for Irish Latin American Studies*, http://www.irlandeses.org/educationtableau.htm.

113 Fr Patrick O'Grady, *Poverty in Argentina: Labour and Capital* (Burns & Oates, London, 1897).

114 The first Irish-Argentine Pallottine, Fr Tomás Dunleavy, was from Mercedes. The information on the two O'Grady priests was supplied to me by Fr Donal McCarthy, archivist, Pallottine Fathers, Sandyford Road, Dublin 16.

115 Anthony M. Canning SCA, 'South America', in Patrick Corish (ed.), *A History of Irish Catholicism*, vol. 6 (Gill & Macmillan, Dublin, 1971), p. 22.

116 O'Neill, *Apuntes Historicos Palotinos* for general background; on 4 July 1976, the scene of a massacre in which three Pallottine priests (all had studied at Thurles) and two seminarians lost their lives at the hands of a military 'death squad'; ibid., pp. 241–4.

117 Interview with Rev. Mother M. Dominick, 'The New Orphanage and the Nuns', *TSC*, 3 March 1899; 'The New Irish Orphanage', *TSC*, 17 March 1899; 'Inauguration of the New Irish Orphanage', *TSC*, 24 March 1899; 'Progress of the New Institution', *TSC*, 7 April 1899.

118 Roger, 'The Children of the Diaspora'; Keogh, *La Independencia de Irlanda*, pp. 66–7.

119 'Las Hermanas de la Misericordia', *TSC: Número del Centenario, 1875–1975*, pp. 79–82; Roger, 'The Children of the Diaspora'.

120 See John W. O'Malley, *Vatican I: The Council and Making of the Ultramontane Church* (Harvard University Press, Cambridge, MA, 2018).

121 There is an extensive literature on this subject. The following book charts the arrival and spread of one of the most influential of the continental orders in nineteenth-century Ireland: Brendan McConvery, *The Redemptorists in Ireland 1851–2011* (Columba Press, Dublin, 2012).

122 Emmet Larkin, *The Historical Dimensions of Irish Catholicism* (Catholic University of America Press, Washington DC, 1997), pp. 57–89.

123 This was confirmed to me by Juan José Delaney during our many conversations in Buenos Aires and on our trips by car to Mercedes, Venado Tuerto and San Antonio de Areco.

124 Bulfin, *Tales of the Pampas* (LOLA, Buenos Aires, 1997) (Introduction by Susan Wilkinson); this edition also publishes the stories in Spanish, *Cuentos de la Pampa*.

125 Toni Morrison, *The Origin of Others* (Harvard University Press, Cambridge, MA, 2017); see also her *Race* (Vintage, London, 1988); 'Toni Morrison Obituary', *Guardian*, 6 August 2019, https://www.theguardian.com/books/2019/aug/06/toni-morrison-obituary.

126 Declan Kiberd, *Inventing Ireland: The Literature of the Modern Nation* (Jonathan Cape, London, 1995); Roy Foster, *Modern Ireland 1600–1972* (Allen Lane, London, 1988); and Roy Foster, *W.B. Yeats: A life. The Apprentice Mage, 1865–1914*, vol. 1 (Oxford University Press, Oxford, 1997); Philip O'Leary, *The Prose Literature of the Gaelic Revival 1881–1921* (Pennsylvania State University Press, University Park, 1994).

127 Gearóid Ó Tuathaigh, 'Language, Ideology and National Identity', in Joe Cleary and Clare Connolly (eds), *The Cambridge Companion to Modern Irish Culture* (Cambridge University Press, Cambridge, 2006), pp. 46 ff; Patrick Maume, 'Douglas Hyde (Dubhglas de híde)', *Dictionary of Irish Biography*, https://www.dib.ie/biography/hyde-douglas-de-hide-dubhghlas-a4185.

128 He told the first meeting of the Gaelic League in Buenos Aires that he remembered as a child in the United States hearing his parents speaking 'the old language'. Although born in the US, he declared his fidelity to Gaelic ideals to be as strong as if he had been born under Irish skies. 'The Gaelic League', *TSC*, 19 May 1899.

129 Coghlan, *Los Irlandeses en la Argentina*, p. 250, refers to a Peter Dinneen who was born in Cork and came to Argentina in 1890. He had married Mary Ann Hennessy, from Bandon, in 1881. They had five children. He died in La Plata in 1933.

130 In 1907, MacManus married Elsa O'Rourke, a sister of Annie, the wife of William Bulfin. He remained on the left wing of Irish-Argentine politics. As a prominent member of the Irish Catholic Association, MacManus remained a thorn in the side of the general body

of its members – stretching back to 1910 when there had been a civil war over, among other things, the disposal of Irish-held property in the capital. It was a bitter and an unseemly affair, during which MacManus was accused of having 'tipped the bowler hat' of one of the leading Irish-Argentine patricians – a gesture of great disrespect and not the action of a gentleman. MacManus, between 17 March 1912 and July 1913, published an impressive journal, *Fianna*. He remained active in Irish-Argentine politics during the Irish war of independence and civil war. See Laura P.Z. Izarra, 'Locations and Identities in Irish Diasporic Narratives', *Hungarian Journal of English and American Studies (HJEAS)*, vol. 10, nos. 1/2, 2004, pp. 341–52, www.jstor.org/stable/41274286. His brother, Seumas MacManus, had a long association with Notre Dame University. He was a primary school teacher and first secretary of the Gaelic League in County Donegal. He was also a founder member of the 1798 committee in Mountcharles and a strong supporter of Arthur Griffith. His first marriage in 1901 was to the writer Anna Johnston (Ethna Carbery). She died in 1902. Among his publications are: *Donegal Fairy Stories* (1900) and *The Donegal Wonder Book* (1926); he also published *The Story of the Irish Race* (The Irish Publishing Company, New York, 1921) and *Rocky Road to Dublin* (Macmillan, New York, 1938). In 1911, he married Catalina Violante Páez, the daughter of a former president of Venezuela. See Helen Meehan, 'Seumas MacManus', *Dictionary of Irish Biography*, https://www.dib.ie/node/21471/revisions/118159/view?destination=/node/21471/revisions.

131 His family had estancias in both Uruguay and Argentina.

132 Murray, *The Story of the Irish in Argentina*, p. 308. He lists those elected to the committee at the first meeting as J.E. O'Curry, president; Patrick Conway, vice-president; D. Suffern, treasurer; James Savage, pro-treasurer, Michael O'Breen, secretary; and Pádraic (Patrick) MacManus, pro-secretary.

133 I met the Irish estanciero Mateo Kelly, from San Antonio de Areco, on a number of occasions. He was ninety-eight in 2016 when I last saw him. He told me that he had never gone to Ireland because he would not ever set foot on English soil because of what had happened to his grandfather and grand-uncle in Ireland. He told me that they had both been sentenced to be deported. When they got to Liverpool, a friendly ship's captain unshackled them and his grandfather escaped to Argentina in 1847 while his grand-uncle also evaded capture and got to Australia.

134 He is listed as attending the third meeting of the league on 2 July 1899.

135 'The Gaelic League', *TSC*, 19 May 1899. Santiago Ussher was born on 11 November 1867 in San Andrés de Giles. He was ordained a diocesan priest on 22 December 1894. He worked in the chancery of the archbishop of Buenos Aires for most of his life and was a leading spokesman for Irish-Argentines. He died on 23 March 1960. His brother, Tomás, was a Salesian priest (died 3 August 1950) and three of his sisters were Salesian nuns: Maria Juana (b. 1870) was superior of St Mary's College, Malvinas, from 1908 to the 1930s; Catalina and Anna were also teachers in the Salesian order. See William Ussher obituary, *TSC,* 25 January 1907, and his wife Anne's obituary, *TSC*, 16 November 1900. See also Santiago Ussher, *The Ussher-Walsh Family Album* (Buenos Aires, 1933). This was updated by the family and published in an extended edition. I am grateful to the Kelly family, Temperley, for giving me access to this family history.

136 'The Gaelic League', *TSC*, 19 May 1899.

137 'Buenos Aires Gaelic League', *TSC*, 9 June 1899.

138 'From the Old Land in the Old Tongue', *TSC*, 14 November 1899.

139 'The Gaelic League's Christmas Box – £100 Sterling', *TSC*, 1 December 1899.

140 David Suffern (1853–1924) was a member of a wealthy Irish-Argentine estanciero family, with lands in Argentina and Uruguay. His father, also David, came to Argentina in 1841,

and became a successful estanciero. A collection of Suffern family papers is to be found in the Rare Books and Special Collections, Hesburgh Libraries, University of Notre Dame, https://goo.gl/2XF3Y2; I am grateful to Aedin Clements and Erika R. Hosselkus for their help during my visit.

141 MacNeill continued: 'Although we never met until tonight, we are old emotional acquaintances because of the work we are both engaged in, and for some time we have been looking with respect and favour at the work you were doing to bring help to your native land in the sacred cause of the language. We would be pleased if it were possible for you to remain among us for ever, and we would also be pleased if our Argentinian fellow Gaels were to come to us to work shoulder to shoulder to make Ireland Gaelic as she should be.' *Freeman's Journal*, 4 September 1902.

142 *Freeman's Journal*, 4 September 1902; I am grateful to Prof. Matthew MacNamara for his translation from Irish of the two speeches.

143 J.J. Lee, 'Patrick Henry Pearse', *Dictionary of Irish Biography*, https://www.dib.ie/biography/pearse-patrick-henry-a7247.

144 Bulfin, *Rambles in Eirinn*.

145 Owen McGee, *Arthur Griffith* (Merrion Press, Dublin, 2015), pp. 119–21.

146 See Keogh, *La Independencia de Irlanda,* pp. 69–150; see also Brian Maye, 'Rambles in Ireland – and Argentina', *Irish Times*, 2 December 2013.

147 Pádraig Puirséal, 'Eamonn Bulfin', *Irish Press*, 7 January 1969.

148 His sisters, Catalina, Mary, Aileen and Anita, also developed strong nationalist views and were active in the nationalist movement between 1919 and 1923.

149 For a more detailed account of the events, see Keogh, *La Independencia de Irlanda*, pp. 179–204.

150 Roger Casement, who had returned from Germany by U-boat to try to stop the rising, stood trial and was hanged in Brixton Prison on 3 August 1916. Laura Izarra, 'Rumours of "The Insurrection in Dublin" across the South Atlantic', *ABEI Journal*, no. 18, November 2016, pp. 25–40; Thomas Kent, Castle Lyons, County Cork, was condemned to death by court martial following a gunfight with the RIC. He was executed by firing squad on 9 May 1916.

151 I explain the complex sequence of events regarding his Argentine passport in *La Independencia de Irlanda*, pp. 190–3.

152 Keogh, *La Independencia de Irlanda*, letter reproduced in that volume. See also 'Took Part in 1916 Rising', *Offaly Independent*, 4 January 1969, pp. 147–204.

153 Document no. 36, *Documents on Irish Foreign Policy*, vol. 1, June 1920, Dáil Éireann Report on the Propaganda Department, http://www.difp.ie/docs/1919/Message-to-the-Free-Nations-of-the-World/2.htm.

154 See Charles Townshend, *The Republic: The Fight for Irish Independence, 1918–1923* (Penguin Books, London, 2014).

155 See the following by Dermot Keogh: *Ireland and Europe 1919–1989* (Hibernian University Press, Dublin and Cork, 1990), pp. 5–24; *The Vatican, the Bishops and Irish Politics* (Cambridge University Press, Cambridge, 1986), pp. 29–75; 'Origins of Irish Diplomacy in Europe, 1919–1921', *Études Irlandaises*, no. 7, Nouvelle Serie, December 1982, pp. 145–64; 'The Treaty Split and the Paris Irish Race Convention', *Études Irlandaises*, no. 12, December 1987, pp. 165–70. See also Kennedy, '"In Spite of All Impediments"'; Gerard Keown, *First of the Small Nations: The Beginnings of Irish Foreign Policy in the Interwar Years* (Oxford University Press, Oxford, 2016), pp. 36–111.

156 Martin Maguire, *The Civil Service and the Revolution in Ireland 1918–1938: 'Shaking the Blood-Stained hand of Mr Collins'* (Manchester University Press, Manchester and New York, 2008), p. 52 ff.

157 The other holders of that office were: Arthur Griffith (26 August 1921–9 January 1922); George Gavan Duffy (10 January 1922–25 July 1922); Arthur Griffith (25 July 1922–12 August 1922); and Desmond Fitzgerald (30 August 1922–23 June 1927).

158 Keogh, 'Origins of Irish Diplomacy in Europe, 1919–1921', pp. 145–64; *Ireland and Europe, 1919–1948* (Gill & Macmillan, Dublin, 1988), p. 256 (published in paperback: *Ireland and Europe 1919–1989* [Hibernian University Press, Cork and Dublin 1989]), p. 340; *The Vatican, the Bishops and Irish Politics* (Cambridge University Press, Cambridge, 1986), p. 316 (reissued 2005); *Jews in Twentieth-Century Ireland: Refugees, Anti-Semitism and the Holocaust* (Cork University Press, Cork, 1998); 'The Catholic Church, the Holy See and the 1916 Rising', in Gabriel Doherty and Dermot Keogh (eds), *1916: The Long Revolution* (Mercier Press, Cork, 2007), pp. 250–309; (with Ann Keogh) *Sir Bertram Windle: The Honan Bequest and the Modernisation of University College Cork, 1904–1919* (Cork University Press, Cork, 2010). See also Jérôme aan de Wiel, *The Irish Factor, 1899–1919: Ireland's Strategic and Diplomatic Importance for Foreign Powers* (Irish Academic Press, Dublin, 2008); Jérôme aan de Wiel, 'Europe and the Irish Crisis, 1900–1917', in Gabriel Doherty and Dermot Keogh (eds), *1916: The Long Revolution* (Mercier Press, Cork and Dublin, 2007).

159 See Dave Hannigan, *De Valera in America: The Rebel President's 1919 Campaign* (The O'Brien Press, Dublin, 2008).

160 One of the most important books published in this general area in recent years is Bruce Nelson's *Irish Nationalists and the Making of the Irish Race* (Princeton University Press, Princeton, 2012); see also Patrick McCartan, *With De Valera in America* (Fitzpatrick Ltd., Dublin, 1932); Éamon de Valera, *Ireland's Request to the Government of the United States of America* (Melbourne, 1921); Katherine O'Doherty, *Assignment America: de Valera's Mission to the United States* (De Tanko Publishers, New York, 1957); Michael G. Malouf, 'With Dev in America: Sinn Féin and Recognition Politics, 1919–21', *Intervention: International Journal of Postcolonial Studies*, vol. 4, no. 1, April 2002, pp. 22–44; M. Carroll, *American Opinion and the Irish Question 1910–1923* (Gill & Macmillan, Dublin, 1978); Francis M. Carroll, *Money for Ireland: Finance, Diplomacy, Politics and the First Dáil Éireann Loans, 1916–1936* (Praeger, Westport, CT, 2002); Francis M. Carroll, *The American Commission on Irish Independence, 1919: The Diary, Correspondence, and Report* (Irish Manuscripts Commission, Dublin, 1985); F.M. Carroll, 'De Valera and the Americans: The Early Years, 1916–1923', *The Canadian Journal of Irish Studies*, vol. 8, no. 1, 1982, pp. 36–54, https://doi.org/10.2307/25512548; James P. Walsh, 'De Valera in the United States, 1919', *Records of the American Catholic Historical Society of Philadelphia*, vol. 73, nos. 3/4, 1962, pp. 92–107, https://www.jstor.org/stable/44210437; Tim Pat Coogan, Éamon de Valera: The Man Who Was Ireland (HarperCollins, New York, 1995); Diarmaid Ferriter, *Judging Dev: A Reassessment of the Life and Legacy of Éamon de Valera* (Royal Irish Academy, Dublin, 2007); Ronan Fanning, Éamon de Valera: A Will to Power (Harvard University Press, Cambridge, MA, 2016); T Ryle Dwyer, *Big Fellow, Long Fellow: A Joint Biography of Collins and de Valera* (Gill & Macmillan, Dublin 1999); David McCullagh, *De Valera: Rise 1882–1932* (Gill & Macmillan, Dublin, 2017); John Bowman, *De Valera and the Ulster Question, 1917–1973* (Oxford University Press, Oxford, 1989); John P. O'Carroll et al. (eds), *De Valera and His Times* (Cork University Press, Cork, 1986); Robert Schmuhl, *Ireland's Exiled Children: America and the Easter Rising* (Oxford University Press, Oxford, 2016); Miriam Nyhan Grey, *Ireland's Allies: America and the 1916 Easter Rising* (UCD Press, Dublin, 2016); Deirdre McMahon, *Republicans and Imperialists* (Yale University Press, New Haven and London, 1984); 'Éamon de Valera and the Irish Americans', in Woodrow Wilson Occasional papers, Series no. 2, 1986; Joseph Lee and Marion R. Casey (eds), *Making the*

Irish American: History and Heritage of the Irish in the United States (New York University Press, New York, 2007).

161 Keogh, *La Independencia de Irlanda*, p. 220 ff.

162 De Valera to Bulfin, 6 May 1919, Eamonn Bulfin pension file, Irish military archives, http://mspcsearch.militaryarchives.ie/docs/files//PDF_Pensions/R1/MSP34REF1098 EAMONN%20BULFIN/WMSP34REF1098EAMONNBULFIN.pdf.

163 Keogh, *La Independencia de Irlanda*, pp. 222–3.

164 Kennedy, '"Mr Blythe, I Think, Hears from Him Occasionally"', pp. 44–6.

165 Eamonn Bulfin's *Libreta de Enrolamiento*, Bulfin family archives.

166 Kelly, *The Ruling Few*, pp. 109–41.

167 Ibid., pp. 19–22.

168 Ibid., p. 116.

169 Ibid., pp. 116–23.

170 That world is beautifully portrayed in Constance Backhouse, *Gauchos e Institutrices: Una Autobiografía* (Createspace Independent Publishing, Amazon, 2017).

171 Kelly, *The Ruling Few*, pp. 109–41.

172 Norberto Galasso, *Don Hipólito: Vida de Hipólito Yrigoyen* (Colihue, Buenos Aires, 2013), p. 65.

173 Ibid., pp. 113–14.

174 Ibid., p. 122.

175 Educated at Balliol, Oxford, he had served in Peking for five years before being sent to Argentina.

176 Ibid., pp. 123, 129.

177 Kennedy, '"Mr Blythe, I Think, Hears from Him Occasionally"', pp. 47–9.

178 Diarmuid Ó hÉigeartaigh to Bulfin, 3 April 1920, Eamonn Bulfin family scrapbook.

179 Ibid.

180 Silvia Elena Kenny de Cavanagh told me that matters became so heated at one meeting of the ICA that MacManus had tipped her father's bowler hat over his eyes – a studied insult which could only have been done by a cad.

181 Helen Meehan, 'The McManus Brothers', *Donegal Annual*, no. 46, 1994, p. 12; see also 'The late Mr. and Mrs. MacManus – Funeral in Donegal', *Derry People*, 16 February 1929.

182 The group Comité Argentino pro Libertad in Irlanda sent a long report to Éamon de Valera on 4 May 1921; see Laurence Ginnell papers, P4/A1-P4/A2, Mullingar Public Library.

183 Keogh, *La Independencia de Irlanda*, p. 253; see also Eamonn Bulfin to Military Service Pensions Board, 10 December 1935, file MSP34REF1098, military archives, Cathal Brugha Barracks, Dublin (see also file W34D427, Eamonn Bulfin).

184 FO371/4417 A6540/6540/2, NA, London.

185 'Brilliant Scenes at St. Paul's Monastery Golden Jubilee', *TSC*, 1 October 1920.

186 Report sent to President Éamon de Valera, 4 May 1921, Comité Argentino pro Libertad in Irlanda, Laurence Ginnell papers, County Library, Mullingar, p. 26.

187 'This Morning at the Irish Church', *TSC*, 29 October 1920.

188 *TSC*, 5 November 1920.

189 *TSC*, 12 November 1920.

190 Report sent to President Éamon de Valera, 4 May 1921, Comité Argentino pro Libertad in Irlanda, Laurence Ginnell papers, County Library, Mullingar, pp. 24–5.

191 Macleay reported that one of the masses for 'MacSweeney' [*sic*] was advertised as being also for 'other "patriots and martyrs", among whom Murphy [not identified?] and Asshe [*sic*, Thomas Ashe] were mentioned', FO371/4417 A8533/6540/2, NA, London.

192 FO371/4417 A8533/6540/2, NA, London. In Peru, Elvira García y García published a strong letter in *La Prensa* on 4 November 1920: 'And so McSwiney [*sic*], dead and sanctified

in the heart of his Church, which has followed day by day the course of his tortures, is converted into a symbol and at the same time a powerful weapon, which he would not have been had he retained his liberty, which might have been interpreted as a sign of weakness on the part of the English Government.' This led to a rebuttal of her arguments by F.W. Manners, secretary to the British legation in Lima. See FO395/314 P1348/1348/151, NA, London.

193   Gerry White and Brendan O'Shea, *The Burning of Cork* (Mercier Press, Cork, 2006).

194   At the time, Argentina had withdrawn from the League of Nations because it was opposed to the restriction of membership. It became active again in the league in 1933. Manley O. Hudson, 'The Argentine Republic and the League of Nations', *The American Journal of International Law*, vol. 28, no. 1, 1934, pp. 125–33, https://doi.org/10.2307/2190304; Konstantin D. Magliveras, 'The Withdrawal from the League of Nations Revisited', *Penn State International Law Review*, vol. 10, no. 1, January 1991, https://elibrary.law.psu.edu/cgi/viewcontent.cgi?article=1281&context=psilr.

195   NA/FO371/A/5663 4452/272/45.

196   Ibid.

197   Ibid.

198   The book was published by Bruce Humphries Inc. Boston, 1946.

199   Bulfin to Collins, 17 March 1921, Bulfin's signature was in Irish using the old Irish script. The letter was addressed to Michael Collins, but he used the Irish form of his first name in salutation, *A Mhicíl, a Chara*. FO371/5663 A4452/272/45, NA, London.

200   Report of the Irish White Cross to 31 August 1922, see p. 79 ff, https://archive.org/details/reportofirishwhiooirisrich/page/10/mode/2up.

201   Apart from Ussher and the provincial of the Passionist community, Fr Thomas [Tomás] O'Grady, the other members of the committee were Fr Constantine Bermingham, provincial of the Passionists (treasurer), and members Henry Grace CM, Fr John M. Sheehy and Fr James Doyle PSS.

202   Editorial, *The Standard*, 10 June 1921.

203   Logue to Fr Thomas O'Grady, 15 July 1921, Pallottine archives, box 63 (Ussher papers), Belgrano, Buenos Aires.

204   Ussher letter, 4 January 1922, see *TSC*, 6 January 1922.

205   Keiko Inoue, 'Sinn Féin Propaganda and the "Partition Election", 1921', *Studia Hibernica*, no. 30, 1998, pp. 47–61, www.jstor.org/stable/20495089.

206   Sheila M. Lawlor, 'Ireland from Truce to Treaty: War or Peace? July to October 1921', *Irish Historical Studies*, vol. 22, no. 85, 1980, pp. 49–64, www.jstor.org/stable/30006713.

207   Francis J. Costello, 'The Role of Propaganda in the Anglo-Irish War 1919–1921', *The Canadian Journal of Irish Studies*, vol. 14, no. 2, 1989, pp. 5–24; Giovanni Costigan, 'The Anglo-Irish Conflict, 1919–1922: A War of Independence or Systematized Murder?', *University Review*, vol. 5, no. 1, 1968, pp. 64–86, www.jstor.org/stable/25504818; Mary MacDiarmada, 'Art O'Brien, London Envoy of Dáil Éireann, 1919–1922: A Diplomat "in the Citadel of the Enemy's Authority"', *Irish Studies in International Affairs*, vol. 30, 2019, pp. 59–71; Emmet O'Connor, 'Communists, Russia, and the IRA, 1920–1923', *The Historical Journal*, vol. 46, no. 1, 2003, pp. 115–31, www.jstor.org/stable/3133597.

208   Fr Thomas O'Grady to Ussher, 18 July 1921, Pallottine archives, box 63 (Ussher papers), Belgrano, Buenos Aires.

209   NA/FO371/5663 A5268/272/45.

210   This statement was picked up by the British government and relayed to Macleay. It was sent by Elsham Holmes, one of the London correspondents for *La Nación*; see FO372, A5152/52522. London received a copy of the text from Macleay. Bisham Holmes was identified as the journalist who had sent the text to *La Nación*. The British envoy considered

the text significant in view of the fact that de Valera had refused to make any statement in London on the eve of his conference with the British prime minister, Lloyd George, NA/FO371/5524/A5252.

211 He sometimes signed his name in Irish, Labhras Mac Fhionnghail.

212 See Keogh, *La Independencia de Irlanda*, pp. 292–6.

213 D.H. Akenson, 'Was de Valera a Republican?', *The Review of Politics*, vol. 33, no. 2, 1971, pp. 233–53, www.jstor.org/stable/1406252.

214 For full text of document, see https://archive.org/stream/op1256876-1001#mode/2up.

215 NA/FO 371/5524 A5759/5152/2.

216 Macleay to London, 28 July 1921, A5525/5151/2, NA, London; see also 'Envoy in Argentina 1921', Section B of catalogue, items 29, 30 and 31, in Laurence Ginnell papers, County Library, Mullingar, County Westmeath. I am grateful to Ms Paula O'Donovan, County Librarian, Westmeath, and all the library staff for helping me access this collection.

217 NA/FO 371/5524 A5524/5152/2.

218 Ibid.

219 'Mr Ginnell Again', *Freeman's Journal*, 5 August 1921.

220 NA/FO371/5524 A6768/5152/2.

221 Ibid.

222 In a telegram to Dáil Éireann, Ginnell wrote that a 'High Mass for Ireland at the Passionist Church, Buenos Ayhres, was attended by immense congregation on official invitation and "Te Deum" commemorating reconquest from English. Irish only foreign flag in church', *Freeman's Journal*, 18 August 1921. This may have been a separate ceremony to the one in Santo Domingo church.

223 FO371/5524 A6768/5152/2, NA, London.

224 Ibid.

225 The meeting was reported in the *Freeman's Journal* on 22 August 1921.

226 Macleay to Foreign Office, 20 August 1921 A6094/5152/2, telegram no 121.

227 NA/FO371/5574 A6928/6785/51. The news of such a meeting was greeted with incredulity by the British minister in Brazil, Sir John Tilley; having read press reports of the meeting to the Brazilian minister for foreign affairs, he replied that the report must have been 'an invention of the Press'.

228 NA/FO371/5524 A 6327/51.

229 NA/ FO371/5524 A6096/5152/2.

230 Ginnell to Dublin, 3 March 1922, NAI/DFA/ES 216.

231 It was not uncommon then to refer to a Catholic priest as Mr; Alfred MacConastair was a Passionist priest in Buenos Aires in the 1920s; he wrote a book called *Lily of the Marshes: The Story of Maria Goretti* (Macmillan, Dublin, 1951).

232 Eamonn Bulfin chronology, in Patrick J. Little Witness Statement, no. 1769, https://www.militaryarchives.ie/collections/online-collections/bureau-of-military-history-1913-1921/reels/bmh/BMH.WS1769.pdf.

233 Galería Güemes is an *art nouveau* building situated on Calle Florida. When it opened in 1915, it had six and eight floors rising in two wings, served by fourteen lifts. It had 350 offices, seventy luxury apartments, two restaurants, and cafés, etc., in the three basements, https://en.wikipedia.org/wiki/Galer%C3%ADa_G%C3%BCemes.

234 NA/FO371/5524 A6920/5152.

235 Ginnell to Dublin, 3 March 1922, DFA/ES 216.

236 Carroll, *America and the Making of an Independent Ireland*, p. 75.

237 NA/ FO371/5524 A6491/5152/2.

238 Little was born on 17 June 1884 in Dundrum, County Dublin. His father, Philip Francis, was born in Canada and was a former leader of the Liberal party in Newfoundland and

served as premier, attorney general and high court judge before coming to Ireland. There he supported the Irish Parliamentary Party. P.J. Little studied at Clongowes and at UCD. He was active in the Literary and Historical Society and was the editor of a number of Sinn Féin papers between 1915 and 1926. He sided with de Valera in the civil war. He held a number of ministerial posts in the Fianna Fáil governments, being minister for posts and telegraphs between 1939 and 1948. From April to December 1921, he was a diplomatic representative of Dáil Éireann in South Africa and in Argentina. He was also a Brazilian representative at the Irish Race Conference in Paris in January 1922. See Marie Coleman, 'Patrick John ('P.J.') Little', *Dictionary of Irish Biography*, https://www.dib.ie/biography/little-patrick-john-p-j-a4851.

239 Little also signed his reports Pádraig Mac Caoilte and the pseudonym 'Microbes and Co.'.

240 NA/FO371/5574 A8288/6787/51.

241 NA/FO371/5574 A 6785/6785/51.

242 NA/FO371/5574 A8288/6787/51.

243 NA/FO371/5524 A6749/5152/2.

244 NA/FO371/5524 A7502/5152/2.

245 Ginnell to Dublin, 3 March 1922, NAI/DFA/ES 216.

246 Eamonn Bulfin chronology, in Patrick J. Little Witness Statement, no. 1769, https://www.militaryarchives.ie/collections/online-collections/bureau-of-military-history-1913-1921/reels/bmh/BMH.WS1769.pdf.

247 NA/FO371/5524 A8259/5152/2.

248 Eamonn Bulfin chronology, in Patrick J. Little Witness Statement, no. 1769.

249 Ibid.

250 Ibid.

251 Ginnell to Dublin, 3 March 1922, NAI/DFA/ES 216.

252 Eamonn Bulfin chronology, in Patrick J. Little Witness Statement, no. 1769.

253 Patrick J. Little to the Department of Foreign Affairs, 4 December 1921, DFA/ES 216.

254 Text of Articles of Agreement of a Treaty between Great Britain and Ireland, signed in London, on 6 December 1921. The site provides biographies of the signatories and secretaries, https://www.difp.ie/volume-1/1921/final-text-of-the-articles-of-agreement-for-a-treaty-between-great-britain-and-ireland-as-signed/214/#section-documentpage.

255 Ibid.

256 Ibid.

257 Ibid.

258 Eamonn Bulfin chronology, in Patrick J. Little Witness Statement, no. 1769.

259 The Irish Race Convention was an assembly of representatives from different parts of the world which met in Chicago in 1881 and in Dublin in 1896 but did not meet again until 1916 and then in 1918, 1919 and 1921. After Paris, in 1922, it did not meet until 1947 and the last time was in 1994.

260 Dermot Keogh, 'The Treaty Split and the Paris Irish Race Convention', *Études Irlandaises*, no. 12, December 1987, pp. 165–70; see Diarmuid Coffey, 'Report on the Irish Race Conference in Paris' (other delegates Michael Hayes, Douglas Hyde and Eoin MacNeill), February 1922, no. 239, NAI/DFA/ES, box 11, file 77, *Documents on Irish Foreign Policy* (*DIFP*), vol. 1, http://www.difp.ie/docs/1922/Irish-Race-Convention-Paris/239.htm; George Gavan Duffy, Foreign Office memorandum no. 1, 25 January 1922, Dublin, *DIFP*, vol. 1, http://www.difp.ie/docs/volume/1/1922/227.htm.

261 For coverage of the event, see, in particular, the *Freeman's Journal* for 21 January, 7 February and 15 March 1922.

262 Bowen had been at school in Stonyhurst College with Oliver St John Gogarty.

263 Little to Robert Brennan, 4 December 1921, *Documents on Irish Foreign Policy*, vol. 1, no. 120, DFA ES box 32, file 216(4), https://www.difp.ie/docs/1921/Argentina/120.htm.

264 Text of 'Distinguished Irishmen in South America: A Short Review', *Sunday Independent*, 12 March 1922.

265 'The Irish Race Convention', *TSC*, 23 December 1921.

266 Ginnell to Dublin, 3 March 1922, DFA/ES 216.

267 'Irish Republican Government Loan', *TSC*, 10 February 1922.

268 Eamonn Bulfin chronology, in Patrick J. Little witness statement, no. 1769.

269 Colum Kenny, *The Enigma of Arthur Griffith: 'Father of Us All'* (Merrion Press, Dublin, 2020), pp. 226–34.

270 *Dáil Éireann Debates*, vol. 1, no. 1, 9 September 1922, https://www.oireachtas.ie/ga/ debates/debate/dail/1922-09-09/3/.

271 I provide a detailed account of Ginnell's mission in Argentina in my *La Independencia de Irlanda*, pp. 291–356.

272 'Laurence Ginnell RIP', obituary, *TSC*, 27 April 1923.

273 David McCullagh, *De Valera: Rise, 1882–1932* (Gill Books, Dublin, 2017), vol. 1, pp. 327–76.

274 'Death of Mr. Eamonn Bulfin', *Offaly Independent*, 4 January 1969.

275 The quoted phrase is taken from the final line of Czeslaw Milosz' poem 'Capri', in the collection *Facing the River* (Ecco Press, New Jersey, 1995), p. 12.

CHAPTER 2 Building Diplomatic Relations from the Irish Civil War to the Fall of Juan Domingo Perón and the Cuban Revolution

1 Keown, *First of the Small Nations*, pp. 1–178. This survey makes one reference to Argentina in relation to the Bulfin mission. There is no reference to Argentina for the period 1922–32.

2 Dermot Keogh, *Ireland and the Vatican: The Politics of Church and State 1922–1960* (Cork University Press, Cork 1995), see early chapters.

3 NAI/DFA/313/24d, confidential reports, 22 July 1958.

4 Profiles of three editors: Gerald and Frank Foley, and Fr Miguel Quinn, *TSC: Número del Centenario, 1875–1975*, p. 14.

5 In 1929, he returned to Ireland and died in 1933 in County Mayo.

6 Born in Carmen de Areco on 25 October 1870, he studied with the Passionist Fathers at Salto and Capitán Sarmiento. He entered the national seminary at Villa Devoto and was ordained on 22 December 1894. Suffering from poor health throughout his life, he first worked in Córdoba and later in the pampas as chaplain at an orphanage in San Nicolás de Arroyos, 61 kilometres from Rosario. He worked closely with Frs Edmundo Flannery and Juan Morgan Sheehy. In 1904, he became chaplain to the Sisters of Mercy School, Santa Brígida, in Buenos Aires. He wrote and helped edit the *Hibernian Argentine Review. TSC: Numero del Centenario, 1875–1975*, p. 13.

7 I am grateful to Luis and Juan José Delaney for their reminiscences. The importance of *TSC* was also confirmed in my interviews with many other Irish-Argentines of an older generation.

8 A comparative study of the three newspapers on the evolution of Irish nationalism before and after independence is a subject which deserves to be tackled. I have been unable to locate statistics for the circulations and readership of any of the three papers.

9 This estimate was provided by a correspondent in 'Impressions of the Pilgrimage', *TSC*, 21 March 1924.

10 Victor O'Carolan was born in Ireland in 1884. He entered the Passionist order and was ordained in 1908. He came to Argentina soon after ordination and worked there until his death in 1969. He was superior of the Passionists in Buenos Aires. He also worked in Capitán Sarmiento and gave retreats throughout the country. During the post-1916 period and the

war of independence, he was very active raising funds for the victims of British violence in Ireland. The photo (see Fig. 2.1) was signed at the back 'An Irish pilgrimage train on the Argentine Pampa, bearing the loved name of President DE Valera – March 16 1924'. And 'greetings to Mrs Roughan from Rev. Victor O'Carolan CP, Retiro de San Pablo Capitán Sarmiento FCCA, Argentina July 22 1925'. Also copy of same annotated by Fr O'Carolan on reverse 'Viva De Valera written on an Irish-Argentine pilgrimage train in Buenos Aires, March 16, 1924, put there by a priest. It is a British railway!' UCD archives, Éamon de Valera papers, P150. In the Seán T. O'Kelly papers, NLI MS 48,500/11 there are photos of an open-air meeting in which de Valera was present. Signed on back: 'TO Miss N[elly] Ryan from Fr Victor O'Carolan C.P.'

11 'Success of the Pilgrimage', editorial, *TSC*, 21 March 1924.

12 'The Irish Elections', *TSC*, 26 February 1932.

13 'The Supreme Pontiff and President de Valera Honour our Irish-Argentine Community', *TSC*, 25 March 1932.

14 In the Gothic style, it was 170 feet long, 87 feet in height and 55 feet in width. The tower, reaching to 210 feet, was – in settlement of an old score – a foot higher than the nearby bishop's cathedral; and it had twenty-five bells, the largest of which weighed four tons. The stained-glass windows depicted Irish saints. The organ, built in Germany, had four keyboards and seventy-two registers. It was the largest organ in the Argentine Republic. 'Irish Church in Argentina', *Irish Press*, 7 March 1932.

15 'Inauguration festivities at Mercedes', *TSC*, 25 March 1932.

16 'The Supreme Pontiff and President de Valera Honour our Irish-Argentine Community', *TSC*, 25 March 1932.

17 'The Dublin Congress', *TSC*, 22 January 1932.

18 This was published as *A Short Account of Irish Catholic Action in Argentina* (The Southern Cross Publishing Company, Buenos Aires, 1932).

19 'The Dublin Congress', *TSC*, 22 January 1932.

20 The first-class return trip to Southampton was 2,543.50 pesos and second class was 1,298.50 pesos. The first-class boat and train from Southampton to Dublin, with hotel in London (with dinner and breakfast), was 63 pesos, and 48 pesos second class. Each pilgrim had to make his or her own arrangements for lodgings in Dublin during the congress. 'The Dublin Congress', *TSC*, 22 January 1932.

21 'Demonstration in Honour of Monsignor Canon James M. Ussher', *TSC*, 27 May 1932; on Saturday, 21 May, Ussher was the guest of honour at St Bridget's where he celebrated mass and attended a reception. He was given gifts of a tableau based on the life of St Patrick. Both the Argentine and Irish national anthems were sung at the event; 'Adieu to Monsignor Ussher at St Bridget's', *TSC*, 27 May 1932.

22 Ussher's brother, Thomas, a Salesian priest, also joined the pilgrims in Dublin from Rome where he was a delegate to elect a new superior general. Also participating were Mgr Daniel Figueros (PP San Nicolás); Rev. Richard J. Carty, Irish Chaplain; Rev. James Campion, CP; Rev. Michael Fox, CC; Rev. Benedict O'Connor, CP; Rev. Albert Montes Revilla, PP; Rev. Bernard Geraghty, CP; Rev. Michael P. Walsh, PSM; Fr Richard Gearty; Mrs M.K. de O'Rourke; Mrs. M. Murphy; Miss Susana O'Farrell; Mrs. B. Cormac; Miss T. Quinn; Miss N. O'Farrell; Mrs O'Farrell; Mr Patrick Joseph Rattigan; Mr Martin McGann; Mr Patrick Cole; Dr Michael Z. O'Farrell; and Mr J. O'Neill. 'On Board the *Asturias*', *TSC*, 1 July 1932.

23 'The Dublin Eucharistic Congress', *TSC*, 15 April 1932.

24 'The Irish Argentine Pilgrims Set Sail', *TSC*, 27 May 1932; and see also 'Congress Week', *TSC*, 17 June 1932.

25 'The Irish Argentine Pilgrims Set Sail', *TSC*, 27 May 1932.

26 Roscommon Memorial Church, which was opened in 1903, was built from the proceeds of an international fundraising campaign. Fr T.H. Cummins and Richard Gearty, parish priest of San Antonio de Areco, spent twelve months in the United States helping to raise funds. In Argentina, both men raised £2,000, which was one third of the cost of the building.

27 '"At Home" in Honour of Monsignor Ussher', *TSC*, 7 October 1932.

28 Ibid.

29 'News from Our Pilgrims', *TSC*, 1 July 1932.

30 '"At Home" in honour of Monsignor Ussher', *TSC*, 7 October 1932.

31 'President with Argentine Pilgrims', *TSC*, 15 July 1932; and see also 'The Dublin Eucharistic Congress', *TSC*, 29 July 1932.

32 Juan B. de Lemoine, Argentine Consulate, Dublin, to Dr Carlos Saavedra Lamas, 28 June 1932, expediente 4/1932, División Política, Ministerio de Relaciones Exteriores y Culto, Archivo de la Cancillería, Buenos Aires.

33 'Pilgrims Visit Republican Plot', *Irish Press*, 18 June 1932.

34 'News from Our Pilgrims', *TSC*, 1 July 1932.

35 'The Dublin Eucharistic Congress', *TSC*, 29 July 1932.

36 'Celebration at Bodenstown', *Irish Times*, 20 June 1932.

37 Ibid.

38 'Priest Colonists of the Plain of the Plate', *Irish Independent*, 27 June 1932; R.J. Gearty, 'A Short Account of Irish Catholic Action in Argentina', in Patrick Boylan (ed.), *Thirty-First International Eucharistic Congress, Dublin: Section Meeting Papers and Addresses*, vol. 2 (Dublin, 1932), p. 27. See 'Tribute to Work for Catholic Action: Irish in Argentina', *Irish Press*, 24 June 1932; 'Ireland's Glory in South America', *Irish Independent*, 24 June 1932; and 'Ireland and Argentina', *Anglo-Celt*, 2 July 1932.

39 'Argentine Farewell: Enthusiasm at Pilgrims' Farewell Dinner', *Irish Press*, 28 June 1932, and 'The Argentine Pilgrims', *Irish Independent*, 28 June 1932.

40 'The Dublin Eucharistic Congress', *TSC*, 29 July 1932.

41 'News from Our Pilgrims', *TSC*, 1 July 1932.

42 'The Late Laurence Ginnell', *TSC*, 12 August 1932, and 'Irish and Argentine Flags at Grave: Visit Recalled', *Irish Press*, 6 July 1932.

43 See commentary on history of the church by Fr Gerry Shannon, https://www.youtube.com/watch?v=y4RBk7vbpww.

44 'Irish Argentine Delegation Welcomed to Roscommon', *TSC*, 26 August 1932.

45 '"At Home" in Honour of Monsignor Ussher', *TSC*, 7 October 1932.

46 E.T. Long [introduction by Fr C.C. Martindale SJ], *Latin America and the Eucharistic Congress of 1934* (Burns, Oates & Washbourne, London, 1934).

47 Afterwards, an unspent balance of 6,819.90 pesos remained. 'Eucharistic Congress Notes', *TSC*, 7 December 1934.

48 'Sixth Eucharist Assembly of the Irish Section', *TSC*, 7 September 1934.

49 'Last Sunday's Open-Air Mass: Record Gathering', *TSC*, 28 September 1934.

50 'The Catholicism of Argentina', *TSC*, 12 October 1934.

51 *The Southern Cross*, Eucharistic Congress Special Edition, 5 October 1934.

52 Eoin Devereux, 'John Hayes (1887–1957), Founder of Muintir na Tíre', *Old Limerick Journal*, http://www.limerickcity.ie/media/Media,4113,en.pdf; see also Fr Mark Tierney, *The Story of Muintir na Tíre: The First Seventy Years* (Muintir na Tíre, Tipperary, 2004); Stephen Rynne, *Father John Hayes: Founder of Muintir na Tíre, People of the Land* (Clonmore & Reynolds, Dublin, 1960).

53 'Fr Hayes' Farewell Address by Radio', *TSC*, 9 November 1934. He said on radio that 'no other nation in the short time [he had been in Argentina] could win the affection of a stranger and leave impressions so sacred'.

54 'Erin, the Tear and the Smile in Thine Eye', *TSC*, 7 September 1934; see also John Ryan, 'The Founder of Muintir na Tíre: John M. Canon Hayes 1887–1957', *Studies: An Irish Quarterly Review*, vol. 46, no. 183, autumn 1957, pp. 312–21.

55 File: Escritos Varios de Monseñor Ussher, box 63, Pallottine archives, St Patrick's, Belgrano, Buenos Aires.

56 I am grateful to Fr Thomas Murray, archivist, diocese of Ardagh and Clonmacnois, for sending on this excerpt from the diary of Bishop McNamee, archive, diocese of Ardagh and Clonmacnois, Longford.

57 Michael J. O'Doherty was archbishop of Manila, Philippines, from 1916 until his death in 1949. He was born in Charlestown, County Mayo, on 30 July 1874. He was appointed rector of the Irish College in Salamanca in 1904. He was succeeded by his brother, Denis, in that post.

58 'Where the Bishops are Staying', *TSC*, 14 September 1934.

59 He was bishop of Ardagh and Clonmacnois from 1927 until 1966; his diocese extended into seven counties – Longford, Leitrim, Westmeath, Offaly, Cavan, Roscommon and Sligo – many of them counties of high emigration to Argentina.

60 McNamee diary entry.

61 Richard Gearty died in San Antonio de Areco in summer 1938. He had been educated at Summerhill College, Sligo, and ordained for the diocese of Elphin. He had been parish priest of Roscommon before going to the United States and Argentina. 'Irish Priest Dies in Argentina', *Leitrim Observer*, 27 August 1938.

62 I am grateful to Fr Thomas Murray, archivist, diocese of Ardagh and Clonmacnois, for sending on this excerpt from the diary of Bishop McNamee, archive, diocese of Ardagh and Clonmacnois, Longford. I have corrected the spelling of Palermo in the text.

63 'Eucharistic Congress: Christ of the Andes', *Irish Independent*, 22 November 1934.

64 Bishop McNamee diary.

65 See *TSC*, 19 October 1934.

66 'Eucharistic Congress', *Anglo-Celt*, 20 October 1934.

67 Bishop McNamee diary.

68 'Irish Prelates Visit the Camp', *TSC*, 19 October 1934.

69 Bishop McNamee diary.

70 'Fr Hayes' Farewell Address by Radio', *TSC*, 9 November 1934.

71 Hayes to Ussher, 10 April 1935, Escritos Varios de Monseñor Ussher, box 63, Pallottine archives, St Patrick's, Belgrano, Buenos Aires.

72 Alfredo's parents were Patricio José Leaden and Brígida Ussher. He had two uncles who were priests, Santiago and Tomás Ussher. Three of their sisters were nuns in the María Auxiliadora order. Alfredo's brother, Guillermo, became a Salesian priest (1941) and later an auxiliary bishop of Buenos Aires (1975); Alfredo was educated by the Irish Sisters of Mercy in Clonmacnoise College, San Antonio de Areco. Studying in the Pallottine preparatory college in Rawson from 1932, he went to Ireland in 1934. He studied with the Pallottines at Thurles from 1934 until 1938 where he did his novitiate and studied philosophy. He went to Rome and studied at the Gregorian. In 1941 – Italy having entered the war the previous year – Alfredo made the dangerous journey through Italy, France and Spain. He made his way to Lisbon and returned to Buenos Aires. After completing his studies, he was ordained in December 1942.

73 Escritos Varios de Monseñor Ussher, box 63, Pallottine archives, St Patrick's, Belgrano, Buenos Aires.

74 Ibid. Hayes was given hospitality by Alfredo's parents.

75 'An Irish Consulate', *TSC*, 9 November 1934.

76 'A Message from the President of Argentina', *Irish Press*, 10 December 1934.

77 Archbishop Gilmartin of Tuam wrote on 13 April 1935 to Ussher hoping that the congress would bring about a greater closeness between the two countries: 'I cannot tell you how delighted I was to read all about the celebration and St Patrick's Day in Buenos Aires and the Argentine. You are much more enthusiastic than we are in the old country and it is a good lesson to us to know the Catholic vitality – which distinguishes your people.' File: Escritos Varios de Monseñor Ussher, box 63, Pallottine archives, St Patrick's, Belgrano, Buenos Aires.

78 The first lines of the letter read: 'I am instructed by the President, Minister for External Affairs, to reply to your letter of 2 November last and to express regret for the long delay in replying.' File: Escritos Varios de Monseñor Ussher, box 63, Pallottine archives, St Patrick's, Belgrano, Buenos Aires.

79 File: Escritos Varios de Monseñor Ussher, box 63, Pallottine archives, St Patrick's, Belgrano, Buenos Aires.

80 Ibid.

81 Deirdre McMahon, *Republicans and Imperialists: Anglo-Irish Relations in the 1930s* (Yale University Press, New Haven, 1984); Paul Canning, *British Policy towards Ireland 1921–1941* (Clarendon Press, Oxford, 1985); Paul Canning, 'The Impact of Éamon de Valera: Domestic Causes of the Anglo-Irish Economic War', *Albion: A Quarterly Journal Concerned with British Studies*, vol. 15, no. 3, 1983, pp. 179–205; Donal Lowry, 'The Captive Dominion: Imperial Realities behind Irish Diplomacy, 1922–1949', *Irish Historical Studies*, vol. 36, no. 142, pp. 202–26; Kevin O'Rourke, '"Burn Everything British but Their Coal": The Anglo-Irish Economic War of the 1930s', *The Journal of Economic History*, vol. 51, no. 2, 1991, pp. 357–66; Thomas Mohr, 'Law without Loyalty: The Abolition of the Irish Appeal to the Privy Council', *Irish Jurist*, New Series, vol. 37, 2002, pp. 187–226; Deirdre McMahon, 'The Chief Justice and the Governor General Controversy in 1932', *Irish Jurist*, New Series, vol. 17, no. 1, 1983, pp. 145–67; Paul Canning, 'Yet Another Failure for Appeasement? The Case of the Irish Ports', *The International History Review*, vol. 4, no. 3, 1982, pp. 371–92.

82 Thomas E. Hachey, 'Irish Nationalism and the British Connection', in Thomas E. Hachey and Lawrence J. McCaffrey (eds), *Perspectives on Irish Nationalism* (University Press of Kentucky, Lexington, 1989), pp. 121–38; Kennedy, '"Nobody Knows and Ever Shall Know from Me That I Have Written It": Joseph Walshe, Éamon de Valera and the Execution of Irish Foreign Policy, 1932–8', *Irish Studies International Affairs*, vol. 14, pp. 165–83.

83 Dermot Keogh, 'The Constitutional Revolution: An Analysis of the Making of the Constitution', in Frank Litton (ed.), *The Constitution of Ireland 1937–1987*, a special issue of *Administration*, vol. 35, no. 4, 1987, pp. 4–83; and [with Andrew McCarthy], *The Making of the Irish Constitution 1937: Bunreacht na hÉireann* (Mercier Press, Cork, 2007).

84 Patrick Keatinge, 'Ireland and the League of Nations', *Studies: An Irish Quarterly Review*, vol. 59, no. 234, summer 1970, p. 142.

85 Cian McMahon, 'Irish Free State Newspapers and the Abyssinian Crisis, 1935–6', *Irish Historical Studies*, vol. 36, no. 143, 2009, pp. 368–88.

86 Dermot Keogh, *Ireland and Europe 1919–1989: A Diplomatic and Political History* (Hibernian University Press, Cork and Dublin, 1990), pp. 63–97.

87 See Michael Kennedy, *Ireland and the League of Nations 1919–1946* (Four Courts Press, Dublin, 1996), pp. 177–84; see also his entry 'Seán (John Ernest) Lester', *Dictionary of Irish Biography* (Cambridge University Press, Cambridge, 2009), pp. 469–71; see also Yannick Wehrli, 'Seán Lester, Ireland and Latin America in the League of Nations', *Irish Migration Studies in Latin America*, http://www.irlandeses.org/0903wehrli.htm; de Valera made reference to the Chaco dispute when he addressed the league on 26 September 1932 having taken over the presidency of the council. See Anon, *Peace and War: Speeches by Mr de Valera on International Affairs* (M.H. Gill & Son Ltd, Dublin, 1944), p. 7; Martha Kavanagh, 'The Irish Free State and Collective Security, 1930–6', *Irish Studies in International Affairs*, vol. 15, 2004, pp. 103–22; Keatinge, 'Ireland and the League of Nations', pp. 133–47.

88 See Douglas Gageby, *The Last Secretary General: Seán Lester and the League of Nations* (Town House, Dublin, 1999), p. 34; Paul McNamara, *Seán Lester, Poland and the Nazi Takeover of Danzig* (Irish Academic Press, Dublin and Portland, 2009); Marit Fosse and John Fox, *Seán Lester: The Guardian of a Small Flickering Light* (Hamilton Books, n.p., 2015).

89 https://en.mercopress.com/2009/04/28/bolivia-and-paraguay-seal-peace-and-limits–74-years-after-the-chaco-war; Bruce W. Farcau, *The Chaco War: Bolivia and Paraguay, 1932–1935* (Praeger, Westport, Connecticut and London, 1996); James M. Malloy, *Bolivia: The Uncompleted Revolution* (University of Pittsburgh Press, Pittsburgh, 1970), p. 72 ff.

90 See Keogh, *Ireland and Europe 1919–1989*, chapters 3 to 6; Keogh, *Twentieth Century Ireland*, pp. 110–60; Keogh, *Ireland and the Vatican*; Keogh and O'Driscoll (eds), *Ireland in World War Two*; O'Driscoll, *Ireland, Germany and the Nazis*; Donal Ó Drisceoil, *Censorship in Ireland, 1939–1945: Neutrality, Politics and Society* (Cork University Press, Cork, 1996).

91 During the 1930s, Argentina went through *la década infame* (infamous decade) – a series of military interventions and rule by an alliance of estancieros and oligarchs, known as the *Concordancia*.

92 'Neutral Policy for Argentina', *Irish Press*, 7 June 1943.

93 'Will Burn Wheat instead of Coal' [United Press report], *Irish Press*, 24 July 1943.

94 Keogh, *Ireland and Europe*, pp. 171–6; see also Whelan, *Ireland's Revolutionary Diplomat*, pp. 208–22.

95 Both Miguel Quinn and his successor, Juan Santos Gaynor, were Argentine-born but nonetheless educated within two orders which were predominantly run by Irishmen. Born in San Andrés de Giles on 1 November 1905, Gaynor joined the Pallottine order and was sent to the seminary in Thurles, County Tipperary. Later, he did a doctorate at the Gregorian, in Rome. Ordained in 1928, he returned to Argentina where he did parish work in Rawson, Suipacha and in St Patrick's, in Buenos Aires. Gaynor combined his work as editor of the paper with that of a teacher, preacher and administrator. Between 1951 and 1964, he was an inspector general of religious instruction in schools, a professor of theology in *El Instituto de Cultura Superior Religiosa*, and a professor of English literature in the *Escuela Nacional de Lenguas Vivas*. In 1958, the Juan S. Gaynor Foundation was established in Belgrano. Having been appointed consultor general of his congregation, he moved to Rome in 1958 and died in Ireland on 10 July 1963. He is buried in Thurles, County Tipperary. 'Rev. Juan Santo Gaynor', *TSC: Numero del Centenario, 1875–1975*, p. 14; see also O'Neill, *Apuntes Históricos Palotinos*, pp. 279–80.

96 Having worked through the files of the Ministry of Foreign Affairs and Worship, in Buenos Aires, up to the 1950s, I have found very little of substance other than a flurry of interest in 1932 relating to the change of government and de Valera's early Anglo-Irish policy.

97 Matthew Farrell (1803–60), the president's grandfather, came from County Longford.

98 See 'Gestiones para Establecer una Representación Diplomática en Irlanda', 'Irlanda', expediente, 3/1945, caja 17, Ministerio de Relaciones Exteriores y Culto, Archivo Histórico de la Cancillería Argentina, Buenos Aires.

99 Ibid.

100 Dermot Keogh, 'Éamon de Valera and Hitler: An Analysis of International Reaction to the Visit to the German Minister, May 1945', *Irish Studies in International Affairs*, vol. 3, no. 1, 1989, pp. 69–92; see also Dermot Keogh, 'He Kept an Eye on Us', *Irish Times*, 25 September 1999, a review of Martin S. Quigley, *A US Spy in Ireland: The Truth behind Irish 'Neutrality' during the Second World War* (Roberts Rinehart, Lanham, MD, 1999); see also his *Peace without Hiroshima: Secret Action at the Vatican in the Spring of 1945* (Madison Books, Lanham, MD, 1991).

101 'Herr Hitler May be Alive and either in Argentina or the Antarctic', *Irish Press*, 18 July 1945.

102 Richard J. Evans, *The Hitler Conspiracies* (Oxford University Press, Oxford, 2020), see pp. 171–3, 177–9 and 181–7. On Perón and the Nazis, see Uki Goñi, *The Real Odessa: How Perón Brought the Nazi War Criminals to Argentina* (Granta Books, London, 2002).

103 See Claudio Gustavo Meunier and Oscar Rimondi, *Alas de Trueno* [Wings of Thunder] (C.G. Gustavo, Buenos Aires, 2004).

104 Keogh, 'Éamon de Valera and Hitler', pp. 69–92.

105 See 'Gestiones para Establecer una Representación Diplomática en Irlanda'.

106 See Mariano Ben Plotkin, *Mañana es San Perón: A Cultural History of Perón's Argentina* (SR Books, Wilmington, DE, 2003), pp. 3–134.

107 Ibid., p. 310.

108 'Editorial', *Irish Press*, 19 September 1946.

109 As secretary of the Department of External Affairs in 1935, Walshe had written to Mgr Ussher with the news that de Valera believed it was time to open diplomatic relations with Argentina.

110 The director of the political division, Ricardo Bunge, acknowledged receipt of the letter on 13 July. Nothing on the file reveals that the Castiñeiras letter was shown to the foreign minister, Dr Bramuglia. Castiñeiras to Bramuglia, 13 June 1946, 'Irlanda', expediente 2, Irlanda 2/946, Ministerio de Relaciones Exteriores y Culto, Archivo Histórico de la Cancillería Argentina, Buenos Aires.

111 Ibid.

112 Patrick Keatinge, *The Formulation of Irish Foreign Policy* (Institute of Public Administration, Dublin, 1973), Table 2, p. 306.

113 George Gavan Duffy (1882–1951) was an Irish diplomat, politician, barrister and judge. He was a plenipotentiary at the treaty talks in London in 1921. He reluctantly signed the agreement but later resigned from government where he had been minister for foreign affairs from January to July 1922. He was appointed a judge of the High Court in 1936. In 1946, he was appointed president of the High Court. See Gerard Hogan, 'George Gavan Duffy', *Dictionary of Irish Biography*, https://www.dib.ie/biography/duffy-george-gavan-a2810.

114 Sheridan wrote in a familiar style, addressing the judge as 'My dear Gavan Duffy'. Neither man had been in touch since their schooldays: 'This letter will appear to you like a voice from the dead. My earlier recollection of you was at one of the famous academies at Stonyhurst when you carried off all the most important prizes. That was in the year 1898 and I have followed your career with such interest and was delighted when you were appointed to the Supreme Court of Ireland. The right man in the right place.' (The middle of this file is burnt through, as if a cigarette or candle had been left on top of it, and regrettably much of the text of the letter has been lost.)

115 NAI/D/T 41036: The Department of External Affairs received a request in September 1946 from the Chilean consul general in Dublin, Eduardo F. Hunter, to have de Valera attend the inauguration of their new president, Gabriel González Videla. In correspondence with Iveagh House, he stressed the 'strong ties of friendship' between the two countries, 'feelings which have existed since the early days of independence because of General Bernardo O'Higgins Riquelme, our National Hero, and even before that, with his august father before him, Don Ambrosio O'Higgins, an Irishman, Governor General of Chile and Viceroy of Perú, the greatest statesman Chile ever had in Colonial days, and also that of other Irishmen, who participated patriotically and so conspicuously in Chilean emancipation, such as Mackenna, O'Brien, Lynch, etc.' NAI/DFA, 410/38.

116 See Kevin C. Kearns, *Ireland's Arctic Siege: The Big Freeze of 1947* (Gill & Macmillan, Dublin, 2011).

117   Michael Kennedy, 'Leopold Harding Kerney', *Dictionary of Irish Biography*, https://www. dib.ie/biography/kerney-leopold-harding-a4524.

118   NAI/D/T 14064, Memorandum for government, 19 April 1947.

119   Whelan, *Ireland's Revolutionary Diplomat*, p. 233; I am grateful to Dr Whelan and Niall Kerney for providing me with a copy of the 22-page report completed by Kerney on 28 June 1947 (p. 14 missing).

120   NAI/D/T 14064, Government decision G.C.4/353, item 5, 29.4.1947.

121   De Valera to Bramuglia, 22 April 1947, 'Irlanda', expediente 2, Irlanda 2/946, Ministerio de Relaciones Exteriores y Culto, Archivo Histórico de la Cancillería Argentina, Buenos Aires.

122   In mid-May, Kerney's delegation was in Santiago, Chile, where he met the president, Señor Gabriel González Videla, and the country's foreign minister. Kerney apologised to the president, on behalf of de Valera, for the latter's unavailability to attend his inauguration the previous year. On 24 July, Consul General Hunter wrote to Iveagh House that Kerney's visit had 'served as a first step to establish direct diplomatic relations with my country, which I trust will lead in the very near future, as is the desire of my government and the mission I have been entrusted with, the success of which rests entirely on the part of Your Excellency, to establish a permanent Irish diplomatic representative to Chile'. NAI/DFA, 410/38.

123   *TSC*, 2 May 1947.

124   'Kerney Press Conference', *Irish Press*, 5 June 1947.

125   Leopold Kerney report, Dublin, 19 June 1947, Leopold Kerney papers (LKPA), in family possession.

126   LKPA, Kerney report for 1 May 1947.

127   Ibid.

128   See *TSC* on 9, 16, 23, 30 May and 6 June.

129   LKPA, Kerney report, 19 June 1947.

130   Quoted in Kerney report, 31 May 1947.

131   Whelan, *Ireland's Revolutionary Diplomat*, p. 235; O'Carolan was a Passionist and had been in Argentina for a few decades. He remained an enthusiastic supporter of Éamon de Valera.

132   Quoted in Kerney report, 31 May 1947.

133   LKPA, Kerney report for 26 May 1947.

134   Ibid.

135   *TSC*, 6 June 1947.

136   Ibid.

137   *Irish Press*, 14 June 1947.

138   NAI/DFA/313/24, Murphy report, 22 March 1948.

139   Ibid. Emphasis in original.

140   Horan gave this profile of the wealthier Irish-Argentines: 'What of the attitude of the Irish-Argentine towards Ireland. With the landed oligarchy Ireland counts for very little, if at all. Indeed one has the impression that as a class that section of the community would almost prefer to pass as British and not Irish. During the Second World War they had no sympathy whatever with our policy of neutrality. Neither had they any sympathy with Argentina's own policy of neutrality which she was able to maintain, despite great pressure from the United States, right up to the 26th January, 1944, when she broke off relations with Germany and Japan, though she did not actually declare war on those powers until March 1945. No doubt too they would have taken the view that our neutrality was similar to that of Argentina, which was, on the whole, anti-Ally and pro-Axis.' Horan report, NAI/DFA/313/24d, confidential reports, 22 July 1958.

141   Ibid.

142   'Irlanda', expediente 2, Irlanda 2/946, Ministerio de Relaciones Exteriores y Culto, Archivo Histórico de la Cancillería Argentina, Buenos Aires.

143 *Irish Press,* 21 June 1947.

144 'Irlanda', expediente 2, Irlanda 2/946, Ministerio de Relaciones Exteriores y Culto, Archivo Histórico de la Cancillería Argentina, Buenos Aires.

145 Ibid.

146 'Envoys Exchange Notes at US Ceremony', *Irish Press,* 6 August 1947; see also *Irish Independent,* 6 August 1947.

147 'Irlanda', expediente 2, Irlanda 2/946, Ministerio de Relaciones Exteriores y Culto, Archivo Histórico de la Cancillería Argentina, Buenos Aires.

148 A past pupil of the Christian Brothers O'Connell's School in Dublin, he began his career in 1913 in the departments of National Health Insurance, Education and Inland Revenue.

149 'Mr Matthew Murphy Obituary', *Irish Press,* 30 December 1967.

150 'Young Violinist in Debut: Olinda von Kap-Herr Proves an Intelligent Player', *New York Times,* 8 December 1928.

151 'Arrival of Mr Matthew Murphy', *TSC,* 5 December 1947; see also Dermot Keogh, 'Diplomatic Snapshots: The Irish Consul in San Francisco, 1933–1947', in Donald Jordan and Timothy J. O'Keefe (eds), *The Irish in the San Francisco Bay Area: Essays on Good Fortune* (the Executive Council of the Irish Literary and Historical Society, San Francisco, 2005), pp. 220–44.

152 Stephen Kelly, 'A Policy of Futility: Éamon de Valera's Anti-Partition Campaign, 1948–1951', *Études d'Histoire et de Civilisation,* vol. 36, no. 2, 2011, https://journals.openedition.org/etudesirlandaises/2348.

153 MacBride wrote a memoir on his early years and time in politics between 1904 and 1951. Caitriona Lawlor (ed.), *Seán MacBride: That Day's Struggle: A Memoir 1904–1951* (Currach Press, Dublin, 2005), pp. 130–228.

154 Dermot Keogh, *Twentieth Century Ireland,* pp. 186 and 424.

155 Whelan, *Ireland and the Marshall Plan*; for background to Irish–US relations, see by same author: *De Valera and Roosevelt: Irish and American Diplomacy in Times of Crisis, 1932–1939* (Cambridge University Press, Cambridge, 2020).

156 Wylie, *Ireland and the Cold War,* pp. 198–224.

157 Dermot Keogh, *Ireland and the Vatican: The Policy and Diplomacy of Church–State Relations, 1922–1960* (Cork University Press, Cork, 1995), pp. 225–64.

158 My book *Ireland and the Vatican* throws light on official thinking during the 1950s and the policy nexus between church and state relating to foreign policy. For a more general view of the global links between Marian devotion, the Cold War and the defeat of communism, see Peter Jan Margry (ed.), *Cold War Mary: Ideologies, Politics, and Marian Devotional Culture* (Leuven University Press, Leuven, 2020).

159 Keogh, *Twentieth Century Ireland,* pp. 190–1.

160 Seán Nunan, a member of the generation who had served in 1919 with de Valera in the United States, replaced him and remained in that post until 1955.

161 In MacBride's published memoirs, there are four references in the index to his wife. None are very informative and reveal little of the personality of Kid Bulfin or of her dynamism. She ran a farm and a jam-making factory to support the family through difficult times. Lawlor (ed.), *Seán MacBride,* pp. 62, 100, 105, 111.

162 MacBride explained in his memoirs that there had been a number of incidents before the change of government where letters of credence addressed to the king of England had been opened in Dublin. That had led to 'acrimonious correspondence' with Buckingham Palace. At cabinet, MacBride explained what he had done and there was approval for his actions: 'They all said that it was about time we put an end to this nonsense of presenting letters of credence to Buckingham Palace.' Lawlor (ed.), *Seán MacBride,* pp. 157–8.

163 The Republic of Ireland Act 1948, which was signed into law on 21 December 1948, came into force on 18 April 1949. The power was vested in the president of Ireland to hold the executive authority, subject to the advice of the Irish government, in external relations.

164 Nicholas Nolan minute, 3 August 1948, doc. 107, NAI, TSCH/3/S6070A: Crowe et al., *Documents on Irish Foreign Policy*, vol. IX, 1948–1951 (RIA, Dublin, 2014), pp. 125–6.

165 'Argentina's Envoy', *Sunday Independent*, 1 August 1948.

166 'WELCOME', *TSC*, 19 December 1947.

167 'La Llegada del Ministro Irlandés', *TSC*, 26 December 1947.

168 'Ussher's Speech', *TSC*, 4 January 1947.

169 Ibid.

170 Ibid.

171 'Thanksgiving at Holy Cross', *TSC*, 2 January 1947.

172 'The Arrival of the Irish Minister', *TSC*, 26 December 1947.

173 These words were taken from Eduardo Clancy, 'José María Dunphy: "These are the times that try men's souls"', unpublished essay sent to me by the author.

174 Jan-Werner Müller, *What Is Populism?* (Penguin Books, London, 2017), pp. 44–9, 114. Emphasis in original.

175 NAI/DFA/313/24, Murphy report, 5 November 1950.

176 Ibid.

177 Murphy did admit that the workers were loyal to her: 'Every worker recently gave up 2 days' pay to the fund last month in respect of the 17 August and 17 October (San Martin Day and Loyalty Day) and had to line up for hours outside banks to pay it and give particulars of salary and wages etc.' NAI, DFA/313/24, Murphy report, 5 November 1950.

178 NAI, DFA/313/24, Murphy report, 5 November 1950.

179 Ibid.

180 The journey in the nineteenth century between Ireland and Buenos Aires was an endurance test of many weeks. But before the invention of jet engines, travel to Argentina from Europe presented its own challenges. In 1956, Br O'Connell described his plane journey from New York to Buenos Aires: Idlewild to Panama, to Guaquil in Ecuador, to Taltara [?] in Peru, then to Lima and on to Santiago in Chile. He then flew in a Douglas propellor plane through, rather than over, the Andes: 'As we were approaching the mountain range, the weather was changing and our plane was being tossed around; at one moment it seemed to shoot up vertically and would come down so rapidly that I thought it must hit the mountain. All this time a storm of snow and hurricane winds were battering our plane all over the place, now and again I looked out only to see outside the steel-like masses of rock against which I thought we should be battered. The few passengers were all sick and badly shaken, one could feel the efforts the captain was making to control an aircraft as helpless almost as a feather in the circumstances. What a relief when we got out from those treacherous mountain passes.' O'Connor memoir (unnumbered, but see final two pages).

181 NAI/DFA/313/24B.

182 Rock, *The British in Argentina*, pp. 304–6.

183 Guillermo David, National Library, Buenos Aires, has written an important paper on this topic in which he identifies the roles of Guillermo Patricio Kelly, John William Cooke, José Luis Nell, Joe Baxter and Rodolfo Walsh. Cooke was the son of Juan Isaac Cooke, a minister for foreign affairs in the Farrell government. John William was a national deputy at twenty-four, also a writer, a journalist and a Perón loyalist, who after the leader's exile became a leader of the Peronist resistance to military repression. He met with Ernesto 'Che' Guevara Lynch in 1960. Guillermo Patricio Kelly experienced terms in prison on many occasions for his militant activities. He died in 2005 after a lifetime of revolutionary

activity and having survived being tortured during the civilian military dictatorship. In this paper, David also mentions José Luis Nell, Lucía María Cullen, Miguel Fitzgerald, Santiago MacGuire, Aníbal Ford, Santiago Ulises Murphy, Heber O'Neill Velázquez, Patricio Calloway, Jorge Patricio Dillon, Gastón Dillon, Gloria Kehoe Wilson, Silva Hynes, Patricia Teresa Flynn, Valeria Dixon, Norma Kennedy and Vicki Walsh. See Guillermo David, 'Irlandeses Peronistas', paper given at SILAS conference, Pontifical Catholic University, Santiago, Chile, December 2018.

184 For background to these reforms, see Plotkin, *Mañana es San Perón*, pp. 85 ff; see also Lucretia L. Ilsley, 'The Argentine Constitutional Revision of 1949', *The Journal of Politics*, vol. 14, no. 2, 1952, pp. 224–40.

185 Lila M. Caimari, *Perón y la Iglesia Católica: Religión, Estado y Sociedad en la Argentina (1943–1955)* (Ariel Historia, Buenos Aires, 1994); see reviews of her book by Émile Poulat, 'Archives De Sciences Sociales Des Religions', *Archives De Sciences Sociales Des Religions*, vol. 41, no. 94, 1996, pp. 61–2, www.jstor.org/stable/30128691, and David Rock in *The Hispanic American Historical Review*, vol. 77, no. 4, 1997, pp. 753–4, https://doi.org/10.2307/2517041. See also Plotkin, *Mañana es San Perón*.

186 NAI/DFA/313/24B; because of his fear that the diplomatic bag would be opened in Buenos Aires, Murphy regularly took the precaution of sending his report from Montevideo, Uruguay.

187 Plotkin, *Mañana es San Perón*, p. 33.

188 Emir Rodríguez Monegal et al., 'Borges and Politics', *Diacritics*, vol. 8, no. 4, 1978, p. 64, www.jstor.org/stable/464739. In 1948, Borges' sister Norah and mother Doña Leonor Azevedo de Borges were arrested on Calle Florida as part of a group who were singing the national anthem and handing out anti-government pamphlets. As the protesters did not have a permit to hold a meeting, the judge sent them to jail for a month. Borges' mother, who was sixty, was put under house arrest.

189 Alfie Byrne was lord mayor of Dublin between 1930 and 1939. He had a long career as an alderman in Dublin Corporation, as a nationalist MP at Westminster and later as a TD in Dáil Éireann. He was regularly seen cycling around the city, chatting to people and dispensing lollipops to children.

190 NAI/DFA/313/24B.

191 NAI/DFA/313/24B. His report of 19 February gave details of his interview on 10 December 1951 with the foreign minister, Jerónimo Remorino. The report, which he had sent independently, never reached Dublin and the chargé believed it had been intercepted by the Argentine authorities.

192 NAI/DFA, 313/24A, Murphy report, 23 June 1952.

193 NAI/DFA, 313/24A, Murphy report, 26 June 1952.

194 The Irish legation bought a wreath for 800 pesos. Other diplomatic missions spent up to 3,000 pesos on flowers.

195 NAI/DFA, 313/24A, Murphy report, 5 September 1952.

196 Ibid.

197 Ibid.

198 Dennis Gilbert, *The Oligarchy and the Old Regime in Latin America, 1880–1970* (Rowman & Littlefield, Lanham and London, 2017), p. 27; see also fictional account by Beatriz Guido, *El Incendio y las Vísperas* (Editorial Losada, Buenos Aires, 1964).

199 See Jason Wilson, *Buenos Aires: A Cultural and Literary History* (Signal Books, Oxford, 2007), p. 104; Joseph A. Page, *Perón: A Biography* (Random House, New York, 1983), see Chapter 30.

200 Robert D. Crassweller, *Perón and the Enigmas of Argentina* (Norton, New York and London, 1987), pp. 294–6.

201 Flavia Fiorucci, 'Between Institutional Survival and Intellectual Commitment: The Case of the Argentine Society of Writers during Perón's Rule (1945–1955)', *The Americas*, vol. 62, no. 4, April 2006, p. 614.

202 In Australia, where Cold War tensions split the Labour Party in 1955, a breakaway Democratic Labour Party was set up in 1957. That served as an example of what might happen to the Peronist movement. See Brenda Niall, *Mannix* (Text Publishing, Melbourne, 2015), pp. 284–316.

203 John Murray, 'Perón and the Church', *Studies: An Irish Quarterly Review*, vol. 44, no. 175, 1955, pp. 257–70, https://www.jstor.org/stable/30098658; see also David F. D'Amico, 'Religious Liberty in Argentina during the First Perón Regime, 1943–1955', *Church History*, vol. 46, no. 4, 1977, pp. 490–503, https://doi.org/10.2307/3164442. Those two articles capture the range of publications which appeared during and in the aftermath of the overthrow of Perón.

204 Müller, *What Is Populism?*, p. 114.

205 Horacio Verbitsky, *Cristo Vence: La Iglesia en la Argentina: Un Siglo de Historia Política (1884–1983)*. Tomo 1: *De Roca a Perón* (Editorial Sudamericana, Buenos Aires, 2007).

206 NAI/DFA/410/72/16.

207 Ibid.

208 This classical reference refers to Emperor Tiberius' withdrawal from Rome in AD 26, after twelve years in power, to the island of Capri where he reigned for a further eleven years. There, according to his biographer, Suetonius, he led a life of heavy drinking and debauchery. Murphy, with his classical formation, reverted to the Tiberius reference in order to infer that Perón, based on salacious rumour, was behaving in a like fashion.

209 Murphy to Secretary, 19 November 1954, NAI, DFA/410/72/16.

210 'Letter to Gen. Perón', *The Times* (London), 24 November 1954.

211 A number of the bishops were not in the country to sign the joint pastoral.

212 'Police Break up Demonstration', *Cork Examiner*, 29 November 1955.

213 NAI/DFA313/24B, Murphy to Iveagh House, 21 December 1955.

214 Perón went to the city airport at the time of the mass to greet a triumphant Pascual Pérez, who had won the world flyweight title in Japan on 26 November. The boxer later defeated Yoshio Shirai in Tokyo on 30 May 1955, having first taken the world flyweight title from him in a bout on 26 November 1954. Deemed to be among the top three flyweight champions ever, he had also won gold in 1948 in the London Olympics. (A tango, 'The Great Champion', had been composed in his honour.)

215 NAI/DFA313/24B, Murphy to Iveagh House, 21 December 1954.

216 Austen Ivereigh, *Catholicism and Politics in Argentina, 1810–1960* (St Martin's Press, New York, 1995), p. 175.

217 'Perón and the Church, *Irish Independent*, 11 December 1954.

218 NAI/DFA313/24B, Murphy to Iveagh House, 21 December 1954.

219 Ibid. The journalistic source was convinced that his poor mental health dated back to a fall from his motorcycle. He also knew that Perón had large assets abroad. The fact that he was rushing through so many items convinced Murphy's source that the general was about to quit power. Argentina without Perón would be 'chaos', according to the same source.

220 NAI,/DFA/410/72/16, Murphy to Secretary, 30 December 1954.

221 An article in *The Tablet*, 11 December 1954, noted that in the past the government had submitted the names of teachers of religion to the local bishop for approval. The new decree changed that system of appointment as it 'curtails the executive power's exclusive authority'.

222 'New Argentine Rebuff to Catholics', *The Times* (London), 3 December 1954.

223 'Perón Government Lifts Moral Ban', *Irish Press*, 31 December 1954; this was also reported by *The Times* (London) on the same day.

224 NAI/DFA/410/72/16, Cremin to Secretary, 26 January 1955.

225 NAI/DFA/410/72/16, Cremin to Secretary, 4 January 1955.

226 NAI/DFA/410/72/16, Cremin to Secretary, 26 January 1955.

227 NAI/DFA/410/72/16, Murphy to Secretary, 3 February 1955. This report was sent from Iveagh House to Murphy in Buenos Aires on 19 March.

228 Michael A. Burdick, *For God and the Fatherland: Religion and Politics in Argentina* (State University of New York, New York, 1995), p. 63 ff.

229 Bernardo Furlong is listed as secretary of the ICA in 1955.

230 NAI/DFA313/24B, Murphy to Iveagh House, 21 December 1955.

231 It is most unlikely, in my view, that any of the Christian Brothers at that time in Buenos Aires were Argentine citizens.

232 NAI/DFA/410/72/16, Murphy to Secretary, 3 January 1955.

233 NAI/DFA/410/72/16, Murphy to Secretary, 21 April 1955. The report was sent on to Cremin at the Holy See.

234 'Relay of Mass Drowned by Noise', *Irish Independent*, 7 May 1955.

235 Verbitsky, *Cristo Vence*, Tomo I, p. 274.

236 Ibid.

237 'Arrests in Argentina', *Irish Independent*, 9 May 1955.

238 'Perón Driving for Head-on Clash', *Catholic Herald*, 10 May 1955. Many clergy rounded up by the Argentine police early in May were released in the third week of that month: 'Argentina Releases 16 Catholic Leaders', *Irish Press*, 19 May 1955.

239 There are divergent views on the birthplace of Fr Michael Fox. One source states that he was born in Castletown-Geoghegan, County Westmeath. He spent his priestly life of over fifty years in Argentina. His final parish was in Rosario, where he is buried under the main altar of his church there. He died in the 1990s. He revisited his home town in Ireland in 1956, the year the local hurlers won the senior county championship. Some of the above information was received from his cousin, Fr Christopher Fox, and from his book, *Painted Butterflies: Memories of a Missionary* (Choice Publishing, Drogheda, 2015), pp. 189–90. According to the *Irish Press*, 6 June 1955, Fr Fox was born in Argentina. (This is more likely.) His father was Michael Fox, Loughavalley, County Westmeath. Both his maternal grandparents were from Westmeath. At the age of two, he was taken to Ireland and educated at St Finian's College, Mullingar. He studied in the Latin American College, Rome, and was ordained in 1926. He was a brother of Mrs J. Flynn, Adamstown, Castletown-Geoghegan, and Sr Mary Thaddeus, Holy Faith Convent, Glasnevin, Dublin. Fox's arrest was reported in the *Irish Independent* on 3 May 1955, stating that he was charged with creating a disturbance. The same edition had an editorial entitled 'Perón's Attack on the Church'. Fr Gaynor, the editor of *TSC*, told Murphy that Fox had been born in Argentina and taken to Ireland at the age of two, where he was educated. He became a secular priest and was stationed at Castletown-Geoghegan, Mullingar, for a time. His brothers and sisters still lived there. Murphy was told that Fox was 'a close friend of our President [Seán T. O'Kelly] and Mr de Valera'. The latter once served his mass at Croagh Patrick. Murphy was asked to have this brought to the attention of the Argentinian foreign minister. Gaynor felt that by Murphy calling upon the minister, it would set wheels in motion that might result in his release.

240 NAI/DFA/410/72/16, Murphy to Secretary, 12 May 1955.

241 Ibid.

242 Ibid.

243 Ibid.

244 NAI/DFA/410/72/16, Murphy to Secretary, 26 May 1955. This report was sent to Cremin at the Holy See.

245 'Danger of Excommunication', *Cork Examiner*, 4 June 1955.

246 One official in Iveagh House minuted: 'I am not sure that his [Murphy's] contacts with the foreign office are close enough on that account to ensure the success of a delicate intervention of this type.'

247 Ibid.

248 'Fr Fox Freed in S. America', *Irish Press*, 10 June 1955.

249 'Westmeath Priest Jailed', *Longford Leader*, 11 June 1955.

250 'Ireland Never to Follow Mexico or Argentina', *Connacht Sentinel*, 7 June 1955.

251 'Catholics to Defy Argentine Police', *New York Times*, 9 June 1955.

252 'Perón Learned from His Masters', *The Standard*, 10 June 1955; 'Dictator Shows True Colours in the Argentine', *Irish Press*, 13 June 1955.

253 NAI/DFA/410/72/16, Murphy to Secretary, 13 (*sic*) June 1955. This report has to have been written after 16 June. It was sent by special airmail and therefore was more openly critical than what he would send by post or through the diplomatic bag. There is no mention of the role played at the cathedral by the Irish Christian Brothers in the Newman annals. That is not surprising given the fear that such a source might be seized in a police raid on the school. See Newman Christian Brothers house annals, 1945 – 22 October 1983, Newman College, San Isidro, Buenos Aires. (I am grateful to Br Tom O'Connell, Newman College, and Br John Burke, former principal, Newman College, now at Christian Brothers Province Centre, Griffith Avenue, Dublin 9.) But a former brother who taught in Newman during the 1970s told me that two members of the order, Tony Gallagher and Atty O'Brien, had set out earlier in the morning from the school, which was near the cathedral, the former armed with a hurley and the latter with a hammer. The crowds were so dense that they were not able to get through. It is my view that Murphy was correct and that a number of other Christian Brothers were in the cathedral and ready to defend it if necessary.

254 Told to me by a former Christian Brother who taught in Newman in the 1970s. The superior in Newman was Br Lawlor, from Thurles, County Tipperary. Others on the staff at the time were Br Kearney, Cork, Br Ryan, Tipperary, Br O'Reilly, Dublin, and Br Kelly, Waterford.

255 Verbitsky, *Cristo Vence*, Tomo 1, p. 291 ff.

256 'Expelled Bishop on Way to Rome', *Irish Press*, 16 June 1955.

257 NAI/DFA/410/72/16, Cremin to Secretary, 18 June 1955. In a later report, 20 June, Cremin reflected on the claim by Perón that the *patronato* justified him in removing from his functions a particular ecclesiastic. The *patronato* was, under Canons 1448–71, a traditional right which some countries, and in particular some Latin American countries, claimed to enjoy in relation to nominations to church benefices and sees. That is claimed to be a legacy derived from Spain. This gives the government some say in the appointment of bishops. But the *patronato* did not confer the right to remove a bishop. The ambassador said firmly that such a view was 'far-fetched and entirely ignores the realities of the present-day situation in this matter'. See NAI/DFA/410/72/16, Cremin to Secretary, 20 June 1955.

258 NAI/DFA/410/72/16, Murphy to Secretary, 17 June 1955.

259 Ibid.

260 Christian Brothers house annals, p. 77.

261 The events received detailed and prominent coverage in the Irish newspapers. See, for example, *Irish Independent*, 17 June 1955, where it was the lead story.

262 Christian Brothers house annals, p. 77.

263 NAI/DFA/410/72/16, Murphy to Secretary, 17 June 1955.

264 Ibid.

265 Ibid.

266 Ibid.

267 Ibid. Murphy had great difficulty sending that report to Dublin, being informed that no cables in code would be accepted by any of the companies and he was given no guarantee as to when it might be sent. By whatever route, it did arrive in Iveagh House.

268 'Sack Argentine Churches: First Eyewitness Story of Burnings', *Chicago Daily Tribune*, 18 June 1955.

269 See *Irish Press*, *Irish Independent*, *Irish Times* and *Cork Examiner* for 17, 18 and 20 June, which led with reports from Argentina, as did the evening papers, the *Herald* and the *Evening Echo*. During the following week, all Irish papers provided extensive coverage of what was happening in Argentina.

270 'Maynooth Message to Argentina', *Irish Press*, 30 June 1955.

271 'Knock Pilgrims Prayed for Argentina', *Irish Independent*, 2 July 1955.

272 There is an oral tradition in the Pallottines that another of their priests, Fr Luis Brady, was arrested in his parish in Suipacha. He was taken from his rectory to the jail across the plaza. When asked by the local police if there was anything that they could do to make him comfortable, he asked that his bed be brought from the rectory. The police duly obliged. Source: Fr Donal McCarthy to author, 6 May 2016.

273 Fr Tomás O'Donnell, Pallottine, Mercedes, email to author, 24 August 2019.

274 Fr Tony Stakelum, 'Let Us Remember Fr Peter Davern', manuscript article, Pallottine archives, Sandyford Road, Dundrum, Dublin 16; I am grateful to the Pallottine archivist Fr Donal McCarthy for providing me with this reference.

275 *Irish Press*, 7 September 1955.

276 NAI/DFA/410/72/16, Murphy to Secretary, 17 June 1955.

277 NAI/DFA/410/72/16, Murphy to Secretary, 28 June 1955.

278 Ibid.

279 Ibid.

280 NAI/DFA 313/24C. Each of the twelve appeared in civilian clothes in their new passports which were to act as identity papers during the church–state crisis. Horan, reporting on 16 May 1956, confirmed that Murphy had sent a list of those names to Iveagh House, noting that all were already in possession of Irish passports and that the new documents had been issued on the understanding that they 'would be used only in Argentina for identification purposes'. Horan was instructed not to recall the new passports in case of a recrudescence of anti-clerical violence and it was important 'to be prepared for that contingency'.

281 Kenneth P. Serbin, 'Church–State Reciprocity in Contemporary Brazil: The Convening of the International Eucharistic Congress of 1955 in Rio Janeiro', Kellogg Institute, Working Paper 229, August 1996, https://kellogg.nd.edu/sites/default/files/old_files/documents/229.pdf.

282 NAI/DFA/410/72/16.

283 ARCH/12/ Papal Nuncio in Ireland, Alberto Levame to D'Alton, 3 July 1955, Argentina folder (Cardinal D'Alton papers), Cardinal Tomás Ó Fiaich Library & Archive (hereafter CÓFLA).

284 Cardinal Francis Spellman of New York had also applied for a visa. The Argentinian ambassadors in Dublin and Washington, Murphy was told, had been instructed to represent that position to the respective foreign ministries. NAI, DFA/410/72/16.

285 CÓFLA ARCH/12, undated press release, Argentina folder (Cardinal D'Alton papers), Cardinal Tomás Ó Fiaich Library & Archive. See also NAI/DFA/410/72/16, Murphy to Secretary, 14 July 1955.

286 Cardinal John D'Alton to Fr Walsh, Provincial of Pallottines, Argentina, from Ara Coeli, 3 September 1955, box 24, Pallottine archives, St Patrick's, Belgrano, Buenos Aires.

287 Christian Brothers house annals, p. 79.

288 Rock, *The British in Argentina*, pp. 316–17.

289 Christian Brothers house annals, p. 79.

290 In English, *cuervo* means raven. The use of the word was pejorative.

291 My translation of Mugica's words are not literal. Quoted in Araceli Bellotta, 'El Cura de las Villas', *Todo es Historia*, no. 361, August, 1997, p. 11.

292 NAI/D/T 14064.

293 Conor Cruise O'Brien, 'Ireland in International Affairs', in Owen Dudley Edwards (ed.), *Conor Cruise O'Brien Introduces Ireland* (McGraw-Hill Books, New York, 1969), p. 129.

294 Ronan Fanning, 'The Evolution of Irish Foreign Policy', in Kennedy and Morrison Skelly (eds), *Irish Foreign Policy 1919–1966*, pp. 322–3.

295 Conor Cruise O'Brien, *To Katanga and Back: A UN Case History* (Hutchinson, London, 1962), p. 12 ff.

296 Aoife Bhreatnach, 'Frank Aiken: European Federation and United Nations Internation-alism', *Irish Studies in International Affairs*, vol 13, 2002, pp. 237–49.

297 Noel Dorr, 'Frank Aiken at the United Nations: Some Personal Recollections', in Bryce Evans and Stephen Kelly (eds), *Frank Aiken: Nationalist and Internationalist* (Irish Academic Press, Newbridge, Ireland, 2014), p. 210.

298 O'Brien, 'Ireland in International Affairs', p. 130.

299 Keogh, *Twentieth Century Ireland*, pp. 241–5.

300 Horan had wide diplomatic experience. He was posted to the consulate in New York between August 1943 and June 1945. Having spent two years in Iveagh House as head of the consular section, he served as *chargé ad interim* at Lisbon during August and September 1947 and as secretary to the legation in Paris from February 1947 to September 1949. He spent two further years in headquarters as a counsellor in charge of the consular section. In April 1952, he was made chief of protocol. He then served in Spain before taking up his position in Buenos Aires. NAI/D/T 14064, profile of Timothy Joseph Horan.

301 NAI/DFA 313/24C.

302 Ibid.

303 Pacho O'Donnell, *Breve Historia Argentina: De la Conquista a los Kirchner* (Aguilar, Buenos Aires, 2014), pp. 252–3.

304 Details of the massacre are in Michael McCaughan, *Rodolfo Walsh: Periodista, Escritor y Revolucionario, 1927–1977* (LOM Ediciones, Santiago, Chile, 2015), pp. 57–9.

305 Rodolfo Walsh, *Operación Masacre* (De La Flor, Buenos Aires, 1984). See also the film of the same name made in 1973, directed and written by Jorge Cedrón.

306 O'Donnell, *Breve Historia Argentina* (Aguilar, Buenos Aires, 2014), p. 250.

307 Horan report 18 July 1957, NAI/DFA 31324C.

308 NAI/DFA 313/24C.

309 Rock, *The British in Argentina*, pp. 334–5.

310 NAI/DFA 313/24C.

311 Scott Mainwaring and Anibal Pérez Liñán, *Democracies and Dictatorships in Latin America: Emergence, Survival and Fall* (Cambridge University Press, New York, 2013), pp. 136–9.

CHAPTER 3 Rediscovering Latin America: Irish missionary 'soft power' and Irish diplomacy in Argentina, 1962–74

1 Mary Daly, *Sixties Ireland: Reshaping the Economy, State and Society* (Cambridge University Press, Cambridge, 2016).

2 O'Driscoll, *Ireland, West Germany and the New Europe 1949–73*.

3 Dermot Keogh and Aoife Keogh, 'Ireland and European Integration: From the Treaty of Rome to Membership', in Mark Callanan (ed.), *Foundations of an Ever Closer Union: An Irish Perspective on the Fifty Years since the Treaty of Rome* (Institute of Public Administration, Dublin, 2007), pp. 6–50.

4   Quoted in Michael Kennedy, 'Frederick H. Boland', *Dictionary of Irish Biography*, https://www.dib.ie/biography/boland-frederick-h-a0761.

5   See O'Sullivan, *Ireland, Africa and the End of Empire*, pp. 35–56. This book is an outstanding synthesis of Irish foreign policy towards Africa over two decades.

6   David O'Donoghue, *The Irish Army in the Congo 1960–1964: The Far Battalions* (Irish Academic Press, 2006).

7   See https://www.military.ie/en/overseas-deployments/past-missions/african-missions/.

8   The Irish public were invited to read a range of literature dealing with missionary activity on that continent, *Africa, Far East, The Word*, etc. As a child, I remember putting an old penny in a slot on a collection box and as the penny dropped into it the statue of St Martin de Porres bowed his head. (A Peruvian Dominican lay brother beatified in 1837 and canonised in 1962.) In my primary school in Dublin, I brought in a penny a month for 'the black babies'. See Fiona Bateman, 'The Spiritual Empire: Irish Catholic Missionary Discourse in the Twentieth Century', PhD thesis, NUI Galway, 2003.

9   O'Sullivan, *Ireland, Africa and the End of Empire*, p. 15.

10 O'Sullivan's *Ireland, Africa and the End of Empire* is an exemplary study of this subject.

11 Tom Commins was born in October 1913 and educated at Rockwell College. He entered the civil service in 1933, serving in the departments of Agriculture, Supplies and Industry and Commerce. He entered the Department of External Affairs in May 1946 as commercial secretary to the legation in Washington. In 1948, he was recalled to headquarters as counsellor in charge of the European Recovery Programme. He was counsellor in Paris from August 1954 to September 1955 before being posted to Lisbon. NAI/D/T/S14064B.

12 The agrément was received in Dublin on 21 October and he took up his post in spring 1960. Born in Waterford on 23 September 1914, he joined the Department of External Affairs in March 1934. Married with five children, he had served at headquarters in the early years of his career. In September 1954, he had been appointed counsellor to the Holy See, and counsellor to Canberra in 1959. NAI/DT/S14064C.

13 NAI/DFA/313/24G.

14 John F. Kennedy Library, https://www.jfklibrary.org/events-and-awards/forums/past-forums/transcripts/50th-anniversary-of-the-bay-of-pigs-invasion.

15 NAI/DFA/313/24G.

16 Ibid.

17 Ibid.

18 Seán Ó hÉideáin, who had served as a third secretary in Buenos Aires in 1951 and 1952, was sent to act as chargé d'affaires. He would be appointed ambassador to Argentina in 1977.

19 NAI/DT/S14064C.

20 NAI/D/T/2014, S14064B.

21 The class roll book from the North Monastery School carries his name in Irish as Mícheál Leon Scantelberí. He was born on 6 December 1917 at Weaver's Point, Crosshaven, County Cork. The roll also notes that he had won a 'college Entrance Schol. UCC'.

22 A future president of UCC, Tadgh Ó Ciaracáin (Tadgh Carey) had also won a UCC college exhibition (scholarship); I am grateful to Tony Duggan for this information.

23 This anecdote was mentioned to me frequently during my researches by a number of retired diplomats, one being Ambassador Bernard Davenport.

24 Dorr, 'Some Personal Recollections', in Evans and Kelly (eds), *Frank Aiken*, pp. 224–9.

25 Guevara had an Irish grandmother, Ana Isabel Lynch.

26 Richard Goodwin memorandum for President Kennedy, 22 August 1961, https://goo.gl/vuuUB6.

27 NAI/DFA 313/24G.

28 'Journalist who Interviewed Che and Taught Fidel to Make Irish Coffee', *Guardian*, 1 January 2013, https://www.theguardian.com/media/greenslade/2013/jan/01/che-guevara-ireland; 'When Che Guevara Walked on Irish Soil', https://www.irishecho.com/2012/04/when-che-guevara-walked-on-irish-soil/.

29 'What is Ireland Doing Putting Che Guevara on a Stamp?', *Irish Times*, 9 October 2017, https://www.irishtimes.com/news/ireland/irish-news/what-is-ireland-doing-putting-che-guevara-on-a-stamp-1.3249319.

30 While on an extended visit to Buenos Aires in 2017, many Irish-Argentines complained to me about the Irish government having put Guevara on a postage stamp. His receiving a panel in the travelling exhibition on the Irish in Latin America was greeted with similar scepticism.

31 NAI/D/T/2014, S14064C.

32 Since an Irish mission had been opened in Buenos Aires in 1919, successive diplomats had tried to bring about greater unity within the balkanised Irish-Argentine community. Eamonn Bulfin and Laurence Ginnell in late 1921 set up an organisation which did not survive the closing down of the Dáil Éireann mission in 1922. Geography, personality conflicts, feuds and political divisions had kept different Irish groups apart since the 1890s. The Irish Catholic Association remained the single most important unifying force throughout the decades but there was also the need for an umbrella organisation.

33 José E. Richards, '*La Federación de Sociedades Argentino-Irlandeses: Su Origen y Desenvolvimiento*', *TSC: Número del Centenario, 1875-1975*, pp. 59-61. I am grateful to Juan José Delaney for helping me make the connection with the federation.

34 My thanks to Mr Jimmy Ussher for arranging for Ann and me to consult the archives in December 2018 at the Fahy Club, Av. Congreso 2931, Buenos Aires. I was given access to two sets of minute books: 1) *Acta de la Asamblea Constitutiva de la Federación de Sociedades Irlandesas de la República Argentina* (from date of foundation in 1963 to 30 November 1989); 2) *Actas de Consejo Directivo*, 8 November 1978 to 1993 (two minute books).

35 There were soon further additions to the members: Shamrock Concert and Dance and the Sociedad Irlandesa Mercedina. The honorary presidents were nominated by Christian Brothers of Ireland, Passionist Fathers and Pallottine Fathers. I was given access to the minutes of the Asamblea Ordinaria and of the Consejo Directivo from the early 1960s to the early 1990s. On 30 November 1976, the following members of the executive committee, or *Consejo Directorio*, were present at a general assembly of the federation: Juan M Clancy, Ambrosio Geoghegan, A.G. McLoughlin, Eduardo A. Coghlan, Ernesto Enright, Guillermo P. Ford, Thelma McLoughlin and J.E. Rossiter. The associations represented at the general assembly were Irish Chaplains' Association; Hurling Club; *The Southern Cross*; Ladies of St Joseph Society; Sisters of Mercy; St Patrick's House; Association of Fahy Past Pupils; Passionist Fathers; Pallottine Fathers; Irish Race Society, Junín; Argentine-Irish Cultural Institute; San Antonio de Areco Association; Mercedes Association; and the Asociación Socorros Hospitalarios.

36 *Acta de la Asamblea Constitutiva de la Federación de Sociedades Irlandesas de la República Argentina*, 1 September 1961.

37 Minute book of *Consejo Directivo*, Federation Room, Fahy Club, Av. Congreso 2931, Buenos Aires.

38 See *Registro de Asistentes, Asamblea Ordinaria*, Federation Room, Fahy Club, Av. Congreso 2931, Buenos Aires.

39 Juan José Delaney, *What, Che? Integration, Adaptation, and Assimilation of the Irish-Argentine Community through Its Languages and Literature* (USAL, Buenos Aires, 2017), p. 126 ff.

40 Lazaro Droznes, *Cantando Como la Cigarra: Vida y Canciones de María Elena Walsh* (Unitexto, Buenos Aires, 2014); Sara Facio, *María Elena Walsh* (La Azotea, Buenos Aires, 1999); see also María Elena Walsh, *Novios de Antaño* (Seix Barral, Buenos Aires, 1990).

41 Rodolfo Walsh, *Los Irlandeses* (El Aleph Editors, Barcelona, 2007); also *Cuentos Completos* (Ediciones de la Flor, Buenos Aires, 2013); see also McCaughan, *Rodolfo Walsh*, p. 167 ff.

42 I am relying here on the work of Samuel L. Bailey, *Immigration in the Lands of Promise: Italians in Buenos Aires and New York City, 1870 to 1914* (Cornell University Press, Ithaca, 1999), pp. 10–24.

43 In 1975, *The Southern Cross* celebrated its centenary with a special supplement subsidised by the Irish embassy – a rich source on which to base a study of Irish-Argentine identity. *TSC: Número del Centenario, 1875–1975*, 104 pages.

44 NAI/DFA/2001/43/207/ [old file number, 313/24J].

45 '1916 Commemoration Mass at the Metropolitan Cathedral', *TSC*, 15 April 1966.

46 The Richards last visited Ireland in 1939 on honeymoon and were stranded by the outbreak of war. They returned to Buenos Aires via the US.

47 'Off to Ireland', *TSC*, 8 April 1966.

48 Howlin was a hotel and restaurant owner in Buenos Aires.

49 'Imperishable Memories of Ireland', *TSC*, 20 April 1966.

50 'Bust of San Martín in Dublin', *TSC*, 22 April 1966; see also 'Argentina's Gift to Ireland Marks Two Jubilees', *Irish Press*, 15 April 1966. The text of Richards' address, together with a photograph of both himself and Seán Lemass, is reprinted in *A Record of Ireland's Commemoration of the 1916 Rising* (Department of Foreign Affairs, Dublin, 1966), pp. 58–9.

51 'Argentina's Gift to Irish Nation', *Cork Examiner*, 15 April 1966; see also *Irish Independent*, 15 April 1966.

52 'Argentina's Gift to Ireland Marks Two Jubilees', *Irish Press*, 15 April 1966.

53 'The President', *Cork Examiner*, 19 April 1966.

54 Dr Richards told de Valera that Ireland was held in very high regard in Argentina and that her constitution 'had not just been translated into Spanish and studied in their universities but was also considered, especially by Catholic authors, as unique in the world'. It was, he said, admired on account of its provisions regarding religious tolerance that they found reflected the spirit which existed in Ireland. 'Imperishable Memories of Ireland', *TSC*, 20 April 1966.

55 S. Blanke, 'US Religious Interest Groups and Central America, 1973–1990'; see Chapter 2: 'Mission to Latin America', pp. 34–5, http://webdoc.sub.gwdg.de/ebook/diss/2003/fu-berlin/2003/122/Kapitel2.pdf.

56 Peter Hebblethwaite, *John XIII: Pope of the Council* (Geoffrey Chapman, London, 1985), p. 463.

57 Renato Poblete, 'From Medellin to Puebla: Notes for Reflection', *Journal of Interamerican Studies and World Affairs*, vol. 21, no. 1, Special Issue: The Church and Politics in Latin America (February 1979), pp. 31–44; see also Phillip Berryman, *Liberation Theology* (Temple University Press, Philadelphia, 1987). For further references, see bibliography.

58 Peter Hebblethwaite, *Paul VI: The First Modern Pope* (HarperCollins, London, 1993), p. 556.

59 Associated with the University of Cambridge and the Dominican order in the 1960s, its contents were influenced by Marx and Wittgenstein. Its influential members included Terry Eagleton, Herbert McCabe and Denys Turner.

60 See Philip Pettit, *The Gentle Revolution: Crisis in the Universities* (Scepter Books, Dublin, 1969).

61 I worked for the *Irish Press* between 1970 and 1976. Andy Pollok worked for the *Irish Times*, and Brian Trench for *Hibernia*. All three of us shared an interest in Latin America and wrote articles on the region, as did Peadar Kirby.

62 Obituary, 'Fr Joe Dunn (1930–1996)', *Irish Times*, 1 August 1996. See also his books: *No Tigers in Africa: Recollections and Reflections on 25 Years of Radharc* (Columba Press, Dublin, 1986); *No Lions in the Hierarchy: An Anthology of Sorts* (Columba Press, Dublin 1994); *No Vipers in the Vatican: A Second Anthology of Sorts* (Columba Press, Dublin, 1996).

63 See https://radharc.ie/product/ref-no-0145-who-is-for-liberation/.

64 Among the other documentaries produced by Radharc were the following: *Trinidad: Single or Return* (1976), *Where the Pope is a Communist and the Bishop a Guerrilla* (Guatemala, 1984), *A Matter of Life and Debt* (Chile et al. 1988), *A Parish in Perú* (1976), *Left, Right, Human Right* (Chile, 1982), *Adiós to Zapata* (Mexico, 1987), *A New Way of Living the Church* (Mexico, 1987), *The Black Irish* (Montserrat, West Indies, 1976), *The Exemplary Revolution* (Nicaragua, 1980), *Church and State in Nicaragua* (1988) and *Grenada, Oct '83: The End of Revolution*.

65 Obituary for Sally O'Neill, *Irish Times*, 20 April 2019.

66 The Irish Missionary Union (IMU) (founded 1970) and the Conference of Religious of Ireland (CORI) amalgamated in June 2016 to form the Association of Missionaries and Religious of Ireland (AMRI). CORI was set up in 1983 as the Conference of Major Religious Superiors (CMRS) but changed its name to the Conference of Religious of Ireland in the 1990s.

67 Kirby, *Ireland and Latin America*, pp. 138–9. During the pandemic in 2020/1, it proved very difficult to get more detailed figures including a breakdown of male and female missionaries.

68 The numbers of legionaries to Latin America was significant. Among the most famous was Alphonsus (Alfie) Lamb, who worked in many countries between 1953 and his death on 21 January 1959. He is buried in the vault of the Irish Christian Brothers in Recoleta, Buenos Aires. See Hilde Firtel, *Alfie Lambe: Envoy Extraordinaire* (Praedicanda Publications, Dublin, 2012).

69 The superior of the Columban Fathers, Fr Jeremias Dennehy, received an urgent request from the Holy See in 1950 to send Irish missionaries to Latin America. The order chose Argentina as their first mission and sent Fr Jaime Loughran and Fr Murphy, both with extensive experience in China, to visit Colombia, Ecuador and Peru on their way to Buenos Aires. Murphy fell ill and died in Lima. He was replaced by Fr Juan McFadden. They travelled via Santiago, Chile, to Argentina, where they met the papal nuncio, Mgr Zain, who was a friend of Loughran's from China. Zain encouraged both men to visit Cardenal Caro, who immediately invited the Columbans to work in Santiago. Before setting out for Buenos Aires, they wrote to Dennehy giving details of Caro's offer. In Argentina, they learned from their superior that that offer had been accepted. Instead of working in Argentina, Fr Jaime Loughran founded the Columban mission in three parishes in Santiago. Another parish, in the diocese of Iquique, was incorporated at a later date.

70 I am grateful to the archivist for the Columban Fathers, Barbara Scally, for supplying archival material on the history of the Columbans in Argentina: Argentine Collection, Ref. IE: CFCA AR, 1 box. See also Peru Collection, Ref. IE: CFCA PEI, 1950–2013, and Chile, Ref. IE: CFCA CLA.

71 Edward Walsh email to author, 16 April 2107. My gratitude for this information to this former Dominican who worked in northern Argentina. After writing the section, I received a first draft of his memoir which will, when completed, serve as a history of the mission and provide very valuable information on pastoral life in the north of Argentina in the 1960s and 1970s. Received draft 19 December 2020.

72 Mary O'Byrne, who worked as a Dominican sister in Buenos Aires, helped me find answers to a number of questions. She has written an important study on the Dominican mission in Argentina: *Strands from a Tapestry: A Story of Dominican Sisters in Latin America*

(Dominican Publications, Dublin, 2001). Her work contains appendices with lists of the Dominican priests and sisters who worked in Argentina and in Latin America, see pp. 272–5.

73 O'Byrne, *Strands from a Tapestry*, pp. 23–82. My thanks to the author and other sisters in the order for their help.

74 Ibid., pp. 59–111.

75 I am grateful to Fr Edward Hogan, archivist, Society of African Missions, Blackrock, Cork, for the following references: Fr J.A. Craven, 'Mission to Argentina', *Far East*, March/April 1967, pp. 5–7; Fr Tony Gill, 'Missionary Mail', *African Mission*, September/October 1967, pp. 6–7; Fr Tony Gill, 'The Cosquin Valley', *African Mission*, March/April 1969, pp. 13–14; Fr Tony Gill, 'El Tinkunaku: A South American Town (Province of Salta) that has Christ as its Lord Mayor', *African Mission*, November/December 1974, pp. 5–7; and Fr Seán Healy, 'The SMA in Argentina', *African Mission*, summer 1983, pp. 10–11.

76 Angelelli published a letter in defence of Fr Gill when he was arrested in 1975. The text was published in *TSC* in June 1984.

77 My thanks to Fr Michael O'Sullivan for this information; He himself worked in Chile, Mexico and Central America. Other Jesuits who worked in Latin America were: John Sweeney (Mexico); Kevin O'Higgins (Paraguay); John Leonard (Paraguay); Henry Grant (Paraguay); Brendan Rumley (Paraguay and Peru); Jimmy McPolin (El Salvador); and Rory Halpin (El Salvador).

78 Neil Doogan and Tony Coote were later ordained. Tony Coote worked in Mexico and Neil Doogan in Ecuador and Nicaragua, where he was working in 2020.

79 Ivan Illich, 'The Seamy Side of Charity', *America*, 21 January 1967, http://www.america magazine.org/content/article.cfm?article_id=12003.

80 Background on the church in Latin America in English can be found in the following volumes: J. Lloyd Mecham, *Church and State in Latin America* (University of North Carolina, Chapel Hill, 1966); Dan H. Levine (editor and contributor), *Religion and Political Conflict in Latin America* (University of North Carolina Press, Chapel Hill, 1986); *Churches and Politics in Latin America* (Sage Publications, London, 1980); Scott Mainwaring and Alexander Wilde (eds), *The Progressive Church in Latin America* (Notre Dame University Press, Notre Dame, IN, 1989); Dermot Keogh (ed.), *Church and Politics in Latin America* (Macmillan, New York, 1990). See also Enrique Dussel, *Historia de la Iglesia en América Latina* (Mundo Negro, Mexico, D.F. 1983). A full list of works cited is to be found in the bibliography.

81 'Military Concordat (1957) and Update (1992)', http://www.concordatwatch.eu/topic-31391.843.

82 This changed the original structure, which dated back to the beginning of the twentieth century. Catholic chaplains formed an integral part of the Argentine armed forces and, according to canon law, were under the jurisdiction of the local bishop in whose diocese their barracks were located.

83 The Irish Dominicans had a mission in Corrientes in Tortolo's diocese. The bishop, on a visit to their house, told one of the Irish priests to cut his beard off, to which he replied: 'You are my bishop, not my barber.'

84 Stephen Gregory and Daniel Timerman, 'Rituals of the Modern State: The Case of Torture in Argentina', *Dialectical Anthropology*, vol. 11, no. 1, 1986, pp. 63–71, https://www.jstor.org/stable/29790171. Emilio Mignone cites a work by a military chaplain, Marcial Castro Castillo, *Fuerzas Armadas: Etica y Repression* (Editorial Nuevo Order, Buenos Aires, 1979) in his book, *Witness to the Truth: The Complicity of Church and Dictatorship in Argentina, 1976–1983* (Orbis books, Maryknoll, New York, 1988), pp. 15–16.

85 A fragment of his diaries for the period has survived and has been published. Lucas Bilbao and Ariel Lede, *Profeta del Genocidio: El Vicariato Castrense y los Diarios del Obispo Bonamín en la Última Dictator* (Editorial Sudamericana, Buenos Aires, 2016) (con prólogo de Horacio Verbitsky), see p. 251 ff.

86 Emilio Mignone, *Witness to the Truth: The Complicity of Church and Dictatorship in Argentina, 1976–1983* (Orbis Books, Maryknoll, New York, 1988), pp. 6–8 and 16–17. Spanish edition: *Iglesia y Dictadura: El Papel de la Iglesia a la Luz de Sus Relaciones con el Régimen Militar* (Ediciones del Pensamiento Nacional, Buenos Aires, 1986); Mignone noted that the Holy See elevated the vicariate to a military ordinate on 21 July 1986, giving it the status of a diocese and, at the same time, raising twenty-eight other vicariates around the world to the same status. (There are twelve in the Americas, nine in Europe, three in Africa, three in Asia and two in Oceania. Mignone considered that measure by the Holy See to have been 'a grave mistake').

87 José Comblin, *The Church and the National Security State* (Orbis Books, New York, 1979); see, in particular, pages 64 to 98 for the historical origins and a definition of the 'national security state'.

88 See Gustavo Morello, *The Catholic Church and Argentina's Dirty War* (Oxford University Press, New York, 2015). This book, focusing largely on the 'disappearance' of Fr James Weeks and five seminarians from the La Salette missionary house in Cordoba on 3 August 1976, parallels the case of Fr Patrick Rice. The book is a model of outstanding scholarship. See also Horacio Verbitsky, *Doble Juego: La Argentina Católica y Militar* (Editorial Sudamericana, Buenos Aires, 2006), and José Pablo Martín, *Ruptura Ideológica del Catolicismo Argentine: 36 Entrevistas entre 1988 y 1992* (Universidad Nacional de General Sarmiento, Buenos Aires, 2013).

89 Rice wrote on the front cover: '*Editamos aquí una cronica de la disertación sobre el Tema Tercer Mundo y Compromiso Cristiano de* [We edited here a dissertation on the theme of the Third World and Christian Commitment by] *los padres J.C. Gorosito y J.C. De Zan en el Rotary Club Paraná 9 (centro) y llevada a cabo en session del día 24/VIII/70*. (Los Editores Ediciones 'Libreria selecta SRL', Paraná, 1970).

90 See José Pablo Martín, *Movimiento de Sacerdotes para el Tercer Mundo, un Debate Argentine* (Cellett, Buenos Aires, 2010). For further insight into the divisions within the Argentine church, see his *Ruptura Ideológica del Catolicismo Argentine*. The movement was formed after the Second Vatican Council and ended on 24 March 1976. In 1970, the movement had 524 members in Argentina or 9 per cent of the total number of priests in the country. Of the priests between ages thirty and forty, 20 per cent were members of the movement. Horacio Verbitsky, preface, in Martín, *Ruptura Ideológica del Catolicismo Argentino*, pp. 11–15.

91 Paoli was ordained in 1940. He was active in the Italian resistance and was part of the escape line for Jews in his area. He gave distinguished service during the building up of Catholic Action in post-war Italy, working closely in Rome with Mgr Giovanni Batista Montini, later Paul VI. Paoli was attracted to the new order of the Little Brothers of Charles de Foucauld, and completed his novitiate for the fraternity in El Abiodh, in Algeria. Returning to Italy, he worked in Sardinia among coalminers.

92 He had lived among the Bedouin peoples. Ordained at forty-three in 1901, he spent the remainder of his life among Moslems. He was beatified on 13 November 2005.

93 See film, *Regreso a Fortín Olmos*.

94 Notes supplied to me by Patrick in a curriculum vitae prepared in 2007.

95 Patricio Rice y Juanín Pilatti, 'Fraternidades de Santa Fe, Fortín Olmos y Reconquista', in Patricio Rice y Luis Torres (eds), *En Medio de la Tempestad: Los Hermanitos del Evangelio en Argentina (1959–1977)* (Doble Clic Editoras, Buenos Aires, 2007), p. 89.

96 This website has a number of links on the background and the career of Bishop Angelelli: http://www.elortiba.org/old/angelelli.html.

97 Julio Saquero, in Rice y Torres (eds), *En Medio de la Tempestad*, pp. 223–9.

98 Patricio Rice y Luis Torres (eds), *En Medio de la Tempestad*, pp. 89–90.

99 Already suffering from Parkinson's, he made his wishes to remain in Buenos Aires known to his superiors and to his friend, the taoiseach, Jack Lynch. An oral source told me it was believed in Iveagh House at the time that the meeting between the two men was the reason the government reversed its decision and allowed Skentelbery to remain in his position in Buenos Aires until a few months before his retirement in 1973.

100 I confirmed that they met at that time but I have not found a minute of the meeting. It might be described as having taken place 'off the record'.

101 Despite having developed Parkinson's disease, he led an active if not relaxed professional life, swimming to help combat the illness every morning in the Jockey Club.

102 For a critical view of that guerrilla movement, see Richard Gillespie, *Soldiers of Perón: Argentina's Montoneros* (Clarendon Press, Oxford, 1982).

103 It is not possible here to describe in detail the rise of the revolutionary left in Argentina during the 1960s. Michael McCaughan provides a good background in his *Rodolfo Walsh*, see p. 167 ff.

104 The Montoneros also held Aramburu responsible for the execution in June 1956 of eighteen military personnel who took part in the abortive coup.

105 'Body of Argentina's Kidnapped Ex-President Found', *New York Times*, 18 July 1970, http://www.nytimes.com/1970/07/18/archives/body-of-argentinas-kidnapped-expresident-found.html

106 NAI/DFA/2003/17/257 [old file number, 313/24K].

107 See David Rock, *Argentina 1516–1987: From Spanish Colonization to Alfonsín* (University of California Press, Berkeley, 1987), pp. 349–51; Gillespie, *Soldiers of Perón*, pp. 47–8; and María José Moyano, *Argentina's Lost Patrol: Armed Struggle 1969–1979* (Yale University Press, New Haven, 1995), pp. 11–41.

108 Seamus Heaney, 'The Cure at Troy', quoted in Frank Ormsby (ed.), *Rage for Order: Poetry on the Northern Ireland Troubles* (The Blackstaff Press, Belfast, 1992), pp. 318–19.

109 Eavan Boland, 'The Death of Reason', in *In a Time of Violence* (Norton, New York and London, 1992), p. 9.

110 From 23 September 1973 to 20 January 1977, he was made secretary of state, serving under both Nixon and, from 9 August 1974, Gerald Ford.

111 Seymour M. Hersh, *The Price of Power: Kissinger in the Nixon White House* (Summit Books, New York, 1983).

112 For a general overview of US policy, see David M.K. Sheinin, *Argentina and the United States: An Alliance Contained* (The University of Georgia Press, Athens and London, 2006), pp. 150–80.

113 NAI/DFA/2003/17/257 [old file number, 313/24K].

114 Joseph Grunwald, 'The Alliance for Progress', *Proceedings of the Academy of Political Science*, vol. 27, no. 4, 1964, pp. 78–93, https://www.jstor.org/stable/i249935; Robert M. Smetherman and Bobbie B. Smetherman, 'The Alliance for Progress: Promises Unfulfilled', *The American Journal of Economics and Sociology*, vol. 31, no. 1, 1972, pp. 79–85, https://www.jstor.org/stable/3485582; Michael Dunne, 'Kennedy's Alliance for Progress: Countering Revolution in Latin America. Part I: From the White House to the Charter of Punta Del Este', *International Affairs (Royal Institute of International Affairs 1944–)*, vol. 89, no. 6, 2013, pp. 1389–409, https://www.jstor.org/stable/24538448.

115 NAI/DFA/2003/17/257 [old file number, 313/24K].

116 Keogh and Aoife Keogh, 'Ireland and European Integration', pp. 6–50.

117 Garret FitzGerald, *All in a Life: An Autobiography* (Gill & Macmillan, Dublin, 1991), pp. 146–95.

118 'Espionage Fears as Soviet Embassy Opened in Dublin', *Irish Times*, 2 January 2004. This decision was taken against strong objections from the minister for defence, Patrick Donegan, who claimed that 'three out of four embassy personnel, including spouses, would have "an intelligence function"'. FitzGerald countered by saying that Ireland was 'the only country in the European Community that had no diplomatic relations with the Soviet Union'. 'Failure to have relations will place Ireland in an inferior and parochial position vis-à-vis our European partners,' he added. See also Micheál Ó Corcora and Ronald J. Hill, 'The Soviet Union in Irish Foreign Policy', *International Affairs (Royal Institute of International Affairs 1944–)*, vol. 58, no. 2, spring 1982, pp. 254–70; Michael Joseph Quinn, 'Irish–Soviet Diplomatic and Friendship Relations, 1919–80', PhD thesis (2014), National University of Ireland, Maynooth.

119 FitzGerald, *All in a Life*, pp. 152–3.

120 Ibid. pp. 180–1.

121 The Spanish embassy in Lisbon was burned. Spain withdrew 'for consultation' its ambassadors from the Netherlands, Norway, West and East Germany and the Holy See. It withdrew its ambassador from Portugal unconditionally. Among the fifteen European countries to recall their ambassadors for consultation were Norway, Italy, Belgium, Sweden, United Kingdom and West and East Germany. The French ambassador was on leave and did not hurry back to Madrid and neither did the Canadian ambassador.

122 Three were members of the Basque separatist group, ETA, and two were in the communist revolutionary organisation, FRAP. (As I [Dermot Keogh] did not agree with the death penalty, I urged FitzGerald at the time to withdraw the Irish ambassador. In retrospect, I now accept that his decision not to do so was the correct one.)

123 It would also have created a precedent. In Irish diplomacy, it was the consistent view that an ambassador should remain at her or his post irrespective of the difficult conditions of service. Had such a precedent been set in 1975, it would have been difficult not to withdraw the Irish ambassador in London during various crises in Anglo-Irish relations or when, in other countries, a democratic government was replaced by a repressive authoritarian regime.

124 FitzGerald, *All in a Life*, pp. 180–1.

125 I first saw this correspondence in Bernard Davenport's apartment in Florence in 2017.

126 This may be a reference to the concern Matthew Murphy had in the early 1950s about the diplomatic bag being opened and correspondence screened by the Argentine authorities. See Chapter 3.

127 It was the practice for embassies to send multiple carbon copies of a confidential report to Iveagh House. In the case of the embassy in Buenos Aires, many of those multiple copies remained on the 'confidential reports'. That meant that, outside the section, those reports had gone uncirculated and possibly unread in some cases.

128 NAI/DFA/2004/7/300 [old file number 313/24L].

129 Bernard Davenport email to author, 26 July 2017.

130 FitzGerald, *All in a Life*, pp. 118–21. In FitzGerald's account of the three-day meeting, involving senior DFA officials and ambassadors, there is no mention of Latin America. A contribution from Davenport would have been valuable. But despite being chargé, his ranking precluded him from being invited. FitzGerald, who wrote that such a conference had never previously been held, was not entirely accurate in that observation. De Valera, as taoiseach and minister for external affairs, called a meeting of ambassadors after the Second World War, to review Ireland's options in the new world order.

131   When referring to 'not the only person to think so', the minister was unquestionably pointing to the secretary of the Department of Foreign Affairs, Hugh McCann. DFA/2004/7/300 [old file number 313/24L].

132   Davenport told me when I met him in Florence that he had sent many technical reports on Argentine agriculture and on its national economy which had been passed on directly to the departments of Finance and Industry and Commerce. I failed to locate those reports in the national archives.

133   NAI/DFA/2004/7/300 [old file number 313/24L], Davenport report, 26 January 1973.

134   Ibid.

135   NAI/DFA/2004/7/300 [old file number 313/24L], Davenport report, 16 February 1973.

136   Ibid.

137   Ibid.

138   NAI/DFA/2004/7/300 [old file number 313/24L], Profile of Peronism, 7 March 1973.

139   Ibid.

140   Ibid.

141   Davenport told me that the back window of the ambassadorial car was shattered by a rock as he was caught in the crossfire between the two rival Peronist factions. Conversations with the former envoy, Florence, October 2017.

142   NAI/DFA/2004/7/300 [old file number 313/24L], Davenport report, 5 June 1973.

143   Ibid.

144   He received detailed accounts of the bloody events and gun battles which accompanied his awaited arrival from the Associated Press agency chief Bill Anderson and from his United Press counterpart, Bob Sullivan. Dermot Keogh meetings with Bernard Davenport, Florence, October 2017.

145   NAI/DFA/2004/7/300 [old file number 313/24L], Davenport report, 16 July 1972.

146   Crassweller, *Perón and the Enigmas of Argentina*, pp. 354–61.

147   Ibid.

148   NAI/DFA/2004/7/300 [old file number 313/24L], Davenport report, 16 July 1972.

149   NAI/DFA/2004/7/300 [old file number 313/24L], Davenport report, 24 September 1973.

150   NAI/DFA/2004/7/300 [old file number 313/24L], Davenport report, 24 September 1973.

151   Gillespie, *Soldiers of Perón*, pp. 144–5.

152   His report, dated 31 December, was submitted on his return to Dublin, NAI/DFA/2004/7/300 [old file number 313/24L].

153   NAI/DFA/2004/7/300 [old file number 313/24L], Davenport report, 12 December 1973.

154   NAI/DFA/2004/7/300 [old file number 313/24L].

155   Quoted in Seyom Brown, *Faces of Power: Constancy and Change in United States Foreign Policy from Truman to Obama* (Columbia University Press, New York, 2015), 3rd edn, p. 273 ff.

156   NAI/DFA/2004/7/300 [old file number 313/24L], Davenport report, 13 September 1973.

157   Ibid.

158   NAI/DFA/2004/7/300 [old file number 313/24L], Davenport report, 31 December 1973: Davenport's estimate of deaths in the coup and its aftermath was far too high. At best, it reflected the contemporary speculation in diplomatic circles in Buenos Aires and the gravity with which events in Chile were viewed by the ambassadors. The US historian Peter Kornbluh wrote that in October 1973 the CIA 'obtained a "highly secretive" summary on post-coup repression prepared for the new military Junta. The document became the basis for a special secret briefing paper titled "Chilean Executions" prepared for Secretary of State Henry Kissinger. In the six weeks following the coup, according to the report, the military had massacred approximately 1,500 civilians. Of those, some 320–360 were summarily executed by firing squad while in custody, or shot on sight in the street. The summary

estimated that more than 13,500 Chilean citizens had been quickly rounded up through raids and mass arrests ...' The CIA report also noted that there were approximately twenty detention camps scattered throughout the country, the existence or whereabouts of many not known to the public. The National Stadium was an exception ... Kornbluh wrote that 'during a ruthless seventeen-year dictatorship, the Chilean military were responsible for the murder, disappearance and death by torture of some 3,197 citizens'. See Peter Kornbluh, *The Pinochet File: A Declassified Dossier on Atrocity and Accountability* (The New Press, New York and London, 2013), pp. 161–2, 555. See also the Report of the Chilean National Commission on Truth and Reconciliation, posted by USIP Library on 4 October 2002. Source: *Report of the Chilean National Commission on Truth and Reconciliation* (Notre Dame, IN: University of Notre Dame Press, 1993), vol. I/II, Foreword, pp. xxi–xxii. Note: Digitised and posted by permission of the University of Notre Dame Press, 22 February 2000. See also United States Institute of Peace, Washington DC, https://www.usip.org/publications/1990/05/truth-commission-chile-90.

159 Human Rights Watch, Chile, *When Tyrants Tremble: The Pinochet Case*, October 1999, vol. 11, no. 1 (B), https://www.hrw.org/reports/1999/chile/.

160 Françoise de Menthon, extracts from her diary, 15 October 1973 to 3 February 1974, http://solidaridadconchile.org/?p=42.

161 The Swedish ambassador, Harald Edelstam, and his staff also saved many lives. He was expelled from Chile. See film *The Black Pimpernel*, directed by Ulf Hutberg, 2007, and Marcia Esparza and Carla de Ycata, *Remembering the Rescuers of Victims of Human Rights Crimes in Latin America* (Lexington Books, Lanham, MD, 2016). Sweden admitted 30,000 Chilean refugees between 1973 and 1990. The Italian embassy also played an important role as a sanctuary. See Nanni Moretti film *Santiago, Italia*, released in 2018, https://www.arte.tv/en/videos/088255-000-A/nanni-moretti-s-new-film-santiago-italia/.

162 See Enrico Calamai, *Niente Asilo Politico: Diplomazia, Diritti Umani e Desaparecidos* (Feltrinelli, Milan, 2016).

163 As background to the Catholic response in the US to the coup in Chile and the abuse of human rights in Latin America, see Thomas E. Quigley, 'The Chilean Coup, the Church and the Human Rights Movement', *America: The Jesuit Review*, 11 February 2002, https://www.americamagazine.org/issue/360/article/chilean-coup-church-and-human-rights-movement (Quigley was at the time a policy adviser for the Office of International Justice and Peace of the US Conference of Catholic Bishops, Washington DC).

164 See Keogh, *Jews in Twentieth Century Ireland*; Frank Callanan, 'We never let them in', *Irish Times*, 16 May 1998.

165 See 'Resettlement in Ireland of Refugees from Chile' (February–April 1974), National Archives of Ireland, 2005/7/445, S 19123, quoted in Claire Healy, '"Foreigners of this Kind": Chilean Refugees in Ireland, 1973–1990', *Irish Migration Studies in Latin America*, vol. 4, no. 4, October 2006, https://www.irlandeses.org/0610healy3.htm.

166 'Adiós, No; Tan solo un "Hasta Luego"', *The Southern Cross*, 4 January 1974.

167 He was in Argentina to report on two terrorist attacks on St Patrick's Day 1992 and on 18 July 1994 [see p. 365].

168 'Economist and Diplomat who Lived Life to Full', obituary, *Irish Times*, 7 July 2018, https://www.irishtimes.com/life-and-style/people/economist-and-diplomat-who-lived-life-to-full-1.3555275.

CHAPTER 4 Irish Diplomats Witness Military Dictatorship, Repression and Disappearances: A divided Argentina and 'history from below'

1 Lennon remained in Ireland from mid-November 1975 until mid-July 1976. He left Buenos Aires in the middle of December 1976, retiring the following month.

2　On arrival in Iveagh House, Davenport told me that there was neither a desk nor a job waiting for him.

3　Born in Dundalk in 1915, he was educated at the local Christian Brothers school. He entered the Department of External Affairs as first secretary in 1947, having previously served as administrative officer in the Office of Public Works and the Department of Finance. He became a counsellor in 1951, and was posted as counsellor to Paris in 1956. In 1961, he became envoy extraordinary and minister plenipotentiary to Portugal. In 1962, he moved to the Irish embassy in the Netherlands, which also was accredited to Denmark. In 1967, he was transferred to Madrid. Three years later he became the permanent representative of Ireland in Geneva to the European Office of the United Nations and to the intergovernmental agencies related to the United Nations. His last posting before retirement was Buenos Aires from 1974 to 1977. He was married with five children.

4　This judgement is based on a number of sources. The personnel files in the Department of Foreign Affairs, if opened, may reveal a lively correspondence on this topic written in code between Lennon and his superiors in Iveagh House. Through marriage, Lennon was related to the minister for defence, Patrick Donegan.

5　She was born on the feast of Our Lady of Fátima – 13 May 1957. Her document registers her date of birth as the 18th.

6　Fátima told me that her father was a trade union organiser in Tucumán working with sugar cane cutters and factory workers. Her parents split up and she came with her mother, her three sisters and one brother to Villa 31. She wrote an account of her contacts with Fr Mugica in 'Haciendo Memoria de Carlos Mugica', an essay completed on 3 May 2020.

7　See also Fátima Cabrera, 'Las Villas Miserias de Capital Federal: Padre Carlos Mugica', in Rice y Torres (eds), *En Medio de la Tempestad*, pp. 128–31.

8　Composed by Héctor Pedro Blomberg, it was a *valsecito criollo* which was made famous by the singer and friend of the composer Ignacio Corsini.

9　https://www.periodicovas.com/villa–31-la-historia-de-galleta/.

10　This account of Cabrera and Alfaro's work is based on Fátima Edelmira Cabrera, *Denuncia de Fátima Edelmira Cabrera (ex pareja)*, 29 January 1999, by Fátima Cabrera, Carpeta Liberados, Legajo CONADEP no. 6976 – Patrick Rice and Fátima Cabrera, Fondo Documental del Archivo Nacional de la Memoria, ex-ESMA.

11　Fátima Cabrera, 'Recordando de Carlos Mugica', in Rice y Torres, *En Medio de la Tempestad*, pp. 128–31.

12　The writer V.S. Naipaul met Mugica in 1972 and wrote a critical profile of the priest who he learned later was 'one of the patrons of the guerrillas'. He wrote: 'He was a big man, busy and serious and frowning. The black leather jacket he was wearing bulked out his arms and chest. His hair was thin and his eyes were angry ... He said, with some irony, that he also "happened to be" Peronist, and then he added, irony quite overtaking him, touched at the end with a little rage, that as a Peronist he was not as concerned as some people were with economic growth.' Naipaul pressed him on that apparent contradiction between being a Peronist and not being concerned with economic growth: 'Mugica became enraged. He said he had better things to do, and he wasn't going to waste his time talking to a norteamericano, an American ... "I can talk to you for five years, and still you wouldn't understand Peronism."' V.S. Naipaul, 'Argentina: Living with Cruelty', *New York Review of Books*, 30 January 1992, http://www.nybooks.com/articles/1992/01/30/argentina-living-with-cruelty/.

13　Cabrera, 'Recordando de Carlos Mugica'.

14　See María Sucarrat, *El Inocente: Vida, Passion y Muerte de Carlos Mugica* (Octubre Editorial, Buenos Aires, 2017) (*Nueva Edición*), p. 354 ff. This volume contains material from the archive of the Jesuit Fr José María 'Pichi' Meisegeier which is in Córdoba. The Jesuit took over Mugica's parish after he was murdered.

15 On 10 May 2014, President Cristina Fernández de Kirchner unveiled a monument in honour of the murdered priest designed by Alejandro Marmo – the same artist who cast the two ten-storey-high portraits of Evita on the side of the Department of Health at the opposite end of Avenida 9 de Julio reminiscent of the Che Guevara image in the Plaza de la Revolución in Havana. 'Giant Evita Perón Statue Unveiled in Buenos Aires', *Telegraph*, 27 July 2011, https://www.telegraph.co.uk/news/worldnews/southamerica/argentina/8665460/Giant-Evita-Peron-statue-unveiled-in-Buenos-Aires.html. The Guevara statue, based on an Alberto Korda photograph, was sculpted by Enrique Ávila González.

16 For a general history of the area, see Demian Konfino, *Villa 31: Historia de un Amor Invisible* (Editorial Punto de Encuentro, Buenos Aires, 2012).

17 http://www.marcha.org.ar/dia-de-la-memoria-la-dignidad-villera/.

18 The holiday commemorates the death of Gen. Manuel Belgrano – a lawyer, economist, politician and military leader who took part in the wars of independence and is credited with creating the national flag.

19 For a dramatic description of the president's last days and hours, see Crassweller, *Perón and the Enigmas of Argentina*, pp. 366–8.

20 NAI/DFA, 2005/4/70, 313/24M, Lennon to Dublin, 1 July 1974.

21 'Death of Perón', *Irish Press*, 2 and 3 July 1974.

22 DT/15361B, NAI/DT.

23 Ibid.

24 Ibid.

25 Ibid.

26 Montoneros, too, passed the coffin, giving the V for victory sign. See Page, *Perón: A Biography*, pp. 492–4.

27 NAI/DFA, 2005/4/70 [313/24M], Lennon to Dublin, 5 and 10 July 1974.

28 An idiomatic expression for 'true friendship'.

29 According to the Irish legend, Gráinne fell in love with Diarmuid and ran away from the older Fionn to be with him. Lennon has picked up on the local gossip that the president and her minister were lovers.

30 NAI/DFA, 2005/4/70 [313/24M], Lennon to Dublin, 10 July 1974.

31 Ibid.

32 NAI/DFA, 2005/4/70 [313/24M], Lennon to Dublin, 9 September 1974.

33 NAI/DFA, 2011/39/1249, Ambassador Lennon to Secretary, 15 November 1974.

34 The Triple A was a flag of convenience for right-wing death squads. It was allegedly formally organised by José López Rega in 1973. According to the Truth Commission CONADEP report, *Nunca Más*, the Triple A killed 1,122 people. See Ignacio González Janzen, *La Tríple A: AAA* (Editorial Contrapunto, Buenos Aires, 1986).

35 NAI/DFA, 2005/4/70 [313/24M], Lennon to Dublin, 4 October 1974.

36 NAI/DFA, 2005/4/70 [313/24M], Lennon to Dublin, 14 October 1974.

37 NAI/DFA, 2005/4/70 [313/24M], Lennon to Dublin, 22 July 1974.

38 Harman had studied at the Christian Brothers school, Coláiste Mhuire, and went on to University College Dublin where he studied psychology. He joined the diplomatic service in October 1974. After a year in the political division, he was posted to Buenos Aires in November 1975.

39 Harman was related by marriage to Fr Alfredo Kelly, a Pallottine, who died in the massacre in St Patrick's, Belgrano, on 4 July 1976. He was posted to Buenos Aires from 14 November 1975 to December 1978. During his subsequent career, he was four years in the political division in Dublin before moving to the London embassy as first secretary, serving as press and information officer. He returned to Dublin where he worked between 1986 and 1993. That year, he was named ambassador and head of delegation to the OSCE, Vienna. In 1998, he

was made ambassador and permanent representative to the Council of Europe, Strasbourg. In 2003, he was made ambassador to Russia (and also to Belarus, Kazakhstan, Kyrgystan, Tajikistan, Uzbekistan and Turkmenistan). He was made ambassador to Spain in 2009. He returned to Argentina as ambassador in October 2014 and retired on 1 December 2017, having strengthened greatly the cultural, educational and diplomatic links between the two countries.

40 The nuncio had service in Nicaragua (1952–4), United States (1954–61) and India (1961–4). For most of the remainder of the 1960s, he remained at the Holy See before being posted in 1969 to Jerusalem and Palestine. He also served as pro-nuncio in Cyprus in 1973.

41 See biographical details, https://en.wikipedia.org/wiki/Patrick_Coveney.

42 Conversations with Archbishop Patrick Coveney, Parochial House, Crosshaven, County Cork, January 2013.

43 Bissonnet reports, mid-February and 14 March 1975, Political Affairs – Policy and Background – Internal Policy Trends – Argentina, file no. dossier 20-ARG-1-4, CO121, vol. 7, from 1 November 1974 to 15 February 1977, Acc. no. 288281, Canadian National Archives, Ottawa.

44 Bissonnet reports, mid-February and 14 March 1975.

45 The nuncio took particular care to fill the archbishopric of Buenos Aires and the most important of the fourteen archbishoprics in the country. There were forty-eight dioceses, a military vicariate and, counting auxiliary bishops, eighty bishops in the country.

46 'Cardinal Raúl Primatesta, Confidant of John Paul II, Blamed for Complicity with the Argentine Junta', *The Independent*, 5 May 2006, https://www.independent.co.uk/news/obituaries/cardinal-raul-francisco-primatesta-6101772.html.

47 Bissonnet reports, 3 November 1975, Political Affairs – Policy and Background – Internal Policy Trends – Argentina, file no. dossier 20-ARG-1-4, CO121, vol. 7, from 1 November 1974 to 15 February 1977, Acc. no. 288281, Canadian National Archives, Ottawa.

48 Bissonnet reports, 5 December 1975, Political Affairs – Policy and Background – Internal Policy Trends – Argentina, file no. dossier 20-ARG-1-4, CO121, vol. 7, from 1 November 1974 to 15 February 1977, Acc. no. 288281, Canadian National Archives, Ottawa.

49 According to the then editor of the *Buenos Aires Herald*, Robert J. Cox, the nunciature had once been 'an Argentine ruling family's sumptuous house'. Donated to the Roman Catholic Church, it was dark and gloomy inside and 'the dark room, with its heavy drapes and bulky furniture, was like a tomb'. David Cox (foreword by Robert J. Cox), *Dirty Secrets, Dirty War: Buenos Aires, Argentina, 1976–1983. The Exile of Editor Robert J. Cox* (Evening Post Publishing Company, Charleston, SC, with Joggling Board Press, 2008), p. 76.

50 They also played tennis at the nunciature.

51 Claudio Uriarte, *Almirante Cero: Biografía no Autorizada de Emilio Eduardo Massera* (Planeta, Buenos Aires, 2011), p. 209; he described Laghi as a 'person more political than religious'.

52 Horacio Verbitsky has written extensively on the history of Argentina. Among his publications are the following: *The Flight: Confessions of an Argentine Dirty Warrior. A Firsthand Account of Atrocity*, published in Spanish as *El Vuelo* (Planeta, Buenos Aires, 1995). In order to understand his interpretation of the role of the Catholic Church in Argentina, see his other works: *La Violencia Evangélica: De Lonardi al Cordobazo, 1955–1969* (Editorial Sudamericana, Buenos Aires, 2008); *Vigilia de Armas: Del Cordobazo de 1969 al 23 de Marzo de 1976* (Editorial Sudamericana, Buenos Aires, 2009); *La Mano Izquierda de Dios: La Última Dictadura, 1976–1983* (Editorial Sudamericana, Buenos Aires, 2010); *El Silencio: De Paulo VI a Bergoglio. Las Relaciones Secretas de la Iglesia con la ESMA* (Editorial Sudamericana, Buenos Aires, 2005); *Cristo Vence: De Roca a Perón* (Sudamericana, Buenos

Aires, 2007); *Civiles y Militares: Memoria Secreta de la Transición* (Editorial Contrapunto, Buenos Aires, 1987); and *Rodolfo Walsh y la Prensa Clandestina, 1976–1978* (República Argentina: Ediciones de la Urraca, Buenos Aires, 1985); see also Diana Ortiz, *The Blindfold's Eyes: My Journey from Torture to Truth* (Orbis Books, Maryknoll, New York, 2004).

53 Pio Laghi served as apostolic delegate to the United States from 10 December 1980 until 26 March 1984 when he was given the title apostolic pro-nuncio after the Holy See and the United States set up diplomatic relations. He remained in Washington until he was recalled to Rome in 1990 where he served as prefect of the Congregation for Catholic Education for Seminaries and Institutes of Study.

54 See Marcos Novaro y Vicente Palermo, *La Dictadura Military 1976–8: Del Golpe de Estado a la Restauración Democrática* [Historia Argentina], vol. 9 (Paidós, Buenos Aires, 2003), pp. 17–66. For an excellent review of the days leading up to the coup d'état, see Gabriela Saidon, *La Farsa: Los 48 Dias previos al Golpe* (Planeta, Buenos Aires, 2016).

55 NAI/DFA, 2011/39/1249, Ambassador Lennon to Secretary, 17 November 1975.

56 NAI/DFA, 2011/39/1249, Justin Harman, chargé d'affaires a.i. [*ad interim*] to Secretary, 19 January 1976. My emphasis.

57 NAI/DFA, 2011/39/1249, Justin Harman, chargé d'affaires a.i. to Secretary, 8 March 1976.

58 Ambassador Hill to Assistant Secretary of State William D. Rogers, 16 March 1976, Department of State, INR/IL historical files, box 16, Buenos Aires. Secret: Document 38, Foreign Relations of the United States, 1969–76, vol. E-11, Part 2, Documents on South America, 1973–1976, https://history.state.gov/historicaldocuments/frus1969-76ve11p2/d38.

59 Conversations with Archbishop Patrick Coveney, Parochial House, Crosshaven, County Cork, January 2013.

60 Grace Livingstone, *Britain and the Dictatorships of Argentina and Chile, 1973–82: Foreign Policy, Corporations and Social Movements* (Palgrave Macmillan, Switzerland, 2018), p. 130.

61 Footnote to Document 38, Foreign Relations of the United States, 1969–76, vol. E-11, Part 2, Documents on South America, 1973–1976, https://history.state.gov/historicaldocuments/frus1969-76ve11p2/d38.

62 Saidon, *La Farsa*, p. 239.

63 http://futbolydictadura.blogspot.com/2008/11/el-precepto_17.html.

64 Saidon, *La Farsa*, p. 253.

65 Justin Harman email to author, 6 September 2017. The armed guard was to prevent people successfully entering the Colombian embassy to seek sanctuary.

66 NAI/DFA/2011/39/1249, Harman to Minister [cable], received 25 March 1976.

67 NAI/DFA, 2012/59/2215.

68 Justin Harman email to author, 6 September 2017;

69 http://www.goal.com/es-ar/news/4465/retro/2016/03/24/4707124/el-amistoso-que-la-selecci%C3%B3n-argentina-jug%C3%B3-ante-polonia-el.

70 Raanan Rein, *Argentine Jews or Jewish Argentines? Essays on Ethnicity, Identity and Diaspora* (Brill, Leiden and Boston, 2010), p. 229.

71 Justin Harman email to author, 6 September 2017.

72 'Junta Takes Over in Argentina', *Guardian*, 25 March 1976, https://www.theguardian.com/world/2016/mar/25/argentina-junta-coup-videla-peron-1976-archive.

73 *La Nación*, 25 March 1976, https://www.educ.ar/recursos/129451/la-nacion-25-de-marzo-de-1976.

74 The Argentine ambassador's note stated that the new government's actions had been necessitated by the 'public institutional, social and administrative chaos which existed in the republic' and that the new administration would be 'characterised by the full rule of law, within a framework of order and observance of human dignity and it will respect all freedoms compatible with the demands of national recovery'.

75 NAI/DFA/2011/39/1249, cable traffic between Irish embassy in Buenos Aires and Iveagh House and between the Irish government and her EEC counterparts at the level of political directors.

76 Ibid.

77 Livingstone, *Britain and the Dictatorships of Argentina and Chile*, pp. 131–2. The day before the coup, the British government had sent a message to the Argentine foreign ministry offering secret talks on the Falklands. The top priority of the Foreign Office, according to Livingstone, was to recognise the regime 'as soon as practicable'. That was to prevent the Argentine military leaders from making the British offer public.

78 This detailed report noted that in 1955, following the overthrow of Perón by General Lonardi, there were large street demonstrations in favour of the new regime, the demolition of statues and book-burning. NAI/DFA, 2012/59/2215, Harman to Minister, 30 March 1976, 'Political Reports from Buenos Aires', January 1975 to November 1982.

79 Ibid.

80 Ibid.

81 Jerry W. Knudson, 'Veil of Silence: The Argentine Press and the Dirty War, 1976–1983', *Latin American Perspectives*, vol. 24, no. 6, 1997, pp. 93–112, www.jstor.org/stable/2634308.

82 That judgement was very much wide of the mark. Franklin A. 'Tex' Harris, a human rights officer at the US embassy from autumn 1977, was one of a number of foreign diplomats in Buenos Aires who would later gain international recognition for dealing courageously with hundreds of families who lost loved ones at the hands of that 'moderate' civilian military government. For a sympathetic profile of Harris, see William Michael Schmidli, *The Fate of Freedom Elsewhere: Human Rights and US Cold War Policy towards Argentina* (Cornell University Press, Cornell, 2013), p. 120 ff.

83 Document 41, Hill to Department of State, 29 March 1976. Source: National Archives, RG 59, Central Foreign Policy File, D760119-0409. Foreign Relations of the United States 1969–76, vol. E-11, Part 2, Documents on South America, 1973–1976. National Archives, RG 59, Central Foreign Policy File, D760119-0409.

84 Colm Tóibín, 'Don't Abandon Me', a review of Edwin Williamson, *Borges: A Life* (Penguin, London, 2005), in *London Review of Books*, vol. 28 no. 9, 11 May 2006, pp. 19–26, https://www.lrb.co.uk/v28/n09/colm-toibin/dont-abandon-me.

85 See Jayson McNamara's documentary *Messenger on a White Horse* (2018), https://www.youtube.com/watch?v=UdeYlLRkq7c (trailer).

86 Alfredo Leaden, already mentioned in Chapter 2, was born in Buenos Aires in 1919. His father Guillermo and mother Brígida Ussher had three sons and five daughters. Two were priests, Alfredo (a Pallottine) and Guillermo (Marist), the latter becoming the auxiliary bishop of Buenos Aires. Alfredo went to the Sisters of Mercy School Clonmacnoise, San Antonio de Areco, and later the Pallottines at Mercedes. He entered the Pallottine preparatory school (minor seminary) in 1932 and went to Thurles in Ireland, where he studied philosophy. In 1937, he went to Rome to begin his theological studies. When Italy entered the war in 1942, he made his way to Lisbon and returned to Buenos Aires where he studied at the Jesuit-run Colegio Máximo. Ordained on 19 December 1942, he was assigned to the Fahy Institute. He was rector in Mercedes from 1947 to 1953; parish priest of Rawson from 1953 until 1958; parish priest in St Patrick's, Belgrano, Buenos Aires, from 1958 to 1966 and of Castelar from 1966 to 1970. He was master of novices from 1970 to 1972 and provincial delegate from 1972 until his murder on 4 July 1976. See *William Ussher and Anne Walsh, and Their Descendants*, compiled originally by Mgr Santiago Ussher in 1933 and updated in 1991. In possession of the Kelly family, Temperley, province of Buenos Aires.

87 Alfredo Leaden to Patrick Dwyer, 17 April 1976: Fr Donal McCarthy, 'History of the Pallottines in Argentina' (unpublished manuscript).

88 https://www.intelligence.gov/argentina-declassification-project/history.

89 Report of an Amnesty International Mission to Argentina, 6–15 November 1976 (Amnesty International, London, March 1977), pp. 13–16.

90 Ibid.

91 Ibid.

92 Ibid.

93 NAI/DFA/2011/39/1249, Harman to Minister, 20 May 1976. See J. Patrice McSherry, *Predatory States: Operation Condor and Covert War in Latin America* (Rowman & Littlefield Publishers, Lanham, 2005); see, in particular, pp. 1–68 and 241–56.

94 In July 1976, at least twenty Uruguayan refugees were abducted in Buenos Aires by armed men. Former Uruguayan senator Héctor Gutiérrez Ruiz was one of a number of Uruguayans killed on 20 May 1976. Another body found in the same burnt-out car was that of the former Uruguayan senator, Zelmar Michelini. The bodies of two other Uruguayan activists were also found in the car. Rice told me in 2008 that, in his view, the death of the two Uruguayan senators was a brutal way of saying to all foreign refugees, missionaries and human rights activists working in the country that they did not have immunity from disappearance, torture and summary justice.

95 In a detailed report on refugees in Argentina, Harman wrote that there was a need for urgent action to relocate immediately between 800 and 1,000 political refugees. NAI/DFA/2011/39/1249, Harman to Minister, 26 May 1976, NAI/DFA/2011/39/1249. Underlining in original.

96 https://www.nytimes.com/1976/06/04/archives/torres-expresident-of-bolivia-found-murdered-in-argentina-man-of.html.

97 NAI/DFA/2011/39/1249, Harman to Minister, 26 May 1976, NAI/DFA/2011/39/1249.

98 There is a vast literature on the conflict in Argentina. I cite many texts in the course of this study. I have interviewed many survivors. What follows is a selection of some of the texts read in the preparation of this work. Some have been cited earlier: Federico Finchelstein, *The Ideological Origins of the Dirty War: Fascism, Populism, and Dictatorship in Twentieth Century Argentina* (Oxford University Press, Oxford and New York, 2014); Martin Edward Andersen, *Dossier Secreto: Argentina's Desaparecidos and the Myth of the 'Dirty War'* (Westview Press, Bounlder, 1993); Eduardo Luis Duhalde, *El Estado Terrorista Argentino* (Colihue, Buenos Aires, 2013); Marguerite Feitlowitz, *A Lexicon of Terror: Argentina and the Legacy of Torture* (Oxford University Press, Oxford, 1998); see also Ulises Gorini, *La Rebelión de las Madres: Historia de las Madres de Plaza de Mayo* (Ediciones Biblioteca Nacional, Buenos Aires, 2105), vols 1 and 2; David M.K. Sheinin, *Ordinary Argentinians in the Dirty War* (University Press of Florida, Gainesville, 2012); Miguel Steuermann et al., *Testimonios de una Semana de Horror* (Cultura de la Nación, Buenos Aires, 1995).

99 Following Patrick Rice's funeral in July 2010, I visited that building in the ESMA. The perpetrators had, following its use as a detention centre, attempted to disguise and cover up their evil deeds. Alterations had been made to the interior of the building to confuse those who had survived detention there. Upon their return they found doors and windows and stairs changed. But that did little to fool anyone who had been detained there.

In the basement, there was a workshop where detainees were set to work using their professional or trade skills. Printers, for example, were used to make forged identity documents for the military. It was a bizarre world. In the loft, prisoners were chained and tortured. On the floor below, some officers had their living quarters. It could not have been possible for the officers to miss the naked and hooded figures of the prisoners being taken from the floor below to the floor above their living rooms. Neither would the officers billeted there have been able to avoid hearing the screams of those being tortured and interrogated day and night.

100 Museum and Site of Memory ESMA, https://www.argentina.gob.ar/derechoshumanos/
     museo-sitio-de-memoria-esma/en.

101 Vincent Druliolle, 'Remembering and its Place in Post Dictatorship Argentina', in Francesca
     Lessa and Vincent Druliolle, *The Memory of State Terror in the Southern Cone: Argentina,
     Chile, and Uruguay* (Palgrave Macmillan, New York, 2011), pp. 27–9.

102 After the fall of the civilian military dictatorship, the democratic government of
     President Raúl Alfonsín set up the Comisión Nacional sobre la Desaparición de Personas
     (CONADEP) on 15 December 1983. That Truth Commission reported on 20 September
     1984 that the number of clandestine detention centres in the country was 340. That number
     was later calculated, following further investigations, at 520.

103 Informe de Investigación RUVTE-ILID de 2015 (El Programa Regisro Unificado de
     Víctimas del Terrorismo de Estado), Anexo V, 'Criterios de Clasificación', p. 1575 ff, https://
     www.argentina.gob.ar/sitiosdememoria/ruvte/informe; I am grateful to Paula Eugenía
     Donadio and Amy Rice Cabrera for this information. See also https://www.argentina.
     gob.ar/sites/default/files/6._anexo_v_listado_de_ccd-investigacion_ruvte-ilid.pdf;see
     Comisión Nacional sobre la Desaparición de Personas (CONADEP), *Nunca Más* (Eudeba,
     Buenos Aires, 2015), p. 59 ff.

104 Rita Arditti, *Searching for Life: The Grandmothers of the Plaza de Mayo and the Disappeared
     Children of Argentina* (University of California Press, Berkeley, 1999), pp. 16–17.

105 An English translation was published in 2005.

106 Horacio Verbitsky, *The Flight: Confessions of an Argentine Dirty Warrior. A Firsthand
     Account of Atrocity* (The New Press, London and New York, 1996 and 2005); published
     in Spanish as *El Vuelo* (Planeta, Buenos Aires, 1995). Based on the confessions in 1993 of
     the retired navy officer Adolfo Scilingo, it remains the only inside account – by a serving
     member of the Argentine forces – of how live political dissidents were pushed out of
     aeroplanes to their death in the River Plate.

107 The history of the Argentine military vicariate has yet to be written. Only then will it be
     possible to answer whether or not any military chaplains resisted the prevailing culture
     of death and opposed the use of torture and the death flights. Gustavo Morello's study is
     among the best available for an examination of the Argentine church during the civilian
     military dictatorship. He makes use of the categories of progressive and anti-secular or
     institutional to describe opposing poles in the Catholic Church in Argentina in the period.
     See Morello, *The Catholic Church and Argentina's Dirty War*, p. 181 ff.

108 Verbitsky, *The Flight*, pp. 11–47.

109 Emilio Mignone became a personal friend after I invited him to visit Ireland in 1989 to
     deliver an annual lecture at University College Cork in honour of Jean Donovan who was
     murdered in El Salvador on 2 December 1980. Her death is the subject of the documentary,
     Roses in December, directed by Bernard Stone and Ana Carrigan. The text of Mignone's
     lecture was published in Dermot Keogh (ed.), *Witness to the Truth: Church and Dictatorship
     in Latin America* (Hibernian University Press, Cork and Dublin 1989). See Michael T.
     Kaufman, 'Emilio F. Mignone, 76, Dies; Argentine Rights Campaigner', *New York Times*,
     25 December 1998; see also Mario del Carril [Introduction Hilda Sabato], *La Vida de
     Emilio Mignone: Justicia, Catolicismo y Derechos Humanos* (Emecé, Buenos Aires, 2011).
     In 2003, New York University's International Center for Transnational Justice and the
     Center for Human Rights and Global Justice established an annual lecture in his honour.
     The Argentine government established an annual international human rights prize in his
     honour in 2007.

110 Mignone, *Witness to the Truth*; Emilio Mignone, *500 Años de Evangelización en América
     Latina* (IDEAS, Ediciones Letra Buena, Buenos Aires, 1992).

111 Horacio Verbitsky, *El Silencio: De Paulo VI a Bergoglio: Las Relaciones de la Iglesia con la ESMA* (Editorial Sudamericana, Buenos Aires, 2005), pp. 51–3.

112 Mignone told me that was his theory in Cork, 1989.

113 Verbitsky, *El Silencio*, pp. 51–61.

114 Iain Guest, *Behind the Disappearances: Argentina's Dirty War against Human Rights and the United Nations* (University of Pennsylvania Press, Philadelphia, 1990), pp. 10–11.

115 See Phil Davison, 'Revelations of the Flight Torment a Nation: Argentina – How the "Disappeared Ones" Died', *Independent*, 14 May 1995: 'Nineteen years later, as a wall of military silence finally begins to crumble, Mignone believes he finally knows his daughter's fate. "She was almost certainly interrogated for a few days, drugged, carried on to a military plane and dumped alive over the Rio de la Plata or the Atlantic," he said.'

116 Verbitsky, *El Silencio*, pp. 55–60 and 102–8; see also Verbitsky, *La Mano Izquierda de Dios*, vol. iv, pp. 88–127; 'La Historia Secreta del Candidato Bergoglio: Papabilidades', *Página 12*, 10 April 2005.

117 '"Dirty War" Victim Rejects Pope's Connection to Kidnapping', *New York Times*, 21 March 2013, http://www.nytimes.com/2013/03/22/world/americas/jesuit-priest-rejects-popes-connection-to-kidnapping.html?_r=0.

118 'Argentina "Dirty War" Accusations Haunt Pope Francis', BBC News, 15 March 2013, http://www.bbc.com/news/world-europe-21794798. The report quoted Graciela Yorio as continuing to uphold the views of her late brother. The role played by Fr Jorge Bergoglio during this period in Argentine history is beyond the scope of this current study. The work of Horacio Verbitsky has already been cited. See also his article 'Papabilidades', *Página 12*, 10 April 2005. In relation to his role as Jesuit provincial and his actions during the civilian military dictatorship, the following may be of interest: Elisabetta Piqué, *Francisco: Vida y Revolución* (La Esfera de los Libros, Buenos Aires, 2015), pp. 84–5. She wrote that Mr Verbitsky refused to be interviewed by her for her biography of Francis 1, p. 85. See Nello Scavo, *La Lista de Bergoglio: Los Salvados por Francisco durante la Dictatura. Una Historia no Contada* (Editorial Claritiana, Buenos Aires, 2013). Adolfo Pérez Esquivel has written a prologue entitled 'Bergoglio Ayudó a los Perseguidos' ('Bergoglio Helped the Persecuted'), pp. 7–11. See also Marcelo Larraquy, *Recen por Él: La Historia jamás contada del Hombre que Desafía los Secretos del Vaticano* (Editorial Sudamericana, Buenos Aires, 2014), p. 84 ff. See also Sergio Rubin y Francesca Ambrogetti, *El Jesuita: La Historia de Francisco, el Papa Argentino* (Vergara, Buenos Aires, 2010), p. 84 ff; Jorge Mario Bergoglio y Abraham Skorka, *On Heaven and Earth: Pope Francis on Faith, Family and the Church in the 21st Century* (Bloomsbury, London, 2013); and Jimmy Burns, *Francis* (Constable, London, 2016).

119 Katryn Sikkink, *Mixed Signals: US Human Rights Policy and Latin* America (Cornell University Press, Ithaca and London, 2004), pp. xiv–xv; see also the National Security Archive, Washington DC, https://nsarchive2.gwu.edu/NSAEBB/NSAEBB104/index.htm; see also full text, Argentina Project, US Secretary of State, transcript, 6 June 1976; the participants were: Kissinger; Under-Secretary Rogers; Under-Secretary Maw; Luigi R. Einaudi, notetaker; Anthony Hervas, interpreter for Guzzetti, Ambassador Carasales, Ambassador Pereyra and Mr Estrada, https://foia.state.gov/Search/results.aspx?searchText=+Guzzetti&beginDate=&endDate=&publishedBeginDate=&publishedEndDate=&caseNumber=.

120 On 6 October 1976, Admiral Guzzetti was told by Charles Robinson, a senior State Department official, that 'the problem is that the United States is an idealistic and moral country and its citizens have great difficulty in comprehending the kinds of problems faced by Argentina today. There is a tendency to apply our moral standards abroad and Argentina must understand the reaction of Congress with regard to loans and military assistance. The

American people, right or wrong, have the perception that today there exists in Argentina a pattern of gross violations of human rights'. The US ambassador in Buenos Aires, Robert Hill, had consistently put pressure on the Argentine government to stop the human rights abuses. Hill, having met Admiral Guzzetti upon his return from the US, was disconcerted. He was convinced that the Argentine foreign minister expected to receive warnings on his government's human rights practices: 'He has returned in a state of jubilation, convinced that there is no real problem with the USG [government] over that issue.' In another cable, Hill had reported that the ambassador's concerns over human rights had been dismissed by President Jorge Videla: 'The president said he had been gratified when Guzzetti reported to him that secretary of state Kissinger understood their problem and had said he hoped they could get terrorism under control as quickly as possible.' Videla told Hill that he had the impression that senior officers of the US government understood the situation faced by the Argentine government 'but junior bureaucrats do not'. The ambassador assured Videla that that was not the case. Hill added: 'If security forces continue to kill people to tune of brass band, I concluded, this will not be possible.'

'Kissinger Approved Argentinian "Dirty War"', *Guardian*, 6 December 2003, https://www.theguardian.com/world/2003/dec/06/argentina.usa; see also 'America's Role in Argentina's Dirty War', *New York Times*, 17 March 2016, https://www.nytimes.com/2016/03/17/opinion/americas-role-in-argentinas-dirty-war.html?_r=0. President Obama visited Argentina on the fortieth anniversary of the coup of 1976, in March 2016. He used the occasion to announce that he would move to declassify American military, intelligence and law enforcement records that could reveal what the United States government knew about Argentina's conflict in the 1970s and 1980s. The Holy See, in October 2016, also announced that it would open the files in its archives on the civilian military dictatorship 'in the service of truth, justice and peace'.

121 The Irish diplomat Justin Harman reported on 6 October 1976 that Guzzetti's shocking remarks had been circulated at a meeting of EEC counsellors. Antibodies or no, the same meeting heard that the wife of the first secretary of the Swedish embassy 'had been very nearly killed in a recent attack ... [apparently] by the right wing because of Sweden's policy of accepting refugees'. NA/DFA/2006/131/103, Harman to Minister, 6 October 1976 [Political Situation in Argentina, March 1976 – November 1976].

122 Guzzetti served as minister for foreign affairs from March 1976 until May 1977. On 7 May 1977, Montoneros shot him in a hospital waiting room in Buenos Aires. He survived as a mute quadriplegic. He died in 1988. See Cynthia J. Arnson (ed.), *Argentina–United States Bilateral Relations* (Woodrow Wilson Center, Washington DC, 2004), https://www.wilsoncenter.org/publication/argentina-united-states-bilateral-relations-historical-perspective-and-future-challeng-0; see also Carlos Osorio and Kathleen Costar (eds), *Kissinger to the Argentine Generals in 1976: National Security Archive Briefing Book*, no. 133, posted 27 August 2004, https://nsarchive2.gwu.edu/NSAEBB/NSAEBB133/, and Arturo J. Aldama (ed.), *Violence and the Body: Race, Gender and the State* (University of Indiana Press, Bloomington, 2003), p. 390.

123 Victoria Fortuna, *Moving Otherwise: Dance, Violence, and Memory in Buenos Aires* (Oxford University Press, Oxford, 2019), p. 80.

124 Mgr Coveney served in Buenos Aires between 1972 and 1976.

125 The register in the Irish College, Rome, records that Kevin Mullen was born in Mountnugent, County Cavan, on 26 February 1939. His parents were Michael Joseph Mullen and Catherine (Kitty) Coffey. He attended secondary school at St Finian's College, Mullingar (five years), studied in Maynooth (three years), and arrived in the Irish College on 12 October 1960. He was ordained a deacon on 27 October 1963, and a priest

on 22 November 1964. Returning to his diocese of Meath, he was assigned to teach in the college he had attended and he also did parish work. He was frequently called upon to help out at the nunciature. He was in residence in Dunboyne, close to the nunciature. He was then called to Rome, entering the *Accademia Ecclesiastica* in 1969. He was later assigned to Bangkok, Thailand, for two years. Mullen was then sent to Bangladesh on a short assignment and later to Damascus. See TSC, 25 June 1976. (I am grateful to Fr Albert McDonnell, vice rector, Irish College, Rome, and to his brother, Mgr Austin Mullen, for the information in this brief profile.)

126 Cardinal Seán Brady of Armagh was a classmate both at Maynooth and in the Irish College, Rome. He recalled that he had displayed considerable physical and moral courage early in his career, smuggling letters of dissidents out of Damascus, Syria.

127 Mgr Austin Mullen email to author, 4 February 2013.

128 Kevin Mullen told this anecdote to Professor Matthew MacNamara in Paris while he was serving at the nunciature there.

129 Both Cox and Mullen lived close to each other on Avenida Alvear where the nunciature was situated.

130 While there is no reference to Mullen in her family memoir, the book is a jewel of its kind. See Maud Daverio de Cox, *Testimonios del Antiguo Pueblo de San Martín: Las Costumbres, la Educación, los 'Ingleses' y el 'Progreso'* (Prosa Editores, Buenos Aires, 2017).

131 Cox, *Dirty Secrets, Dirty War*, pp. 206–7.

132 NAI/DFA/2011/39/1249, Harman to Minister, 25 June 1976.

133 NAI/DFA/2011/39/1249.

134 NAI/DFA, 2011/39/1249, Justin Harman, chargé d'affaires a.i., to Secretary, 25 June 1976.

135 Horacio Verbitsky, *Doble Juego: La Argentina Católica y Militar* (Editorial Sudamericana, Buenos Aires, 2006), pp. 200–1.

136 Hughes was transferred to Montevideo. He did not wish to leave, but his superiors gave him no option as his life was in danger.

137 Eugenio Delaney declined to offer any views on those he worked with, in particular Fr Richards; Eugenio Delaney email to author, 18 July 2018.

138 Eugenio Delaney email to author, 10 June 2014.

139 'Pasionistas Víctimas de un Ataque Terrista: Bomba en Nazaret', *TSC*, 27 August 1976.

140 Diego Martínez, 'La Otra Cara de la Iglesia', *Página 12*, 9 December 2007, https://www.pagina12.com.ar/diario/elpais/1-95949-2007-12-09.html.

141 The couple married on 7 April 1948. Born in 1927, she was the daughter of Samuel Alejandro Hartridge Parkes, an Anglo-Argentine professor of physics and once Argentine ambassador to Turkey.

142 Gabriel Seisdedos, *El Honor de Dios: Mártires Paolotinos. La Historia Silenciada de un Crimen Impune* (Ciudad Nueva, Buenos Aires, 2011), p. 250.

143 I am grateful to Fr Donal McCarthy, Pallottine archivist, Dublin, for most of this information regarding the three priests' contacts with Ireland (letter to author, 22 September 2018). I also found information in the Pallottine archives in St Patrick's, Belgrano, Buenos Aires.

144 'A Red Carpet for Father Kentenich at Los Cerrillos Airport [Chile], 21 June 2017, https://www.schoenstatt.org/en/kentenich-en/2017/06/a-red-carpet-for-father-kentenich-at-los-cerrillos-airport/.

145 Seisdedos, *El Honor de Dios*, p. 66 ff.

146 Discussions with Juan José Delaney, Buenos Aires, 2016.

147 Ibid.

148 Verbitsky, *La Mano Izquierda de Dios*, pp. 63–4.

149 Kelly's diary, which has been translated into English but remains unpublished, provides an invaluable insight into the mindset of the priests living through difficult months of the dictatorship. Fr Donal McCarthy, archivist, Pallottine House, Sandyford, Dublin, gave me a digital copy of this document and many other documents relating to the order's work in Argentina.

150 Fr Donal McCarthy, 'History of the Pallottines in Argentina' (unpublished), Cornelius (Connie) Ryan letters.

151 Eduardo Kimel, *La Masacre de San Patricio* (Ediciones Dialéctica, Buenos Aires, n.d.) (Prólogo de Pérez Esquivel), pp. 23–4.

152 Sergio Lucero, *Juntos Vivieron y Juntos Murieron: La Entrega de los Cinco Palotinos* (Editorial Claretiana, Buenos Aires, 2016), p. 22.

153 Verbitsky, *La Mano Izquierda de Dios*, pp. 63–4.

154 There is another account which names two youths. 'El Horrendo Crimen de los Cinco Religiosos Palotinos', *El Periodista de Buenos Aires*, no. 32, 19 al 25 de Abril, 1980, p. 27.

155 Ibid. According to a source cited in the article, they talked to a person who had a friend working in the police station 37. The policemen in the patrol car who had gone to the scene within days had received death threats. The police chief responded by making six or seven copies of the names of those who were in the black Peugeot that night. He distributed the copies to different people and let it be known that 'if a hair on the head of a single policeman in the patrol car on that night was touched, the list would be made public'.

156 This important detail is found in Patrick Rice, Carlos Bustos and Pablo Gazzarri, *Death and Violence in Argentina* (Catholic Institute for International Relations (CIIR), London) reproduced in Spanish in Rice y Torres, *En Medio de la Tempestad*, pp. 188–9.

157 Verbitsky, *La Mano Izquierda de Dios*, pp. 61–4.

158 Seisdedos, *El Honor de Dios*, p. 143.

159 NAI/DFA/2006/131/103, Harman telegram, 5[?] July 1976 [Political Situation in Argentina, March 1976–November 1976]; the *Irish Times*, on 3 July 1976, had carried a short report entitled '25 Police Killed in Argentina'. It gave details of a bomb, placed by a guerrilla, in the dining room of the federal police security department in Buenos Aires, killing over twenty policemen. On 5 July, the same paper reported: 'Priests of Irish Descent Massacred in Argentina'. The latter was believed to have been an act of reprisal and vengeance ordered by Massera for the attack on the barracks. (Discussions with Fr Tom O'Donnell, PP, Mercedes, Argentina, May 2014.)

160 This is speculation on my part.

161 Fr Kelly's father Jack had died in 1955.

162 Related to me by Sr Dymphna Tipper OP. She recalled with great emotion being in the congregation as those airs were played. She also mentioned that mourners were requested not to go up to the open coffins, so disfigured were the remains. She also remembered that Bishop Leaden sat during the mass close to the coffin of his murdered brother, Alfredo. Phone conversation 18 January 2021.

163 My thanks to Fr Tomás O'Donnell for information on the families of the murdered Pallottines and on the funeral services (email to author, 8 May 2020).

164 The mourners would have included parishioners with the surnames Aspel, Ballesty, Brady, Brennan, Brown, Burke, Byrne, Carmody, Casey, Clavin, Dalton, Dillon, Doherty, Donnelly, Duffy, Dunleavy, Dunne, Flynn, Ganley, Gardiner, Garrahan, Haughton, Hayes, Healy, Hoare, Horan, Horn, Kilmeate, Langan, Lawless, Lawlor, Lennard, Lennon, Lucy, Lynch, Macdonnell, Mallone, Mannion, Moran, Morrow, Moughty, Murphy, Murtagh, O'Reilly, Pierce, Shanahan, Slaven, Sheehan, Smith, Tyrell and Wynne.

165 Barbeito was buried in his home town of Avellaneda and Barletti in San Antonio de Areco.

166 I don't have a copy of the text of that letter sent by the Conferencia Episcopal Argentina (Argentine Episcopal Conference), on 7 July to the civilian military government.

167 'Who Benefits?', *Buenos Aires Herald*, 5 July 1976.

168 There was a drop-off in the sales of *TSC* during those years, the letters page reflecting the hostility of a number of its readers to the editor's consistent anti-government stance on human rights issues. Because of Fr Richards' editorial line, he ran foul of a number of prominent members of the Federation of Irish Societies. The federation had a partial share in the ownership of the paper together with the Pallottines and the Passionists.

169 This verbatim quotation was reproduced in *TSC*, 16 July 1976: '*Se ha querido callar esas voces (la de los asesinados) pero sus voces son mas fuertes aun desde sus tumbas. Nada ni nadie podra acallar la voz de la Iglesia.*'

170 Based on accounts by Frs Patrick Dwyer and Donal F. McCarthy, 'History of the Pallottines in Argentina', Pallottine archives, Dublin.

171 Meeting with Bishop Guillermo Leaden, Marist House, Buenos Aires, 2016.

172 Bissonnet to Ottawa, [?] July 1976, Political Affairs – Policy and Background – Internal Policy Trends – Argentina, file no. dossier 20-ARG-1-4, CO121, vol. 7, from 1 November 1974 to 15 February 1977, Acc. no. 288281, Canadian National Archives, Ottawa. The US ambassador, Hill, had reported that he had been informed by an 'officer attached to presidential staff, on highest degree of confidentiality, that five churchmen plus three nuns were executed by members of army intelligence service (SIE)'. According to the same source, Mario Firmenich, the senior Montonero leader, had been allegedly responsible for the assassination of President Aramburu and the recent bombing of federal police headquarters. That source claimed that Firmenich was 'hiding in St. Patrick's church ... [and] ... was alleged to be under protection of clergy'. SIE had gone to capture him but found that he had left. They killed the five Pallottines. There was another unconfirmed report that the killings were the work of the federal police rather than the army. While unable to confirm either report, 'we accept the probability that killings were action of some element of the GOA security forces'. The report said it was also quite possible that the action could have been carried out by 'lower level members of the security forces without orders from their superiors'. But Hill found it not implausible 'that churchmen could have been assisting an extremist to evade capture'. At an Independence Day reception on 5 July, Cardinal Aramburu commented to Hill that the 'church must pay its toll'. Argentina Project, US Secretary of State [virtual reading room documents search results], https://foia.state.gov/Search/results.aspx?searchText=Patrick+Rice&beginDate=&endDate=&publishedBeginDate=&publishedEndDate=&caseNumber=.

173 Harman reported the speculation that Barletti, one of the murdered Pallottines, was 'in fact in some way connected with the leftist movement'. He had heard that he had been arrested in June but later released. The Irish diplomat was duty bound to report what he had heard in this regard. (It is my hypothesis that he may have been a member of Cristianos para la Liberación, of which Fr Carlos Bustos was a founder member. NAI/DFA/2006/131/103.

174 Lucero, *Juntos Vivieron y Juntos Murieron*, p. 24.

CHAPTER 5 Irish Diplomacy and the Disappearance, Torture and Illegal Detention of Fr Patrick Rice and Fátima Cabrera

1 Raúl Zurita, *INRI* (Marick Press, Grosse Pointe Farms, Michigan, 2018), p. 129.

2 NAI/DFA/2011/39/1249, Ambassador Lennon to Minister, 2 August 1976.

3 On 9 August 1976, the Cuban diplomat Jesús Cejas Arias was kidnapped in the Belgrano area together with a colleague, Crescencio Galañena Hernández. They were taken to a clandestine detention centre, Automotive Orletti, tortured and their bodies were hidden in a 200-litre

metal drum. Cejas Arias' remains were discovered in 2013 and returned to Cuba for burial. The remains of Galañena Hernández were also found near the other body in Virreyes, San Fernando, the province of Buenos Aires. Cuba Confidential, 'Argentina Turns Over Body of Cuban Diplomat Killed in 1976', https://cubaconfidential.wordpress.com/tag/cuban-diplomat/.

4   NAI/DFA, 2011/39/1249, Ambassador Lennon to Secretary, 19 August 1976.

5   Roberto Favre, 'Los Mártires Asuncionistas Carlos Antonio Di Pietro y Raúl Eduardo Rodriguez', http://confar.org.ar/wp1/wp-content/uploads/2016/07/martires_ asuncionistas.pdf.

6   Besides Sr Terence O'Keeffe, other Irish Dominicans were Dymphna Tipper and Brigid Fahy. Mary O'Byrne arrived in 1977. See O'Byrne, *Strands from a Tapestry*, pp. 79–81. The nuns had given Rice permission to hold classes in the school for catechists from Soldati, as it was much safer to do so there since the *villa* was under constant surveillance and disappearances were frequent.

7   'Irish Priest Abducted', *Buenos Aires Herald*, 13 October 1976. This article stated that the community originally lived in Villa Soldati, which was also known as Villa Fátima. Later, a number moved to a house in La Boca. More recently, they moved to Floresta to be nearer the *villa*. In fact, the Little Brothers had for a time communities in La Boca, Villa Soldati and Calle Malabia.

8   A contemporary account of the disappearance of members of the Little Brothers is to be found in the US Department of State memorandum, April 1978, entitled 'Repression of a Religious Community in Argentina: The Continuing "Secret Detention" of Fathers Gazzarri, Silva and Bustos in Buenos Aires', Argentina Project, US Department of State, https://foia. state.gov/documents/Argentina/0000A6C3.pdf.

9   Rice y Torres, *En Medio de la Tempestad*, pp. 135–7; see also Domingo Bresci, *MSTM: Historia de un Compromiso. A Cincuenta Años Del Movimiento De Sacerdotes Para El Tercer Mundo* (GES Comunicación, Buenos Aires, 2018), pp. 328–30; see also María Soledad, 'Movimiento de Sacerdotes para el Tercer Mundo y Servicios de Inteligencia: 1969–1970', *Sociedad y Religión: Sociología, Antropología e Historia de la Religión en el Cono Sur*, vol. xx, no. 30–1, 2008, pp. 171–89.

10   The town is 170 kilometres south-east of La Rioja.

11   An Irish priest, Fr Tony Gill, worked for a number of years with Bishop Angelelli. He was a Dubliner and a member of the Society of African Missions (SMA). He was very popular in his parish as he cycled around on an old bike. He was arrested with another priest, Padre Enri Praolini, allegedly for being connected to the guerrillas. See Antonio Puigjané, *Con un Oído en el Evangelio y el otro en el Pueblo*, quoted in Roberto Rojo, *Angelelli: La Vida por los Pobres* (Nexo Ediciones, La Rioja, 2001), pp. 234–6. That episode may have occurred in 1973. He was expelled from Argentina and deported back to Ireland in December 1975. When flying from La Rioja to Buenos Aires en route to Ireland, he was sitting beside Carlos Ménem, the governor of La Rioja and future president of Argentina. Unfortunately, my efforts to have a conversation with Fr Gill to clarify the events and timeline have proven to be unsuccessful. The order's archivist, Fr Edward Hogan, has helped me to fill in the missing dates.

12   Rice y Torres, *En Medio de la Tempestad*, p. 136.

13   'Dos Muertes como Mensaje a Angelelli', *Pagina 12*, https://www.pagina12.com.ar/diario/ elpais/1-201200-2012-08-16.html; and 'Los Discípulos del Obispo Angelelli', *Página 12*, https://www.pagina12.com.ar/diario/elpais/1-260238-2014-11-20.html.

14   See *Nunca Más*, National Commission on the Disappearance of Persons (CONADEP), 1984; see also Renata Keller, 'The Martyrdom of Monseñor Angelelli', *Journal of Religion and Society*, vol. 12, 2010, pp. 4–21; Rojo, *Angelelli: La Vida por los Pobres*; Luis O. Liberti,

Monseñor Enrique Angelelli (Editorial Guadalupe, Buenos Aires, 2005); Ricardo Mercado Luna, *Enrique Angelelli: Obispo de La Rioja. Aportes para una Historia de Fé, Compromiso y Martirio* (Grupo Nexo Editor, La Rioja, 2010).

15 Rice y Torres, *En Medio de la Tempestad*, pp. 136–7.

16 After he came back from La Rioja, Rice told Fátima Cabrera, then a catechist in Soldati, that he had found a central focus for his future life's work – the promotion of human rights.

17 Rice y Torres, *En Medio de la Tempestad*, p. 137.

18 The text was published in Spanish in *En Medio de la Tempestad* (see pp. 184–93). Besides the Angelelli case, the report also detailed the circumstances in which many members of the clergy were disappeared and kidnapped. It was a remarkable first draft of history directly implicating the Argentine authorities in disappearances and killings. There is a copy of the CIIR text on file in the DFA.

19 John Simpson and Jana Bennett, *The Disappeared and the Mothers of the Plaza: The Story of the 11,000 Argentinians who Vanished* (St Martin's Press, New York, 1985), p. 181.

20 Morello, *The Catholic Church and Argentina's Dirty War.*

21 Fr Weeks continued to minister in Peru, Bolivia and Argentina for the remainder of his working life. He died on 30 March 2015.

22 'Los Obispos Riojanos Celebraron los Procesamientos por el Asesinato de Angelelli', *Página 12*, 25 November 2011.

23 'Tres ex Generals y un Obispo Muerto', *Página 12*, 25 November 2011.

24 'Evidence from Francis Helps Convict Bishop's Junta-era Killers', *The Tablet*, 8 July 2014, http://www.thetablet.co.uk/news/954/123/evidence-from-francis-helps-convict-bishop-s-junta-era-killers; 'Argentina Military Officers Convicted of Bishop's Murder', http://www.bbc.com/news/world-latin-america-28172088 (5 July 2014); 'Argentina Recalls the Murder of Mgr Angelelli who was Opposed to Dictatorship', http://www.fides.org/en/news/38283-AMERICA_ARGENTINA_Argentina_recalls_the_murder_of_Mgr_Angelelli_who_was_opposed_to_dictatorship#.WNgQpPnyuck (5 August 2015).

25 'Francisco Delcaró Beato al Obispo Angelelli, Asesinado por la Dictadura Militar', *La Nación*, 8 June 2018, https://goo.gl/aMJx4q.

26 Fr Tony Gill and Fátima Cabrera attended the ceremonies. The bishop's elevation was not welcomed by all Catholics. '"The Beatification of Satanelli" – Patron of Communist Terrorists and Road Accidents', *Rorate Caeli*, https://rorate-caeli.blogspot.com/2019/04/the-beatification-of-satanelli-patron.html; 'A New Vileness: The Beatification of Bishop Angelelli', *One Peter 5 – 1P5*, 14 June 2018, https://onepeterfive.com/vileness-beatification-angelelli/.

27 NAI/DFA, 2011/39/1249, Ambassador Lennon to Secretary, 3 September 1976.

28 Address by Pope Paul VI on 27 September 1976 when receiving new Argentine ambassador, http://www.vatican.va/content/paul-vi/en/speeches/1976/documents/hf_p-vi_spe_19760927_ambasciatore-argentina.html. See also André Dupuy, *La Diplomatie du Saint Siège après le IIe Concile du Vatican: Le Pontificat de Paul VI 1963–1978* (Téqui, Paris, n.d.), p. 281.

29 Kimel, *La Masacre de San Patricio*, pp. 88–9.

30 NAI/DFA, 2011/39/1249, Ambassador Lennon to Secretary, 11 October 1976.

31 Fátima Cabrera email to author, 5 March 2019.

32 As the right of public assembly was banned under the dictatorship for more than three people, it was common at that time in Argentina to meet under cover of church, sporting or community events.

33 Information from Fátima Cabrera and her daughter Amy, email and phone conversations, 11 February 2019.

34 Unknown to Rice, around 2 October an Irish Pallottine priest was mistaken for him and detained while purchasing medicine in a pharmacy in Belgrano, Buenos Aires.

35 Cabrera (who was introduced in chapters 4 and 5) was going to her mother's house.

36 In the confusion as they were being kidnapped, Cabrera tried to tell Rice that her real name was Fátima. He found that confusing as the chapel was in Barrio Fátima and he concluded incorrectly that she had given him another false name.

37 Patrick Rice testimony, case 2450, Argentina, Inter-American Commission on Human Rights (IACHR), letter, 9 April 1978, http://www.cidh.org/annualrep/78eng/Argentina.2450.htm.

38 Conor O'Clery, 'Priest Describes his Torture in Argentina', *Irish Times*, 8 December 1976.

39 Accounts of the disappearance of Fátima Cabrera and Patrick Rice have been published in a number of books: see Miron Varouhakis, *Shadow of Heroes* (Xlibris-LLC, Bloomington, IN, 2010), p. 82 ff; Penny Lernoux, *Cry of the People: The Struggle for Human Rights in Latin America. The Catholic Church in Conflict with US Policy* (Penguin Books, New York, 1982); Tim Pat Coogan, *Wherever Green Is Worn: The Story of the Irish Diaspora* (Palgrave, London, 2001), p. 624; William T. Cavanaugh, *Torture and Eucharist* (Blackwell Publishing, Oxford, 1998), p. 54; Michael Newton, *The Encyclopaedia of Kidnappings* (Facts on File Inc., New York, 2002), p. 248; Burdick, *For God and the Fatherland*, references p. 155; Iain Guest, *Behind Argentina's Dirty War against Human Rights and the United Nations* (University of Pennsylvania Press, Philadelphia, 1990), p. 40.

40 Ibid.

41 See Case 2450 Argentina, Inter-American Commission on Human Rights (Organisation of American States), Rice letter to Commission, 9 April 1978, http://www.cidh.org/annualrep/78eng/Argentina.2450.htm.

42 Diego Martinez, 'Un Luchador Consecuente' ['A Fighter of Great Consistency'], *Pagina 12*, 9 July 2011, http://www.pagina12.com.ar/diario/elpais/1-149174-2010-07-09.html.

43 Patrick Rice submission to the Inter-American Commission on Human Rights, 9 April 1978, http://www.cidh.org/annualrep/78eng/Argentina.2450.htm.

44 O'Clery, 'Priest Describes His Torture in Argentina', op. cit.

45 See https://www.cij.gov.ar/nota-8749-Superintendencia-de-Seguridad-Federal-y--Garage-Azopardo-.html; https://www.suteba.org.ar/mas-datos-del-centro-clandestino-garage-azopardo-4992.html.

46 The terrible thing, Fátima told me, was that the building had been greatly modified since it was used as a torture centre and that, up to a short time before they discovered its exact location, it was being used as an office where people went to have their identity cards and passports issued. The building was no longer in the control of the federal police. Source: My discussion with Fátima. See also 'Garage Azopardo', https://readtheplaque.com/plaque/garage-azopardo.

47 See poem, http://english.emory.edu/classes/paintings&poems/auden.html.

48 O'Clery, 'Priest Describes His Torture in Argentina', op. cit.

49 Conversations with Fátima Rice, 2000–19. See also Rice y Torres, *En Medio de la Tempestad*, for relevant information throughout the volume. While both Fátima Cabrera and Patrick Rice were being tortured, Doña Blanca, Fátima's mother, visited the police station to enquire about the whereabouts of her daughter. She recalled seeing a blond man there who may have been the navy commander Alfredo Astiz, who was based at the ESMA. There, she was given no information. Her family had contacts in the military but those sources did not yield any results. She was obliged to travel to Tucumán, where her daughter was born, to get documentation necessary to process the disappearance complaint with the police. She told me of her long and terrifying journey of eighteen hours, travelling alone during a state of siege when the bus was stopped and searched a number of times. The military took passengers

away. When she arrived in Tucumán, she found soldiers posted all around the main square. She got back to Buenos Aires with the documentation and went on a round of the different police stations. Again she learned nothing and continued to live in a macabre world where the military had literally power over life and death. Conversations with Doña Blanca, Buenos Aires, 2000–7.

50 Fátima Cabrera, 'Debo Agradecer a Dios ser una Sobreviviente', in Rice y Torres, *En Medio de la Tempestad*, pp. 149–52.

51 Ibid.

52 Patrick Rice submission to the Inter-American Commission on Human Rights, 9 April 1978, http://www.cidh.org/annualrep/78eng/Argentina.2450.htm.

53 Conversations with Fátima Cabrera, Buenos Aires, 2010; see also Rice y Torres, *En Medio de la Tempestad*, p. 52.

54 Fátima Cabrera account sent to me by email from her daughter, Amy, 7 February 2019; also Conversation with Fátima Cabrera, Cork, September 2018.

55 Inter-American Commission on Human Rights, Case 2450, Rice letter, 9 April 1978, http://www.cidh.org/annualrep/78eng/Argentina.2450.htm

56 Conversation with Fátima Cabrera, Cork, September 2018.

57 Patrick Rice, 'Una Entrega Generosa y Creative en Medio de la Violencia Represiva', in Rice y Torres, *En Medio de la Tempestad*, p. 133.

58 Ibid.

59 Document outlining case including Patrick Rice and Fátima Cabrera against six people: five policemen and one member of the military; see p. 36 ff of the documentation.

60 Ibid.

61 The telephone number of the ambassador's residence was quite well known to members of the Irish-Argentine community. Because of the danger in which he lived, he would have given his fellow priests numbers to call in the event of an emergency: embassy, nunciature, Dominican Sisters and the *Southern Cross* and *Buenos Aires Herald*. Information based on conversations with Patrick Rice. See Washington Uranga, 'Por la Memoria del Cura Barrendero Mauricio Silva', *Pagina 12*, 8 October 2007, http://www.pagina12.com.ar/diario/elpais/1-92647-2007-10-08.html; see also Jerry Ryan, 'Two Priests in a Dirty War: Mauricio Silva and Christian von Wernich Show Us Two Faces of the Church in Argentina', *National Catholic Reporter*, 11 July 2008.

62 He became a frequent visitor to the embassy in the following weeks, liaising with Harman and the ambassador. There, Kratzer wrote that he found 'verdadera solidaridad' (authentic solidarity). On every visit to the Irish embassy, he met Harman and Ambassador James Wilfred Lennon (aka Wilfie); '*el propio embajador*' ('the ambassador himself'), he wrote later, used to take him in his car and drop him many blocks away so as to lessen the risk of his being picked up. Juan José Kratzer, 'Una Vida Evangélica más Radical', in Rice y Torres, *En Medio de la Tempestad*, p. 160. In 2016, I spoke to Juan Kratzer by phone while we were both in Buenos Aires. In 1977, Kratzer was on a death list. He got to the nunciature and was supplied with a travel document and an airline ticket. Taken under cover in the nunciature car to the airport, he was escorted to the plane and he made good his escape.

63 Kratzer, after being forced to leave his native Argentina, worked in Italy as a psychiatric nurse. He later married Arturo Paoli's niece and lived in Savona until his death from brain cancer in 2017. When I spoke at length to Kratzer on the phone in 2016, he told me that the nuncio was able to provide him with a copy of the document that they had given to him in 1977. Additional information also supplied by Justin Harman.

64 NAI/DFA, 2012/59/2236, Guido Doglione, for Prior François Élidia, Little Brothers of Charles de Foucauld, mid-October 1976. Replying on 26 October, FitzGerald said: 'The

Irish embassy has been most concerned with Fr Rice's welfare and has expressed this concern to the Argentinian authorities at the highest level. The embassy is at present pressing the Argentinian authorities for the reasons for Fr Rice's detention and, in the continuing absence of charges against him, for his release.'

65 Rice y Torres, *En Medio de la Tempestad*, p. 207.

66 Iveagh House had already contacted the local gardaí at Fermoy, the town nearest to the farm where Rice's parents and brothers and sister lived. Sergeant Twomey immediately visited the Rice home at Curraghmore, and informed his father, William, of his son's 'disappearance'. His father wrote on 13 October: 'I hope you will be able to find out his whereabouts and communicate with us immediately as we (his mother and myself and family) are very worried for his safety.' I am very grateful to the DFA archivist Ms Maureen Sweeney for her assistance in locating this consular file, NAI/DFA, 2012/59/2236, which was released to the National Archives in January 2013.

67 Patrick Rice file, Holy See [N. 2559/76], p. 151.

68 Sr Terence was from Ballykearney, Mitchelstown, County Cork; she taught in Eccles Street, Cabra and Muckross. She had a sister in the order, Sr Berenice. Her brother, Fr Gerard, was a Dominican priest.

69 Informed of this by Patrick's sister, Kathleen.

70 Phone interview with Sr Dymphna Tipper, November 2018. In a phone conversation on 18 January 2021, Sr Dymphna remembered that his name was Carlos and described him as a fine, tall, bearded man, which exactly fits the description of Fr Bustos.

71 Conversation with Sr Dymphna Tipper. See also O'Byrne, *Strands from a Tapestry*, p. 79; I am very grateful to Sr Mary O'Byrne for her help and for introducing me to other members of her community who have served in Argentina. Sr Dymphna Tipper had a clear recollection of the events and provided other details to me in a phone conversation on 18 January 2021.

72 My friend, the late Michael Geraghty, who was living in Buenos Aires at the time, told me that that had happened.

73 Patrick Rice file, Holy See; 'Irish Priest Abducted', *Buenos Aires Herald*, 13 October 1976; 'La Embajada Irlandesa Denunció el Secustro de un Sacerdote Obrero', *La Razón*, 14 October 1976.

74 'Concern over Fate of Missing Irish Priest in Argentina', *Irish Times*, 14 October 1976.

75 'Irish Priest Kidnapped by Gunmen in Argentina' (Reuters, Buenos Aires, 13 October 1976), *The Times* (London), 14 October 1976.

76 *Washington Post*, 14 October 1976.

77 On 20 August 1976, thirty prisoners, in the custody of the federal police, were taken by truck to Fátima, near the city of Pilar, in the province of Buenos Aires. They were machine-gunned and their bodies dynamited. The remains were spread over a radius of thirty metres. This has become known as the Massacre of Fátima or Pilar. Rice brought me to visit that site in 2006 on the thirtieth anniversary of the massacre when a plaque was unveiled to those who had been murdered. Conversations with Patrick Rice, 2000–6.

78 Audio of testimony given by Fátima Cabrera at the trial of six officials, Tribunales de Comodoro Py, Buenos Aires, 11 December 2018, https://drive.google.com/file/d/1qSTv4vf-Xwx2I32xzsNKFptD9jaLw3Eb/view?usp=sharing.

79 Ibid.

80 Seisdedos may not have been his real name. The Italian consul, Enrico Calami, speculated that that was the case. I have been unable to find him on any list of Ministry of Foreign Affairs employees.

81 NAI/DFA, 2012/59/2236. (The signatures on the telegram indicate that it was circulated widely in the department.)

82 'Irish Priest Arrested in Argentina', *Irish Times*, 15 October 1976.

83 'Kidnapped Priest Held by Police', *Irish Press*, 15 October 1976.

84 The same day, the Irish consulate general in New York requested information regarding the case: 'some inquiries received here from media'. Telegram from consulate general, New York, 15 October 1976, NAI/DFA, 2012/59/2236.

85 Pio Laghi to Cardinal Jean Villot, 15 October 1976, Patrick Rice file, Holy See, pp. 3–4, 170–1. The second copy on pages 170–1 has less text redacted; this confirms that Fauret was referring to Weeks and the kidnapped seminarians. Fauret makes reference to 'detained in Córdoba, and were released being able to remain freely in the country or go to the USA, while the fifth, of Chilean nationality, was expelled from Argentina because he had entered Argentina illegally'. Fauret neglected to inform Laghi that Weeks and his confrères had been badly tortured while in custody.

86 'Argentina Holds a Priest on Subversion Charge' (Reuters, 16 October 1976), *New York Times*, 17 October 1976. Rice, in his testimony before the 44th session of the Inter-American Commission on Human Rights in June 1978, stated: 'I would present the news item that appeared in the newspaper LA NACION on Thursday, October 14, 1976, page 18. On October 18, 1976, the Foreign Minister of Argentina, Rear Admiral César A. Guzzetti, acknowledged that I had been "arrested by the police" (see the copy of LA NACION).' Inter-American Commission on Human Rights, case 2450, Argentina, http://www.cidh.org/annualrep/78eng/Argentina.2450.htm.

87 Lennon received a number of versions as to why Rice had been held. The first came from his fellow priests who, according to Lennon in his report on 22 October, 'had only hearsay evidence' that Rice had been abducted 'after a prayer meeting by armed men in unnumbered cars'. The second version, given to the nuncio by the minister of the interior, was 'that he was seen by a police sergeant putting subversive propaganda under doors and then arrested by the policeman who identified himself at time of arrest'. The third version, given to the ambassador by the under-secretary at the foreign ministry, Captain Alarra, 'was that he was arrested by police who identified themselves, while assisting a girl to distribute subversive literature'. Lennon received a fourth version of the arrest on 19 October from the chief of protocol at the Ministry of Foreign Affairs and Worship. The latter was substantially in agreement with the third version 'except that in this case an off-duty policeman was the arresting officer and Fr Rice was allegedly assisting a girl, a known guerrilla, to paste posters on a wall, claiming that the ERP was the only legitimate Argentine Army'. 'Three posters had been hung, I was told,' the ambassador wrote. Lennon to Secretary, Department of Foreign Affairs, 22 October 1976, NAI/DFA [343/393], 2012/59/2236.

88 Des Nix, 'Envoy Applies to Have Irish Priest Freed', *Irish Press*, 18 October 1976.

89 An *oblea* can be a 'sticker' one gets in a car park.

90 Fátima Cabrera told me in September 2018 during a meeting in Cork that she was carrying anti-military leaflets which, when confronted, she immediately threw away under the cover of darkness.

91 Harguindeguy to Pio Laghi, 27 October 1976. (It is not clear whether that was the date sent or received.) The letter gave the nuncio details of Rice's parents' names, his identity card number, that he lived in Villafañe and worked as carpenter/joiner on a construction site situated on Avenida La Plata and Pedro Goyena. It recorded that he had links with Arturo Paoli (described as a 'prominent member of the movement of priests for the third world') since 1974 and that he was active in Santa Fe province where he worked at Fortín Olmos with the Little Brothers of Jesus (*sic*). The letter also mentions the activities of that group in the province of Tucumán. It claimed that the Archbishop of Tucumán, Blas (Victorio) Conrero, did not want them in his diocese. The minister also knew that Rice had been in Suriyaco,

in Rioja, which was a spiritual retreat house for priests for the third world, the majority of whom – Rice included – were foreigners. See Patrick Rice File, Archive of the Holy See, pp. 154–5; released to his wife, Fátima Cabrera, on instructions from Pope Francis I, in 2018.

92 See Case 2450 Argentina, Inter-American Commission on Human Rights (Organisation of American States), http://www.cidh.org/annualrep/78eng/Argentina.2450.htm.

93 Conversation with Fátima Cabrera, Cork, September 2018.

94 Ironically, Rice did not have the faculties to celebrate mass in jail in 1976. Von Wernich retained full faculties despite the charges brought against him. He continued to be permitted to celebrate mass while in jail and on trial for complicity in seven murders, forty-two kidnappings and thirty-one instances of torture.

95 That daughter was later disappeared, as was one of Mainer's sons, Pablo Joaquín (Pecos). Source: Fátima Cabrera.

96 I heard Lucy Mainer recount at the trial of Fr Christian Von Wernich in La Plata in 2007 the details of her meeting with Rice. He attended as many sessions of the trial as he could. Another priest, Rev. Rubén Capitanio, who had been in the seminary with Von Wernich, testified and condemned the Catholic Church in Argentina for complicity in the atrocities committed during the 'dirty war'. He told the panel of three judges: 'The attitude of the church was scandalously close to the dictatorship ... to such an extent that I would say it was of a sinful degree.' The church, he added, 'was like a mother that did not look for her children; it did not kill anybody, but it did not save anybody, either ... Many men and women of the church, bishops as well, have come to agree with my way of looking at the reality of the church's role [and] we have much to be sorry for.' Alexei Barrionuevo, 'Argentine Church Faces "Dirty War" Past', *New York Times*, 17 September 2007, http://www.nytimes.com/2007/09/17/world/americas/17church.html. Von Wernich had fled to Chile where he worked under an alias. When the amnesty laws, passed at the end of military rule, were struck down, and deemed to be unconstitutional in 2003, he was extradited to Argentina the same year. There was outrage over his particular case because he was accused of gaining privileged information in his pastoral role as a priest and passing it on to the authorities. Survivors claimed that the former prison chaplain, who had served in that role between 1976 and 1983, had gained the confidence of prisoners and then passed on information to the military authorities. Witnesses said that he had even attended several torture sessions and had given absolution to the interrogators, saying that they had been doing God's work. He accused those who testified against him as having been influenced by the devil – 'responsible for malice' and 'the father of evil and lies'. On 9 October 2007, after a three-month trial, Von Wernich (69) was sentenced to life imprisonment. See BBC report, '"Dirty War" Priest Gets Life Term', 10 October 2007, http://news.bbc.co.uk/2/hi/americas/7035294.stm. For video of verdict and for the full text of the judgement, see http://juicioavonwernich.wordpress.com. See Pablo Morosi, 'Condenaron a Reclusión Perpetua a Von Wernich', *La Nacion*, 10 October 2007, http://www.lanacion.com.ar/951794-condenaron-a-reclusion-perpetua-a-von-wernich; also 'Reclusión Perpetua para Von Wernich', *Clarin*, 9 October 2007, http://edant.clarin.com/diario/2007/10/09/um/m-01515747.htm. The same edition carried a report that the Argentinian Episcopal Conference stated that any member of the Catholic Church who participated in violent acts of repression acted on their own responsibility. The statement was issued under the chairmanship of the archbishop of Buenos Aires, Jorge Bergoglio.

97 At a break in the trial, Rice introduced himself to her and they had an emotional reunion in the courthouse. Other observers at the trial, from the History Department, University College Cork, were Dr Hiram Morgan and Dr Lawrence Geary. The woman witness did not name the particular prison in which the mass was celebrated; it was in federal police headquarters.

98 John McEntee, 'Fr Rice Tells of Prison Nightmare', *Irish Press*, 8 December 1976.

99 Conor O'Clery, 'Priest Describes His Torture in Argentina', *Irish Times*, 8 December 1976.

100 While bad syntax, its meaning was very apparent to Rice. See O'Byrne, *Strands from a Tapestry*, p. 80.

101 Lennon sent a more detailed report of the prison visit in the diplomatic bag on 22 October: 'When we saw him on the 18th instant, he more or less confirmed this version [of his kidnapping] – he had been abducted after a prayer meeting by armed men in unnumbered car.' The ambassador added: 'Unfortunately, he could not speak Irish. There were two police present at the interview both of whom disclaimed any knowledge of English – a disclaim I doubt.' NAI/DFA, 2012/59/2236.

102 Conversations with Patrick Rice, 2000–10.

103 NAI/DFA, 2012/59/2236. Ambassador Lennon said in the same report that one of the British vice consuls had called to obtain details of the kidnapping: 'They have several citizens, some with dual nationality, in detention or missing. They aim in such cases at expulsion as early as possible, a line which is also followed by the USA. The Nuncio told me that he believes expulsion is the best solution.'

104 Philip Molloy, 'Envoy Can't Speak about Jailed Priest', *Irish Press*, 19 October 1976.

105 Two minutes in nunciature papers, p. 167 and p. 164, Patrick Rice papers, Holy See.

106 NAI/DFA, 2012/59/2236, Secretary to Ambassador Lennon, 18 October 1976 [telegram].

107 Ibid.

108 Nunciature papers, p. 167 and p. 164, Patrick Rice papers, Holy See.

109 'Notes for information of the Minister [Garret FitzGerald]', 1 November 1976, NAI/DFA, 2012/59/2236.

110 NAI/DFA, 2012/59/2236.

111 NAI/DFA, 2012/59/2236, Joe Small memorandum of meeting with Ambassador Del Carril, 19 October 1976.

112 Ibid.

113 'Irish Columban Priests Recall Stories of Chile Following the Pinochet Coup', *Irish Times*, 26 October 1998, http://www.irishtimes.com/news/irish-columban-priests-recall-stories-of-chile-following-the-pinochet-coup-1.207314; see also Alo Connaughton, 'Mission in Pinochet's Chile: A Memoir', *Irish Migration Studies in Latin America*, http://www.irlandeses.org/imsla2011_7_04_10_Alo_Connaughton.htm; see also Teresita Durkan, *Reflections of a Life: Ó Mhuigheó go Valparaíso* (Veritas Publications, Dublin, 1999).

114 Sheila Cassidy, 'Blood Cries Out', *Guardian*, 4 November 1998, https://www.theguardian.com/world/1998/nov/04/pinochet.chile.

115 See her personal account in Sheila Cassidy, *Audacity to Believe* (Darton, Longman & Todd, London, 2011). Her biography was first published in 1978.

116 The foreign ministry archives in Buenos Aires support the view that del Carril worked very hard to protect lives in Santiago after the takeover by Pinochet. He wrote to Alberto J. Vignes, the Argentine foreign minister, on 21 September 1973 on behalf of a Uruguayan citizen, Eduardo Marichal, to grant him asylum in Argentina, http://desclasificacion.cancilleria.gov.ar/userfiles/documentos//MOU_URUGUAY/41AH096_020.pdf.

117 Joe Small, memorandum of meeting with Ambassador del Carril, 19 October 1976, NAI/DFA, 2012/59/2236.

118 Ibid.

119 Livingstone, *Britain and the Dictatorships of Argentina and Chile, 1973–82*, p. 72.

120 Robert Graham, 'British Policy towards Latin America', in Victor Bulmer-Thomas (ed.), *Britain and Latin America: A Changing Relationship* (The Royal Institute of International Affairs and Cambridge University Press, Cambridge, 1989), p. 63.

121 See also Michael D. Wilkinson, 'The Chile Solidarity Campaign and British Government Policy towards Chile, 1973–1990', *European Review of Latin American and Caribbean Studies*, no. 52, June 1992, p. 65.

122 Ambassador Lennon to Secretary, 18 October 1976 [telegram], NAI/DFA, 2012/59/2236.

123 Ibid.

124 'Envoy Attempts to Free Irish Priest', *Irish Times*, 20 October 1976.

125 Weeks, as explained in the previous chapter, was a missionary of the Order of Our Lady of Lasalette, who had been imprisoned two months before in Córdoba together with five seminarians. Deported in mid-August following the intervention of the US government, his case set a strong precedent which the Irish embassy thought might be followed in the Rice case.

126 'Irish Priest May Be Deported', *Irish Press*, 20 October 1976.

127 'Embassy Push for Decision on Priest', *Irish Press*, 21 October 1976.

128 'Imprisoned Priest now in Penitentiary', *Irish Times*, 22 October 1976; 'Priest Moved', *Irish Press*, 22 October 1976.

129 Ambassador Lennon to Secretary of Department of Foreign Affairs, 22 October 1976, NAI/DFA, 2012/59/2236.

130 NAI/DFA, 2012/59/2236.

131 Harman agreed that, due to the fact that all correspondence from prison had to be in Spanish, the embassy had undertaken to translate letters to his parents into English and forward them to Ireland. In turn, the embassy would provide him with the general gist of his parents' letters. Harman sent letters to Mr and Mrs Rice in the early part of November 1976. NAI/DFA, 2012/59/2236, Harman to Small, 25 November 1976.

132 NAI/DFA, 2012/59/2236, Harman to Rice parents, 25 October 1976.

133 NAI/DFA, 2012/59/2236, Telegram from Washington [Ambassador J.G. Molloy], 28 October 1976.

134 NAI/DFA, 2012/59/2236, Telegram from Iveagh House to Washington Embassy, 29 October 1976.

135 NAI/DFA, 2012/59/2236.

136 It was four weeks before Rice's right foot, infected as a result of the torture, was treated.

137 '"I'm Innocent," says Fr Rice', *Irish Press*, 30 October 1976.

138 On the occasion of that visit, Rice probably gave Harman a letter in Spanish, dated 12 November, which he asked him to translate and send to his parents and family. The letter had to get through the prison censor. Therefore, it was necessary to read between the lines. It serves as a factual description of prison routine without any reference to the omnipresent sense of menace or violence. Without the help of the embassy or the media in Ireland, Rice wrote: 'I feel the situation would be a thousand times worse and I even doubt that I would be writing this letter. However all that is over now, and I have a lot of hope that things will be settled up soon. Up to now they have not brought any charges against me, and I am held (as they say here) at the disposition of the government, that is to say [until] the Argentine government has decided otherwise. This is the case with a lot of people who are being held prisoner at the moment'. He then gave a description of the prison. It was quite new and about an hour from Buenos Aires. There were fourteen blocks. There were forty cells in each block with two in each cell – a group of eighty overall: 'They get up at 6.30, have breakfast of bread and milk at 7.30 and have 2 hours recreation in the fresh air where the 80 are out together.' Prisoners were back in their cells at 10.30 and had lunch at midday of some meat with salad and bread. That was followed by two hours of recreation and dinner at 7.30. They were then sent back to the cells. Rice added: 'In general the food is good and they have a canteen where we can buy things.' He wrote that visits were restricted to direct

relatives once a week for two hours. Special permission was required for anyone else to visit: 'We are in the cells for 20 hours a day and we spend the time reading, writing or chatting with a cellmate.' No work was allowed. He was not allowed to be given a copy of the Bible. There were five priests in jail with him but they were in different blocks. Each Monday, they were allowed to meet together 'and we celebrate Mass'. He mentioned that he could not write in English and that he could not receive any correspondence in English. Therefore, he did not get any of the letters sent to him by his parents or family. About the general situation, he wrote: 'The news from outside is very sad. There is a lot of violence every day. I hope the situation gets better soon.' Asking for his family, he ended: 'Really I will never forget this month, especially the first three days. With the help of God everything will work out in the end. At the moment it isn't easy to get used to being closed in and to the prison discipline. When I get out I will probably have to leave Argentina. From here I will go for a while to Ireland and after that God only knows. I hope everything will work out soon.' The reference in the letter to 'the first three days' was a veiled way of speaking of his torture. Justin Harman's translation was sent to Rice's parents. His mother, Amy, copied it by hand and sent it to Fr Vincent Twomey SVD, a former confrère and close friend of Rice who was very anxious to hear news of his situation. I am grateful to him for supplying me with a copy on 14 October 2019.

139 'Jorge Taiana: De la Militancia a la Diplomacia', *La Nación*, 5 June 2005, https://www.lanacion.com.ar/710134-jorge-taiana-de-la-militancia-a-la-diplomacia. He also became friends with the concert pianist Miguel Ángel Estrella, who was later jailed and tortured in Uruguay for twenty-seven months between 1978 and 1980. Carol A. Hess, 'Miguel Ángel Estrella: (Classical) Music for the People, Dictatorship, and Memory', in Patricia Ann Hall (ed.), *The Oxford Handbook of Music Censorship* (Oxford University Press, Oxford, 2018), pp. 333–5; and 'Pianista Argentine Toco en la Cárcel donde fue Torturado', *Gaceta Mercantil*, 2 June 2012, http://www.gacetamercantil.com/notas/17743/.

140 A minute addressed to Joe Small on 1 November 1976, read: 'Yes. Fr Rice was first held in police custody from 11th to 22nd Oct. approx.; then transferred to Villa Devoto Prison and then to a third detention place at a Political prison on or about 29th October. The name of this prison does not appear to be yet available to us.' The minute left out that Rice had been abducted on 11 October, transferred on the 12th to a clandestine prison under the control of the armed forces, where he had been tortured, and then released back into the custody of the federal police. NAI/DFA, 2012/59/2236.

141 Ibid.

142 *Dáil Éireann Debates*, vol. 293, no. 8, 4 November 1976, https://www.oireachtas.ie/en/debates/debate/dail/1976-11-04/10/.

143 Ibid.

144 NAI/DFA, 2012/59/2236.

145 Ibid. Harman reported that as regards a lawyer for Rice, the embassy had not appointed anybody. They intended avoiding having to do so unless it became absolutely essential: 'It will be understood that the current climate here is most unfavourable for any Argentine professional to be seen openly defending any individual suspected of subversion.' He sent copies of two letters which he had sent to Mr and Mrs Rice. He also gave the full address of the prison: Unidad 9, Calle 10 y 76, Casilla de Correo 65, La Plata, Prov. De Buenos Aires.

146 NAI/DFA, 2012/59/2236.

147 Ibid.; see also 'Irish Envoy Pleads for Jail Priest', *Irish Independent*, 11 November 1976.

148 'Pleas for Priest', *Irish Times*, 13 November 1976.

149 NAI/DFA, 2012/59/2236.

150 Antoinette Lawlor, letter, *Irish Times*, 20 November 1976.

151   *Irish Times*, 23 November 1976.

152   NAI/DFA, 2012/59/2236.

153   Ibid.

154   Ibid., Harman to Assistant Secretary, Joe Small, 25 November 1976.

155   Diplomatic Correspondent, 'Irish Priest to be Freed from Argentine Jail', *Irish Times*, 2 December 1976.

156   NAI/DFA, 2012/59/2236, Minute by Small to Secretary Rigney, 1 December 1976.

157   NAI/DFA, 2012/59/2236.

158   Diplomatic Correspondent, 'Irish Priest to be Freed from Argentine Jail', *Irish Times*, 2 December 1976.

159   'Fr Rice Soon to be Freed', *Irish Press*, 2 December 1976.

160   'Expelled Irish Priest Flying Home', *Irish Times*, 4 December 1976.

161   'Argentina Deports Irish Priest' (Reuters/AP report), *Irish Times*, 4 December 1976; see also 'Argentina to Deport Irish Catholic Priest' (AP report), *Washington Post*, 3 December 1978.

162   Conversations with Patrick Rice, 2000–10.

163   'Argentina to Deport Irish Catholic Priest' (AP report), *Washington Post*, 3 December 1976.

164   The post had arrived at the embassy for him during his months of captivity. On 25 December and on 7 January 1977, Harman sent on to him, through Iveagh House, further bundles of supportive correspondence.

165   NAI/DFA, 2012/59/2236.

166   Jean Sheridan, 'Fr Rice is Home "Without a Penny,"' *Irish Press*, 6 December 1976.

167   *Irish Times*, 6 December 1976.

168   Denis Reading, '"Stop or be Shot," Cork-born Priest was Told', *Cork Examiner*, 6 December 1976.

169   Donal Musgrave, 'Expelled Priest to Speak at Amnesty Press Conference', *Irish Times*, 6 December 1976.

170   David Watts, 'Tortured Priest Speaks of "Total War" in Argentina', *The Times* (London), 8 December 1976.

171   *Daily Telegraph*, 8 December 1976.

172   Conor O'Clery, 'Priest Describes His Torture in Argentina', *Irish Times*, 8 December 1976.

173   Ibid.

174   John McEntee, 'Fr Rice Tells of Prison Nightmare', *Irish Press*, 8 December 1976.

175   Conor O'Clery, 'Priest Describes His Torture in Argentina', *Irish Times*, 8 December 1976.

176   John McEntee, 'Fr Rice Tells of Prison Nightmare', *Irish Press*, 8 December 1976.

177   *Cork Examiner*, 9 December 1976.

178   Walter Schwarz, 'Spain Erupts into Fury', *Guardian*, 29 September 1975, https://www.theguardian.com/world/1975/sep/29/spain.walterschwarz.

179   Ibid.

180   FitzGerald, *All in a Life*, pp. 180–1.

181   DFA/2009/120/98, Human Rights in Argentina, 1 November 1976 to 25 January 1979. Other documents on the file include a note from Michael Daly, head of Chancery, British embassy, Dublin, dated 2 January 1976, addressed to Jeremy Craig. It detailed the facts of Dr Sheila Cassidy's arrest. There was also a copy of the British government statement issued on 30 December 1975.

182   Dennis Kennedy, 'FitzGerald Meets Soviet Leaders', *Irish Times*, 16 December 1976.

183   *Dáil Éireann Debates*, 16 December 1976, https://www.oireachtas.ie/en/debates/debate/dail/1976-12-16/45/.

184   'Ambassador Stays in Argentina', *Cork Examiner*, 17 December 1976.

185 'Irish Embassy to the Vatican to be Closed', 4 November 2011, https://www.rte.ie/news/2011/1103/308258-embassies/.

186 The underlying reason for the closure of the Irish embassy to the Holy See was, in my view – and this is merely speculation – a protest at the failure of the Vatican to cooperate with state inquiries into clerical involvement in child sexual abuse in Ireland.

187 'Irish Community Say Goodbye to Ambassador Lennon', *TSC*, 17 December 1976. When he'd begun his posting, he'd presented a new Irish flag to the cathedral at Luján to be placed in the shrine of the Virgin.

188 'Profile of an Ambassador', *TSC*, 17 December 1976.

189 'Fr Patrick Rice', *TSC*, 17 December 1976.

190 NAI/DFA, 2012/59/2236, Harman to Secretary, 11 January 1977.

191 Ibid.

192 Ibid.

CHAPTER 6 Ireland and the Denunciation of Human Rights Abuses in Argentina, 1977–9: Mgr Kevin Mullen – 'I just keep coming up against a stone wall'

1 'Carter and Human Rights, 1977–1981', Office of the Historian, https://history.state.gov/milestones/1977-1980/human-rights.

2 President Carter called her 'a champion of oppressed people around the world'. 'Patricia Derian, Diplomat Who Made Human Rights a Priority, Dies at 86', *New York Times*, 20 May 2016, https://www.nytimes.com/2016/05/21/us/patricia-derian-diplomat-who-made-human-rights-a-priority-dies-at-86.html; 'Patricia Derian, Activist who was President Carter's Human Rights Chief, dies at 86', *Washington Post*, 20 May 2016, https://www.washingtonpost.com/national/patricia-derian-activist-who-was-president-carters-human-rights-chief-dies-at–86/2016/05/20/ba2c1ec6-1d11-11e6-b6e0-c53b7ef63b45_story.html?utm_term=.e5835f512720; *La Nación* wrote appreciatively that she had been 'actively involved in the visit that the Inter-American Commission on Human Rights made to the country in 1979, and in 1985 had returned to Argentina to testify at the trial of nine retired military officers, including three former presidents, who were charged with the murder and disappearance of 9,000 Argentines'. 'Murió Patricia Derian, la Funcionaria de EE.UU. que se Enfrentó a Massera en la ESMA durante la Dictadura', *La Nación*, 21 May 2016. During the ceremony where she received her award in 2006, she demonstrated what her work in Argentina meant to her by returning to the Mothers of the Plaza de Mayo the handkerchiefs that they had given her when she first visited Buenos Aires in 1977. 'Fearless in the Face of Massera', *Buenos Aires Herald*, 21 May 2016.

3 'Patricia Derian, Diplomat Who Made Human Rights a Priority, Dies at 86'.

4 Text of Jimmy Carter's speech on the thirtieth anniversary of the Universal Declaration of Human Rights, https://www.presidency.ucsb.edu/documents/universal-declaration-human-rights-remarks-white-house-meeting-commemorating-the-30th.

5 David M.K. Sheinin, *Argentina and the United States: An Alliance Contained* (The University of Georgia Press, Athens and London, 2006), p. 167.

6 Ibid., pp. 165–6.

7 Déaglán de Bréadún, 'Carter's Staff Did Not Take North "Seriously"', *Irish Times*, 31 December 2009, https://www.irishtimes.com/news/carter-s-staff-did-not-take-north-seriously-1.796527. On 30 August 1977, Carter issued a statement on Northern Ireland, an area on which his predecessors had remained mute. See text at https://www.presidency.ucsb.edu/documents/northern-ireland-statement-us-policy. See also Luke Devoy, 'The British Response to American Interest in Northern Ireland, 1976–1979', *Irish Studies in International Affairs*, vol. 25, 2014, pp. 221–38.

8   Joseph E. Thompson, *American Policy and Northern Ireland: A Saga of Peacebuilding* (Praeger, Westport, CT, London, 2001); Thomas K. Robb, *Jimmy Carter and the Anglo-American 'Special Relationship'* (Edinburgh University Press, Edinburgh, 2017), p. 49 ff, www.jstor.org/stable/10.3366/j.ctt1g051bg.7; Luke Devoy, 'The British Response to American Interest in Northern Ireland, 1976–79', *Irish Studies in International Affairs*, vol. 25, 2014, pp. 221–38.

9   There were a number of high-level staff changes in the Department of Foreign Affairs: Robert McDonagh replaced Paul Keating as secretary in February. Popular and hard-working, he was more attuned to the calm style of the former minister for foreign affairs. On 14 May 2015, the *Irish Times* described him when he died as a 'distinguished and fair-minded former chief of foreign affairs', adding: 'It was Bob who advised [Patrick] Hillery [minister of external affairs, 1969–1973] not to pursue a proposal initiated by his predecessor Frank Aiken in the Assembly of the Council of Europe, to insert in the European Convention on Human Rights a clause prohibiting discrimination in housing and employment. Bob was much less at home with Hillery's successor Garret FitzGerald whose scattershot style was not to his taste.' Andrew O'Rourke took over as secretary when McDonagh became ambassador to Italy in December 1978, http://www.irishtimes.com/life-and-style/people/distinguished-and-fair-minded-former-chief-of-foreign-affairs-1.2214004. See also Charles Lysaght, 'Obituary: Bob McDonagh', *Irish Independent*, 8 April 2017.

10 'Former Senior Diplomat Padraic McKernan Dies', *Irish Times*, 27 January 2010.

11 Obituary: 'Jeremy Craig: Diplomat Played Key Role for Ireland in EEC, UN and Middle East', *Irish Times*, 26 March 2016, https://www.irishtimes.com/life-and-style/people/jeremy-craig-diplomat-played-key-role-for-ireland-in-eec-un-and-middle-east-1.2586942.

12 Julia LaBua, 'Outside the Public Eye: How the Carter Administration Used "Quiet Diplomacy" to Impact Human Rights in Argentina', *Iowa Historical Review*, vol. 1, no. 1, 2007, pp. 131–9, http://ir.uiowa.edu/iowa-historical-review/vol1/iss1/7.

13 F.A. 'Tex' Harris, *Fighting the 'Dirty War': Argentina, 1977*, https://afsa.org/sites/default/files/harris-fighting-the-dirty-war.pdf.

14 'Nuevo Embajador de Irlanda en la Argentina', *TSC*, 4 February 1977. The ambassador's brother Eustas was a priest in the Dominican Order, which had priests working in the north of Argentina.

15 Ó hÉideáin spent part of his annual leave every summer training with *An Fórsa Cosanta Áitiúil* (FCA).

16 This was based on the findings of a mission which visited the country from 6 to 15 November 1976. The British Liberal MP Lord Averbury led the team which was made up of US Congressman Fr Robert Drinan SJ and Patricia Kenney of AI. For general background on international reaction to repression in Argentina, see David Weissbrodt and Maria Luisa Bartolomei, 'The Effectiveness of International Human Rights Pressures: The Case of Argentina, 1976–1983', *Scholarly Repository, University of Minnesota Law School*, vol. 75, 1991, p. 1009, http://scholarship.law.umn.edu/faculty_articles/264.

17 In Buenos Aires, the most frequently cited were: La Atómica, near Ezeiza airport; La Escuela de Mecánica de la Armada (Navy Mechanical School) (ESMA); Campo de Mayo (army garrison); Superintendencia de Seguridad Federal, also known as the Coordinación Federal (central police headquarters); Repartición 1 y 59, La Plata (in reality, it was under the command of the Cuerpo de Infantería, province of Buenos Aires/1 and 60); Regimento No 1 de Infantería Patricios; and Brigada de Investigaciones de Banfield (Pozo de Banfield). In Córdoba, Campo de la Rivera, La Perla was the most frequently named. In Tucumán, the Amnesty mission was told of Famaillá, Fronterita, Santa Lucía, Las Mesadas and La Escuela de Policía and Escuela. *Report of an Amnesty International Mission to Argentina, 6–15 November 1976* (Amnesty International, London, March 1977), pp. 32–3.

18 Ibid., pp. 30–1. The account was taken from a December press conference in London and also from other interviews directly with Amnesty International.

19 Ibid., pp. 32–4, 48–50.

20 Ibid. The Jesuit Robert Drinan, who was a member of the AI delegation, said on 23 March at a press conference in Washington DC that the decision of the Carter administration to prohibit the provision of military assistance to a nation engaged in the systematic violation of the human rights of its citizens was not 'a tactical judgment but a moral commitment'. He also stated that the AI mission had been subject to 'intense surveillance' during its time in Argentina. At least twenty plain-clothes police had followed them wherever they went, questioning and intimidating a number of people whom they met, he said. One woman had disappeared after talking to the mission only to be released twenty-four hours later without any explanation for her detention. Another woman had been held for two weeks after talking to one of the team. Having met more than a hundred members of the families of the disappeared, the mission learned that they (the families) were left 'completely in the dark as to the physical well-being and whereabouts of their relatives'. The refusal to release the names of the disappeared was 'a singularly outrageous action', Drinan said. Congressman Bob Drinan's statement upon release of the report of an Amnesty International mission to Argentina, 23 March 1977, box 350 (Folder 1), Drinan papers, Argentina folder, Burns Library, Boston College, Boston MA. The secretary general of AI, Martin Ennals, said in the preface that policemen 'intimidated and even detained a number of people whom they met', and that their presence 'seriously limited their freedom of inquiry'. When the delegation visited two refugee centres, they were accompanied by four Ford Falcons containing sixteen armed men (p. 6).

21 NAI/DFA/2011/39/1249.

22 Cox, *Dirty Secrets, Dirty War*, pp. 75–7.

23 Given the hierarchical nature of diplomatic life, the papal nuncio, Pio Laghi, almost certainly had sight in advance of the text. I have no documentary evidence to support this view, but in the hierarchical world of Vatican diplomacy, it is improbable that a subordinate would give a sermon of such sensitivity without first clearing the text with the nuncio.

24 The European Court of Human Rights ruled in 1978 that fourteen men from Northern Ireland had been subject to inhuman and degrading treatment but not torture. Colm Keena, 'Treatment of "Hooded Men" Not Torture, Human Rights Court Told', *Irish Times*, 20 March 2018.

25 'En una Homilía se Condenó la Violencia', *La Opinión*, 20 March 1977; see also 'Buenos Aires Celebra la Memoria de San Patricio', *TSC*, 25 March 1977.

26 See 'Buenos Aires Celebra la Memoria de San Patricio', *TSC*, 25 March 1977.

27 *TSC* reproduced the sermon in full. See also the short account of the sermon: 'En una Homilía se Condenó la Violencia', *La Opinión*, 20 March 1977.

28 NAI/DFA, 2009/120/97, Ambassador Ó hÉideáin to Secretary, 29 January 1979.

29 NAI/DFA/2011/39/1249.

30 NAI/DFA/2011/39/1249. For an overview of the international human rights campaign against Argentina, see Weissbrodt and Bartolomei, 'The Effectiveness of International Human Rights Pressures', pp. 1009–35.

31 See text, http://www.historyisaweapon.com/defcon1/walshopenletterargjunta.html. The death of his Montonero daughter María Victoria in a gun battle in 1976 had inspired him in December that year to write a 'Letter to My Friends' ('*Carta a Mis Amigos*'). See McCaughan, *Rodolfo Walsh*, p. 224 ff.

32 Ibid., p. 243 ff.

33 See speech by Eduardo Jozami, director, 'Instalación de la "Carat Abierta de un Escritor a la Junta Military" en la ex-ESMA', Centro Cultural de la Memoria Haroldo Conti, April

2012, http://conti.derhuman.jus.gov.ar/2012/04/noticias-inauguracion-instalacion-carta-abierta.shtml; 'Carta Abierta pro la Memoria de Walsh', *Página 12*, 26 March 2012, https://www.pagina12.com.ar/diario/elpais/1-190444-2012-03-26.html. The artist León Ferrari's son Ariel was imprisoned in the ESMA and disappeared. The pianist Miguel Angel Estrella also attended the dedication. In 2017, the National Library in Buenos Aires mounted an exhibition devoted to Rodolfo Walsh. It was supported by the Irish ambassador to Buenos Aires, Justin Harman. See n.a., *Rodolfo Walsh: Los Oficios de la Palabra* (Biblioteca Nacional Mariano Moreno, Buenos Aires, 2017).

34 Carter proposed in early March halving US military aid to Argentina because of his concerns over human rights. (Uruguay and Ethiopia were also to receive cuts in military aid.) In reaction, the junta rejected the remaining $15 million as proof of their displeasure.

35 I had a number of conversations with Derian when I invited her to lecture in 1989 at University College Cork. She told me of her Argentine experiences. For a review of certain key documents relating to US–Argentine relations during the 'dirty war', see the National Security Archive selection, http://nsarchive.gwu.edu/NSAEBB/NSAEBB85/; http://nsarchive.gwu.edu/NSAEBB/NSAEBB73/. See also Charles Stuart Kennedy interview with Patricia Derian, 12 March 1996, The Association for Diplomatic Studies and Training, Foreign Affairs Oral History Project, http://adst.org/wp-content/uploads/2013/12/Derian-Patricia.1996I.pdf, pp. 48–9. See also 'Carter Aide in Argentina to Gauge Rights Impact', *Washington Post*, 31 March 1977, https://www.washingtonpost.com/archive/politics/1977/03/31/carter-aide-in-argentina-to-gauge-rights-impact/7352a3e5-5e6b-483b-9d6a-df4983caaeba/.

36 She was accompanied by two US embassy officials, Fernando Rondón and Robert S. Steven.

37 Memorandum of conversation between the papal nuncio, Monsignor Pio Laghi, and Patricia Derian at the nunciature, Buenos Aires, 29 March 1977, https://www.archives.gov/files/argentina/data/docid-33064660.pdf. Fernando Rondón and Robert S. Steven, American embassy, Buenos Aires, were also present. Ambassador Hill circulated a summary of the interview on 29 March 1977. See Argentina Project, US Secretary of State, https://foia.state.gov/Search/results.aspx?searchText=Pio+Laghi&beginDate=&endDate=&publishedBeginDate=&publishedEndDate=&caseNumber=.

38 Videla had told the nuncio the previous week on a visit to the nunciature: 'Many of the military were men with grave problems of conscience which they brought to the military chaplains … At the same time, they believed that they were doing what was necessary.' Laghi also said there was guilt 'in the leaders of the country; they knew that they have committed evil in human rights matters and do not need to be told of their guilt by visitors. That would be "rubbing salt into the wounds"'.

39 Derian interview with Pio Laghi, 29 March 1977. Over two months later, on 10 May, the nuncio told the US ambassador Robert Hill that Videla 'was well intentioned' but did not have 'political sensitivity' and showed a lack of leadership. He told Hill, who was about to end his term as ambassador, that Admiral Massera had informed him (Laghi) that he had been approached by 'hardliners recently who asked him to lead a take-over of the government from President Videla'. He said he had refused 'because he did not have sufficient support within the military to carry out such a scheme'. Laghi's view was that the Massera alternative was far worse. Regarding the nuncio's standing, Hill reported to Washington that he was 'unhappy with the comments' that had been 'circulating to the effect that he might not return and that Nunciatura would function indefinitely with a chargé'. Argentina Project, US State Department, US Hill telegram, 26 April 1977, https://foia.state.gov/Search/results.aspx?searchText=Admiral+Massera&beginDate=&endDate=&publishedBeginDate=&publishedEndDate=&caseNumber=.

40 Derian report, ibid. My emphasis.

41 Ibid.

42 John L. Allen, 'Vatican Diplomat Pio Laghi Dead at 86', *National Catholic Reporter*, 12 January 2009, https://www.ncronline.org/news/vatican-diplomat-pio-laghi-dead-86. 'Cardinal Pio Laghi', *Guardian*, 23 January 2009, https://www.theguardian.com/world/2009/jan/23/obituary-pio-laghi. Perhaps Laghi was most successful in his role in 1979 as coordinator of the mediation by Pope John Paul II and the Holy See between Chile and Argentina over the Beagle Channel conflict. War that year was very narrowly averted even if it took a few decades to arrive at a final settlement. Julio Algañaraz, 'El Halcón de la Pag', *Clarín*, 20 December 1978. Irish diplomats monitored carefully that conflict in Buenos Aires and at the Irish embassy to the Holy See. See NAI/DFA/2008/79/83.

43 Jayson McNamara (director), *El Mensajero* (documental, Argentina y Australia, 2017).

44 Robert Cox, 'The Courage of Kevin Mullen', *Buenos Aires Herald*, 1 February 2014.

45 Cox, *Dirty Secrets, Dirty War*, p. 75.

46 Cox, 'The Courage of Kevin Mullen'.

47 Ibid. Prof. Gustavo Morello had catalogued the numbers of Catholic activists affected by the violence in *Católicos y Violencia Política en Argentina entre 1969 y 1980*, https://www.academia.edu/4281536/Catolicos_y_violencia_politica_en_Argentina_entre_1969_y_1980.

48 Cox, 'The Courage of Kevin Mullen'.

49 Mullen told the US diplomat that the authorities suspected the murdered Bishop Angelelli of being a Marxist and also the bishop of Neuquen, Jaime de Nevares. See US embassy memorandum, 2 December 1977, recording the conversation in the American Club between the two men, https://www.archives.gov/files/argentina/data/docid–33064660.pdf.

50 Gloria Kehoe Wilson, *Pico de Paloma y otros Escritos* (Corregidor, Buenos Aires, 2004); I am grateful to Juan José Delaney for this reference.

51 Richards also went to the office of Archbishop Tortolo, the vicar-general of the military vicariate, to inquire about Gloria's whereabouts. Tortolo sent him to his secretary, Mgr Emilio Grasselli, who showed Richards a file containing the names of 2,100 missing people. 'Beside the names on some of these files there was a cross, meaning that the person had been confirmed dead,' the priest said. See Uki Goñi, 'Role of Vatican in Argentina's Dirty War' (1995), https://www.irlandeses.org/uki1995.htm.

52 *TSC*, 24 June 1977.

53 *TSC*, 8 July 1977.

54 I never met Federico Jesús Richards. He was born in 1921 into an Irish family. He joined the Passionist order in 1938 and was ordained in 1945. His brother Pedro was also a Passionist priest – he coordinated the Christian Family Movement in Argentina. Federico Richards studied philosophy in Vicente López and theology at Retiro San Pablo, near Capitán Sarmiento. He worked after ordination in Montevideo, returning to Buenos Aires in 1955. In 1964, he took charge of the house of studies in San Miguel. He became editor of *The Southern Cross* in 1969, a position he held for nearly two decades. In parallel with his journalistic work, he was active in the pastoral and intellectual life of Holy Cross. During the civilian military government after 1976, one source told me the following: Richards was requested (date not known) to meet a senior police officer of his acquaintance. They spoke briefly in his office in the police station. As the officer excused himself to leave the room for a few minutes, he told Richards in his absence to read the file left on his desk. Richards, on opening the file, was shocked to read an order for his own disappearance. When the police officer returned to the room, nothing further was said about the content of the file and Richards left with the certain knowledge that he had been placed on an official death list.

55 This is an area yet to be researched. It was the case that an extensive interview given by him to *Humor* brought him into conflict with his superiors. See 'Padre Federico Richards', *Humor*, no. 80, April 1982, pp. 71–6, https://issuu.com/revistahumor/docs/reportaje_padre_richards._humor_n__. Richards stepped down from the editorship of *TSC* in April 1978 due to the pressure of the job and ill health. The full circumstances of his sabbatical have yet to be chronicled. He spent some time recuperating and studying in Rome, returning to his editorial duties on 15 May 1979. He continued in that post until his death in Buenos Aires in 1999.

56 'Pope Francis Orders Vatican to Open Files on Argentine Dictatorship', *Guardian*, 29 April 2015.

57 Argentina Project, US State Department, US diplomatic reports from Rome, Madrid and Buenos Aires [one document], 28 October 1977, https://foia.state.gov/Search/results.aspx ?searchText=Admiral+Massera&beginDate=&endDate=&publishedBeginDate=&publish edEndDate=&caseNumber=.

58 In 1966, sixty representatives from across Latin America met in Montevideo and made a commitment to promote the non-violent transformation of society. A second meeting in Medellin, Colombia, gave birth to SERPAJ under the direction of Esquivel.

59 See Charles Stuart Kennedy interview with Patricia Derian, 12 March 1996, The Association for Diplomatic Studies and Training, Foreign Affairs Oral History Project, http://adst.org/wp-content/uploads/2013/12/Derian-Patricia.1996I.pdf, pp. 51–2.

60 Leora Margelovich, 'The "Cleansing" of the Dirty War: How Argentina Mimicked and Developed the Human Rights Violations of Nazi Germany' (20 May 2016), https://macaulay.cuny.edu/eportfolios/lmargelovich/2016/05/20/7/.

61 Ibid., pp. 169–71.

62 David K. Sheinin, *Argentina and the United States: An Alliance Contained* (University of Georgia Press, Athens and London, 2006), pp. 155–6.

63 Born in Bar, Ukraine, into a Jewish family, he escaped the pogroms when he was five and arrived in 1928 in Buenos Aires. They lived in a Jewish area of the city. His father died when he was twelve. Fluent in Spanish, and later in English, he worked as a journalist, with wide experience in covering Latin American politics.

64 Mauricio Schoijet, 'The Timerman Affair, Argentina, and the United States', *Crime and Social Justice*, no. 20, 1983, pp. 16–36, www.jstor.org/stable/29766206.

65 Cox, *Dirty Secrets, Dirty War*, pp. 99–100.

66 Ibid., p. 100.

67 Besides criticising the Argentine military, he expressed deep disappointment in the leadership of DAIA, the Delegación de Asociaciones Israelitas de Argentina, for remaining silent during his illegal detention which had lasted over a year – only issuing a statement upon his release from jail. Jacobo Timerman, *Prisoner without a Name, Cell without a Number* (Penguin Books, London, 1981). See also Mark Falcoff, 'The Timerman Case', *Commentary*, vol. 72, no. 1, July 1981, pp. 15–23.

68 'Murió el Periodista Jacobo Timerman', *La Nación*, 12 November 1999, https://www.lanacion.com.ar/160880-murio-el-periodista-jacobo-timerman; 'Timerman, un Hombre de las Dos Argentinas', *Página 12*, https://www.pagina12.com.ar/1999/99-11/99-11-12/pag03.htm.

69 In 1996, both organisations were merged into *La Conferencia Argentina de Religiosas y Religiosos* (CONFER), http://confar.org.ar/50-anos-de-confar/.

70 Mullen conversation with William H. Heller, US embassy counsellor, 2 December 1977, https://www.archives.gov/files/argentina/data/docid-33064660.pdf.

71 A number of bishops refused to be silenced, two of whom, Enrique Angelelli of La Rioja and Carlos Horacio Ponce de León of San Nicolás, were murdered on 4 August 1976 and 11 July

1977 respectively. Other bishops who refused to be silenced were: the bishop of Neuquén, Jáime de Nevares, Bishop Jorge Novack of Quilmes and Bishop Miguel Heseyne of Viedma. Jeffrey Klaiber, SJ, *The Church, Dictatorships, and Democracy in Latin America* (Wipe & Stock, Eugene, OR, 2009), pp. 66–91.

72 María Adela de Antokoletz (Hija), *Desovillando la Historia* (Ediciones Baobab, Buenos Aires, 2014), pp. 18–20. The author's brother Daniel, a lawyer, was disappeared in ESMA in November 1976. Their mother, Mariá Adela Gard de Antokoletz, was a founder member of the Madres de Plaza de Mayo Linéa Fundadora. This description of the history of the organisation is based on a daughter's reconstruction of her mother's recollections. I also had conversations with the author, Buenos Aires, December 2018 and in Cork, May 2019.

73 Feitlowitz, *A Lexicon of Terror*, pp. 253–6. This source provides a detailed account of Grasselli's record. See also Centro de Estudios Legales y Sociales (CELS) annual report, 2000 (Eudeba, Buenos Aires, 2000), pp. 43–4. Many of the hundreds of family members who visited Grasselli did not believe that he wrote up over 2,500 filing cards with details of each case. They remained convinced in court that Grasselli already had the details before their visits. He admitted in court that he had sometimes had the assistance of military officers. His offices in the Stella Maris church grounds were right beside military headquarters, in Edificio Libertad. See 'El Cura de las Fichas de Desaparecidos', *Página 12*, 29 August 2014. (The priest's name is spelled variously with one s or two.)

74 See Ulises Gorini, *La Rebelión de las Madres: Historia de las Madres de Plaza de Mayo 1976–1983* (Ediciones Biblioteca Nacional, Buenos Aires, 2015), vol. 1, and Ulices Gorini, *La otra Lucha: Historia de las Madres de Plaza de Mayo 1983–1986* (Ediciones Biblioteca Nacional, Buenos Aires, 2015), vol. 2.

75 Arditti, *Searching for Life*.

76 'Falleció el Padre Bernardo Hughes' (with interview from *Página 12*, 9 December 2007), https://www.pagina12.com.ar/diario/elpais/1-95949-2007-12-09.html; *Comunicar Colonia Caroya*, https://fm-comunicar.com.ar/noticia/3839/fallecio-el-padre-bernardo-hughes.

77 Taurozzi, *Los Pasionistas en Argentina y Uruguay*, pp. 306–8.

78 Sam Ferguson, 'Argentina's "Blond Angel of Death" Convicted for Role in Dirty War', *The Christian Science Monitor*, 27 October 2011; Astiz was also convicted of six counts of homicide, torture and kidnapping, including the disappearance of the writer and Montonero, Rodolfo Walsh.

79 See Ulises Gorini (Prólogo de Osvaldo Bayer), *La Rebelión de las Madres: Historia de las Madres de Plaza de Mayo*, vols 1 and 2 (Ediciones Biblioteca Nacional, Buenos Aires, 2015).

80 Diana Beatriz Viñoles, *Biografía de Alice Domon (1937–1977): Las Religiosas Francesas Desaparecidas* (Editora Patria Grande, Buenos Aires, 2014), p. 348.

81 Ibid. Sr Alice Domon was from Charquemont, Doubs, France. She was sent to Argentina in 1967. She worked in an industrial part of Buenos Aires, in Hurlingham and Morón. She taught children with a mental disability and did pastoral work, collaborating closely with Fr Ismael Calcagno (parish priest of Morón). He was a cousin-in-law of General Jorge Rafael Videla. Sr Léonie Duquet came to Argentina in the early 1970s. She worked in San Pablo de Ramos Mejia, south of Buenos Aires. The two nuns knew the dictator personally and had taught one of his sons who had a disability. When the coup d'état took place in 1976, Domon went to Corrientes and in 1971 to work with the *Ligas Agrarias* which had been formed to help small cotton producers. She returned to Buenos Aires after the coup d'état to work in the area of human rights, living with Sr Léonie. They ministered in poor areas and, when the Mothers of the Plaza de Mayo were formed in April 1977, they forged a very close bond with the leaders and became active in the organisation. At the time of their disappearance, they were helping in a national and international publicity campaign to force the government in Argentina to reveal the whereabouts of the disappeared and the dead.

82 US embassy report, Buenos Aires, 20 December 1977, http://foia.state.gov/documents/argentina/0000A5E4.pdf.

83 Feitlowitz, *A Lexicon of Terror*, p. 215. See also *Gariwo: Garden of the Righteous Worldwide*, https://en.gariwo.net/righteous/dictatorships-in-latin-america/alice-domon-7614.html. See also 'Disparitions: Un Ancien Agent Français mis en Cause', *Le Figaro*, 6 February 2007, https://www.lefigaro.fr/international/2007/02/06/01003-20070206ARTFIG90202-disparitions_un_ancien_agent_francais_mis_en_cause.php.

84 In 2000, Alberto Marquardt premiered the film, *Yo, Sor Alice*.

85 In another version of this meeting, Cox wrote: '[Mullen gestured] with his hand that their bodies had been cut open at the chest so that they would sink faster. "How do you know this?" Maud asked: "Maud, there is such a thing as a confession for those who repent. I have sent what I was told to the Vatican."' Cox, *Dirty Secrets, Dirty War*, p. 207.

86 Cox, 'The Courage of Kevin Mullen'.

87 Rice received treatment from the psychiatrist Prof. Robert Daly, University College Cork (UCC), to help him recover from the trauma of torture and imprisonment.

88 Rice included in his praise the Irish ambassador and diplomats in London. Rice to FitzGerald, 15 January 1977, NAI/DFA 2008/79/81 [old file number 305/229/18/2/1]. The letter shows all the signs of having been written under great strain. I have silently corrected the spelling.

89 Ibid.

90 Fátima Cabrera had not given him her correct name. Using an alias when attending a meeting during the dictatorship was a common practice for security reasons. If a person was picked up by the police returning from a meeting, they could not reveal the identities of those in attendance even under torture as they did not know their names.

91 Rice knew she had a partner (*novio*), Alberto Cayetano Alfaro, and therefore described her in his letter as being married. In 1974 Alfaro and Cabrera were living together '*ya como pareja*' ('already as a couple'), to use Fátima Cabrera's own words. See Rice y Torres, *En Medio de la Tempestad*, pp. 149–52.

92 Fátima Edelmira Cabrera, *Denuncia de Fátima Edelmira Cabrera (ex pareja)*, 29 January 1999 by Fátima Cabrera, Carpeta Liberados, Legajo CONADEP no. 6976 – Patrick Rice and Fátima Cabrera, Fondo Documental del Archivo Nacional de la Memoria, ex-ESMA.

93 NAI/DFA 2008/79/81 [old file number 305/229/18/2/1], Rice to FitzGerald, 15 January 1977.

94 NAI/DFA 2008/79/81 [old file number 305/229/18/2/1].

95 A member of the Movement of Third World Priests (MSTM) and a founder member of Cristianos para la Liberación, he was believed to have been taken to the ESMA where he was tortured and later dumped alive from a plane over the River Plate.

96 Alan McGregor, 'Thousands Killed in Argentine Terror', *The Times* (London), 22 February 1977. The editor of the *Buenos Aires Herald*, Robert Cox, when he was imprisoned in 1977 also saw a giant swastika painted on the wall of the federal police headquarters.

97 'Argentina Tactics Highlighted', *Irish Times*, 22 February 1977.

98 The accuracy of Rice's testimony was later confirmed by the Delegación de Asociaciones Israelitas Argentinas (DAIA): 'The 1976–1983 military dictatorship that institutionalized widespread terror by Task Groups also centralized the anti-semitic actions, that form unofficial "paramilitary" actions turned into the so-called "special treatment" in the concentration camps and in an outstanding over-representation of Jewish people among the number of victims. Cruelty while in detention, special treatment in torture sessions, specific interrogations and the usage of Nazi terminology and symbols were some of the expressions of the new stage of anti-Semitism in Argentina.' Marisa Braylan et al., *Report on Anti-Semitism in Argentina 1998* (DAIA, Buenos Aires, n.d.), pp. 15–16. See also Marisa Braylan et al., *Report on the Situation of the Jewish Detainees-Disappeared during the Genocide*

Perpetrated in Argentina (DAIA, Buenos Aires, 1999). The Barcelona-based Commission of Solidarity with Relatives of the Disappeared (Cosofam), in a 196-page report in 1999, wrote that 'Jews represented more than 12 per cent of the victims of the military regime while constituting under 1 per cent [or 300,000] of Argentina's population'. The group identified 1,296 Jewish victims by name who were among the disappeared. The report also said that Rabbi Alexander Schindler, Union of American Hebrew Congregations, obtained a promise from the US Department of State in 1976 to provide, if necessary, 100,000 visas to Jewish refugees from Argentina. During the civilian military dictatorship, the Jewish leadership in Buenos Aires faced the dilemma of whether or not to speak out and risk an even fiercer anti-Semitic backlash. Uki Goñi, 'Jews Targeted in Argentina's Dirty War', *Guardian*, 24 March 1999, https://www.theguardian.com/theguardian/1999/mar/24/guardianweekly.guardianweekly1. For a background to the history of the Jews in Argentina, see Haim Avni, *Argentina and the Jews: A History of Jewish Immigration* (University of Alabama Press, Tuscaloosa and London, 1991); Ricardo Feierstein, *Historia de los Judíos Argentinos* (Galerna, Buenos Aires, 2006). See also AMIA, *Comunidad Judía de Buenos Aires 1894–1994* (AMIA, Buenos Aires, 1995). Although members of the Jewish community wielded considerable influence in a number of occupations, the community in Argentina was not that large. In 1888, there were 76,385 Jews in the country, 229,605 by 1909, 275,000 in 1960 and about 181,000 in 2014, or 0.43 per cent of the population. A two-volume DAIA study on Argentine-Nazi-Fascist links between 1933 and 1949 has unearthed a wealth of primary sources on that important theme: *Proyecto testimonio: Revelaciones de los Archivos Argentinos sobre la Política Oficial en la Era Nazi-Fascista* (Planeta, Buenos Aires, 1998), vols. I and II.

99 NAI/DFA 2008/79/81 [old file number 305/229/18/2/1].

100 NAI/DFA, 2012/59/2236.

101 NAI/DFA 2008/79/81 [old file number 305/229/18/2/1].

102 On 11 March, the ambassador wrote to the secretary, and for the attention of Rigney, enclosing Rice's letter to Harman of 9 February. He identified Kratzer as the source 'of the interesting item of information in my telex no C4 to the effect that Srta. Cabrera's mother and family are hostile to her daughter's friends and blame them for her imprisonment. Await instructions'. He also included information based on a conversation between Harman and Gloria Genoud, a friend of Rice who had recently arrived from London. Harman got the impression from Genoud that Rice 'is becoming increasingly worried about the case of Srta. Cabrera'. Rice told her that the Cabrera family had not made contact with the embassy. Harman said to her that she might tell Rice, as he was now in England and Ireland, that 'it would be normal for him to maintain contact with the department in Dublin'. NAI/DFA 2008/79/81 [old file number 305/229/18/2/1].

103 Anon., *Gritar el Evangelio con la Vida: Mauricio Silva Barrendero*, https://www.scribd.com/document/268636232/Mauricio-Silva-Barrendero-Fragmentos.

104 João Cara, 'La Lucha por Mauricio', in Rice y Torres (eds), *En Medio de la Tempestad*, pp. 173–9.

105 María Soledad Catoggio, *Los Desaparecidos de la Iglesia: El Clero Contestatario Frente a la Dictadura* (Siglo Veintiuno Ediciones, Buenos Aires, 2016), pp. 141–2.

106 After Silva's disappearance, Marta Garaygochea went underground. She slept in both the Constitución and Retiro railway stations and on the street. Warned that the police were looking for her and that she might place others in danger, she went to Córdoba and remained there with a friend from November 1977 to March 1978. She continued her work in Bolivia, Ecuador and Venezuela. She returned to Buenos Aires with the return of democracy in 1983. Marta Garaygochea, 'El Ultimo Tiempo de la Fraternidad de Malabia', in Rice y Torres (eds), *En Medio de la Tempestad*, pp. 177–9.

107 João Cara, in Rice y Torres (eds), *En Medio de la Tempestad*, pp. 174–5.

108 Yvonne Thayer report, 27 June 1977, US Embassy, Buenos Aires, Argentina Project, US Department of State, https://foia.state.gov/Search/results.aspx?searchText=Fr+Patrick+Rice&beginDate=&endDate=&publishedBeginDate=&publishedEndDate=&caseNumber=.

109 He was survived by his younger brother Jesús, who was also a Little Brother. The latter spent much of his life running a boys' home in Caracas, Venezuela. Henri de Solan, a Little Brother who had gone to work in the province of Corrientes, was taken in September 1976. He spent twelve months in detention before finally being accused of giving the use of a typewriter to a government opposition group. When the case fell through, he was deported to his native France in February 1978. US embassy document, Buenos Aires, AR042A R, 25 June 1978, http://foia.state.gov/documents/Argentina/0000A6C3.pdf.

110 A statue of the hero of the wars of independence in Buenos Aires was erected in 1919 in Buenos Aires. (A replica was placed in Dublin's docklands in 2012.)

111 He replaced Massera as a member of the ruling junta on 15 September 1978 and held the position until 11 September 1981. Convicted of serious crimes in 1985, he was sentenced to eight years in jail.

112 'Here to Honour Argentina's Irish Naval Hero', *Irish Independent*, 20 June 1977.

113 NAI/DFA, 2012/59/2236.

114 For text of address, see *Irish Independent*, 23 June 1977.

115 See photograph, *Irish Press*, 23 June 1977; see also *Western Journal*, 1 July 1977. The past pupils of the Fahy Institute, Moreno, also arranged to have a plaque unveiled in July 1977 in honour of Fr Dominic Fahy, at his birthplace, in Loughrea, County Galway. See *Connacht Tribune*, 15 July 1977; the plaque was unveiled in Loughrea Cathedral, on Sunday, 31 July 1977.

116 'Priest Adds to Protest at Argentine Visit', *Irish Times*, 23 June 1977; see also *Evening Herald*, 23 June 1977.

117 NAI/DFA, 2012/59/2236.

118 Rear Admiral Laurio H. Destéfani was the author of *The Malvinas, the South Georgias and the South Sandwich Islands: The Conflict with Britain* (Edipress, Buenos Aires, 1982) and *Historia Maritima Argentina/Armada Argentina* (Cuántica Editora, Buenos Aires, 1982).

119 NAI/DFA/2009/120/97, Political Situation in Argentina, Dec 76 to Sept 79.

120 Ibid.

121 He argued further that Ireland needed the support of Argentina in international organisations. Moreover, he mentioned that 'also the English claim Brown. His wife was an Englishwoman and she described him as an Englishman by origin on the very public memorial over his tomb in Recoleta Cemetery in Buenos Aires. Brown went on record as saying he was not an Englishman (see the biography of Guillermo Brown by Felipe Bosch, p. 245). As reported already, Admiral Massera expressed the view publicly at the beginning of March 1977 that Brown was an Irishman with the traditional courage of his race (see *La Razón*, 3 March 1977). But that is not the only view in the field. The daily paper *La Nación* in a piece on the British queen's coronation recently considered Brown British and was taken to task once more in the columns of the Irish-Argentine weekly *The Southern Cross* on 24 June 1977 by Dr José Richards writing under his pen-name Irish Porteño, and quoting the historian Dr Eduardo A. Coghlan's letter of refutation of 9 January 1976 in the same *La Nación*: 'It would be regrettable indeed if by failing to participate substantially in the current bicentennial celebration Ireland should now let Brown go to the British by default.' NAI/DFA/2009/120/97, Political Situation in Argentina, Dec 76 to Sept 79.

122 Rice wrote on 18 August to O'Kennedy that he had been instructed by the Irish embassy to send all correspondence to Iveagh House. He reminded the minister of the dangers of being

a prisoner in an Argentine jail. He cited the case of one prisoner in La Plata Jail who had been so ill-treated that he was totally paralysed and his mental faculties greatly impaired. NAI/DFA 2008/79/81 [old file number 305/229/18/2/1].

123 NAI/DFA 2008/79/81 [old file number 305/229/18/2/1], Rice to FitzGerald, 7 July 1977; Rice again repeated the error that Cabrera was twenty-one.

124 NAI/DFA 2008/79/81 [old file number 305/229/18/2/1], Jeremy Craig memorandum, 9 July 1977.

125 Ibid. Emphases in original.

126 NAI/DFA 2008/79/81 [old file number 305/229/18/2/1].

127 NAI/DFA 2008/79/81 [old file number 305/229/18/2/1], Rice to O'Kennedy, 18 August 1977.

128 In Spanish, the phrase is usually written thus: *La Esperanza es lo último se pierde* ('Hope is the last to go' or 'Where there is life there is hope').

129 NAI/DFA 2008/79/81 [old file number 305/229/18/2/1].

130 Ibid.

131 Ibid.

132 Ibid.

133 Ibid.

134 Ibid.

135 Ibid.

136 NAI/DFA, 2009/120/97, Ambassador Ó hÉidáin to Secretary, 19 November 1977.

137 Ibid. On 3 November, the papal nuncio, Pio Laghi, thanked the Irish ambassador for the 'eighteen bottles of special Irish whiskey (fifteen-year-old John Jameson) for use at the forthcoming dinner which the Diplomatic Corps is offering in honour of the ruling military junta. In my own name and on behalf of our colleagues in the corps I wish to express to Your Excellency profound gratitude for such a generous and thoughtful initiative.' Leaping forward, on 2 March 1979, the Irish ambassador and the commander-in-chief of the navy and then a member of the ruling junta, Admiral Armando Lambuschini, both laid wreaths at the monument of Admiral Brown. Lambruschini said in his speech that 'Brown wished for a country, he made one and defended it. Our task is of another dimension, we have a country and have the duty to defend it'. NAI/DFA, 2009/120/97, Irish Ambassador to Secretary, 29 March 1979.

138 'In Honor of Raoul Wallenberg', *International Journal on World Peace*, vol. 6, no. 1, January–March 1989, pp. 92–8, www.jstor.org/stable/20751329.

139 Calamai, *Niente Asilo Político*, pp. 109–86.

140 Juan Miguel María Halvey was born on 19 March 1957. He was arrested on 8 October 1975, in Nicolás Avellaneda High School, and charged with distributing subversive literature. He was first acquitted but the court of appeal later found him guilty. He was sentenced to two years in prison, expiring on 7 October 1977. He met Patrick Rice when they were both in La Plata Prison. Rice mentioned the case to the embassy on one occasion. Halvey's grandfather, Michael Joseph Halvey, was born on 4 November 1891 in Mount Bellew, County Galway. While Halvey was in jail, his widowed mother applied to get him an Irish passport. She felt he would be safer with his relatives in Galway than in Buenos Aires. His application was supported by an Irish Pallottine parish priest. On a visit to the Irish embassy, his mother was told that the embassy would not 'consider it opportune' to intervene in any way before the expiry of the boy's sentence. Halvey was released with twenty-two others on 15 November 1977. It is presumed that he went to Ireland with his mother.

On 6 January 1977, the Irish embassy reported on the case of Santiago Ryan who had been abducted on 7 April 1976. His father was Irish and therefore he was eligible for an

Irish passport. A member of the Communist Party for thirty-five years, he had worked in the printing department of a well-known Buenos Aires publishing house for thirty-seven years. His wife pleaded with the embassy 'to do all in your power' to locate her husband's whereabouts. She said five habeas corpus writs had been issued but with no result. She was also going to appeal to the Russian and Italian consulates as Ryan's mother was Italian. Justin Harman told Sra. Ryan that because her husband was an Argentine citizen, the Irish embassy 'could take no official action on his case'. She knew that but wanted to leave the details in case there was anything they could do presumably on an informal basis. From his British counterpart, Harman learned that they could on occasion informally express to the foreign ministry that a certain individual was, under their law, also a British citizen and that they would wish to maintain a 'semi-interest' in the case. But such an intervention in a dual-nationality case was only considered by the British where 'this concerned detention (i.e. when it is known where the person is being detained) and not in the case of disappearances'. Harman expressed doubt that Ryan was still alive. He did not recommend any action as it might 'lessen our credit with the Foreign Ministry in future cases of more direct concern to us'. I read this file in the Irish embassy archive in Buenos Aires.

141 NAI/DFA 2008/79/81 [old file number 305/229/18/2/1].

142 Ibid.

143 This information was sent to the department by the ambassador on 3 March 1978 following a meeting with the ICF representative. NAI/DFA 2008/79/81 [old file number 305/229/18/2/1].

144 NAI/DFA 2008/79/81 [old file number 305/229/18/2/1].

145 Ibid.

146 NAI/DFA 2008/79/82, letter from Patrick Rice, 760 Irving St., N.E., Washington DC, April [?] 1978; Patrick also asked for his regards to be passed on to John Neville and to the minister.

147 Conversations with Doña Blanca in early 2000s, particularly in 2005 and 2006.

148 Conversations with Fátima Cabrera over many decades.

149 Argentina Project, US Department of State, Ambassador Castro's report 19 June 1978, https://foia.state.gov/Search/results.aspx?searchText=World+cup+in+argentina&beginD ate=&endDate=&publishedBeginDate=&publishedEndDate=&caseNumber=.

150 Ibid.

151 See Uriarte, *Almirante Cero*, p. 283.

152 Ambassador Castro added in the report already quoted: 'My only concern is that Kissinger's repeated high praise for Argentina's action in wiping out terrorism and his stress on the importance of Argentina may have gone to some considerable extent to his hosts' heads. Despite his disclaimers that the methods used in fighting terrorism must not be perpetuated, there is some danger that Argentines may use Kissinger's laudatory statements as justification for hardening their human rights stance.' Argentina Project, US Department of State, Castro report, 27 June 1978, https://foia.state.gov/Search/results.aspx?searchTex t=World+cup+in+argentina&beginDate=&endDate=&publishedBeginDate=&publishe dEndDate=&caseNumber=.

153 Gareth Bland, 'In Celebration of Holland's Underappreciated 1978 Masters', 12 January 2015, https://thesefootballtimes.co/2015/12/01/in-celebration-of-hollands-underappreciated-1978-masters/.

154 Elgy Gillespie, 'Opium of the People', *Irish Times*, 23 December 1978.

155 NAI/DFA, 2009/120/97, Summary of discussions of ambassadors of the Nine, sent by Irish Ambassador to Secretary, 12 July 1978.

156 The couple had first met at the Irish Argentine Encuentro in Monte in 1977. Carmen Casey was a classical guitarist and lute player.

157 Harman's sister Joan and the editor of *TSC*, Fr Federico Richards, were among the guests. Dr John Scanlan played the organ at the ceremony.

158 Séamus Timoney (1926–91), http://www.ucd.ie/merrionstreet/1970_timoney.html. See also Maurice Roche, 'The Secrets of Opus Dei', *Magill*, 30 April, 1983, https://magill.ie/archive/secrets-opus-dei.

159 The Irish army bought a single prototype but never adopted the model for its own use. I am grateful to Col. Dan Harvey for this information.

160 Timoney refers to the vehicle as an AFC.

161 NAI/DFA/2009/120/97, Political Situation in Argentina, Dec 76 to Sept 79.

162 The ambassador said he knew the late Colonel Séamus Timoney and Mrs Timoney when he was resident in Galway some years before.

163 NAI/DFA/2009/120/97, Political Situation in Argentina, Dec 76 to Sept 79.

164 Ibid.

165 Ibid.

166 Ibid.

167 NAI/DFA, 2009/120/97, Irish Ambassador to Secretary, 23 November 1978.

168 Ibid.

169 Clipping on file NAI/DFA, 2009/120/97; also photograph clipping from the *Buenos Aires Herald*, 4 November 1978, and *La Nación*, 5 November 1978.

170 NAI/DFA, 2009/120/97, Mgr Kevin Mullen to Irish Ambassador, 21 December 1978.

171 F. Allen Harris report, 27 December 1978, Argentine Project, US Department of State, https://foia.state.gov/Search/results.aspx?searchText=Kevin+Mullen&beginDate=&endDate=&publishedBeginDate=&publishedEndDate=&caseNumber=.

172 The ambassador did not record the nature, location or date of the said meeting. Perhaps Mullen did not go into such detail.

173 Following the bombing of the dining room at federal police headquarters in Moreno on 2 July 1976 in which twenty-four people were killed and more than seventy injured, General Edmundo René Ojeda was made chief of the Policía Federal Argentina (PFA), a post he held until 1978 when he took a break. He resumed his position in 1979. He replaced Arturo Amador Corbetta. In that position, Ojeda was suspected of having been involved in *la masacre de Fátima*. In the early morning of 20 August 1976, twenty men and ten women were taken by lorry to a remote place, on a dirt road that joins the village of Fátima, near Pilar, with provincial route 6. It was known in those times as a *zona liberada* – an area exclusively under the control of the military. Tied and blindfolded, they were shot at a metre's distance. The bodies were piled together, explosives attached, and then blown up. There were teenagers among the executed. Ojeda was allegedly implicated in the massacre but died before he could be brought to trial. On 18 June 2008, a tribunal in Buenos Aires sentenced two officers to life imprisonment for the massacre. A third officer was acquitted but that verdict was appealed.

174 Amy Rice Cabrera kindly supplied me with the following information about Edmundo René Ojeda: he died before the restoration of the judicial process in 2004 to examine the human rights abuses during the civilian military dictatorship.

175 NAI/DFA, 2009/120/97, Ambassador Ó hÉideáin to Secretary, 29 January 1979.

176 Ibid.

177 Ibid.

178 Mullen named the two priest founders of Cristianos para la Liberación as Carlos Bustos and Pablo Gazzarr (27 November 1976). He said they were disappeared in 1976 and presumed dead. The US document misspelled Pablo Gazzarri's name. As seen earlier, he was disappeared on 27 November 1976. Bustos disappeared on 8 April 1977.

179 Memorandum of conversation with Mgr Kevin Mullen, US Embassy, Buenos Aires, 8 February 1979 (copy supplied by Jerome Mullen, 4 April 2021). In the memorandum, Kevin Mullen spelled Fr Gazzarri's name as Gazzar.

180 'Mons Kelvin (*sic*) Mullen, Su Cambio de Destino', *TSC*, 22 December 1978.

181 I have been unsuccessful in my efforts to recover this report.

182 NAI/DFA, 2009/120/97, Ambassador Ó hÉideáin to Secretary, 29 January 1979.

183 Ibid.

184 NAI/DFA, 2009/120/97.

185 The remains of Jesús Cejas and Crescencio Galañena were returned to relatives on 1 November 2012 and 1 July 2013 respectively. Mundo Latino made the film *Más Allá del Dolor* in 2019, https://cubasi.cu/en/cuba/item/8662-argentina-pays-tribute-to-cuban-diplomats-missing-here.

186 He was the author of *La Hora de Argentina* (El Ateneo Editorial, Buenos Aires, 1974).

187 Holmberg was conservative in her political views. She had approved of the overthrow of the Peronist government by the military in March 1976.

188 Massera may also have met the Montonero leader in Villa Wanda, Arezzo, owned by the head of the masonic P2 lodge, Licio Gelli.

189 CIA cable 18 January 1979, National Security Archive, Washington DC, https://nsarchive.gwu.edu/document/19320-national-security-archive-doc-18-cia-cable.

190 Marina Franco and Carlos Pérez, 'Between Urgency and Strategy: Argentine Exiles in Paris, 1976–1983', *Latin American Perspectives*, vol. 34, no. 4, 2007, pp. 50–67, www.jstor.org/stable/27648033.

191 Andrea Basconi, *Elena Holmberg: La Mujer que Sabía Demasiado. El Crimen que Desnuda la Interna de la Dictadura Militar* (Editorial Sudamericana, Buenos Aires, 2012), p. 132 ff. The Argentine diplomat Gregorio Dupont, a friend of Holmberg, testified in the process inquiring into her disappearance and murder in which he allegedly implicated Massera. There was an alleged link between his testimony and the death of his brother Marcelo, who worked in public relations. He was abducted on 30 September 1982 having complained to a friend that he was being followed by a dark Ford Falcon car. His body was found on 7 October 1982.

192 Told to me by Maud Cox during a visit to their apartment in December 2018 with Ann and Ambassador Justin Harman. Maud said that she had been surrounded by soldiers with guns cocked and she had bustled her way through to the shop on the other side. She was not sure whether it was a warning or a kidnap attempt.

193 Cox, *Dirty Secrets, Dirty War*, pp. 206–7.

194 Roy Greenslade, 'Cox, Hero of Argentinian Journalism, Gets Honorary Citizenship at Last', *Guardian*, 2 August 2010. Cox donated his papers to Duke University, https://archives.lib.duke.edu/catalog/coxrobert.

195 Email from Mgr Austin Mullen to author, 4 February 2013.

196 Ambassador Justin Harman and Jerome Mullen interviewed Hermana María Fé Rodríguez López, in Santiago, Spain, in summer 2018. They kindly provided me with this paragraph based on their interview.

197 I am grateful to Fr Albert McDonnell, vice rector, Irish College, Rome, for helping me with details of the profile of Mgr Mullen. I am also grateful to Mgr Austin Mullen and his brother Jerome for the help they gave me when researching this section of the book.

198 Mgr Austin Mullen email to author, 5 February 2013.

199 Ibid.

200 Archbishop Jan Pawlowski to Jerome Mullen, 25 July 2019, Segreteria di Stato, Sezione per il Personale di Ruolo Diplomatico della Santa Sede. I am grateful to Jerome Mullen for a copy of this letter.

201 Héctor was forced to leave Buenos Aires. He lobbied for his father's release in New York and in Washington. His nemesis was Jorge Espil, the Argentine ambassador. See Héctor Timerman's letter to *New York Times*, 19 April 1981, in which he challenged Ambassador Aja Espil's claims in a letter to the same paper that the Argentine courts were open 'to any person'. 'That is a lie,' Timerman wrote. In 2007, Héctor Timerman became the Argentine ambassador to Washington. He held that post until 2010. He was Argentine minister of foreign affairs, international trade and worship from June 2010 to 10 December 2015. See Nora Boustany, 'An Ambassador Born of the "Dirty Wars"', *Washington Post*, 8 April 2008, http://www.washingtonpost.com/wp-dyn/content/article/2008/04/07/AR2008040702546.html.

202 Rice also brought both their cases before the European Parliament, the International Red Cross, Amnesty International and the UN Commission on Human Rights in Geneva.

203 Inter-American Commission on Human Rights, details of complaint lodged by Patrick Rice about the detention of Fátima Cabrera and himself, http://www.cidh.org/annualrep/78eng/Argentina.2450.htm.

204 Conversations with Rice in Buenos Aires and in Cork. He told me that he narrowly escaped being arrested during the military coup staged during the OAS meeting in La Paz on 31 October 1979.

205 Margaret Swedish and Marie Dennis, *Like Grains of Wheat: A Spirituality of Solidarity* (Orbis Books, Maryknoll, New York, 2004). Scott Wright, who worked in El Salvador in the early 1980s, tells his own story in Chapter 4 of *Like Grains of Wheat*. Wright became a friend of Patrick Rice.

206 Born in 1920, he took a law degree at the University of Buenos Aires in 1945 and a juris doctorate degree in 1969.

207 'Falleció Ayer el ex Embajador Aja Espil', 1 September 2005, https://www.lanacion.com.ar/politica/fallecio-ayer-el-ex-embajador-aja-espil-nid734933.

208 Fr Peter Hinde, O. Carm., email to author, 22 August 2019. Fr Hinde died of Covid-19 in 2020, https://cruxnow.com/church-in-the-americas/2020/11/recently-honored-carmelite-father-peter-hinde-dies-of-covid-19.

209 Colman McCarthy, 'Mass at St Matthew's Drives Argentines from Church', *Washington Post*, 1 June 1979.

210 Ibid.

211 Signed statement by Ruth M. Fitzpatrick and Elizabeth Campbell, RSM (Religious Sisters of Mercy); it was distributed to the press after the protest. Copy in Patrick Rice file, the Holy See.

212 McCarthy, 'Mass at St Matthew's'.

213 Ibid.

214 Fr Peter Hinde to author. There is a copy of the text of O'Malley's sermon in the archives of the Holy See. See also copy of Spanish text in Rice y Torres, *En Medio de la Tempestad*, pp. 250–5. Copies of the following leaflets were also put on the same file: 'Where Are Our Children … Where Are Our Mothers'; prayer by Fr Carlos Mugica and statement by the Organisation for Christian Action on Argentina; incomplete letter addressed to Bishop Thomas C. Kelly, OP; statement by Ruth McDonough Fitzpatrick and Elizabeth Campbell; and press clippings. See Holy See, Patrick Rice file, Argentina 721, 6 June 1979, Archivio del Consilium pro Publicis Ecclesiae Negotiis.

215 McCarthy, 'Mass at St Matthew's'.

216 Ibid.

217 Ibid.

218 Ibid. The following year, the Argentine embassy organised a mass for El Día de la Revolución in the chapel of the US army at Fort Lesley J. McNair.

219 Uriarte, *Almirante Cero*, p. 335.

220 Rice told me of this episode on two occasions when I was staying with him in Buenos Aires. And when I had a meeting with Horacio Verbitsky in Buenos Aires in 2016, he also related to me details of that event. I have been unable to find any written report of this episode in Washington DC or in Buenos Aires.

221 In Verbitsky, *Doble Juego*, pp. 194–5, he wrote that Massera was unable to complete his lecture. But another source states that he did so (see footnote immediately below).

222 Uriarte, *Almirante Cero*, p. 335.

223 David Pion-Berlin, 'The Fall of Military Rule in Argentina, 1976–1983', *Journal of Interamerican Studies and World Affairs*, vol. 27, no. 2, 1985, pp. 55–76, www.jstor.org/stable/165718.

CHAPTER 7 Irish Foreign Policy, Irish-Argentines and War in the Falklands/Malvinas

1   The phrase 'end of history' featured in the title of an essay by Francis Fukuyama; see *The National Interest*, vol. 16, 1989, pp. 3–18. His book *The End of History and the Last Man* (Free Press, New York, 1992) further developed his argument that the victory of liberal democracy and the fall of the Soviet Union and the end of the Cold War was not just the terminus of a particular period but the end of history. While Fukuyama correctly identified the significance of those years as a decisive turning point in history, the years following demonstrated the longevity of *homo historicus*. Events in the Caribbean and Central and Latin America demonstrated time and again that history was not at an end – and nowhere was that more evident than in the Anglo-Argentine Falklands/Malvinas crisis of 1982.

2   The term 'Reagan doctrine' suggested a homogeneity of approach by Washington towards anti-communist armed resistance which did not exist in reality, there being significant differences between levels of US military support to the mujahedeen in Afghanistan and anti-regime resistance in Cambodia, Mozambique, Angola and Nicaragua. See Chester Pach, 'The Reagan Doctrine: Principle, Pragmatism, and Policy', *Presidential Studies Quarterly*, vol. 36, no. 1, 2006, pp. 75–88, www.jstor.org/stable/27552748.

3   https://goo.gl/eAb8s2.

4   This article first appeared in *Commentary*, vol. 68, no. 5, November 1979, pp. 34–45. https://www.commentarymagazine.com/articles/dictatorships-double-standards/. See also Jeane J. Kirkpatrick, *Dictatorships and Double Standards: Rationalism and Reason in Politics* (Simon & Schuster, New York, 1982), pp. 32–90; and her *Making War to Keep Peace* (HarperCollins, New York, 2007); Seymour Maxwell Ginger, 'The Reagan–Kirkpatrick Policies and the United Nations', *Foreign Affairs*, vol. 62, no. 2, winter 1983, pp. 436–57. For a critique of President Reagan's regional policies, see Walter LaFeber, *Inevitable Revolutions: The United States in Central America* (Norton, New York, 1982), pp. 271–317.

5   See obituaries in the *Guardian* and *New York Times*, 9 December 2006.

6   Nicholas Henderson, *Mandarin: The Diaries of an Ambassador* (Weidenfeld & Nicolson, London, 1994), pp. 451–2.

7   Sally-Ann Treharne, *Reagan and Thatcher's Special Relationship: Latin America and Anglo-American Relations* (Edinburgh University Press, Edinburgh, 2015), pp. 40–1.

8   Dermot Keogh, 'El Salvador and the United States', *Millennium: Journal of International Studies*, vol. 13, no. 2, summer 1984, pp. 153–83.

9   Dermot Keogh, *Romero: Church and State in El Salvador* (Dominican Publications, Dublin, 1981).

10 Simon Carswell, 'Emotional Return to El Salvador for President Higgins', *Irish Times*, https://www.irishtimes.com/news/world/europe/emotional-return-to-el-salvador-for-president-higgins-1.1571154.

11 Five members of El Salvador's National Guard murdered four Catholic missionaries near the airport in San Salvador on 2 December 1980. They were Maryknoll sisters Maura Clarke and Ita Ford, an Ursuline sister, Dorothy Kazel, and a lay missionary, Jean Donovan. The latter had studied at UCC during her junior year abroad.

12 'Dublin Protest over Reagan Visit', *New York Times*, 27 May 1984, https://www.nytimes.com/1984/05/27/world/dublin-protest-over-reagan-visit.html.

13 Ibid.

14 Ryle Dwyer, 'Reagan Visit was a Focus of Protests', *Irish Examiner*, 29 December 2014, https://www.irishexaminer.com/viewpoints/analysis/national-archives–1984-reagan-visit-was-a-focus-of-protests-304253.html.

15 For background see, Noel Dorr, *Sunningdale: The Search for Peace in Northern Ireland* (Royal Irish Academy, Dublin, 2017); and his *A Small State at the Top Table: Memories of Ireland on the UN Security Council, 1981–2* (Institute of Public Administration, Dublin, 2011), p. 137. See also Stephen Kelly, *'A Failed Political Entity': Charles Haughey and the Northern Ireland Question, 1945–1992* (Merrion Press, Dublin, 2016).

16 Dorr, *A Small State at the Top Table*, p. 137; press conference transcript, https://www.margaretthatcher.org/document/104456. See also Stephen Kelly, 'Love/Hate: The Haughey–Thatcher Relationship Revisited', *Irish Times*, 24 December 2014, https://goo.gl/mvXEKG; and Kelly's '"The Totality of Relationships": The Haughey–Thatcher Relationship and the Anglo-Irish Summit Meeting, 8 December 1980', *Éire-Ireland*, vol. 51, nos. 3 and 4, fall/winter 2016, pp. 244–73.

17 Frank Sheridan (ed.), *David Goodall: A Memoir. The Making of the Anglo-Irish Agreement of 1985* (NUI, Dublin, 2021), p. 189.

18 Stephen Kelly, quoting H.A.J. Staples of the British embassy in Dublin, in 'Love/Hate: The Haughey–Thatcher Relationship Revisited'.

19 See article by Conor Cruise O'Brien, *Irish Times*, 24 August 1982, in which he coined the acronym; see also 'The creation of "GUBU", a Term that would Define the Haughey Era', *Irish Times*, 20 December 2008.

20 Wooing away Irish-American support from traditional groups like NORAID, he helped build a 'Friends of Ireland' group led by the house speaker, Tip O'Neill. The latter was one of the 'Four Horsemen', along with Senators Ted Kennedy, Daniel Moynihan and New York governor Hugh Carey.

21 Frank Sheridan (ed.), *A Memoir by David Goodall*, p. 191.

22 Ibid., p. 157.

23 NAI/D/T, 2011/127-96 [old file number S14064C], P. O'Sullivan minute, Department of Taoiseach, 6 November 1981.

24 Statement on his retirement at Iveagh House, https://www.dfa.ie/annualreport/2016/my-year-2016/colin-wrafter/.

25 South Georgia has an Irish connection. The County Kerry explorer Tom Crean was a member of the ill-fated Shackleton expedition to the Antarctic in 1915. One of a crew of six, he rowed in 1915 about 1,500 kilometres in seventeen days from Elephant Island to South Georgia and then trekked across the island (48 km) to find help at a whaling station for the other stranded explorers. South Georgia is best known for the fact that Shackleton died and was buried there in 1921 while staging his third attempt to cross the Antarctic continent.

26 Donal Corcoran, 'Why Did Britain and Argentina Go to War over the Falkland Islands/Malvinas?' MA thesis (minor), University College Cork, 2005, pp. 8–10.

27 Malcolm N. Shaw, 'The Heritage of States: The Principle of *Uti Possidetis Juris* Today', *British Yearbook of International Law*, vol 67, no. 1, January 1997, pp. 75–154; Fozia Lone, '*Uti Possidetis Juris*', Oxford Bibliographies, http://www.oxfordbibliographies.com/view/document/obo-9780199796953/obo-9780199796953-0065.xml.

28 Lowell S. Gustafson, *The Sovereignty Dispute over the Falkland/Malvinas Islands* (Oxford University Press, New York, 1988), p. 56, quoted in Corcoran, 'Why Did Britain and Argentina Go to War?' p. 9.

29 Fitzgerald, a mechanical engineer and professional pilot, was the son of Irish-born parents. Elizabeth Fitzgerald, nee Lawler, was born in 1861, in Lansdowne Road, Dublin. She came from a family of Catholic lawyers and was educated at Loreto, Dublin, before going in 1912 to Buenos Aires. There she met her future husband, Vourchier Crawford Fitzgerald, who was born in 1863 in Birr, County Offaly. Interviews with Miguel Fitzgerald and his mother Elizabeth, *TSC*, 18 September 1964.

30 Interview in *TSC*, 18 September 1964.

31 NAI/DFA/313/24I. See also Miguel Lawler Fitzgerald, *Rumbo y Fé* (Lápiz en Mano, Buenos Aires, n.d.). I am grateful to Br John Burke for loaning me his signed copy of this volume. Skentelbery sent a clipping from *El Cronista* which wrote that Fitzgerald's flight had caught the imagination of the leaders of the different political parties, inspiring them to sink their differences and combine together in a national movement for the recovery of the Malvinas/Falklands.

32 Interview in *TSC*, 18 September 1964.

33 Ibid.

34 Ibid.

35 NAI/DFA/313/24I.

36 For list of UN actions and resolutions, see http://www.staff.city.ac.uk/p.willetts/SAC/UN/UN-LIST.HTM#R1514. For historical background, see Peter Willetts, 'The United Nations, Self-Determination and the Falkland Islands', text of talk, Falkland Islands Chamber of Commerce, Port Stanley, 8 March 2013, http://www.staff.city.ac.uk/p.willetts/SAC/COMMENTS/PW080313.HTM.

37 Corcoran, 'Why Did Britain and Argentina Go to War?' See Chapter 2.

38 Undated DFA minute, circa July 1976, NLI/DFA/2006/131/19.

39 Ibid.

40 NLI/DFA/2006/131/19.

41 Born in Dublin in 1916 and raised in west Cork, he studied modern languages at Cambridge, served with the Royal Irish Fusiliers in Africa and Burma during the Second World War and served in Nyasaland, now Malawi, before being posted as governor to the Falklands/Malvinas. A champion of islanders' rights, he was a strong voice in favour of keeping the islands British – a view which ran counter to the predominant policy option canvassed in the 1960s and 1970s by the Foreign and Commonwealth Office.

42 For a detailed review of British policy, together with documents, see S.R. Ashton and Wm. Roger Louis (eds), *East of Suez and the Commonwealth 1964–1971. Part III, Dependent Territories, Africa, Economics Race* (The Stationery Office, London, 2004), p. 135 ff. See also interview with David Michael Summerhayes, who served in Buenos Aires as a diplomat prior to the war (dates recorded: April, June and July 2003), https://www.chu.cam.ac.uk/media/uploads/files/Summerhayes.pdf.

43 When the plane returned to Buenos Aires, all were freed but three spent a brief period in jail. In 1977, the leader, Dardo Cabo, by then a member of the Montoneros guerrillas, was disappeared and murdered by the armed forces. In July 2009, the Peronist government of the province of Buenos Aires honoured the survivors of the group and granted them a special pension. 'Pensions for Argentine Members of Failed Attempt to Capture the Falklands in 1966', *MercoPress*, 22 July 2009, https://en.mercopress.com/2009/07/22/pensions-for-argentine-members-of-failed-attempt-to-capture-the-falklands-i.

44 See *Guardian*, 29 September 1966; also 'That Little Chap in the Hat', *Guardian*, 17 June 1999, https://www.theguardian.com/theguardian/1999/jun/17/features11.g2.

45 Anglo-Argentinean discussions, FCO42/46, no. 231, 21 September 1967, in Ashton and Louis, *East of Suez and the Commonwealth 1964–1971*, pp. 150–1.

46 Haskard to Foreign and Commonwealth Office, 21 October 1967, FCO 42/67, No. 1; Ashton and Louis, *East of Suez and the Commonwealth 1964–1971*, pp. 152–5.

47 Max Hastings, *The Battle for the Falklands* (Pan Macmillan, London, 1967), pp. 22–8.

48 Ashton and Louis, *East of Suez and the Commonwealth 1964–1971*, pp. 52–3, 160–1, 169–82.

49 'Secret Plan to Persuade "Reactionary" Falklands to Accept Argentinian Rule', *Guardian*, 29 November 2001, https://www.theguardian.com/uk/2001/nov/29/falklands.argentina.

50 NAI/DFA/2006/131/19.

51 Obituary for Sir Cosmo Haskard, *The Times* (London), 4 March 2017, https://www.thetimes.co.uk/article/sir-cosmo-haskard-zgzv8czwt?t=ie.

52 Julian Haskard's tribute to his father, 28 February 2017, https://www.fiassociation.com/article.php/807.

53 British briefing note, 20 January 1976, NLI/DFA/2006/131/19.

54 Editorial by Robert Cox, *Buenos Aires Herald*, 6 January 1976, NLI/DFA/2006/131/19.

55 NAI/DFA/2006/131/19.

56 'Argentine Navy Fires at UK Ship, 5 February 1976, NLI/DFA/2006/131/19.

57 *The Times* (London), 13 March 1976, NLI/DFA/2006/131/19.

58 Ivor Richards set out the British case to the United Nations in a letter dated 3 March 1976, NAI/DFA/2006/131/19.

59 NAI/DFA/2006/131/19.

60 For information on UN and Falklands/Malvinas, see UN records, https://search.archives.un.org/falklands-malvinas-policy-statements.

61 NAI/DFA/2006/131/19.

62 Ibid.

63 Ibid. For text of resolution, see https://treaties.un.org/doc/source/docs/A_RES_31_49-Eng.pdf.

64 Livingstone, *Britain and the Dictatorships of Argentina and Chile, 1973–82*, pp. 186–200.

65 Although these two historical cases are distinct, there are parallels with what would emerge as the Sino-British joint declaration on Hong Kong signed in December 1984. The transfer to China of the sovereignty of Hong Kong took place on 1 July 1997. Rumours of those talks had also reached the Falkland islanders.

66 In 1982, there were at least two Irish citizens working as teachers in Port Stanley and there were about a dozen other Irish passport-holders among the inhabitants.

67 This complex series of events is clearly outlined in Lawrence Freedman, *The Official History of the Falklands Campaign. Vol. I: The Origins of the Falklands War* (Routledge, London, 2004), pp. 99–152.

68 Ibid., p. 158.

69 The cost of refitting would be £2.5 million and running costs of the ship ran at £2 million a year. Moreover, the British Antarctic Survey announced a decision, based on budgetary cuts, to close its station on South Georgia, 1,300 kilometres south-east of the Falklands/Malvinas. But those decisions were misread by the Argentines as a lack of resolve on the part of the British to remain in the South Atlantic. Freedman, *The Official History of the Falklands Campaign*, vol. 1, p. 199.

70 Nick Barker, *Beyond Endurance: An Epic of Whitehall and the South Atlantic Conflict* (Leo Cooper, London, 1997), pp. 76–88.

71 Ibid., pp. 28, 45. The British mission in Buenos Aires was upgraded in 1980. The head of mission at chargé rank was promoted to ambassador.

72 'Obituary: Captain Nicholas Barker', *Independent*, 9 April 1997, https://www.independent.co.uk/news/people/obituary-captain-nicholas-barker-1266075.html.

73 Barker, *Beyond Endurance*, pp. 28–9.

74 Freedman, *The Official History of the Falklands Campaign*, vol. 1, p. 139.

75 Nicholas J. White, 'The Business and the Politics of Decolonization: The British Experience in the Twentieth Century', *The Economic History Review*, vol. 53, no. 3, 2000, pp. 544–64; Stephen Brooke, 'Review of Stephen Howe's *Anticolonialism in British Politics: The Left and the End of Empire, 1918–1964*', *Albion: A Quarterly Journal Concerned with British Studies*, vol. 28, no. 1, 1996, pp. 166–8, www.jstor.org/stable/4052012.

76 I am grateful to Jeff Kildea for drawing my attention to this reference, https://en.m.wikipedia.org/wiki/Indonesian_invasion_of_East_Timor.

77 Gerlof D. Homan, 'The United States and the Netherlands East Indies: The Evolution of American Anticolonialism', *Pacific Historical Review*, vol. 53, no. 4, 1984, pp. 423–46, www.jstor.org/stable/3639414.

78 Daniele Schweimler, 'Scrap Dealer Who Accidentally Set Off the Falklands War', http://news.bbc.co.uk/2/hi/8599404.stm.

79 Dorr, *A Small State at the Top Table*, p. 126.

80 'La Movilización del 30 de Marzo de 1982 y el Marzo Caliente de 2017', *La Palabra Caliente*, https://lapalabracaliente.wordpress.com/2017/03/29/la-movilizacion-del-30-de-marzo-de-1982-y-el-marzo-caliente-de-2017/.

81 Alfredo Astiz, an intelligence officer responsible in December 1977 for the kidnapping at Holy Cross of the Mothers of the Plaza de Mayo, was prominent in the taking of the island.

82 'Foreign Secretary Resigns in Britain in Falkland Crisis', *New York Times*, 6 April 1982, https://www.nytimes.com/1982/04/06/world/foreign-secretary-resigns-britain-falkland-crisis-text-carrington-letter-page-a6.html.

83 For an evolution of British policy towards Argentina and the Falklands, see Livingstone, *Britain and the Dictatorships of Argentina and Chile, 1973–1982*, p. 205 ff; David Rock, *The British in Argentina*, pp. 339–66.

84 See Freedman, *The Official History of the Falklands Campaign*, vols 1 and 2; Lawrence Freedman and Virginia Gamba-Stonehouse, *Signals of War: The Falklands Conflict of 1982* (Princeton University Press, Princeton, 2016); D. George Boyce, *The Falklands War* (Palgrave Macmillan, New York, 2005); Jimmy Burns, *The Land that Lost Its Heroes: How Argentina Lost the Falklands War* (Bloomsbury, London, 2002); Paul Eddy and Magnus Linklater [*Sunday Times* Insight Team], *Falklands War* (Andre Deutsch, London, 1982); Peter J. Beck, 'Cooperative Confrontation in the Falkland Islands Dispute: The Anglo-Argentine Search for a Way Forward', *Journal of Interamerican Studies and World Affairs*, vol. 24, no. 1, February 1982, pp. 37–58; Peter Beck, *The Falkland Islands as an International Problem* (Routledge, London, 1988); Duncan Anderson, *The Falklands War, 1982* (Osprey, Oxford, 2002); Carlos Büsser, *Malvinas: La Guerra Inconclusa* (Ediciónes Fernández Reguera, Buenos Aires, 1987); Juan Bautista Yofre, *1982: Los Documentos Secretos de la Guerra de Malvinas-Falklands y el Derrumbe del Proceso* (Editorial Sudamericana, Buenos Aires, 2011); Federico G. Lorenz, *Malvinas: Una Guerra Argentina* (Editorial Sudamericana, Buenos Aires, 2009).

85 Lisa L. Martin, 'Institutions and Cooperation: Sanctions during the Falkland Islands Conflict', *International Security*, vol. 16, no. 4, spring 1992, pp. 150–1.

86 Tom Ruys, Oliver Corten and Alexandra Hofer (eds), *The Use of Force in International Law: A Case-based Approach* (Oxford University Press, Oxford, 2018), see Introduction, and Part I, Chapter 30 on Falklands/Malvinas episode.

87 Sir Anthony Parsons, 'The Falklands Crisis in the United Nations, 31 March–14 June 1982', *International Affairs*, vol. 59, no. 2, spring 1983, pp. 169–78.

88 Ibid.

89 Dorr, *A Small State at the Top Table*, p. 138.

90 On 11 April 1982, an article in the *Sunday Independent* reported that Dorr had acted beyond his instructions and not consulted Dublin when voting for the British motion. That view was not accurate and was strongly disputed by Iveagh House.

91 Phone discussion with Colin Wrafter and email, 29 May 2020.

92 Discussion with Br John Burke, January 2020; see also Christian Brothers house annals, 2 May 1982.

93 Conversation with John Michel, Buenos Aires, 2016.

94 Lead story, *TSC*, 19 March 1982.

95 NAI/DFA/2012/40/1. The Irish-Argentine community at San Miguel del Monte said in a statement that the 'recuperation of our Malvinas islands and the Irish vote in the Security Council of the UN were impossible to reconcile with the profound sense of national sovereignty of every act of remembering Admiral Brown', *La Prensa*, 15 April 1982. Other letters and articles in the press came from the following: Guillermo A. Dunne, 7 April 1982; Enrique Moore, 16 April 1982: 'it is lamentable that the Irish government has again falen (*sic*) short in international desisions (*sic*) and I have absolute certenty (*sic*) that if this issue would have being (*sic*) put to the Irish people they would have flatly reyected (*sic*) your actual governments (*sic*) position'; María Cecilia Hecker Doyle, 10 April 1982; Federico A. Rossiter, 14 April 1982; Guillermo, Eduardo, Roberto and Juan C. Quinn, 6 April 1982; Guillermo A. Carracedo, vice-president, Cereals Export Centre.

96 *TSC*, 16 April 1982. There was also a letter from Guillermo P. Ford, a former president of the Irish Federation, expressing his full support for the statement that had been issued.

97 NAI/DFA/2012/40/5.

98 Christian Brothers house annals, 23 April 1982.

99 Br John Burke told me that one brother in particular was in contact with Haughey.

100 See *Irish Press*, 12 April 1982. Santa Brígida may have been the other college to have been given police protection.

101 Christian Brothers house annals, 3 September 1982.

102 NAI/DFA/2012/40/5.

103 Ibid.

104 'Irish Caught Up in Falklands Invasion Crisis, *Irish Press*, 3 April 1982.

105 NAI/DFA/2012/40/5.

106 NAI/DFA/2012/40/5; and the excellent overview by Cesar N. Caviedes, 'Conflict over the Falkland Islands: A Never-Ending Story?', *Latin American Research Review*, vol. 29, no. 2, 1994, pp. 172–87, www.jstor.org/stable/2503598.

107 Ibid.

108 Ibid.

109 While the letters sent to Ambassador Walshe were numerous, I have not surveyed members of the Irish-Argentine community to discover how widespread the pro-invasion sentiments were in Buenos Aires and in the different towns of the camp.

110 NAI/DFA/2012/40/1; telex of letter sent to Dublin on 6 April 1982, see NAI/ DFA/2012/40/5.

111 Ibid.

112 Ibid.

113 Ibid.

114 Ibid.

115 *TSC*, 9 April 1982.

116 Ibid.

117 NAI/DFA/2012/40/1.

118   Arnd Schneider, 'Organizing Ethnicity: Three Episodes in the Politics of Italian Associations in Argentina, 1947–1989, *Canadian Journal of Latin American and Caribbean Studies*, vol. 25, no. 50, 2000, pp. 195–228; and see 'Malvinas: The Italian Collectivity Shows Solidarity with the Argentine People', *Tribuna Italiana*, 14 April 1982.

119   Among those present were: the president, John Scanlan, Doreen Furlong, Guillermo Howlin, Maria Scally de Herrera, Ina H. de Moore, Juan Clancy, Alfredo McLoughlin, Francisco Cavanagh, Carlos Brady and Santiago M. Quaine.

120   In Spanish, the name was *Federación de Sociedades Irlandesas de la República Argentina*.

121   Minutes of board of directors, Federation of Irish Societies of the Republic of Argentina, 6 April 1982, *acta* no. 123, p. 66 (Federation archive, Fahy Club, Buenos Aires).

122   *TSC*, 16 April 1982.

123   NAI/DFA/2012/40/1, John J. Scanlan, Federation of Irish-Argentine Societies to Irish Ambassador, Buenos Aires, 7 April 1982.

124   NAI/DFA/2012/40/5.

125   Ibid.

126   This was an unusual procedural departure. The cabinet minutes traditionally only recorded *decisions*.

127   Paul Lewis, 'EEC to Embargo Argentine Imports', *New York Times*, 15 April 1982, https://goo.gl/oZR44T.

128   'Irish "Would Take Up Arms"', *Irish Independent*, 12 April 1982; 'Argentina Trade Ban: Warning of Anti-Irish Moves', *Irish Press*, 12 April 1982.

129   Discussions with Patrick McKernan, 1983.

130   NAI/DFA/2012/40/5.

131   Ibid.

132   'A No Equivocarse', *TSC*, 16 April 1982.

133   Christian Brothers house annals, 24 April 1982.

134   21 April 1982, European Parliament Debate, *Official Journal*, no. 1-284/149.

135   Déaglán de Bréadún, 'Major Rift in Relations after British Sank *Belgrano*', *Irish Times*, 28 December 2012; Jon Begley, 'The Literature of the Falklands/Malvinas War', *The Edinburgh Companion to Twentieth-Century British and American War Literature* (Edinburgh University Press, Edinburgh, 2012), pp. 231–40; Lawrence Freedman, 'Bridgehead Revisited: The Literature of the Falklands', *International Affairs*, vol. 59, no. 3, summer 1983, pp. 445–52.

136   Among those captured was Lieutenant Commander Alfredo Astiz, wanted for questioning by the Swedish and French governments over the murder of a Swedish woman and the kidnapping, torture and disappearance of two French nuns. According to the Geneva Convention for prisoners of war, Astiz avoided being investigated by the Swedish and French governments. He was in the end deported by the British government back home. Lawrence Freedman and Virginia Gamba-Stonehouse, *Signals of War*, p. 323 ff; and Freedman, *The Official History of the Falklands Campaign*, vol. 2, pp. 249–60.

137   *TSC*, 23 April 1982.

138   NAI/DFA/2012/59/66.

139   Ibid.

140   Ibid.

141   'The Day "Sharelga" was Sunk by a Sub!', *Drogheda Independent*, 5 September 2012, https://www.independent.ie/regionals/droghedaindependent/lifestyle/the-day-sharelga-was-sunk-by-a-sub-27169745.html. See also *Hansard*, 18 June 1985, Statement by the Prime Minister: 'The Irish trawler Sharelga sank on 18 April 1982, some 30 miles east of Dublin. The Coastguard at Anglesey picked up a distress call just after 12.20. A Royal

Navy submarine was involved, but, for reasons of operational security, no further details can be given. The Ministry of Defence has accepted liability for the incident and agreed to pay fair and reasonable compensation.' http://hansard.millbanksystems.com/written_answers/1985/jun/18/sharelga-sinking.

142 DFA/NAI/2012/59/66; copy of telex version of 'non-paper' on this file.

143 Ibid.

144 *TSC*, 30 April 1982.

145 Interview with O'Sullivan, *TSC*, 28 May 1982.

146 NAI/DFA/2012/59/66.

147 *TSC*, 23 April 1982.

148 Ibid.

149 For a detailed chronology on the crisis, see 'The Falklands War: A Chronology of Events', *The History Press*, https://www.thehistorypress.co.uk/articles/the-falklands-war-a-chronology-of-events/.

150 Charles Lysaght, 'Obituary: Former British Ambassador to Dublin Leonard Figg', *Irish Independent*, 14 September 2014. It is unclear whether Figg's remarks quoted in the document were comments made to Lysaght or are quotes from one of Figg's diplomatic reports.

151 De Bréadún, 'Major Rift in Relations'.

152 For general reading see: Max Hastings and Simon Jenkins, *The Battle for the Falklands* (Pan Books, London, 1983); Desmond Rice and Arthur Gavshon, *The Sinking of the Belgrano* (Secker & Warburg, London, 1984); Alejandro Debat and Luis Lorenzano, *Argentina, the Malvinas and the End of Military Rule* (Verso Books, London, 1982); Simon Collier, 'The First Falklands War? Argentine Attitudes', *International Affairs*, vol. 59, no. 3, summer 1983, pp. 457–64; Jeane J. Kirkpatrick, 'My Falklands War and Theirs', *The National Interest*, no. 18, winter 1989/90, pp. 11–20; Geoffrey Edwards, 'Europe and the Falkland Islands Crisis 1982', *Journal of Common Market Studies*, vol. 22, no. 4, June 1984, p. 292; Thomas M. Franck, 'Dulce et Decorum Est: The Strategic Role of Legal Principles in the Falklands War', *The American Journal of International Law*, vol. 77, no. 1, January 1983, pp. 109–24; Duncan Campbell, 'The Chile Connection', *New Statesman*, 25 January 1985, pp. 8–10; David C. Gompert, Hans Binnendijk and Bonny Lin, *Blinders, Blunders, and Wars: What America and China Can Learn* (Rand Corporation, New York, 2014), pp. 151–60; Jean Houbert, 'The Falklands: A Hiccup of Decolonisation', *Current Research on Peace and Violence*, vol. 5, no. 1, 1982, pp. 1–25; Richard J. Regan, *Just War* (Catholic University of America Press, Washington DC, 2013), pp. 154–62.

153 NAI/DFA/2012/59/66.

154 Ibid.

155 On the sinking of the *Sharelga*, Power described Britain as being no better than a hit-and-run driver over her conduct in failing to surface her submarine after colliding with the Clogherhead trawler; see *Drogheda Independent*, 7 May 1982.

156 Power was quoted in the *Evening Herald* on 4 May as saying: 'the government would now take a neutral stance on the Falklands crisis following the sinking of the General Belgrano'.

157 See Eamonn O'Kane, *Britain, Ireland and Northern Ireland since 1980: The Totality of Relationships* (Routledge, London and New York, 2007), p. 28; and Dorr, *A Small State at the Top Table*, p. 184.

158 Michael Brophy, 'Power Politics is all in the Timing', *Irish Independent*, 5 May 1982.

159 'The Belgrano Inquiry', http://belgranoinquiry.com/. See also 'Gotcha! How the Sun Reaped Spoils Of War', *Guardian*, 7 April 2002, https://www.theguardian.com/business/2002/apr/07/pressandpublishing.media.

160 J.J. Power letter, *Irish Times*, 31 January 2012.

161 NAI/DFA/2012/40/6.

162 Ibid. Transcript of Haughey's RTÉ television interview, 4 May 1982.

163 Julian Amery, Obituary, *London Independent*, https://www.independent.co.uk/incoming/lord-amery-of-lustleigh-obituary-5601769.html.

164 Dorr, *A Small State at the Top Table*, pp. 119–260.

165 For an overview of the British position, see text of a British government document, entitled 'The Falkland Islands: Negotiations for a Peaceful Settlement' with two appendices (issued on 21 May 1982), *New York Times*, 21 May 1982, https://www.nytimes.com/1982/05/21/world/text-of-british-government-document-on-the-falkland-islands-negotiations.html.

166 See Dorr, *A Small State at the Top Table*, p. 183.

167 Based on an oral source. Patrick McKernan told me that that was the case in 1983.

168 The US secretary of state, Alexander Haig, wrote to Gerard Collins on 5 May asking to 'avoid any move that would suggest lessened solidarity with Britain while we're in this most critical phase', NAI/DFA/2012/59/66.

169 See Dorr, *A Small State at the Top Table*, p. 179 ff.

170 John Bew, 'Irish Ambassador "Boring and Long-Winded"', *Irish Times*, 1 August 2013, https://goo.gl/ne5Yho. Sir Anthony Parsons also wrote of Dorr: 'Everyone else spoke in favour of the Secretary General. Dorr was "his usual sententious self but this time his claptrap was harmless"'. See Freedman, *The Official History of the Falklands Campaign*, vol. 2, p. 367. Freedman, who wrote the official British history of the Falklands/Malvinas war, did not subject that judgement to any objective test. In my view, a diary entry written in the heat of battle was not a considered or balanced view of Dorr nor of the domestic political climate in which he exercised his professional duties.

171 Michael Lillis, who was a senior Irish diplomat at the time of the Falklands/Malvinas crisis, argued in 2014 in a review of the Dorr book that the government decisions on 4 May were, in his opinion, 'destructive of any remaining hope of restoring a dialogue with Mrs Thatcher [on Northern Ireland]'. Mr Lillis wrote further that 'few ambassadors to the United Nations ... have faced situations as uncomfortable as Noel Dorr did' on 4 May when he received instructions 'delivered in public and without consultation with him', which were 'clearly contrary to the national interest of Ireland where our most pressing challenge [Northern Ireland] was concerned'. While Mr Lillis admired 'the indefatigable devotion and energy of Noel Dorr and his tiny team in New York as they pursued their Sisyphean task day and night during those tumultuous weeks', he concluded that, because the government decisions were so much at variance with Irish national interests, both Dorr and the secretary of the department, Seán Donlon, should 'at a minimum have requested the Taoiseach and their minister [Gerard Collins] for transfers to other responsibilities'. Mr Lillis, in his review of Noel Dorr's book, was very critical of Ireland's identification with the authoritarian regimes of Latin America: Michael Lillis, 'Mr Haughey's Dud Exocet' [reviewing Noel Dorr's book], *Dublin Review of Books*, no. 98, March 2018, https://drb.ie/articles/mr-haugheys-dud-exocet/. I am grateful to Michael Lillis for sending me references to his writing in this area. Now that the archives covering those events are in the public domain, Mr Lillis might consider writing a follow-up essay on the events of those crowded months. His wide knowledge of Spain and Latin America would, in the light of the availability of Irish, British and other national archives, add greatly to the growing body of literature on such a contested field of history. Mr Lillis is the co-author with Ronan Fanning of the valuable volume *The Lives of Eliza Lynch: Scandal and Courage* (Gill & Macmillan, Dublin, 2009). He has also written 'The True Origins of Eliza Lynch', *Irish Times*, 11 March 2014, https://www.irishtimes.com/culture/heritage/the-true-origins-of-eliza-lynch-1.1719349. At a

seminar in Trinity College on 13 April 2012, Noel Dorr said: 'I don't think I feel inclined to apologise for whatever efforts we made in our time to try to avert a war.' He described as 'clumsy' the 4 May government statement. He said he had successfully recommended the replacement of the phrase 'immediate meeting' of the Security Council with 'immediately seek a meeting'. He added: 'You may say that's parsing on the head of a pin but then that's the way wars are averted.' Marie O'Halloran, 'Former Diplomat Defends Irish Stance on Falklands War', *Irish Times*, 14 April 2012. See also Michael Kennedy's review of Dorr's book *A Small State at the Top Table* in *Studies: An Irish Quarterly Review*, vol. 101, no. 402, summer 2012, pp. 242–4, https://www.jstor.org/stable/23333122.

172　As mentioned before, I knew Patrick McKernan personally. We had extensive conversations, beginning in 1983, on Ireland and the Falklands/Malvinas crisis.

173　Conversations with Patrick McKernan, 1983.

174　Ibid.

175　Geoffrey Edwards, 'Europe and the Falkland Islands Crisis, 1982', *Journal of Common Market Studies*, vol. 22, no. 4, June 1984, p. 307, quoted in Lisa Martin, 'Institutions and Cooperation: Sanctions during the Falkland Islands Conflict', *International Security*, vol. 16, no. 4, spring 1992, p. 165, www.jstor.org/stable/2539190.

176　Martin, 'Institutions and Cooperation'.

177　Martin, 'Institutions and Cooperation', pp. 164–72.

178　For a good overview, see Michael E. Brown et al. (eds), *The Perils of Anarchy: Contemporary Realism and International Security* (MIT Press, Cambridge, MA, 1995), p. 484 ff.

179　*Dáil Éireann Debates*, 18 May 1982, https://www.oireachtas.ie/en/debates/debate/dail/1982-05-18/20/#spk_212.

180　Conversations with Patrick McKernan in 1983.

181　O'Kane, *Britain, Ireland and Northern Ireland since 1980*, p. 29.

182　Freedman, *The Official History of the Falklands Campaign*, vol. 2, p. 501. See also letter from Tom Cleary, chairman of An Bord Bainne, to the taoiseach on 4 August 1982, 'in relation to the backlash we were receiving in the UK as a consequence of the policy of the Irish government in relation to the Falklands dispute'. He said his staff had worked hard to contain the effects of this and in time he felt the adverse reaction would wear itself out. Together with IRA bombings in London, the climate makes the role of a company marketing 'high-profile' Irish products extremely difficult. The board had several cancellations of promotions they were organising. He said that a sustained period of the current climate would do irreparable damage to this business which had been built up over twenty years at very considerable cost. Haughey replied on 13 September that his department had undertaken a fresh consideration of the issues raised by firms exporting to Britain. The conclusion reached was that 'while firms and agencies had experienced adverse reaction of varying intensity, the permanent effect on Irish export businesses was likely to be limited to the loss of a relatively small number of orders', NAI/DFA/2012/59/66.

183　There had been a controversy over previous Irish fixtures against Argentina. In 1974, the Irish soccer team toured Latin America, playing against Brazil and Chile. The latter game, held in the national stadium in Santiago where hundreds of prisoners had been detained, interrogated, and in some cases killed, was the first international fixture in that venue since the military coup d'état on 11 September 1973. Eamon Dunphy, a well-known football pundit, was then a member of the team. The Irish government, and the foreign minister, refused requests to intervene to stop the team from travelling. See 'How Dunphy Landed in Hot Water', *Irish Independent*, 9 January 2005, and Eamon Dunphy, *The Rocky Road* (Penguin, Dublin, 2013), pp. 225–30.

184　'El XI de Fútbol de Irlanda no Juega Aquí', *TSC*, 21 May 1982.

185   *TSC*, 28 May 1982.

186   'A Comedy of Errors: Ireland's Ill-Fated South American Tour', *Irish Times*, 4 June 2014 https://goo.gl/xi3ahy.

187   Having received mailbags of critical letters during April, the Irish embassy was showered from 5 May with letters of congratulation and high praise for the revised stance of the Irish government on the Falklands/Malvinas crisis. Arturo S. Moore congratulated Walshe on 18 May 'on the courageous and chivalrous position taken by the Irish delegation by withdrawing its support from the country that attacks us'. The president of the Catholic Association of Saint Patrick in Rosario wrote on 6 May stating that because of the policy change, 'Ireland has thus repaired the damage to her prestige in this country. Ireland, too, has demonstrated to Argentina that she exercises a sovereign independent opinion on matters of world importance. Congratulations and heartfelt thanks, Prime Minister Haughey, and members of your government.' NAI/DFA/2012/40/1.

188   Some five other journalists, mostly working for the BBC, had Irish passports to gain access to Buenos Aires and used RTÉ airtime to broadcast. The presence of those journalists – particularly after the arrest on 13 April of Simon Winchester (*Sunday Times*) and two colleagues, Ian Mather and Tony Prime (both of *The Observer*) – was a source of concern for the Irish embassy. Imprisoned in Tierra del Fuego for eleven weeks, they were released on bail of about $20,000. Winchester published *Prison Diary, Argentina*, in 1984 based on his experiences.

189   The issue on 30 April 1982 is listed as no. 5502 and that on 14 May is given as 5503.

190   *TSC*, 15 May 1982.

191   Christian Brothers house annals, 4 May 1982.

192   Ibid., 17 May 1982.

193   NAI/DFA/2012/40/3.

194   NAI/DFA/2012/40/1.

195   *TSC*, 21 May 1982.

196   NAI/DFA/2012/40/6; minutes of board of directors, Federation of Irish Societies of the Republic of Argentina, 7 May 1982, *acta* no. 123, pp. 70–1 [Federation archive, Fahy Club, Buenos Aires]. It is likely that there was a meeting on the 7th – the following day the letter was sent to Haughey and a covering letter to the ambassador.

197   NAI/DFA/2012/40/1; copy also on NAI/DFA/2012/40/6.

198   At my request, Br Burke made an enquiry in Newman College among the older Christian Brothers. They could not remember the exact date, but the general feeling was that the visit had taken place in the mid-1960s when Haughey was minister for agriculture between 1964 and 1966. There was no reference to the visit in the Newman house chronicle. Prof. Gary Murphy confirmed the date of this visit to be September/October 1967 when Haughey and his wife Maureen visted Argentina together with Brazil, Chile and Perú.

199   NAI/DFA/2012/40/6.

200   Ibid.

201   Ibid.

202   Ibid.

203   Ibid.

204   Ibid.

205   Ibid.

206   Ibid.

207   NAI/DFA/2012/40/6 and NAI/DFA/2012/40/7.

208   'Doloroso Despertar', *TSC*, 21 May 1982.

209 An editorial on Northern Ireland claimed that Éamon de Valera was one of the few men *'que lograban sacarlo a Winston Churchill de sus cajillas'* (to drive Churchill up the walls), *TSC*, 28 May 1982.

210 *TSC*, 28 May 1982.

211 *TSC*, 11 June 1982.

212 When Scanlan informed the ambassador of the contents of the reply, Walshe complained about his not having been sent a copy. The Department of the Taoiseach supplied a copy on request to Iveagh House and it was sent on to Buenos Aires.

213 NAI/DFA/2012/59/16, Scanlan to Seán Aylward, private secretary to Charles Haughey, 10 June 1982 and reply on 25 June.

214 Ambassador Walshe was taken aback that the Aylward/Haughey correspondence with Scanlan was not sent through the Department of Foreign Affairs. It was sent by normal post.

215 A note in *TSC* on 11 June announced that the federation had launched an appeal to fund an open letter in the three principal Irish daily newspapers to thank Ireland for its independent stance in favour of Argentina over the crisis in the South Atlantic.

216 Minutes of board of directors, Federation of Irish Societies of the Republic of Argentina, 1 June 1982, *acta* no. 125, p. 71 [Federation archive, Fahy Club, Buenos Aires].

217 *TSC*, 11 June 1982.

218 The breakthrough came with the signing with Chile of a treaty of peace and friendship in 1984.

219 Between 28 May and 2 June 1982, the pope had visited the United Kingdom. His visit to Buenos Aires was to counterbalance his trip to Britain, coming as he did as an emissary of peace.

220 *New York Times*, 27 October 1982.

221 For an overall view of the writing on the Falklands/Malvinas crisis in 1982, see Begley, 'The Literature of the Falklands/Malvinas War'; also Freedman, 'Bridgehead Revisited'.

222 This is an area of research which ought to be undertaken. Ronnie Quinn is the only Irish-Argentine I found who wrote a book on the 1982 conflict which is a combination of fact and fiction: see *El Raro Privilegio* (Editorial Dunken, Buenos Aires, 2012). I am grateful to him for sending me a copy of this work.

223 *TSC*, 23 July 1982; the event is covered in great detail on pages 1 and 5.

224 The Santa Ursula Seed Firm, supported by other industries, schools and individuals, was the largest donor. The fund was oversubscribed in two weeks.

225 NAI/DFA/2012/40/3. At the bottom of the advertisement was the following: 'Note: The cost of this Open Letter has been defrayed by the contributions of Irish nationals and Argentine nationals of Irish descent all resident in Argentina.'

226 Castlereagh was chief secretary of Ireland during the 1798 rebellion.

227 *TSC*, 9 July 1982. The same paper, on 16 July, carried a front-page picture of Ronnie Quinn and Robert Lavignone at the Hurling Club. They had served in the Falklands/Malvinas during the war.

228 'The Sun does not Shine on the Irish', *Irish Press*, 26 June 1982.

229 Haughey had faced an electoral battle in Dublin West for a seat vacated by the Fine Gael TD Richard Burke who had become a commissioner in Brussels on the nomination of the taoiseach. The gamble to win the seat for Fianna Fáil backfired. Polling took place on 25 May 1982 and Fine Gael retained the seat, leaving Haughey still the leader of a minority government.

230 *TSC*, 20 November 1983.

231 That was not the first time an Irish monument had been attacked. The previous year, a bust of Admiral Brown had to be recovered from the lake at San Miguel del Monte, the article noted.

232 *TSC*, 13 August 1984.

CHAPTER 8 The Aftermath of Dictatorship, Human Rights and the Evolution of Irish Policy towards Latin America

1 This document, dated 24 November 1982, was part report and mostly a general essay on Argentine history, politics and society. It was written at a time when Ambassador Walshe had lived through a particularly intense year of war in the South Atlantic with all the attendant pressures brought to bear on both himself and the third secretary, Colin Wrafter, living as they were under a civilian military dictatorship. Ambassador Walshe produced a *tour d'horizon* of Argentine society and history, offering explanations of the history of the country based, in part, on ethnocentric judgements on southern Italian immigrants and their culture. My use of the document is confined to his description of a dinner party and his predictions about the future political development of the country. A copy of this document was kindly given to me in 2013.

2 Ibid.

3 Ibid.

4 Ibid.

5 Freedman, *The Official History of the Falklands Campaign. Vol. 2: War and Diplomacy*, p. 598.

6 Ibid.

7 Emilio Mignone, the director of the Centro de Estudios Legales y Sociales (CELS), estimated that the number killed was 20,000 and that the number rose to 30,000 if those who were disappeared and reappeared were included. See Arditti, *Searching for Life*, pp. 43–4.

8 https://www.usip.org/publications/1983/12/truth-commission-argentina.

9 Vincent Druliolle, 'Remembering and Its Place in Post Dictatorship Argentina', in Lessa and Druliolle, *The Memory of State Terror in the Southern Cone*, pp. 27–9.

10 A Swedish girl, Dagmar Hagelin (17), was another Astiz victim. Mistaken for a Montonero in the house of a friend, she was shot and kidnapped on 27 January 1977 by an Astiz-led snatch squad. Taken to the ESMA, she was tortured and disappeared. 'Jorge Acosta and the Murder of Dagmar Hagelin', http://www.yendor.com/vanished/junta/acosta.html.

11 'Argentina "Angel of Death" Alfredo Astiz Convicted', *BBC News*, http://www.bbc.com/news/world-latin-america-15472396. For an overview of the trials of those involved in disappearances, see Louise Mallinder, *Amnesty, Human Rights and Political Transitions* (Hart Publishing, Oxford and Portland, 2008), p. 310 ff., and also Leigh A. Payne, *Unsettling Accounts: Neither Truth nor Reconciliation in Confessions of State Violence* (Duke University Press, Durham and London, 2008), p. 84 ff.

12 Tom Hennigan, '"Blond Angel of Death" Gets Life in Jail', *Irish Times*, 28 October 2011, https://www.irishtimes.com/news/blond-angel-of-death-gets-life-in-jail-1.632912.

13 There are three Spanish-speaking countries in the Caribbean: Cuba, Dominican Republic and Puerto Rico. By adding all the fourteen Caribbean countries, the professional challenge for the two diplomats in Buenos Aires became all the more daunting.

14 Sean Ó hÉideáin did serve from November 1961 to August 1962 to fill in for the late ambassador who died on 3 November 1960 (see Appendix).

15 Many countries – West Germany, France, Italy, Sweden, etc. – helped during the Chilean and Argentine dictatorship to get political refugees out of both countries on travel documents provided by the respective embassies and consulates. Ireland failed to have a similar policy of openness. The case of Fátima Cabrera illustrates the closed-mindedness of the Department

of Justice to pleas to grant her a visa notwithstanding the fact she had a paid return ticket to Buenos Aires, a sponsor in Ireland, and a guarantee that she would not be a burden on the state. While the countries mentioned above provided asylum to Argentines in their hundreds, I have found no evidence that a single visa was issued by the Irish government for other than a short-term stay.

16 Ireland opened diplomatic relations with Venezuela in 1980 to which the Irish ambassador in Buenos Aires was accredited. The Irish embassy in Mexico took over that role in 1999.

17 In the Caribbean, Cuba is accredited to the Irish embassy in Mexico. The Irish embassy in Ottawa was listed as looking after consular affairs in Jamaica. Trinidad and Tobago was the responsibility of the permanent mission to the UN in New York. The Irish embassy in Washington DC handled consular work for many of the other island states in the Caribbean.

18 Meetings of first secretaries have been mentioned already in the text.

19 See Latin America Trade Forum policy publication, *Ireland and Latin America: Looking to the Future. Strategy and Proposals for Trade Growth* (Dublin, July 2015).

20 Department of Foreign Affairs and Trade organigram, https://www.dfa.ie/about-us/who-we-are/our-structures/.

21 https://www.ireland.ie/media/ireland/stories/globaldiaspora/Global-Ireland-in-English.pdf.

22 Successive Chilean governments did not appreciate the failure of Ireland to reciprocate until 2018. In the margins of the visit to Santiago by President Michael D. Higgins in 2012, Irish officials were told of pressures to transfer resources to open new Chilean diplomatic missions in other locations. That aside indicated official irritation in Santiago over the tardiness of the Irish government to open a resident mission in that country. It became abundantly clear that unless a resident Irish diplomatic mission was opened in Santiago, the Chilean embassy in Dublin might be closed.

23 Rice explained his approach to human rights in 'The Disappeared: A New Challenge to Christian Faith in Latin America', in Keogh (ed.), *Church and Politics in Latin America*, pp. 372–97.

24 Betty Campbell was a co-founder of Tabor House and Community for Contemplative Political Action in Washington DC. She has lived in Ciudad Juárez, Mexico, since 1995.

25 http://www.desaparecidos.org/fedefam/eng.html.

26 Guest, *Behind the Disappearances*, pp. 214–15.

27 Ibid., pp. 376–7.

28 Conversations with Fátima Cabrera in Buenos Aires and in Ireland.

29 See 'Story of Alicia Emelina Panameno de Garcia', http://www.embracingelsalvador.org/alicia-de-garcia/.

30 Four US citizens – three nuns and a laywoman – were murdered in San Salvador on 2 December 1980. They were Sisters Dorothy Kazel, Ita Ford and Maura Clark, and laywoman Jean Donovan. A memorial lecture in honour of Jean Donovan was established in UCC in the 1980s where she had studied during her 'junior year abroad'.

31 U2's lead singer Bono wrote a song in 1986, 'Mothers of the Disappeared', in tribute to the CoMadres and to a similar group in Nicaragua. It was included on the *Joshua Tree* album.

32 Fátima Cabrera, 'Debo Agradecer a Dios ser una Sobreviviente', in Rice y Torres, *En Medio de la Tempestad*, pp. 149–52. When Fátima Cabrera and Patrick Rice met, as the former pointed out above, the notion of their becoming a couple was not even in question. They celebrated the fact that they were both still alive. Cabrera told me on more than one occasion that she felt she owed her life to Rice because of the international campaign that he had waged on her behalf. When Cabrera announced that she was going to go with Rice to Caracas, Doña Blanca said that her daughter could go and when things did not work out she

was welcome to return home in a few months. But the couple married in Caracas, where they had two children. I visited them there in 1987. They had a third child when they returned to live in Buenos Aires. All lived happily together until Rice's untimely death on 7 July 2010.

33 Fátima Cabrera's sister died in mysterious circumstances. She was either killed or she committed suicide.

34 Jesús died in 2016.

35 Cabrera, 'Debo Agradecer a Dios ser una Sobreviviente'.

36 Patrick Rice curriculum vitae.

37 'Former Priest Who Devoted His Life to Promoting Human Rights', Obituary, *Irish Times*, 17 July 2010, https://www.irishtimes.com/life-and-style/people/former-priest-who-devoted-his-life-to-promoting-human-rights-1.623269.

38 See the following works by Dermot Keogh: *Romero: Church and State in El Salvador* (Dominican Publications, Dublin, 1981), p. 170; *Central America: Human Rights and US Foreign Policy* (Cork University Press, Cork, 1985), p. 168; *Church and Politics in Latin America* (Macmillan, London, 1990), p. 430; 'El Salvador and the United States', *Millennium: Journal of International Studies*, vol. 13, no. 2, summer 1984, pp. 153, 183. See also Mignone, *Witness to the Truth*.

39 Aldo Etchegoyen was a Methodist bishop emeritus and founder member of the Permanent Assembly of Human Rights from 1975. He was president of the Methodist Council of Latin America and the Caribbean (CIEMAL) for the period 1983 and 1989 and general secretary between 2001 and 2008. Between 1990 and 1997, he was president of the Council of Methodist Bishops of Latin America.

40 Federico José Pagura (1923–2016), Methodist bishop emeritus, was one of ten co-presidents of the World Council of Churches from 1998 until 2004. He helped Chilean refugees after 1973 and was a founder member of the Ecumenical Movement for Human Rights in 1976. During the dictatorship, he joined in the silent vigils of the Mothers of the Plaza de Mayo. He was interested in poetry and was the author of many tangos where he composed the words for social purposes such as *Tememos Esperanza* (We Have Hope). In 2003, the Argentine Congress included him in their list of 'Most Noteworthy' of the country.

41 Padre Raúl Reynaldo Troncoso was born in Rafaela, province of Santa Fe, in 1937. He was a member of the Movement of Third World Priests. He was imprisoned between 1976 and 1981.

42 Elías Musse was born in 1940 in Villa Italia, Tandil, province of Buenos Aires. He was the son of Lebanese parents. Ordained in 1960, he went from Buenos Aires to study with the Jesuits in Chile. He was a founder member of the Movement of Third World Priests. He was imprisoned from 8 June 1976 until 1982, freed by the intervention of Pope John Paul II on his visit to Argentina: https://lanotadigital.com.ar/2010/07/15/cura-de-victoria-testimonio-en-una-causa-por-crimenes-de-la-dictadura/.

43 See University of Minnesota, Human Rights Library, http://www1.umn.edu/humanrts/instree/d4deidrb.htm. See also at the same site: http://www1.umn.edu/humanrts/edumat/studyguides/religion.html.

44 I travelled to Buenos Aires with my wife Ann to be present at the event. I do not have transcripts of what was said on that occasion but I did take notes.

45 This is based on my notes and memory of the event.

46 https://turismo.buenosaires.gob.ar/en/otros-establecimientos/memorial-museum-former-esma.

47 See 'La Memoria que Vive en Lugar del Horror', *Pagina 12*, 27 December 2010.

48 In 2008, the municipality of Buenos Aires declared that 14 June would henceforth be known as 'The Day of the Street Cleaner' in memory of Mauricio. A book was published in Silva's

honour: *Cry the Gospel by One's Life: Mauricio Silva, Street Cleaner*. The Nobel Prize winner Adolfo Pérez Esquivel was one of about 200 people who attended the ceremony in Mauricio Silva's honour. See Ryan, 'Two Priests in a Dirty War'.

49 Hannah Arendt, *Eichmann in Jerusalem: A Report on the Banality of Evil* (Penguin, London, 1994).

50 This is based on my notes and newspaper clippings gathered of the occasion.

51 That struggle takes many forms. Throughout Buenos Aires, handmade memory tiles – marking the locations where victims of state terror were killed or disappeared – are mounted on walls or inscribed in the paving stones around the city. The Parque de la Memoria, opened in November 2007, is situated on the Costanera Norte, beside the River Plate made infamous by the *vuelos de la muerte* (death flights) in which between 1,500 and 2,000 people were murdered. The figure may have been as high as 4,000.

52 President Robinson visited Chile, Argentina and Brazil.

53 President McAleese visited Argentina, Chile and Brazil.

54 As a Labour Party senator and TD, he had been very active in opposing human rights violations in Chile during the military dictatorship of General Augusto Pinochet. He was also involved in the campaign to secure permission for Chilean refugees to settle in Ireland. In 1982, he was held at gunpoint in San Salvador by then government authorities and deported to neighbouring Nicaragua. He made a presidential visit to El Salvador in 2013. In 1989, President Daniel Ortega of Nicaragua visited Ireland where he received a warm welcome in Galway, the home town of President Higgins. Higgins was an international election observer during the Chilean national plebiscite in 1988. He was honoured by the Chilean government in January 2016 for 'his brave and generous humanitarian help that contributed to save thousands of lives of the Chilean people and also foreigners persecuted by the dictatorship'. Simon Carswell, 'Emotional Return to El Salvador for President Higgins', *Irish Times*, 24 October 2013.

55 President Michael D. Higgins, speech at the opening of an exhibition on the Irish in Latin America, Havana, 16 February 2017, https://president.ie/en/media-library/speeches/speech-at-the-opening-of-an-exhibition-on-the-irish-in-latin-america-1.

56 https://goo.gl/HRRcqB.

57 President Michael D. Higgins, Buenos Aires, 12 October 2012, https://goo.gl/uDtfFK.

58 Tom Hennigan, 'Higgins Salutes Argentina Diaspora', *Irish Times*, 13 October 2012, https://www.irishtimes.com/news/higgins-salutes-argentina-diaspora-1.742440. The desire for closer relations between Ireland and the countries of Latin America was a constant theme on his three state visits to that region.

Bibliography

PRIMARY SOURCES

National Archives of Ireland (NAI)
Dáil Éireann Papers: Departments of Foreign Affairs, Propaganda/Publicity and
    Finance
Files relating to Latin America
Eamonn Bulfin reports from Buenos Aires, 1920/1
Frank W. Egan reports from Chile, 1920/2
Michael Collins files

Irish Department of Foreign Affairs and Trade (DFAT)
(The department changed its name in 1971 from the Department of External Affairs to
    the Department of Foreign Affairs. In 2011, it became the Department of Foreign
    Affairs and Trade.)
Confidential and political reports from Irish missions in Argentina, Australia, Britain,
    Canada, France, the Holy See, Italy, Spain, Portugal and the United States

Files of Irish embassy, Buenos Aires
Argentine embassy files returned to NAI

Iveagh House files on Argentina
Confidential reports, 1948–83
Human rights files from Irish embassy, Buenos Aires
Patrick Rice files, 1976–83
Fátima Cabrera files, 1976–7

Falklands/Malvinas files
Files relating to Chilean refugees (including files in DFA)
El Salvador files
Personal correspondence with archives section, DFAT

Files from other Irish missions
Britain
Canada
France

Germany
Holy See
Italy
Portugal
Spain
United States of America

Department of the Taoiseach (D/T)
Files on ambassadorial appointments to Argentina and related files
Files relating to Chilean refugees
General files

Irish Embassy, Buenos Aires
(Edificio Bluesky, Avenida del Libertador 1068, Recoleta)
Embassy files relating to the period of the civilian military dictatorship, 1976–83
Miscellaneous working files relating to embassy's contact with Irish-Argentine societies

Archivo Histórico de la Cancillería, Buenos Aires, Argentina
(Rafael Obligado s/n entre Ericsson y Edison, Puerto Nuevo, Terminal 5, Dársena F)
https://www.cancilleria.gob.ar/es/institucional/patrimonio/archivo-historico-de-
    cancilleria
Ministerio de Relaciones Exteriores Comercio Internacional y Culto

Diplomática y Consular
Argentine relations with Britain and Ireland in late nineteenth and early twentieth
    centuries, on immigration, the *Dresden* episode and aftermath, and the government
Archivo Cancillería, caja 443, 1890, serie: diplomática y consular
1916–18 consular files, Dublin and London
Administration and political files, England, boxes 1681 and 1682
1921–1950s: Political Division, Irish-Argentine files
Argentine embassy, Dublin: firmas de condolencia de autoridades y particulares (Perón
    book of condolences)
(Files of the Argentine embassies in Dublin, London and Washington were not
    available at the time I was doing my research.)

Hotel de Inmigrantes Archive, Buenos Aires
List of *Dresden* passengers, 1889
Photographs
https://www.afar.com/places/hotel-de-inmigrantes-buenos-aires

Archives of the Holy See and of the Nunciature, Buenos Aires
Documents in the possession of the Holy See relating to the victims of the civilian
    military government in Argentina (1976–83) were opened in 2018 under direction

from Pope Francis I. Those eligible to see the material were victims of state repression or surviving members of their families.

Some 195 pages of redacted papers relating to Patrick Rice were released to his widow, Fátima Cabrera, in 2018. (I am grateful to her for allowing me to consult that material.) The documents are from the following sources:

Segretaria di stato: relevant documents from consiglio per gli affair pubblici della chiesa

Correspondence and memoranda: the apostolic nunciature, Buenos Aires

Correspondence: the apostolic nunciature, Washington DC

Correspondence: the Argentine cancillería and interior ministry

British National Archive, Kew, London, UK (TNA)

British Foreign and Commonwealth Office

Files relating to the period 1919 to 1922

FO FO371/3758

FO 371/5574

FO371/4549

FO371/5663

FO371/5524

FO371/4417

FO395/314

FO395/5663

http://www.nationalarchives.gov.uk/

Laurence Ginnell files, UK (TNA)

Prosecution of Laurence Ginnell MP; seditious and treasonable speeches, 1917, Westport, County Mayo; no action pending further instructions (ref. WO 35/99/5)

File 162, 219 folios: Laurence Ginnell MP, political activities; activity key suspects fortnight to 15 February 1918 (reference CO 904/202/9)

Prosecution of Reverend Father O'Flanagan, Laurence Ginnell, MP, Louis Walsh and P.J. McCrann; seditious speeches, 1917, Termonbarry and Strokestown, County Roscommon; no further action, ecclesiastical authorities informed (ref. WO 35/95/20)

Eamonn Bulfin files, UK (TNA)

Dublin Castle, Sinn Féin activities (WO 35/206/20), UK (TNA), Kew, London

Prosecution of E.A. Morkan, Eamonn Bulfin and F. Bulfin; possession of seditious literature and bomb, 1918, Derrinlough and Birr; internment and deportation orders (ref. WO 35/101/19)

US Department of State and Office of the Director of National Intelligence

President Barack Obama releases files relating to Argentine military dictatorship between 1976 and 1983, https://nsarchive.gwu.edu/briefing-book/southern-cone/2016-03-18/obama-brings-declassified-diplomacy-argentina

See also: 'National Declassification Center Releases Records relating to human rights abuses in Argentina', https://www.archives.gov/argentina/humanrights

The Office of the Director of National Intelligence has posted the US–Argentine collection as a whole, which can be found at: intel.gov/argentina

Additional information and links to the documents can be found here: https://aotus.blogs.archives.gov/2019/04/12/declassification-diplomacy-the-united-states-declassification-project-for-argentina/

Related documents are available to download from this ZIP file: https://www.archives.gov/files/argentina/data/argentina-human-rights.zip

US National Archives, Maryland

Argentina Declassification Project, Overview and Origins and Responsive Records https://www.intel.gov/argentina-declassification-project/records

The National Declassification Center Releases Records Relating to Human Rights Abuses in Argentina: https://www.archives.gov/argentina/humanrights

US Department of State
General files on US and Argentina

US Department of State, Virtual Reading Room Documents Search

Search terms, Patrick Rice, Kevin Mullen, Patricia Derian, Pio Laghi, Emilio Mignone: https://foia.state.gov/Search/Search.aspx

https://nsarchive.gwu.edu/events/argentine-dirty-war-1976-1983

https://nsarchive.gwu.edu/briefing-book/southern-cone/2017-04-27/trump-continues-us-declassified-diplomacy-argentina

Lifting of Pinochet's immunity renews focus on operation Condor: https://nsarchive2.gwu.edu//NSAEBB/NSAEBB125/index.htm

Library and Archives, Canada (LAC), Ottawa

Political affairs; social affairs; internal security; political prisoners in Argentina, 1976–83: http://www.bac-lac.gc.ca/ENG/Pages/home.aspx

PERSONAL PAPERS

National Library of Ireland

Seán T. O'Kelly papers
http://www.nli.ie/pdfs/mss%20lists/oceallaigh.pdf
MSS 27,672-27734 (accession no. 4096)

James O'Mara papers
http://sources.nli.ie/Record/MS_UR_078596
MS 21,546

Douglas Hyde papers
http://catalogue.nli.ie/Collection/vtls000651854/CollectionList?ui=standard
http://catalogue.nli.ie/Collection/vtls000651854

William Bulfin papers
http://catalogue.nli.ie/Search/Results?lookfor=bulfin%2C+william&type=AllFields
    &submit=FIND
http://sources.nli.ie/Record/MS_UR_010676
http://sources.nli.ie/Record/MS_UR_078906
MS 13,812, 13,813, 13,815, 13,818

Laurence Ginnell papers
http://catalogue.nli.ie/Collection/vtls000623943/HierarchyTree?recordID=vt
    ls000624214
NLI MS 49,810/10/6

Laurence Ginnell (1852–1923) papers (Westmeath County Council Library Service,
    Mullingar)
Extensive collection of letters, photographs and documents relating to his work as a
    Sinn Féin envoy in Argentina between July 1921 and March 1922
Laurence Ginnell papers in family possession, Mullingar
Alice Ginnell diary and notebook
Laurence Ginnell correspondence

William Bulfin papers – in family possession
(Ms Jeanne Winder and Michael Bulfin, Dublin)
Correspondence between William Bulfin and his wife, Annie O'Rourke
Manuscripts of William Bulfin, including note fragments for book, *Rambles in Éirinn*
Photographs of William Bulfin
(The bulk of his papers are in the National Library of Ireland)

Eamonn Bulfin papers – in family possession
(Ms Jeanne Winder and Michael Bulfin, Dublin)
Uncatalogued collection of correspondence covering Eamonn Bulfin's life from his
    time as a schoolboy in St Enda's to his role in the 1916 Rising, his sentencing to
    death, internment and return to Ireland, December 1916. Bulfin's engagement in
    Sinn Féin and friendship with Michael Collins. His role as Sinn Féin envoy in
    Argentina, 1919–22

Album following chronology of his life (probably assembled by his wife)
   Letters from Patrick Pearse, Michael Collins, etc.
   Miscellaneous files
   Photographs

Leopold Kerney Private Archives (LKPA) (family possession)
LKPA, Argentina files, 1947

Trinity College Dublin
Douglas Hyde papers
President of Ireland, Mary Robinson, 'Douglas Hyde (1860–1949): The Trinity
   connection – quatercentenary discourse, 11.5.1992'
https://www.tcd.ie/Secretary/FellowsScholars/discourses/discourses/1992_M.T.W
   %20Robinson%20on%20D.%20Hyde.pdf

Michael Davitt papers

NUI, Galway, James Hardiman Library
Muintir na Tíre papers (transferred to NUIG in 2018)
https://digital.library.nuigalway.ie/islandora/object/nuigalway:muintir
P134/12/1/3/1: scrap album of Canon John Hayes' trip to attend Eucharistic Congress
   in Buenos Aires, Argentina, 1934 (I am grateful to Dr Mary Harris for locating this
   file for me)

Gaelic League papers

University College Cork, Special Collections, UCC
Daniel Florence O'Leary letters
The Southern Cross, 1875 (microfilm)

University College Dublin Archives
Éamon de Valera papers, P150
Correspondence
Photographs
https://www.ucd.ie/archives/t4media/p0150-devalera-eamon-descriptive-catalogue.
   pdf

Desmond and Mabel FitzGerald papers, P80
https://www.ucd.ie/archives/t4media/p0080-fitzgerald-desmond-descriptive-
   catalogue.PDF

Garret FitzGerald Papers (Minister for Foreign Affairs, 1973–7), P215
https://www.ucd.ie/archives/t4media/p0215-fitzgerald-garret-descriptive-catalogue.
   PDF

University of Notre Dame Archives, South Bend, Indiana
Suffern family papers
Eva Perón letters
http://archives.nd.edu/

Boston College, Burns Library, Chestnut Hill, Boston
https://libguides.bc.edu/Burns
Robert F. Drinan papers
https://library.bc.edu/finding-aids/CA1986-001-finding-aid.pdf
Graham Greene papers
https://library.bc.edu/finding-aids/MS1995-003-finding-aid.pdf

Patrick Rice and Fátima Cabrera Rice Archives, Virrey Cevallos 1758, 1135 Buenos Aires
Large collection of uncatalogued personal and professional papers covering Rice's
    life in Argentina from 1970 until his death in 2010. It is difficult to overstate the
    historical importance of this archive.

Ministerio de Justicia y Derechos Humanos, Archivio Nacional de la Memoria, ex-ESMA, Avenida Libertador 8151, Buenos Aires
https://turismo.buenosaires.gob.ar/en/otros-establecimientos/memorial-museum-
    former-esma
Sergio Kuchevasky, presidente Archivio Nacional de la Memoria, secretaria de
    Derechos Humanos y Pluralismo Cultural, on 14 December 2018, supplied fifty-
    one pages of documents, file CONADEP no. 6976, to Fátima Cabrera. The folder
    contains:

1) Sworn testimony by Patrick Rice in Argentine embassy, Caracas, on 26
    July 1984, for the Comisión Nacional sobre Desaparición de Personas,
    Buenos Aires. The statement covers his enforced disappearance, illegal
    detention, torture and release. Sixteen pages plus related documents;

2) Statement by Fátima Edelmira Cabrera, on 29 January 1999, on the
    disappearance of her ex-partner, Alberto Cayetano Alfaro;

3) Three submissions to the courts by Fátima Cabrera, 22 December
    2004, 8 June 2008, and 4 March 2016, regarding her illegal detention,
    disappearance and torture.

Patrick Rice and Fátima Cabrera case. Trial began on 3 December 2019 and ended two
    years later
Audio of Fátima Cabrera's evidence, given on 11 December 2019
https://drive.google.com/file/d/1qSTv4vf-Xwx2I32xzsNKFptD9jaLw3Eb/view?usp=
    sharing

Report on the investigation into the victims of enforced disappearances and
assassinations, caused by the repressive actions of the state, clandestine detention
centres and other places of clandestine detention
https://www.argentina.gob.ar/sitiosdememoria/ruvte/informe

Listado de centros clandestinos de detención, Anexo V [List of clandestine centres of
detention (CCDs)]
https://www.argentina.gob.ar/sites/default/files/6._anexo_v_listado_de_ccd-
investigacion_ruvte-ilid.pdf

Buenos Aires Archdioceses (Conferencia Episcopal Argentina)

In 2016, I was permitted to see one file on Colectividad Irlandesa (short file with a
copy of the constitution of the Federation of the Irish Argentine Societies). In 2017,
Pope Francis I requested that a protocol be drawn up for the consultation of files held
in that archive relating to the victim (him/herself) or the surviving family members of
repression during the civilian military dictatorship, 1976–83.

During that period the archdiocese received over 3,000 letters from the families of
the disappeared. The Rice family requested access to those files in 2018 and passed on a
copy of the released documents to me. That collection was made up of correspondence
with the nuncio regarding the Rice case together with letters from government
departments.

(The archdiocesan archive was burned down in 1955 in the course of a Peronist
street demonstration, together with a number of nearby churches.)

Inter-American Commission on Human Rights (Organisation of American States)

Patrick Rice case, initiated in May 1977 (Argentine government referred to Case 2450
Argentina). This file contains detailed correspondence of Rice's kidnapping, torture
and release. See his letter of 9 April 1978 to the Inter-American Commission on
Human Rights and the commission's notes and correspondence with the Argentine
government. Rice gave evidence on 9 January 1978 at the 44th session of the Inter-
American Commission. Findings in favour of Rice were approved on 18 November
1978 at the 605th meeting of the commission.
http://www.cidh.org/annualrep/78eng/Argentina.2450.htm

Irish-Argentine Societies and Institutions

Federation of Irish-Argentine Societies [Federación de Sociedades Argentino
Irlandesas]
Fahy Club, Av. Congreso 2931 Buenos Aires
(visit arranged by James Ussher)
Articles of association
Executive council minute books
Annual General Assembly minute books

Irish Catholic Association [La Asociación Católica Irlandesa] and The Southern Cross *Archive (Colegio Santa Brígida, Av. Gaona 2085, C1416DRI CABA)*
Irish Catholic Association archives
The Southern Cross, in hard copy
Complete series of *Fianna* and *The Argentine Review* (which incorporated *The Hiberno-Argentine Review*)
A small collection of letters relating to the working of *TSC*
A library of older books on Irish history, culture and literature which were in the office of *TSC*
The Southern Cross photographic collection, which I saw in 2010 in the former editorial office, Riobamba 451 4C, Buenos Aires, is not in the archival collection and neither is there the microfilm of the newspaper.

The Kelly Family, Temperley, Buenos Aires
The Ussher-Walsh Family Album, Arbol Genealógica del matrimonio de Irlandeses, William Ussher y Anne Walsh, y sus descendientes. Compiled by Mgr Santiago Ussher, Buenos Aires, 11 November 1933; revised and updated by Juan José Ussher Móran, Córdoba, 23 November 1991

Silvia Elena Kenny de Cavanagh (Buenos Aires)
Miscellaneous papers and books

Irish Catholic and Irish Missionary Sources
All Hallows Missionary College, Dublin (1842–1915)
Before the college closed in 2016, I consulted the archives relating to Latin America which consisted of letters from former students in the nineteenth century to the rector. I copied and digitised a collection of letters from alumni working in Argentina.

See sources online
Past All Hallows ordination and graduation posters from 1852 to 2015 (there are missing years)
Annuals – contain letters from Fr Dominic Fahy OP
(1842–1912), incomplete
1848–51; 1855–8; 1860–3; 1896; 1899; 1902–3; 1906; 1907; 1909–12, etc.

Irish Christian Brothers' Archive, Buenos Aires
https://www.cardenal-newman.edu/
Newman College House Annals 1945–22 October 1983
Handwritten memoir by the late Br David O'Connor, mainly about Ireland
but it also contains interesting passages about his time teaching in Argentina from the 1950s. He died in 1994 aged eighty-nine. He is buried in Buenos Aires. (Copy supplied by Br John Burke.)

Interviews with Bros Tom O'Connell and Seán Hayes in Buenos Aires and John
Bourke in Dublin and Cork

Archives of the Pallottine Fathers, St Patrick's, Belgrano, Echeverría 3900,
C1430BTL CABA
Over thirty boxes of partially sorted but uncatalogued material relating to the
missionary and educational activities of the order in Argentina dating back to the
nineteenth century. The files are not arranged in any particular subject order. The
collection is most valuable. Each item has been cited only by reference to the box
number.

Part of Mgr Santiago Ussher's archive is included in the collection. Among the
material cited is the following:

Files relating to the writing of Ussher's biography of Fr Dominic Fahy together with
photocopies of original documents which he collected in Ireland, Rome, the
United States and Argentina
Files relating to Ussher's time as chairperson of the Irish White Cross between 1921 and
1922
Correspondence, together with memorabilia, relating to Ussher's visit as head of an
Argentine delegation to the Eucharistic Congress, Dublin, 1932
Correspondence relating to the Eucharistic Congress in Buenos Aires in 1934 and
details of Irish participation
Letter to Ussher in 1935 from the secretary of the Department of Foreign Affairs, Joseph
Walshe, relaying de Valera's commitment to open an Irish legation in Buenos Aires

Pallottine Provincial Archives, Sandyford Road, Dundrum, Dublin 16
Fr Donal McCarthy, who retired as archivist in 2021, generously made his extensive
draft history of the Pallottines in Argentina available to me in digital form.

- History of the Pallottines in Argentina between 1959 and 1978. (His digital
  copy also includes profiles of the priests who served in Argentina.)
- Files relating to the history of the order's mission in Argentina and of the
  priests who served there from the nineteenth to the twentieth century.
- An English translation of Fr Alfredo Kelly's diary. He was one of the five
  Pallottines who was murdered on 4 July 1976. I did not read the original
  Spanish version.

Fr Tomás O'Donnell, who has been in Argentina since 1976, deposited in the Dundrum
archives documents and articles of his late confrère, Fr Juan Santos Gaynor, who
was the editor of *The Southern Cross* between 1939 and 1958.

Fr McCarthy, at my request, sent copies of a large collection of photographs relating to the Pallottine mission in Argentina. Fr O'Donnell also supplied information and photographs to me from the Pallottine archive in Mercedes.

Passionist Fathers, Holy Cross, Estados Unidos 3150, Buenos Aires
I visited Holy Cross on each of nearly twenty visits to Buenos Aires since 2000 and worked in the archives on a number of occasions. My most extensive visit was as the guest of the late Fr Michael Egan in 2010. While I did not visit the archives on that occasion, he gave access to his private collections of books and pamphlets. He very kindly gave me two books by Mgr Santiago Ussher and other printed material. In 2016, I sought permission to see the archives and was given access to the personal papers of Fr Federico Richards. When I requested to see the *Holy Cross Chronicle*, a journal of events kept in each Passionist monastery, I was told that it was not available for consultation. Mariano Galazzi kindly made a digital copy of the *Holy Cross Chronicle*, 1949–98, available to me.

Passionist Fathers, Mount Argus, Dublin
Provincial archives and historical documents on the mission to Argentina from the late nineteenth century
https://passionistarchives.ie/index.php/contact

Congregation of the Sisters of Mercy Archives
Letters relating to work of the order in Buenos Aires in the nineteenth century
https://sistersofmercy.ie/archives

Oblate (OMI) Provincial Archives, Dublin
Nine letters written in the late 1880s from Fr Matthew Gaughren in Argentina to Fr Tatin in England

Pontifical Irish College, Rome
https://www.irishcollege.org/archive/
Paul Cullen papers and Cullen supplements guide
https://www.irishcollege.org/wp-content/uploads/2011/02/Cullen-Papers-in-the-Irish-College-Rome.pdf
https://www.irishcollege.org/wp-content/uploads/2011/02/Cullen-Supplements.pdf

Michael O'Riordan papers (1857–1919), rector from 1905 to 1919
John Hagan papers, rector from 1919 to 1930
https://www.irishcollege.org/wp-content/uploads/2011/02/Hagan-Introduction.pdf

Dublin Archdiocesan Archives
Archbishop Daniel Murray (1832–52) papers
Cardinal Paul Cullen (1852–78) papers

Archbishop William Walsh (1885–1921) papers
Archbishop Edward Byrne (1921–40) papers
Archbishop John Charles McQuaid (1940–71) papers
Nineteenth-century letters relating to the supplying of priests for the missionary movement in Argentina
https://dublindiocese.ie/archives/

Diocese of Ardagh and Clonmacnois
Bishop James Joseph McNamee's diary during his visit as part of the Irish delegation to the Eucharistic Congress, in Buenos Aires, in 1934 https://ardaghdiocese.org/

Cardinal Tomás Ó Fiaich Library & Archive (CÓFLA)
Cardinal Michael Logue papers
Cardinal Joseph MacRory papers
Cardinal John D'Alton papers (Arch/12/ D'Alton, Argentina file)
http://www.ofiaich.ie/

Latin American Newspaper Digital Archive (LAN)
Covers many leading nineteenth- and twentieth-century newspapers in Argentina, Brazil, Chile, Cuba, Guatemala, Mexico, Peru, Venezuela and elsewhere
https://guides.library.yale.edu/Latnewspapers

IRISH NEWSPAPERS

Irish newspapers online digital collection
Irish Times online

THESES

María Mónica Brown, 'La Inmigración Irlandesa en la Provincial de Buenos Aires el Partido de Mercedes' [no date], Municipal Library, Mercedes
Patrick McKenna, 'Nineteenth-Century Irish Emigration to, and Settlement in, Argentina', MA Geography thesis, NUI Maynooth, 1994

ORAL SOURCES

John Burke
John Clancy
Eduardo and Salomé Clancy

Archbishop Patrick Coveney
Bernard and Fiamma Davenport
Juan José Delaney

Luis Delaney
Patricia (Patt) Derian
Michael Egan
Diana Englebert Moody
Michel Geraghty
Justin Harman
Mateo Kelly
Silvia Elena Kenny de Cavanagh
Sergio Kiernan
Roberto Landaburu
Bishop Guillermo Leaden
Mgr Austin Mullen
Jerome Mullen

Emilio Mignone
Patrick McKernan
Br Tom O'Connell
Fr Tomás O'Donnell
Paula Ortiz
Veronica Repetti
Patrick Rice, Fátima Cabrera Rice,
   and Amy, Blanca and Carlos Rice
   Cabrera
Jimmy Ussher
Horacio Verbitsky
Colin Wrafter
Fr Santiago Whelan

BOOKS AND ARTICLES

Akenson, Donald H., *God's Peoples: Covenant and Land in South Africa, Israel, and Ulster* (Cornell University Press, Ithaca, 1992)

— *Conor: A Biography of Conor Cruise O'Brien* (Cornell University Press, Ithaca, 1994)

— *If the Irish Ran the World: Montserrat, 1630–1730* (Liverpool University Press, London, 1997)

— *Irish History of Civilization*, vols. I & II (McGill-Queens University, Montreal, 2005)

— *Irish in Ontario: A Study in Rural History* (McGill-Queen's University Press, Kingston, 1984)

— *United States and Ireland* (Harvard University Press, Cambridge, MA, 1973)

Albarracín, Julia, *Making Immigrants in Modern Argentina* (University of Notre Dame Press, Notre Dame, Indiana, 2020)

Amnesty International, *Testimony on Secret Detention Camps in Argentina* (Amnesty International, London, 1977)

Anctil, Pierre and Tōnu Onu, *A Reluctant Welcome for Jewish People: Voices in Le Devoir's Editorials, 1910–1947* (University of Ottawa Press, Ottawa, 2019)

Andersen, Martin Edward, *Dossier Secreto: Argentina's Desaparecidos and the Myth of the 'Dirty War'* (Westview Press, Boulder, Colorado, 1993)

Anderson, Benedict, *Imagined Communities: Reflections on the Origin and Spread of Nationalism* (Verso, London, 1991)

Anderson, Duncan, *The Falklands War, 1982* (Osprey, Oxford, 2002)

Anon., *A Record of Ireland's Commemoration of the 1916 Rising* (Department of External Affairs, Dublin, 1966)

Arditti, Rita, *Searching for Life: The Grandmothers of the Plaza de Mayo and the Disappeared Children of Argentina* (University of California Press, Berkeley, 1999)

Arendt, Hannah, *Eichmann in Jerusalem: A Report on the Banality of Evil* (Penguin, London, 1994)

Arnson, Cynthia J. (ed.), *Argentina–United States Bilateral Relations* (Woodrow Wilson Center, Washington DC, 2004)

Ashton, S.R., and Wm. Roger Louis, *East of Suez and the Commonwealth, 1964–1971. Part III: Dependent Territories, Africa, Economics Race* (The Stationery Office, London, 2004)

Avni, Haim, *Argentina and the Jews: A History of Jewish Immigration* (University of Alabama Press, Tuscaloosa and London, 1991)

Baily, Samuel L., *Immigrants in the Lands of Promise: Italians in Buenos Aires and New York City, 1870 to 1914* (Cornell University Press, Ithaca and London, 1999)

Baily, Samuel L., and Eduardo José Míguez (eds), *Mass Migration to Modern Latin America* (Scholarly Resources Inc., Delaware, 2003)

Barker, Nick, *Beyond Endurance: An Epic of Whitehall and the South Atlantic Conflict* (Leo Cooper, London, 1997)

Barr, Colin, *Ireland's Empire: The Irish Catholic Church in the English-Speaking World, 1829–1914* (Cambridge University Press, Cambridge, 2000)

Bartlett, Thomas (ed.), *The Cambridge History of Ireland, 1880 to the Present* (Cambridge University Press, Cambridge, 2019)

Basconi, Andrea, *Elena Holmberg: La Mujer que Sabía Demasiado: El Crimen que Desnuda la Interna de la Dictadura Militar* (Editorial Sudamericana, Buenos Aires, 2012)

Bauman, Zygmunt, *Modernity and the Holocaust* (Polity Press, Cambridge, 2017)

—*Globalization: The Human Consequences* (Polity Press, Cambridge, 2017)

— *Identity: Conversations with Benedetto Vecchi* (Polity Press, Cambridge, 2013)

— *Liquid Modernity* (Polity Press, Cambridge, 2017)

— *Liquid Times: Living in an Age of Uncertainty* (Polity Press, Cambridge, 2016)

Beck, Peter, *The Falkland Islands as an International Problem* (Routledge, London, 1988)

Beeson, Trevor, and Jenny Pearce, *A Vision of Hope: The Churches and Change in Latin America* (Collins, London, 1984)

Begley, Jon, 'The Literature of the Falklands/Malvinas War', *The Edinburgh Companion to Twentieth-Century British and American War Literature* (Edinburgh University Press, Edinburgh, 2012)

Beiner, Guy, *Forgetful Remembrance: Social Forgetting and Vernacular Historiography of a Rebellion in Ulster* (Oxford University Press, Oxford and New York, 2018)

— *Remembering the Year of the French: Irish Folk History and Social Memory* (University of Wisconsin Press, Madison, 2007)

— 'A Short History of Irish Memory in the Long Twentieth Century', in Thomas Bartlett (ed.), *The Cambridge History of Ireland, 1880 to the Present* (Cambridge University Press, Cambridge, 2018), pp. 708–25

— 'Ritual, Identity and Nation: When the Historian Becomes the High Priest of Commemoration', in Richard Grayson and Feargal McGarry, *Remembering 1916: The Easter Rising, the Somme and the Politics of Memory in Ireland* (Cambridge University Press, Cambridge, 2016), pp. 24–42

Bellotta, Araceli, 'El Cura de las Villas', *Todo es Historia* (Buenos Aires), no. 391, August 1997, pp. 8–26

Bergoglio, Jorge Mario, and Abraham Skorka, *On Heaven and Earth: Pope Francis on Faith, Family and the Church in the 21st Century* (Bloomsbury, London, 2010)

Berryman, Philip, *The Religious Roots of Rebellion: Christians in the Central American Revolutions* (SCM Press, London, 1984)

Bethell, Leslie (ed.), *Argentina since Independence* (Cambridge University Press, Cambridge, 1963)

Bew, Paul, *Land and the National Question in Ireland, 1858–82* (Humanities Press, Atlantic Highlands, NJ, 1979)

Bielenberg, Andy, *The Irish Diaspora* (Routledge, London, 2015)

Bigo, Piero, *The Church and Third World Revolution* (Orbis, Maryknoll, New York, 1974)

Bilbao, Lucas, and Ariel Lede, *Profeta del Genocidio: El Vicariato Castrense y los Diarios del Obispo Bonamín en la Última Dictator* (Editorial Sudamericana, Buenos Aires, 2016)

Blasier, Cole, *The Hovering Giant: US Responses to Revolutionary Change in Latin America* (University of Pittsburg Press, Pittsburg, 1976)

— *The Giant's Rival: The USSR and Latin America* (Pittsburg University Press, Pittsburg, 1983)

Borges, Jorge Luis, *On Argentina* (Penguin, London, 2010)

Bowman, John, *De Valera and the Ulster Question, 1917–1973* (Oxford University Press, Oxford, 1989)

Boyce, D. George, *The Falklands War* (Palgrave Macmillan, New York, 2005)

Boyle, Valerie (ed.), *A South American Adventure: Letters from George Reid, 1867–1870* (Valerie Boyle, London, 1999)

Braylan, Marisa, et al., *Report on Anti-Semitism in Argentina, 1998* (DAIA, Buenos Aires, n.d.)

Bresci, Domingo, *Historia de un Compromiso: MSTM. A Cincuenta Años del Movimiento de Sacerdotes para el Tercer Mundo. Sociedad y Religión. Los Desafíos Actuales* (GES Comunicación, Buenos Aires, 2018)

Broderick, Eugene, *John Hearne: Architect of the 1937 Constitution of Ireland* (Irish Academic Press, Dublin, 2017)

Brown, Michael E., et al. (eds), *The Perils of Anarchy: Contemporary Realism and International Security* (The MIT Press, Cambridge, MA, 1995)

Brown, Seyom, *Faces of Power: Constancy and Change in United States Foreign Policy from Truman to Obama* (Columbia University Press, New York, 2015)

Bulfin, William, *Tales of the Pampas* (T. Fisher Unwin, London, 1902); bilingual edition with introduction by Susan Wilkinson (LOLA, Buenos Aires, 1997); revised edition with an introduction by Juan José Delaney (Corregidor, Buenos Aires, 2014)

— *Rambles in Éirinn* (M.H. Gill, Dublin and Waterford, 1907)

Bulmer-Thomas, Victor (ed.), *Britain and Latin America: A Changing Relationship* (The Royal Institute of International Affairs and Cambridge University Press, Cambridge, 1989)

Burdick, Michael A., *For God and the Fatherland: Religion and Politics in Argentina* (State University of New York Press, Albany, 1995)

Burns, Jimmy, *Francis: Pope of Good Promise* (Constable, London, 2016)

— *Maradona: The Hand of God* (Bloomsbury Publishing, London, 2021)

— *The Land that Lost Its Heroes: How Argentina Lost the Falklands War* (Bloomsbury, London, 2002)

Burns, William J., *The Back Channel: American Diplomacy in a Disordered World* (Hurst & Co., London, 2019)

Büsser, Carlos, *Malvinas, la Guerra Inconclusa* (Ediciones Fernández Reguera, Buenos Aires, 1987)

Caimari, Lila M., *Perón y la Iglesia Católica: Religión, Estado y Sociedad en la Argentina (1943–1955)* (Ariel Historia, Buenos Aires, 1994)

Calamai, Enrico, *Niente Asilo Politico: Diplomazia, Diritti Umani e Desaparecidos* (Feltrinelli, Milan, 2016)

Campbell, Malcolm, *Ireland's New Worlds: Immigrants, Politics, and Society in the United States and Australia, 1915–1922* (University of Wisconsin Press, Madison, 2008)

Canning, Anthony M., SCA, 'South America', in Patrick Corish (ed.), *A History of Irish Catholicism*, vol. 6 (Gill & Macmillan, Dublin, 1971), pp. 1–27

Canning, Paul, *British Policy towards Ireland, 1921–1941* (Clarendon Press, Oxford, 1985)

Carroll, Francis M., *Money for Ireland: Finance, Diplomacy, Politics and the First Dáil Éireann Loans, 1919–1936* (Praeger, Westport, 2002)

— *The American Commission on Irish Independence, 1919: The Diary, Correspondence, and Report* (Irish Manuscripts Commission, Dublin, 1985)

— *America and the Making of an Independent Ireland* (New York University Press, New York, 2021)

Carroll, Joseph T., *Ireland in the War Years, 1939–1945* (David & Charles, Newton Abbot, 1975)

Cassidy, Sheila, *Audacity to Believe* (Darton, Longman & Todd, London, 2011)

Catoggio, María Soledad, *Los Desaparecidos de la Iglesia: El Clero Contestatario Frente a la Dictadura* (Siglo Veintiuno Ediciones, Buenos Aires, 2016)

Cavanaugh, William T., *Torture and Eucharist* (Blackwell Publishing Ltd., Oxford, 1998)

Cleary, Edward L., *Crisis and Change: The Church in Latin America Today* (Orbis, Maryknoll, New York, 1985)

Cleary, Joe, and Claire Connolly (eds), *The Cambridge Companion to Modern Irish Culture* (Cambridge University Press, Cambridge, 2006)

Coghlan, Eduardo A., *Los Irlandeses en la Argentina: Su Actuación y Descendencia* (no publisher, Buenos Aires, 1987)

— *Andanzas de un Irlandés en el Campo Porteño 1845–1864* (Ediciones Culturales Argentinas, Buenos Aires, 1981)

— *El Aporte de los Irlandeses a la Formación de la Nación Argentina* (A. Casares, Buenos Aires, 1982)

— 'Orígenes y Evolución de la Colectividad Hiberno-Argentina', *The Southern Cross*, centenary edition, 1975

Collier, Simon, 'The First Falklands War? Argentine Attitudes', *International Affairs*, vol. 59, no. 3, summer 1983, pp. 457–64

Collins, Neil, *The Splendid Cause: The Missionary Society of St Columbanus, 1916–1954* (Columba Press, Dublin, 2009)

Comblin, José, *The Church and the National Security State* (Orbis, Maryknoll, New York, 1979)

CONADEP (Comisión Nacional sobre la Desaparición de Personas / National Commission on the Disappearance of Persons), *Nunca Más* (Buenos Aires, 1984)

Coogan, Tim Pat, *Wherever Green Is Worn: The Story of the Irish Diaspora* (Palgrave, London, 2001)

— *Éamon de Valera: The Man Who Was Ireland* (HarperCollins, New York, 1995)

Costello, Gerald, M*ission to Latin America: The Successes and Failures of a Twentieth-Century Crusade* (Orbis, Maryknoll, New York, 1979)

Cotter, Gertrude, 'Britain and Perón's Argentina, 1946–1955', MA thesis, University College Cork, 1989

Cox, David [foreword by Robert J. Cox], *Dirty Secrets, Dirty War: Buenos Aires, Argentina, 1976–1983: The Exile of Editor Robert J. Cox* (Evening Post Publishing Company, Charleston, SC, with Joggling Board Press, 2008)

Crassweller, Robert D., *Perón and the Enigmas of Argentina* (W.W. Norton, New York, 1987)

Crawford, Kathryn Lee, 'Due Obedience and the Rights of Victims: Argentina's Transition to Democracy', *Human Rights Quarterly*, vol. 12, no. 1, February 1990, pp. 17–52

Crowley, John, Donal Ó Drisceoil and Mike Murphy, *Atlas of the Irish Revolution* (Cork University Press, Cork, 2017)

— *Atlas of the Great Irish Famine, 1845–52* (Cork University Press, Cork, 2012)

Cruset, María Eugenia, *Nacionalismos y Diásporas: Los Casos Vasco e Irlandés en Argentina, 1862–1922* (Ediciones Lauburu, La Plata, 2015)

DAIA (Delegación de Asociaciones Israelitas Argentinas), *Proyecto Testimonio: Revelaciones de los Archivos Argentinos sobre la Política Oficial en la Era Nazi-Fascista*, vols. I & II (Planeta, Buenos Aires, 1998)

Daly, Mary E., *Sixties Ireland: Reshaping the Economy, State and Society, 1957–1973* (Cambridge University Press, Cambridge, 2016)

— *Famine in Ireland* (Dublin Historical Association, Dundalgan Press, 1986)

— *Industrial Development and Irish National Identity, 1922–1939* (Syracuse University Press, Syracuse, NY, 1992)

Dávid, Guillermo (ed.), *Rodolfo Walsh* (Biblioteca Nacional Mariano Moreno, Buenos Aires, 2017) [catálogo] de Antokoletz, María Adela (Hija), *Desovillando la Historia* (Ediciones Baobab, Buenos Aires, 2014)

Debat, Alejandro, and Luis Lorenzano, *The Malvinas and the End of Military Rule* (Verso Books, London, 1982)

de Courcy Ireland, John, *The Admiral from Mayo: A Life of Almirante William Brown of Foxford, Father of the Argentine Navy* (E. Burke, Dublin, 1995)

de Cox, Maud Daverio, *Testimonios del Antiguo Pueblo de San Martín: Las Costumbres, la Educación, los 'Ingleses' y el 'Progreso'* (Prosa Editores, Buenos Aires, 2017)

de Eguileor, Jorge Ochoa, and Eduardo Valdés, *¿Dónde Durmieron Nuestros Abuelos? Los Hoteles de Inmigrantes en la Capital Federal* (Fundación Urbe, Buenos Aires, 1991)

de Janvry, Alain, *The Agrarian Question and Reformism in Latin America* (Johns Hopkins University Press, Baltimore and London, 1981)

DeLaney, Jeane, *Identity and Nationalism in Modern Argentina: Defending the True Nation* (University of Notre Dame Press, Notre Dame, 2020)

Delaney, Juan José, *Marco Denevi y la Sacra Ceremonia de la Escritura: Una Biografía Literaria* (Corregidor, Buenos Aires, 2006)

— *What, Che? Integration, Adaptation and Assimilation of the Irish-Argentine Community through its Language and Literature* (USAL, Buenos Aires, 2017)

— *Borges and Irish Writing* (Ediciones El Gato Negro: Embajada de Irlanda, Buenos Aires, 2018)

— 'La Diáspora Irlandesa en Argentina', *Todo es Historia* (Buenos Aires), vol. 39, no. 471, October 2006, pp. 6–29

— 'Lengua y Literatura de los Irlandeses en la Argentina', *Signos Universitarios: Revista de la Universidad del Salvador*, vol. 22, no. 39, 2003, pp. 137–54

— 'Irish Porteño Literature', in Mícheál Ó hAodha and Máirtín Ó Catháin (eds), *New Perspectives on the Irish Abroad: The Silent People?* (Lexington Books, New York, 2014), pp. 145–60

— 'Irish-Porteño Identity in Rodolfo J. Walsh's Writing' [manuscript], in *Memoria de Theophilus Flynn* (Corregidor, Buenos Aires, 2012)

— *Tréboles del Sur* (Grupo Editorial Latinoamericano, Buenos Aires, 1994)

— *Papeles del Desierto, 1974–2004* (Ediciones el Gato Negro, Buenos Aires, 2012)

— *Moira Sullivan* (Corregidor, Buenos Aires, 1999)

— *La carcajada: Cuentos* (Literamérica, Buenos Aires, 1974)

de la Poer Beresford, Marcus, *Marshal William Carr Beresford* (Irish Academic Press, Dublin 2019)

del Carril, Mario, *La Vida de Emilio Mignone: Justicia, Catolicismo y Derechos Humanos* [with introduction by Hilda Sábato] (Emecé, Buenos Aires, 2011

de Meneses, Filipe Ribeiro, 'Investigating Portugal, Salazar and the New State: The Work of the Irish Legation in Lisbon, 1942–1945', *Contemporary European History*, vol. 11, no. 3, August 2002, pp. 391–408

— 'Meeting Salazar: Irish Dignitaries and Diplomats in Portugal, 1942–60', *Archivium Hibernicum*, vol. 64, 2011, pp. 323–48

Devoto, Fernando, *Historia de la Inmigración en la Argentina* (Editorial Sudamericana, Buenos Aires, 2009)

Donnelly, James S. Jr., *The Land and the People of Nineteenth-Century Cork: The Rural Economy and the Land Question* (Routledge & Kegan Paul, London, 1987)

Dooley, Terence, *The Land for the People: The Land Question in Independent Ireland* (UCD Press, Dublin, 2004)

Doorley, Michael, *Irish-American Diaspora Nationalism: The Friends of Irish Freedom, 1916–1935* (Four Courts Press, Dublin, 2005)

Dorr, Noel, *The Search for Peace in Northern Ireland: Sunningdale* (Royal Irish Academy, Dublin, 2017)

— *A Small State at the Top Table: Memories of Ireland and the UN Security Council, 1981–2* (Institute of Public Administration, Dublin, 2011)

Doyle, Aidan, *A History of the Irish Language: From the Norman Invasion to Independence* (Oxford University Press, Oxford, 2015)

Droznes, Lazaro, *Cantando como la Cigarra: Vida y Canciones de María Elena Walsh* (Unitexto, Buenos Aires, 2014)

Druliolle, Vincent, 'Remembering and Its Place in Post-Dictatorship Argentina', in Francesca Lessa and Vincent Druliolle (eds), *The Memory of State Terrorism in the Southern Cone: Argentina, Chile, and Uruguay* (Palgrave Macmillan, New York, 2011), pp. 27–9

Duhalde, Eduardo Luis, *El Estado Terrorista Argentino* (Colihue, Buenos Aires, 2013)

Dunn, Joe, *No Tigers in Africa: Recollections and Reflections on 25 Years of Radharc* (Columba Press, Dublin, 1986)

— *No Lions in the Hierarchy: An Anthology of Sorts* (Columba Press, Dublin 1994)

— *No Vipers in the Vatican: A Second Anthology of Sorts* (Columba Press, Dublin, 1996)

Dunphy, Eamon, *The Rocky Road* (Penguin, Dublin, 2013)

Dupuy, André, *La Diplomatie du Saint Siège après le IIe Concile du Vatican: Le Pontificat de Paul VI 1963–1978* (Téqui, Paris, no date)

Dussel, Enrique, *Historia de la Iglesia en América Latina: Coloniaje y liberación, 1492–1983* (Mundo Negro, Mexico, DF, 1983) [English translation: *A History of the Church in Latin America: Colonialism to Liberalism* (William B. Eerdmann, Grand Rapids, 1981)]

— *History and the Theology of Liberation: A Latin American Perspective* (Orbis, Maryknoll, New York, 1976)

Dwyer, T. Ryle, *Irish Neutrality and the USA, 1939–1947* (Gill & Macmillan, Dublin, 1977)

— *Strained Relations: Ireland at Peace and the USA at War, 1941–1945* (Gill & Macmillan, Dublin, 1988)

— *Guests of the State: The Story of Allied and Axis Servicemen Interned in Ireland during the Second World War* (Brandon, Dingle, 1994)

— *Big Fellow, Long Fellow: A Joint Biography of Collins and de Valera* (Gill & Macmillan, Dublin 1999)

Eddy, Paul, and *Sunday Times* Insight Team, *Falklands War* (Andre Deutsch, London, 1982)

Espacio Memoria y Derechos Humanos [ex-ESMA], *Donde Hubo Muerte, Hoy Hay Vida* (ex-ESMA, Buenos Aires, 2016)

Esparza, Marcia, and Carla de Ycata, *Remembering the Rescuers of Victims of Human Rights Crimes in Latin America* (Lexington Books, Lanham, MD, 2016)

— 'Locations and Identities in Irish Diasporic Narratives', *Hungarian Journal of English and American Studies (HJEAS)*, vol. 10, nos. 1/2, 2004, pp. 341–52

Esteban Semino Museo Ediciones, 'Saint Michael's Estancia' [Healy family] (Gráfica Infinito, Las Heras, 2010)

Evans, Richard J., *The Hitler Conspiracies* (Oxford University Press, New York, 2020)

Facio, Sara, *María Elena Walsh* (La Azotea, Buenos Aires, 1999)

Fanning, Bryan, *Histories of the Irish Future* (Bloomsbury Academic, London, 2015)

Fanning, Charles, *New Perspectives on the Irish Diaspora* (Southern Illinois University Press, Carbondale, 2000)

Fanning, Ronan, *Fatal Path: British Government and Irish Revolution 1910–1922* (Faber & Faber, London, 2013)

— *Éamon de Valera: A Will to Power* (Harvard University Press, Cambridge, MA, 2016)

— with Michael Lillis, *The Lives of Eliza Lynch: Scandal and Courage* (Gill & Macmillan, Dublin, 2009)

— 'Irish Neutrality: An Historical Review', *Irish Studies in International Affairs*, vol. 1, no. 3, 1982, pp. 27–38

— 'The United States and Irish Participation in NATO: The Debate of 1950', *Irish Studies in International Affairs*, vol. 1, no. 1, 1979, pp. 39–48

Fanning, Tim, *Paisanos: The Forgotten Irish Who Changed the Face of Latin America* (Gill Books, Dublin, 2016) [Spanish translation: *Paisanos: Los Irlandes Olvidados que Cambiaron la Faz de Latinoamérica* (Editorial Sudamericana, Buenos Aires, 2017)

— *Don Juan O'Brien: An Irish Adventurer in Nineteenth-Century South America* (Cork University Press, Cork, 2020)

Farrell, Patricia María Gaudino, *La Asociación Católica Irlandesa y los Irlandeses en la Argentina* (Asociación Católica Irlandesa, Buenos Aires, 2009)

Feierstein, Ricardo, *Historia de los Judíos Argentinos* (Galerna, Buenos Aires, 2006)

Feitlowitz, Marguerite, *A Lexicon of Terror: Argentina and the Legacies of Torture* (Oxford University Press, Oxford, 2011)

Ferrari, Jorge N., 'Las "Latas" de Esquila', *Círculo Numismático de Rosario*, boletín no. 4, 1974, pp. 3–33

Ferriter, Diarmaid, *Occasions of Sin: Sex and Society in Modern Ireland* (Profile Books, London, 2012)

— *Judging Dev: A Reassessment of the Life and Legacy of Éamon de Valera* (Royal Irish Academy, Dublin, 2007)

— *Between Two Hells: The Irish Civil War* (Profile Books, London, 2021)

Finchelstein, Federico, *The Ideological Origins of the Dirty War: Fascism, Populism, and Dictatorship in Twentieth-Century Argentina* (Oxford University Press, Oxford and New York, 2014)

Fishburn, Evelyn, 'The Concept of "Civilization and Barbarism" in Sarmiento's "Facundo": A Reappraisal', *Ibero-Amerikanisches Archiv*, vol. 5, no. 4, 1979, pp. 301–8, www.jstor.org/stable/43392270

FitzGerald, Garret, *All in a Life. Garret FitzGerald: An Autobiography* (Gill & Macmillan, Dublin, 1991)

Fitzgerald, Maurice, *Protectionism to Liberalisation: Ireland and the EEC, 1957 to 1966* (Ashgate, Aldershot, 2000)

Fitzpatrick, David, *Oceans of Consolation: Personal Accounts of Irish Migration to Australia* (Cornell University Press, Ithaca and London, 1994)

Foley, Tadhg, et al. (eds), *Ireland and India: Colonies, Culture and Empire* (Irish Academic Press, Dublin, 2006)

Forristal, Desmond, *The Bridge at Lo Wu: A Life of Sr Eamonn O'Sullivan* (Veritas, Dublin, 1987)

Fortuna, Victoria, *Moving Otherwise: Dance, Violence, and Memory in Buenos Aires* (Oxford University Press, Oxford, 2019)

Foster, Roy, *Modern Ireland 1600–1972* (Allen Lane, London, 1988)

— *W.B. Yeats: A Life. The Apprentice Mage, 1865–1914*, vol. I (Oxford University Press, Oxford, 1997)

Fox, Christopher, *Painted Butterflies: Memories of a Missionary* (Choice Publishing, Drogheda, 2015)

Freedman, Lawrence, *The Official History of the Falklands Campaign*, vols I & II (Routledge, London, 2007)

— 'Bridgehead Revisited: The Literature of the Falklands', *International Affairs*, vol. 59, no. 3, summer 1983, pp. 445–52

— with Virginia Gamba-Stonehouse, *Signals of War: The Falklands Conflict of 1982* (Princeton University Press, Princeton, New Jersey, 2016)

Fukuyama, Francis, *The End of History and the Last Man* (Free Press, New York, 1992)

Gageby, Douglas, *The Last Secretary General: Seán Lester and the League of Nations* (Town House Dublin, Dublin, 1999)

Galazzi, Mariano, *Los Irlandeses en Sudamérica* (Elaleph, Buenos Aires, 2009)

Galeano, Eduardo, *Open Veins in Latin America: Five Centuries of the Pillage of a Continent* (Monthly Review Press, New York and London, 1973)

Gatti, Gabriel, *Surviving Forced Disappearance in Argentina and Uruguay: Identity and Meaning* (Palgrave Macmillan, New York, 2014)

Gearty, R.J., 'A Short Account of Irish Catholic Action in Argentina', in Patrick Boylan (ed.), *Thirty-First International Eucharistic Congress, Dublin: Section Meeting Papers and Addresses*, vol. 2 (Dublin, 1932)

Geary, Laurence M., and Andrew McCarthy (eds), *Ireland, Australia and New Zealand: History, Politics and Culture* (Irish Academic Press, Dublin, 2008)

Gerchunoff, Alberto, *The Jewish Gauchos of the Pampas* (University of New Mexico Press, Albuquerque, 1998) [made into a film in 1975, *Los Gauchos Judíos*, directed by Juan José Jusid]

Gerchunoff, Pablo, *La Caída 1955* (Memoria Crítica, Buenos Aires, 2018)

Gheerbrant, Alain, *The Rebel Church in Latin America* (Penguin, London, 1974)

Gibney, John, Michael Kennedy and Kate O'Malley, *Ireland: A Voice among the Nations* (Royal Irish Academy, Dublin, 2019)

Gilbert, Dennis, *The Oligarchy and the Old Regime in Latin America, 1880–1970* (Rowman & Littlefield, Lanham, MD, and London, 2017)

Gill, Anthony, *Rendering unto Caesar: The Catholic Church and the State in Latin America* (University of Chicago Press, Chicago, 1998)

Gillespie, Richard, *Soldiers of Perón: Argentina's Montoneros* (Oxford University Press, Oxford, 1982)

Gilroy, Paul, *Black Atlantic: Modernity and Double Consciousness* (Harvard University Press, Harvard, 1993)

— *'There Ain't no Black in the Union Jack': The Cultural Politics of Race and Nation* (Routledge, London, 2002)

— *Postcolonial Melancholia* (Columbia University Press, New York, 2005)

Girvin, Brian, *The Emergency: Neutral Ireland 1939–1945* (Macmillan, London, 2006)

Gompert, David C., Hans Binnendijk and Bonny Lin, *Blinders, Blunders, and Wars: What America and China Can Learn* (RAND Corporation, New York, 2014)

Goñi, Uki, *The Real Odessa: How Perón Brought the Nazi War Criminals to Argentina* (Granta Books, London, 2002)

Gorini, Ulises, *La Rebelión de las Madres: Historia de las Madres de Plaza de Mayo, 1976–1983*, vol. I (Ediciones Biblioteca Nacional, Buenos Aires, 2015)

— *La otra Lucha: Historia de las Madres de Plaza de Mayo, 1983–1986*, vol. II (Ediciones Biblioteca Nacional, Buenos Aires, 2015)

Gott, Richard, *Guerrilla Movements in Latin America* (Nelson, London, 1970)

Graham-Yooll, Andrew, *Forgotten Colony: A History of the English-Speaking Communities in Argentina* (Hutchinson, London, 1981)

— *State of Fear: Memories of Argentina's Nightmare* (Hippocrene Books, London, 1986)

— *Matter of Fear: Portrait of an Argentinian Exile* (L. Hill, Westport, CT, 1981)

— *Committed Observer: Memoirs of a Journalist* (J. Libbey, London, 1995)

— *Goodbye Buenos Aires: Novela* (Shoestring Press, Nottingham, 1999)

Gray, Breda, *Women and the Irish Diaspora* (Routledge, London, 2004)

Gregory, Ian N., Niall A. Cunningham, C.D. Lloyd, Ian G. Shuttleworth and Paul S. Ell (eds), *Troubled Geographies: A Spatial History of Religion and Society in Ireland* (Indiana University Press, Bloomington, 2013)

Gribben, Arthur, *The Great Famine and the Irish Diaspora in America* (University of Massachusetts Press, Amherst, 1999)

Guest, Iain, *Behind Argentina's Dirty War against Human Rights and the United Nations* (University of Pennsylvania Press, Philadelphia, 1990)

Guido, Beatriz, *El Incendio y las Vísperas* (Editorial Losada, Buenos Aires, 1964)

Güiraldes, Ricardo, *Don Segundo Sombra* (GZ Editores, Buenos Aires, 2008)

Gustafson, Lowell S., *The Sovereignty Dispute over the Falkland (Malvinas) Islands* (Oxford University Press, New York, 1988)

Gutiérrez, Gustavo, *Las Casas: In Search of the Poor of Jesus Christ* (Orbis, Maryknoll, New York, 1993)

— *God of Life* (Orbis, Maryknoll, New York, 1991)

— *A Theology of Liberation History, Politics and Salvation* (Orbis, Maryknoll, New York, 1973)

Hachey, Thomas E., and Lawrence J. McCaffrey (eds), *Perspectives on Irish Nationalism* (University Press of Kentucky, Lexington, 1989)

Hall, Patricia Ann (ed.), *The Oxford Handbook of Music Censorship* (Oxford University Press, Oxford, 2018)

Hand, Paul, '"This Is Not a Place for Delicate or Nervous or Impatient Diplomats": The Irish Legation in Perón's Argentina, 1948–55', *Irish Studies in International Affairs*, vol. 16, 2005, pp. 175–92

Hannigan, Dave, *De Valera in America: The Rebel President's 1919 Campaign* (The O'Brien Press, Dublin, 2008)

Hanon, Maxine, *Diccionario de Británicos en Buenos Aires* [primera época] (Gutten Press, Buenos Aires, 2005)

Harkness, David W., *Restless Dominion: The Irish Free State and the British Commonwealth of Nations, 1921–31* (Gill & Macmillan, Dublin, 1969)

Harman, Justin, and Verónica Repetti, *Irlandeses en la Ciudad de Buenos Aires* (Asociación Civil Rumbo Sur, Buenos Aires, 2018)

Harris, Mary N., 'Irish Historical Writing on Latin America and on Irish Links with Latin America', in Csaba Lévai (ed.), *Europe and the World in European Historiography* (Edizioni Plus, Università di Pisa, Pisa, Italy, 2006)

— 'Irish Images of Religious Conflict in Mexico in the 1920s', in Mary N. Harris (ed.), *Sights and Insights: Interactive Images of Europe and the Wider World* (Edizioni Plus, Università di Pisa, Pisa, Italy, 2007)

— with Csaba Lévai, *Europe and Its Empires* (Edizioni Plus, Università di Pisa, Pisa, Italy, 2008)

Hastings, Max, and Simon Jenkins, *The Battle for the Falklands* (Pan Books, London, 1983)

Healy, Claire, '"Foreigners of this Kind": Chilean Refugees in Ireland, 1973–1990', *Society for Irish Latin American Studies*, 2006, https://www.irlandeses.org/0610healy1.htm

Henderson, Nicholas, *Mandarin: The Diaries of an Ambassador* (Weidenfeld & Nicolson, London, 1994)

Hersh, Seymour M., *The Price of Power: Kissinger in the Nixon White House* (Summit Books, New York, 1983)

Hickey, Raymond, and Carolina P. Amador-Moreno (eds), *Irish Identities: Sociolinguistic Perspectives* (De Gruyter Mouton, New York, 2020)

Higgins, Michael D., *Renewing the Republic* (Liberties Press, Dublin, 2012)

— 'Reflecting on Irish Migrations: Some Issues for the Social Sciences', *American Journal of Irish Studies*, vol. 9, 2012, pp. 139–50

— 'Liam O'Flaherty and Peadar O'Donnell: Images of Rural Community', *The Crane Bag*, vol. 9, no. 1, 1985, pp. 41–8

— and John P. Gibbons, 'Shopkeeper-Graziers and Land Agitation in Ireland, 1895–1900', in P.J. Drudy (ed.), *Ireland: Land, Politics and People* (Cambridge University Press, Cambridge, 1983), pp. 93–118

— *When Ideas Matter: Speeches for an Ethical Republic* (Head of Zeus, London, 2016)

— *Renewing the Republic* (Liberties Press, Dublin, 2011)

— *Causes for Concern: Irish Politics, Culture and Society* (Liberties Press, Dublin, 2007)

— *The Betrayal* (Salmon, Galway, 1990)

— *The Season of Fire* (Brandon, Dingle, 1993)

— *An Arid Season* (New Island Books, Dublin, 2004)

— *New and Selected Poems* (Liberties Press, Dublin, 2011)

— 'The Prophets Are Weeping', poem published in *The Galway Review*, February 2015

— 'Of Saturdays Made Holy', poem published on 1 May 2020, https://president.ie/en/diary/details/president-publishes-may-day-poem

Hodges, Donald C., *Argentina 1943–1976: The National Revolution and Resistance* (University of New Mexico Press, Albuquerque, 1976)

Hogan, Edmund, *The Irish Missionary Movement: A Historical Survey, 1830–1980* (Gill & Macmillan, Dublin, 1992)

— *Catholic Missionaries and Liberia* (Cork University Press, Cork, 1981)

Holfter, Gisela, and Bettina Migge (eds), *Ireland in the European Eye* (Royal Irish Academy, Dublin, 2019)

Holmes, Michael, and Denis Holmes (eds), *Ireland and India: Connections, Comparisons, Contrasts* (Folens, Dublin, 1997)

Hora, Roy, *The Landowners of the Argentine Pampas: A Social and Political History, 1860–1945* (Oxford University Press, Oxford, 2001)

Houtard, François, and Emile Pin, *The Church and the Latin American Revolution* (Sheed & Ward, New York, 1965)

Howe, Stephen, *Ireland and Empire: Colonial Legacies in Irish History and Culture* (Oxford University Press, Oxford, 2000)

Hoy, Suellen, and Margaret MacCurtain, *From Dublin to New Orleans: The Journey of Nora and Alice* (Attic Press, Dublin, 1994)

Hull, Mark, *Irish Secrets: German Espionage in Ireland, 1939–45* (Irish Academic Press, Dublin and Portland OR, 2003)

Humphreys, R.A. (ed.), *The Detached Recollections of General D.F. O'Leary 1800–1854* (Athlone Press, London, 1969)

Ignatiev, Noel, *How the Irish Became White* (Routledge, New York and London, 1995)

Izarra, Laura, *Narrativas de la Diáspora Irlandesa bajo la Cruz del Sur* (Corregidor, Buenos Aires, 2010)

— 'Rumours of "The Insurrection in Dublin" across the South Atlantic', *ABEI Journal*, no. 18, November 2016 [São Paulo, Brazil], pp. 25–40

— 'Reinventing Brazil: New Readings and Renewal in the Narratives of Irish Travellers', *Irish Migration Studies in Latin America*, vol. 4, no. 3, July 2006

Jakubs, Deborah, 'The Anglo-Argentines: Work, Family and Identity, 1860–1914', in Oliver Marshall, *English-Speaking Communities in Latin America* (St Martin's Press, New York, 2000), pp. 135–57

James, Daniel, *Resistance and Integration: Peronism and the Argentine Working Class, 1946–1976* (Cambridge University Press, Cambridge, 1988)

Janzen, Ignacio González, *La Triple A: AAA* (Editorial Contrapunto, Buenos Aires, 1986)

Jelin, Elizabeth, *La Lucha por el Pasado: Como Construimos la Memoria Social* (Siglo Veintiuno Editores, Buenos Aires, 2017)

Jones, Dick, *Welsh Settlement in Patagonia: A Brief Guide* (Dick Jones, Trelew, 1996)

Jordan, Anthony J., *Major John MacBride, 1865–1916* (Westport Historical Society, Westport, CT, 1991)

Karush, Matthew B., and Oscar Chamosa (eds), *The New Cultural History of Peronism: Power and Identity in Mid-Twentieth-Century Argentina* (Duke University Press, Durham and London, 2010)

Kearns, Kevin C., *Ireland's Arctic Siege: The Big Freeze of 1947* (Gill & Macmillan, Dublin, 2011)

Keatinge, Patrick, *The Formulation of Irish Foreign Policy* (Institute of Public Administration, Dublin, 1973)

— *A Place among the Nations* (Institute of Public Administration, Dublin, 1978)

— *A Singular Stance: Irish Neutrality in the 1980s* (Institute of Public Administration, Dublin, 1984)

Kehoe Wilson, Gloria, *Pico de Paloma y otros Escritos* (Corregidor, Buenos Aires, 2004)

Kelly, David, *The Ruling Few, or the Human Background to Diplomacy* (Hollis & Carter, London, 1952)

Kelly, Helen, *Irish 'Ingleses': The Irish Immigrant Experience in Argentina, 1840–1920* (Irish Academic Press, Dublin, 2009)

Kelly, Stephen, *'A Failed Political Entity': Charles Haughey and the Northern Ireland Question, 1945–1992* (Merrion Press, Dublin, 2016)

Kennedy, Michael, *Ireland and the League of Nations, 1919–1946* (Four Courts Press, Dublin, 1996)

— 'Seán (John Ernest) Lester', *Dictionary of Irish Biography* (Cambridge University Press, Cambridge, 2009), pp. 469–71

— '"Publishing a Secret History": The Documents on Irish Foreign Policy Project', *Irish Studies in International Affairs*, vol. 9, 1998, pp. 103–17

— 'Establishing and Operating a Diplomatic Documents Publishing Project', *Irish Studies in International Affairs*, vol. 15, 2004, pp. 191–204

— '"In Spite of All Impediments": The Early Years of the Irish Diplomatic Service', *History Ireland*, vol. 7, no. 1, 1999, pp. 18–21

— '"Nobody Knows and Ever Shall Know from Me That I Have Written It": Joseph Walshe, Éamon de Valera and the Execution of Irish Foreign Policy, 1932–8', *Irish Studies in International Affairs*, vol. 14, 2003, pp. 165–83

— with Deirdre McMahon (eds), *Obligations and Responsibilities: Ireland at the United Nations, 1955–2005* (Institute for Public Administration, Dublin, 2006)

— '"It Is a Disadvantage to Be Represented by a Woman": The Experiences of Women in the Irish Diplomatic Service', *Irish Studies in International Affairs*, no. 13, 2002, pp. 215–35

— '"Mr Blythe, I Think, Hears from Him Occasionally": The Experiences of Irish Diplomats in Latin America, 1919–23', in Kennedy and Joseph Skelly (eds), *Irish Foreign Policy 1919–66* (Four Courts Press, Dublin, 2000), pp. 44–6

Kenny, Colum, *The Enigma of Arthur Griffith: 'Father of Us All'* (Merrion Press, Dublin, 2020)

Kenny, Kevin, *The American Irish: A History* (Longman, New York, 2000)

— *New Directions in Irish-American History* (University of Wisconsin Press, Madison, 2003)

— *Diaspora: A Very Short History* (Oxford University Press, Oxford, 2013)

Keogh, Dermot, *La Independencia de Irlanda: La Conexión Argentina* (Ediciones Universidad del Salvador, Buenos Aires, 2016)

— (ed.), *Church and Politics in Latin America* (Macmillan, New York, 1990)

— *The Vatican, the Bishops and Irish Politics* (Cambridge University Press, Cambridge, 1986)

— *Jews in Twentieth-Century Ireland: Refugees, Antisemitism and the Holocaust* (Cork University Press, Cork, 1998)

— *Ireland and the Vatican: The Politics and Diplomacy of Church–State Relations* (Cork University Press, Cork, 1995)

— with Mervyn O'Driscoll (eds), *Ireland in World War Two: Diplomacy and Survival* (Mercier Press, Cork, 2004)

— *Ireland and Europe 1919–1939: A Diplomatic and Political History* (Hibernian University Press, Cork and Dublin, 1990)

— *Twentieth-Century Ireland: Revolution and State Building* (Gill & Macmillan, Dublin, 1994)

— with Andrew McCarthy, *The Making of the Irish Constitution 1937: Bunreacht na hÉireann* (Mercier Press, Cork 2007)

— 'The Constitutional Revolution: An Analysis of the Making of the Constitution', in Frank Litton (ed.), *The Constitution of Ireland, 1937–1987*, a special issue of *Administration*, vol. 35, no. 4, 1987, pp. 4–83

— 'Éamon de Valera and Hitler: An Analysis of International Reaction to the Visit to the German Minister, May 1945', *Irish Studies in International Affairs*, vol. 3, no. 1, 1989, pp. 69–92

— 'Origins of Irish Diplomacy in Europe, 1919–1921', *Études Irlandaises*, no. 7, December 1982, pp. 145–64

— 'The Treaty Split and the Paris Irish Race Convention', *Études Irlandaises*, no. 12, December 1987, pp. 165–70

— (ed.), *Central America, Human Rights and US Foreign Policy* (Hibernian University Press, Cork and Dublin, 1985)

— (ed.), *Witness to the Truth: Church and Dictatorship in Latin America* (Hibernian University Press, Cork and Dublin, 1989)

— 'Argentina and the Falklands (Malvinas): The Irish Connection', in Alastair Hennessy and J. King (eds), *The Land that England Lost: Argentina and Britain, a Special Relationship* (I.B. Tauris, London, 1992)

— 'El Salvador: Tragédia en El Cafetal', *Historia 16*, año VI, no. 59, 1981, pp. 11–22

— 'El Salvador and the United States', *Millennium: Journal of International Studies*, vol. 13, no. 2, summer 1984, pp. 153–83

— 'Mannix, Memory and Irish Independence', in Val Noone and Rachel Naughton (eds), *Daniel Mannix: His Legacy* (Melbourne Diocesan Historical Commission, Melbourne, 2014), pp. 35–94

Keogh, Niall, *Con Cremin* (Mercier Press, Cork and Dublin, 2006)

Keown, Gerard, *First of the Small Nations: The Beginnings of Irish Foreign Policy in the Inter-War Years, 1919–1932* (Oxford University Press, Oxford, 2016)

— 'The Irish Race Conference, 1922, Reconsidered', *Irish Historical Studies*, vol. 32, no. 127, 2001, pp. 365–76

Kiberd, Declan, *Inventing Ireland: The Literature of the Modern Nation* (Jonathan Cape, London, 1995)

— *After Ireland: Writing the Nation from Beckett to the Present* (Harvard University Press, Harvard, 2018)

— *Irish Classics* (Harvard University Press, Harvard, 2001)

— with P.J. Mathews, *Handbook of the Irish Revival: An Anthology of Irish Cultural and Political Writings 1891–1922* (Abbey Theatre Press, Dublin, 2015)

Kiernan, Colm, *Ireland and Australia* (Angus & Robertson, North Ryde, New South Wales, 1984)

Kiernan, Sergio, *Delirios Argentinos: Las Ideas más Extrañas de Nuestra Política* (Marea, Buenos Aires, 2006)

Kildea, Jeff, *Anzacs and Ireland* (University of New South Wales Press and Cork University Press, Sydney and Cork, 2013)

Kimel, Eduardo Gabriel, *La Masacre de San Patricio* (Ediciones Dialéctica, Buenos Aires, n.d.) [Prólogo de Pérez Esquivel]

Kirby, Peadar, *Lessons in Liberation* (Dominican Publications, Dublin, 1981)

— *Ireland and Latin America: Links and Lessons* (Dominican Publications, Dublin, 1992)

— with Barry Cannon, *Civil Society and the State in Left-led Latin America: Challenges and Limitations to Democratisation* (Zed Books, London, 2012)

Kirkpatrick, Jeane J., *Dictatorships and Double Standards: Rationalism and Reason in Politics* (Simon & Schuster, New York, 1982)

— *Making War to Keep Peace* (HarperCollins, New York 2007)

Konfino, Demian, *Villa 31: Historia de un Amor Invisible* (Editorial Punto de Encuentro, Buenos Aires, 2012)

Kornblum, Peter, *The Pinochet File: A Declassified Dossier on Atrocity and Accountability* (The New Press, New York, 2013)

LaFeber, Walter, *Inevitable Revolutions: The United States in Central America* (Norton, New York, 1982)

— *America, Russia, and the Cold War, 1945–1992* (McGraw-Hill, New York, 1993)

— *Panama Canal: The Crisis in Historical Perspective* (Oxford University Press, New York, 1989)

— with Lloyd C. Gardner and Thomas J. McCormick, *American Century: A History of the United States since the 1890s*

Landaburu, Roberto E., *Irlandeses, Eduardo Casey, Vida y Obra* (Fondo Editorial Mutual Venado Tuerto, 1995)

— *Irlandeses en la Pampa Gringa: Curas y Ovejeros* (Corregidor, Buenos Aires, 2006)

Landsberger, Henry A. (ed.), *The Church and Social Change in Latin America* (University of Notre Dame Press, Notre Dame, Indiana, 1970)

— *Latin American Peasant Movements* (Cornell University Press, Ithaca and London, 1969)

Larkin, Emmet, *The Historical Dimensions of Irish Catholicism* (The Catholic University of America, Washington DC, 1997)

Larraquy, Marcelo, *Recen por Él: Francisco* (Editorial Sudamericana, Buenos Aires, 2014)

Lauren, Paul Gordon, *The Evolution of International Human Rights* (University of Pennsylvania Press, Philadelphia, 1998)

Lawler Fitzgerald, Miguel, *Rumbo y Fé* (Lápiz en Mano, Buenos Aires, no date)

Leach, Daniel, *Fugitive Ireland: European Minority Nationalists and Irish Political Asylum, 1937–2008* (Four Courts Press, Dublin, 2009)

Lee, Joseph, *Ireland, 1912–1985: Politics and Society* (Cambridge University Press, Cambridge, 1989)

— *The Modernisation of Irish Society 1848–1918* (Gill & Macmillan, Dublin, 1973)

— with Marion R. Casey (eds), *Making the Irish American: History and Heritage of the Irish in the United States* (New York University Press, New York, 2007)

Leith, Ian, *Caithness to Patagonia: Distant Lands and Close Relatives* (Whittles Publishing, Dunbeath, 2016)

Lernoux, Penny, *Cry of the People: The Struggle for Human Rights in Latin America: The Catholic Church in Conflict with US Policy* (Penguin Books, New York, 1982)

Lessa, Francesca, *Memory and Transitional Justice in Argentina and Uruguay: Against Impunity* (Palgrave Macmillan, New York, 2013)

— with Vincent Druliolle, *The Memory of State Terror in the Southern Cone: Argentina, Chile, and Uruguay* (Palgrave Macmillan, New York, 2011)

Levey, Cara, *Fragile Memory, Shifting Impunity: Commemoration and Contestation in Post-Dictatorship Argentina and Uruguay* (Peter Lang, Oxford, 2016)

Levine, Daniel H., *Religion and Politics in Latin America: The Catholic Church in Venezuela and Colombia* (Princeton University Press, New Jersey, 1981)

— (ed.), *Churches and Politics in Latin America* (Sage Publications, London, 1980)

— (editor and contributor), *Religion and Political Conflict in Latin America* (University of North Carolina Press, Chapel Hill, 1986)

Lewis, Paul H., *The Crisis of Argentine Capitalism* (University of North Carolina Press, Chapel Hill and London, 1990)

Liberti, Luis O., *Monseñor Enrique Angelelli* (Editorial Guadalupe, Buenos Aires, 2005)

Lieuwen, Edwin, *Arms and Politics in Latin America* (Praeger, London and New York, 1961)

Lillis, Michael, 'Mr Haughey's Dud Exocet', Review of Noel Dorr's *A Small State at the Top Table: Memories of Ireland on the UN Security Council, 1981–82, Dublin Review of Books*, no. 98, March 2018, http://www.drb.ie/articles/mr-haugheys-dud-exocet

Limerick, Patricia Nelson, *The Legacy of Conquest: The Unbroken Past of the American West* (Norton, New York, 1988)

Livingstone, Grace, *Britain and the Dictatorships of Argentina and Chile, 1973–82* (Palgrave Macmillan, Switzerland, 2018)

Lorenz, Federico G., *Malvinas, una Guerra Argentina* (Editorial Sudamericana, Buenos Aires, 2009)

Loveman, Brian, and Thomas M. Davies Jr, *The Politics of Antipolitics: The Military in Latin America* (University of Nebraska Press, London and Nebraska, 1978)

Lucero, Sergio, *Juntos Vivieron y Juntos Murieron: La Entrega de los Cinco Palotinos* (Editorial Claretiana, Buenos Aires, 2016)

Luna, Ricardo Mercado, *Enrique Angelelli, Obispo de La Rioja: Aportes para una Historia de Fé, Compromiso y Martirio* (Nexo Grupo Editor, La Rioja, 2010)

MacDiarmada, Mary, 'Art O'Brien: London Envoy of Dáil Éireann, 1919–1922: A Diplomat "in the Citadel of the Enemy's Authority"', *Irish Studies in International Affairs*, vol. 30, 2019, pp. 59–71

— *Art O'Brien and Irish Nationalism in London, 1900–25* (Four Courts Press, Dublin, 2020)

MacErlean, John, 'Irish Jesuits in Foreign Missions from 1574 to 1773', *The Irish Jesuit Directory*, Dublin, 1930, pp. 127–38

Maguire, Martin, *The Civil Service and the Revolution in Ireland, 1912–1938: 'Shaking the Blood-Stained Hand of Mr Collins'* (Manchester University Press, Manchester and New York, 2008)

Mainwaring, Scott, and Alexander Wilde (eds), *The Progressive Church in Latin America* (University of Notre Dame Press, Notre Dame, Indiana, 1989)

Malouf, Michael G., *Transatlantic Solidarities: Irish Nationalism and Caribbean Poetics* (University of Virginia Press, Charlottesville, 2009)

— 'With Dev in America: Sinn Féin and Recognition Politics, 1919–21', *Interventions: International Journal of Postcolonial Studies*, vol. 4, no. 1, April 2002, pp. 22–44

Mansergh, Diana (ed.) [foreword by J.J. Lee], *Nationalism and Independence: Selected Irish Papers by Nicholas Mansergh* (Cork University Press, Cork, 1997)

Mansergh, Martin (ed.), *Legacy of History for Making Peace in Ireland: Lectures and Commemorative Addresses* (Mercier Press, Cork, 2003)

Mansergh, Nicholas, *The Irish Question, 1840–1921: A Commentary on Anglo-Irish Relations and on Social and Political Forces in Ireland in the Age of Reform and Revolution* (University of Toronto Press, Toronto, 1965)

— *Unresolved Question: The Anglo-Irish Settlement and Its Undoing, 1912–72* (Yale University Press, New Haven, 1991)

— *Survey of British Commonwealth Affairs* (Oxford University Press, London and New York, 1952–8)

— *Britain and Ireland* (Longmans, Green & Co., London and New York, 1942)

— *The Commonwealth Experience* (Weidenfeld & Nicolson, London, 1969)

— (ed.), *Spirit of the Nation: The Speeches and Statements of Charles J. Haughey, 1957–1986* (Mercier Press, Cork, 1986)

Margry, Peter Jan (ed.), *Cold War Mary: Ideologies, Politics, Marian Devotional Culture* (Leuven University Press, Leuven, 2020)

Martín, José Pablo, *Ruptura Ideológica del Catolicismo Argentino: 36 Entrevistas entre 1988 y 1992* (Universidad Nacional de General Sarmiento, Buenos Aires, 2013)

Martin, Lisa L., 'Institutions and Cooperation: Sanctions during the Falkland Islands Conflict', *International Security*, vol. 16, no. 4, spring 1992, pp. 143–78

Martin, Micheál, *Freedom to Choose: Cork and Party Politics in Ireland, 1918–1932* (Collins Press, Cork, 2009)

Mártinez, Tomás Eloy, *The Perón Novel* (Pantheon Books, New York, 1988)

Matthews, Abraham, *Crónica de la Colonia Galesa de la Patagonia* (Edición Alfonsina, Buenos Aires, n.d.)

McCaffrey, Lawrence John, *The Irish Catholic Diaspora in America* (Catholic University of America, Washington DC, 1997)

McCartan, Patrick, *With de Valera in America* (Fitzpatrick Ltd., Dublin, 1932)

McCaughan, Michael, *Rodolfo Walsh: Periodista, Escritor y Revolucionario, 1927–1977* (Lom Ediciones, Santiago, Chile, 2015) [earlier edition, Latin America Bureau, London, 2002)

McConvery, Brendan, *The Redemptorists in Ireland, 1851–2011* (Columba Press, Dublin, 2012)

McCormick, Thomas J., *America's Half Century: United States Foreign Policy in the Cold War* (Johns Hopkins University Press, Baltimore, 1989)

McCracken, Donal P. (ed.), *The Irish in Southern Africa, 1795–1910* (Ireland and Southern Africa Project, Durban 1992)

— *The Irish Pro-Boers, 1877–1902* (Perskokor, Johannesburg, 1989)

— 'Imperial Running Dogs or Wild Geese Reporters? Irish Journalists in South Africa', *Historia*, vol. 58, no. 1, 2013, pp. 122–38

— *MacBride's Brigade: Irish Commandos in the Anglo-Boer War* (Four Courts Press, Dublin, 1999)

McCullagh, David, *De Valera: Rise, 1882–1932*, vol. I (Gill & Macmillan, Dublin, 2017)

— *De Valera: Rule, 1932–1975* (Gill, Dublin, 2018)

McDonagh, Maeve, *Freedom of Information Law* (Round Hall, Dublin, 2015)

McEvoy, Gabriela, *La Experiencia Invisible: Inmigrantes Irlandeses en el Perú* (Universidad del Perú, Lima, 2018)

McGarry, Fergal, *Irish Politics and the Spanish Civil War* (Cork University Press, Cork, 1999)

McGee, Owen, *A History of Ireland in International Relations* (Irish Academic Press, Newbridge, 2020)

— *Arthur Griffith* (Merrion Press, Dublin, 2015)

McLoughlin, Barry, and Emmet O'Connor, *In Spanish Trenches: The Mind and Deeds of the Irish Who Fought for the Republic in the Spanish Civil War* (UCD Press, Dublin, 2020)

McMahon, Deirdre, *Republicans and Imperialists: Anglo-Irish Relations in the 1930s* (Yale University Press, New Haven, 1984)

McNamara, Robert, *Britain, Nasser and the Balance of Power in the Middle East, 1952–1967: From the Egyptian Revolution to the Six Day War* (Frank Cass, London and Portland, 2003)

McSherry, J. Patrice, *Predatory States: Operation Condor and Covert War in Latin America* (Rowman & Littlefield, Lanham, 2005)

— *Chilean New Song: The Political Power of Music, 1960s–1973* (Temple University Press, Philadelphia, 2015)

Mecham, Lloyd J., *Church and State in Latin America* (University of North Carolina, Chapel Hill, 1966)

Meunier, Claudio Gustavo, and Oscar Rimondi, *Alas de Trueno* [Wings of Thunder] (C.G. Gustavo, Buenos Aires, 2004)

Mignone, Emilio, *Witness to the Truth: The Complicity of Church and Dictatorship in Argentina, 1976–1983* (Orbis, Maryknoll, New York, 1988) [Spanish edition: *Iglesia y Dictadura: El Papel de la Iglesia a la Luz de Sus Relaciones con el Régimen Militar* (Ediciones del Pensamiento Nacional, Buenos Aires, 1986)]

Miller, Rory David (ed.), *Ireland and the Middle East: Trade, Society and Peace* (Irish Academic Press, Dublin, 2007)

— 'The Look of the Irish: Irish Jews and the Zionist Project, 1900–1948', *Jewish Historical Studies*, vol. 43, 2011, pp. 189–211, https://www.jstor.org/stable/29780152

— *Britain, Palestine and Empire: The Mandate Years* (Routledge, New York and London, 2016)

— *Ireland and the Palestine Question: 1948–2004* (Irish Academic Press, Dublin 2005)

— 'Frank Aiken, the UN and the Six Day War, June 1967', *Irish Studies in International Affairs*, vol. 14, 2003, pp. 57–73

Miller, Rory M., *Britain and Latin America in the 19th and 20th Centuries* (Longman, London, 1993)

Moody, Theo W., *The Londonderry Plantation, 1609–41* (William Bullan, Belfast, 1939)

Morello, Gustavo, *The Catholic Church and Argentina's Dirty War* (Oxford University Press, New York, 2015)

Morgan, Hiram, 'Hugh O'Neill and the Nine Years War in Tudor Ireland', *The Historical Journal*, vol. 36, no. 1, March 1993, pp. 21–37

— 'On the Pig's Back: Subaltern Imperialism, Anti-Colonialism and the Irish Rise to Globalism', https://www.academia.edu/36924242/on_the_pigs_back_subaltern_imperialism_anti-colonialism_and_the_irish_rise_to_globalism

Morrison, Toni, *The Origin of Others* (Harvard University Press, Cambridge, MA, 2017)

— *Race* (Vintage, London, 1988)

Moyano, María José, *Argentina's Lost Patrol: Armed Struggle 1969–1979* (Yale University Press, New Haven, 1995)

Mulhall, Marion, *Between the Amazon and Andes: or, Ten Years of a Lady's Travels in the Pampas, Gran Chaco, Paraguay and Matto Grosso* (E. Stanford, London, 1881)

— *Beginnings or Glimpses of Vanished Civilizations* (Longmans, Green & Co., London, 1909)

Müller, Jan-Werner, *Contesting Democracy: Political Ideas in Twentieth-Century Europe* (Yale University Press, New Haven and London, 2015)

— *What Is Populism?* (Penguin Books, London, 2017)

Murray, Edmundo, *Devenir Irlandés: Narrativas Íntimas de la Emigración Irlandesa a la Argentina, 1844–1912* (Eudeba, Buenos Aires, 2004) [See also revised and updated edition in English: *Becoming Irlandés: Private Narratives of the Irish Emigration to Argentina, 1844–1912* (LOLA, Buenos Aires, 2006)]

— *Becoming Gauchos Inglese: Diasporic Models in Irish-Argentine Literature* (Mausel & Co., Bethesda, Dublin and Palo Alto, 2009)

Murray, Thomas, *The Story of the Irish in Argentina* (P.J. Kennedy & Sons, New York, 1919) [Revised edition, Juan José Delaney and Michael Geraghty (eds) (Cork University Press, 2011) and (Corregidor, Buenos Aires, 2012)]

Nagai, Kaori, *Empire of Analogies: Kipling, India and Ireland* (Cork University Press, Cork, 2006)

Naipaul, V.S., *The Return of Eva Perón with the Killings in Trinidad* (André Deutsch, London, 1980)

— 'Argentina: Living with Cruelty', *New York Review of Books*, 30 January 1992

Nelson, Bruce, *Irish Nationalists and the Making of the Irish Race* (Princeton University Press, Princeton, 2012)

Nevin, Kathleen, *You'll Never Go Back* (Cardinal Press, Maynooth, 1999; first edition, Bruce Humphries Inc., Boston, 1946)

Newton, Michael, *The Encyclopedia of Kidnappings* (Facts on File Inc., New York, 2002)

Niall, Brenda, *Mannix* (Text Publishing Company, Melbourne, 2016)

Nolan, Aengus, *Joseph Walshe: Irish Foreign Policy 1922–1946* (Mercier Press, Cork and Dublin, 2008)

Novaro, Marcos, y Vicente Palermo, *La Dictadura Militar, 1976–1983: Del Golpe de Estado a la Restauración Democrática (Historia Argentina)*, vol. IX (Paidós, Buenos Aires, 2003)

Nowlan, Kevin B., and T. Desmond Williams (eds), *Ireland in the War Years and After, 1939–51* (Notre Dame University Press, Notre Dame, 1970)

Nyhan Grey, Miriam, *Ireland's Allies: America and the 1916 Easter Rising* (UCD Press, Dublin, 2016)

O'Brien, Sarah, *The Irish in Argentina: Linguistic Diasporas, Narrative and Performance* (Palgrave Macmillan, London, 2017)

O'Byrne, Mary, *Strands from a Tapestry: A Story of Dominican Sisters in Latin America* (Dominican Publications, Dublin, 2001)

O'Carroll, John P., et al. (eds), *De Valera and His Times* (Cork University Press, Cork, 1986)

Ó Ceallaigh, Seán T., *Seán T: Scéal a Bheatha á Insint ag Seán T. Ó Ceallaigh, arna chur in eagar ag Prionsias Ó Conluain* (O'Gorman, Galway, 1963)

O'Connor, Emmet, *Big Jim Larkin: Hero or Wrecker?* (UCD Press, Dublin, 2015)

— *Reds and the Green: Ireland, Russia and the Communist Internationals, 1919–1943* (UCD Press, Dublin, 2004)

— *James Larkin* (Cork University Press, Cork 2002)

— *Syndicalism in Ireland, 1917–1923* (Cork University Press, Cork, 1988)

— 'Communists, Russia, and the IRA, 1920–1923', *The Historical Journal*, vol. 46, no. 1, 2003, pp. 115–31

O'Dantonio, William V., and Fredrick B. Pike (eds), *Religion, Revolution and Reform* (Praeger, New York, 1964)

O'Donnell, Pacho, *Breve Historia Argentina de la Conquista a los Kirchner* (Aguilar, Buenos Aires, 2014)

O'Donnell, Santiago, and Mariano Melamed, *Derechos Humanos: La Historia del CELS. De Mignone a Verbitsky. De Videla a Cristina* (Editorial Sudamericana, Buenos Aires, 2015)

Ó Drisceoil, Donal, *Censorship in Ireland, 1939–1945: Neutrality, Politics and Society* (Cork University Press, Cork, 1996)

O'Driscoll, Mervyn, *Ireland, Germany and the Nazis: Politics and Diplomacy, 1919–1939* (Four Courts Press, Dublin 2004)

— *Ireland, West Germany and the New Europe, 1949–1973: Best Friend and Ally?* (Manchester University Press, Manchester, 2018)

— *Ireland through European Eyes: Western Europe, the EEC and Ireland, 1945–1973* (Cork University Press, Cork, 2013)

O'Farrell, Patrick James, *The Irish in Australia: 1788 to the Present* (Cork University Press, Cork, 2001)

— *Vanished Kingdoms: Irish in Australia and New Zealand: A Personal Excursion* (New South Wales University Press, Kensington, NSW, 1990)

Ó Giolláin, Diarmuid, *Locating Irish Folklore: Tradition, Modernity, Identity* (Cork University Press, Cork, 2000)

— 'Folk Culture', in Joe Cleary and Claire Connolly (eds), *The Cambridge Companion to Modern Irish Culture* (Cambridge University Press, Cambridge, 2006), pp. 225–44

O'Halpin, Eunan, *Defending Ireland: The Irish State and Its Enemies since 1922* (Oxford University Press, Oxford, 2000)

— *Spying on Ireland: British Intelligence and Irish Neutrality during the Second World War* (Oxford University Press, Oxford, 2008)

Ó hAodha, Mícheál, *Narratives of the Occluded Irish Diaspora: Subversive Voices* (Lang, Oxford and Berlin, 2012)

O'Kane, Eamonn, *Britain, Ireland and Northern Ireland since 1980: The Totality of Relationships* (Routledge, London and New York, 2007)

O'Leary, Daniel Florencio, *Bolívar and the War of Independence* (University of Texas Press, Austin, 1970)

O'Leary, Philip, *The Prose Literature of the Gaelic Revival, 1881–1921* (Pennsylvania State University Press, University Park, 1994)

Oliveri, Mario, *The Representatives: The Real Nature and Function of Papal Legates* (Van Duren, Gerrards Cross, London, 1980)

O'Malley, John W., *Vatican I: The Council and Making of the Ultramontane Church* (Harvard University Press, Cambridge, MA, 2018)

O'Malley, Kate, *Ireland, India and Empire: Indo-Irish Radical Connections, 1919–1964* (Manchester University Press, Manchester, 2009)

— 'Ireland and India: Post-Independence Diplomacy', *Irish Studies in International Affairs*, vol. 22, 2011, pp. 145–62

O'Neill, Kevin, *Apuntes Históricos Palotinos* (Editora Pallotti, Buenos Aires, 1995)

Ortiz, Diana, *The Blindfold's Eyes: My Journey from Torture to Truth* (Orbis, Maryknoll, New York, 2004)

Ó Siochrú, Micheál et al. (eds), *Ireland 1641: Contexts and Reactions* (Manchester University Press, Manchester, 2013)

O'Sullivan, Kevin, *Ireland, Africa and the End of Empire: Small State Identity in the Cold War, 1955–75* (Manchester University Press, Manchester, 2014)

— 'Humanitarian Encounters: Biafra, NGOs and Imaginings of the Third World in Britain and Ireland, 1967–70', in Lasse Heerten and Dirk Moses (eds), *Postcolonial Conflict and the Question of Genocide: The Nigeria–Biafra War, 1967–1970* (Routledge, Abingdon, 2017), pp. 259–77

— '"The cause of nationality is sacred in ... Africa as in Ireland": Ireland and Sub-Saharan Africa at the United Nations, 1960–75', in Michael Kennedy and Deirdre McMahon (eds), *Obligations and Responsibilities: Ireland at the United Nations 1955–2005* (Institute of Public Administration, Dublin, 2005)

— 'Between Internationalism and Empire: Ireland, the "Like-minded" Group, and the Search for a New International Order, 1974–82', *International History Review*, vol. 37, no. 5, 2015, pp. 1083–1101

— with Michael Holmes et al., *The Poor Relations: Irish Foreign Policy and the Third World* (Trócaire with Gill & Macmillan, Dublin, 1993)

Ó Tuathaigh, Gearóid, 'Language, Ideology and National Identity', in Joe Cleary and Claire Connolly (eds), *The Cambridge Companion to Modern Irish Culture* (Cambridge University Press, Cambridge, 2006), pp. 42–58

Owen, Geraint Dyfnallt, *Crisis in Chubut: A Chapter in the History of the Welsh Colony in Patagonia* (C. Davies, Swansea, 1977)

Page, Joseph A., *Perón: A Biography* (Random House, New York, 1983)

Palleiro, María Inés (compiladora), *San Patricio en Buenos Aires: Narrativa, Celebraciones y Migración* (Universidad de Buenos Aires, Editorial de la Facultad de Filosofía y Letras, 2011)

Paoli, Arturo, *El Trabajo y la Paz* (Latinoamérica Libros, Buenos Aires, 1966)

— *Gesù Amore: Meditazioni e Colloqui* (Borla, Torino, 1967)

— *Dialogo della Liberazione* (Morcelliana, Brescia, 1969), translated into English as *Freedom to Be Free* (Orbis, Maryknoll, New York, 1973)

— *Las Bienaventuranzas: Un Estilo de Vida* (Cantabria Sal Terrae, Maliaño, 2008)

— *Un Encuentro Difícil: La Parábola del Buen Samaritano* (San Pablo, Madrid, 2002)

— *La Raíz del Hombre: Meditaciones sobre el Evangelio de Lucas* (PPC, Madrid, 1998)

— *Se Hace Camino al Andar* (San Pablo, Madrid, 1995)

— *Construyendo la Verdad* (Ediciones Sígueme, Salamanca, 1992)

— *El Silencio, Plenitud de la Palabra* (Ediciones Paulinas, Madrid, 1992)

— *Creando Fraternidad: Confrontaciones, Encuentros con el Evangelio* (Ediciones Sígueme, Salamanca, 1984)

— *Gritarán las Piedras: El Rostro Nuevo del ser Cristiano Desde la Experiencia Latinoamericana* (Ediciones Sígueme, Salamanca, 1982)

— *Buscando Libertad: Castidad, Obediencia, Pobreza* (Editorial Sal Terrae, Santander, 1981)

— *'Pan y Vino' Tierra: Del Exilio a la Comunión* (Editorial Sal Terrae, Santander, 1980)

— *El Rostro del Hermano* (Ediciones Sígueme, Salamanca, 1979)

— *La Contemplación* (Ediciones Paulinas, Bogotá, 1978)

— *El Grito de la Tierra* (Ediciones Sígueme, Salamanca, 1977)

— *La Perspectiva Política de San Lucas* (Siglo Veintiuno Editores, Mexico, 1976)

— *El Rostro de tu Hermano* (Ediciones Paulinas, Bogotá, 1976)

— *La Espada y la Cruz* (Cuernavaca Centro Intercultural de Documentación, Cuernavaca, 1971)

— *Diálogo de la Liberación* (Ediciones Carlos Lohlé, Buenos Aires, 1970)

— *Encuentro con el Evangelio* (Latinoamérica Libros, Buenos Aires, 1968)

— *La Persona, el Mundo y Dios* (Ediciones Carlos Lohlé, Buenos Aires, 1967)

— *La Construcción del Reino* (Latinoamérica Libros, Buenos Aires, 1966)

— *Diálogo entre Católicos y Marxistas* (Latinoamérica Libros, Buenos Aires, 1966)

— *El Trabajo y la Paz* (Latinoamérica Libros, 1966)

— *El Encuentro* (Latinoamérica Libros, Buenos Aires, 1964)

Parsons, Sir Anthony, 'The Falklands Crisis in the United Nations, 31 March–14 June 1982', *International Affairs*, vol. 59, no. 2, spring 1983, pp. 169–78

Peart, Barbara, *Tia Barbarita: Memories of Barbara Peart* (Houghton Mifflin Company, Boston and New York, 1934)

Perlmutter, Amos, *The Military and Politics in Modern Times* (Yale University Press, New Haven, 1977)

Petersen, Lucas, *El traductor del Ulises, Salas Subirat: La desconocida historia del Argentino que tradujo la obra maestra de Joyce* (Editorial Sudaméricana, Buenos Aires, 2016)

Pierce, David, *Light, Freedom and Song: A Cultural History of Modern Irish Writing* (Yale University Press, New Haven and London, 2005)

Piqué, Elisabetta, *Francisco: Vida y Revolución* (La Esfera de Los Libros, Buenos Aires, 2013)

Plotkin, Mariano Ben, *Mañana es San Perón: A Cultural History of Perón's Argentina* (SR Books, Wilmington, 2003) [Spanish edition, *Mañana es San Perón: Propaganda, Rituales Políticos y Educación en el Régimen Peronista (1946–1955)* (Ariel Historia, Buenos Aires, 1994)]

Pope Atkins, G., *Latin America in the International Political System* (Free Press, New York, 1977)

Power, Samantha, *The Education of an Idealist: A Memoir* (Dey Street Books, New York, 2019)

— *Chasing the Flame: Sergio Vieira de Mello and the Fight to Save the World* (Penguin Press, New York, 2008)

— *Problems from Hell: America and the Age of Genocide* (Basic Books, New York, 2002)

— with Graham Allison (eds), *Realizing Human Rights: Moving from Inspiration to Impact* (St Martin's Press, New York, 2000)

Quigley, Martin S., *A US Spy in Ireland: The Truth behind Irish 'Neutrality' during the Second World War* (Roberts Rinehart, Lanham, MD, 1999)

— *Peace without Hiroshima: Secret Action at the Vatican in the Spring of 1945* (Madison Books, Seattle, 1991)

Ragendorfer, Ricardo, *Los Doblados: Las Infiltraciones del Batallón 601 en la Guerrilla Argentina* (Editorial Sudamericana, Buenos Aires, 2016)

Reese, Thomas J., *Inside the Vatican* (Harvard University Press, Cambridge, MA, 1996)

Reid, Richard, *Not Just Ned: A True History of the Irish in Australia* (National Museum of Australia Press, Canberra, 2011)

Rein, Raanan, *Argentine Jews or Jewish Argentines? Essays on Ethnicity, Identity and Diaspora* (Brill, Leiden and Boston, 2010)

Rice, Desmond, and Arthur Gavshon, *The Sinking of the Belgrano* (Secker & Warburg, London, 1984)

Rice, Patricio [Patrick], y Luis Torres (eds), *En Medio de la Tempestad: Los Hermanitos del Evangelio en Argentina, 1959–1977* (Doble Clic Editoras, Buenos Aires, 2007)

Robb, Thomas K., *Embracing the Special Relationship, 1977–8: Jimmy Carter and the Anglo-American Special Relationship* (Edinburgh University Press, Edinburgh, 2017)

Rock, David, *The British in Argentina: Commerce, Settlers and Power, 1800–2000* (Palgrave Macmillan, Switzerland, 2019)

— *Argentina, 1516–1987: From Spanish Colonization to Alfonsín* (University of California Press, Berkeley, 1987)

Rojo, Roberto, *Angelelli: La Vida por los Pobres* (Nexo Ediciones, La Rioja, 2001)

Rotker, Susana, *Captive Women: Oblivion and Memory in Argentina* (University of Minnesota Press, Minneapolis, 2002)

Rubin, Sergio, and Francesca Ambrogetti, *El Jesuita: La Historia de Francisco, el Papa Argentino* (Vergaga, Buenos Aires, 2013)

Ruys, Tom, Oliver Corten and Alexandra Hofer (eds), *The Use of Force in International Law: A Case-Based Approach* (Oxford University Press, Oxford, 2018)

Ryan, David, *US–Sandinista Diplomatic Relations: Voice of Intolerance* (Palgrave Macmillan, London and New York, 1995)

Rynne, Stephen, *Father John Hayes: Founder of Muintir na Tíre, People of the Land* (Clonmore and Reynolds, Dublin, 1960)

Sábato, Hilda, and Juan Carlos Korol, *Cómo fue la inmigración Irlandesa en Argentina* (Editorial Plus Ultra, Buenos Aires, 1981)

Saidon, Gabriela, *La Farsa: Los 48 Dias Previos al Golpe* (Planeta, Buenos Aires, 2016)

Sarmiento, Domingo Faustino, *Facundo: Civilisación y Barbarie en las Pampas Argentinas* (Alianza Editorial, Madrid, 1970 and Penguin, London, 1998 [English trans])

Scavo, Nello, *La Lista de Bergoglio: Los Salvados por Francisco durante la Dictadura – La Historia no Contada* [prólogo Adolfo Pérez Esquivel] (Editorial Claretiana, Buenos Aires, 2013)

Schmidli, William Michael, *The Fate of Freedom Elsewhere: Human Rights and US Cold War Policy towards Argentina* (Cornell University Press, Cornell, 2013)

Schmuhl, Robert, *Ireland's Exiled Children: America and the Easter Rising* (Oxford University Press, Oxford, 2016)

Sheinin, David M.K., *Ordinary Argentinians in the Dirty War* (University Press of Florida, Gainesville, 2012)

— *Argentina and the United States: An Alliance Contained* (The University of Georgia Press, Athens, GA, and London, 2006)

Sheridan, Frank (ed.), *A Memoir by David Goodall: The Making of the Anglo-Irish Agreement of 1985* (NUI, Dublin, 2021)

Sikkink, Katryn, *Mixed Signals: US Human Rights Policy and Latin America* (Cornell University Press, Ithaca and London, 2004)

Simson, John, and Jana Bennett, *The Disappeared and the Mothers of the Plaza: The Story of the 11,000 Argentinians who Vanished* (St Martin's Press, New York, 1985)

Skidmore, Thomas, and Peter H. Smith, *Modern Latin America* (Oxford University Press, Oxford, 1984)

Slaby, Alexandra, *Histoire de l'Irlande de 1912 à nos Jour* (Éditions Tallandier, Paris, 2016)

Smith, Brian H., *The Church and Politics in Chile: Challenge to Modern Catholicism* (Princeton University Press, New Jersey, 1982)

Smith, F.B., *Ireland, England, and Australia: Essays in Honour of Oliver MacDonagh* (Australian National University, Canberra, 1990)

Speight, Patrick, *Irish-Argentine Identities in an Age of Political Challenge and Change, 1875–1983* (Peter Lang, Oxford, 2019)

Steuermann, Miguel et al., *Testimonios de una Semana de Horror* (Ediciones JAI, Buenos Aires, 1995)

Stewart, Iain A.D., *From Caledonia to the Pampas: Two Accounts by Early Scottish Emigrants to the Argentine* (Tuckwell Press, East Lothian, 2000)

Sucarrat, María, *El Inocente: Vida, Pasíon y Muerte de Carlos Mugica* (Octubre Editorial, Buenos Aires, 2017) [nueva edición]

Swedish, Margaret, and Marie Dennis, *Like Grains of Wheat: A Spirituality of Solidarity* (Orbis, Maryknoll, New York, 2004)

Taurozzi, Susana, *Los Pasionistas en Argentina y Uruguay: 100 Años* (Misioneros Pasionistas, Buenos Aires, 2006)

The Southern Cross (*La Cruz del Sur*), *Número del Centenario, 1875–1975* (TSC, Buenos Aires, 1975)

— *La Cruz del Sur: 1875–2000 Cientoveinticinco Años Latiendo, Uniendo e Informando con la Comunidad Argentina Irlandesa* (TSC, Buenos Aires, 2000)

Thompson, Joseph E., *American Policy and Northern Ireland: A Saga of Peacebuilding* (Praeger, Westport, CT, London, 2001)

Thomson, Basil, *Ramón Writes* (Buenos Aires Herald, Buenos Aires, 1979)

Tierney, Fr Mark, *The Story of Muintir na Tíre: The First Seventy Years, 1931–2001* (Muintir na Tíre, Tipperary, 2004)

Timerman, Jacobo, *Prisoner without a Name, Cell without a Number* (Penguin Books, London, 1981)

Tóibín, Colm, *The Trial of the Generals: Selected Journalism 1980–1990* (Raven Art Press, Dublin, 1990)

— *The Story of the Night* (Picador, London, 1996)

'Toni Morrison Obituary', *Guardian*, 6 August 2019

Tonra, Ben, et al. (eds), *Ireland in International Affairs: Interests, Institutions and Identities. Essays in Honour of Professor N.P. Keatinge* (Institute of Public Administration, Dublin, 2002)

Townshend, Charles, *The Republic: The Fight for Irish Independence, 1918–1923* (Penguin Books, London, 2014)

Truettner, William H., *The West as America: Reinterpreting Images of the Frontier* (Smithsonian Institution Press, Washington and London, 1991)

Uriarte, Claudio, *Almirante Cero: Biografía no Autorizada de Emilio Eduardo Massera* (Planeta, Buenos Aires, 2011)

Ussher, Santiago, *Father Fahy: A Biography of Anthony Fahy, OP, Irish Missionary in Argentina, 1805–1871* (Archdiocese of Buenos Aires, Buenos Aires, 1951)

— *Los Capellanes Irlandeses en la Colectividad Hiberno: Argentina durante el Siglo XIX* (n.p., Buenos Aires, 1954)

— *Las Hermanas de la Misericordia, 1865–1956* (Buenos Aires, 1955)

— *The Ussher-Walsh Family Album* (Buenos Aires, 1933) [privately printed and updated by family, *c.* 2010]

Varouhakis, Miron, *Shadow of Heroes: The Journey of a Doctor and a Journalist in the Lives of Ordinary People who Became Victims of Torture* (Author Solutions, Bloomington, Indiana, 2010)

Vasconcelos, José, *La Raza Cósmica / The Cosmic Race* (Johns Hopkins University Press, Baltimore, 1997)

Verbitsky, Horacio, et al., *The Flight: Confessions of an Argentine Dirty Warrior. A Firsthand Account of Atrocity*; published in Spanish as *El Vuelo* (Planeta, Buenos Aires, 1995); see all his citations at http://www.peronlibros.com.ar/autores/1486/verbitsky_horacio

— *Cristo Vence: De Roca a Perón* (Editorial Sudamericana, Buenos Aires, 2007)

— *La Violencia Evangélica: De Lonardi al Cordobazo, 1955–1969* (Editorial Sudamericana, Buenos Aires, 2008)

— *Vigilia de Armas: Del Cordobazo de 1969 al 23 de Marzo de 1976* (Editorial Sudamericana, Buenos Aires, 2009)

— *La Mano Izquierda de Dios: La Última Dictadura, 1976–1983* (Editorial Sudamericana, Buenos Aires, 2010)

— *Doble Juego: La Argentina Católica y Militar* (Editorial Sudamericana, Buenos Aires, 2006)

— *El Silencio: De Paulo VI a Bergoglio: Las Relaciones Secretas de la Iglesia con la ESMA* (Editorial Sudamericana, Buenos Aires, 2005)

— *Civiles y Militares: Memoria Secreta de la Transición* (Editorial Contrapunto, Buenos Aires, 1987)

— *Rodolfo Walsh y la Prensa Clandestina, 1976–1978* (República Argentina, Ediciones de la Urraca, Buenos Aires, 1985)

— *Ezeiza* (Planeta, Buenos Aires, 1995)

— *Malvinas: La Última Batalla de la Tercera Guerra Mundial* (Editorial Sudamericana, Buenos Aires, 2002)

— with Juan Pablo Bohoslavsky (eds), *The Economic Accomplices to the Argentine Dictatorship: Outstanding Debts* (Cambridge University Press, New York, 2016)

Vigil, Marís López [preface by Jon Sobrino], *Oscar Romero: Memories in Mosaic* (CAFOD, London, 2000)

Viñoles, Diana Beatriz, *Biografía de Alice Domon, 1937–1977: Las Religiosas Francesas Desaparecidas* (Editora Patria Grande, Buenos Aires, 2014)

Wall, Sinéad, *Irish Diasporic Narratives in Argentina: A Reconsideration of Home, Identity and Belonging* (Peter Lang, Oxford, 2017)

Walsh, María Elena, *Novios de Antaño* (Seix Barral, Buenos Aires, 1990)

Walsh, Rodolfo, *Cuentos Completos* (Ediciones de la Flor, Buenos Aires, 2013)

— *Operación Massacre* [con un prólogo de Osvaldo Bayer] (Planeta, Buenos Aires, 1994)

— *Violento Oficio de Escribir: Obra Periodística, 1953–1977* (Planeta, Buenos Aires, 1995)

— *Years of Dictatorship in Argentina, March 1976 – March 1977: An Open Letter to the Military Junta* (Committee to Save Rodolfo Walsh, London, 1977)

— *Quién Mató a Rosendo?* (Editorial Tiempo Contemporáneo, Buenos Aires, 1969)

— *Los Irlandeses* (El Aleph Editores, Barcelona, 2007)

Whelan, Barry, *Ireland's Revolutionary Diplomat: A Biography of Leopold Kerney* (Notre Dame University Press, Notre Dame, IN, 2019)

Whelan, Bernadette, *Ireland and the Marshall Plan, 1947–1957* (Four Courts Press, Dublin, 2000)

— *American Government in Ireland: A History of the US Consular Service 1790–1913* (Manchester University Press/Palgrave, Manchester, 2010)

— *United States Foreign Policy and Ireland: From Empire to Independence, 1913–1929* (Four Courts Press, Dublin, 2006)

— 'American Propaganda and Ireland during World War One: The Work of the Committee of Public Information', *Irish Studies Review*, vol. 25, no. 2, 2017, pp. 1–29

— 'The Wilson Administration and the 1916 Rising', in Ruán O'Donnell (ed.), *The Impact of the 1916 Rising: Among the Nations* (Irish Academic Press, Dublin and Portland, OR, 2006), pp. 91–119

— with Mary O'Dowd and Gerardine Meaney, *Reading the Irish Woman: Studies in Cultural Encounters and Exchanges, 1714–1960* (Liverpool University Press, Liverpool, 2013)

— with Michael Holmes and Nicholas Rees, *The Poor Relation: Irish Foreign Policy and the Third World* (Trócaire / Gill & Macmillan, Dublin, 1993)

White, Gerry, and Brendan O'Shea, *The Burning of Cork* (Mercier Press, Cork, 2006)

Whyte, John H., *Church and State in Modern Ireland, 1923–1979* (Gill & Macmillan, Dublin, 1980)

— *American Government in Ireland, 1790–1913* (Manchester University Press, Manchester, 2016)

— *United States Foreign Policy and Ireland: From Empire to Independence, 1913–1929* (Four Courts Press, Dublin, 2006)

— 'The New World and the Old: American Marshall Planners in Ireland, 1947–57', *Irish Studies in International Affairs*, vol. 12, 2001, pp. 179–89, https://www.jstor.org/stable/30002065

— 'Recognition of the Irish Free State, 1924: The Diplomatic Context to the Appointment of Timothy Smiddy as the First Irish Minister to the US', *Irish Studies in International Affairs*, vol. 26, 2015, pp. 121–5

Wilkerson, Isabel, *Caste: The Lies that Divide Us* (Allen Lane, London, 2020)

— *The Warmth of Other Suns: The Epic Story of America's Great Migration* (Random House, New York, 2010)

Wilkinson, Susan, *Recollections of an Irish-born Doctor in Nineteenth-Century Argentina: Arthur Pageitt Greene (1848–1933)* (Memoir Club, Tyne & Wear, 2015)

— *The Mimosa: The Life and Time of the Ship that Sailed to Patagonia* (Y Lolfa Cyf, Talybont, 2015)

— 'Arthur Pageitt Greene (1848–1933): Recollections of an Irish-born Doctor in Nineteenth-Century Argentina', *Irish Migration Studies in Latin America*, vol. 6, no. 3, November 2008, http://www.irlandeses.org/0811.pdf

Williams, Bryn, *La Colonia Galesa de Patagonia* [*The Welsh Colony in Patagonia 1865–2000*] (Llanrwst, Dyffryn, 2000)

Wills, Clair, *That Neutral Island: A Cultural History of Ireland during the Second World War* (Faber & Faber, London, 2007)

Wilson, Jason, *Buenos Aires: A Cultural and Literary History* (Signal Books, Oxford, 2007)

Winchester, Simon, *Prison Diary: Argentina* (Chatto & Windus, London, 1984)

Wright, Scott, *Oscar Romero and the Communion of Saints* (Orbis, Maryknoll, New York, 2009)

Wylie, Paula, *Ireland and the Cold War: Diplomacy and Recognition, 1949–63* (Irish Academic Press, Dublin, 2006)

Yofre, Juan Bautista, *1982: Los Documentos Secretos de la Guerra de Malvinas-Falklands y el Derrumbe del Proceso* (Editorial Sudamericana, Buenos Aires, 2011)

Zurita, Raúl, *INRI* (Marick Press, Grosse Pointe Farms, Michigan, 2018)

Index

Illustrations are indicated by page numbers in **bold**.